PRINCIPLES OF ECONOMICS

Moore McDowell • Rodney Thom • Ivan Pastine
Robert Frank • Ben Bernanke

Third European Edition

PRINCIPLES OF ECONOMICS

Moore McDowell • Rodney Thom • Ivan Pastine
Robert Frank • Ben Bernanke

Third European Edition

McGraw Hill Education

London Boston Burr Ridge, IL Dubuque, IA Madison, WI New York San Francisco
St. Louis Bangkok Bogotá Caracas Kuala Lumpur Lisbon Madrid Mexico City Milan
Montreal New Delhi Santiago Seoul Singapore Sydney Taipei Toronto

Principles of Microeconomics
Moore McDowell, Rodney Thom, Ivan Pastine, Robert Frank and Ben Bernanke
ISBN-13 9780077143336
ISBN-10 0077143337

Published by McGraw-Hill Education
Shoppenhangers Road
Maidenhead
Berkshire
SL6 2QL
Telephone: 44 (0) 1628 502 500
Fax: 44 (0) 1628 770 224
Website: www.mheducation.co.uk

British Library Cataloguing in Publication Data
A catalogue record for this book is available from the British Library

Library of Congress Cataloguing in Publication Data
The Library of Congress data for this book has been applied for from the Library of Congress

Executive Editor: Natalie Jacobs
Commissioning Editor: Rebecca Birtwistle
Development Editor: Kiera Jamison
Marketing Manager: Vanessa Boddington
Senior Production Editor: James Bishop

Text design by Hardlines
Cover design by Adam Renvoize
Printed and bound by Ashford Colour Press Ltd

ISBN-13 9780077143336
ISBN-10 0077143337

DEDICATION

For Nuala – MMcD

For Susan – RT

For Tuvana – IP

Brief Table of Contents

Detailed Table of Contents

Preface

The fact that people must make choices, and sometimes unpleasant ones, is central to what economics is about. It applies to writers of textbooks in economics as well as to the rest of the world. The first choice in the case of a textbook concerns the approach taken to getting ideas across to different types of students. This in turn reflects the reasons for which students are taking the economics course for which the text is being used and also the abilities of the target student body, especially where mathematics is an issue. The second concerns the breadth of the subject matter the text covers. Here the choice is between an attempt to cover all the bases adequately or make sure that the more important bases are covered more fully. Compromise is inevitable, especially given cost and length constraints. Again, this is hardly surprising, trade-offs are at the heart of rational decision-making in economics.

In many, perhaps most, introductory courses the instructor is dealing with two types of student and, therefore, has two different goals. The first group comprises students whose interest in economics is just as part of a broad educational curriculum. Some of these students may never take another economics course. For them the imperative is to give them a good understanding of basic economics principles that will enable them to understand more clearly the world in which they will live, and to retain these insights. The second group comprises students progressing to a degree where economics is a major component. For this group the aim of an introductory course will be to provide a firm foundation and the tools of the trade for going further with the discipline.

The authors of this text start from the proposition that, while very few undergraduate students of economics proceed to a PhD and become professional economists, an understanding of basic economics is of immense value in everyday life. We believe that this obvious fact should inform how economics is taught at the introductory level. In developing a European version of the original US text written by Robert Frank and Ben Bernanke, an ongoing process now leading to a third edition, we have adhered to the philosophy that informed the original text in Europe, as in the USA. An abiding concern of many academic economists was this: to judge by what is retained afterwards, many students finish introductory courses without having really learned and understood the most important basic economic principles. The problem is that these courses frequently try to teach students far too much. It seems to us that what is more important is to teach core principles and techniques well, rather than to cover all possible fields of economics at a superficial level. As will be explained below, this has led us to curtail material from the second edition. We continue, however to remind students continually of those basic principles of economics that, in the words of Frank and Bernanke, 'do most of the heavy lifting in economics'. These are:

1. ***The Scarcity Principle*** Having more of one good thing usually means having less of another.
2. ***The Cost–Benefit Principle*** Take no action unless its marginal benefit is at least as great as its marginal cost.
3. ***The Incentive Principle*** Cost–benefit comparisons are relevant not only for identifying the decisions that rational people should make, but also for predicting the actual decisions they do make.
4. ***The Principle of Comparative Advantage*** Everyone does best when each concentrates on the activity for which he or she is relatively most productive.

Scarcity

Cost–Benefit Analysis

Incentives Matter

Comparative Advantage

Increasing Opportunity Cost

5. ***The Principle of Increasing Opportunity Cost*** Use the resources with the lowest opportunity cost before turning to those with higher opportunity costs.

Efficiency

6. ***The Efficiency Principle*** Efficiency is an important social goal because when the economic 'pie' grows larger, everyone can have a larger slice.

Equilibrium

7. ***The Equilibrium Principle*** A market in equilibrium leaves no unexploited opportunities for individuals but may not exploit all gains achievable through collective action.

We continue to use and develop the idea of the 'economic naturalist'. This means using basic economic principles to understand and explain what you see in the world around you, and to resolve some apparent paradoxes. For example, we don't fit child safety restraints in planes, but we do in cars. Do we not care about children in planes?

In the second edition we moved the emphasis of the text somewhat from the needs of the first category of students described above to those of the second group. This decision was taken because of the difference in the academic programme structures in European countries from those in the USA. We added some additional theoretical analysis (for example, an expanded use of simple game theory) and we included some rigorous explanations using mathematics rather than relying on graphs or intuition alone. This shift in emphasis is maintained in the third edition, but in a way that permits instructors to avoid using more rigorous techniques where appropriate for their students.

However, while increasing the technical content we have always been guided by the need to preserve the major advantage the original text had over other texts we had seen. This was the emphasis on getting ideas across in a fashion that captures the reader's attention and makes a lasting contribution to basic understanding of the economics underpinnings of ordinary life. Not only is this important in terms of imparting an understanding of economics as a subject and as a guide to policy, but we believe that it is very important that students who progress with economics should develop a sense of economic intuition as well as mastering technical aspects of the discipline.

CHANGES IN THE THIRD EDITION

The years since the publication of the second edition have seen enormous upheavals in economies across Europe and around the globe. Students entering economics courses today are eager to learn how economic theory can help them understand these dramatic events. This provides a useful opportunity to engage students with economics, and so we have udpated most of the economic naturalists from the second edition.

In most sections we have reduced the word count significantly, making the core ideas more accessible. Using the very helpful reviewer feedback, we have also made significant changes in the material and presentation in both the micro and macro sections of the text. We have also, we think, improved the graphical exposition of material in both sections, and, of course, we have updated data tables where appropriate. Reviewer opinion was divided on the use of in-chapter mathematics in presenting material, rather than confining mathematical treatment to chapter appendices. In general we have left the use of maths as it was in the last edition.

MICROECONOMICS

We have retained most of the changes to content and organisation introduced in the second edition, while amending some the material where potential improvements have been suggested by reviewers and users of the text.

The treatment of oligopoly has been extended with formal models being developed in appendices.

We have included a new final chapter in the micro section. This deals with the role of financial sector problems in the 'Great Contraction' of 2008–2010, for many people something that appears to have resulted from the spectacular collapse of Lehman Brothers. Our emphasis in this chapter is on using ideas from microeconomics (poor incentives, risk, opportunism, asymmetrical information, efficient markets, regulatory failure) and applying them to help students:

a) understand how the financial structures got into trouble
b) see clearly that the various ideas and concepts developed in microeconomics really do help explain reality and improve policy
c) reinforce the idea that good macroeconomics, in theory and practice, requires a consistent microeconomics foundation, thus bridging the pedagogic chasm that seems to separate the two branches of economics analysis for many students.

The international trade chapter from the first edition has not been re-introduced, but remains available in the Online Learning Centre that accompanies this text.

MACROECONOMICS

As in the microeconomics sections, we have retained most of the changes introduced in the second edition. The modular presentation allows instructors to move from Part 7, dealing with measurement issues relating to GDP, the price level and the labour market, to either long-run (Part 8, The Economy in the Long Run) or short-run (Part 9, The Economy in the Short Run) analysis with no loss of continuity. Part 8 uses the Solow model to present a comprehensive analysis of long-run growth and productivity, while Part 9 presents a three-stage treatment of Keynesian macroeconomics in which analysis of the real and monetary sectors is integrated into the IS-LM model to provide a platform for discussion of the fiscal and monetary chapters. These latter chapters have been updated to deal with policy responses to the recent economic and financial crisis with particular emphasis on deficit control, bail-outs and quantitative easing.

In response to requests from users of the second edition, we have introduced new material in Chapter 28, which now introduces the New Keynesian Phillips curve. This permits a more in-depth discussion of the role of expectations in macroeconomics and the interaction between policy and expectations

Chapter 29 presents a self-contained discussion of exchange rate determination that can be used whenever an instructor thinks it best to introduce this important subject. The chapter also integrates trade and capital flows into the IS-LM model and presents a discussion of stabilisation policy in the open economy.

APPROACH

A key feature of the text is what we call 'economic naturalism'. By using examples and posing problems we seek to provide answers to questions that should encourage readers to look at the world through the eyes of an economist. Here are a few examples.

Microeconomics:
Why do airline ticket prices rise when most people fly, while strawberry prices fall when people eat more strawberries?
Sales of lipstick are said to increase when times are tough. Is lipstick an inferior good?
How does subsidising fuel prices make a country poorer?

Macroeconomics:
Is economic growth always good for you?

Why did the Bank of England cut interest rates nine times between December 2007 and March 2009?
Greece and Ireland: How did it all go wrong?

WHY THIS RATHER THAN ANOTHER TEXT?

In addition to the pedagogic approach already described, we believe that this text differs significantly from others in respect of the emphasis on modern economic analysis.

- **Modern microeconomics:** Economic surplus is more central to the presentation of economics in this than in any other text. This concept underlies the argument for economic efficiency as an important social goal. Instead of dwelling on the problem of equity versus efficiency in policy making, we stress that efficiency (maximising surplus) permits the achievement of other goals. We analyse rational decision making in a way that identifies the common decision pitfalls identified by 2002 Nobel Laureate Daniel Kahneman and others – such as the tendency to ignore implicit costs, the tendency not to ignore sunk costs, and the tendency to confuse average and marginal costs and benefits. We introduce the student to the elements of game theory, and show how powerful an approach it can be to explaining otherwise baffling problems. We introduce the Coase theorem, and use it to explain and to question aspects of legal and regulatory policy. The text also introduces students to the economics of information, something that is widely ignored as an area of economics in its own right in many other texts.
- **Modern macroeconomics:** Recent developments have renewed interest in cyclical fluctuations without challenging the importance of such long-run issues as growth, productivity, the evolution of real wages, and capital formation. Our treatment of these issues is organised as follows:
  - **A two-chapter treatment of long-run issues**, followed by a modern treatment of short-term fluctuations and stabilisation policy, emphasising the important distinction between short- and long-run behaviour of the economy.
  - Consistent with both media reporting and public perception we **treat the interest rate rather than the money supply** as the primary instrument of central bank policy.
  - A **more realistic treatment of aggregate demand and aggregate supply** which relates output to inflation rather than to the price level, sidestepping the necessity of a separate derivation of the link between the output gap and inflation.
- This book places a **heavy emphasis on globalisation**, starting with an analysis of its effects on real wage inequality and progressing to such issues as the benefits of trade, the causes and effects of protectionism, the role of capital flows in domestic capital formation, the link between exchange rates and monetary policy, and the sources of speculative attacks on currencies.

THE CHALLENGE

The world is a more competitive place now than it was when we started teaching in the 1970s. In arena after arena, business as usual is no longer good enough. Football players used to drink beer and go fishing during the off season, but they now lift weights and ride exercise bicycles. Academics at the start of their careers used to take life easy or make DIY repairs to their houses at weekends, but the current crop can now be found most weekends at their computers. The competition for student attention has grown similarly more intense. There are many tempting courses in the typical college curriculum and even more tempting diversions outside the classroom. Students are freer than ever to pick and choose.

Yet many academic economists seem to operate under the illusion that most students arrive at college with a burning desire to become economics majors. And many of us do not yet seem to have recognised that students' cognitive abilities and powers of concentration are scarce resources. To hold our ground, we must become not only more selective in what we teach, but also more effective as advocates for our discipline. We must persuade students that we offer something of value. A well-conceived and well-executed introductory course in economics can teach our students more about society and human behaviour in a single term than virtually any other course in the university. This course can and should be an intellectual adventure of the first order. Not all students who take the kind of course we envisioned when writing this book will go on to become economics majors, of course. But many will, and even those who do not will leave with a sense of admiration for the power of economic ideas.

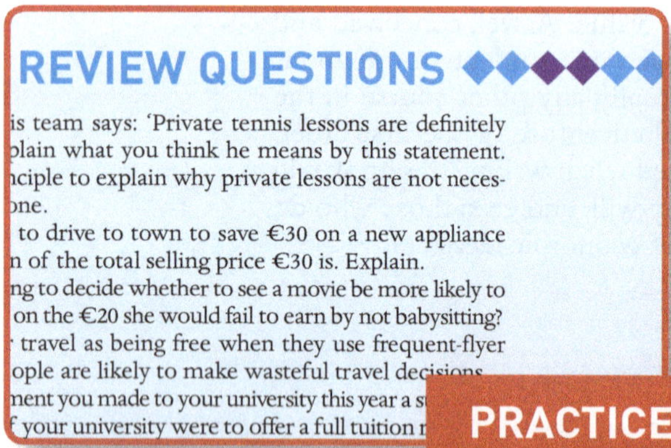

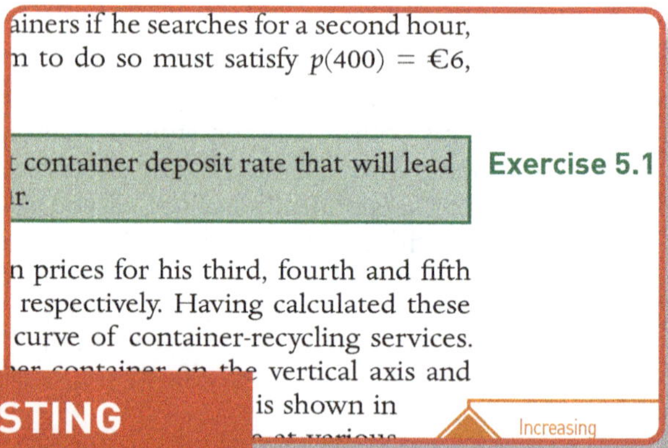

PRACTICE & TESTING

Exercises feature throughout the chapters, to enable you to practise the techniques you have been taught and apply the methodology to real-world situations. Each chapter ends with a set of **Review questions** and **Problems**, ranging in difficulty to consolidate learning. These questions are all integrated into Connect, through which your lecturer can set homework assignments. A **Self-Quiz and Study** tool is also available on Connect. This provides questions to assess your knowledge and then recommends specific readings, supplementary materials and additional practice work.

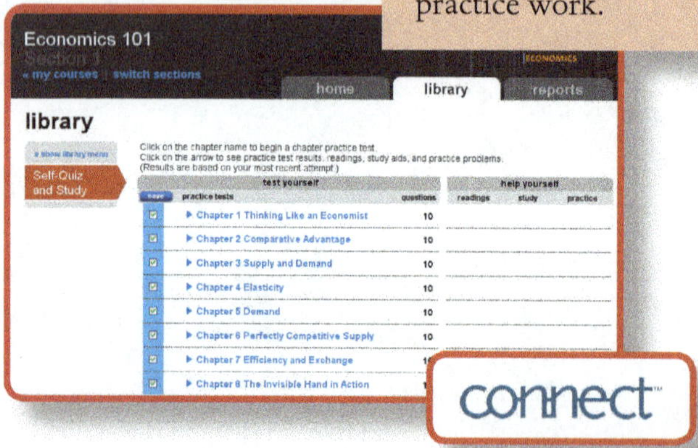

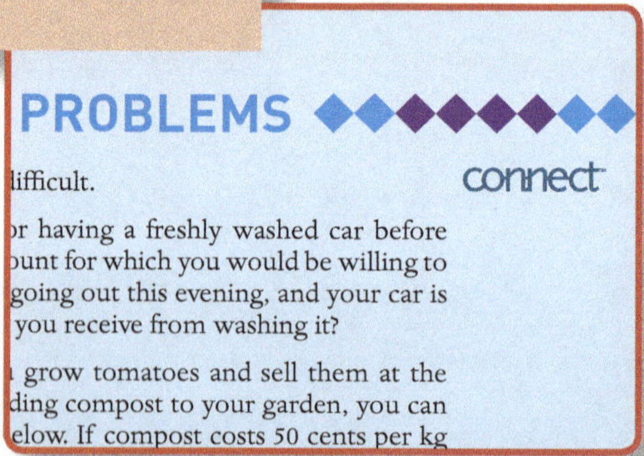

Economic Naturalist 1.1
Adobe supplies its Acrobat Reader soft
internet. Why is this?

And not only Acrobat Reader: you can also downloac
wants to make profits, but gives away its products free
Adobe or equivalent products. In the case of the Rea
extension) created with Adobe Writer. Most users hav
do so it for a variety of reasons to do with security
it . . . but they also require that th
As with a telephone, it's of little u
sell the Writer programme profit

Example 4.5 Should Eric consume more

Eric gets a total of 1,000 utils
400 utils per week from his co
price of oranges is €1 each,
True or false: Eric should con

Eric spends €100 per week
utils/week)/(€100/week) = 1
utils/week)/(€50/week) = 8
might be tempted to respond
higher than for oranges, he sh

APPLICATION

Each chapter cements your understanding of economic theory by showing you how it operates in practice. **Examples** discuss theory in practical contexts. **Economic Naturalist boxes** apply economic perspectives to real-world situations, encouraging you to 'think like an economist'. You will find further Economic Naturalists on the supporting website. Connect also provides helpful tools to relate what is learnt in the book to real life. The prisoner's dilemma (below) explains all about this classic game in one of the many **videos** available.

connect

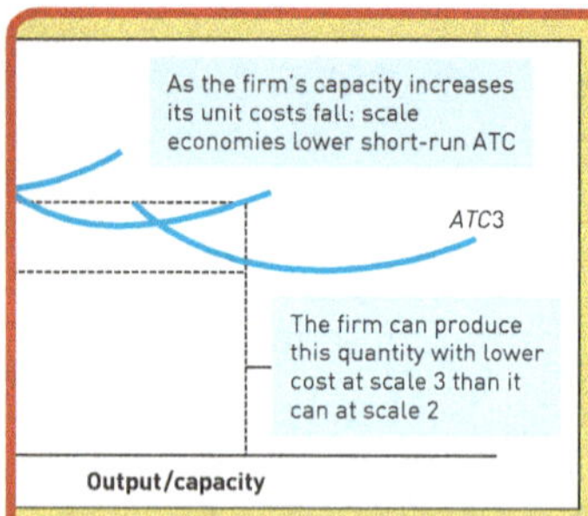

Figure 5.5 Long-run Average Cost and Scale Economies

The glass bottle company's ATC with one, two and three production lines: if it produces the quantity indicated with two production lines it is experiencing diminishing returns at scale 2. But if it can expand to three lines its unit costs will fall. It is taking advantage of scale economies and the diminishing returns problem at scale 2 have been avoided.

…, a firm may be able to reduce its costs in the lo…
…he short run diminishing returns cause the firm's…

…hich starts on page 158.) The other way in which a … is by changing the technology of production. To … **production function**, which … it uses. The glass bottle firm's … two factors of production, …ss its energy and silica inputs …hen depends on its usage of …e represented as a function of

production function the technical relation between inputs in a production process and the outputs it produces

$$Q = f(K, L)$$

…pital and labour employed in the firm to produce …m can smoothly substitute capital for labour or …u change the proportions

AIDING UNDERSTANDING

Each chapter offers extensive pedagogy to aid your understanding of the topics being taught. This includes **Learning objectives** and **Key terms** to outline your aims and clarify essential ideas, and detailed **Figures** and **Tables** to help you visualise economic models and important concepts. **Summaries** and **Recaps** link what you have learned in previous sections to new material and reinforce the topics discussed in each chapter to ensure you have acquired a solid understanding. **Maths boxes** are strategically placed, allowing you to dip in and out of more advanced maths content as you wish.

Maths Box 5.1
Why a marginal cost curve must cut … a mathematical proof

Recall that average cost is total cost divided by the …

$$AC = T…$$

where Q is the number of units being produced.

Now consider the slope of average cost, dAC/dQ … appendix to Chapter 1 we have

SUMMARY

- Economics is the study of … and of the results of th… behaviour begins with the … defined goals and try to a… goals, people normally fac… limited, having more of o… good thing.
- Our focus in this chapter … alternative courses of acti…

RECAP

Applying the rational spending rule

Application of the rational spending rule highlight… in explaining differences in consumption pattern… and across time. The rule also highlights the fact… income are what matter. The demand for a good f… the real price of a complement rises.

Online Resources

Please visit **www.mheducation.co.uk/textbooks/mcdowell3** today.

ONLINE LEARNING CENTRE (OLC)

After completing each chapter, log on to the supporting Online Learning Centre website. Take advantage of the study tools offered to reinforce the material you have read in the text, and to develop your knowledge of economics in a fun and effective way.

Resources for students include:

- Multiple-choice quizzes
- Graphing tool
- In-chapter solutions
- Glossary

Also available for lecturers:

- Lecture outlines
- Solutions to questions
- Naturalist exercises
- Artwork
- Testbank
- PowerPoint slides
- UK data section

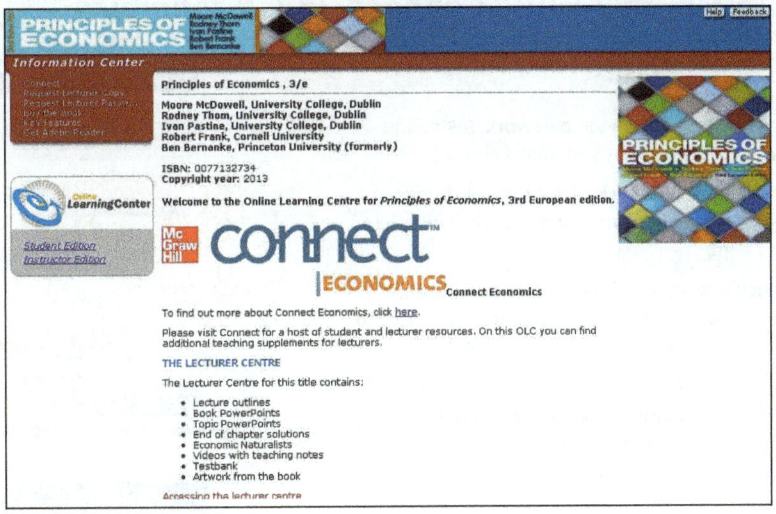

TEST BANK AVAILABLE IN MCGRAW-HILL EZ TEST ONLINE

A test bank of over 1800 questions is available to lecturers adopting this book for their module. A range of questions is provided for each chapter including multiple choice, true or false, and short answer or essay questions. The questions are identified by type, difficulty and topic to help you to select questions that best suit your needs and are accessible through an easy-to-use online testing tool, **McGraw-Hill EZ Test Online**.

McGraw-Hill EZ Test Online is accessible to busy academics virtually anywhere – in their office, at home or while travelling – and eliminates the need for software installation. Lecturers can choose from question banks associated with their adopted textbook or easily create their own questions. They also have access to hundreds of banks and thousands of questions created for other McGraw-Hill titles. Multiple versions of tests can be saved for delivery on paper or online through WebCT, Blackboard and other course management systems. When created and delivered though EZ Test Online, students' tests can be immediately marked, saving lecturers time and providing prompt results to students. To register for this FREE resource, visit **www.eztestonline.com**.

Less managing. More teaching. Greater learning.

INSTRUCTORS...

Would you like your **students** to show up for class **more prepared**? *(Let's face it, class is much more fun if everyone is engaged and prepared...)*

Want an **easy way to assign** homework online and track student **progress**? *(Less time grading means more time teaching...)*

Want an **instant view** of student or class performance? *(No more wondering if students understand...)*

Need to **collect data and generate reports** required for administration or accreditation? *(Say goodbye to manually tracking student learning outcomes...)*

Want to **record and post your lectures** for students to view online?

With McGraw-Hill's *Connect*™ *Plus Economics*,

INSTRUCTORS GET:

- Simple **assignment management**, allowing you to spend more time teaching.
- **Auto-graded** assignments, quizzes and tests.
- **Detailed Visual Reporting** where student and section results can be viewed and analysed.
- Sophisticated **online testing** capability.
- A **filtering and reporting** function that allows you to easily assign and report on materials that are correlated to accreditation standards, learning outcomes, and Bloom's taxonomy.
- An easy-to-use **lecture capture** tool.
- The option to **upload course documents** for student access.

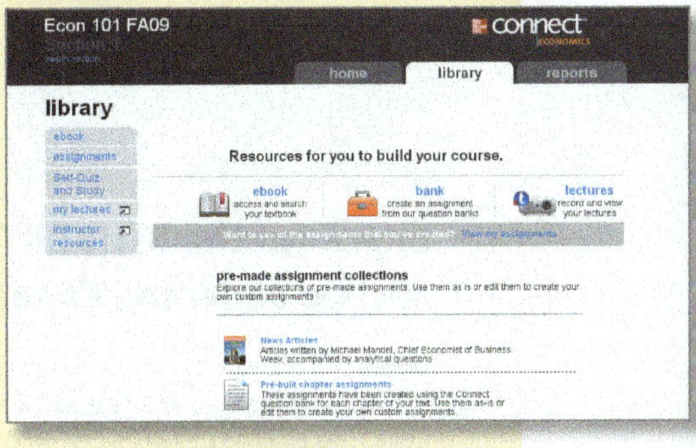

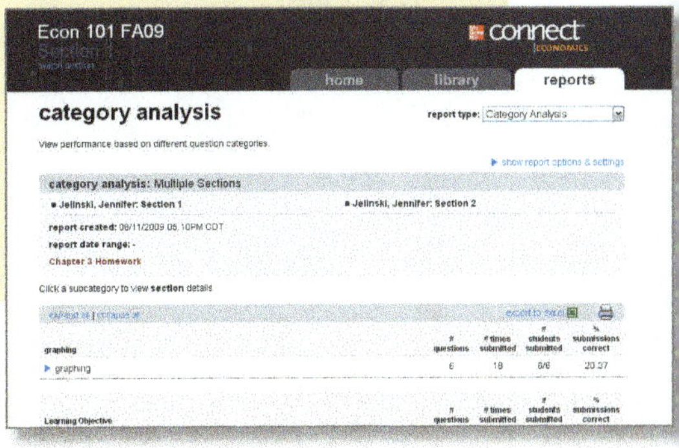

Q: Want an online, **searchable version** of your textbook?

Wish your textbook could be **available online** while you're doing your assignments?

A: *Connect™ Plus Economics* eBook

If you choose to use *Connect™ Plus Economics*, you have an affordable and searchable online version of your book integrated with your other online tools.

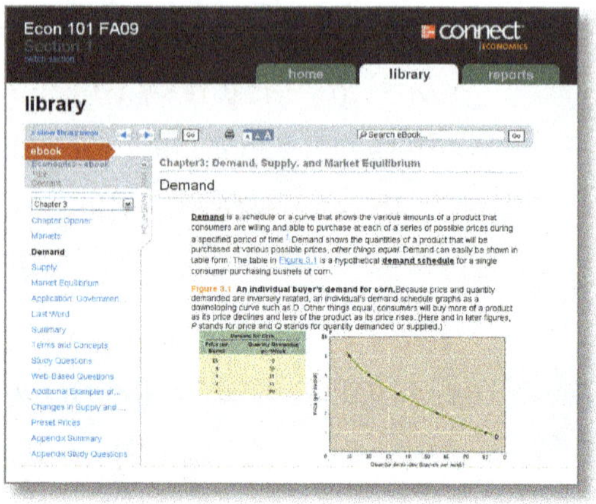

Connect™ Plus Economics eBook offers features like:

- Topic search
- Direct links from assignments
- Adjustable text size
- Jump to page number
- Print by section

Q: Want to get more **value** from your textbook purchase?

Think learning economics should be a bit more **interesting**?

A: Check out the STUDENT RESOURCES section under the *Connect™* Library tab.

Here you'll find a wealth of resources designed to help you achieve your goals in the course. Every student has different needs, so explore the STUDENT RESOURCES to find the materials best suited to you.

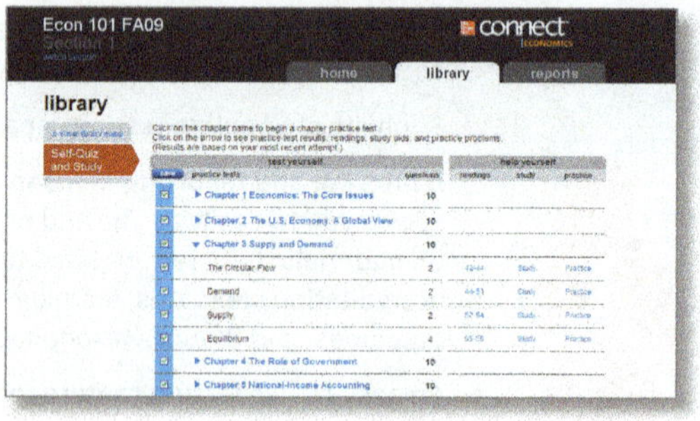

Acknowledgements

PUBLISHER'S ACKNOWLEDGEMENTS

Our thanks go to the following reviewers for their comments at various stages in the text's development:

Maher Asal, University West
Anna Mikaela Backman, Jönköping International Business School
Tiziana Brancaccio, University College Dublin
John Cullinan, University of Limerick
Kevin Denny, University College Dublin
Alex Dickson, University of Strathclyde
Vasco Gabriel, University of Surrey
Chunxia Jiang, Middlesex University Business School
Kari Kristinsson, Iceland University
Paola Manzini, University of St Andrews
Matthew Olczak, Aston University
Philipp Reiss, Maastricht University
John Sheehan, University College Dublin
Yontem Sonmez, University of Central Lancashire
Alan Sutherland, University of St Andrews

We would also like to thank the following people for their comments at various stages of developing the previous edition:

Javad Amid, Uppsala University
Ali Ataullah, Loughborough University
Maria Brouwer, Amsterdam School of Economics
Graham Cookson, King's College London
Rob Gillanders, University College Dublin
Keith Gray, Coventry University
Robert Hamilton, Loughborough University
Anthony Heyes, Royal Holloway, University of London
Richard Ledward, Staffordshire University
Oliver Marnet, Aberystwyth University
Johanna Palmberg, Jönköping International Business School
Keith Pilbeam, City University London
Odile Poulsen, University of East Anglia
Philip Reiss, Maastricht University
Gerard Turley, National University of Ireland, Galway
Cornelis Van Walbeek, University of Cape Town
Perihan Yavash, Coventry University

We would also like to thank all those who contributed to the development of the first edition, and those who offered their feedback in the form of survey responses, as this feedback has also been very useful to us in the development of this new edition.

AUTHORS' ACKNOWLEDGEMENTS

We must also gratefully acknowledge the help we have received from several colleagues in UCD. John Sheehan and Kevin Denny have used the earlier editions in giving micro principles courses, and Frank Walsh has used them for macro principles and all have assisted us with comments and suggestions. We are deeply indebted to Sarah Parlane for her careful reviewing and amendment of some of the proposed new material in the third edition. Brendan Walsh and David Madden have supplied a steady stream of suggestions and comments on proposed economic naturalists, always witty, sometimes constructive. And Cormac Ó Gráda kept us straight on Giffen Goods.

Over the last few years, in dealing with this and previous editions, we have been ably, cheerfully, and forgivingly supported by some very professional and pleasant people at McGraw-Hill. In recent times those most closely involved have been Kiera Jamison, Natalie Jacobs and Hannah Cooper. We are greatly indebted to them for help and for keeping our noses to the grindstone without too much pain. In the past, Emily Jefferson, Caroline Prodger and Mark Kavanagh gave us great support. To all of these, our sincere thanks.

Every effort has been made to trace and acknowledge ownership of copyright and to clear permission for material reproduced in this book. The publishers will be pleased to make suitable arrangements to clear permission with any copyright holders whom it has not been possible to contact.

Part 1

Introduction

Economics differs from many other fields of study in that it is not a collection of settled facts, to be copied down and memorised. Mark Twain said that nothing is older than yesterday's newspaper, and the same can be said of yesterday's economic statistics.

If economics is not a set of durable facts, then what is it? Fundamentally, it is a way of *thinking about the world*. Over many years economists have developed some simple but widely applicable principles that help us to understand almost any economic situation (and a multitude of situations that at first sight might not appear to be concerned with economics), from the relatively simple ones such as economic decisions that individuals make every day to the workings of highly complex markets, such as international financial markets. The principal objective of this book is to help you learn these principles and how to apply them to a variety of economic questions and issues.

The three chapters of Part 1 lay out the basic economic principles that will be used throughout the book. Chapter 1 introduces the notion of scarcity – the unavoidable fact that, although our needs and wants are boundless, the resources available to satisfy them are limited. The chapter goes on to show that decisions about actions based on comparing the costs and benefits of those actions is a useful in dealing with the inevitable trade-offs that scarcity creates. Chapter 1 then discusses several important decision pitfalls and concludes by introducing the concept of *economic naturalism*. Chapter 2 goes beyond individual decision making to consider trade, among both individuals and countries. Trade permits people (or countries) to specialise in the production of particular goods and services, which in turn enhances productivity and raises standards of living. Finally, Chapter 3, a long chapter, looks at how markets work. It presents an overview of the concepts of supply and demand, perhaps the most basic and familiar tools used by economists. It also looks at one of the core concepts in economics, elasticity, the proportionate response of a dependent variable to a change in an independent or causative variable, and how this is measured.

Chapter 1 Thinking Like an Economist

A witty saying proves nothing. — *Voltaire*

Learning Objectives

After studying this chapter you should be able to:

1. Explain the concepts of scarcity and choice, the cost–benefit principle and the importance of incentives;
2. Assess and identify properly costs and benefits;
3. Understand the concept of economic rationality;
4. Understand why what happens 'at the margin' is important;
5. Distinguish between positive and normative statements in economics.

A health warning: thinking (and then speaking) like an economist can make you very unpopular. Partly this is because economists seem to take a lot of pleasure in puncturing other people's balloons (that is, demonstrating that what their victims hold to be self-evident is far from being true). More importantly, economics as a discipline teaches you to think about problems, and solutions to problems, in a way that others find challenging to their way of thinking.

Consider the following policy issue. It is taken as almost an article of faith by teaching professionals that smaller classes are better, in terms of educational outcomes, particularly at the primary (elementary) level. Children, it is said, do better, controlling for other factors, if they are taught in smaller classes. The result is consistent pressure on governments in many countries to spend more to enable class sizes to be reduced.

Most people, parents included, would agree with the class size proposition, and not just because teachers continually argue along these lines. Everyday experience supports the concept of better classroom experience and consequent educational outcomes being linked to smaller class sizes.

An economist considering this issue would be likely to ask some hard questions. The first would be 'What evidence exists to support the proposition that reducing class sizes, all other things being equal, generally improves educational outcomes?' The economist would ask what accepted metric exists that permits objective evaluation of outcomes and comparison of results. If you can't objectively measure outcomes and make comparisons over time or across schools on a common basis, the proposition cannot be demonstrated to be correct. If the accepted metric demonstrates outcome differences statistically related to class size the economist would agree that there is support for the proposition. If not, the economist would be likely to point out that the pressure for smaller classes may reflect the fact that teachers may have a vested interest in pushing for smaller classes as a means of reducing the pressure of work.[1]

People, unfortunately, tend to respond to this in exactly the same way as most people did a few hundred years ago when informed that the Earth was not flat: common sense supported the flat Earth hypothesis. A common response is that it is plainly silly even to question the class size hypothesis. People do not like being told that their 'common sense' is incorrect.

The economist's approach is, first, based on confronting a hypothesis with evidence before conditionally accepting it. This, of course, is exactly what physicists, geologists, astronomers and cosmologists do. It is why economics can credibly seek to be regarded as a science.

Second, an economist will always look at motivation. The economist argues that people tend to behave in a self-interested fashion and respond to incentives. They will combine to press for changes that improve their economic welfare. They may even persuade themselves that what they are seeking is to everyone else's advantage. They are, however, unlikely to combine to press for changes that will reduce their economic welfare. Trades unions do not seek lower wages for their members if unemployment rises. But imputing self-interest to people who are making arguments based on hypotheses about the general good is certain to cause outrage.

Incentives Matter

There are, of course, exceptions to this. Individual altruism exists. Most people would accept that Mother Teresa of Calcutta sought primarily to improve the lot of the poor in Calcutta, not to become an international celebrity. People do combine to achieve ends that do not coincide with group self-interest. They may in some cases be spectacularly wrong-headed in the remedies they support (for example, urging motorists to switch to bio-fuels), but most environmentalists seeking to avert global warming are not doing so in order to earn a living.

Returning to the subject of class size, the next issue for economists would be the cost of reducing class sizes, and whether the cost incurred is warranted by the expected benefits. That, of course, may require putting some monetary value on levels of educational achievement. Unfortunately, where health and education are concerned, this approach tends to call forth Oscar Wilde's observation about knowing the price of everything and the value of nothing. But the economist's question is motivated by the fact that there is a social cost involved in putting more money into healthcare or education: the value of the things that can't be done as a consequence.

Finally, the economist is likely to suggest that we should stop reducing class sizes in any case well before further reductions have no effect on outcomes. The economist will talk about 'marginal', or 'incremental', costs, and 'marginal', or 'incremental', benefits. The economist will suggest that additional funding to reduce class sizes or to reduce road deaths or to improve the health status of the population should not continue beyond the point where marginal costs equal marginal benefits, even if total benefits could be increased. Try that out on a road safety lobbyist! An acceptable level of deaths on the roads?

Cost-Benefit Analysis

[1] Economists interested in this question have to depend on the research undertaken by educational experts – in particular, educational psychologists. They, too, have been active in questioning this conventional wisdom about reducing class sizes, following a similar research methodology. A highly readable survey of the issues and problems, which argues for very limited evidence of significant gains unless class sizes are reduced below 20, is Bennett, N., 'Annotation: Class Size and the Quality of Educational Outcomes', *Journal of Child Psychology and Psychiatry*, 36(6), 1998, pp. 797–804.

ECONOMICS: STUDYING CHOICE IN A WORLD OF SCARCITY

No matter how rich a country is and, for most of us, at any rate, as individuals no matter how rich we are, *scarcity* is a fundamental fact of life. There is never enough time, money or energy to do everything we want to do or have everything we would like to have. Scarcity simply means we must choose, and sometimes make hard choices. **Economics** is the study of how people make choices under conditions of scarcity, and of the results of those choices for society.

economics the study of how people make choices under conditions of scarcity and of the results of those choices for society

A parent with a young child going into the educational system might definitely prefer schools with a class size of 20 rather than a class size of 30, everything else being equal. But suppose fees were payable, and that the fees in a small-class school were significantly higher than in a large-class size school. Income is limited. Therefore you must choose. If you choose small class sizes you will have to give up something as a result. Your choice will in the end come down to the relative importance of competing demands on that income. If you had a menu of schools with different class sizes to choose from, with fees reflecting class size, you could choose any one of them. In doing so you are trading off other things you might do with your income against perceived benefits from class size.

Scarcity

That such trade-offs are widespread and important is one of the core principles of economics. We call it the **Scarcity Principle**, because the simple fact of scarcity makes trade-offs necessary. Another name for the scarcity principle is the **No-Free-Lunch Principle** (which comes from the observation that even lunches that are given to you are never really free – somebody, somehow, always has to pay for them).

Scarcity Principle (also called the **No-Free-Lunch Principle**) although we have boundless needs and wants, the resources available to us are limited, so having more of one good thing usually means having less of another; hence the cliché, 'There ain't no such thing as a free lunch', sometimes reduced to the acronym TANSTAAFL

Cost–Benefit Principle an individual (or a firm, or a society) should take an action if, and only if, the extra benefits from taking that action are at least as great as the extra costs

Inherent in the idea of a trade-off is the fact that choice involves compromise between competing interests. Economists resolve such trade-offs by using *cost–benefit analysis*, which is based on the disarmingly simple principle that an action should be taken if, and only if, its benefits exceed its costs. We call this statement the **Cost–Benefit Principle**, and it, too, is one of the core principles of economics.

With the Cost–Benefit Principle in mind, let us think about our class-size question again. Imagine that classrooms come in only two sizes – 40-seat lecture rooms and 20-seat seminar rooms – and that your university currently offers introductory economics courses to classes of 40 students.

Question: Should administrators reduce the class size to 20 students?

Answer: Reduce if, and only if, the value of the improvement in instruction outweighs its additional cost.

This rule sounds simple, but to apply it we need some way to *measure* the relevant costs and benefits – a task that is often difficult in practice. If we make a few simplifying assumptions, however, we can see how the analysis might work. On the cost side, the primary expense of reducing class size from 40 to 20 is that we will now need two teachers instead of one. We'll also need two smaller classrooms rather than a single big one, and this too may add slightly to the expense of the move. For the sake of discussion, suppose that the cost with a class size of 20 turns out to be €1,000 per student more than the cost per student when the class size is 40. Should administrators switch to the smaller class size? If they apply the cost–benefit principle, they will realise that the reduction in class size makes sense only if the *value of attending the smaller class is at least €1,000 per student greater than the value of attending the larger class.*

Would you (or your family) be willing to pay an extra €1,000 for a smaller economics class? If not, and if other students feel the same way, then sticking with the larger class size makes sense. But if you and others would be willing to pay the extra tuition fees, then reducing the class size to 20 makes good economic sense.

Notice that the 'best' class size, from an economics point of view, will generally not be the same as the 'best' size from the point of view of an educational psychologist. The difference arises because the economics definition of 'best' takes into account both the benefits *and* the costs of different class sizes. The psychologist ignores costs and looks only at the learning benefits of different class sizes.

In practice, of course, different people will feel differently about the value of smaller classes. People with high incomes, for example, tend to be willing to pay more for the advantage, which helps to explain why average class size is smaller, and tuition fees higher, at private schools whose students come predominantly from high-income families.

Scarcity and the trade-offs that result also apply to resources other than money. Bill Gates is one of the richest men on Earth. He has enough money to buy more houses, cars and other goods than he could possibly use. Yet Gates, like the rest of us, has only 24 hours in his day and a limited amount of energy. So even he confronts trade-offs, in that any activity he pursues – whether it be building his business empire or redecorating his mansion – uses up time and energy that he could otherwise spend on other things.

APPLYING THE COST–BENEFIT PRINCIPLE

rational person someone with well-defined goals, who fulfils those goals as best she can

In studying choice under scarcity, we shall usually begin with the premise that people are **rational**, meaning they have well-defined goals and try to fulfil them as best they can. The Cost–Benefit Principle illustrated in our class-size example is a fundamental tool for the study of how rational people make choices.

Often the only real difficulty in applying the cost–benefit rule is to come up with reasonable measures of the relevant benefits and costs. Only in rare instances will exact money measures be conveniently available. But the cost–benefit framework can lend structure to your thinking even when no relevant market data are available.

To illustrate how we proceed in such cases, the following example asks you to decide whether to perform an action whose cost is described only in vague, qualitative terms.

Example 1.1 Should you walk to the centre of town to save €10 on a €25 computer game?

Imagine you are about to buy a €25 computer game at the nearby college book shop when a friend tells you that the same game is on sale at a city-centre store for only €15. If the store in question is a 30-minute walk away, where should you buy the game?

The Cost–Benefit Principle tells us that you should buy it from the store in the city centre if the benefit of doing so exceeds the cost. Here, the benefit of buying elsewhere is exactly €10, since that is the amount you will save on the purchase price of the game. The cost of buying in the city centre is the money value you assign to the time and trouble it takes to make the trip. But how do we estimate that money value?

Imagine that a stranger has offered to pay you to do an errand that involves the same walk to the centre of town (perhaps to drop off a letter for her at the post office). If she offered you a payment of, say, €1,000, would you accept? If so, we know that your cost of walking to the centre of town and back must be less than €1,000. Now imagine her offer being reduced in small increments until you finally refuse the last offer. For example, if you would agree to walk there and back for €9.00 but not for €8.99, then your cost of making the trip is €9.00. In this case, you should buy the game in the town centre, because the €10 you'll save (your benefit) is greater than your €9.00 cost of making the trip.

But suppose, alternatively, that your cost of making the trip had been greater than €10. In that case, your best bet would have been to buy the game from the nearby college book shop. Confronted with this choice, different people may choose differently, depending on how costly they think it is to make the trip into town. But although there is no uniquely correct choice, many people who are asked what they would do in this situation say they would buy the game from the city-centre store.

ECONOMIC SURPLUS

Suppose again that in Example 1.1 your 'cost' of making the trip to the city centre was €9. Compared with the alternative of buying the game at the college store, buying it elsewhere resulted in an **economic surplus** of €1, the difference between the benefit of making the trip and its cost. In general, your goal as an economic decision maker is to choose those actions that generate the largest possible economic surplus. This means taking all actions that yield a positive total economic surplus, which is just another way of restating the Cost–Benefit Principle.

economic surplus the economic surplus from taking any action is the benefit of taking that action minus its cost

The fact that your best choice was to buy the game in the city doesn't imply that you *enjoy* making the trip. It simply means that the trip to town is less unpleasant than the prospect of paying €10 extra for the game. Once again, you've faced a trade-off – in this case, the choice between a cheaper game and the free time gained by avoiding the trip.

OPPORTUNITY COST

Suppose now that the time required for the trip is the only time you have left to study for a difficult test the next day. In such a case, we say that the **opportunity cost** of making the trip – that is, the value of what you must sacrifice to walk to the city centre and back – is high, and you are more likely to decide against making the trip.

opportunity cost the opportunity cost of an activity is the value of the next best alternative that must be forgone in order to undertake the activity

If watching a movie on TV, the movie is the most valuable opportunity that conflicts with the trip to the city centre, the opportunity cost of making the trip is the money value you place on watching the movie – that is, the largest amount you'd be willing to pay to avoid missing it. Note that the opportunity cost of making the trip is not the combined value of *all* possible activities you could have pursued, but only the value of your *best* alternative – the one you would have chosen had you not made the trip.

Increasing Opportunity Cost

Throughout the text we will pose exercises like Exercise 1.1. You will find that pausing to answer them will help you to master key concepts in economics. Because doing these exercises isn't very costly (indeed, many students report that they are actually fun), the Cost–Benefit Principle indicates that it's well worth your while to do them.

Exercise 1.1

You would again save €10 by buying the game in the city rather than at the college store, but your cost of making the trip is now €12, not €9. How much economic surplus would you get from buying the game in the city? Where should you buy it?

THE ROLE OF ECONOMIC MODELS

Non-economists sometimes attack the economist's cost–benefit model on the grounds that people in the real world never conduct complicated mental comparisons between costs and benefits of hypothetical options until a winner emerges before deciding whether to make trips to town. But this criticism betrays a fundamental misunderstanding of how abstract models can help to explain and predict human behaviour. Economists know perfectly well that people don't conduct hypothetical mental 'auctions' between options when they make simple decisions. All the Cost–Benefit Principle really says is that a rational decision is one that is explicitly or implicitly based on a *weighing of costs and benefits*.

Most of us make sensible decisions most of the time, without being consciously aware that we are weighing costs and benefits, just as most people ride a bike without being consciously aware of what keeps them from falling off. Through trial and error, we gradually learn what kinds of choices tend to work best in different contexts, just as bicycle riders internalise the relevant laws of physics, usually without being conscious of them.

The Cost–Benefit Principle is an abstract model of how an idealised rational individual would choose among competing alternatives. (By 'abstract model' we mean a simplified description that captures the essential elements of a situation and allows us to analyse them in a logical way.) A computer model of a complex phenomenon such as climate change, which must ignore many details and include only the major forces at work, is an example of an abstract model.

A model is to an economist in many ways what a laboratory experiment is to a physical scientist. Supposing you climbed the Leaning Tower of Pisa to test Newton's theory of gravity by dropping a feather and a kilogram of lead, you would observe that the lead fell faster and hit the ground first, and might conclude that gravity affects metals to a greater degree than it does organic material. A physicist would demonstrate that this is not the case by creating a vacuum and repeating the experiment. We live in a real world where air pressure and resistance affect how objects fall. We create a simplified world to test the gravity hypothesis by removing the pressure and resistance effects. Would you agree with someone who said that there is little value in talking about the workings of gravity because in the real world we don't live in a vacuum?

RECAP

Cost–benefit analysis

Scarcity is a basic fact of economic life. Having more of one good thing almost always means having less of another (the Scarcity Principle). The Cost–Benefit Principle holds that an individual (or a firm, or a society) should take an action if, and only if, the extra benefit from taking the action is at least as great as the extra cost. The benefit of taking any action minus the cost of taking the action is called the *economic surplus* from that action. Hence the Cost–Benefit Principle suggests that we take only those actions that create additional economic surplus.

FOUR IMPORTANT DECISION PITFALLS[2]

Knowing that rational people tend to compare costs and benefits enables economists to predict the likely behaviour of people in the aggregate. However, there are some pitfalls of which you need to be aware in analysing how rational choices are made. People who think they are behaving rationally sometimes get it wrong. People are not born with an infallible instinct for weighing the relevant costs and benefits of many daily decisions. Indeed, one of the rewards of studying economics is that it can improve the quality of your decisions.

[2] The examples in this section reflect the work of Daniel Kahneman and the late Amos Tversky. Kahneman was awarded the 2003 Nobel Prize in Economics for his efforts to integrate insights from psychology into economics.

PITFALL 1: MEASURING COSTS AND BENEFITS AS PROPORTIONS RATHER THAN ABSOLUTE MONEY AMOUNTS

Should you walk 3 km to save €10 on a €1,000 laptop?

Example 1.2

You are about to buy a €1,000 laptop computer at the nearby college store when you are told that the same computer is on sale at a city-centre store for only €990. If the latter is half an hour's walk away, where should you buy the computer?

Assuming that the laptop is light enough to carry without effort, the structure of this example is exactly the same as that of Example 1.1 – the only difference being that the price of the laptop is dramatically higher than the price of the computer game. If you were prepared to walk into town to save €10 on a computer game, logically you should walk into town to buy the computer. But would you? When real people are asked what they would do in these situations, most say they would walk to town to buy the game but would buy the laptop at the college store. When asked to explain, most of them say something like: 'The trip was worth it for the game because you save 40 per cent, but not worth it for the laptop because you save only €10 out of €1,000, or 1 per cent.'

From a standard economics perspective this is faulty reasoning. The benefit of the trip to town is not the *proportion* you save on the original price. Rather, it is the *absolute money amount* you save. Since the cost and benefit of walking to the city to buy the laptop is exactly the same as for the computer game, the economic surplus from making both trips must be exactly the same. And this means that a rational decision maker would make the same decision in both cases. Yet, as noted, most people choose differently.

Exercise 1.2

Which is more valuable, saving £100 on a £2,000 plane ticket from London to Tokyo or saving £90 on a £200 plane ticket from London to Paris?

PITFALL 2: IGNORING OPPORTUNITY COSTS

In the story, *Silver Blaze*, Sherlock Holmes, Arthur Conan Doyle's legendary detective, is called on to investigate the theft of an expensive racehorse from its stable. A Scotland Yard inspector assigned to the case asks Holmes whether some particular aspect of the crime requires further study. 'Yes,' Holmes replies, and describes 'the curious incident of the dog in the night-time'. 'The dog did nothing in the night-time,' responds the puzzled inspector. Holmes realised that this was precisely the problem. It indicated that, when Silver Blaze was stolen, the watchdog knew the thief.

Like the Scotland Yard policeman, many of us tend to overlook the implicit value of activities that fail to happen. As discussed earlier, however, intelligent decisions require taking the value of *forgone opportunities* properly into account.

The opportunity cost of an activity, once again, is the value of the best alternative that must be forgone in order to engage in that activity. If buying a computer game in the town means not watching a movie, then the value to you of watching that movie is an opportunity cost of the trip. Many people make bad decisions because they tend to ignore the value of such forgone opportunities. To avoid overlooking opportunity costs, economists often translate questions like 'Should I walk to the pub?' into ones like 'Should I walk to the pub or watch the end of the movie on TV?'

How should you use your father's frequent-flyer points?

Example 1.3

As you contemplate what to do next summer you think about going to the United States, where you hope to work and make next year's pocket money. You expect to make €600 after all costs in the United States. The round-trip airfare to New York is €800. Your father tells you that he has accumulated sufficient frequent-flyer points to buy you the return ticket. However, you now hear that your sister is to be married in Nairobi in at the end of the summer. Your attendance is non-negotiable. The cost of a package return ticket to Nairobi and accommodation is €700. You could use the points instead to cover the cost of the Nairobi trip. Which should you use the points for? The Cost–Benefit Principle tells us that you should go to New York if the benefits of the trip exceed its costs. If it were not for the complication of the frequent-flyer points, solving this problem would be a straightforward matter of comparing your benefit from the summer in the United States with all the relevant costs. And since your airfare exceeds the net amount you expect to earn you would not go to New York.

But what about the possibility of using your frequent-flyer coupon to make the trip? Using it for that purpose might make the flight to New York seem free, suggesting you would reap an economic surplus of €600 by making the trip. But doing so would also mean you would have to pay €700 for your airfare and accommodation costs for Nairobi. So the opportunity cost of using your coupon to go to New York is really €700. If you use the points to go to New York, the trip still ends up being a loser, because the cost, €700, exceeds the benefit by €100.

We cannot emphasise strongly enough that the key to using the concept of opportunity cost correctly lies in recognising precisely what taking a given action *prevents us from doing*. Exercise 1.3 illustrates this point by modifying the details of Example 1.3 slightly.

Exercise 1.3 The same as Example 1.3, except that now the frequent-flyer coupon expires before the date for the wedding, so your only chance to use it will be for the New York trip. Should you use your coupon?

PITFALL 3: FAILURE TO IGNORE SUNK COSTS

In another common pitfall people are influenced by costs they ought to ignore. The only costs that should influence a decision about whether to take an action are those that we can *avoid by not taking the action*. As a practical matter, however, many decision makers appear to be influenced by **sunk costs** – costs that are beyond recovery at the moment a decision is made. For example, money spent on a non-transferable, non-refundable airline ticket is a sunk cost.

sunk cost a cost that is beyond recovery at the moment a decision must be made

Because sunk costs must be borne *whether or not an action is taken*, they are irrelevant to the decision of whether to take the action. The sunk cost pitfall (the mistake of being influenced by sunk costs) is illustrated clearly in Example 1.4.

Example 1.4 How much should you eat at an all-you-can-eat restaurant?

The Rajput, an Indian restaurant in Berlin, offers an all-you-can-eat lunch buffet for €15. Customers pay €15 at the door, and no matter how many times they refill their plates, there is no additional charge. One day, as a goodwill gesture, the owner of the restaurant tells 20 randomly selected guests that their lunch is on the house. The remaining guests pay the usual price. If all diners are rational, will there be any difference in the average quantity of food consumed by people in these two groups?

Having eaten their first helping, diners in each group confront the following question: 'Should I go back for another helping?' For rational diners, if the benefit of doing so exceeds the cost, the answer is yes; otherwise it is no. Note that at the moment of decision about a second helping, the €15 charge for the lunch is a sunk cost. Those who paid it have no way to recover it. Thus, for both groups, the (extra) cost of another helping is exactly zero. And since the people who received the free lunch were chosen at random, there is no reason to suppose that their appetites or incomes are different from those of other diners. The benefit of another helping thus should be the same, on average, for people in both groups. And since their respective costs and benefits of an additional helping are the same, the two groups should eat the same number of helpings, on average.

Psychologists and economists have experimental evidence, however, that people in such groups do not eat similar amounts.[3] In particular, those who have had to pay tend to eat substantially more than those who eat for free. People who have to pay seem somehow determined to 'get their money's worth', implicitly to minimising the average cost per mouthful, hardly very intelligent. Would you take your car out for a long drive on a motorway just to lower your average fuel consumption per 100 km?

The fact that the cost–benefit criterion failed the test of prediction in this example does nothing to invalidate its advice about what people *should* do. If you are letting sunk costs influence your decisions, you can do better by changing your behaviour.

PITFALL 4: FAILURE TO UNDERSTAND THE AVERAGE–MARGINAL DISTINCTION

In many situations, the issue is not whether to pursue the activity at all, but rather the *extent* to which it should be pursued. We can apply the Cost–Benefit Principle in such situations by repeatedly asking the question 'Should I increase the level at which I am currently pursuing the activity?'

In attempting to answer this question, the focus should always be on the benefit and cost of an *additional* unit of activity. To emphasise this focus, economists refer to the cost of an additional unit of activity as the **marginal cost** of the activity. Similarly, the benefit of an additional unit of the activity is the **marginal benefit** of the activity.

marginal cost the increase in total cost that results from carrying out one additional unit of an activity

marginal benefit the increase in total benefit that results from carrying out one additional unit of an activity

When the problem is to discover the proper level at which to pursue an activity, the cost–benefit rule is to keep increasing the level as long as the marginal benefit of the activity exceeds its marginal cost. As Example 1.5 illustrates, however, people often fail to apply this rule correctly.

Should the European Space Agency (ESA) expand the Ariane programme from four launches per year to five? — Example 1.5

Suppose it has been estimated by the economists working for the ESA that the gains from the programme are currently €12 billion per year (an average of €3 billion per launch) and that its costs are currently €10 billion per year (an average of €2.5 billion per launch). On the basis of these estimates, the ESA sends its chief economist to Brussels to persuade the Commission to provide increased EU funding to expand the launch vehicle programme. Should the Commission agree?

To discover whether expanding the programme makes economic sense, we must compare the marginal cost of a launch with its marginal benefit. The economists' estimates, however, tell us only the **average cost** and **average benefit** of the programme – which are, respectively, the total cost of the programme divided by the number of launches and the total benefit divided by the number of launches. Knowing the average benefit and average cost per launch for all satellites launched thus far is simply not useful for deciding whether to expand the programme. Of course, the average cost of the launches undertaken so far *might* be the same as the cost of adding another launch. But it might also be either higher or lower than the marginal cost of a launch. The same statement holds true regarding average and marginal benefits.

average cost the total cost of undertaking n units of an activity divided by n

average benefit the total benefit of undertaking n units of an activity divided by n

[3] See, for example, Thaler (1980).

Table 1.1 Total Cost and Satellite Launches

Number of launches (1)	Total cost (€ billion) (2)	Average cost (€ billion) (3)
0	0	0
1	2.0	2.0
2	4.25	2.125
3	6.75	2.25
4	10.0	2.50
5	15.0	3.0

Suppose, for the sake of discussion, that the benefit of an additional launch is in fact the same as the average benefit per launch thus far, €3 billion. Should the ESA add another launch? Not if the cost of adding the fifth launch would be more than €3 billion. And the fact that the average cost per launch is only €2.5 billion simply does not tell us anything about the marginal cost of the fifth launch.

Suppose, for example, that the relationship between the number of satellites launched and the total cost of the programme is as described in Table 1.1. The average cost per launch (column (3)) when there are four launches would then be €10 billion/4 = €2.5 billion per launch. But note that, in column (2) of Table 1.1, adding a fifth launch would raise costs from €10 billion to €15 billion, making the marginal cost of the fifth launch €5 billion. So if the benefit of an additional launch is €3 billion, increasing the number of launches from four to five would make absolutely no economic sense.

Example 1.6 illustrates how to apply the Cost–Benefit Principle correctly in this case.

Example 1.6 How many space vehicles should the ESA launch?

The ESA must decide how many vehicles to launch. The benefit of each launch is estimated to be €3 billion, and the total cost of the programme again depends on the number of launches, in the manner shown in Table 1.1. How many vehicles should be launched?

The ESA should continue to launch satellites as long as the marginal benefit of the programme exceeds its marginal cost. In Example 1.6, the marginal benefit is constant at €3 billion per launch, regardless of the number of launches. The ESA should thus keep launching as long as the marginal cost per launch is less than or equal to €3 billion (Table 1.2).

Applying the definition of marginal cost to the total cost entries in column (2) of Table 1.1 yields the marginal cost values in column (4) of Table 1.2. (Because marginal cost is the change in total cost that results when we change the number of launches by one, we place each marginal cost entry midway between the rows showing the corresponding total cost entries.) Thus, for example, the marginal cost of increasing the number of launches from one to two is €2.25 billion, the difference between the €4.25 billion total cost of two launches and the €2 billion total cost of one launch.

As we see from a comparison of the €3 billion marginal benefit per launch with the marginal cost entries in column (4) of Table 1.2, the first three launches satisfy the cost–benefit test, but the fourth and fifth launches do not. The ESA should thus launch three space satellites. The Commission should actually reduce its funding.

Exercise 1.4 If the marginal benefit of each launch had been not €3 billion but €4.5 billion, how many satellites should the ESA have launched?

Table 1.2 Marginal Cost and Satellite Launches

Number of launches (1)	Total cost (€ billion) (2)	Average cost (€ billion) (3)	Marginal cost (€ billion) (4)
0	0	0	
			2.0
1	2.0	2.0	
			2.25
2	4.25	2.125	
			2.5
3	6.75	2.25	
			3.25
4	10.0	2.5	
			5.0
5	15.0	3.0	

The cost–benefit framework emphasises that the only relevant costs and benefits in deciding whether to pursue an activity further are *marginal* costs and benefits – measures that correspond to the *increment* of activity under consideration. In many contexts, however, people seem more inclined to compare the *average* cost and benefit of the activity.

Examples 1.2–1.4 make the point that people *sometimes* choose irrationally. This, we stress, is not to suggest that people *generally* make irrational choices. On the contrary, most people appear to choose sensibly most of the time, especially when their decisions are important or familiar ones. Rational choice thus offers not only useful advice about making better decisions, but also a basis for predicting and explaining human behaviour.

RECAP

Four important decision pitfalls

1. **The pitfall of measuring costs or benefits proportionally** Many decision makers treat a change in cost or benefit as insignificant if it constitutes only a small proportion of the original amount. *Absolute money amounts*, not proportions, should be employed to measure costs and benefits.
2. **The pitfall of ignoring opportunity costs** When performing a cost–benefit analysis of an action, it is important to account for all relevant *opportunity costs*, defined as the values of the most highly valued alternatives that must be forgone in order to carry out the action. A resource (such as a frequent-flyer coupon) may have a high opportunity cost, even if you originally got it 'for free', if its best alternative use has high value. The identical resource may have a low opportunity cost, however, if it has no good alternative uses.
3. **The pitfall of not ignoring sunk costs** When deciding whether to perform an action, it is important to ignore *sunk costs* – those costs that cannot be avoided even if the action is not taken. Even though a ticket to a concert may have cost you €100, if you have already bought it and cannot sell it to anyone else, the €100 is a sunk cost and should not influence your decision about whether to go to the concert.
4. **The pitfall of using average instead of marginal costs and benefits** Decision makers often have ready information about the total cost and benefit of an activity, and from this it is simple to compute the activity's average cost and benefit. A common mistake is to conclude that an activity should be increased if its average benefit exceeds its average cost. The Cost–Benefit Principle tells us that the level of an activity should be increased if, and only if, its *marginal* benefit exceeds its *marginal* cost.

Some costs and benefits, especially marginal costs and benefits and opportunity costs, are important for decision making, while others, such as sunk costs and average costs and benefits, are essentially irrelevant. This conclusion is implicit in our original statement of the Cost–Benefit Principle. Yet so important are the pitfalls of using proportions instead of absolute money amounts, of ignoring opportunity costs, of taking sunk costs into account, and of confusing average and marginal costs and benefits that we enumerate these pitfalls separately as one of the core ideas for repeated emphasis.

The *Not-All-Costs-and-Benefits-Matter-Equally Principle* is that some costs and benefits (for example, opportunity costs and marginal costs and benefits) matter in making decisions, whereas others (for example, sunk costs and average costs and benefits) don't.

ECONOMICS: MICRO AND MACRO

microeconomics the study of individual choice under scarcity, and its implications for the behaviour of prices and quantities in individual markets

macroeconomics the study of the performance of national economies and the policies that governments use to try to improve that performance

By convention, we use the term **microeconomics** to describe the study of individual choices and of group behaviour in individual markets. **Macroeconomics**, by contrast, is the study of the performance of national economies and of the policies that governments use to try to improve that performance. Macroeconomics tries to understand the determinants of such things as the national unemployment rate, the overall price level and the total value of national output.

Our focus in this chapter is on issues that face the individual decision maker, whether that individual confronts a personal decision, a family decision, a business decision, a government policy decision, or indeed any other type of decision. Further on, we shall consider economic models of groups of individuals, such as all buyers or all sellers in a specific market. Later still, we shall turn to broader economic issues and measures.

No matter which of these levels is our focus, however, our thinking will be shaped by the fact that although economic needs and wants are effectively unlimited, the material and human resources that can be used to satisfy them are finite. Clear thinking about economic problems must therefore always take into account the idea of *trade-offs* – the idea that having more of one good thing usually means having less of another. Our economy and our society are shaped to a substantial degree by the choices people have made when faced with such trade-offs.

THE APPROACH OF THIS TEXT

In planning an introductory economics course the scarcity principle applies just as strongly as elsewhere. Inevitably we have to select from a virtually inexhaustible set of topics and issues that might be covered in an introductory course, since we have only limited time in which to cover them. There is no free lunch: covering some topics inevitably means omitting others.

All textbook authors are necessarily forced to pick and choose. It is our firm view that many, perhaps most, introductory textbooks try to cover far too much. A relatively short list of the discipline's core ideas can explain a great deal of the behaviour and events we see in the world around us. So rather than cover a large number of ideas at a superficial level, our strategy is to focus on this short list of core ideas, returning to each entry again and again, in many different contexts. This strategy will enable you to internalise these ideas remarkably well in the brief span of a single course. The benefit of learning a small number of important ideas well will far outweigh the cost of having to ignore a host of other, less important ideas.[4]

So far, we've already encountered three core ideas: the Scarcity Principle, the Cost–Benefit Principle and the principle that not all costs and benefits matter equally. As these core ideas re-emerge in the course of our discussions, we shall call your attention to them. And shortly after a *new* core idea appears, we shall highlight it by formally restating it.

A second important element in the philosophy of this text is our belief in the importance of active learning. In the same way that you can learn Spanish only by speaking and writing it, or tennis only by playing the game, you can learn economics only by *doing* economics. And because we want you to learn how to do economics, rather than just to read or listen passively as the authors or your instructor does economics, we shall make every effort to encourage you to stay actively involved.

For example, instead of just telling you about an idea, we shall usually first motivate the idea by showing you how it works in the context of a specific example. Often, these examples will be followed by exercises for you to try, as well as applications that show the relevance of the idea to real life. Try working the exercises *before* looking at the answers.

Think critically about the applications: Do you see how they illustrate the point being made? Do they give you new insight into the issue? Work the problems at the end of the chapters, and take extra care with those relating to points that you do not fully understand. Apply economic principles to the world around you. (We shall say more about this when we discuss economic naturalism below.) Finally, when you come across an idea or example that you find interesting, tell a friend about it. You'll be surprised to discover how much the mere act of explaining it helps you understand and remember the underlying principle. The more actively you can become engaged in the learning process, the more effective your learning will be.

ECONOMIC NATURALISM

With the rudiments of the cost–benefit framework under your belt, you are now in a position to become an 'economic naturalist', someone who uses insights from economics to help make sense of observations from everyday life. During a walk in the woods in early April the novice may see only trees, whereas the biology student notices many different species of trees and understands why some are already in leaf while others still lie dormant. Likewise, the novice may notice that in some animal species males are much larger than females, but the biology student knows that such a pattern occurs only in species in which males take several mates. Natural selection favours larger males in those species because their greater size helps them obtain access to females. By contrast, males tend to be roughly the same size as females in monogamous species, in which there is much less fighting for mates.

In similar fashion, learning a few simple economic principles enables us to see the mundane details of ordinary human existence in a new light. Whereas the uninitiated often fail even to notice these details, the economic naturalist not only sees them, but

[4] The famous Australian economist, W. Max Corden, a charming and brilliant teacher as well as a prolific and innovative researcher, was fond of saying to graduate students at a seminar series at Nuffield College, Oxford, that if you couldn't explain something by using the basic tools and concepts of supply and demand it probably wasn't worth explaining in the first place.

becomes actively engaged in the attempt to understand them. Let us consider a few examples of questions that economic naturalists might pose for themselves.

Economic Naturalist 1.1 illustrates a case in which the *benefit* of a product depends on the number of other people who own that product. As the next example demonstrates, the *cost* of a product may also depend on the number of others who own it.

Economic Naturalist 1.1
Adobe supplies its Acrobat Reader software to anyone free of charge from the internet. Why is this?

And not only Acrobat Reader: you can also download the Adobe Flashplayer at no charge. Adobe wants to make profits, but gives away its products free of charge? The answer lies in why people use Adobe or equivalent products. In the case of the Reader, it is to be able to receive files (*.pdf file extension) created with Adobe Writer. Most users have little use for Writer, and those who value it do so it for a variety of reasons to do with security and replication. They are willing to pay for it . . . but they also require that those to whom documents are to be sent can receive and read them. As with a telephone, it's of little use if there are very few people able to receive a call. To be able to sell the Writer programme profitably, Adobe adopts a strategy designed to ensure that as many people as possible can read Acrobat files. The same applies to videos and Flashplayer.

Economic Naturalist 1.2
Why can you not buy a Jaguar without air-conditioning?

If you lived in the Scottish Highlands you would have little use for air-conditioning in your car, even in what passes for summer up there. But if you decided to buy a Jaguar, or a Saab (and many other up-market cars), you would find that climate control is standard, as are things like cruise control. If you bought a Fiat Punto you could get one without these add-ons, but would expect to pay more to buy the same car with the add-ons. So why do Saab or Jaguar not offer this choice? Most buyers of these cars with price tags of anything up to €100,000, depending on the country in Europe, have high incomes, so the makers believe that the overwhelming majority of them would have chosen to order climate control etc., had it been sold as an option. Because of the savings made possible when *all* cars are produced with the same equipment, it would have actually cost more to supply cars for the few who would want them without climate control. Buyers of the least expensive makes of car have much lower incomes on average and many have more pressing alternative uses for their money than to pay for air-conditioning for their cars, even in hot climates. The market for cars without add-ons is larger, so inexpensive marques continue to offer cars at lower prices but without add-ons.

The insights afforded by Economic Naturalist 1.2 suggest an answer to the following strange question.

Economic Naturalist 1.3
Why do the keypad buttons on drive-in automatic teller machines (ATMs) have Braille dots?

Braille dots are common in America and Europe on, for example, the buttons in lifts (elevators) and similar places. Braille keypads enable blind people to participate more fully in the normal flow of daily activity. Indeed, equality and access regulations have reinforced this in order to facilitate blind people in everyday life. Curiously, in North America it is common to find them on the key-pads at drive-in ATMs outside banks. Their usefulness in these circumstances is a little unclear, since blind people cannot drive automobiles on public roads. Why, then, do the manufacturers of automatic teller machines install Braille dots on the machines at drive-in locations?

The answer to this riddle is that once the keypad moulds have been manufactured, the cost of producing buttons with Braille dots is no higher than the cost of producing smooth buttons. Making both would require separate sets of moulds and two different types of inventory. If the patrons of drive-in machines found buttons with Braille dots harder to use, there might be a reason to incur these extra costs. But since the dots pose no difficulty for sighted users, the best and cheapest solution is to produce only keypads with dots.

Economic Naturalist 1.3 was suggested by Cornell student Bill Tjoa, in response to the following assignment.

Exercise 1.6

In 500 words or fewer, use cost–benefit analysis to explain some pattern of events behaviour you have observed in your own environment.

There is probably no more useful step you can take in your study of economics than to perform several versions of the assignment in Exercise 1.6. Students who do so almost invariably become lifelong economic naturalists. Their mastery of economic concepts not only does not decay with the passage of time; it actually grows stronger. We urge you, in the strongest possible terms, to make this investment!

A CAUTIONARY NOTE: ECONOMISTS AND ECONOMICS

We have argued that economics has a legitimate claim to be considered as a science. Any scientist will have personal views as to how the world might be improved, and these will usually reflect the body of knowledge that constitutes the science concerned as well as the scientist's own ethical views. To take global warming as an example, a climatologist can use the results of the empirical and theoretical investigation of climate change to predict the consequences of different levels of greenhouse gases on average temperatures over the next century. In so doing the climatologist is engaging in *positive* scientific analysis. The climatologist may be asked, what can be done about this? As a scientist, his answer should follow this general form. If you wish to reduce climate change by such and such an amount you will have to reduce emissions by so much per annum. Notice that the response avoids the question of what *ought* to be done. Our climate change scientist is still engaging in positive science: his answer (assuming the truth is being told) does not reflect his values, but reflects only the conclusions of his science. A key test of this is whether in principle his answer can be falsified.

Suppose, however, the climatologist had answered: we must ban all use of private cars. This means choosing (implicitly) a level of emissions reductions and a mechanism to achieve it, and will reflect the chooser's values, priorities and willingness to impose costs on others and the value placed on reductions in climate change. His response is not a positive one, but a *normative* one. Conclusions based on tastes or values cannot be subjected to scientific verification or falsification.

Economists are often called on to advise on economic policy or to comment in the media on economic events and developments. In so far as their involvement is based on using economics to demonstrate cause and effect, options that are open, and consequences of proposed actions, economists are engaging in 'positive' economics. Once they stray beyond this, they are making 'normative' economics statements. The critical test is whether there is an express or implied 'ought' in the statement. If there is, the statement may be economics in the sense of a conclusion as to economic policy, but it is normative economics, not positive economics.

In practice, it may be difficult for a non-economist to see when an economist is speaking positively or normatively (and this applies to climatologists, too), so that the listener may believe that what is said is in some sense objectively true while in reality it reflects the values of the speaker as much as the science involved. Scientists, including economists, frequently use (abuse?) their scientific knowledge to advance their ethical views on the basis that their statements reflect the conclusions of science: 'I am Sir Oracle and when I ope my lips let no dog bark' (Shakespeare: *Merchant of Venice*, I (i)).

SUMMARY

- Economics is the study of how people make choices under conditions of scarcity and of the results of those choices for society. Economic analysis of human behaviour begins with the assumption that people are *rational* – that they have well-defined goals and try to achieve them as best they can. In trying to achieve their goals, people normally face trade-offs: because material and human resources are limited, having more of one good thing means making do with less of some other good thing.
- Our focus in this chapter has been on how rational people make choices among alternative courses of action. Our basic tool for analysing these decisions is *cost–benefit analysis*. The Cost–Benefit Principle says that a person should take an action if, and only if, the benefit of that action is at least as great as its cost. The benefit of an action is defined as the largest money amount the person would be willing to pay in order to take the action. The cost of an action is defined as the money value of everything the person must give up in order to take the action.
- Often the question is not whether to pursue an activity but rather how many units of it to pursue. In these cases, the rational person pursues additional units as long as the marginal benefit of the activity (the benefit from pursuing an additional unit of it) exceeds its marginal cost (the cost of pursuing an additional unit of it).
- In using the cost–benefit framework, we need not presume that people *choose rationally* all the time. Indeed, we identified four common pitfalls that plague decision makers in all walks of life: a tendency to treat small proportional changes as insignificant, and/or to ignore opportunity costs, and/or not to ignore sunk costs, and/or to confuse average and marginal costs and benefits.
- *Microeconomics* is the study of individual choices and of group behaviour in individual markets, while *macroeconomics* is the study of the performance of national economies and of the policies that governments use to try to improve economic performance.
- *Statements may be positive or normative.* Positive economics consists in the conclusions of economics that are independent of the ethical value system of the economist. Normative economics consists in statements in economics that reflect or are based on the ethical value system of the economist, implicitly, explicitly or by omission.

REVIEW QUESTIONS

1. A friend of yours on the tennis team says: 'Private tennis lessons are definitely better than group lessons.' Explain what you think he means by this statement. Then use the Cost–Benefit Principle to explain why private lessons are not necessarily the best choice for everyone.
2. True or false: Your willingness to drive to town to save €30 on a new appliance should depend on what fraction of the total selling price €30 is. Explain.
3. Why might someone who is trying to decide whether to see a movie be more likely to focus on the €9 ticket price than on the €20 she would fail to earn by not babysitting?
4. Many people think of their air travel as being free when they use frequent-flyer coupons. Explain why these people are likely to make wasteful travel decisions.
5. Is the non-refundable tuition payment you made to your university this year a sunk cost? How would your answer differ if your university were to offer a full tuition refund to any student who dropped out of school during the first two months of the semester?

PROBLEMS

Problems marked with an asterisk (*) are more difficult.

connect

1. The most you would be willing to pay for having a freshly washed car before going out on a date is €6. The smallest amount for which you would be willing to wash someone else's car is €3.50. You are going out this evening, and your car is dirty. How much economic surplus would you receive from washing it?

2. To earn extra money in the summer, you grow tomatoes and sell them at the farmers' market for 30 cents per kg. By adding compost to your garden, you can increase your yield as shown in the table below. If compost costs 50 cents per kg and your goal is to make as much money as possible, how many kilograms of compost should you add?

Kg of compost	Kg of tomatoes
0	100
1	120
2	125
3	128
4	130
5	131
6	131.5

3. Residents of your city are charged a fixed weekly fee of €6 for garbage collection. They are allowed to put out as many bins as they wish. The average household disposes of three bins of garbage per week under this plan. Now suppose that your city changes to a 'tag' system. Each bin to be collected must have a tag affixed to it. The tags cost €2 each and are not reusable. What effect do you think the introduction of the tag system will have on the total quantity of garbage collected in your city? Explain briefly.

4. Once a week, Smith purchases a six-pack of cola and puts it in his refrigerator for his two children. He invariably discovers that all six cans are gone on the first day. Jones also purchases a six-pack of cola once a week for his two children but, unlike

Smith, he tells them that each may drink no more than three cans. If the children use cost–benefit analysis each time they decide whether to drink a can of cola, explain why the cola lasts much longer at Jones' house than at Smith's.

5. Tom is a mushroom farmer. He invests all his spare cash in additional mushrooms, which grow on otherwise useless land behind his barn. The mushrooms double in weight during their first year, after which time they are harvested and sold at a constant price per kilogram. Tom's friend Dick asks Tom for a loan of €200, which he promises to repay after one year. How much interest will Dick have to pay Tom in order for Tom to recover his opportunity cost of making the loan? Explain briefly.

6. Suppose that in the last few seconds you devoted to Question 1 in your physics exam you earned 4 extra points, while in the last few seconds you devoted to Question 2 you earned 10 extra points. You earned a total of 48 and 12 points, respectively, on the two questions, and the total time you spent on each was the same. If you could take the exam again, how – if at all – should you reallocate your time between these questions?

7. Martha and Sarah have the same preferences and incomes. Just as Martha arrived at the theatre to see a play, she discovered that she had lost the €10 ticket she had purchased earlier. Sarah had also just arrived at the theatre planning to buy a ticket to see the same play when she discovered that she had lost a €10 note from her purse. If both Martha and Sarah are rational and both still have enough money to pay for a ticket, is one of them more likely than the other to go ahead and see the play anyway?

8.* You and your friend Joe have identical tastes. At 2 pm, you go to the local Ticketmaster outlet and buy a €30 ticket to a football match to be played that night 50 km away. Joe plans to attend the same game, but because he cannot get to the Ticketmaster outlet, he plans to buy his ticket at the game. Tickets sold at the game cost only €25, because they carry no Ticketmaster surcharge. (Many people nonetheless pay the higher price at Ticketmaster, to be sure of getting good seats.) At 4 pm, an unexpected snowstorm begins, making the prospect of the 50 km drive much less attractive than before (but assuring the availability of good seats). If both you and Joe are rational, is one of you more likely to attend the game than the other?

9.* For each long-distance call anywhere in the continental United States, a new phone service will charge users 30 cents per minute for the first 2 minutes and 2 cents per minute for additional minutes in each call. Tom's current phone service charges 10 cents per minute for all calls, and his calls are never shorter than 7 minutes. If Tom's dorm switches to the new phone service, what will happen to the average length of his calls?

10.* The meal plan at university A lets students eat as much as they like for a fixed fee of €500 per semester. The average student there eats 250 kg of food per semester. University B charges €500 for a book of meal tickets that entitles the student to eat 250 kg of food per semester. If the student eats more than 250 kg, he or she pays €2 for each additional kilogram; if the student eats less, he or she gets a €2 per kg refund. If students are rational, at which university will average food consumption be higher? Explain briefly.

REFERENCES

Thaler, R. (1980) 'Towards a positive theory of consumer choice', *Journal of Economic Behaviour and Organization*, 1(1).

Appendix A

WORKING WITH EQUATIONS, GRAPHS AND TABLES

Although many of the examples and most of the end-of-chapter problems in this book are quantitative, none requires mathematical skills beyond rudimentary high-school algebra and geometry. In this brief appendix we shall review some of the skills you will need for dealing with these examples and problems.

One important skill is to be able to read simple verbal descriptions and translate the information they provide into the relevant equations or graphs. You will also need to be able to translate information given in tabular form into an equation or graph, and sometimes you will need to translate graphical information into a table or equation. The following examples illustrate all the tools you will need.

USING A VERBAL DESCRIPTION TO CONSTRUCT AN EQUATION

We begin with an example that shows how to construct a long-distance telephone billing equation from a verbal description of the billing plan.

Example 1A.1 Your long-distance telephone plan charges you €5 per month plus 10 cents per minute for long-distance calls. Write an equation that describes your monthly telephone bill.

An **equation** is a simple mathematical expression that describes the relationship between two or more **variables**, or quantities that are free to assume different values in some range. The most common type of equation we shall work with contains two types of variable: **dependent variable** and **independent variable**. In this example, the dependent variable is the money amount of your monthly telephone bill, and the independent variable is the variable on which your bill depends – namely, the volume of long-distance calls you make during the month. Your bill also depends on the €5 monthly fee and the 10 cents per minute charge. But, in this example, those amounts are **constants**, not variables. A constant, also called a **parameter**, is a quantity in an equation that is fixed in value, not free to vary. As the terms suggest, the dependent variable describes an outcome that depends on the value taken by the independent variable.

Once you have identified the dependent variable and the independent variable, choose simple symbols to represent them. In algebra courses, *X* is typically used to represent the independent variable and *Y* the dependent variable. Many people find it easier to remember what the variables stand for, however, if they choose symbols that are linked in some straightforward way to the quantities

equation a mathematical expression that describes the relationship between two or more variables

variable a quantity that is free to take a range of different values

dependent variable a variable in an equation whose value is determined by the value taken by another variable in the equation

independent variable a variable in an equation whose value determines the value taken by another variable in the equation

constant (or parameter) a quantity that is fixed in value that the variables represent. Thus, in this example, we might use B to represent your monthly *bill* in money terms and T to represent the total *time* in minutes you spent during the month on long-distance calls.

Having identified the relevant variables and chosen symbols to represent them, you are now in a position to write the equation that links them:

$$B = 5 + 0.10T \tag{1A.1}$$

where B is your monthly long-distance bill in money terms and T is your monthly total long-distance calling time in minutes. The fixed monthly fee (5) and the charge per minute (0.10) are parameters in this equation. Note the importance of being clear about the units of measure. Because B represents the monthly bill, we must also express the fixed monthly fee and the per-minute monetary charge, which is why the latter number appears in Eq. (1A.1) as 0.10 rather than 10. Equation (1A.1) follows the normal convention in which the dependent variable appears by itself on the left-hand side while the independent variable or variables and constants appear on the right-hand side.

Once we have the equation for the monthly bill, we can use it to calculate how much you will owe as a function of your monthly volume of long-distance calls. For example, if you make 32 minutes of calls, you can calculate your monthly bill by simply substituting 32 minutes for T in Eq. (1A.1):

$$B = 5 + 0.10(32) = 8.20 \tag{1A.2}$$

Your monthly bill when you make 32 minutes of calls is thus equal to €8.20.

Exercise 1A.1 Under the monthly billing plan described in Example 1A.1, how much would you owe for a month during which you made 45 minutes of long-distance calls?

GRAPHING THE EQUATION OF A STRAIGHT LINE

Example 1A.2 shows how to portray the billing plan described in Example 1A.1 as a graph.

Example 1A.2 Construct a graph that portrays the monthly long-distance telephone billing plan described in Example 1A.1, putting your telephone charges, in money per month, on the vertical axis, and your total volume of calls, in minutes per month, on the horizontal axis.

The first step in responding to this instruction is the one we just took, namely to translate the verbal description of the billing plan into an equation. When graphing an equation, the normal convention is to use the vertical axis to represent the dependent variable and the horizontal axis to represent the independent variable. In Fig. 1A.1, we therefore put B on the vertical axis and T on the horizontal axis. One way to construct the graph shown in Fig. 1A.1 is to begin by plotting the monthly bill values that correspond to several different total amounts of long-distance calls. For example, someone who makes 10 minutes of calls during the month would have a bill of $B = 5 + 0.10(10) =$ €6. Thus, in Fig. 1A.1 the value of 10 minutes per month on the horizontal axis corresponds to a bill of €6 per month on the vertical axis (point A). Someone who makes 30 minutes of long-distance calls during the month will have a monthly bill of $B = 5 + 0.10(30) =$ €8, so the value of 30 minutes per month on the horizontal axis corresponds to €8 per month on the vertical axis (point C). Similarly, someone who makes 70 minutes of long-distance calls during the month will have a monthly bill of $B = 5 + 0.10(70) =$ €12, so the value of 70 minutes on the horizontal axis corresponds to €12 on the vertical axis (point D). The line joining these points is the graph of the monthly billing in Eq. (1A.1).

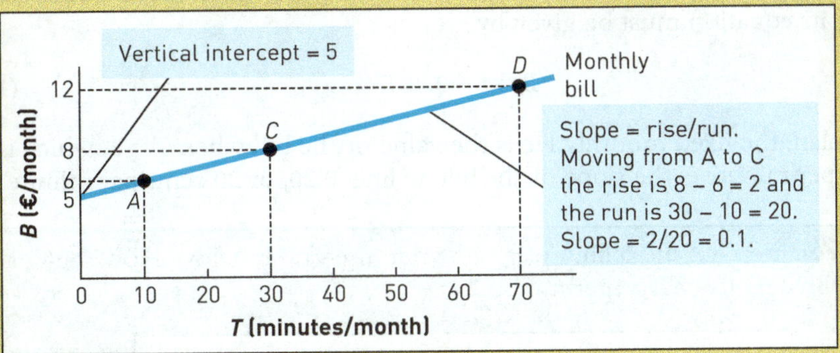

Figure 1A.1 The Monthly Telephone Bill in Example 1A.1

The graph of the equation $B = 5 + 0.10T$ is the straight line shown. Its vertical intercept is 5, and its slope is 0.10.

As shown in Fig. 1A.1, the graph of the equation $B = 5 + 0.10T$ is a straight line. The parameter 5 is the **vertical intercept** of the line – the value of B when $T = 0$, or the point at which the line intersects the vertical axis. The parameter 0.10 is the **slope** of the line, which is the ratio of the **rise** of the line to the corresponding **run**. The ratio rise/run is simply the vertical distance between any two points on the line divided by the horizontal distance between those points. For example, if we choose points A and C in Fig. 1A.1, the rise is $8 - 6 = 2$ and the corresponding run is $30 - 10 = 20$, so rise/run $= 2/20 = 0.10$. More generally, for the graph of any equation $Y = a + bX$, the parameter a is the vertical intercept and the parameter b is the slope.

vertical intercept in a straight line, the value taken by the dependent variable when the independent variable equals zero

slope in a straight line, the ratio of the vertical distance the straight line travels between any two points (**rise**) to the corresponding horizontal distance (**run**)

DERIVING THE EQUATION OF A STRAIGHT LINE FROM ITS GRAPH

Example 1A.3 shows how to derive the equation for a straight line from a graph of the line.

Example 1A.3

Figure 1A.2 shows the graph of the monthly billing plan for a new long-distance plan. What is the equation for this graph? How much is the fixed monthly fee under this plan? How much is the charge per minute?

The slope of the line shown in Fig. 1A.2 is the rise between any two points divided by the corresponding run. For points A and C, rise $= 12 - 8 = 4$, and run $= 40 - 20 = 20$,

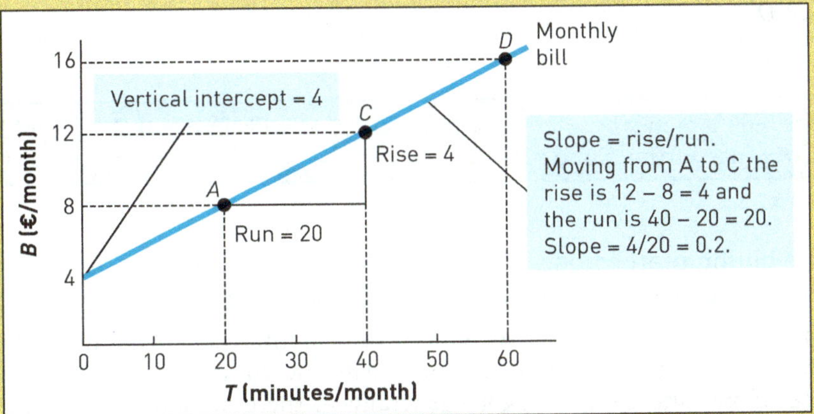

Figure 1A.2 Another Monthly Long-Distance Plan

The vertical distance between points A and C is $12 - 8 = 4$ units, and the horizontal distance between points A and C is $40 - 20 = 20$, so the slope of the line is $4/20 = 1/5 = 0.20$. The vertical intercept (the value of B when $T = 0$) is 4. so the equation for the billing plan shown is $B = 4 + 0.20T$.

so the slope equals rise/run = $4/20 = 1/5 = 0.20$. And since the horizontal intercept of the line is 4, its equation must be given by

$$B = 4 + 0.20T \tag{1A.3}$$

Under this plan, the fixed monthly fee is the value of the bill when $T = 0$, which is €4. The charge per minute is the slope of the billing line, 0.20, or 20 cents per minute.

Exercise 1A.2 Write the equation for the billing plan shown in the graph below. How much is its fixed monthly fee? Its charge per minute?

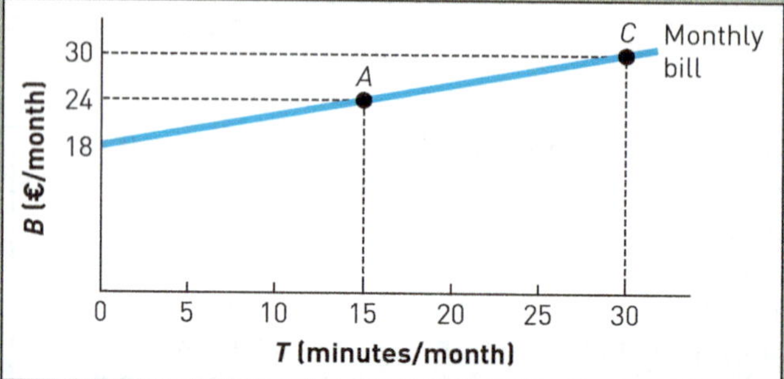

CHANGES IN THE VERTICAL INTERCEPT AND SLOPE

Examples 1A.4 and 1A.5 and Exercises 1A.3 and 1A.4 provide practice in seeing how a line shifts with a change in its vertical intercept or slope.

Example 1A.4 Show how the billing plan whose graph is in Fig. 1A.2 would change if the monthly fixed fee were increased from €4 to €8.

An increase in the monthly fixed fee from €4 to €8 would increase the vertical intercept of the billing plan by €4 but would leave its slope unchanged. An increase in the fixed fee thus leads to a parallel upward shift in the billing plan by €4, as shown in Fig. 1A.3. For any given number of minutes of long-distance calls, the monthly charge on the new bill will be €4 higher than on the old bill. Thus 20 minutes of calls per month costs €8 under the original plan (point A) but €12 under the new plan (point A'). And 40 minutes costs €12 under the original plan (point C), €16 under the new plan (point C'); and 60 minutes costs €16 under the original plan (point D), €20 under the new plan (point D').

Exercise 1A.3 Show how the billing plan whose graph is in Fig. 1A.2 would change if the monthly fixed fee were reduced from €4 to €2.

Example 1A.5 Show how the billing plan whose graph is in Fig. 1A.2 would change if the charge per minute were increased from 20 cents to 40 cents.

Because the monthly fixed fee is unchanged, the vertical intercept of the new billing plan continues to be 4. But the slope of the new plan, shown in Fig. 1A.4, is 0.40, or twice the slope of the original plan. More generally, in the equation $Y = a + bX$, an increase in b makes the slope of the graph of the equation steeper.

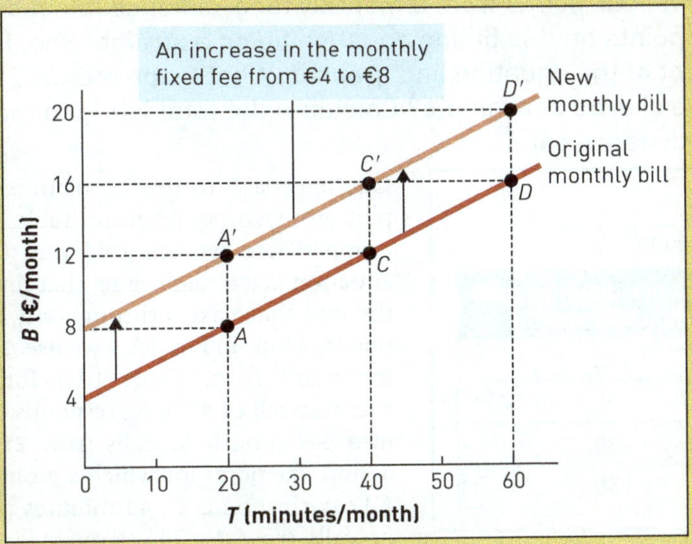

Figure 1A.3 The Effect of an Increase in the Vertical Intercept

An increase in the vertical intercept of a straight line produces an upward parallel shift in the line.

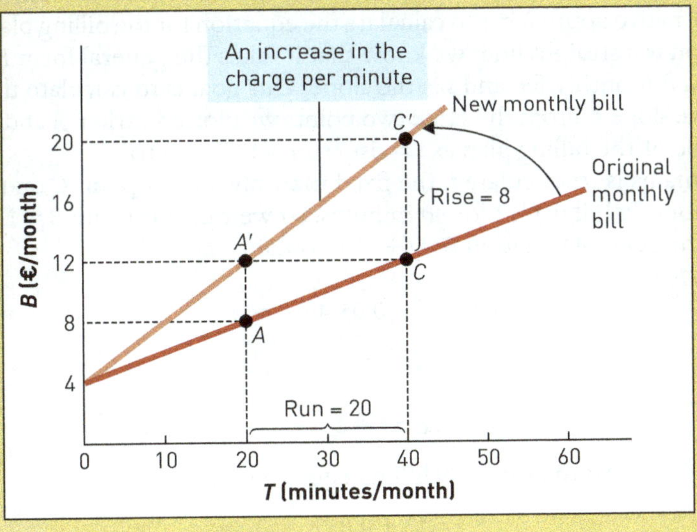

Figure 1A.4 The Effect of an Increase in the Charge per Minute

Because the fixed monthly fee continues to be €4, the vertical intercept of the new plan is the same as that of the original plan. With the new charge per minute of 40 cents, the slope of the billing plan rises from 0.20 to 0.40.

Exercise 1A.4

Show how the billing plan whose graph is in Fig. 1A.2 would change if the charge per minute were reduced from 20 cents to 10 cents.

Exercise 1A.4 illustrates the general rule that in an equation $Y = a + bX$, a reduction in b makes the slope of the graph of the equation less steep.

CONSTRUCTING EQUATIONS AND GRAPHS FROM TABLES

Example 1A.6 and Exercise 1A.5 show how to transform tabular information into an equation or graph.

Example 1A.6 Table 1A.1 shows four points from a monthly long-distance telephone billing equation. If all points on this billing equation lie on a straight line, find the vertical intercept of the equation and graph it. What is the monthly fixed fee? What is the charge per minute? Calculate the total bill for a month with 1 hour of long-distance calls.

Table 1A.1

Points on a Long-Distance Billing Plan

Long-distance bill (€/month)	Total long-distance calls (minutes/month)
10.50	10
11.00	20
11.50	30
12.00	40

One approach to this problem is simply to plot any two points from Table 1A.1 on a graph. Since we are told that the billing equation is a straight line, that line must be the one that passes through any two of its points. Thus, in Fig. 1A.5 we use A to denote the point from Table 1A.1 for which a monthly bill of €11 corresponds to 20 minutes per month of calls (row 2) and C to denote the point for which a monthly bill of €12 corresponds to 40 minutes per month of calls (row 4). The straight line passing through these points is the graph of the billing equation.

Unless you have a steady hand, however, or use extremely large graph paper, the method of extending a line between two points on the billing plan is unlikely to be very accurate. An alternative approach is to calculate the equation for the billing plan directly. Since the equation is a straight line, we know that it takes the general form $B = f + sT$, where f is the fixed monthly fee and s is the slope. Our goal is to calculate the vertical intercept f and the slope s. From the same two points we plotted earlier, A and C, we can calculate the slope of the billing plan as $s = \text{rise}/\text{run} = 1/20 = 0.05$.

So all that remains is to calculate f, the fixed monthly fee. At point C on the billing plan, the total monthly bill is €12 for 40 minutes, so we can substitute $B = 12$, $s = 0.05$ and $T = 40$ into the general equation $B = f + sT$ to obtain

$$12 = f + 0.05(40) \qquad (1A.4)$$

or

$$12 = f + 2 \qquad (1A.5)$$

which solves for $f = 10$. So the monthly billing equation must be

$$B = 10 + 0.05T \qquad (1A.6)$$

Figure 1A.5 Plotting the Monthly Billing Equation from a Sample of Points

Point A is taken from row 2, Table 1a.1, and point C from row 4. The monthly billing plan is the straight line that passes through these points.

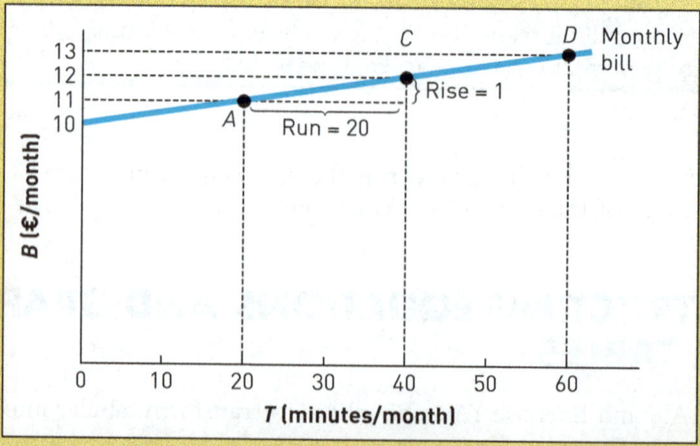

For this billing equation, the fixed fee is €10 per month, the calling charge is 5 cents per minute (€0.05 / minute), and the total bill for a month with 1 hour of long-distance calls is $B = 10 + 0.05(60) =$ €13, just as shown in Fig. 1A.5.

Exercise 1A.5

The table below shows four points from a monthly long-distance telephone billing plan.

Long-distance bill (€/month)	Total long-distance calls (minutes/month)
20.00	10
30.00	20
40.00	30
50.00	40

If all points on this billing plan lie on a straight line, find the vertical intercept of the corresponding equation without graphing it. What is the monthly fixed fee? What is the charge per minute? How much would the charges be for 1 hour of long-distance calls per month?

Appendix B

ELEMENTS OF CALCULUS FOR USE IN ECONOMICS

WHY USE CALCULUS?

Graphs may be considered as a pictorial description of the relationship between the variables on the axes. As such, they are limited in their ability to treat the relationship in an exact and unambiguous fashion, since they depend on the accuracy with which the graphical account of the relationship is drawn. They also suffer from the unavoidable restriction that even the most exact graphical description is in reality limited to portraying properly the relationship between two variables in a tractable fashion.

This means that a normal graph can show only the relationship between two variables, X and Y, while holding all other factors that might affect the relationship constant. Take, for example, the well-established relationships between temperature, price and consumption of ice cream. Any competent marketing study would easily show that in any location the quantity of ice cream sold on a given day will be inversely related to the unit price at which it is sold. Or, as an economist would put it, the demand curve for ice cream has a negative slope (Fig. 1B.1). Here, following the convention in economics, and in defiance of the mathematical tradition, the consumption of ice cream, the dependent or endogenous variable, is shown on the horizontal axis, while the unit price, the independent, causative or exogenous variable, is shown on the vertical axis.

The marketing analyst would also produce data indicating that, at any given unit price, the quantity sold would rise with the ambient temperature. Less is sold in winter than in summer, when it is raining than when the sun is splitting the pavement. That relationship is shown by using temperature (in degrees) on the vertical axis and consumption on the horizontal (Fig. 1B.2).

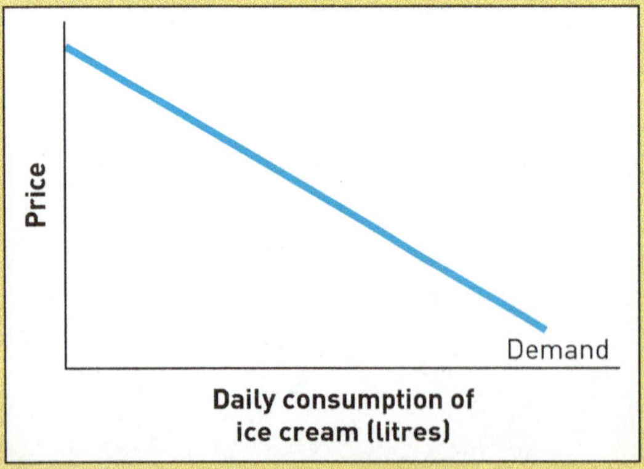

Figure 1B.1 The Demand Curve for Ice Cream
The effect of unit price on consumption.

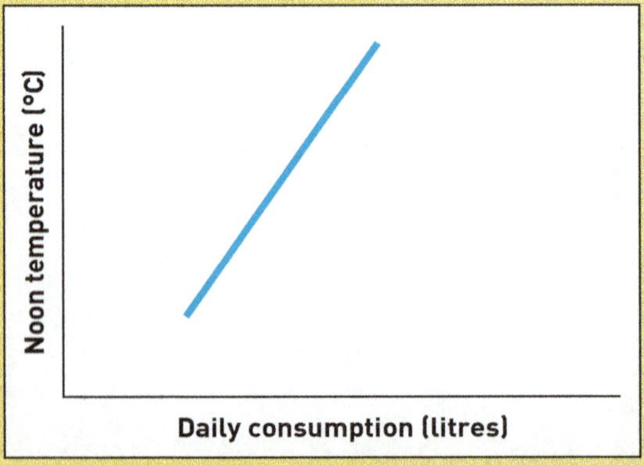

Figure 1B.2 Temperature Effect on Daily Ice Cream Consumption

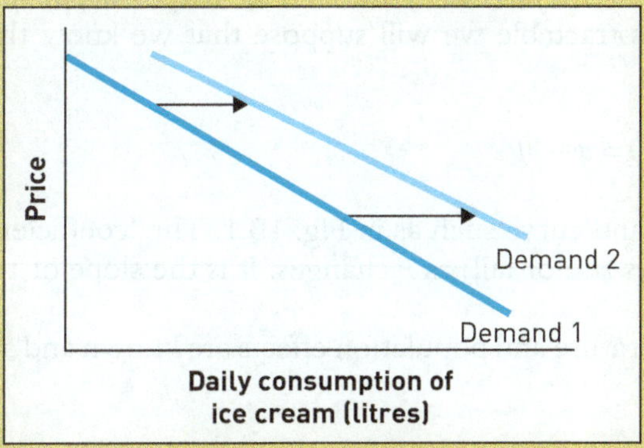

Figure 1B.3 The Demand Curve for Ice Cream
A rise in temperature increases consumption at any price.

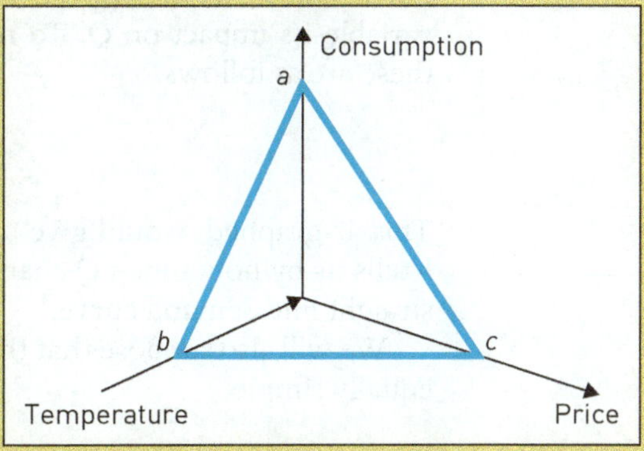

Figure 1B.4 The Surface *abc* shows the Price and Temperature Effects on Consumption, Holding Other Things Constant

Exercise 1B.1

If you were given the information that produced Fig. 1B.2, and wanted to show how the temperature–consumption relationship is affected by a price change, what would you do?

Neither Fig. 1B.1 nor Fig. 1B.2 can deal satisfactorily with the problem that both price and temperature may vary between days, something that makes it difficult to separate the price and temperature effects. As an expedient, when using graphic analysis we assume we know each of the effects from prior information, and adjust one for any change in the other. Thus, if we know the price–consumption relationship (the demand curve), we can shift it to make allowance for a change in temperature (Fig. 1B.3).

In this case, we show a hypothetical demand curve for choc ices at a holiday resort (a) when the noon temperature is 18°C, and (b) when it is 27°C. Suppose, however, we wanted to establish what a small change in price and temperature would do to sales. In practice this approach would not be very helpful, since we would need to be very exact in moving the demand curve to take the temperature effect into account. We could, of course, try to draw a three-dimensional graph, using some form of perspective, as shown in Fig. 1B.4, but measuring the impact of changes using this approach is extremely difficult other than in an inexact fashion.

Even if we did adopt this approach, we could not deal with the following problem. Sales will also be affected by the number of visitors to the holiday resort. Our demand curve shift approach and our three-dimensional graph approach will both be incapable of allowing for a change in the final factor, the number of potential consumers.

DEALING WITH THE PROBLEM

If we use simple mathematical notation, the basis of the problem and its solution become clear. Use Q to represent the volume of sales (in litres – or, if we prefer, in number of choc ices). Let P represent the unit price (e.g. €0.75 per choc ice). Let T be the temperature at noon, and let N be the number of potential customers.

We are saying that Q is a *function* of P, T and N, which we can write as:

$$Q = Q(P,T,N)$$

Furthermore, let us suppose that market analysis has established for each independent variable its impact on Q. To make this tractable we will suppose that we know that these are as follows:

$$Q = a - bP$$

This, if graphed, would give us a demand curve such as in Fig. 1B.1. The 'coefficient' b tells us by how much Q changes (sales rise or fall) as P changes. It is the slope of the straight line demand curve.[5]

We will also suppose that the temperature and population effects are known and are equally simple:

$$Q = cT$$

meaning that, controlling for price, consumption will rise with temperature in a predictable fashion and

$$Q = dN$$

meaning that, controlling for the other factors, more people means more sales. Putting these together, we can write the whole relationship as

$$Q = a - bP + cT + dN$$

Any change in Q from one day to the next will be due to a change in one or more of the independent variables. Use the Greek letter Δ (capital delta, capital D) to mean 'change in':

$$\Delta Q = -b\Delta P + c\Delta T + f\Delta N$$

Now, assuming all this, and assuming we know the changes in price, temperature and population, we can determine the change in sales.

All very simple? Alas, no.

We have made it all very easy by assuming straight-line relationships. That is, the slopes in each case are constant, so that the absolute impact of a large or small change in P, T and N is given; the ratios $\Delta Q/\Delta P$, $\Delta Q/\Delta T$ and $\Delta Q/\Delta N$ are the same whether the change in temperature, price or population is large or small, which is a bit implausible, and regardless of where we measure it from a starting point. There might be a different impact on sales from an increase in temperature from 11°C to 14°C from that of a change from 19°C to 22°C, and the impact of a change from 19°C to 22°C (3°C) in one day might be considerably higher than three times the impact of a change from 19°C to 20°C.

Using straight-line relationships is fine for explanatory purposes in a classroom, or as a rough approximation to likely effects, but real life is more complex, and proper measurement of such effects cannot depend on this method. However, it does point us towards the solution.

Return to the simple demand curve of Fig. 1B.1. It could be written, as already noted, $Q = a - bP$. The value of b tells us the change (in litres) of sales for a change (in cents) of price. Suppose it was in fact $Q = 2{,}000 - 10P$. In this case $\Delta Q/\Delta P = -10$, which is true whether P is 5 cents or 15 cents, and whether the starting price is 75 cents or 65 cents.

[5] Actually, in geometric terms it is the *inverse* of the slope, because slope measures vertical (P) change over horizontal (Q) change, but this need not concern us here.

In this case, holding the other factors constant we could set down in a table the level of sales at various prices (Table 1B.1), and the relationship, if graphed, would give us our straight-line demand curve. At a price of zero and for a given number in the resort, and for a given temperature (ice cream is free) people would consume 2,000 litres a day. At a price of €2 a bar, no ice cream would be sold.

Table 1B.1

Sales at Various Prices

Price (cents per choc ice)	Volume sold (litres)
0	2,000
10	1,900
50	1,500
75	1,250
100	1,000
150	500
200	0

Now, suppose the demand curve was not a straight line, which is more than possible. Suppose it was curved, as in Fig. 1B.5.

Then, remembering what the slope of the curve means (the rate at which sales change as price changes), we see that (a) it changes as we move down the curve, and (b) the impact of a change in price depends on where we start from. To add to our woes, there is no reason to believe that the temperature effect or the population effect is linear (a straight line) either.

HOW DO WE DEAL WITH THIS?

At its simplest, and using a graph, we would measure the slope by getting the slope of a tangent to the curve at the relevant point (Fig. 1B.6). This is unsatisfactory, since we would need to provide the value of the tangent slope at every point on the curve . . . and there is an infinite number of such points; so, operationally, we would have to calculate a large number of tangent slopes in order to make good predictions of price change effects on consumption (or weather or population effects).

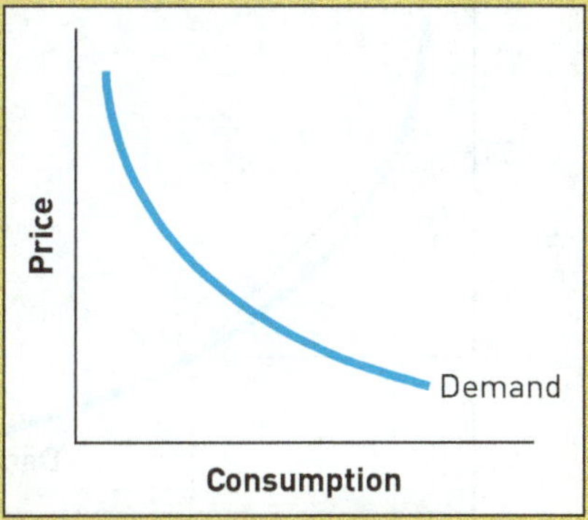

Figure 1B.5 A 'Curved' Demand Curve

THE SOLUTION: USE CALCULUS – DIFFERENTIATING

Go back to the definition of a slope: it is the rate of change of sales (in this example) with respect to the change in price (ignoring the other effects). It is $\Delta Q/\Delta P$. In Fig. 1B.7, starting from a price of 50, if we lower price to 40 we see that sales will rise to 1,650. $\Delta Q/\Delta P$ is 150/10, or 15:1. That is an approximation to, but only an approximation to, the sales increase from any reduction of between 1 cent and 10 cents starting from 50, and not very different from that of a reduction from, say, 48 cents to 47 cents. But it is only an approximation, and will not accurately predict the impact of reducing price by 1 cent at any point in this interval. For that, it would appear we need either tangent values or something else.

We start by noting that if at any point A on the curve if ΔP is very small, $\Delta Q/\Delta P$ will be close to the value of the slope at that point.

If we keep making ΔP smaller and smaller around A, the slope of the straight line approaches that of the tangent at A,

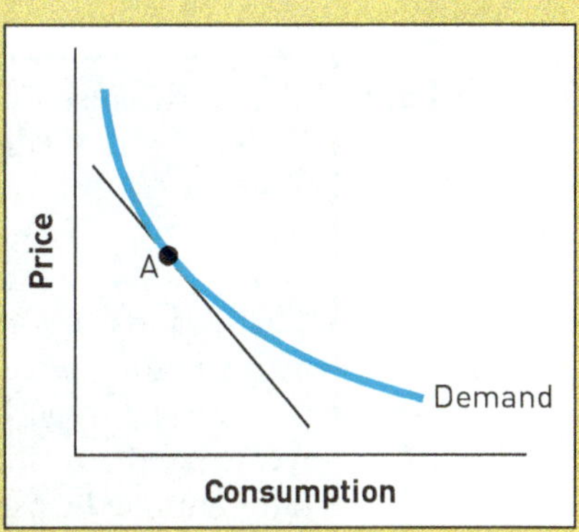

Figure 1B.6 A 'Curved' Demand Curve

The slope at *A* is found by drawing the tangent to the curve at *a* and getting the slope of the tangent.

and eventually coincides with it. The slope of the tangent is the slope of the curve between two points that are infinitely close to each other (coincide). Or the slope of the tangent is given by $\Delta Q \Delta P$ when ΔP and ΔQ are extremely small ($\Delta P \rightarrow 0$).

For any expression $y = y(x)$ the value of $\Delta y/\Delta x$ as $\Delta x \rightarrow 0$ is written dy/dx, and is described as the 'first derivative' of y with respect to x. Obtaining it is done by 'differentiating' y with respect to x.

differentiation finding the slope or rate of change of a function using algebra rather than geometry

The *differential calculus* is the procedure that enables us to obtain the value of dy/dx from the original expression $y = y(x)$, or to **differentiate** y with respect to x.

For simple algebraic functions this turns out to be easy to learn (although we will not prove it here: this is not a rigorous text in mathematics).

Take an expression

$$Y = a + bX + cX^2 + dX^3$$

dY/dX is found by multiplying the coefficient of each X term on the right-hand side by the power of X concerned and reducing that power by 1. Remembering that $X^0 = 1$, and $X^1 = X$ the expression can be rewritten:

$$Y = aX^0 + bX^1 + cX^2 + dX^3$$

$$dY/dX = 0aX^{-1} + 1bX^0 + 2cX^1 + 3dX^2$$

or

$$dY/dX = b + 2cX + 3dX^2$$

So, if we had a non-linear demand curve:

$$Q = 2{,}000 - 350P + 5P^2$$

we can find the slope, dQ/dP, at any point by differentiating Q with respect to P and solving:

$$dQ/dP = -350 + 10P$$

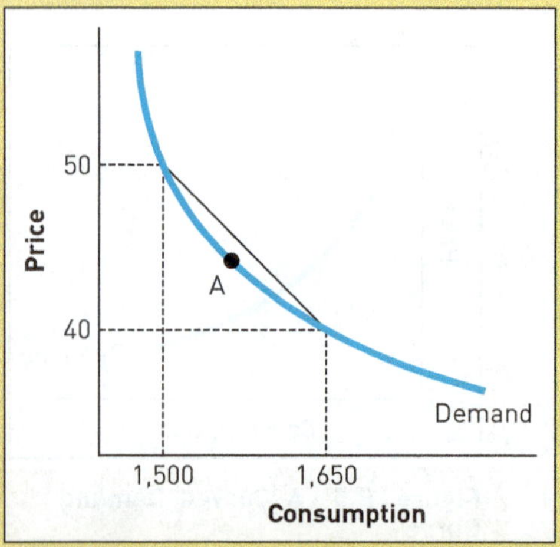

Figure 1B.7 Differentiating

Exercise 1B.2 Obtain this result by the procedure just outlined.

For $P = 1$, $dQ/dP = -340$; for $P = 5$, $dQ/dP = -300$; for $P = 15$, $dQ/dP = -200$

$$\Delta Q = (dQ/dP)\Delta P$$

That is, for a small change in P (e.g. raise price by 1) sales would fall by 350/1 or 350 if the existing price is 1, by 300 if the existing price is 5, and so on.

Now, let us go back to our ice cream example. If all that changed was price, and we wanted to estimate the impact of a price change on sales we would simply differentiate the expression for Q with respect to price and estimate the impact in the same way as we have just done.

But suppose that price, temperature and numbers in town are all changing. How do we estimate the impact of all these on sales?

We start with a small change in notation. In these circumstances, where sales, Q, are dependent on (in this case) three variables, P, T and N, we shall use dQ to mean change in sales, dP change in price, dT change in temperature and dN change in potential number of customers. We shall use the small Greek letter delta δ(d), to indicate the rate of change obtained by differentiating where Q is being differentiated with respect to just one of the variables that determine it (or 'partially differentiated').

Since (if we have properly specified the demand relationship) we know that changes in Q are due to the impact of the three independent variables, we can state this formally:

$$dQ = (\delta Q/\delta P)dp + (\delta Q/\delta T)dT + (\delta Q/\delta N)dN$$

Exactly the same procedure as before is used to obtain the rates of change values; but if you want to isolate the effect of T, for example, you differentiate with respect to T, and any term in the expression not including T is ignored (or treated as being multiplied by T^0, which is the same thing).

Exercise 1B.3

$$Q = 3{,}000 - 15P - 3P^2 + 2.5T - 6T^{1/2} + 15N + 20N^{1/2}$$

(i) Write down the expression for $\delta Q/\delta P$.
(ii) What is $\delta Q/\delta P$ if $P = 50$? What is $\delta Q/\delta T$ if $T = 16$?
(iii) By how much will sales rise if the numbers in town rise from 10,000 to 10,500? (Remember that raising a number to the power of $\frac{1}{2}$ means its square root, and a negative power means the reciprocal of the positive value, i.e. $X^{-1} = 1/X$.)

There are three other useful differentiation rules for economists.

1. Suppose we know that Y is a product of two variables, each of which is a function of X:

$$Y = UV, \text{ where } U = U(X) \text{ and } V = V(X)$$

and we want to find the impact of a change in X on Y.
How do we differentiate Y with respect to X?
The rule is a simple one:

$$dY/dX = UdV/dX + V\,dU/dX$$

This is called the *product chain rule*.

Example

$$Y = UV$$

$$U = 10 - 2X \text{ and } V = -5 + 8X$$

$$dU/dX = -2 \text{ and } dV/dX = 8$$

$$dY/dX = (100 - 2X)(8) + (-5 + 8X)(-2) = 90$$

2. Suppose that $Y = U/V$, where U and V are both functions of X.
The rule is:

$$dY/dX = [(VdU/dX) - (UdV/dX)]/V^2$$

This is the *divisor chain rule*.

Example

$$Y = U/V$$

$$U = 10 + 2X \text{ and } V = 5 + 8X$$

$$\begin{aligned} dY/dX &= 2(5 + 8X) - 8(10 + 2X)(8)]/(5 + 8X)^2 \\ &= 70/(25 - 80X + 64X^2) \end{aligned}$$

3. Finally, suppose that the relation between Y and X is of the form

$$Y = (a + bX)^n = (f(X))^n$$

The rule for deriving dY/dX is:

$$dY/dX = [n(fX)^{n-1}][d(f(X)d(X)]$$

This is the *function chain rule*.

Example

$$Y = (10 + 5X)^2$$

$$dY/dX = 2(10 + 5X)5 = 100 + 50X$$

Exercise 1B.4

(i) Show that the function chain rule is correct in this case by extending the bracket term in the function rule example and differentiating Y with respect to X.

(ii) Show that the divisor chain rule is correct by turning the terms in the example into a product:

$$Y = (10 + 2X)(5 + 8X)^{-1}$$

Chapter 2

Markets, Specialisation and Economic Efficiency

A human being should be able to change a diaper, plan an invasion, butcher a hog, conn a ship, design a building, write a sonnet, balance accounts, build a wall, set a bone, comfort the dying, take orders, give orders, cooperate, act alone, solve equations, analyze a new problem, pitch manure, program a computer, cook a tasty meal, fight efficiently, die gallantly. Specialization is for insects.

Robert A. Heinlein

Learning Objectives

After studying this chapter you should be able to:

1. Explain the difference between absolute and comparative advantage;
2. Understand how comparative advantage enables gains to be made from specialisation and exchange, including international trade even in the face of absolute disadvantage;
3. Understand increasing opportunity cost;
4. Use the concept of the production possibility frontier;
5. Appreciate how comparative advantage can change and be changed;
6. Explain the difference between technical and economic efficiency.

Developed countries, such as are characterised by a much higher degree of specialisation than under-developed countries in the organisation of economic life. Just think about households. In the richer, advanced economies of the Organisation for Economic Co-operation and Development (OECD), the 'club' of advanced economies, households (wage earners) in general consume goods and services that they do not produce, and produce goods or services that they do not consume. In poorer economies we observe widespread household production of goods and services to be consumed within the same households. This is obvious in the agricultural sector where food production for consumption is concerned, but it applies elsewhere too. For example, clothes making and repairing is commonly part of the 'output' of a household, but is consumed within the household (although it may also be sold to other households).

This aspect of OECD household activity, has become more pronounced since the end of the Second World War. Ask yourself how many of today's young adults have the household skills that their parents or grandparents have or had? What has replaced those skills? The answer is goods and services produced outside the household (clothes, pizzas, cleaning) and bought in out of earnings derived from what the household produces and sells to other economic entities.

The same applies to the organisation of production by firms. This is often referred to as 'vertical disintegration of production'. Within manufacturing this can be seen in the trend towards separate production of 'parts' from the assembly of those parts into 'final goods'. Planes, trains and automobiles spring to mind immediately. Specialist firms produce gearboxes for car manufacturers. Boeing and Airbus subcontract purchases of components to other suppliers, as do manufacturers of railway engines. This is another instance of specialisation and exchange replacing within-firm production.

The positive correlation between income levels and specialisation and exchange across countries and over time within countries raises a further question: which is the cause and which is the effect?

Where there is less specialisation the firm or household by definition contains a wider variety of skills. This is common in poorer countries, but rarer in richer ones, where people specialise and hire others to do things for them. Why this difference in skills and employment?

Is it that people in poorer countries are simply too poor to hire others to perform these services? In this chapter we will see that the reverse is actually the case. The point to be made is that people in poorer countries do not provide their own services because they are poor; rather, they are poor largely *because* they provide their own services.

The alternative to a system in which everyone is a jack-of-all-trades is one in which people *specialise* in particular goods and services, and then satisfy their needs by trading among themselves. Economic systems based on specialisation and the exchange of goods and services are generally far more productive than those with less specialisation.

Comparative Advantage

To see why this is the case we shall explore why people choose to exchange goods and services in the first place, rather than having each person produce his or her own food, cars, clothing, shelter and the like.

The reason that specialisation is so productive is the existence of what economists call *comparative advantage*. A person has a comparative advantage at producing a particular good or service – say, haircuts – if that person is *relatively* more efficient at producing haircuts than at producing other goods or services. We can all have more of *every* good and service if each of us specialises in the activities at which we have a comparative advantage.

This chapter will also introduce the *production possibilities curve* (PPC), which is a graphical method of describing the combinations of goods and services that an economy can produce. The development of this tool will allow us to see much more precisely how specialisation enhances the productive capacity of even the simplest economy.

Back, then, to rich and poor countries. If the failure to specialise is the root cause of poverty, why do people not simply specialise? First, the size of the market determines the limits to the benefits from the specialist division of labour. For specialisation to make sense it may be necessary that others specialise at the same time, so as to create a market for the potentially increased supply of goods and services that specialists produce. Inadequate transport infrastructure may drastically limit the size of the potential market. Specialisation may require training or skills that are hard to acquire. It may require capital in the form of dedicated equipment, which is costly to acquire. Thus there is an element of a 'chicken and egg' problem: specialisation increases the value of goods and services being produced (the size of the economy), but the incentive to specialise may depend on the existing size of the economy.

These problems are the concern of what is known as 'development economics' and, interesting as it is, development economics is outside the scope of an introductory text. However, what we are going to look at in this chapter is fundamental to understanding why countries – and people – become better off through specialisation and exchange. To do so, we look at the problem in a simplified and rather abstract fashion, so as to avoid the kind of difficulties just described.

EXCHANGE AND OPPORTUNITY COST

The *Scarcity Principle* reminds us that the opportunity cost of spending more time on any one activity is having less time available to spend on others. As Example 2.1 makes clear, this principle helps explain why everyone can do better by concentrating on those activities at which they perform best *relative* to others.

THE PRINCIPLE OF COMPARATIVE ADVANTAGE

One of the most important insights of modern economics is that when two people (or two nations) have different opportunity costs of performing various tasks, they can always increase the total value of available goods and services by trading with one another. Example 2.1 captures the logic behind this insight by looking at productive efficiency.

Should Paula update her own web page?

Example 2.1

Consider a small community in which Paula is the only professional bicycle mechanic and Beth is the only professional HTML programmer. Paula also happens to be an even better HTML programmer than Beth. If the amount of time each of them takes to perform these tasks is as shown in Table 2.1, and if each regards the two tasks as equally pleasant (or unpleasant), does the fact that Paula can program faster than Beth imply that Paula should update her own web page?

The entries in Table 2.1 show that Paula has an **absolute advantage** over Beth in both activities. While Paula, the mechanic, needs only 20 minutes to update a web page, Beth, the programmer, needs 30 minutes. Paula's advantage over Beth is even greater when the task is fixing bikes: she can complete a repair in only 10 minutes, compared with Beth's 30 minutes.

absolute advantage one person has an absolute advantage over another if an hour spent in performing a task earns more than the other person can earn in an hour at the task

comparative advantage one person has a comparative advantage over another in a task if his or her opportunity cost of performing a task is lower than the other person's opportunity cost

But the fact that Paula is a better programmer than Beth does *not* imply that Paula should update her own web page. Beth has a **comparative advantage** over Paula at programming: she is *relatively* more productive at programming than Paula. Similarly, Paula has a comparative advantage in bicycle repair. (Remember that a person has a comparative advantage at a given task if his or her opportunity cost of performing that task is lower than another person's.)

What is Beth's opportunity cost of updating a web page? Since she takes 30 minutes to update each page – the same amount of time she takes to fix a bicycle – her opportunity cost of updating a web page is one bicycle repair. In other words, by taking the time to update a web page, Beth is effectively giving up the opportunity to do one bicycle repair. Paula, in contrast, can complete two bicycle repairs in the time she takes to update a single web page. For her, the opportunity cost of updating a web page is two bicycle repairs. Paula's opportunity cost of programming, measured in terms of bicycle repairs forgone, is twice as high as Beth's. Thus, Beth has a comparative advantage at programming.

The interesting and important implication of the opportunity cost comparison summarised in Table 2.2 is that the total number of bicycle repairs and web updates accomplished if Paula and Beth both spend part of their time at each activity will always be

Table 2.1 Productivity Information for Paula and Beth

	Time to update a web page (minutes)	Time to complete a bicycle repair (minutes)
Paula	20	10
Beth	30	30

Table 2.2 Opportunity Costs for Paula and Beth

	Opportunity cost of updating a web page	Opportunity cost of a bicycle repair
Paula	2 bicycle repairs	0.5 web page update
Beth	1 bicycle repair	1 web page update

smaller than the number accomplished if each specialises in the activity in which she has a comparative advantage. Suppose, for example, that people in their community demand a total of 16 web page updates per day. If Paula spent half her time updating web pages and the other half repairing bicycles, an eight-hour workday would yield 12 web page updates and 24 bicycle repairs. To complete the remaining four updates, Beth would have to spend two hours programming, which would leave her six hours to repair bicycles. And since she takes 30 minutes to do each repair, she would have time to complete 12 of them. So when the two women try to be jacks-of-all-trades, they end up completing a total of 16 web page updates and 36 bicycle repairs.

Consider what would have happened had each woman specialised in her activity of comparative advantage. Beth could have updated 16 web pages on her own, and Paula could have performed 48 bicycle repairs. Specialisation would have created an additional 12 bicycle repairs out of thin air.

When computing the opportunity cost of one good in terms of another, we must pay close attention to the form in which the productivity information is presented. In Example 2.1, we were told how many minutes each person needed to perform each task. Alternatively, we might be told how many units of each task each person can perform in an hour. Work through Exercise 2.1 to see how to proceed when information is presented in this alternative format.

Exercise 2.1

Consider a small community in which Barbara is the only professional bicycle mechanic and Pat is the only professional HTML programmer. If their productivity rates at the two tasks are as shown in the table, and if each regards the two tasks as equally pleasant (or unpleasant), does the fact that Barbara can program faster than Pat imply that Barbara should update her own web page?

	Productivity in programming (per hour)	Productivity in bicycle repair (per hour)
Pat	2 web page updates	1 repair
Barbara	3 web page updates	3 repairs

The principle illustrated by Example 2.1 is so important that we state it formally as one of the core principles of the course:

The Principle of Comparative Advantage: everyone does best when each person (or each country) concentrates on the activities for which his or her opportunity cost is lowest.

Indeed, the gains made possible from specialisation based on comparative advantage constitute the rationale for *market exchange*. They explain why each person does not devote 10 per cent of his or her time to producing cars, 5 per cent to growing food, 25 per cent to building housing, 0.0001 per cent to performing brain surgery, and so on. By concentrating on those tasks at which we are relatively more productive, we can together produce vastly more than if we all tried to be self-sufficient.

The point here is not that people whose time is valuable should never perform their own services. If that were the case most DIY stores would have many fewer customers. The point is that where time and resources are scarce it is economically efficient to specialise along lines dictated by comparative advantage.

Specialisation and its effects provide ample grist for the economic naturalist. Here is an example from the world of sports.

Economic Naturalist 2.1

What has happened to football (soccer)? They just don't seem to be able to score goals like they used to![1]

Over the last century the standards of athletes and their performances have steadily improved right across the spectrum of sports, as intensive and scientific training and the application of technology have been increasingly used to improve performance. Most observers would agree that professionalism has greatly improved the skills and performances of sports in general. But has it happened in soccer? Consider the following. Look at the scoring record in the World Cup since the 1930s. Between 1930 and 1954 the average number of goals scored in World Cup games rose from 2.88 to 5.36. From 1954 there was a fairly steady decline to 2.21 in 1990. There seems to have been a small recovery since 1990: 2.71 in 1994, 2.67 in 1998. However it fell to 2.52 in 2002, to 2.2 in 2006 and to 2.19 in 2010.

One suggestion was that scoring was harder in recent decades because goalkeepers were getting bigger . . . but no one suggested that they were getting smaller between 1930 and 1954. However, something did happen in the mid-1950s. It became more and more common to put most of a team's effort (in the form of the formation in which players took the field) into defence. The old 3–2–5 formation (five attackers) gave way to 4–3–3 and 4–4–2. For some reason, teams began to shift the weight of specialisation from attack to defence, and this has been maintained to the present, with 4–5–1 not being unknown. On that basis the fall in the average score becomes easy to understand, and when account is taken of the fall in the percentage of attackers, the goal score per attacker may even have risen, consistent with professionalisation. The lower scores, then, reflect not a falling skill among attackers but increased specialisation in defence and a consequent increased ability of teams to defend and selection of players for defensive capability. But what might have driven the move to emphasise and specialise in defence? A possible explanation may lie in the increased amounts of money going into football and the consequent potential cost to a club of losing matches and facing relegation. If teams are risk averse they would be expected to respond to this by putting more effort into specialising in defence and less into attack. What do you think?

SOURCES OF COMPARATIVE ADVANTAGE

At the individual level, comparative advantage often appears to be the result of inborn talent. For instance, some people seem to be naturally gifted at programming computers while others seem to have a special knack for fixing bikes. But comparative advantage is more often the result of education, training or experience. Thus we usually leave the design of kitchens to people with architectural training, the drafting of contracts to people who have studied law and the teaching of physics to people with advanced degrees in that field.

At the national level, comparative advantage may derive from differences in natural resources or from differences in society or culture. The United States, which has a disproportionate share of the world's leading research universities, has a comparative advantage in the design of electronic computing hardware and software. Canada, which

[1] We are indebted to a colleague in University College Dublin's Economics School, David Madden, for suggesting the material for Economic naturalist 2.1.

has one of the world's highest per capita endowments of farm and forest land, has a comparative advantage in the production of agricultural products. Topography and climate explain why Colorado specialises in the skiing industry while Hawaii specialises as an ocean resort.

Seemingly, non-economic factors can also give rise to comparative advantage. For instance, the emergence of English as the *de facto* world language gives English-speaking countries a comparative advantage over non-English-speaking nations in the production of books, movies and popular music. Even a country's institutions may affect the likelihood that it will achieve comparative advantage in a particular pursuit. For example, cultures that encourage entrepreneurship will tend to have a comparative advantage in the introduction of new products, whereas those that promote high standards of care and craftsmanship will tend to have a comparative advantage in the production of high-quality variants of established products.

Economic Naturalist 2.2
How is India's education focus reflected in its trade?

India and China are very similar in some respects. Both have rising populations, raw material deposits, surplus labour from agriculture. Both are successful importers of foreign capital. This suggests that they should export similar products to third countries, on the basis that the fundamental drivers of comparative advantage seem to be similar. However, the composition of exports from the two countries is quite different, implying different areas of comparative advantage. Chinese exports are in the manufactured goods sector, with a steady shift from low-tech, textile-based and simple manufacturing goods to high-end electronic goods. Indian exports in recent years have seen a big increase in internationally traded services in which it has now overtaken China as the main Asian exporter.

The diverging trends can be attributed to the concept that comparative advantage changes and can be influenced by government policy, or is 'endogenous'. India has invested substantial resources in higher education rather than simply providing technical training so as to take advantage of English as India's lingua franca. This has enabled India to double its share of the world market for traded services, which increasingly uses English on a global basis, over the last decade. By selecting a different focus in its education strategy India has created comparative advantage in an area that does not involve head-to-head competition with sectors where China is dominant.

RECAP

Exchange and opportunity cost

Gains from exchange are possible if trading partners have comparative advantages in producing different goods and services. Maximum production is achieved if each person specialises in producing the good or service in which he or she has the lowest opportunity cost (the Principle of Comparative Advantage). Comparative advantage makes specialisation worthwhile even if one trading partner is more productive than others, in absolute terms, in every activity.

COMPARATIVE ADVANTAGE AND PRODUCTION POSSIBILITIES

Comparative advantage and specialisation allow an economy to produce more than if each person tries to produce a little of everything. In this section we gain further insight into the advantages of specialisation by introducing a graph that can be used to describe the various combinations of goods and services that an economy can produce.

THE PRODUCTION POSSIBILITIES CURVE

Imagine a simple island economy in which only two goods are produced: coffee and pine nuts. Production consists either of picking coffee beans that grow on small bushes on the island's central valley floor or of picking pine nuts that grow on trees on the steep hillsides. The more time workers spend picking coffee, the less time they have available for picking nuts. Given how productive workers are at each activity, we could summarise the various combinations of coffee and nuts they can pick each day. This menu of possibilities is known as the **production possibilities curve** (PPC).

> **production possibilities curve** a graph that describes the maximum amount of one good that can be produced for every possible level of production of the other good

To start the analysis, let's simplify further by looking at an economy that has only a single worker who can divide her time between the two activities.

What is the PPC for an economy in which Susan is the only worker? — Example 2.2

Consider a society consisting only of Susan, who allocates her production time between coffee and nuts. She is more productive at picking coffee than at picking nuts. She can pick 2 kg of nuts or 4 kg of coffee in an hour. If she works a total of 6 hours per day, describe her PPC – the graph that displays, for each level of nut production, the maximum amount of coffee that Susan can pick.

The vertical axis in Fig. 2.1 shows Susan's daily production of coffee, and the horizontal axis shows her daily production of nuts. First, suppose she employs her entire workday (6 hours) picking coffee. In that case, since she can pick 4 kg of coffee per hour, she would pick 24 kg per day of coffee and zero kg of nuts. That combination of coffee and nut production is represented by point *A* in Fig. 2.1. It is the vertical intercept of Susan's PPC.

If Susan devotes all her time to picking nuts, since she can pick 2 kg of nuts per hour, her total daily production would be 12 kg of nuts. That combination is represented by point *D* in Fig. 2.1, the horizontal intercept of Susan's PPC. Because Susan's production of each good is exactly proportional to the amount of time she devotes to that good, the remaining points along her production possibilities curve will lie on the straight line that joins *A* and *D*.

For example, suppose that Susan devotes 4 hours each day to picking coffee and 2 hours to picking nuts. She will then end up with (4 hours/day) × (4 kg/hour) × 16 kg of coffee per day and (2 hours/day) × (2 kg/hour) = 4 kg of nuts. This is the point labelled *B* in Fig. 2.1. Alternatively, if she devotes 2 hours to coffee and 4 to nuts, she will get (2 hours/day) × (4 kg/hour) = 8 kg of coffee per day and (4 hours/day) × (2 kg/hour) = 8 kg of nuts. This alternative combination is represented by point *C* in Fig. 2.1.

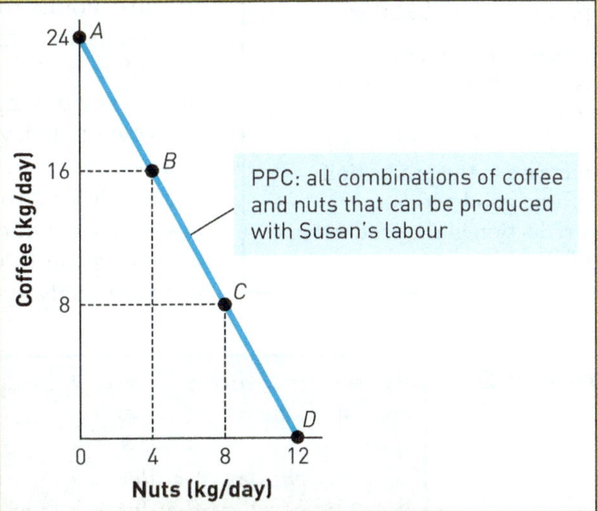

Figure 2.1 Susan's Production Possibilities
For the production relationships given, the PPC is a straight line.

Since Susan's PPC is a straight line, its slope is constant. The absolute value of the slope of Susan's PPC is the ratio of its vertical intercept to its horizontal intercept: (24 kg of coffee/day)/(12 kg of nuts/day) = (2 kg of coffee)/(1 kg of nuts). This ratio means that Susan's *opportunity cost of an additional kilogram of nuts is 2 kg of coffee.*

Note that Susan's opportunity cost (*OC*) of nuts can also be expressed as the following simple formula:

$$\mathrm{OC}_{nuts} = \frac{\text{Loss in coffee}}{\text{Gain in nuts}} \qquad (2.1)$$

where 'loss in coffee' means the amount of coffee given up, and 'gain in nuts' means the corresponding increase in nuts. Likewise, Susan's opportunity cost of coffee can be expressed by this formula:

$$\mathrm{OC}_{coffee} = \frac{\text{Loss in nuts}}{\text{Gain in coffee}} \qquad (2.2)$$

To say that Susan's opportunity cost of an additional kilogram of nuts is 2 kg of coffee is thus equivalent to saying that her opportunity cost of a kilogram of coffee is $\frac{1}{2}$ kg of nuts.

The downward slope of the PPC shown in Fig. 2.1 illustrates the Scarcity Principle – the idea that because our resources are limited, having more of one good thing generally means having to settle for less of another (see Chapter 1). Susan can have an additional kilogram of coffee if she wishes, but only if she is willing to give up half a kilogram of nuts. As Susan is the only person in the economy, her opportunity cost of producing a good is its *price*. Thus the price she has to pay for an additional kilogram of coffee is half a kilogram of nuts; or the price she has to pay for an additional kilogram of nuts is 2 kg of coffee.

Any point that lies either along the PPC or within it is said to be an **attainable point**, meaning that it can be produced with currently available resources. In Fig. 2.2, for example, points *A*, *B*, *C*, *D* and *E* are attainable points. Points that lie outside the PPC are said to be **unattainable**, meaning that they cannot be produced using currently available resources. In Fig. 2.2, *F* is an unattainable point because Susan cannot pick 16 kg of coffee per day *and* 8 kg of nuts. Points that lie within the curve are said to be **inefficient points**, in the sense that existing resources would allow for production of more of at least one good without sacrificing the production of any other good. At *E*, for example, Susan is picking only 8 kg of coffee per day and 4 kg of nuts, which means that she could increase her coffee harvest per day without giving up any nuts (by moving from *E* to *B*) or pick more nuts each day without giving up any coffee (by moving from *E* to *C*). An **efficient point** is one that lies along the PPC. At any such point, more of one good can be produced only by producing less of the other.

attainable point any combination of goods that can be produced using currently available resources

unattainable point any combination of goods that cannot be produced using currently available resources

inefficient point any combination of goods for which currently available resources enable an increase in the production of one good without a reduction in the production of the other

efficient point any combination of goods for which currently available resources do not allow an increase in the production of one good without a reduction in the production of the other

Exercise 2.2

For the PPC shown in Fig. 2.2, state whether the following points are attainable and/or efficient:

a. 20 kg per day of coffee, 4 kg per day of nuts
b. 12 kg per day of coffee, 6 kg per day of nuts
c. 4 kg per day of coffee, 8 kg per day of nuts.

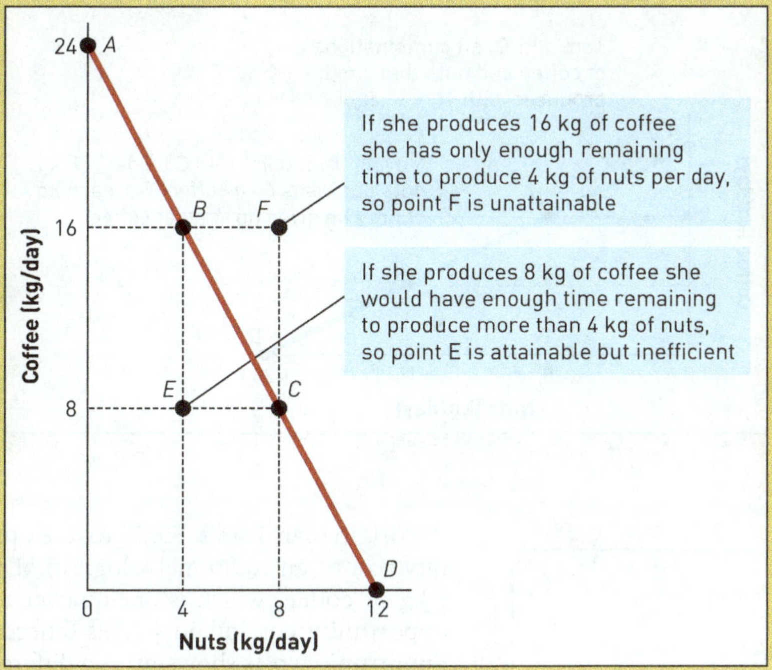

Figure 2.2 Attainable and Efficient Points on Susan's PPC

Points that lie either along the PPC (for example, *A*, *B*, *C* and *D*) or within it (for example, *E*) are said to be attainable. Points that lie outside the PPC (for example, *F*) are unattainable. Points that lie along the PPC are said to be efficient, while those that lie within the PPC are said to be inefficient.

HOW INDIVIDUAL PRODUCTIVITY AFFECTS THE SLOPE AND POSITION OF THE PPC

Now suppose there are two workers, Susan and Tom. The PPC will now reflect both their activities. To see how the slope and position of the PPC depend on an individual's productivity, let us compare Susan's PPC to that of Tom, who is less productive at picking coffee but more productive at picking nuts.

How do changes in productivity affect the opportunity cost of nuts? — Example 2.3

Tom is especially well suited to picking nuts that grow on hillside trees. He can pick 4 kg of nuts or 2 kg of coffee per hour. If Tom were the only person in the economy, describe the economy's PPC.

We can construct Tom's PPC the same way we did Susan's. Note first that if Tom devotes an entire workday (6 hours) to coffee picking, he ends up with (6 hours/day) × (2 kg/hour) = 12 kg of coffee per day and 0 kg of nuts. So the vertical intercept of Tom's PPC is *A* in Fig. 2.3. If instead he devotes all his time to picking nuts, he gets (6 hours/day) × (4 kg/hour) = 24 kg of nuts per day and no coffee. That means that the horizontal intercept of his PPC is *D* in Fig. 2.3. Because Tom's production of each good is proportional to the amount of time he devotes to it, the remaining points on his PPC will lie along the straight line that joins these two extreme points.

For example, if Tom devotes 4 hours each day to picking coffee and 2 hours to picking nuts, he will end up with (4 hours/day) × (2 kg/hour) = 8 kg of coffee per day and (2 hours/day) × (4 kg/hour) = 8 kg of nuts per day. This is the point labelled *B* in Fig. 2.3. Alternatively, if he devotes 2 hours to coffee and 4 to nuts, he will get (2 hours/day) × (2 kg/hour) = 4 kg of coffee per day and (4 hours/day) × (4 kg/hour) = 16 kg of nuts. This alternative combination is represented by point *C* in Fig. 2.3.

How does Tom's PPC compare with Susan's? Note in Fig. 2.4 that because Tom is *absolutely* less productive than Susan at picking coffee, the vertical intercept of his PPC lies closer to the origin than Susan's. By the same token, because Susan is *absolutely* less productive than Tom at picking nuts, the horizontal intercept of her PPC lies closer to

Figure 2.3 Tom's PPC
Tom's opportunity cost of producing 1 kg of nuts is only $\frac{1}{2}$ kg of coffee.

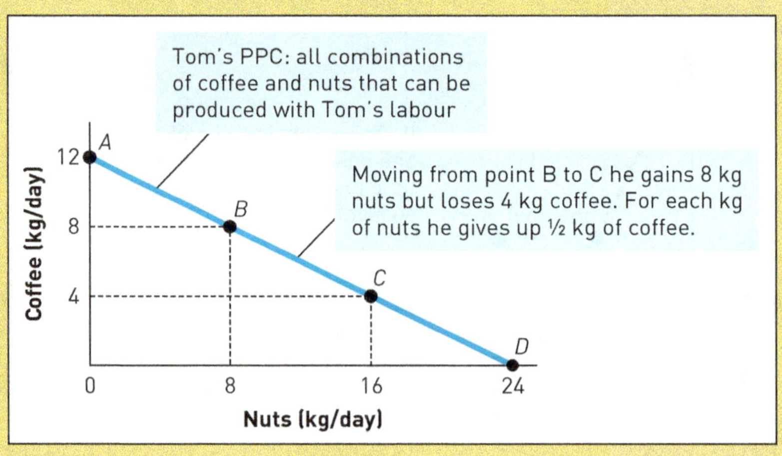

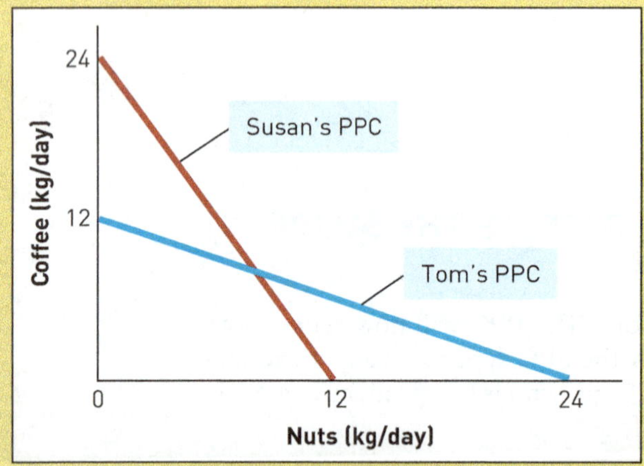

Figure 2.4 Individual PPCs Compared
Tom is less productive in coffee than Susan, but more productive in nuts.

the origin than Tom's. For Tom, the opportunity cost of an additional kilogram of nuts is $\frac{1}{2}$ kg of coffee, which is one-quarter Susan's opportunity cost of nuts. This difference in opportunity costs shows up as a difference in the slopes of their PPCs: the absolute value of the slope of Tom's PPC is $\frac{1}{2}$, whereas Susan's is 2.

In this example, Tom has both an absolute advantage and a comparative advantage over Susan in picking nuts. Susan, for her part, has both an absolute advantage and a comparative advantage over Tom in picking coffee.

We cannot emphasise too strongly that the Principle of Comparative Advantage is a *relative* concept – one that makes sense only when the productivities of two or more people (or countries) are being compared. To cement this idea, work through Exercise 2.3.

Exercise 2.3 Suppose Susan can pick 2 kg of coffee per hour or 4 kg of nuts per hour; Tom can pick 1 kg of coffee per hour and 1 kg of nuts per hour. What is Susan's opportunity cost of picking 1 kg of nuts? What is Tom's opportunity cost of picking 1 kg of nuts? Where does Susan's comparative advantage now lie?

THE GAINS FROM SPECIALISATION

Earlier we saw that a comparative advantage arising from disparities in individual opportunity costs creates gains for everyone (see Examples 2.1 and 2.2). Example 2.4 shows how the same point can be illustrated using PPCs.

Example 2.4 How costly is failure to specialise?

Suppose that in Example 2.3 Susan and Tom had divided their time so that each person's output consisted of half nuts and half coffee. How much of each good would

Tom and Susan have been able to consume? How much could they have consumed if each had specialised in the activity for which he or she enjoyed a comparative advantage?

Since Tom can pick twice as many kg of nuts in an hour as kg of coffee, to pick equal quantities of each he must spend 2 hours picking coffee for every hour he devotes to picking nuts. And since he works a 6-hour day, that means spending 2 hours picking nuts and 4 hours picking coffee. Dividing his time in this way, he will end up with 8 kg of coffee and 8 kg of nuts per day. Similarly, since Susan can pick twice as many kg of coffee in an hour as kg of nuts, to pick equal quantities of each she must spend 2 hours picking nuts for every hour she devotes to picking coffee. And since she too works a 6-hour day, that means spending 2 hours picking coffee and 4 hours picking nuts. So, like Tom, she will end up with 8 kg of coffee per day and 8 kg of nuts (see Fig. 2.5). Their combined daily production will thus be 16 kg of each good. Had they each specialised in their respective activities of comparative advantage, their combined daily production would have been 24 kg of each good.

If they exchange coffee and nuts with one another, each can consume a combination of the two goods that would have been unattainable if exchange had not been possible. For example, Susan can give Tom 12 kg of coffee in exchange for 12 kg of nuts, enabling each to consume 4 kg per day more of each good than when each produced and consumed alone. Note that point *E* in Fig. 2.5, which has 12 kg per day of each good, lies beyond both Tom's and Susan's PPC, yet is easily attainable with specialisation and exchange.

As Exercise 2.4 illustrates, the gains from specialisation grow larger as the difference in opportunity costs increases.

Does it matter how they specialise?

Yes, it does. On the basis of the data used to produce Fig. 2.5 we can show how they should specialise so as to maximise their possible income from coffee and nuts (Fig. 2.6).

Susan has a comparative advantage in coffee, and Tom has a comparative advantage in nuts. Suppose they both devote all their time to nuts. The total they can produce is 36 kg of nuts per day. They decide to reduce nut production in order to produce coffee. Suppose Susan starts to produce coffee (in which she has a comparative advantage). The combined total of coffee and nuts is given by the solid line. When Susan gives all her time to coffee they are producing 24 kg of nuts (Tom being the nut producer) and 24 kg of coffee (the solid lines). They have specialised to reflect comparative advantage. Suppose, however, they decided to let Tom start producing coffee, while Susan produced

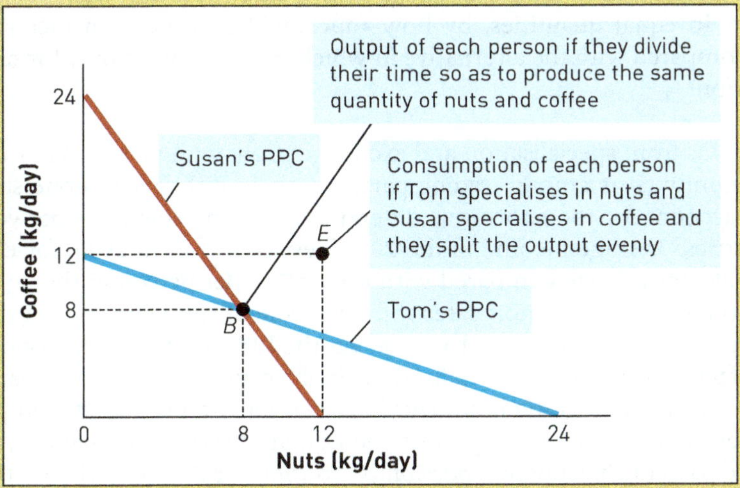

Figure 2.5 Production without Specialisation

When Tom and Susan divide their time so that each produces the same number of kilograms of coffee and nuts, they can produce a total of 16 kg of coffee and 16 kg of nuts each day.

Figure 2.6 Specialisation to Reflect Comparative Advantage

If Susan specialises in coffee, and Tom specialises in nuts, the quantities they can produce together are greater than if they specialise the other way. The solid lines constitute their *production possibility frontier* (PPF) or *production possibility curve* (PPC).

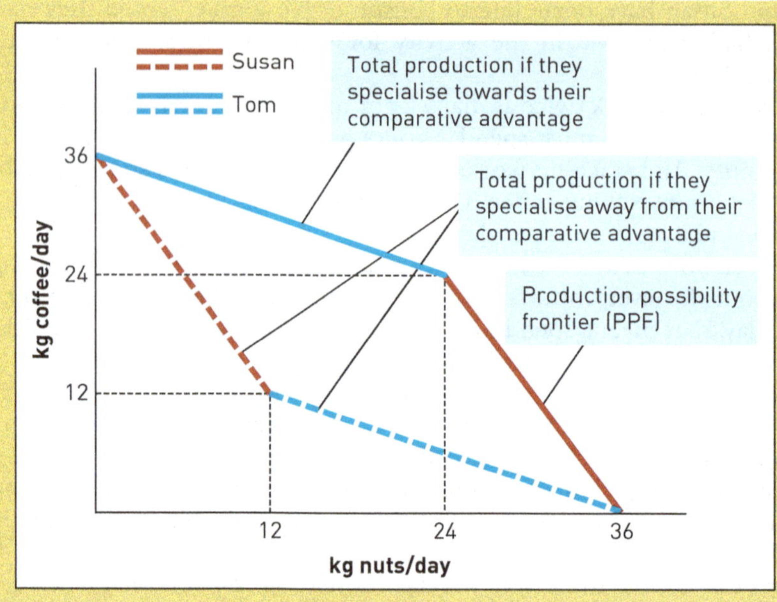

nuts. When Tom was fully occupied producing coffee, and Susan producing nuts, they would produce a total of 12 kg of nuts and 12 kg of coffee (the broken lines).

When they specialise according to comparative advantage the combination of coffee and nuts they can produce is given by the solid line production 'frontier'. This lies outside the alternative 'frontier', implying that specialising according to comparative advantage makes possible higher levels of output of both goods . . . and higher incomes for the two producers. The solid lines constitute their *production possibility curve* (PPC) or *production possibility frontier* (PPF). If they decided that they wanted to produce 6 kg of coffee it would make more sense to use Susan's time producing coffee rather than to use Tom's, since 6 kg of coffee so produced cost them only 3 kg of nuts, while assigning the job of producing 6 kg of coffee to Tom would cost them 12 kg of nuts.

Increasing Opportunity Cost

Exercise 2.4 How do differences in opportunity cost affect the gains from specialisation?

Susan can pick 5 kg of coffee or 1 kg of nuts in an hour. Tom can pick 1 kg of coffee or 5 kg of nuts in an hour. Assuming they again work 6-hour days and want to consume coffee and nuts in equal quantities, by how much will specialisation increase their consumption compared with the alternative in which each produced only for his or her own consumption?

Although the gains from specialisation and exchange grow with increases in the differences in opportunity costs among trading partners, these differences alone still seem insufficient to account for the enormous differences in living standards between rich and poor countries. Average income in the 20 richest countries in 2000, for example, was over €27,000 per person, compared with only €211 per person in the 20 poorest countries. Although we will say more later about the role of specialisation in explaining these differences, we first discuss how to construct the PPC for an entire economy and examine how factors other than specialisation might cause it to shift outwards over time. Because the PPC marks the boundary between what an economy can produce from its own resources and levels of production that are beyond its capability, it is frequently referred to as the 'production possibility frontier', or PPF. We will use the term PPF rather than PPC for the remainder of this chapter.

A PPF FOR A MANY-PERSON ECONOMY

We can use an extension of the Susan and Tom case to build a production possibility curve for an economy with a greater number of workers (Fig. 2.7), in this case, three workers.

We shall say more in a moment about the reasons for this 'bow' shape. But first note that a bow-shaped PPF means that the opportunity cost of producing nuts increases as the economy produces more of them. This pattern of *increasing opportunity cost* persists over the entire length of the PPF. Note, finally, that the same pattern of increasing opportunity cost applies to coffee. Thus, as more coffee is produced, the opportunity cost of producing additional coffee – as measured by the amount of nuts that must be sacrificed – also rises.

Why is the PPF for the multi-person economy bow-shaped? The answer lies in the fact that some resources are relatively well suited to picking nuts while others are relatively well suited to picking coffee. If the economy is initially producing only coffee and wants to begin producing some nuts, which workers will it reassign? Recall Susan and Tom, the two workers discussed in Example 2.4, in which Tom's comparative advantage was picking nuts and Susan's comparative advantage was picking coffee. We showed that it made sense to ask Susan to start producing coffee before asking Tom to do so. If both workers were currently picking coffee and you wanted to reassign one of them to pick nuts instead, whom would you send? Tom would be the clear choice, because his departure would cost the economy only half as much coffee as Susan's and would augment nut production by twice as much.

The principle is the same in any large multi-person economy, except that the range of opportunity cost differences across workers is even greater than in Example 2.4. As we keep reassigning workers from coffee production to nut production, sooner or later we must withdraw even coffee specialists like Susan from coffee production. Indeed, we must eventually reassign others whose opportunity cost of producing nuts is far higher than hers.

The shape of the PPF shown in Fig. 2.7 illustrates the general principle that when resources have different opportunity costs, we should always exploit the resource with the lowest opportunity cost first. We call this the *Low-Hanging-Fruit Principle*, in honour of the fruit picker's rule of picking the most accessible fruit first.

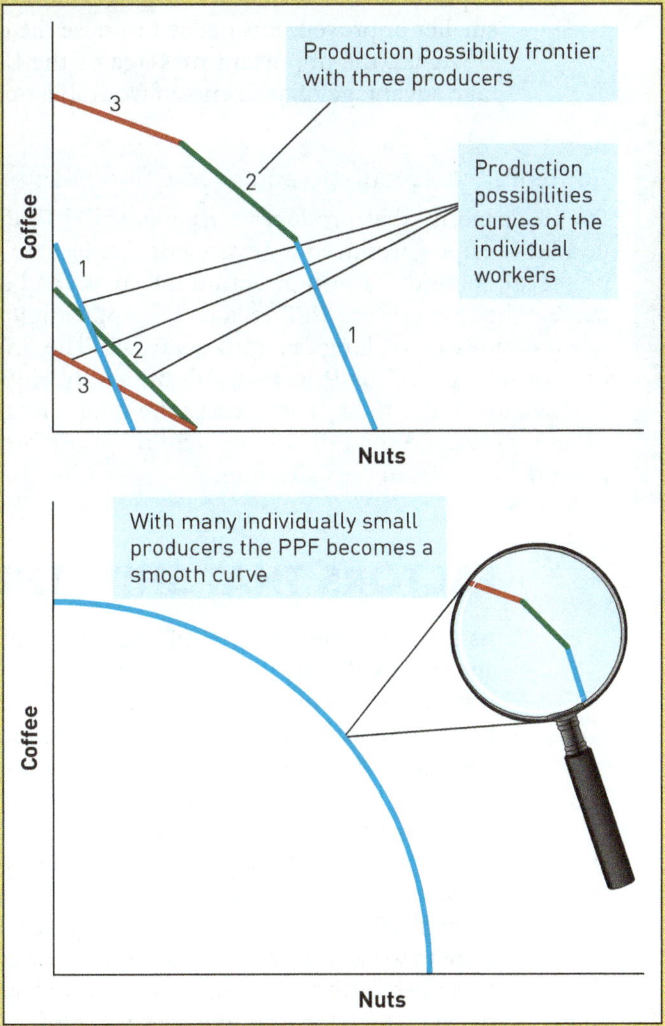

Figure 2.7 The PPF for a Multi-Person Economy

In the upper panel, a three-person economy; in the bottom panel a million-person economy. For an economy with millions of workers, the PPF typically has a gentle outward bow shape.

The Principle of Increasing Opportunity Cost (also called 'The Low-Hanging-Fruit Principle'): in expanding the production of any good, first employ those resources with the lowest opportunity cost, and only afterwards turn to resources with higher opportunity costs.

A note on the logic of the fruit picker's rule

Why should a fruit picker harvest the low-hanging fruit first? This rule makes sense for several reasons. For one, the low-hanging fruit is easier (and hence cheaper) to pick, and if he or she planned on picking only a limited amount of fruit to begin with, they would clearly come out ahead by avoiding the less accessible fruit on the higher branches. But even if they planned on picking all the fruit on the tree, they would do better to start with the lower branches first, because this would enable them to enjoy the revenue from the sale of the fruit sooner.

The fruit picker's job can be likened to the task confronting a new chief executive officer (CEO) who has been hired to reform an inefficient, ailing company. The CEO has limited time and attention, so it makes sense to focus first on the problems that are relatively easy to correct and whose elimination will provide the biggest improvements in performance – the low-hanging fruit. Later on, the CEO can worry about the many smaller improvements needed to raise the company from very good to excellent.

Again, the important message of the Low-Hanging-Fruit Principle is to be sure to take advantage of your most favourable opportunities first.

RECAP

Comparative advantage and production possibilities

For an economy that produces two goods, the PPF describes the maximum amount of one good that can be produced for every possible level of production of the other good. Attainable points are those that lie on or within the curve, and efficient points are those that lie along the curve. The slope of the PPF tells us the opportunity cost of producing an additional unit of the good measured along the horizontal axis. The Principle of Increasing Opportunity Cost, or the Low-Hanging-Fruit Principle, tells us that the slope of the PPF becomes steeper as we move downwards to the right. The greater the differences among individual opportunity costs, the more bow-shaped the PPF will be, and the more bow-shaped the PPF, the greater will be the potential gains from specialisation.

FACTORS THAT SHIFT THE ECONOMY'S PPF

As its name implies, the PPF provides a summary of the production options open to any society. At any given moment, the PPF confronts society with a *trade-off*: the only way people can produce and consume more nuts is to produce and consume less coffee. In the long run, however, it is often possible to increase production of all goods. This is what is meant when people speak of economic growth. As shown in Fig. 2.8, economic growth is an outward shift in the economy's PPF. It can result from increases in the amount of productive resources available or from improvements in knowledge or technology that render existing resources more productive.

What causes the quantity of productive resources to grow in an economy? One factor is *investment* in new factories and equipment. When workers have more and better equipment to work with, their productivity increases, often dramatically. This is surely an important factor behind the differences in living standards between rich and poor countries. According to one study, for example, the value of capital investment per worker in the United States is about $30,000, while in Nepal the corresponding figure is less than $1,000.[2]

Such large differences in capital per worker do not occur all at once. They are a consequence of decades – even centuries – of differences in rates of savings and

[2] Heston and Summers (1991).

investment. Over time, even small differences in rates of investment can translate into extremely large differences in the amount of capital equipment available to each worker. Differences of this sort are often *self-reinforcing*: not only do higher rates of saving and investment cause incomes to grow, but the resulting higher income levels also make it easier to devote additional resources to savings and investment. Over time, then, even small initial productivity advantages from specialisation can translate into very large income gaps.

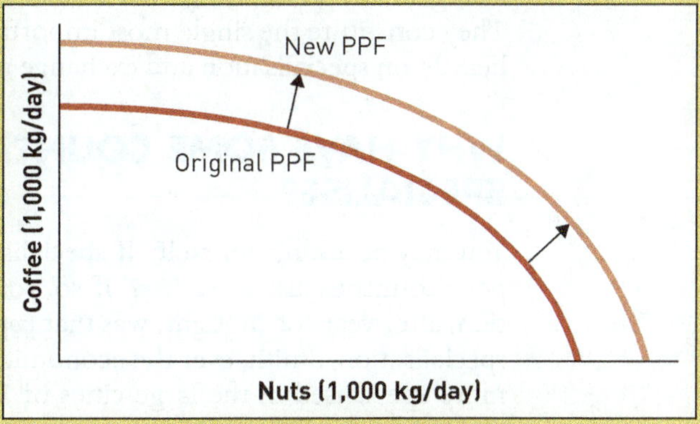

Figure 2.8 Economic Growth: An Outward Shift in the Economy's PPF

Increases in productive resources (such as labour and capital equipment) or improvements in knowledge and technology cause the PPF to shift outwards. They are the main factors that drive economic growth.

Population growth also causes an economy's PPF curve to shift outwards and thus is often listed as one of the sources of economic growth. But because population growth also generates more mouths to feed, it cannot by itself raise a country's standard of living. Indeed it may even cause a decline in the standard of living if existing population densities have already begun to put pressure on available land, water and other scarce resources.

Perhaps the most important source of economic growth is improvements in *knowledge and technology*. As economists have long recognised, such improvements often lead to higher output through increased specialisation. Improvements in technology often occur spontaneously, but more frequently they are directly or indirectly the result of increases in education.

In Exercise 2.4 we discussed a two-person example in which individual differences in opportunity cost led to a threefold gain from specialisation. Real-world gains from specialisation often are far more spectacular than those in the example. One reason is that specialisation not only capitalises on pre-existing differences in individual skills but also deepens those skills through practice and experience. Moreover, it eliminates many of the switching and start-up costs people incur when they move back and forth among numerous tasks. These gains apply not only to people but also to the tools and equipment they use. Breaking a task down into simple steps, each of which can be performed by a different machine, greatly multiplies the productivity of individual workers.

Even in simple settings, these factors can combine to increase productivity hundreds- or even thousands-fold. Adam Smith, the Scottish moral philosopher who is remembered today as the founder of modern economics, was the first to recognise the magnitude of the gains made possible by the division and specialisation of labour. Consider, for instance, his description of work in an eighteenth-century Scottish pin factory:

> One man draws out the wire, another straightens it, a third cuts it, a fourth points it, a fifth grinds it at the top for receiving the head; to make the head requires two or three distinct operations . . . I have seen a small manufactory of this kind where only ten men were employed . . . [who] could, when they exerted themselves, make among them . . . upwards of forty-eight thousand pins in a day. Each person, therefore, making a tenth part of forty-eight thousand pins, might be considered as making four thousand eight hundred pins in a day. But if they had all wrought separately and independently, . . . they certainly could not each of them have made twenty, perhaps not one pin in a day.[3]

[3] This quotation is from Book 1 of Smith's *An Enquiry into the Nature and Causes of the Wealth of Nations*, usually referred to today as *The Wealth of Nations*, originally published in 1776 and frequently said to have launched the discipline of economics (Smith, 1776, book 1).

The gains in productivity that result from specialisation are indeed often prodigious. They constitute the single most important explanation for why societies that don't rely heavily on specialisation and exchange are rapidly becoming relics.

WHY HAVE SOME COUNTRIES BEEN SLOW TO SPECIALISE?

You may be asking yourself, 'If specialisation is such a great thing, why don't people in poor countries just specialise?' If so, you are in good company. Adam Smith's explanation, after years of thought, was that *population density* is an important precondition for specialisation. Smith, ever the economic naturalist, observed that work tended to be far more specialised in the large cities of England in the eighteenth century than in the rural highlands of Scotland:

> In the lone houses and very small villages which are scattered about in so desert a country as the Highlands of Scotland, every farmer must be butcher, baker and brewer for his own family . . . A country carpenter . . . is not only a carpenter, but a joiner, a cabinet maker, and even a carver in wood, as well as a wheelwright, a ploughwright, a cart and wagon maker.[4]

In contrast, each of these same tasks was performed by a different specialist in the large English and Scottish cities of Smith's day. Scottish highlanders would also have specialised had they been able to, but the markets in which they participated were simply too small and fragmented. Of course, high population density by itself provides no guarantee that specialisation will result in rapid economic growth. But especially before the arrival of modern shipping and electronic communications technology, low population density was a definite obstacle to gains from specialisation.

Nepal remains one of the most remote and isolated countries on the planet. In the mid-1960s, its average population density was less than 30 people per km^2. Specialisation was further limited by Nepal's rugged terrain. Exchanging goods and services with residents of other villages was difficult, because the nearest village in most cases could be reached only after trekking for several hours, or even days, over treacherous Himalayan trails. More than any other factor, this extreme isolation accounts for Nepal's long-standing failure to benefit from widespread specialisation.

Population density is by no means the only important factor that influences the degree of specialisation. Specialisation may be severely impeded, for example, by *laws and customs* that limit people's freedom to transact freely with one another. The communist governments of North Korea and the former East Germany (GDR) restricted exchange severely, which helps explain why those countries achieved far less specialisation than South Korea and the former West Germany (FRG), whose governments were far more supportive of specialisation and market exchange.

Finally, specialisation is limited by the *size of the market*. It is worth doing only if a significant quantity of output is to be produced. Hence the 'chicken and egg' problem in a country like Nepal: large-scale production, high productivity and high income depend on division of labour, but division of labour is worthwhile only to the extent that the level of demand for the final products produced by labour warrants it. Because there is little specialisation, Nepal is poor . . . but because it is poor there is little incentive to specialise.

CAN WE HAVE TOO MUCH SPECIALISATION?

The mere fact that specialisation boosts productivity does not mean that more specialisation is always better than less, for specialisation also entails *costs*. For example, most

[4] Smith op. cit., book 1, ch. 2.

people appear to enjoy variety in the work they do, yet variety tends to be one of the first casualties as workplace tasks become ever more narrowly specialised. Indeed, one of Karl Marx's central themes was that the fragmentation of workplace tasks often exacts a heavy psychological toll on workers:

> All means for the development of production . . . mutilate the labourer into a fragment of a man, degrade him to the level of an appendage of a machine, destroy every remnant of charm in his work and turn it into hated toil.[5]

Do the extra goods made possible by specialisation simply come at too high a price? We must certainly acknowledge at least the *potential* for specialisation to proceed too far. Yet specialisation need not entail rigidly segmented, mind-numbingly repetitive work. And it is important to recognise that *failure* to specialise entails costs as well. Those who don't specialise must accept low wages or work extremely long hours.

When all is said and done, we can expect to meet life's financial obligations in the shortest time – thereby freeing up more time to do whatever else we wish – if we concentrate at least a significant proportion of our efforts on those tasks for which we have a comparative advantage. But strange things can affect a country's comparative advantage. See Economic Naturalist 2.3.

Economic Naturalist 2.3
How did branding restore Switzerland's watch-making industry?

Technological advances in the 1970s and 1980s resulted in a major challenge to one of Switzerland's most important industries, making and selling high-quality mechanical watches. The Swiss reputation for very high-quality and expensive time-pieces and the experience of Swiss manufacturers enabled the Swiss industry to produce high-volume, relatively low-cost watches for the mass market as well. The challenge came from electronic watches that became as well designed, as reliable and more accurate that the spring-driven, mechanical watches for which Switzerland was famous. And they cost a fraction of the price because they could be made in low-wage countries in the developing world. This changed comparative advantage and it moved away from Swiss watch production to production of electronic competitors, mostly in Asia. Production in Switzerland fell from nearly 85 millions units in 1974 to about 34 millions in 1983. Then along came Swatch. Instead of producing high-price, spring-based mechanical watches, Swatch produced battery-powered, low-cost mechanical watches in a variety of funky designs, fashion accessories rather than heirlooms, and branded as such. Affordability, disposability and style compatibility were the brand keynotes. Later, electronic watches were added to the range. The amazing success of Swatch in the marketplace meant that its battery-powered watches effectively rescued Swiss mechanical watch-making from the edge of disappearance from the mass market, and did so by using clever design to offset the comparative advantage in the mass market originally held by the upstart LED, etc. time-pieces from southern and eastern Asia . . . another example of endogenous comparative advantage.

COMPARATIVE ADVANTAGE AND THE GAINS FROM INTERNATIONAL TRADE

The logic that leads the individuals in an economy to specialise and exchange goods with one another also leads nations to specialise and trade among themselves. As with individuals, nations can benefit from exchange based on comparative advantage, even though one may be generally more productive than another in absolute terms.

[5] Marx (1867, pp. 708–9).

Economic Naturalist 2.4

If trade between nations is so beneficial, why did the WTO talks collapse so spectacularly in 2003?

The World Trade Organisation, an international body, supports and extends free trade among its member nations It meets every few years to negotiate movements towards increased liberalisation of trade. In the summer of 2003 its members met in Cancun in Mexico, but the talks collapsed with a walk-out by a group of (mainly) southern hemisphere countries in September. The breaking point in the talks was the explicit refusal of the US to abandon agricultural subsidies, and the reluctance of the EU to do much either. These subsidies had the effect of depressing the prices received by countries exporting the commodities affected, as they protected EU and US production. At the same time the EU and US were seeking to liberalise trade in manufactured goods and traded services, and arguing that trade liberalisation was superior to aid in promoting economic development. The walk-out was hardly surprising. However, the question is why did the richer countries want to distort trade rather than allow free trade. The answer was simple. Increased free trade would make both the richer countries and the less-developed countries better off by permitting growth of trade based on comparative advantage. However, in both camps there were winners and losers from freeing trade, and the political clout of potential losers was sufficient to make the negotiators try to continue to shelter the losers from competition. Everyone lost so that the losers did not lose.

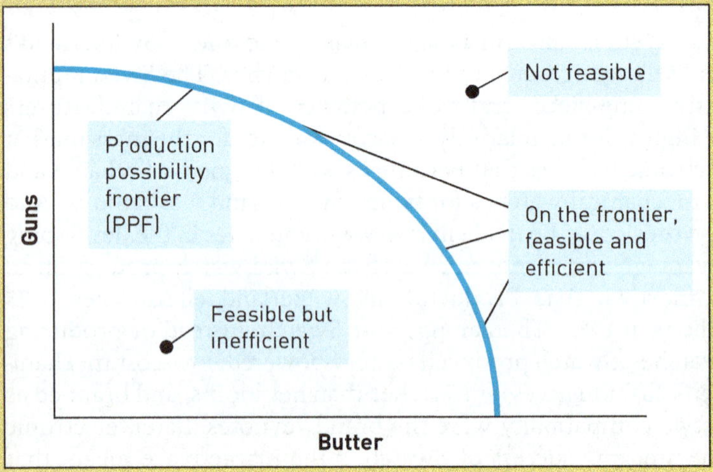

Figure 2.9 Efficient, Inefficient and Impossible Consumption Bundles

Production and consumption within the PPF is inefficient because more of both goods could be produced at no opportunity cost. Consumption of levels of both outside the frontier is not possible from the economy's own resources.

To explain the link between comparative advantage and trade we start with a country's PPF. In this simplified model (Fig. 2.9) we look at an economy that produces and consumes two goods, guns and butter.

Trade permits a country, while it is producing a combination of goods lying along the frontier, to consume a combination lying outside the frontier. This increases economic welfare. In Fig. 2.10 we suppose that the economy is producing and consuming the volumes of the two goods indicated by point *A*. The slope of the PPF at *A* tells us the cost (in guns) of more butter, and the cost of more butter in terms of guns. This is the rate at which the economy can exchange guns and butter from its own resources when it is producing at point *A*. Now suppose the economy is offered the chance to buy or sell the two goods on world markets. World prices are such that guns and butter can be exchanged or traded at prices indicated by the slope of the line *XY*. If the economy now increases production of guns and reduces production of butter (moves to point *B*) it can export guns and import butter to arrive at point *C*. At *C* it is consuming the same amount of guns as at *A* but considerably more butter. Hence economic welfare has increased. Even if consumption does not arrive at *C*, welfare has risen since the potential to consume goods has increased relative to the potential in the absence of trade, because the line *XY* lies on or outside the PPF other than at *B*, and outside it at *A*.

Efficiency

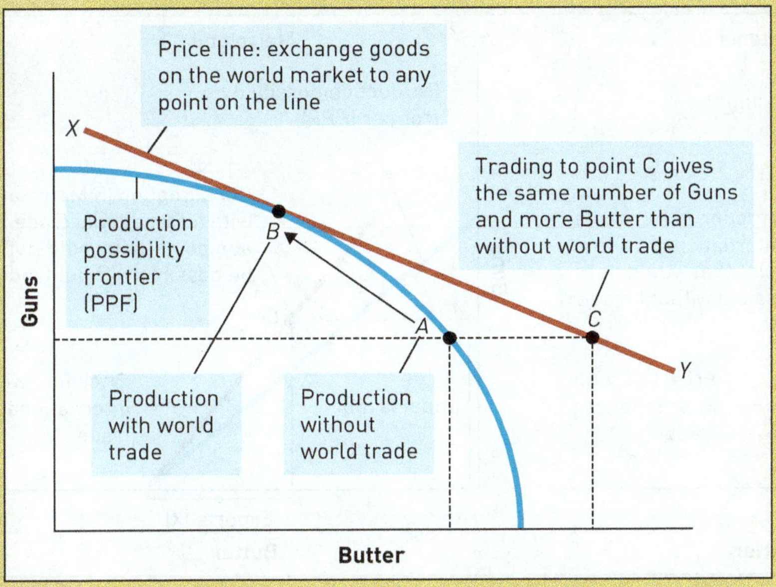

Figure 2.10 Trade and Consumption

When the prices at which a country can trade are different from the opportunity cost of the two goods (the slope of the PPF) the country can increase its total consumption by changing what it produces and exchanging goods at trade prices.

This happens when the opportunity cost of one good in terms of the other in the absence of trade differs from the rate at which the goods can be exchanged through trade. In the absence of trade the country's PPF is both its production and consumption possibility frontier. When trade is possible, trade prices determine its consumption possibilities given its production potential.

Scarcity

Note, however, that trade implies contraction in one industry (butter) and expansion of the other (guns). Obviously this has income implications for people in the two industries. Notice also that the overall gain arises if, and only if, there is a shift of resources and a change in the relative sizes of the two industries. This is why most economists reject the concern expressed by the anti-globalist lobby to the effect that opening up markets in the West to exports from poorer countries should not mean contraction of traditional sectors in the poorer countries. This concern is well meaning but wrong-headed. In order for trade to improve economic welfare, it is necessary that resources be shifted to a growing export sector. If the poor country is fully employed, but at a low income and productivity level, expanding export production means a contraction in the activity in the rest of the economy, and typically in traditional production.

If one country gains from being able to trade, do it and its trading partner both gain? Or does trade mean a gain by one at the expense of the other? The logic of specialisation reflecting comparative advantage suggests the first. Even if one country is less efficient than the other at producing both goods, as with individuals who specialise, both gain from trade.

This is illustrated in Fig. 2.11. Here we have a simplified model with two countries. Ruritania has the same population as Metroland, but is less efficient at producing both guns and butter. To make the story simpler still, we assume straight-line PPFs in both countries. Note that although one country is more efficient than the other in producing both goods, the slopes of the PPFs are different. Metroland has an absolute advantage in producing both, but a comparative advantage in producing butter. Ruritania's comparative advantage is in producing guns.

If there is no trade between them, each is limited in its consumption by its PPF. Now suppose trade is permitted, and the goods can be exchanged as indicated by the red trade exchange rate line. This is steeper than the Metroland PPF, but shallower than the Ruritania PPF. That is, trade is possible and the goods can be exchanged in trade at rates that differ from their opportunity costs in both countries.

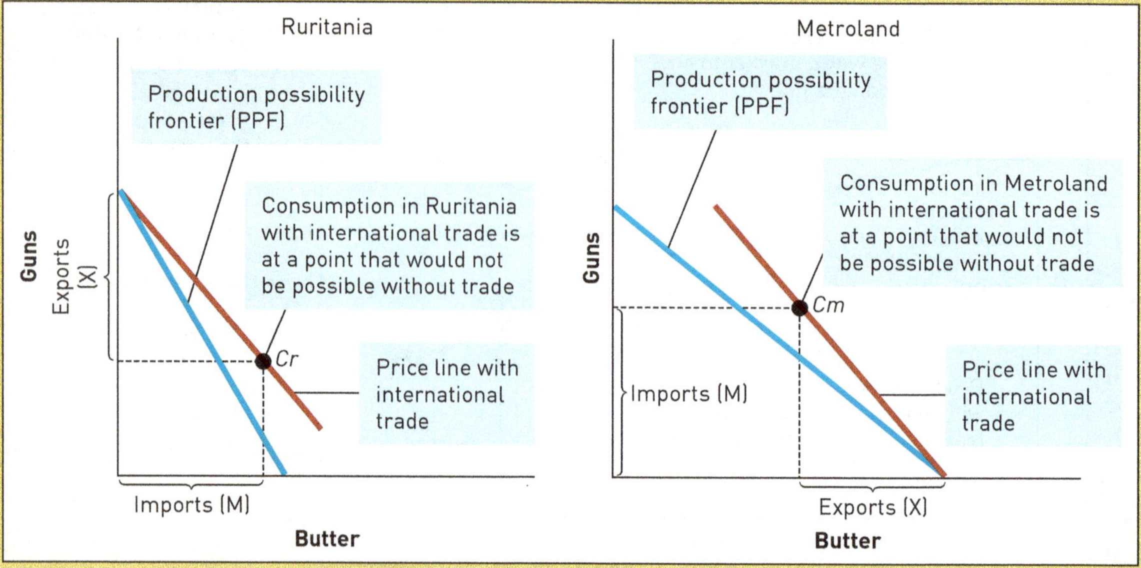

Figure 2.11 Specialisation and the Gain from Trade

When countries specialise according to comparative advantage, and trade accordingly, both can consume at levels in excess of what would be possible if there were no trade.

Ruritania, having specialised in producing guns, exports some of these to Metroland (X on the vertical axis in the left-hand panel) and imports butter from Metroland (M on the horizontal axis). It receives more butter this way than if it had produced the butter by producing fewer guns. Total consumption is at *Cr*, outside Ruritania's PPF. Similarly, Metroland on this basis ends up consuming at *Cm*, also outside its PPF. Both countries have gained from trade.

RECAP

Comparative advantage and international trade

Nations, like individuals, can benefit from exchange, even though one trading partner may be more productive than the other in absolute terms. The greater the difference between domestic opportunity costs and world opportunity costs, the more a nation benefits from exchange with other nations. But expansion in exchange does not guarantee that each individual citizen will do better. In particular, unskilled workers in high-wage countries may be hurt in the short run by the reduction of barriers to trade with low-wage nations.

SUMMARY

- One person has an *absolute* advantage over another in the production of a good if she can produce more of that good than the other person. One person has a *comparative* advantage over another in the production of a good if she is relatively more efficient than the other person at producing that good, meaning that her opportunity cost of producing it is lower than her counterpart's. Specialisation based on comparative advantage is the basis for economic exchange. When each person specialises in the task at which he or she is relatively more efficient, the economic pie is maximised, making possible the largest slice for everyone.

- At the *individual* level, comparative advantage may spring from differences in talent or ability, or from differences in education, training and experience. At the *national* level, sources of comparative advantage include these innate and learned differences, as well as differences in language, culture, institutions, climate, natural resources and a host of other factors.
- The *production possibilities frontier* (PPF), or *production possibilities curve* (PPC), is a simple device for summarising the possible combinations of output that a society can produce if it employs its resources efficiently. In a simple economy that produces only coffee and nuts, a graph of the PPF shows the maximum quantity of coffee production (vertical axis) possible at each level of nut production (horizontal axis). The slope of the PPF at any point represents the opportunity cost of nuts at that point, expressed in kg of coffee.
- All PPFs slope downwards because of the *Scarcity Principle*, which states that the only way a consumer can get more of one good is to settle for less of another. In economies whose workers have different opportunity costs of producing each good, the slope of the PPF becomes steeper as consumers move downwards along the curve. This change in slope illustrates the Principle of Increasing Opportunity Cost (or the Low-Hanging-Fruit Principle), which states that, in expanding the production of any good, a society should first employ those resources that are relatively efficient at producing that good, only afterwards turning to those that are less efficient.
- Factors that cause a country's PPF to shift outwards over time include *investment* in new factories and equipment, *population growth*, and improvements in *knowledge and technology*.
- The same logic that prompts individuals to specialise in their production and exchange goods with one another also leads nations to specialise and trade with one another. On both levels, each trading partner can benefit from an exchange, even though one may be more productive than the other, in absolute terms, for each good. For both individuals and nations, the benefits of exchange tend to be larger the larger are the differences between the trading partners' *opportunity costs*.

REVIEW QUESTIONS

1. Explain what 'having a comparative advantage' in producing a particular good or service means. What does 'having an absolute advantage' in producing a good or service mean?
2. How will a reduction in the number of hours worked each day affect an economy's PPF?
3. How will technological innovations that boost labour productivity affect an economy's PPF?
4. Why does saying that people are poor because they do not specialise make more sense than saying that people perform their own services because they are poor?
5. What factors have helped the United States to become the world's leading exporter of movies, books and popular music?

PROBLEMS

connect

Problems marked with an asterisk (*) are more difficult.

1. Ted can wax 4 cars per day or wash 12 cars. Tom can wax 3 cars per day or wash 6. What is each man's opportunity cost of washing a car? Who has a comparative advantage in washing cars?

2. Ted can wax a car in 20 minutes or wash a car in 60 minutes. Tom can wax a car in 15 minutes or wash a car in 30 minutes. What is each man's opportunity cost of washing a car? Who has a comparative advantage in washing cars?

3. Toby can produce 5 litres of apple cider or 2.5 kg of feta cheese per hour. Kyle can produce 3 litres of apple cider or 1.5 kg of feta cheese per hour. Can Toby and Kyle benefit from specialisation and trade? Explain.

4. Nancy and Bill are auto mechanics. Nancy takes 4 hours to replace a clutch and 2 hours to replace a set of brakes. Bill takes 6 hours to replace a clutch and 2 hours to replace a set of brakes. State whether anyone has an absolute advantage at either task and, for each task, identify who has a comparative advantage.

5. Consider a society consisting only of Helen, who allocates her time between sewing dresses and baking bread. Each hour she devotes to sewing dresses yields 4 dresses, and each hour she devotes to baking bread yields 8 loaves of bread. If Helen works a total of 8 hours per day, graph her PPF.

6. Refer to Problem 5. Which of the points listed below is efficient? Which is attainable?
   a. 28 dresses per day, 16 loaves per day.
   b. 16 dresses per day, 32 loaves per day.
   c. 18 dresses per day, 24 loaves per day.

7. Suppose that in Problem 5 a sewing machine is introduced that enables Helen to sew 8 dresses per hour rather than only 4. Show how this development shifts her PPF.

8. Refer to Problem 7 to explain what is meant by the following statement: 'An increase in productivity with respect to any one good increases our options for producing and consuming all other goods.'

9. Susan can pick 4 kg of coffee in an hour or 2 kg of nuts. Tom can pick 2 kg of coffee in an hour or 4 kg of nuts. Each works 6 hours per day.
   a. What is the maximum number of kg of coffee the two can pick in a day?
   b. What is the maximum number of kg of nuts the two can pick in a day?
   c. If Susan and Tom were picking the maximum number of kg of coffee when they decided that they would like to begin picking 4 kg of nuts per day, who would pick the nuts, and how many kg of coffee would they still be able to pick?
   d. Now suppose that Susan and Tom were picking the maximum number of kg of nuts when they decided that they would like to begin picking 8 kg of coffee per day. Who would pick the coffee, and how many kg of nuts would they still be able to pick?
   e. Would it be possible for Susan and Tom to pick a total of 26 kg of nuts and 20 kg of coffee each day? If so, how much of each good should each person pick?

10.* Refer to the two-person economy described in Problem 9.
   a. Is the point (30 kg of coffee per day, 12 kg of nuts per day) an attainable point? Is it an efficient point? What about the point (24 kg of coffee per day, 24 kg of nuts per day)?
   b. On a graph with kg of coffee per day on the vertical axis and kg of nuts per day on the horizontal axis, show all the points you identified in Problem 9, parts (a)–(e), and in Problem 10(a). Connect these points with straight lines. Is the result the PPF for an economy consisting of Susan and Tom?
   c. Suppose that Susan and Tom could buy or sell coffee and nuts in the world market at a price of €2 per kg for coffee and €2 per kg for nuts. If each person specialised completely in the good for which he or she had a comparative advantage, how much could they earn by selling all their produce?

d. At the prices just described, what is the maximum amount of coffee Susan and Tom could buy in the world market? The maximum amount of nuts? Would it be possible for them to consume 40 kg of nuts and 8 kg of coffee each day?

e. In light of their ability to buy and sell in world markets at the stated prices, show on the same graph all combinations of the two goods it would be possible for them to consume.

REFERENCES

Heston, A. and R. Summers (1991) 'The Penn World Table (Mark 5): An Expanded Set of International Comparisons, 1950–1988', *Quarterly Journal of Economics*, May, pp. 327–68.

Jørgensen, J.G., T. Lüthje and P.J.H. Schröder (2001) 'Trade: The Work-Horse of Integration', Chapter 6 in J.D. Hansen (ed.), *European Integration – An Economic Perspective* (Oxford: Oxford University Press).

Marx, K. (1867) *Das Kapital* (New York: Modern Library).

Smith, A. (1776) *An Enquiry into the Nature and Causes of the Wealth of Nations* (New York: Everyman's Library).

Chapter 3 Markets, Supply, Demand and Elasticity

The entire economic system depends on the fact that people are willing to do unpleasant things in return for money.
Scott Adams

Learning Objectives

After studying this chapter you should be able to:

1. Understand the coordination problem for society;
2. Understand how buyers respond to prices and are affected by changes in incomes and tastes;
3. Understand how producers respond to prices and how their response is affected by changes in costs and technology;
4. Understand and apply the idea of market equilibrium;
5. Show the impact of interventions in the market;
6. Measure and use the concept of elasticity;
7. Understand and comment on different elasticity measures.

If we added up the stocks of food held in supermarkets, convenience stores and restaurants in any large city we would realise that at any point in time what is available would meet likely demand for a couple of days at the most. Little or no food is actually produced within the city. But by and large city populations (in the developed world, at least) eat well. This requires thousands of tonnes of food to be delivered to an enormous number of locations in the city every day.

Few of us, eating in a restaurant, or buying a sandwich, spend much time thinking about the quite extraordinary coordination of people and resources needed make sure that what we eat is actually available. It all happens without being centrally controlled. No central agency is actually making and executing decisions that result in our being able to eat what we eat when we eat it. Yet someone has to decide how much of each type of food gets delivered to *each* of the many restaurants, hospitals, supermarkets and grocery stores in a large city, how and when it is delivered, and how delivery systems are made available.

It is not simply a question of transport logistics, delivering the various commodities as and when demanded. There is also the question of how the different quantities of the enormous number of products consumed come to be produced in the first place. In each case, and in respect of each kilogram or litre being produced, some individual somewhere is making a decision that determines what is produced, and where it goes. Individual decisions, made by people without any detailed knowledge about who needs what, where and when, somehow

Table 3.1 Mean In-patient Waiting Times, days, 2000, for two elective surgery procedures[1]

	Hip replacement	Knee replacement
Australia	163	201
Denmark	112	112
Finland	206	274
Norway	133	160
Netherlands	96	85
Spain	123	148
England	244	281

produce the end result whereby what we wish to buy is available when and where we look for it.

Thousands of individuals must decide what role, if any, they will play in this collective effort. Some people must choose to drive food-delivery trucks rather than trucks that deliver concrete. Others must become the mechanics who fix these trucks rather than carpenters who build houses. Others must become farmers rather than architects or bricklayers. Still others must become chefs in up-market restaurants, or flip burgers at McDonald's, instead of becoming plumbers or electricians.

Despite the almost incomprehensible number and complexity of the tasks involved, somehow the supplying of the city manages to get done remarkably smoothly. Yes, from time to time a supermarket will run out of stuffed olives, or you may sometimes be told that someone else has just ordered the last serving of roast duck. But such events are rarely a problem. For the most part the city's food delivery system functions so smoothly that it attracts virtually no notice.

But things are not always as smoothly organised. Think about finding an apartment to rent. In many cities there are perennial problems affecting the rental housing market. People face chronic problems in finding accommodation. There is a shortage of rented accommodation, and in some cases this shortage has been increasing rather than declining. We are able to buy the kind of food we want where and where we want it, but we may find it very difficult to find accommodation. Housing services and food are both basic requirements of life, and both are needed in any large city. Food and goods and services generally are available in wide variety, and people (at least those with adequate income) are generally satisfied with what they receive and the choices available to them. In contrast, in the rental housing industry, chronic shortages and chronic dissatisfaction are rife among both buyers and sellers.

Think about healthcare. The market for healthcare services is one in which in some European countries does not appear to work as smoothly as in the case of food supplies. This is far from uniform in terms of the length of waiting times (a measure of ability to 'consume' the service when demanded) (Table 3.1[2]). During the 1990s there were several attempts to re-organise the delivery of UK health services, because the tax-financed National Health Service (NHS) was not seen as delivering care as required when required and at reasonable cost.

[1] Source: Siciliani & Hurst, OECD, 2003.

[2] The authors of this study make clear that there are serious problems in defining waiting periods that have to be dealt with in making cross-country comparisons. These figures should be treated as indicating relative performance rather than being taken as highly reliable point estimates.

Adequate availability of, and access to, healthcare is seen as a basic requirement in modern societies, but despite the steady growth in spending per head on healthcare, in some countries this spending does not deliver the level and type of care that people regard as desirable, while in others it does. Complaints about the availability and quality of healthcare seem to be much less common in the Netherlands, France or Germany than they are in Britain.

In the case of healthcare the reason for this difference in performance is the choice of allocation mechanism used to determine what is produced and where it goes. In the case of many countries the allocation of resources to and within healthcare services is determined collectively through a political process. Changes in demands for treatment do not elicit directly a supply response. Resources are rationed leaving increased demands unmet.

The market for rented accommodation is highly regulated, generally in favour of 'tenants' rights' and building standards. By and large these regulations result in tenants having to pay less than the market rent, and/or have tenancy rights that are onerous on the landlords, and/or increase the cost of providing accommodation. When demand rises, supply response is weak. Shortages appear.

In contrast, by and large, producers and sellers of food are not restricted as to the prices they offer, and face a less restrictive regulatory regime in terms of customer rights and physical planning of retail outlets. The allocation of food essentially in the hands of market forces – the forces of supply and demand.

Both economics theory and everyday experience suggest that the seemingly chaotic and unplanned outcomes of market forces can in most, but not all, cases do a better job of allocating economic resources than can (for example) a government agency, even if the agency has the best of intentions.

In this chapter we shall explore how markets allocate food, housing and other goods and services, usually with remarkable efficiency despite the complexity of the tasks. To be sure, markets are by no means perfect, and our stress on their virtues is to some extent an attempt to counteract what most economists view as an under-appreciation by the general public of their remarkable strengths. But in the course of our discussion we shall see why markets function so smoothly most of the time, and why bureaucratic rules and regulations rarely work as well in solving complex economic problems.

To convey an understanding of how and where markets work well (and where this is not the case) is a major goal of this book. In this chapter we provide only a brief introduction and overview. As the course proceeds we shall discuss the economic role of markets in considerably more detail, paying attention to some of the problems of markets as well as their strengths. In the remainder of this chapter we will first look at the problem of 'value' in relation to 'price'. Then we examine at a basic level the relationships between prices and quantities bought and offered for sale, and the idea of a 'reservation price'. This leads to the concept of 'market equilibrium'. Following that we look at those factors that cause prices and quantities bought and sold to change and, how regulation can affect markets. The final part of the chapter deals with measurement of responses in demand and supply to price and income changes under the heading of 'elasticity'.

BUYERS AND SELLERS IN MARKETS

We begin by defining a **market**: the market for any good consists of all the buyers and sellers of that good. So, for example, the market for pizza on a given day in a given place is just the set of buyers and sellers able to buy or sell pizza at that time and place.

market the market for any good consists of all buyers or sellers of that good

Sellers comprise the individuals and companies that sell – or could sell – pizza. Buyers in this market include all individuals who buy – or might buy – pizza. Depending on location and quality you would expect to be able to buy a slice for less than €3 or its equivalent in most countries in Europe.

Where does the market price of pizza come from? More generally, we may ask: 'Why are some goods cheap and others expensive?' Aristotle had no idea. Nor did Plato, nor Copernicus, nor Newton. It is astonishing that, for almost the entire span of human history, not even the most intelligent and creative minds on earth had any real inkling of how to answer that seemingly simple question. Even Adam Smith suffered confusion on this issue.

Smith and other early economists (including Karl Marx) thought that the market price of a good was determined by its *cost of* production. But although costs do affect prices, they cannot explain why one of Pablo Picasso's paintings sells for so much more than one of Jackson Pollock's.

Stanley Jevons and other nineteenth-century economists tried to explain price by focusing on the value people derived from consuming different goods and services. It is plausible that people will pay a lot for a good they value highly. Yet willingness to pay cannot be the whole story. Deprive a person of water in the desert, for example, and he will be dead in a matter of hours, and yet water sells for just a few cents per litre. Human beings can get along perfectly well without gold, yet in 2011 gold fetched over €1,000 per troy ounce.[3]

The answer to the problem is that both production costs and value to users matter. In the late nineteenth century, the British economist Alfred Marshall was among the first to show clearly how *costs* and *value* interact to determine both the prevailing market price for a good, and the amount of it that is bought and sold. Our task in the pages ahead will be to explore Marshall's insights and gain some practice in applying them. As a first step, we introduce the two main components of Marshall's path-breaking analysis: the **demand curve** and the supply curve.

demand curve a schedule or graph showing the quantity of a good that buyers wish to buy at each price

THE DEMAND CURVE

In the pizza market, the demand curve is a simple schedule or graph that tells us how many slices people would be willing to buy at different prices. By convention, economists usually put price on the vertical axis of the demand curve and quantity on the horizontal axis.

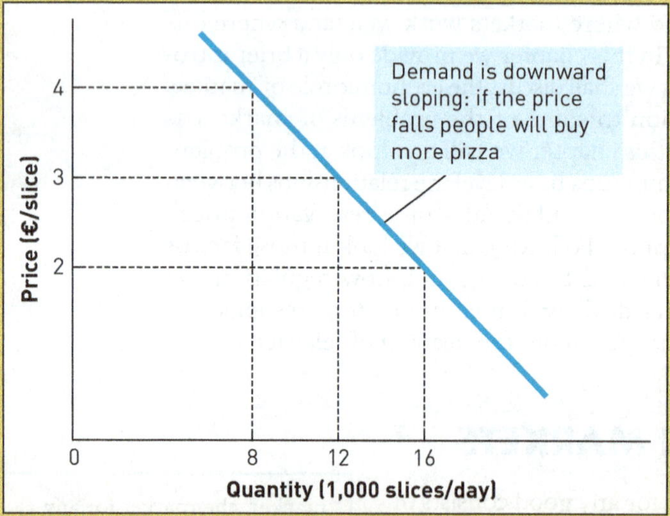

Figure 3.1 The Daily Demand Curve for Pizza
The demand curve for any good is a downward-sloping function of its price.

A fundamental property of the demand curve is that it is *downward-sloping* with respect to price. For example, the demand curve for pizza tells us that as the price of pizza falls, buyers will buy more slices. Thus the daily demand curve for pizza in Manchester or Milan on a given day might look like the curve seen in Fig. 3.1. (Although economists usually refer to demand and supply 'curves', we often draw them as straight lines in examples.)

The demand curve in Fig. 3.1 tells us that when the price of pizza is €2 per slice buyers will want to buy 16,000 slices per day, whereas they will want to buy only 12,000 slices at a price of €3, and only 8,000 at a

[3] The troy ounce is the standard measure of weight for precious metals. Its metric equivalent is approximately 31 grams, and its imperial equivalent is approximately 1.1 ounces avoirdupois.

price of €4. The demand curve for pizza – as for any other good – slopes downward for many reasons. Some have to do with the individual consumer's reactions to price changes: as pizza becomes more expensive, a consumer may switch to chicken sandwiches or other foods that substitute for pizza. This is called the **substitution effect** of a price change. In addition, a price increase reduces the quantity demanded because it reduces a consumer's overall ability to consume. For example, if you have to commute by car to work, and fuel prices rise, you are in a sense poorer. Being poorer, you are likely to spend less on (among other things) fuel for weekend leisure use of your car. This is called the **income effect** of a price change.

substitution effect the change in the quantity demanded of a good that results because buyers switch to substitutes when the price of the good changes

income effect the change in the quantity demanded of a good that results because of a change in real income of purchasers arising from the price change

buyer's reservation price the largest money amount the buyer would be willing to pay for a unit of a good

Another reason that the demand curve slopes downward is that consumers differ in terms of how much they are willing to pay for the good. The Cost–Benefit Principle (Chapter 1) tells us that a given person will buy the good if the expected benefit to be received from it exceeds its cost. The benefit is the **buyer's reservation price**, the highest money amount she (or he) would be willing to pay for the good. The cost to the purchaser is the actual amount that the buyer actually must pay for it, its market price. In most markets, different buyers have different reservation prices. Thus if a good is sold at a high price, it will satisfy the cost–benefit test for fewer buyers than when it sells for a lower price.

To put this same point another way, the downward-sloping demand curve reflects the fact that the reservation price of the marginal buyer declines as the quantity of the good bought increases. Here the marginal buyer is the person who purchases the last unit of the good that is sold. If buyers are currently purchasing 12,000 slices of pizza a day in Fig. 3.1, for example, the reservation price for the buyer of the 12,000th slice must be €3. Similarly, when the quantity sold is 16,000 slices per day, the marginal buyer's reservation price must be only €2.

We defined the demand curve for any good as a schedule telling how much of it consumers wish to purchase at various prices. This is called the *horizontal interpretation* of the demand curve. Using the horizontal interpretation, we start with price on the vertical axis and read the corresponding quantity demanded on the horizontal axis. Thus, at a price of €4 per slice, the demand curve in Fig. 3.1 tells us that the quantity of pizza demanded will be 8,000 slices per day. *It tells us the quantity that will be demanded as a function of the price at which it is made available.*

The demand curve can also be interpreted in a second way, which is to start with quantity on the horizontal axis and then read the marginal buyer's reservation price on the vertical axis. Thus, when the quantity of pizza sold is 8,000 slices per day, the demand curve in Fig. 3.1 tells us that the marginal buyer's reservation price is €4 per slice. This second way of reading the demand curve is called the *vertical interpretation.* This means that the demand curve tells us what the market price will be if any given amount is made available (in this case, if 8,000 slices are offered for sale the price sellers will receive is €4). *It tells us the market price as a function of the available amount.*

Exercise 3.1

In Fig. 3.1, what is the marginal buyer's reservation price when the quantity of pizza sold is 10,000 slices per day? For the same demand curve, what will be the quantity of pizza demanded at a price of €2.50 per slice?

THE SUPPLY CURVE

supply curve a curve or schedule showing the quantity of a good that sellers wish to sell at each price

In the pizza market, the **supply curve** is a schedule or graph that tells us, for any price, the total number of slices that the pizza vendors

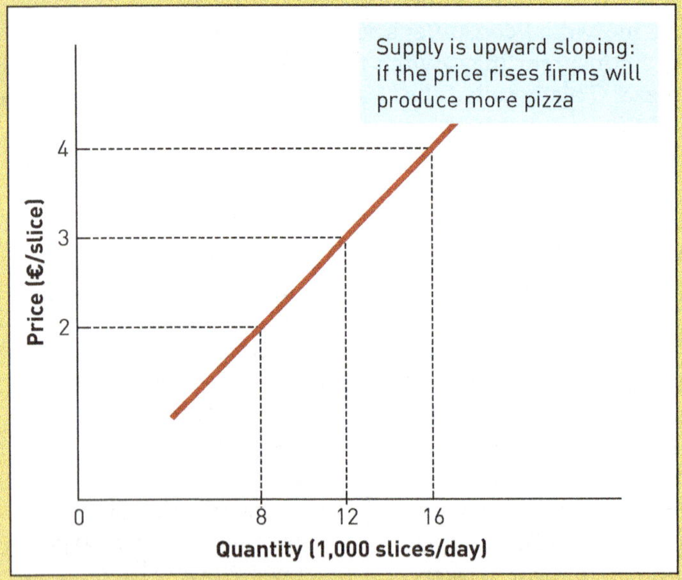

Figure 3.2 The Daily Supply Curve of Pizza
At higher prices, sellers generally offer more units for sale.

would be willing to sell at that price. What does the supply curve of pizza look like? The answer to this question is based on the logical assumption that suppliers should be willing to sell additional slices as long as the price they receive is sufficient to cover their opportunity costs of supplying them. Thus, what you could earn by selling a slice of pizza must be sufficient to compensate you for what you could have earned if you had invested your time and money in some other way.

Sellers usually differ with respect to their opportunity costs of supplying pizza. For those with limited education and work experience, the opportunity cost of selling pizza is relatively low (because typically they have few if any high-paying alternatives). For others the opportunity cost of selling pizza is of moderate value, and for still others – like rock stars and professional athletes – it is prohibitively high. Differences in opportunity cost among people provide one reason for an *upward sloping* daily supply curve of pizza with respect to price. Fig. 3.2, which shows a hypothetical supply curve on a given day.

The upward sloping supply curve may be seen as a consequence of the *Low-Hanging-Fruit Principle*, discussed in Chapter 1. This principle tells us that, as we expand the production of pizza, we turn first to those whose opportunity costs of producing pizza are lowest, and only then to others with higher opportunity costs. It also reflects the fact that if a given producer faces increasing opportunity costs for producing more of a product, it will be necessary to pay more per unit to get more produced.

The supply curve, too, can be interpreted either horizontally or vertically. Under the *horizontal interpretation*, we begin with a price, then go over to the supply curve to read the quantity that sellers wish to sell at that price on the horizontal axis. For instance, at a price of €2 per slice, sellers in Fig. 3.2 wish to sell 8,000 slices per day. *It tells us the quantity that producers will supply as a function of the price they expect to receive.*

Under the *vertical interpretation*, we begin with a quantity, then go up to the supply curve to read the corresponding marginal cost on the vertical axis. Thus, if sellers in Fig. 3.2 are currently supplying 12,000 slices per day, the opportunity cost of the marginal seller is €3 per slice. In other words, the supply curve tells us that the marginal cost of producing the 12,000th slice of pizza is €3. Similarly, when the quantity of pizza supplied is 16,000 slices per day, the marginal cost of producing another slice must be €4. The **seller's reservation price** for selling an additional unit of a good is the *marginal cost* of producing that good. It is the smallest money amount which the seller would accept for selling an additional unit. Under the vertical interpretation the supply curve tells us the sellers' reservation price for any given quantity. *It tells us the amount that will have to be paid to deliver any quantity as a function of quantity.*

> **seller's reservation price** the smallest money amount for which a seller would be willing to sell an additional unit, generally equal to marginal cost

Exercise 3.2 In Fig. 3.2, what is the marginal cost of a slice of pizza when the quantity of pizza sold is 10,000 slices per day? For the same supply curve, what will be the quantity of pizza supplied at a price of €3.50 per slice?

Example 3.1

Samples of points on the demand and supply curves of a pizza market are provided in Table 3.2. Graph the demand and supply curves for this market, and find its equilibrium price and quantity.

The points in Table 3.2 are plotted in Fig. 3.3. and then joined to indicate the supply and demand curves for this market. These curves intersect to yield an *equilibrium price* of €2.50 per slice and an *equilibrium quantity* of 5,000 slices per day. This means a price at which the amount demanded equals the amount being supplied (see below).

Table 3.2 Points along the Demand and Supply Curves of a Pizza Market

Price (€/slice)	Quantity demanded (1,000 slices/day)	Price (€/slice)	Quantity supplied (1,000 slices/day)
1	8	1	2
2	6	2	4
3	4	3	6
4	2	4	8

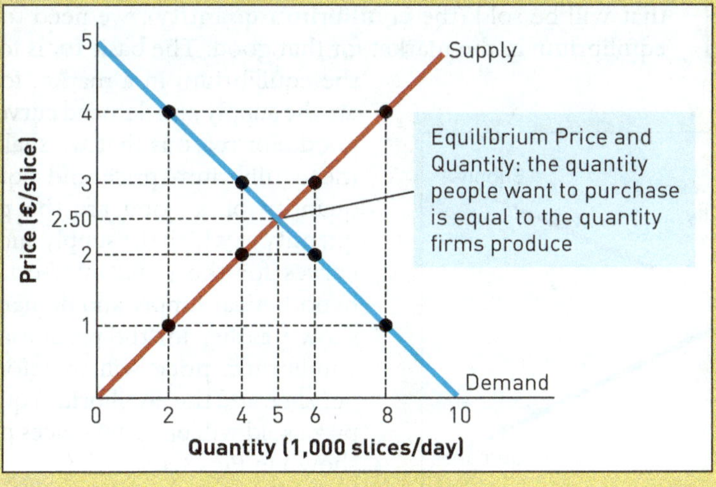

Figure 3.3 Graphing Supply and Demand and Finding the Equilibrium Price and Quantity

To graph the demand and supply curve, plot the relevant points given in Table 3.2 and then join them with a line. The equilibrium price and quantity occur at the intersection of these curves.

RECAP

Demand and supply curves

The *market* for a good consists of the actual and potential buyers and sellers of that good. For any given price, the *demand curve* shows the quantity that demanders would be willing to buy, and the *supply curve* shows the quantity that suppliers of the good would be willing to sell. Suppliers are willing to sell more at higher prices (supply curves slope upward) and demanders are willing to buy less at higher prices (demand curves slope downward).

MARKET EQUILIBRIUM

equilibrium a system is in equilibrium when there is no tendency for it to change

The concept of **equilibrium** is employed in both the physical and social sciences, and it is of central importance in economic analysis. In general, a system is in equilibrium when all forces at work within the system are cancelled by others, resulting in a *stable*, *balanced*, or *unchanging* situation. In physics, for example, a ball hanging from a spring is said to be in equilibrium when the spring has stretched sufficiently that the upward force it exerts on the ball is exactly counterbalanced by the downward force of gravity. The ball does not move. *Its position does not change*. Equilibrium in this sense is a *static* concept. Now consider a falling object. It accelerates and then its speed becomes a constant. This happens when the force of gravity is just offset by the increase in the resistance as it falls though the air. It reaches its terminal velocity. *Its position in space changes at a constant rate*. This is a *dynamic equilibrium*. In economics, a market for a good or service is said to be in equilibrium when no participant in the market has any reason to alter his or her behaviour, so that there is no tendency for production or price in that market to change. This is a *static equilibrium*. If we think about *inflation* – the phenomenon of generally increasing prices for all goods and services – we will realise that the average rate at which prices rise over time is variable. Inflation measures the average rate of increase of prices. When these are such that inflation is constant (the average of prices is rising at a constant rate) we have a *dynamic equilibrium* in prices.

equilibrium price and **equilibrium quantity** the values of price and quantity for which quantity supplied and quantity demanded are equal

If we want to determine the final position of a ball hanging from a spring, we need to find the point at which the forces of gravity and spring tension are balanced and the system is in equilibrium. Similarly, if we want to find the price at which a good will sell (which we will call the **equilibrium price**) and the quantity of it that will be sold (the **equilibrium quantity**), we need to find the equilibrium in the market for that good. The basic tools for finding the equilibrium in a market for a good are the supply and demand curves for that good. For reasons that we shall explain, the equilibrium price and equilibrium quantity of a good are the price and quantity at which the supply and demand curves for the good intersect. For the hypothetical supply and demand curves shown earlier for the pizza market, the equilibrium price will therefore be €3 per slice and the equilibrium quantity of pizza sold will be 12,000 slices per day, as shown in Fig. 3.4.

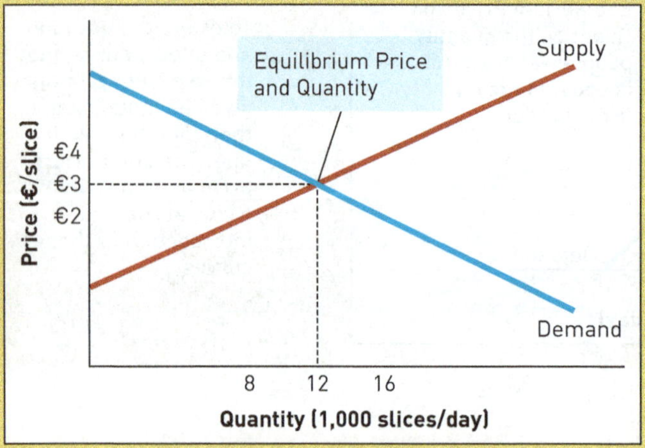

Figure 3.4 The Equilibrium Price and Quantity of Pizza
The equilibrium quantity and price of a product are the values that correspond to the intersection of the supply and demand curves for that product.

In Fig. 3.4, note that at the equilibrium price of €3 per slice, both sellers and buyers are 'satisfied' in the following sense: buyers are buying exactly the quantity of pizza they wish to buy at that price (12,000 slices per day) and sellers are selling exactly the quantity of pizza they wish to sell (also 12,000 slices per day). And since they are satisfied in this sense, *neither buyers nor sellers face any incentives to change their behaviour*.

Note the limited sense of the term 'satisfied' in the definition of **market equilibrium**. It means only that sellers can to sell all they wish to sell at that price. Similarly, it means only that buyers they are able to buy exactly as many units of the good as they wish to at the market price.

market equilibrium occurs in a market when all buyers and sellers are satisfied with their respective quantities at the market price

Note also that if the price of pizza in our market were anything other than €3 per slice, either buyers or sellers would frustrated. Suppose, for example, that the price of pizza were €4 per slice in Fig. 3.5.

At that price, buyers wish to buy only 8,000 slices per day, but sellers wish to sell 16,000. Because no one can force someone to buy a slice of pizza against her wishes, buyers will buy only the 8,000 slices they wish to buy. At any price exceeding the equilibrium price, sellers end up being frustrated. At a price of €4, they are left with an **excess supply** of 8,000 slices per day.

excess supply the amount by which quantity supplied exceeds quantity demanded when the price of a good exceeds the equilibrium price

excess demand the amount by which quantity demanded exceeds quantity supplied when the price of a good lies below the equilibrium price

Conversely, suppose that the price of pizza were less than the equilibrium price – say, €2 per slice. As shown in Fig. 3.5, buyers want to buy 16,000 slices per day at that price, whereas sellers want to sell only 8,000. Because sellers cannot be forced to sell pizza against their wishes, this time it is the buyers who end up being frustrated. At a price of €2 per slice in this example, they experience an **excess demand** of 8,000 slices per day. Would-be buyers are turned away.

An extraordinary feature of markets for goods and services is their automatic tendency to gravitate toward their respective equilibrium prices and quantities. How this happens is implicit in our definitions of excess supply and excess demand. Suppose, for example, that the price of pizza in our hypothetical market was €4 per slice, leading to excess supply, as shown in Fig. 3.5. Sellers are frustrated in the sense of wanting to sell more pizza than buyers wish to buy, and have an incentive to take whatever steps they can to increase their sales. The simplest strategy available to them is to cut their price slightly. Thus, if one seller reduced his price from €4 to, say, €3.95 per slice, he would attract many of the buyers who had been paying €4 per slice for pizza supplied by other sellers. Those sellers, in order to recover their lost business, would then have an incentive to match the price cut. However, even if all sellers lowered their prices to €3.95 per slice, there would still be considerable excess supply. So sellers would face continuing incentives to cut their prices. This pressure to cut prices will not go away until price falls all the way to €3 per slice.

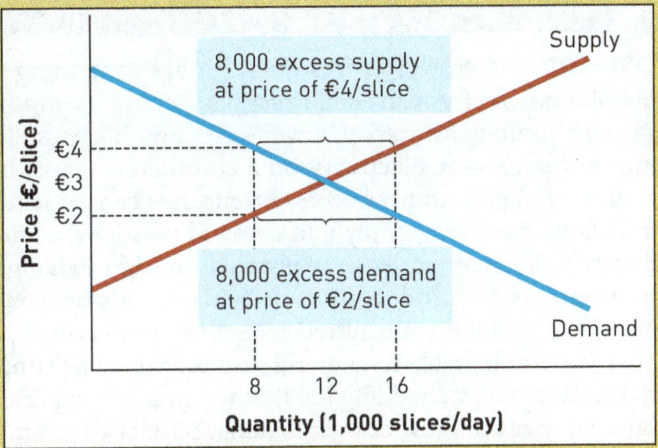

Figure 3.5 Excess Supply and Excess Demand
When price exceeds the equilibrium price, there is excess supply, or surplus, the difference between quantity supplied and quantity demanded. When the price is less than the equilibrium price there is excess demand, or a shortage, the difference between quantity demanded and quantity supplied.

If price starts out less than the equilibrium price – say, €2 per slice – it is buyers who are frustrated. Someone unable to buy as much pizza as desired at a price of €2 per slice has an incentive to offer a higher price, hoping to obtain pizza that would otherwise have been sold to other buyers.[4] And sellers, for their part, will be only too happy to post higher prices as long as queues of frustrated buyers remain.

The upshot is that price has a tendency to gravitate to its equilibrium level under conditions of either excess supply or excess demand. At this level, both buyers and sellers are 'satisfied' in the technical sense of being able to buy or sell precisely the amounts of their choosing.

We emphasise that market equilibrium does not necessarily produce an ideal outcome for all market participants. Thus, in Example 3.1 above, market participants

[4] Unrealistic? Maybe in a pizza parlour where demand exceeds supply, but think about tickets for a rock concert. In any case, the seller has an incentive to raise the price.

are satisfied with the amount of pizza they buy and sell at a price of €2.50 per slice, but for a poor buyer this may be more than he can afford. This means that he can't buy additional pizza without sacrificing other more highly valued purchases.

Indeed, buyers with extremely low incomes often have difficulty purchasing even basic goods and services, which has prompted governments in almost every society to attempt to ease the burdens of the poor. Yet the laws of supply and demand cannot simply be repealed by an act of the legislature. In the next section we will see that when legislators attempt to prevent markets from reaching their equilibrium prices and quantities, they often do more harm than good.

Economic Naturalist 3.1

Why does an increase in demand or an interruption of supply cause few or no problems in the market for cornflakes, but can lead to a virtual collapse in the market for electricity?

Obviously, the answer to this question has something to do with how electricity is produced and distributed, but from an economics perspective its importance lies in highlighting how central to the smooth running of markets inventories are. It's possible to hold stocks of cornflakes; it is virtually impossible to store electricity on a commercial basis. Inventories are both a shock absorber and a source of signals to producers. Inventories can be run down or increased if there is a temporary imbalance between supply and demand (absorb the 'shock'). Changes in inventories signal to producers to increase or decrease production (signal changes in supply relative to demand). In the case of electricity, the product must be, and can only be, consumed as it is produced. Further, the power lines by which it is transmitted are subject to overload problems, while the power stations that produce it are vulnerable to demand surges. If one line supplying a city is interrupted, unless demand is reduced (outages, shedding load) other lines will experience increased demand, and this may trigger safety devices to prevent over-loading. Similar problems can occur at power stations. As a result, a problem in one area can cascade across linked generation and supply systems, as happened in the north-east of the US in August, 2000, when about 50 million people were deprived of supply. The problem started because there was a surge in afternoon demand in Ontario, Canada, at a time when higher summer temperatures across the north-east of the continent had increased demand generally for air-conditioning. Now, think what would have happened if households and suppliers could have responded by running down electricity inventories.

RENT CONTROLS RECONSIDERED

Most European countries have rent controls of some sort, but there are substantial differences in the type and extent of these controls across countries. The experience of cities with and without significant controls has resulted in a widely held view among economists that the controls should be abolished. But controls linger on. They represent an attempt to use the law to suspend the market because legislators feel that they are protecting some people who would be badly hurt by having to pay higher rents. The intention may be good, but, as we shall see, the consequences are usually (a) bad, and (b) the opposite to what was sought in bringing in the legal restrictions on rents.

The case against controls can be easily analysed by using the concepts of the supply curve and the demand curve.

Suppose that in central Paris demand and supply curves for one-bedroom apartments are as shown in Fig. 3.6. This market, left alone, would reach an equilibrium monthly rent of €1,600, at which 20,000 one-bedroom apartments would be rented. Both owners and tenants would be 'satisfied', in the sense that they would not wish to rent either more or fewer units at that price. This would not necessarily mean, of

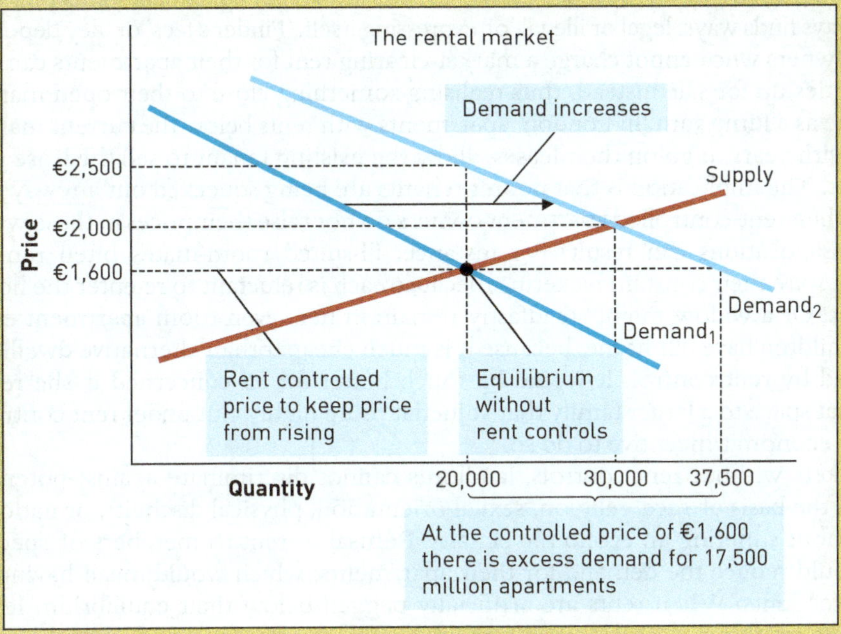

Figure 3.6 An Unregulated Housing Market is hit by Rent Controls

The initial equilibrium monthly rent is €1,600, and 20,000 apartments will be rented. Demand rises. The new equilibrium is a supply of 30,000 apartments at a rent of €2,000. Fixing the rent at €1,600 results in e: excess demand of 17,500 apartments.

course, that all is well and good. Many potential tenants, for example, might simply be unable to afford a rent of €1,600 per month for an apartment in the city.

Now suppose that the demand for apartments to rent increases The new conditions mean that the demand curve shifts to the right: at any rent, more people want accommodation; the market-clearing price for any given amount rises. The consequence would be (a) a rise in the rents paid for apartments, to €2,000 per month and (b) an increase in the number of apartments available to rent to 30,000.

Suppose that, following tenants' complaints about rising rents the city authorities legislated to set the price back to €1,600. The legislative goal is to prevent rents from rising in order to protect existing tenants.

But note in Fig. 3.6 that, when rents for one-bedroom apartments are prevented from rising above €1,600 per month, landlords are willing to supply only 20,000 apartments per month, 10,000 fewer than at the new equilibrium monthly rent of €2,000.[5] At this price tenants would now seek to rent 37,500 apartments. (For example, many people who would have decided to live in the 'banlieus' rather than pay €2,000 a month in central Paris will now choose to live in the city.) So when rents are prevented from rising above €1,600 per month, we see an excess demand for one-bedroom apartments of 17,500. Put another way, the rent controls result in a housing shortage of 17,500 units.

If the housing market were completely unregulated, rents would rise sharply, as would the supply of accommodation. With a legal ceiling on rents many other ways exist, however, in which the pressures of excess demand can make themselves felt. For instance, owners will quickly learn that they are free to spend less on maintaining the quality of their rental units. After all, if there are scores of renters knocking at his door, a landlord has considerable room to manoeuvre. Leaking pipes, peeling paint, broken central heating and other problems are less likely to receive prompt, if any, attention when rents are set well below market-clearing levels.

Reduced availability of apartments and poorer maintenance are not the only difficulties. With an offering of only 20,000 apartments, we see in Fig. 3.6 that there are renters who

[5] You might think this is unrealistic. After all, the number of one-bedroom apartments can't easily be reduced. Actually, this isn't really the case, since they can be converted to other uses, or they can be sold to people who want to own rather than rent.

would be willing to pay as much as €2,500 per month for an apartment. This pressure almost always finds ways, legal or illegal, of expressing itself. 'Finder's fees' or 'key deposits' emerge. Owners who cannot charge a market-clearing rent for their apartments can put the properties up for sale instead, thus realising something close to their open market rental value as a lump sum. In London, apartments with rents below the current market rent, but with years to go on their leases, allow the existing tenant to sell the lease to a new tenant. The implication is that poorer tenants are being squeezed out anyway.

Even when rent-controlled apartment owners do not raise their prices in these ways, serious misallocations can result. For instance, ill-suited room-mates often remain together despite their constant bickering, because each is reluctant to re-enter the housing market. Or a widow might steadfastly remain in her seven-room apartment even after her children have left home, because it is much cheaper than alternative dwellings not covered by rent control. It would be much better for all concerned if she relinquished that space to a larger family that valued it more highly. But under rent controls, she has no economic incentive to do so.

In markets without rent controls, landlords cannot discriminate against potential tenants on the basis of race, religion, sexual orientation, physical disability, or national origin without suffering an economic penalty. Refusal to rent to members of specific groups would reduce the demand for their apartments, which would mean having to accept lower rents. When rents are artificially pegged below their equilibrium level, however, the resulting excess demand for flats enables landlords to engage in discrimination with no further economic penalty.

Rent controls are not the only instance in which governments have attempted to repeal the law of supply and demand in the interest of helping the poor. During the late 1970s, for example, several governments on both sides of the Atlantic tried to hold the prices of oil products (petrol, central heating oil, etc.) below their equilibrium levels out of concern that higher prices imposed unacceptable hardships on low-income households. This was at a time when supply interruptions in global oil markets (the so-called 'second oil shock') had sent prices up from about €15 per barrel to over €30 per barrel. As with controls in the rental housing market, unintended consequences of price controls in the market made the policy an extremely costly way of trying to aid the poor. For example, petrol shortages resulted in long queues at the pumps – a waste not only of valuable time, but also of petrol as cars sat idling or moving slowly up to the pumps for extended periods.

In their opposition to rent controls and similar measures, are economists revealing a total lack of concern for the poor? Although this claim is sometimes made by those who don't understand the issues, or who stand to benefit in some way from government regulations, there is little justification for it. Economists simply realise that there are *much more effective ways to help poor people than to try to give them apartments and other goods at artificially low prices.* One straightforward approach would be to give the poor additional income and let them decide for themselves how to spend it.

PIZZA PRICE CONTROLS?

The sources of the contrast between widespread incidence of rent-controlled housing markets and largely unregulated food markets can be seen more vividly by trying to imagine what would happen if concern for the poor successfully lobbied a city administration to implement price controls on pizza. Suppose, for example, that the supply and demand curves for pizza are as shown in Fig. 3.7, and that the city imposes a **price ceiling** of €2 per slice, making it unlawful to charge more than that amount. At €2 per slice, buyers want to buy 16,000 slices per day, but sellers want to sell only 8,000.

> **price ceiling** a maximum allowable price, specified by law

At a price of €2 per slice, every pizza restaurant in the city will have long queues of buyers trying unsuccessfully to purchase pizza. Frustrated buyers will behave rudely to

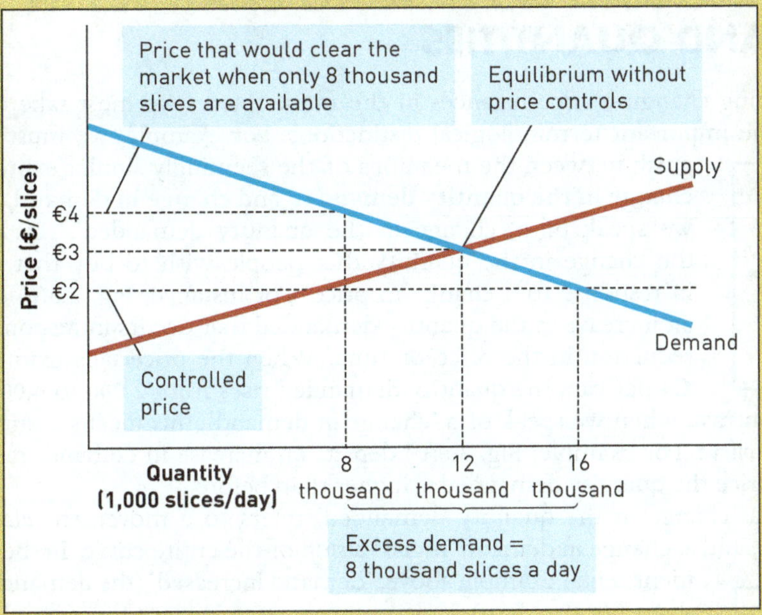

Figure 3.7 Price Controls in the Pizza Market

A price ceiling below the equilibrium price of pizza would result in excess demand for pizza. Supply is less than demand, and the market clearing price, given this supply, is higher than the equilibrium price as well as the controlled ceiling price.

cooks, who will respond in kind. Friends of restaurant managers will begin to get preferential treatment. Devious pricing strategies will begin to emerge (such as the €2 slice of pizza sold in combination with a €5 glass of Pepsi Cola). Pizza will be made from poorer-quality ingredients. Rumours will begin to circulate about sources of black-market pizza. And so on.

The very idea of not being able to buy a pizza seems absurd, yet precisely such things happen routinely in markets in which prices are held below the equilibrium levels. For example, prior to the collapse of communist governments, it was considered normal in those countries for people to queue for hours to buy basic goods, while the politically connected had first choice of those goods that were available.

At one point during the 1970s a shortage of potatoes in Western Europe sent potato prices soaring. Potatoes had a high weighting in the procedure by which inflation was measured in Belgium. (This reflected the Belgian passion for *pommes frites*.) The government sought to hold down the consumer price index (CPI, the measure of inflation) by freezing the price of potatoes. This intervention succeeded in holding down the CPI, but unfortunately potatoes disappeared from the shops as they were exported to the Netherlands, France and Germany where prices were not controlled. So, the price index didn't rise . . . because people couldn't get their hands on potatoes (other than in black-market transactions). *Pommes frites* simply disappeared from menus. The controls were rapidly abandoned.

RECAP

Market equilibrium

Market equilibrium, the situation in which all buyers and sellers are satisfied with their respective quantities at the market price, occurs at the intersection of the supply and demand curves. The corresponding price and quantity are called the *equilibrium price* and the *equilibrium quantity*.

Unless prevented by regulation, prices and quantities are driven toward their equilibrium values by the actions of buyers and sellers. If the price is initially too high, so that there is excess supply, frustrated sellers will cut their price in order to sell more. If the price is initially too low, so that there is excess demand, competition among buyers drives the price upward. This process continues until equilibrium is reached.

PREDICTING AND EXPLAINING CHANGES IN PRICES AND QUANTITIES

When describing changing circumstances in the marketplace, we must take care to recognise some important terminological distinctions. For example, we must distinguish between the meanings of the seemingly similar expressions **change in the quantity demanded** and **change in demand**. When we speak of a 'change in the quantity demanded', this means the change in the quantity that people wish to buy that occurs in response to a change in price. For instance, Fig. 3.8(a) depicts an increase in the quantity demanded that occurs in response to a reduction in the price of tuna. When the price falls from €5 to €4 per can, the quantity demanded rises from 2,000 to 4,000 cans per day. By contrast, when we speak of a 'change in demand', this means a *shift in the* entire *demand curve*. For example, Fig. 3.8(b) depicts an increase in demand, meaning that at every price the quantity demanded is higher than before.

change in the quantity demanded a movement along the demand curve that occurs in response to a change in price

change in demand a shift of the entire demand curve

In summary, a 'change in the quantity demanded' refers to a movement *along* the demand curve, and a 'change in demand' means a *shift* of the entire curve. In the apartment rental example above, 'demand increased' (the demand curve shifted to the right). If no controls were in place there would have been 'an increase in the quantity supplied' (a movement along the supply curve).

A similar terminological distinction applies on the supply side of the market. A **change in supply** means a shift in the entire supply curve, whereas a **change in the quantity supplied** refers to a movement along the supply curve.

change in supply a shift of the entire supply curve

change in the quantity supplied a movement along the supply curve that occurs in response to a change in price

SHIFTS IN DEMAND

To get a better feel for how the supply and demand model enables us to predict and explain price and quantity movements, it is helpful to begin with a few simple examples. Example 3.2 illustrates a shift in demand that results from events outside the particular market itself. The factors that can cause a change/shift in demand include the following:

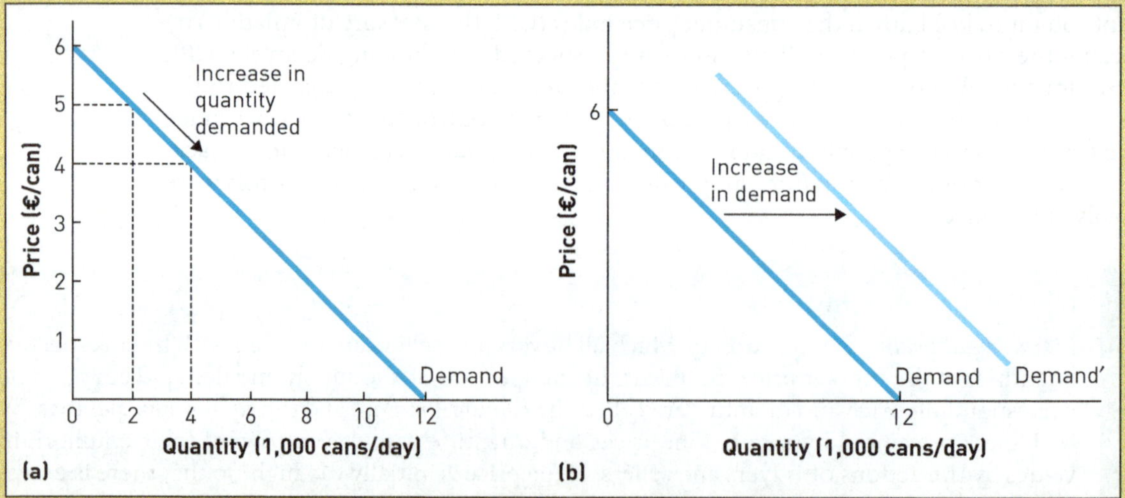

Figure 3.8 An Increase in the Quantity Demanded versus an Increase in Demand

(a) An increase in quantity demanded describes a downward movement along the demand curve as price falls. (b) An increase in demand describes an outward shift of the demand curve.

changes in the prices of complementary and substitute goods; changes in incomes, fashion (changes in taste); expectations.

What will happen to the equilibrium price and quantity of tennis balls if court-rental fees decline?

Example 3.2

Let the initial supply and demand curves for tennis balls be as shown by the curves *S* and *D* in Fig. 3.9, where the resulting equilibrium price and quantity are €1 per ball and 40 million balls per month, respectively. Tennis courts and tennis balls are what economists call **complements**, goods that are more valuable when used *in combination* than when used alone. Tennis balls, for example, would be of little value if there were no tennis courts on which to play. As tennis courts become cheaper to use, people will respond by playing more tennis, and this will increase their demand for tennis balls. A decline in court-rental fees will thus shift the demand curve for tennis balls rightward and upward to *D*′.

> **complements** two goods are complements in consumption if an increase in the price of one causes a leftward shift in the demand curve for the other (or if a decrease causes a rightward shift)

Note in Fig. 3.9 that for the illustrative demand shift shown, the new equilibrium price of tennis balls, €1.40, is higher than the original price, and the new equilibrium quantity, 58 million balls per month, is higher than the original quantity.

In Fig. 3.10 are shown the supply and demand for courier services. The demand for courier services falls as a consequence of the increased use of e-mails. As a result, both

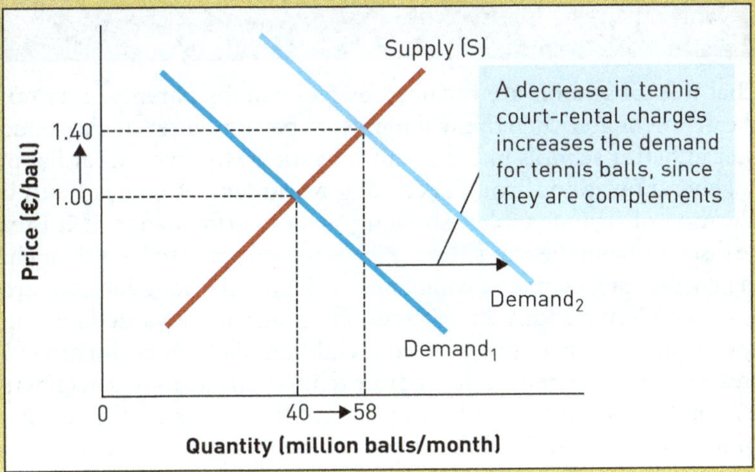

Figure 3.9 The Effect on the Market for Tennis Balls of a Decline in Tennis Court-Rental charges
When the price of a complement falls, demand shifts right, causing equilibrium price and quantity to rise.

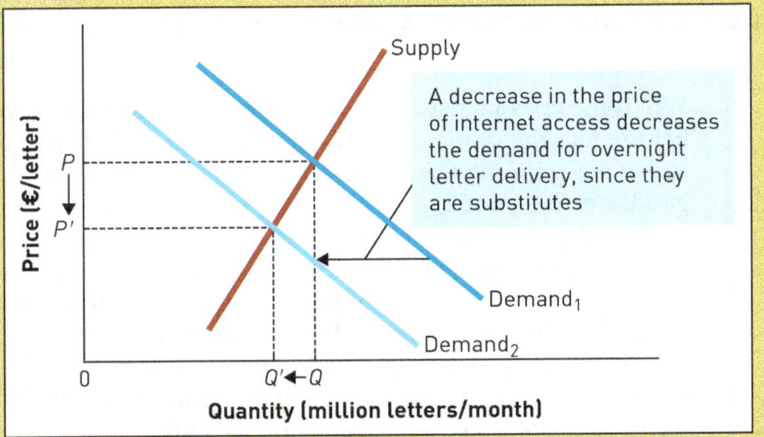

Figure 3.10 The Effect on the Market for Overnight Letter Delivery of a Decline in the Price of Internet Access
When the price of a substitute falls, demand shifts left, causing equilibrium price and quantity to fall.

the new equilibrium price, P', and the new equilibrium quantity, Q', are lower than the initial values, P and Q. Cheaper internet access probably won't put postal services out of business, but it will definitely cost them many customers who can now use secure internet software to exchange documents rather than send them by courier.

substitutes two goods are substitutes in consumption if an increase in the price of one causes a rightward shift in the demand curve for the other (or if a decrease causes a leftward shift)

To summarise, economists define goods as **substitutes** if an increase in the price of one causes a rightward shift in the demand curve for the other. By contrast, goods are complements if an increase in the price of one causes a leftward shift in the demand curve for the other. The concepts of substitutes and complements enable you to answer questions such as that posed in Exercise 3.3.

Exercise 3.3 How will a decline in air fares between Britain and France affect cross-Channel ferry fares and the price of hotel rooms in resort communities in France?

Demand curves are shifted not just by changes in the prices of substitutes and complements but also by other factors that change the amounts that people are willing to pay for a given good or service. One of the most important such factors is income.

Economic Naturalist 3.2
Why does public investment in improving school performance generally end up being enjoyed by the better off?

An obvious reason could be that if local schools are financed by fees paid by parents or by taxes on households in the local school catchment area then the willingness to pay for better-quality education through fees or taxes will result in better schools in better-off localities. However, what happens if the investment is financed by general taxation through central government? A clue is given by the interest in parents in the publication of 'league tables' showing school performance. If it is easy to send a child to a school at some distance from the child's home, parents will apply to have their children accepted by 'better' schools. In general, interest in and willingness/ability to pay for education are positively correlated with income, as is student performance If schools in turn are rewarded for improvements by further investment, they have an incentive to accept children likely to perform well. The schools' and the parents' interests coincide: parents select better schools and schools select better (in expected performance terms) children. Brighter student prospects from outside the locality will obtain places at the expense of less bright-prospect children within the locality . . . which, of course, improves school performance, and the cycle continues. That's not all. Suppose schools are not allowed to select from outside the catchment area. Will that sort out the problem? Actually, no, at least in the longer term. Why? Because parents will migrate to the better school districts, bidding up property prices, so that when the dust settles, the better schools will be serving better-off families!

normal good one whose demand curve shifts rightward when the incomes of buyers increase and leftward when the incomes of buyers decrease

inferior good one whose demand curve shifts leftward when the incomes of buyers increase and rightward when the incomes of buyers decrease

When incomes increase, the demand curves for most goods will behave like the demand curve for conveniently located property, and in recognition of that fact, economists have chosen to call such goods **normal goods**.

Not all goods are normal goods, however. The demand curves for some goods actually shift leftward when income goes up, and such goods are called **inferior goods**. In general, inferior goods are goods for which there exist attractive substitutes that sell for only slightly higher prices. Property in an unsafe, inconveniently located neighbourhood is an example. An increase in income would cause the demand for such property to shift leftward.

Ground or minced beef with high-fat content is another example of an inferior good. For health reasons, most people prefer grades of meat with a low-fat content, and when they do buy high-fat meats it is usually a sign of budgetary pressure. When people in this situation receive higher incomes, they usually switch quickly to leaner grades of meat.

Expectations about the future are another factor that may cause demand curves to shift. If Apple Macintosh users hear a credible rumour, for example, that a cheaper or significantly upgraded model will be introduced next month, the demand curve for the current model is likely to shift leftward.

SHIFTS IN THE SUPPLY CURVE

Because the supply curve is based on costs of production, anything that changes production costs will shift the supply curve, and hence will result in a new equilibrium quantity and price. These include input prices, changes in technology, taxes and subsidies (these also affect demand).

What will happen to the equilibrium price and quantity of bread and other foodstuffs as governments encourage production of renewable energy via ethanol?

Example 3.3

Suppose the initial supply and demand curves for a product like bread are as shown by the curves *S* and *D* in Fig. 3.11, giving an equilibrium price and quantity of €3 per kg and weekly sales of 12,000 kg. As demand for ethanol rises, producers increase their purchases of cereals to produce ethanol. This raises the prices for cereals products will rise. Food producers face higher raw material prices for things like bread. A rise in input prices shifts the supply curve for those products up and to the left. The result is higher prices for the bread, etc., that are produced from these inputs. In the long run, this is expected to spill over to other food products as land and other inputs are switched by farmers to producing raw material for ethanol production and away from producing food.

What will happen to the equilibrium price and number of attic conversions in houses if the wage rate of carpenters falls?

Example 3.4

Suppose that the initial supply and demand curves for attic conversions in houses are as shown by the curves *S* and *D* in Fig. 3.12, resulting in an equilibrium price of €120,000 per house and an equilibrium number of house extensions quantity of 40 houses

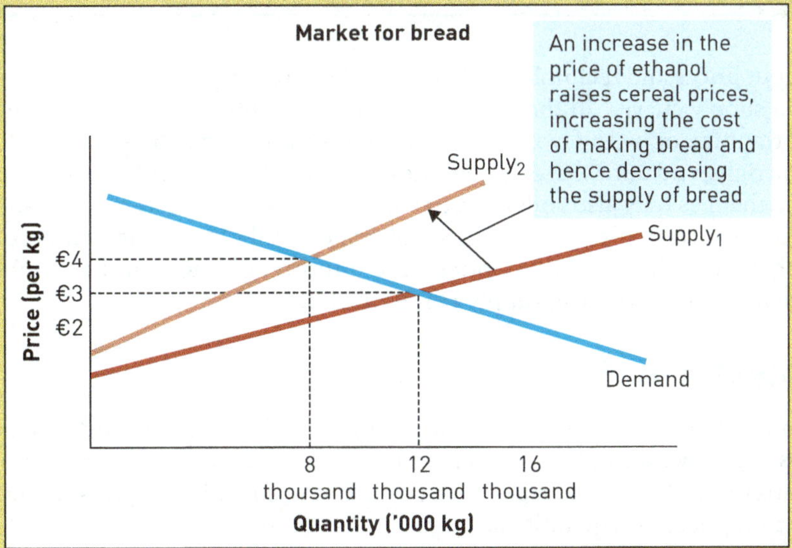

Figure 3.11 The Effect on the Bread Market of an Increase in the Demand for Ethanol as a Fossil Fuel Replacement

When input prices rise, supply shifts left, causing equilibrium price to rise and equilibrium quantity to fall.

Figure 3.12 The Effect on the Market for Attic Conversions of a Decline in Carpenters' Wage Rates

When input prices fall, supply shifts right, causing equilibrium price to fall and equilibrium quantity to rise.

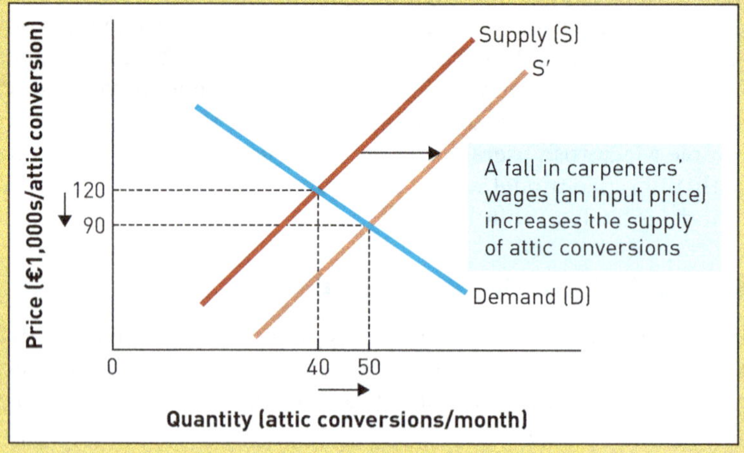

per month. A decline in the wage rate of carpenters reduces the marginal cost of remodelling houses, and this means that, for any given price for an attic conversion, more builders can profitably serve the market than before. Diagrammatically, this means a rightward shift in the supply curve conversion services, from S to S' in Fig. 3.12 (A 'rightward shift' in the supply curve can also be described as a 'downward shift'.)

Because it is safe to assume that carpenters form a very small percentage of the total potential demand side of the market, a fall in their wages will not significantly affect the demand for conversions. Hence we can model the market on the basis that the demand side is unaffected in this case.

We see from Fig. 3.12 that the new equilibrium price, €90,000 per house, is lower than the original price, and the new equilibrium quantity, 50 houses per month, is higher than the original quantity.

Examples 3.4 and 3.5 both involved changes in the cost of an *ingredient*, or *input*, in the production of the good in question – cereals in the case of bread and carpenters' labour in the production of houses. Supply curves also shift when *technology* changes. Exercise 3.4 is a case in point.

Exercise 3.4

Why do professors expect students to undertake more revisions of any work submitted for credit today than they demanded from students thirty years ago?

Changes in input prices and technology are two of the most important factors that give rise to shifts in supply curves. In the case of agricultural commodities, *weather* may be another important factor, with favourable conditions shifting the supply curves of such products to the right, and unfavourable conditions shifting them to the left. Expectations of future price changes may also shift current supply curves, as when the expectation of poor crops from a current drought causes suppliers to withhold supplies from existing stocks in the hope of selling at higher prices in the future. Changes in the number of *sellers* in the market can also cause supply curves to shift.

FOUR SIMPLE RULES

For supply and demand curves that have the conventional slopes (upward-sloping for supply curves, downward-sloping for demand curves), the preceding examples and exercises illustrate the four basic rules that govern how shifts in supply and demand affect equilibrium prices and quantities.

These rules are summarised in Fig. 3.13 (a)–(d).

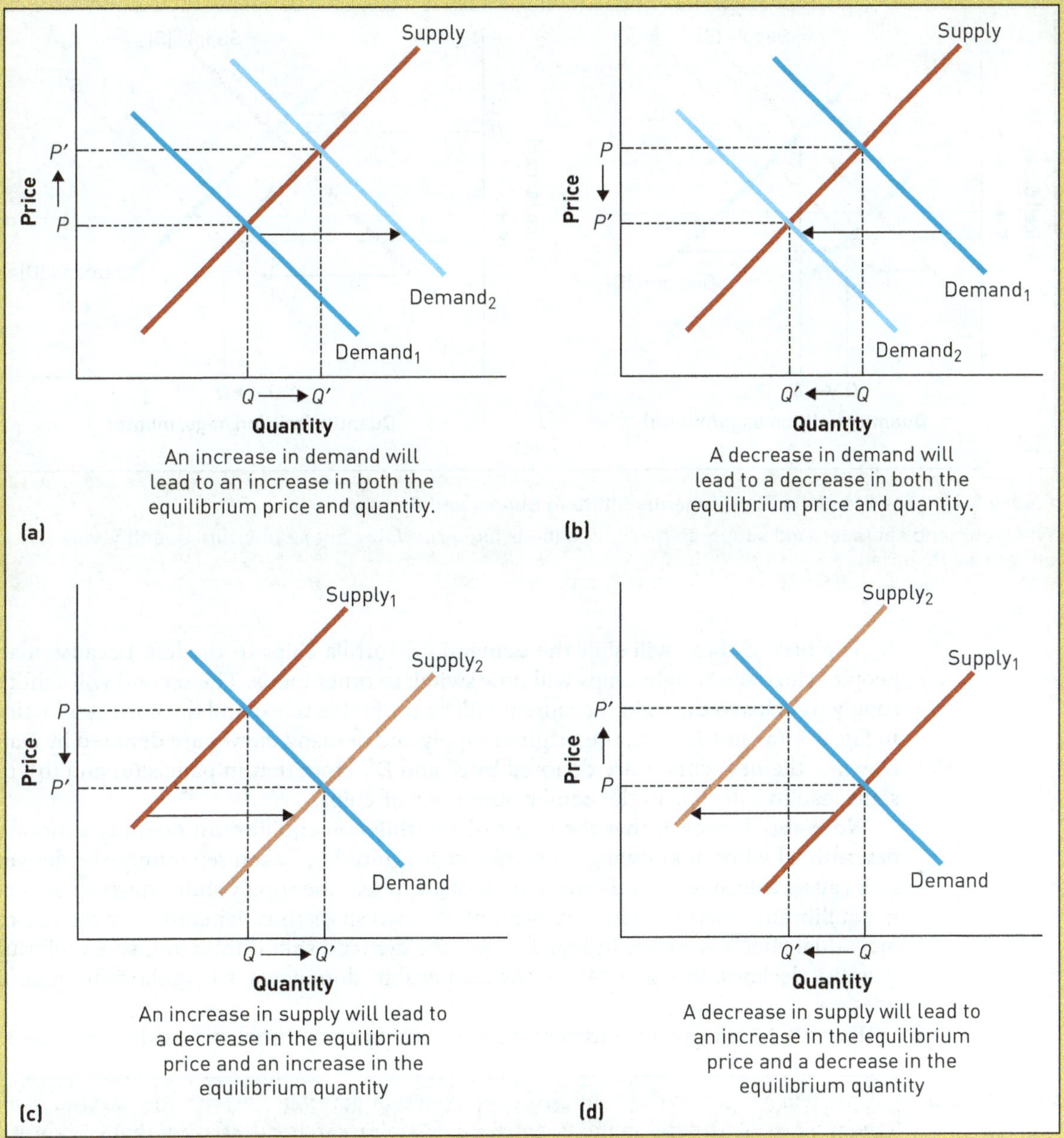

Figure 3.13 Four Rules Governing the Effects of Supply and Demand Shifts

The rules summarised in Fig. 3.13 hold for supply or demand shifts of any magnitude, provided that the curves have their conventional slopes. But as Example 3.5 demonstrates, when both supply and demand curves shift at the same time, the direction in which equilibrium price or quantity changes will depend on the *relative magnitudes* of the shifts.

How do shifts in *both* demand and supply affect equilibrium quantities and prices? **Example 3.5**

What will happen to the equilibrium price and quantity in the corn tortilla chip market if both of the following events occur: (1) researchers prove that the oils in which tortilla chips are fried are harmful to human health; and (2) the price of corn harvesting equipment falls?

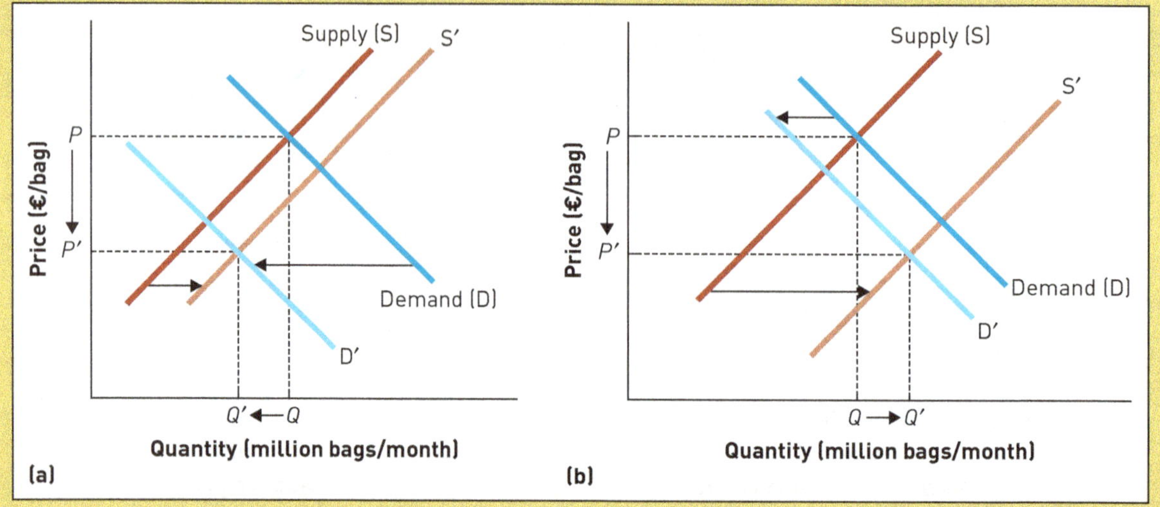

Figure 3.14 The Effects of Simultaneous Shifts in Supply and Demand
When demand shifts left and supply shifts right, equilibrium price falls, but equilibrium quantity may either rise (b) or fall (a).

The first of these will shift the demand for tortilla chips to the left, because many people who once bought chips will now switch to other foods. The second will shift the supply of chips to the right, because it will be profitable to expand the corn production. In Fig. 3.14(a) and 3.14(b), the original supply and demand curves are denoted by *S* and *D*, while the new curves are denoted by *S′* and *D′*. Note that in panels (a) and (b), the shifts lead to a decline in the equilibrium price of chips.

Note also, however, that the effect of the shifts on equilibrium quantity cannot be determined without knowing their relative magnitudes. Taken separately, the demand shift causes a decline in equilibrium quantity, whereas the supply shift causes an increase in equilibrium quantity. The net effect of the two shifts thus depends on which of the individual effects is larger. In Fig. 3.14 (a), the demand shift dominates, so equilibrium quantity declines. In Fig. 3.14 (b), the supply shift dominates, so equilibrium quantity goes up.

Exercise 3.5 asks you to consider a simple variation on the problem posed in Example 3.6.

Exercise 3.5

What will happen to the equilibrium price and quantity in the corn tortilla chip market if both of the following events occur: (1) researchers discover that a vitamin found in corn helps protect against cancer and heart disease; and (2) a swarm of locusts destroys part of the corn crop in the US mid-West?

RECAP

Factors that shift supply and demand

- **Factors that cause an increase (rightward or upward shift) in demand:**
  1. A decrease in the price of complements to the good or service.
  2. An increase in the price of substitutes for the good or service.
  3. An increase in income (for a normal good).
  4. An increased preference by demanders for the good or service.
  5. An increase in the population of potential buyers.
  6. An expectation of higher prices in the future.

  When these factors move in the opposite direction, demand will shift left.

RECAP

- **Factors that cause an increase (rightward or downward shift) in supply:**
  1. A decrease in the cost of materials, labour or other inputs used in the production of the good or service.
  2. An improvement in technology that reduces the cost of producing the good or service.
  3. A improvement in the weather (especially for agricultural products).
  4. An increase in the number of suppliers.
  5. An expectation of lower prices in the future.

When these factors move in the opposite direction, supply will shift left.

Economic Naturalist 3.3

Why do the prices of some goods (such as airline tickets from Europe to the United States) go up during the summer, while others (such as the price of strawberries) go down? And what about supermarket prices for wine, beer and spirits at Christmas?

Seasonal price movements for airline tickets are primarily the result of *seasonal variations in demand*. Thus ticket prices on the North Atlantic routes are highest during the summer months because the demand for tickets is highest during those months.

By contrast, seasonal price movements for strawberries are primarily the result of *seasonal variations in supply*. In the winter months strawberries offered for sale in Europe are for the most part produced under glass or are imported into Europe. The costs involved are higher than in the summer months, when seasonal factors permit production in the open across a large part of Europe.

Drinks prices generally fall at Christmas when demand is higher. This, however, is due to increased competition between retailers for the lucrative Christmas market, when sales are expected to increase at any price level.

Exercise 3.6

Use supply and demand curves to explain the airline tickets and strawberries example from Economic Naturalist 3.3.

MEASURING THE IMPACT OF PRICE CHANGES ON SUPPLY AND DEMAND: ELASTICITY

Conventionally, most police forces and legal systems in Europe and America operate on the basis of penalising the supply of illegal drugs much more severely than the use of those drugs at the individual level. This aspect of 'the war on drugs' has been reinforced in recent years by reducing penalties for, and even in some cases 'decriminalising', drug use, while increasing the penalties for supplying those drugs to users. Many economists have strongly criticised this approach because it fails to take into account the impact of policy on supply and demand, and the consequences of that impact. What is of interest to us here is the fact that the critics of this policy have grounded their criticism on a particular tool of economic analysis of markets, the concept of *elasticity*. It is a good example of how economics can be used to analyse policy problems that might be thought to be outside the area of interest of economists.

The starting point is a view that addictive 'controlled substances' are unlike many other goods that people consume. The difference lies in the response to price change. In the short run, at least, the quantity demanded responds only weakly to changes in their prices. The measure of the change in quantity demanded in response to a change

Figure 3.15 The Effect of Extra Border Policing on the Market for Illicit Drugs

Extra law enforcement shifts supply leftward and reduce the quantity demanded, but they may actually increase the total amount spent on drugs.

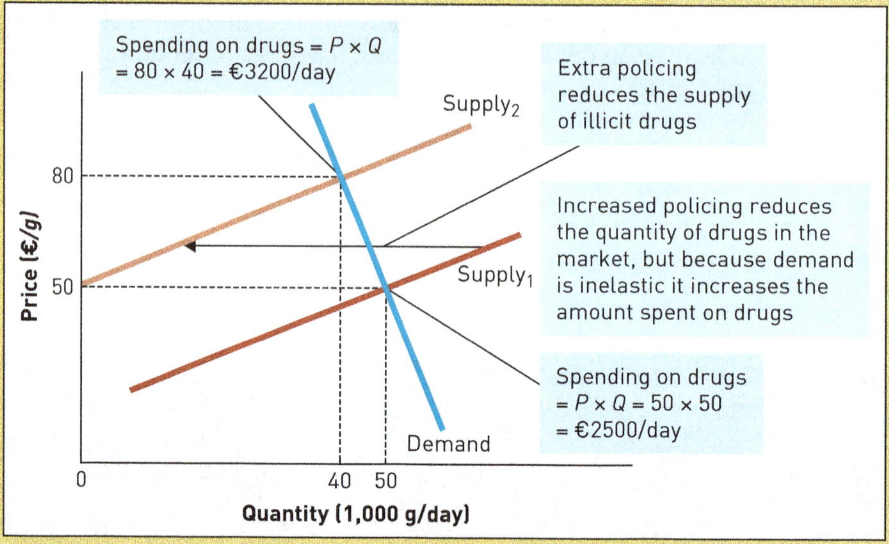

in price in this context is called the price *elasticity* of demand. The assertion that the quantity demanded is relatively non-responsive to the price in the case of, say heroin, may be re-phrased as saying that '*the price elasticity of demand for heroin is low*', or '*the demand for heroin is price inelastic*'. The critics of conventional policy object to the structure of that policy because a low value for price elasticity of demand for addictive substances has serious implications for criminal behaviour in a broader context. Specifically, they argue that it results in increased crime against persons and property.

This is not surprising. Many illicit drug users commit crimes to finance their addiction. This connection between drugs and crime has led to calls for more vigorous efforts to stop the smuggling of illicit drugs. But will interrupting the supply of drugs reduce crime? The immediate effect of reducing the availability of drugs will be to increase the market price of drugs, the consequence of a leftward shift in the supply curve (Fig. 3.15). The quantity consumed will fall. But, argue the critics of conventional policy, the amount of crime drug users commit depends not on the *quantity* of drugs they consume, but rather on their *total expenditure* on drugs. Whether expenditure rises or falls when consumption falls depends on the characteristics of the demand curve.

In Fig. 3.15 the steep slope of the demand curve means that the reduced supply increases spending on drugs. This puts pressure on addicts to increase their ability to pay by increasing their 'income', presumed to be in part at least on crime. So, a drugs shortage can lead to a rise in crimes that yield income to the perpetrators. In addition, addicts who are 'pushers' will have an incentive to try to sell more to finance their own consumption. The empirical basis for this argument is to be found in econometric analysis of some US municipal crime statistics in the 1980s.

Central to the case being made is the issue of what we call *price elasticity of demand*. The concept refers to the responsiveness of quantity demanded to a change in price. If this is low a reduction in supply, as we will see, leads to an increase in price and spending even though the amount of drugs being consumed must by definition fall. Critics of conventional policy argue that this is the case, and, therefore, that crime increases as addicts attempt to finance an increasingly expensive habit. Therefore, they argue, it is better to go after consumers than to concentrate on interrupting supply. It follows that being able to measure price responsiveness is important, and not just for commercial transactions. It can, as in this case, be important for many aspects of policy formulation.

In the first part of this chapter we saw how shifts in supply and demand curves enabled us to predict the *direction of change* in the equilibrium values of price and quantity. An understanding of price elasticity will enable us to make even more precise statements about the *effects of such changes*. In the illicit drugs example just considered, the decrease in supply was expected to lead to an increase in total spending. In many other cases, a decrease in supply will lead to a reduction in total spending. For example, if there was a shortage of apples leading to a fall in the supply of cider in Europe most observers might not expect total spending on cider to rise as its price rose. Why this difference?

The underlying concept used to measure this effect is the *price elasticity of demand*. We shall explore why some goods have higher price elasticity of demand than others, and the implications of that fact for how total spending responds to changes in price. We shall also discuss the *price elasticity of supply* and examine the factors that explain why it takes different values for different goods.

PRICE ELASTICITY OF DEMAND

When the price of a good or service rises, the quantity demanded falls. But to predict the effect of the price increase on total expenditure, we must also know how much quantity falls. The quantity demanded of some goods, such as salt, is not very sensitive to changes in price. Indeed, even if the price of salt were to double, or to fall by half, most people would hardly alter their consumption of it at all. For other goods, however, the quantity demanded is extremely responsive to changes in price.

Price elasticity defined

The **price elasticity of demand** for a good is a measure of the responsiveness of the quantity demanded of that good to changes in its price. Formally, the price elasticity of demand for a good is defined as the percentage change in the quantity demanded that results from a 1 per cent change in its price. For example, if the price of beef falls by 1 per cent and the quantity demanded rises by 2 per cent, then the price elasticity of demand for beef has a value of –2. The minus sign follows from the mathematical result that dividing a positive number by a negative number, or a negative number by a positive number, yields a negative number.

price elasticity of demand percentage change in quantity demanded that results from a 1 per cent change in price

Although the definition just given refers to the response of quantity demanded to a 1 per cent change in price, it can also be adapted to other variations in price, provided that they are relatively small. In such cases, we calculate the price elasticity of demand as the percentage change in quantity demanded divided by the corresponding percentage change in price. Thus, if a 2 per cent reduction in the price of pork led to a 6 per cent increase in the quantity of pork demanded, the price elasticity of demand for pork would be

$$\frac{\text{Percentage change in consumption}}{\text{Percentage change in price}} = \frac{6 \text{ per cent}}{-2 \text{ per cent}} = -3 \quad (3.1)$$

Strictly speaking, as long as demand curves slope downwards, the price elasticity of demand will always be negative (or zero), because price changes are always in the opposite direction from changes in quantity demanded. So for convenience, we can drop the negative sign and speak of price elasticities in terms of absolute value. The demand for a good is said to be **elastic** with respect to price if the absolute value of its price elasticity is greater than 1. It is said to be **inelastic** if the absolute value of its price elasticity is less than 1. Finally, demand is said to be **unit elastic** if the absolute value of its price elasticity is equal to 1 (see Fig. 3.16).

elastic demand is elastic with respect to price if the price elasticity of demand is greater than 1

inelastic demand is inelastic with respect to price if the price elasticity of demand is less than 1

unit elastic demand is unit elastic with respect to price if the price elasticity of demand equals 1

Figure 3.16 Elastic and Inelastic Demand

Demand for a good is called elastic, unit elastic or inelastic with respect to price if the price elasticity is greater than 1, equal to 1, or less than 1, respectively.

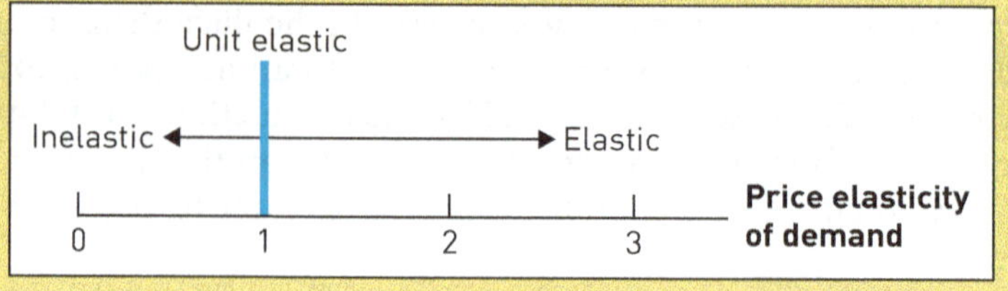

Example 3.6 What is the elasticity of demand for pizza?

When the price of pizza is €1 per slice, buyers wish to purchase 400 slices per day, but when price falls to €0.97 per slice, the quantity demanded rises to 404 slices per day. At the original price, what is the price elasticity of demand for pizza? Is the demand for pizza elastic with respect to price?

In response to a 3 per cent reduction in the price of pizza, the quantity demanded increases by 1 per cent. The price elasticity of demand for pizza is thus (1 per cent)/(3 per cent) = 1/3. So when the initial price of pizza is €1, the demand for pizza is not elastic with respect to price; it is less than 1; it is inelastic.

Exercise 3.7 What is the elasticity of demand for season ski passes?

Suppose the price of a weekly ski pass in Cortina d'Ampezzo is €160, and the ski lift operator sells 10,000 weekly passes at that price. On the advice of an economist, the price is lowered to €152, and weekly sales rise to 12,000 passes, which was predicted by the economist. What did the economist estimate the price elasticity of demand to be when the price was €160? Was demand elastic or inelastic?

Determinants of price elasticity of demand

To understand what determines price elasticity of demand for a good or service first remember that a rational consumer will purchase a unit of good or service only if the purchase passes the cost–benefit test. For instance, consider a good (such as a flat-screen LED TV set for your flat) that you buy only one unit of (if you buy it at all). Suppose that, at the current price, you have decided to buy it. Now imagine that the price goes up by 10 per cent. Will a price increase of this magnitude be likely to make you change your mind? The answer will depend on factors such as the following.

Substitution possibilities

When the price of a product you want to buy goes up significantly, you ask yourself, 'Is there some other good that can do roughly the same job, but for less money?' If the answer is yes, then you can escape the effect of the price increase by simply switching to the substitute product. But if the answer is no, you are more likely to stick with your current purchase.

These observations suggest that the price elasticity of demand will tend to be higher for products for which *close substitutes* are readily available. Salt, for example, has no close substitutes, which is one reason that the demand for it is highly inelastic. Note, however, that while the quantity of salt people demand is highly insensitive to price, the same cannot be said of the demand for any *specific brand* of salt. After all, despite what salt manufacturers say about the special advantages of their own labels, consumers tend to regard one brand of salt as a virtually perfect substitute for another. Thus, if one producer were to raise the price of its salt significantly, many people would simply switch to some other brand.

The vaccine against rabies is a product for which there are essentially no attractive substitutes. A person who is bitten by a rabid animal and does not take the vaccine faces a certain and painful death. So most people in that position would pay any price they could afford rather than do without the vaccine.

Budget share

Suppose the price of key rings suddenly were to double. How would that affect the number of key rings you buy? If you're like most people, it would have no effect at all. Doubling the price of a 25 cent item that you buy only every few years is simply nothing to worry about. By contrast, if the price of the new TV set you were about to buy suddenly doubled, you would definitely want to check out possible substitutes. You might also consider holding on to your current TV for a little longer. *The larger the share of your budget an item accounts for*, the greater is your incentive to look for substitutes when the price of the item rises. High unit price items therefore tend to have higher price elasticities of demand.

Time

The impact of a price change on consumption is affected by the time element in the consumption decision. Cars and fuel prices are an example of this. If you were going to change your car, and fuel prices rose sharply, it is reasonable to suppose you might select a new car that has better fuel economy figures. As a result, the fuel price rise would result in a significant fall in your consumption of fuel. However, if you, for whatever reason, did not contemplate replacing your car for a couple of years your fuel usage would not fall as sharply, being affected only by your usage of the car, and not by its fuel economy. Hence, in the short run, motorists' responses to fuel price changes will be weaker than in the long run. Short-run price elasticity of demand will be lower than long-run. This applies to any good the consumption of which is 'habit formed', meaning that past decisions affect current demand.

As this example illustrates, substitution of one product or service for another takes time. Some substitutions occur in the immediate aftermath of a price increase, but many others take place years or even decades later. For this reason, the price elasticity of demand for any good or service will be higher in the *long run* than in the *short run*.

RECAP

Factors that influence price elasticity

The price elasticity of demand for a good or service tends to be larger when *substitutes* for the good are more readily available, when the good's share in the consumer's budget is *larger* and when consumers have more time to *adjust* to a change in price.

SOME REPRESENTATIVE ELASTICITY ESTIMATES

Table 3.3 shows that the price elasticities of demand for different products often differ substantially – in this sample, ranging from a high of 2.8 for green peas to a low of 0.18 for theatre and opera tickets. This variability is explained in part by the determinants of elasticity just discussed. Patrons of theatre and opera, for example, often tend to have high incomes, implying that the shares of their budgets devoted to these items are likely to be small. What is more, theatre and opera patrons are often highly knowledgeable and enthusiastic about these art forms; for many of them, there are simply no acceptable substitute forms of entertainment (and, of course, listening to a CD does not yield the satisfaction of seeing and being seen at Covent Garden!)

Why is the price elasticity of demand almost 16 times larger for green peas than for theatre and opera performances? The answer cannot be that income effects loom

Table 3.3 Price Elasticity Estimates for Selected Products

Good or service	Price elasticity
Green peas	2.80
Restaurant meals	1.63
Automobiles	1.35
Electricity	1.20
Beer	1.19
Movies	0.87
Air travel (foreign)	0.77
Shoes	0.70
Coffee	0.25
Theatre, opera	0.18

Sources: These short-run elasticity estimates are taken from Houthakker and Taylor (1970); Taylor (1975); Elzinga (1977); Fisher (1996).

any larger for green peas than for theatre tickets. Even though the average consumer of green peas earns much less than the average theatre or opera patron, the share of a typical family's budget devoted to green peas is surely very small. What differentiates green peas from theatre and opera performances is that there are so many more close substitutes for peas than for opera and theatre. The lowly green pea, which is mostly found in the canned goods or frozen foods sections of supermarkets, just does not seem to have inspired a loyal consumer following.

USING PRICE ELASTICITY OF DEMAND

An understanding of the factors affecting price elasticity of demand is necessary both to make sense of consumer behaviour and to design effective public policy. Governments in most countries curb smoking by taxing cigarettes so as to increase their price.

Environmental concerns led the UK Government to commit itself to a steady increase in the real price of fuel by increasing excise tax on oil at a rate in excess of the general inflation rate.

Higher taxes have been (not surprisingly) resisted by the tobacco industry. The tobacco industry has consistently maintained that peer pressure is what encourages teenagers to smoke. Price, they claimed, had little effect. Motorists have resisted the increase in fuel duty, especially when oil prices were rising anyway. They argued that it would have little impact on the environment since fuel usage was very inelastic with respect to price. So forget higher taxes if you want to save the world or deter people from smoking. Demand, they argue, is very price inelastic.

Peer pressure and other social factors are a significant factor in sustaining demand for tobacco. But that does not imply that a higher tax on cigarettes would have little impact on adolescent smoking. For at least some teenage smokers, a higher tax would lead them to choose to spend their money on other things rather than pay the higher prices.

If the tax deters even a small number of smokers directly through its effect on the price of cigarettes, it will also deter others indirectly, by reducing the number of peer role models who smoke. This price effect is actually supported by the evidence of the effects of restrictions on smoking. A restriction (such as bans in pubs) is analytically equivalent to a very high price being charged for smoking when/where restricted. To the extent that people do not fully (if at all) replace smoking not done where prohibited by an equivalent increase in smoking where permitted, the restriction will reduce smoking. In 2004 Ireland introduced a work-place ban on smoking, an initiative that has been followed in many countries in Europe and elsewhere since then. It appears to have had the desired effect of reducing the total consumption of tobacco. This implies that demand is not as price inelastic as you might think.

In 2004 a paper published in the UK gave some interesting results on price elasticity for fuel used for transport. The results of the analysis indicated a price elasticity of demand in the short run of only −0.25, but in the long run of −0.64. Elasticity of fuel used per vehicle in the short run was very low, −0.08, but in the long run −1.1. Elasticity of vehicle usage (km per vehicle) was −0.10 in the short run and −0.30 in the long run. Long-run response to price changes was much more pronounced than short-run response, while shifting to more efficient cars and trucks meant a smaller impact on road usage than on fuel usage.[6]

A GRAPHICAL INTERPRETATION OF PRICE ELASTICITY

For small changes in price, the price elasticity of demand is the proportion by which quantity demanded changes divided by the corresponding proportion by which price changes. This gives us a simple expression for the price elasticity of demand for a good based on minimal information about its demand curve.

To illustrate, let P be the current price of the good and Q the quantity demanded at that price. Let ΔP be a small change in the current price and ΔQ the resulting change in quantity demanded (see Fig. 3.17). The expression $\Delta P/P$ is then the proportionate change in price; and $\Delta Q/Q$ is the corresponding proportionate change in quantity. The formula for price elasticity may then be written as:

$$\text{Price elasticity} = \varepsilon = \frac{\Delta Q/Q}{\Delta P/P} \tag{3.2}$$

Suppose, for example, that 20 units were sold at the original price of 100, and that when the price rose to 105, quantity demanded fell to 15 units. Neglecting the negative sign of the quantity change, we would then have $\Delta Q/Q = 5/20$ and $\Delta P/P = 5/100$, or $\varepsilon = (5/20)/(5/100)$; elasticity is 5.

One attractive feature of this formula is that it has a straightforward graphical interpretation. Thus, if we want to calculate the price elasticity of demand at a point on the demand curve shown in Fig. 3.17, we can begin by rewriting the right-hand side of Eq. (3.2) as $(P/Q) \times (\Delta Q/\Delta P)$. Mathematically, the slope of the demand curve is equal to $\Delta P/\Delta Q$. $\Delta Q/\Delta P$ is the reciprocal of that slope: $\Delta Q/\Delta P = 1/\text{slope}$. So the price elasticity of demand at point A, denoted ε_A, has the following simple formula:

$$\varepsilon_A = \frac{P}{Q} \times \frac{1}{\text{Slope}} \tag{3.3}$$

To demonstrate how convenient this graphical interpretation of elasticity can be, suppose we want to find the price elasticity of demand at point A on the demand curve in Fig. 3.18. The slope of this demand curve is the ratio of its vertical intercept to its horizontal intercept: $20/5 = 4$. So $1/\text{slope} = 1/4$. (Actually, the slope is -4, but we again ignore the minus sign for convenience, since the price elasticity of demand always has the same sign.) The ratio P/Q at point A is $8/3$, so the price elasticity at point A is equal to $(P/Q) \times (1/\text{slope}) = (8/3) \times (1/4) = 2/3$. This means that when the price of the good is 8, a 3 per cent reduction in price will lead to a 2 per cent increase in quantity demanded.

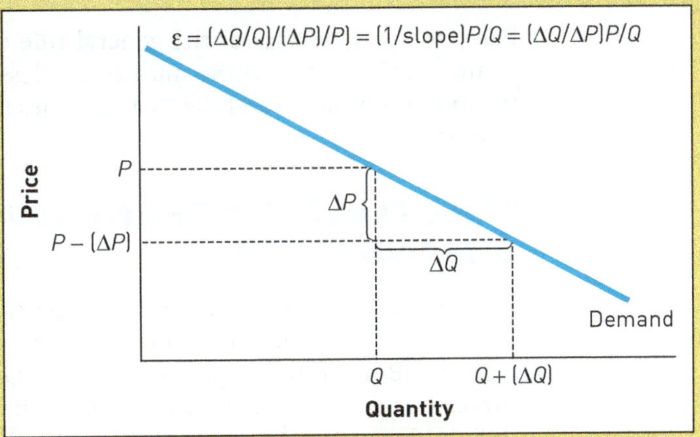

Figure 3.17 A Graphical Interpretation of the Price Elasticity of Demand
The price elasticity of demand at any point along a straight-line demand curve is the ratio of price to quantity at that point times the reciprocal of the slope of the demand curve.

[6] Goodwin, Dargay and Hanly, 2004.

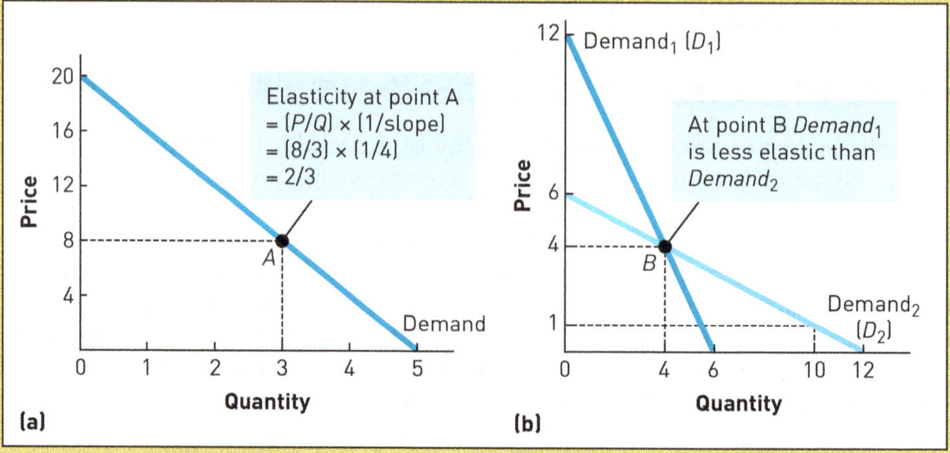

Figure 3.18 Calculating the Price Elasticity of Demand

The price elasticity of demand at A is given by $(P/Q) \times (1/\text{slope}) = (8/3) \times (1/4) = 2/3$. When price and quantity are the same, the price elasticity of demand is always greater for the less steep of two demand curves.

In Fig. 3.18 (a) a demand curve has an elasticity that varies along the curve. At a price of 8, the price elasticity of demand is 2/3. Revenue could be increased by raising the price. Can you explain why? In Fig. 3.18 (b) two demand curves intersect at price = 4. Can you explain why the price elasticity of demand at a price of 4 is higher for D_2 and lower for D_1? See Exercise 3.8.

Exercise 3.8

1: Calculate the price elasticity of demand when $P = 4$ in Fig. 3.18(a).
2: For the demand curves D_1 and D_2 shown in Fig. 3.18(b), calculate the price elasticity of demand when $P = 4$. What is the price elasticity of demand on D_2 when $P = 1$?

Exercise 3.8 (2) illustrates the general rule that if two demand curves have a point in common, the steeper curve must be the less elastic of the two with respect to price at that point. But note carefully that this does not mean that the steeper curve is less elastic at every point.

PRICE ELASTICITY CHANGES ALONG A STRAIGHT-LINE DEMAND CURVE

Price elasticity has a different value at every point along a straight-line demand curve. The slope of a straight-line demand curve is constant, which means that 1/slope is also constant. But the price–quantity ratio, P/Q, declines as we move down the demand curve. The elasticity of demand thus declines steadily as we move downward along a straight-line demand curve.

This pattern makes sense. After all, a price movement of a given absolute size is small in percentage terms when it occurs near the top of the demand curve but large in percentage terms when it occurs near the bottom of the demand curve. The opposite percentage effect applies in the case of a given quantity change. Price elasticity will behalf way down the demand curve. Why?

The graphical interpretation of elasticity makes it easy to see why. Consider, for example, the price elasticity of demand at point A on the demand curve D shown in Fig. 3.19 (a) At that point, the ratio P/Q is equal to $6/3 = 2$. The slope of this demand curve

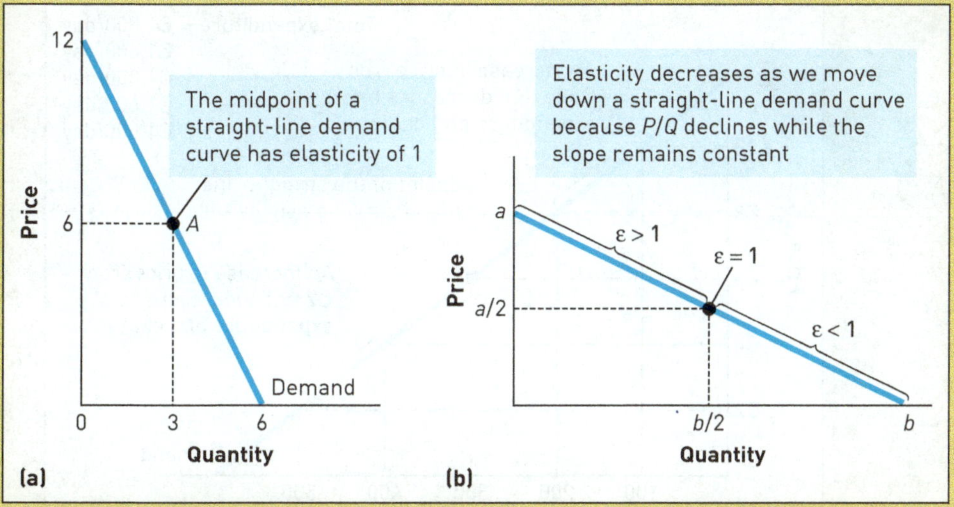

Figure 3.19 Elasticity at the Midpoint of a Straight-Line Demand Curve

is the ratio of its vertical intercept to its horizontal intercept, $12/6 = 2$. So $(1/\text{slope}) = 1/2$ (again, we neglect the negative sign for simplicity). Inserting these values into the graphical elasticity formula yields $\varepsilon_A = (P/Q) \times (1/\text{slope}) = (2) \times (1/2) = 1$. This result holds not just for the particular demand curve shown, but also for any other straight-line demand curve (Fig. 3.19 (b)). Since P/Q declines as we move downward along a straight-line demand curve, price elasticity of demand must be less than 1 at any point below the midpoint.[7]

TWO SPECIAL CASES

There are two important exceptions to the general rule that elasticity declines along straight-line demand curves. Note that the horizontal demand curve in Fig. 3.20(a) has

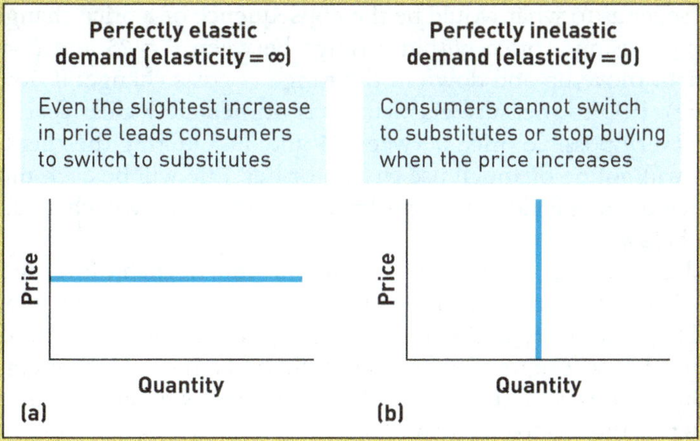

Figure 3.20 Perfectly Elastic and Perfectly Inelastic Demand Curves

The horizontal demand curve (a) is perfectly elastic, or infinitely elastic, at every point. Even the slightest increase in price leads consumers to switch to substitutes. The vertical demand curve (b) is perfectly inelastic at every point. Consumers cannot not switch.

[7] This has to be the case: a point A halfway up the demand curve must refer to a price halfway between zero and the top point of the demand curve. That is, the horizontal line from A to the vertical axis bisects the vertical axis between the origin and the top point of the demand curve. It is a simple theorem from school geometry that the vertical line between A and the horizontal axis must then bisect the horizontal axis between the origin and the bottom point of the demand curve. Hence, the arithmetic result above must always follow with a straight-line demand curve because at this point $P/Q = \Delta P/\Delta Q$.

Figure 3.21 The Demand Curve for Cinema Tickets

An increase in price from €2 to €4 per ticket increases total expenditure on tickets; an increase from €8 to €10 reduces expenditure from €1,600 to €1,000.

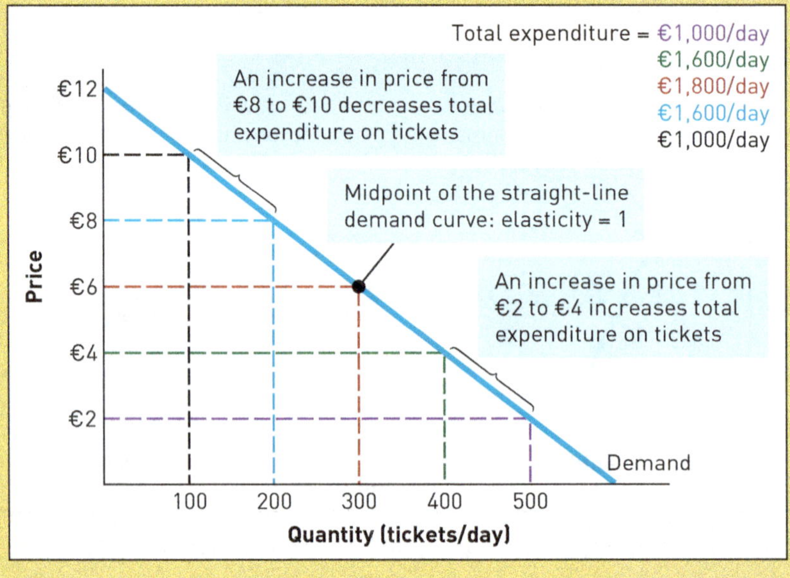

perfectly elastic demand demand is perfectly elastic with respect to price if price elasticity of demand is infinite

perfectly inelastic demand demand is perfectly inelastic with respect to price if price elasticity of demand is zero

a slope of zero, which means that the reciprocal of its slope is infinite. Price elasticity of demand is thus infinite at every point along a horizontal demand curve. Such demand curves are said to be **perfectly elastic**.

In contrast, the demand curve in Fig. 3.21(b) is vertical, which means that its slope is infinite. The reciprocal of its slope is thus equal to zero. Price elasticity of demand is thus exactly zero at every point along the curve. For this reason, vertical demand curves are said to be **perfectly inelastic**.

THE MIDPOINT FORMULA

You are advising a seller as to what would be the consequence of a price change, where what is at stake is choosing a price within a range between $P = 25$ and $P = 30$, and allowing that price to move up and down in the range as costs change. If you use the expression (1/slope). P/Q to measure elasticity it is immediately clear that there is a different value for every possible price between 25 and 30. Offering the client a list of 10 or more values will not be of much use to him or her. Life will be even more complicated if the demand curve is not a straight line, since the slope will change, too (see the technical note below).

What you need is a reliable 'average' value that will yield a reliable 'average' answer to the question: 'What is the price elasticity of demand for my product?' which really means: 'What will happen to my total sales revenue if price changes by so much in that range?' To deal with this we can use the 'midpoint' formula. It can be thought of as an average of the point values over the range. To provide this we generate an estimate using what is known as the 'midpoint formula'.

If the two points in question are (Q_A, P_A) and (Q_B, P_B), this formula is given by

$$\varepsilon = \frac{\Delta Q/(Q_A + Q_B)}{\Delta P/(P_A + P_B)} \tag{3.4}$$

The midpoint formula thus sidesteps the question of which price–quantity pair to use by using averages of the top and bottom price values and an average value for slope.

We will not employ the midpoint formula again in this text. Hereafter, all questions concerning elasticity will employ the measure discussed earlier, which is called *point elasticity*.

Maths Box 3.1

Demand curves, of course, are not always (or even mostly) straight lines. Hence, the slope of the curve will vary along the curve. Hence, when we want to estimate the price elasticity of demand a formulation using the $(\Delta Q/Q)/(\Delta P/P)$ approach will of necessity be an approximation. To deal with this properly we have to use calculus. As a result, in estimating real-world elasticities economists will normally use the first derivative of the demand curve, dP/dQ, as the measure of slope, and define elasticity as

$$\varepsilon = (-)\,(dQ/dP)/(P/Q)$$

For the rest of the discussion in this chapter we shall stay with the $(\Delta Q/Q)/(\Delta P/P)$ approach.

Exercise 3.9

Suppose that you encounter a question like the following in a standardised test in economics (a multiple choice test): *At a price of 3, quantity demanded of a good is 6, while at a price of 4, quantity demanded is 4. What is the price elasticity of demand for this good?* How would you answer it?

RECAP

Calculating price elasticity of demand

The price elasticity of demand for a good is the percentage change in the quantity demanded that results from a 1 per cent change in its price. Mathematically, the elasticity of demand at a point along a demand curve is equal to $(P/Q) \times (1/\text{slope})$, where P and Q represent price and quantity and $(1/\text{slope})$ is the reciprocal of the slope of the demand curve at that point. Demand is elastic with respect to price if the absolute value of its price elasticity exceeds 1; inelastic if price elasticity is less than 1; and unit elastic if price elasticity is equal to 1.

ELASTICITY AND TOTAL EXPENDITURE

Sellers of goods and services will often have a strong interest in being able to answer questions like: 'Will consumers spend more on my product if I sell more units at a lower price or fewer units at a higher price?' As it turns out, the answer to this question depends critically on the price elasticity of demand. To see why, let us first examine how the total amount spent on a good varies with the price of the good.

The total daily expenditure on a good is simply the daily number of units bought times the price for which it sells. The market demand curve for a good tells us the quantity that will be sold at each price. We can thus use the information on the demand curve to show how the total amount spent on a good will vary with its price.

To illustrate, let us calculate how much cinema-goers will spend on tickets each day if the demand curve is as shown in Fig. 3.21 and the price is €2 per ticket. The demand curve tells us that at a price of €2 per ticket, 500 tickets per day will be sold, so total expenditure at that price will be €1,000 per day. If tickets sell not for €2 but for €4 apiece, 400 tickets will be sold each day, so total expenditure at the higher price will be €1,600 per day.

Total expenditure = Total revenue: The euro amount that consumers spend on a product $(P - Q)$ is equal to the euro amount that sellers receive.

Table 3.4

Price (€/ticket)	Total expenditure (€/day)
12	0
10	1,000
8	1,600
6	1,800
4	1,600
2	1,000
0	0

In this example a rise in price resulted in a rise in total sales revenue. But this does not have to be the case The law of demand tells us that when the price of a good rises, people will buy less of it. The two factors that govern total revenue – price and quantity – will thus always move in opposite directions.

So, a rise in price from €8 per ticket to €10 per ticket will cause total expenditure on tickets to go down. Thus people will spend €1,600 per day on tickets at a price of €8, but only €1,000 per day at a price of €10.

The general rule illustrated by Fig. 3.21 is that a price increase will produce an increase in total revenue whenever it is greater, in percentage terms, than the corresponding percentage change in quantity demanded. Conversely, a fall in price will increase total revenue when, in percentage terms it is less than the corresponding increase in quantity sold.

This rule can be illustrated by using another graphical representation of the impact of price changes on total sales revenues. In this case we plot price on the horizontal axis and total expenditure by purchasers (sales revenues of the seller) on the vertical axis. In Fig. 3.22 this is done using the information implicit in the demand curve in Fig. 3.21.

To do this, first in table form we derive the total sales revenues values at the prices on the vertical axis of Fig. 3.22 (Table 3.4). Ideally, we could get values from Fig. 3.18 for a larger number of prices, sufficient to give us a more or less continuous set of values for price and sales revenue or expenditure by purchasers. We then plot these as in Fig. 3.22.

Note that in Fig. 3.22 as the price per ticket increases from 0 to €6, total expenditure increases. But as the price rises from €6 to €12, total expenditure decreases. Total expenditure reaches a maximum of €1,800 per day at a price of €6.

This pattern holds true in general. For a straight-line demand curve, total expenditure is highest at the price that lies *on the midpoint of the demand curve*. Totals sales revenue, therefore, is maximized where price elasticity of demand is unity. This latter result holds true even if the demand curve is not a straight line, although the point at which elasticity is unity will not usually be halfway between the top and bottom of the demand curve in this case.

Figure 3.22 Total Expenditure as a Function of Price

For a good whose demand curve is a straight line, total expenditure reaches a maximum at the price corresponding to the midpoint of the demand curve.

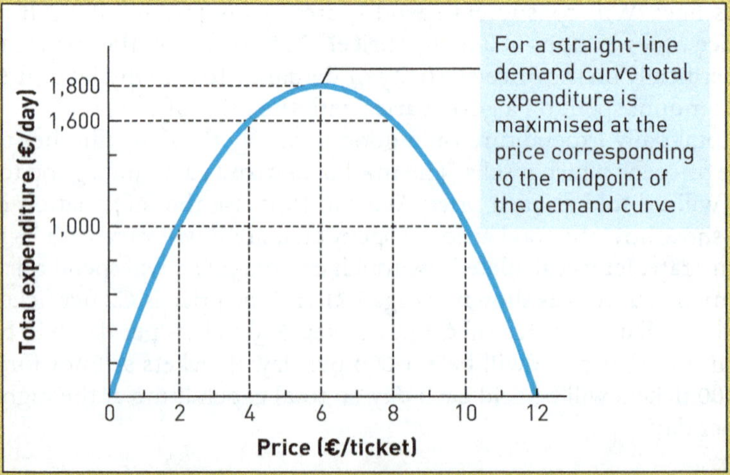

Table 3.5 Elasticity and the Effect of a Price Change on Total Expenditure

If demand is . . .	A price increase will . . .	A price reduction will . . .
elastic [ε > 1]	reduce total expenditure $P \times Q =$ PQ ↓	increase total expenditure $P \times Q =$ PQ ↑
inelastic [ε < 1]	increase total expenditure $P \times Q =$ PQ ↑	reduce total expenditure $P \times Q =$ PQ ↓

When price elasticity is greater than 1, changes in price and changes in total expenditure always move in opposite directions. For a product whose price elasticity of demand is less than 1, price changes and total expenditure changes always move in the same direction.

The relationship between elasticity and the effect of a price change on total revenue is summarised in Table 3.5, where the symbol ε is used to denote elasticity.

INCOME ELASTICITY AND CROSS-PRICE ELASTICITY OF DEMAND

The elasticity of demand for a good can be defined not only with respect to its own price but also with respect to the prices of substitutes or complements, or even to income. For example, the elasticity of demand for peanuts with respect to the price of cashews – also known as the **cross-price elasticity of demand** for peanuts with respect to cashew prices – is the percentage by which the quantity of peanuts demanded changes in response to a 1 per cent change in the price of cashews. The **income elasticity of demand** for peanuts is the percentage by which the quantity demanded of peanuts changes in response to a 1 per cent change in income.

> **cross-price elasticity of demand** the percentage by which the quantity demanded of the first good changes in response to a 1 per cent change in the price of the second
>
> **income elasticity of demand** the percentage by which quantity demanded changes in response to a 1 per cent change in income

Unlike the elasticity of demand for a good with respect to its own price, these other elasticities may be either *positive* or *negative*, so it is important to note their algebraic signs carefully. The income elasticity of demand for inferior goods, for example, is negative, whereas the income elasticity of demand for normal goods is positive. When the cross-price elasticity of demand for two goods is positive – as in our peanuts/cashews example – the two goods are *substitutes*. When it is negative, the two goods are *complements*. The elasticity of demand for tennis racquets with respect to court-rental fees, for example, is less than zero.

Exercise 3.10

Suppose the business manager of a rock band knows that he can sell 5,000 tickets to the band's weekly summer concerts if he sets the price at €20 per ticket. If the elasticity of demand for tickets is equal to 3, will total ticket revenue go up or down in response to a 10 per cent increase in the price of tickets? Show the impact on sales revenue from increasing or decreasing his price by 10 per cent.

RECAP

Cross-price and income elasticities

When the elasticity of demand for one good with respect to the price of another good is positive, the two goods are *substitutes*; when this cross-price elasticity of demand is negative, the two goods are *complements*. A *normal* good has positive income elasticity of demand and an *inferior* good has negative income elasticity of demand.

THE PRICE ELASTICITY OF SUPPLY

On the buyer's side of the market, we use price elasticity of demand to measure the responsiveness of quantity demanded to changes in price. On the seller's side of the market, the analogous measure is **price elasticity of supply**. It is defined as the percentage change in quantity supplied that occurs in response to a 1 per cent change in price. For example, if a 1 per cent increase in the price of peanuts leads to a 2 per cent increase in the quantity supplied, the price elasticity of supply of peanuts would be 2.

price elasticity of supply the percentage change in quantity supplied that occurs in response to a 1 per cent change in price

The mathematical formula for the price elasticity of supply at any point is the same as the corresponding expression for the price elasticity of demand:

$$\text{Price elasticity of supply} = \frac{\Delta Q/Q}{\Delta P/P} \tag{3.5}$$

where P and Q are the price and quantity at that point, P is a small change in the initial price and ΔQ is the resulting change in quantity.

As with the corresponding expression for price elasticity of demand, Eq. (3.5) can be rewritten as $(P/Q) \times (\Delta Q/\Delta P)$. And since $(\Delta Q/\Delta P)$ is the reciprocal of the slope of the supply curve, the right-hand side of Eq. (2.7) is equal to $(P/Q) \times (1/\text{slope}) \times$ the same expression we saw for price elasticity of demand. Price and quantity are always positive, as is the slope of the typical supply curve, which implies that price elasticity of supply will be a positive number at every point.

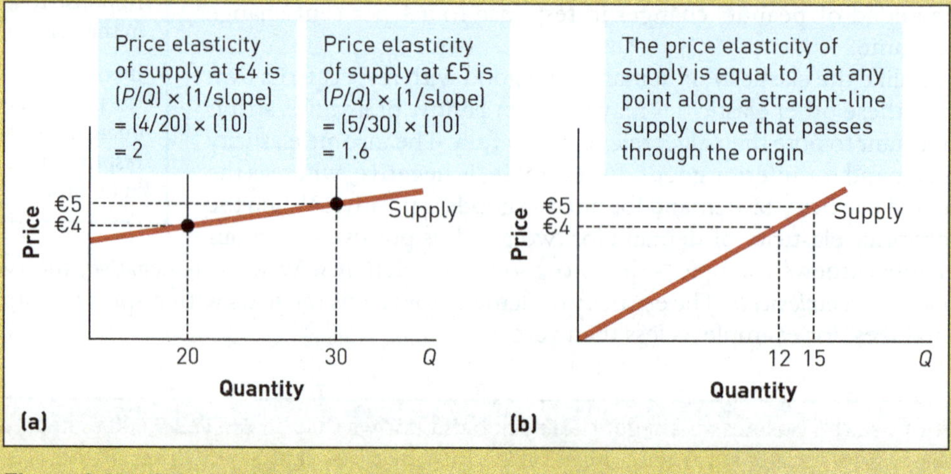

Figure 3.23 Calculating the Price Elasticity of Supply Graphically
Price elasticity of supply is $(P/Q) \times (1/\text{slope})$. The price elasticity of supply is equal to 1 at any point along a straight-line supply curve that passes through the origin.

Consider the supply curve shown in Fig. 3.23(a). The slope of this supply curve is 1/10, so the reciprocal of this slope is 10. Using the formula, this means that the price elasticity of supply at a supply price of 4 is $(4/20) \times (10) = 2$. The corresponding expression at $P = 5$, $(5/30) \times (10) = 1.6$). Elasticity is positive, and declining as P rises because Q rises faster than P along the curve. Elasticity approaches the value for the reciprocal of the slope as P, Q increase. There is an exception to this, which occurs when the supply curve passes through the origin (Fig. 3.23(b)). In this case, the elasticity of supply is positive, but is constant, having the same value at every point on the curve. This is because the value, Q/P, is the same at every point on the curve when it passes through the origin. It is also the same as the reciprocal of the slope. Not only is it constant and positive, therefore, but it is equal to 1.[8] Note the contrast between this result and our earlier finding that price elasticity of demand declines as we move downward along any straight-line demand curve.[9]

On the buyer's side of the market, two important polar cases were demand curves with infinite price elasticity and zero price elasticity. As Example 3.7 and Exercise 3.11 illustrate, analogous polar cases exist on the seller's side of the market.

Example 3.7

What is the elasticity of supply of land within the territory of Hong Kong?

Land in Hong Kong sells in the market for a price, just like steel or wheat or cars or any other product. And the demand for land in Hong Kong is a downward-sloping function of its price. For all practical purposes, however, its supply is completely fixed, at least in the short run (from time to time the administration in Hong Kong has added a bit by landfills). No matter whether its price is high or low, the same amount of it is available in the market. The supply curve of such a good is a *vertical* straight line, and its price elasticity is zero at every price. Supply curves of that type are said to be **perfectly inelastic**.

Whenever additional units of a good can be produced by using the same combination of inputs, purchased at the same prices, as have been used so far, the supply curve of that good will be a horizontal straight line. Such supply curves are said to be **perfectly elastic**.

perfectly inelastic supply supply is perfectly inelastic with respect to price if elasticity is zero

perfectly elastic supply supply is perfectly elastic with respect to price if elasticity of supply is infinite

Exercise 3.11

What is the elasticity of supply of lemonade?

Suppose that the ingredients required to bring a paper cup of lemonade to market and their respective costs are as follows:

Ingredient	Cents
Paper cup	2.0
Lemon	3.8
Sugar	2.0
Water	0.2
Ice	1.0
Labour (30 seconds @ €6/hour)	5.0

Derive the supply curve graphically.

[8] Passing through the origin means that there is no minimum expected price other than zero below which there will be no production at all. This is not always the case.

[9] Technical note:
As with the demand curve, strictly speaking the slope value is based on the first derivative of the supply curve, not on $\Delta P/\Delta Q$. The latter is only an approximation if the supply curve is not a straight line.

Determinants of supply elasticity

The lemonade case was one whose production process was essentially like a cooking recipe. For such cases, we can exactly double our output by doubling each ingredient. If the price of each ingredient remains fixed, the marginal cost of production for such goods will be constant – and hence their horizontal supply curves.

The Hong Kong land example is a contrast in the extreme. The inputs that were used to produce land in Hong Kong – even if we knew what they were – could not be duplicated at any price.

The key to predicting how elastic the supply of a good will be with respect to price is to know the terms on which *additional units* of the inputs involved in producing that good can be acquired. In general, the more easily additional units of these inputs can be acquired, the higher price elasticity of supply will be. The following factors (among others) govern the ease with which additional inputs can be acquired by a producer.

Flexibility of inputs

To the extent that production of a good requires inputs that are also useful for the production of other goods, it is relatively easy to lure additional inputs away from their current uses, making supply of that good relatively elastic with respect to price. Thus the fact that lemonade production requires labour with only minimal skills means that a large pool of workers could shift from other activities to lemonade production if a profitable opportunity arose. Brain surgery, by contrast, requires highly trained and specialised labour, which means that even a large price increase would not increase available supplies, except in the very long run.

Mobility of inputs

If inputs can be easily transported from one site to another, an increase in the price of a product in one market will enable a producer in that market to summon inputs from other markets. For example, the supply of agricultural products in California is made more elastic with respect to price by the fact that thousands of farm workers are willing to migrate northward during the growing season. The supply of entertainment is similarly made more elastic by the willingness of entertainers to hit the road. Circus performers, lounge singers, comedians and even exotic dancers often spend a substantial fraction of their time away from home. For instance, according to a 1996 *New York Times* article, the top exotic dancers 'basically follow the action, so the same entertainers who worked the Indianapolis 500 earlier in the year now headed to Atlanta for the Olympics'.

For most goods, the price elasticity of supply increases each time a new highway is built, or when the telecommunications network improves, or indeed when any other development makes it easier to find and transport inputs from one place to another.

Ability to produce substitute inputs

The inputs required to produce finished diamond gemstones include raw diamond crystal, skilled labour, and elaborate cutting and polishing machinery. In time, the number of people with the requisite skills can be increased, as can the amount of specialised machinery. The number of raw diamond crystals buried in the earth is probably fixed in the same way that Hong Kong land is fixed, but unlike Hong Kong land, rising prices will encourage miners to spend the effort required to find a larger proportion of those crystals. Still, the supply of natural gemstone diamonds tends to be relatively inelastic because of the difficulty of augmenting the number of diamond crystals.

The day is close at hand, however, when gemstone makers will be able to produce synthetic diamond crystals that are indistinguishable from real ones. Indeed, there are already synthetic crystals that fool even highly experienced jewellers. The introduction of a perfect synthetic substitute for natural diamond crystals would increase the price elasticity of supply of diamonds (or, at any rate, the price elasticity of supply of gemstones that look and feel just like diamonds).

Time

Because it takes time for producers to switch from one activity another, and because it takes time to build new machines and factories and train additional skilled workers, the price elasticity of supply will be higher for most goods in the long run than in the short run. In the short run, a manufacturer's inability to augment existing stocks of equipment and skilled labour may make it impossible to expand output beyond a certain limit. But if a shortage of managers was the bottleneck, new MBAs can graduate in only two years. Or if a shortage of legal staff is the problem, new lawyers can be trained in three years. In the long run, firms can always buy new equipment, build new factories and hire additional skilled workers.

The conditions that gave rise to the perfectly elastic supply curve for lemonade in Exercise 3.11 are also satisfied for many other products in the long run. If a product can be copied (in the sense that any company can acquire the design and other technological information required to produce it), and if the inputs needed for its production are used in roughly fixed proportions and are available at fixed market prices, then the long-run supply curve for that product will be horizontal. But many products do not satisfy these conditions, and their supply curves remain steeply upward-sloping, even in the very long run.

Economic Naturalist 3.4
Why might we be concerned that lower food prices could result in a rise in inflation?

The commodity price boom that peaked in mid 2008 collapsed over the next few months. As a result, prices for many staple food crops fell sharply. By the spring of 2009 some observers expressed concerns that this could cause a sharp rise in inflation sparked by rapidly rising food prices. The following is a quotation from an article that appeared in the Lex column of the *Financial Times* in April 2009.

'The cost of corn, soya and wheat has fallen sharply from the levels they reached last summer at the height of the commodity boom. But lower prices mean lower returns per acre, so farmers are cutting plantings of marginally productive land . . . This is [what] investors who worry about a rapid return of inflation fear: low prices lead to under-investment and cuts in productive capacity. When the economy picks up, prices soar because suppliers – in this case, farms – cannot keep up with renewed demand'.

The argument here is represented in terms of shifts in supply and demand curves. It is based on the observation that the short-term capacity to respond to demand changes is often much weaker than the long-run response (price elasticity of supply is lower in the short run than in the long run).

In Figure 3.24 the fall in demand leads to a collapse in prices as the market clears where the lower demand intersects the short-run supply curve (2). Farmers respond by cutting production, taking land out of production (a move along the long-run supply curve) until equilibrium is restored (3) at a price below the original price, but higher than when the demand collapse occurred. Now suppose demand recovers to the old level: prices soar (a move along the new short-run supply curve) (4). Price soars. The fear is that this will trigger demands for higher wages and impart an upward shock to prices in general, or higher inflation, until the old equilibrium is restored. In the meantime we would expect to see prices of the commodities concerned fluctuating (price volatility).

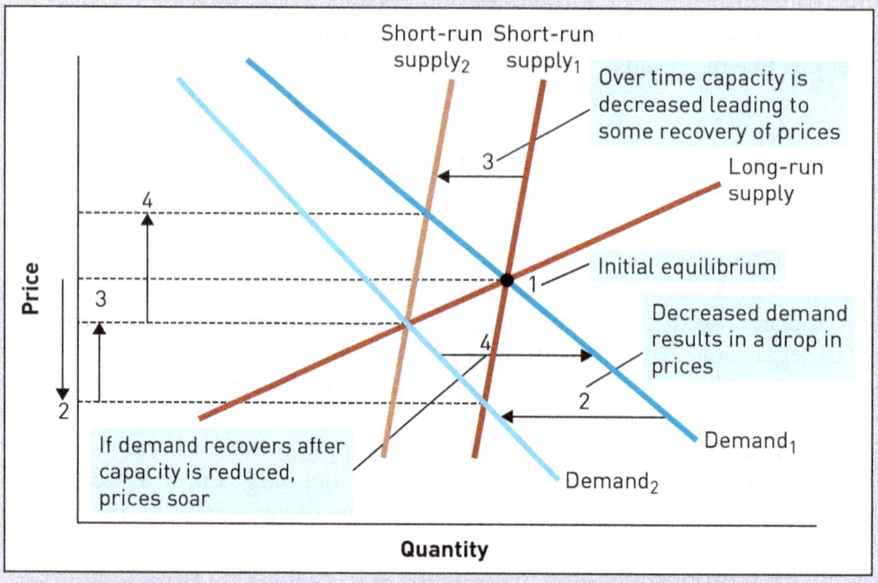

Figure 3.24 A Fall in Demand Causes a Supply Response Leading to Higher Prices Later On

The following chart, based on IMF data for world food commodity prices, suggests that the views expressed in the Lex column were well founded. It shows what happened to commodity prices in the two years after the Lex column was published.

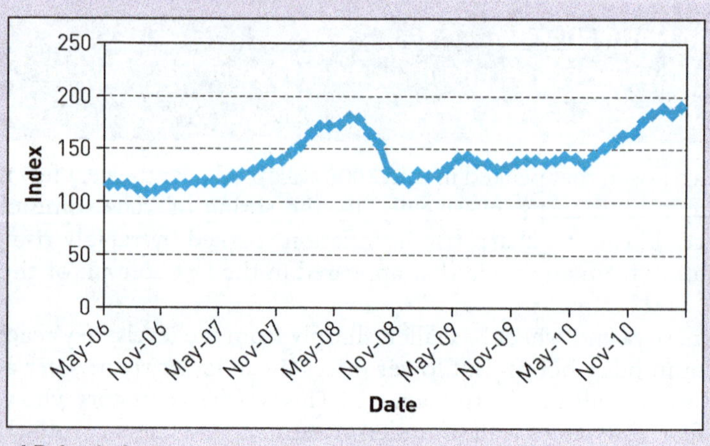

Figure 3.25 Food Price Index

Price volatility is also common in markets in which demand curves fluctuate sharply and supply curves are highly inelastic. One such market was California's unregulated market for wholesale electricity during the summer of 2000. The supply of electricity-generating capacity was essentially fixed in the short run. And because air conditioning accounts for a large share of demand, several spells of unusually warm weather caused demand to shift sharply to the right. Price at one point reached more than four times its highest level from the summer of 1999 (see Economic Naturalist 3.1 above).

Unique and essential inputs: the ultimate supply bottleneck

A football team that consistently wins, or is close to winning its national league, and appears regularly in the European Championship, generates substantial profits as a rule. Suppose you wanted to enter the business as a team owner, at a level at which you could credibly compete for this kind of money, and wanted to do so by building a new team (not by purchasing an existing top-level club). What are the inputs you would need? Talented players, a shrewd and dedicated manager and assistants, trainers, physicians, a stadium, practice facilities, means for transporting players to away games, a marketing staff and so on. And whereas some of these inputs can be acquired at reasonable prices in the marketplace, many others cannot. Indeed, the most important input of all – highly talented players – is in extremely limited supply. This is so because the very definition of talented player is inescapably relative – simply put, such a player is *one who is better than most others*.

Given the huge payoff that accrues to a championship team, it is no surprise that the bidding for the most talented players has become so intense. If there were a long list of superbly talented strikers, each of star quality, Real Madrid would not have had to pay €20 million plus to Manchester United for David Beckham, and then pay Beckham as much as €5 million a year. But, of course, the supply of such players is extremely limited.

Another source of supply bottlenecks arises from the existence of fixed numbers of places and numerical restrictions on promotions and demotions in a football league. It is conceivable that you could produce more and better players by spending more on them. But you can't produce more places at the top of the league. A place in the UK Premiership is an essential input to play against other Premiership clubs. The same applies to Serie A in Italy. There are many hungry football teams in Britain, France, Italy, Spain . . . that would like nothing better than to play in the Champions' League, or at least be promoted to a higher level, where the financial returns are greater.[10] Every team in England would like to get into the Premiership. But no matter how much each is willing to spend, only two or three can succeed in any year. Similar restrictions apply in the Champions' League. The supply of places in the Premiership or the Champions' League is perfectly inelastic with respect to price even in the very long run.

Sports champions are by no means the only important product whose supply elasticity is constrained by the inability to reproduce unique and essential inputs. In the movie industry, for example, although the supply of movies starring Russell Crowe is not perfectly inelastic, there are only so many films he can make each year. Because his films consistently generate huge box-office revenues, scores of film producers want to sign him for their projects. But because there isn't enough of him to go around, his earnings per film can run to millions of dollars.

In the long run, *unique and* essential *inputs* are the only truly significant supply bottleneck. If it were not for the inability to duplicate the services of such inputs, most goods and services would have extremely high price elasticities of supply in the long run.

Economic Naturalist 3.5
Do economists always get it right where elasticity is concerned?

Alas, no, it seems. In a case before the High Court in Dublin in 2011 the effect of changing prices on firms' sales was considered. The firm in question, whose price was regulated, was a ferry service supplier. The regulation was relaxed, and as a result the ticket price for the trip between the mainland and the Aran Islands was increased from €19 to €25 (30 per cent). The ferry firm's sales fell by 5 per cent. It was argued that this suggested a very low price elasticity of demand (these values suggested PED was approximately −0.17). However, while the ferry operator's sales fell by 5 per

[10] You may love the game or hate it, but if you want to know why the game is important, and the economic pressures that affect it, you must read Joe McGinnis, *The Miracle of Castel di Sangro*, Random House, 2000, describing a year in the life of a village team from the Abruzzi that was unexpectedly promoted to Serie B.

cent, this was against an increase in total sales by all operators of 16 per cent, while the other operators also raised their prices.

If higher prices are accompanied by increased sales it must be the case that the market demand curve had shifted to the right. At any price, given the slope of the demand curve, P/Q has to fall (Fig. 3.26) when the demand curve shifts to the right, and this will be all the more the case for the demand curve for a single firm's sales. Hence, conclusions as to the PED for the single firm's sales cannot be made on the basis of observing what happens to sales when both price and the demand curve are changed simultaneously.

In Fig. 3.26 a firm's demand curve is shifted to the right. Sales fall, but the slope of the curve is unchanged when price is increased. The observed change in sales may be thought of as the outcome of two influences: the impact on sales of the price change and the impact of whatever caused the demand curve to shift. PED measures the impact of price alone. The procedure described must underestimate the true PED.

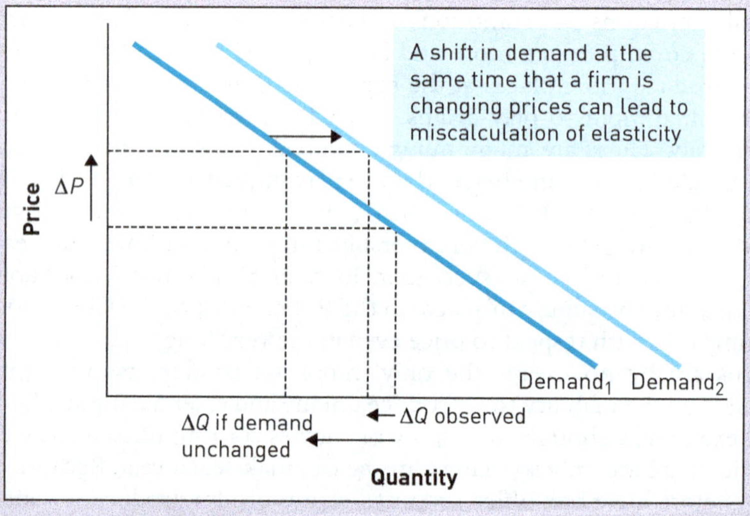

Figure 3.26 An Example of How Elasticity of Demand can be Miscalculated

WHAT MARKETS DELIVER 1: MARKETS AND SOCIAL WELFARE

Most of the material so far in this chapter has stressed the mechanics of how markets work. In the introduction, however, we argued that represent a highly effective system of *allocating resources*. We return to this idea in the last two sections of the chapter, building on what we have established so far.

When a market for a good is in equilibrium, the equilibrium price conveys important information to potential suppliers about the value that potential demanders place on that good. At the same time, the equilibrium price informs potential demanders about the opportunity cost of supplying the good. This rapid, two-way transmission of information is the reason that markets can coordinate an activity as complex as supplying London or Paris with food and drink, even though no one person or organisation oversees the process.

But are the prices and quantities determined in market equilibrium socially optimal, in the sense of maximising total economic surplus? That is, does equilibrium in unregulated markets always maximise the difference between the total benefits and total costs experienced by market participants? As we shall see, the answer is 'it depends': a market that is out of equilibrium, such as the market for rented housing in cities with rent control laws, always creates opportunities for individuals to arrange transactions that will increase their individual economic surplus. As we shall see, however, a market for a good that is in equilibrium makes the largest possible contribution to total economic surplus only when its supply and demand curves fully reflect the costs and benefits associated with the production and consumption of that good.

CASH ON THE TABLE

In economics, we assume that all exchange is purely voluntary. This means that a transaction cannot take place unless the buyer's reservation price for the good exceeds the seller's reservation price. When that condition is met and a transaction takes place, both parties receive an economic surplus. The **buyer's surplus** from the transaction is the difference between the buyer's reservation price and the price actually paid. The **seller's surplus** is the difference between the price received and the seller's reservation price. The **total surplus** from the transaction is the sum of the buyer's surplus and the seller's surplus. It is also equal to the difference between the buyer's reservation price and the seller's reservation price.

buyer's surplus the difference between the buyer's reservation price and the price he or she actually pays

seller's surplus the difference between the price received by the seller and his or her reservation price

total surplus the difference between the buyer's reservation price and the seller's reservation price

'cash on the table' economic metaphor for unexploited gains from exchange

Suppose that there is a potential buyer whose reservation price for an additional slice of pizza is €4 and a potential seller whose reservation price is only €2. If this buyer purchases a slice of pizza from this seller for €3, the total surplus generated by this exchange is €4 – €2 = €2, of which €4 – €3 = €1 is the buyer's surplus and €3 – €2 = €1 is the seller's surplus.

A regulation that prevents the price of a good from reaching its equilibrium level unnecessarily prevents exchanges of this sort from taking place, and in the process reduces total economic surplus. Consider again the effect of price controls imposed in the market for pizza. The demand curve in Fig. 3.27 tells us that if a price ceiling of €2 per slice were imposed, only 8,000 slices of pizza per day would be sold. At that quantity, the vertical interpretations of the supply and demand curves tell us that a buyer would be willing to pay as much as €4 for an additional slice and that a seller would be willing to sell one for as little €2. The difference – €2 per slice – is the additional economic surplus that would result if an additional slice were produced and sold. As noted earlier, an extra slice sold at a price of €3 would result in an additional €1 of economic surplus for both buyer and seller.

When a market is out of equilibrium, it is always possible to identify *mutually beneficial exchanges* of this sort. When people have failed to take advantage of all mutually beneficial exchanges, we often say that there is **'cash on the table'** – the economist's metaphor for unexploited opportunities. When the price in a market is below the equilibrium price, there is cash on the table, because the reservation price of sellers (marginal cost) will always be lower than the reservation price of buyers. In the absence of a law preventing buyers paying more than €2 per slice, restaurant owners would quickly raise their prices and expand their production until the equilibrium price of €3 per slice were reached. At that price, buyers would be able to get precisely the 12,000 slices

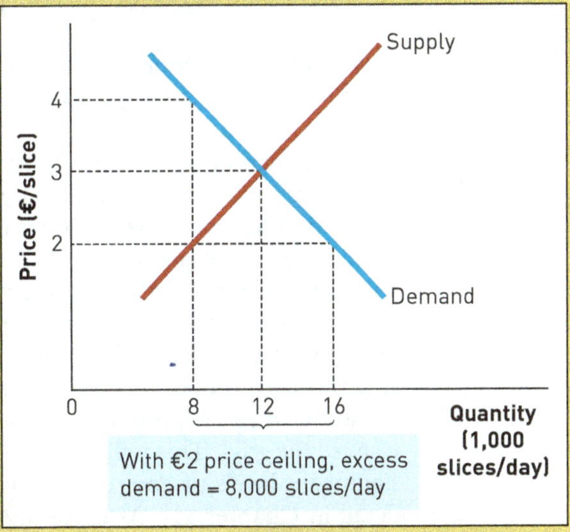

Figure 3.27 Price Controls in the Pizza Market
A price ceiling below the equilibrium price of pizza would result in excess demand for pizza.

of pizza they want to buy each day. All mutually beneficial opportunities for exchange would have been exploited, leaving no more cash on the table.

Buyers and sellers in the marketplace have an uncanny ability to detect the presence of cash on the table. It is almost as if unexploited opportunities gave off some exotic scent triggering neuro-chemical explosions in the olfactory centres of their brains. The desire to scrape cash off the table and into their pockets is what drives sellers in each of any large city's thousands of individual food outlets to work diligently to meet their customers' demands. That they succeed to a far higher degree than participants in the city's rent-controlled housing market is plainly evident. Whatever flaws it might have, the market system moves with considerably greater speed and agility than any centralised allocation mechanisms yet devised. But, as we emphasise in the following section, this does not mean that markets *always* lead to the greatest good for all.

SMART FOR ONE, DUMB FOR ALL

socially optimal quantity the quantity of a good that results in the maximum possible economic surplus from producing and consuming the good

economic efficiency (also called **efficiency**) occurs when all goods and services are produced and consumed at their respective socially optimal levels

The **socially optimal quantity** of any good is the quantity that maximises the total economic surplus that results from producing and consuming the good. From the Cost–Benefit Principle (Chapter 1), we know that we should keep expanding production of the good as long as its marginal benefit is at least as great as its marginal cost. This means that the socially optimal quantity is that level for which the marginal cost and marginal benefit of the good are the same.

When the quantity of a good is less than the socially optimal quantity, boosting its production will increase total economic surplus. By the same token, when the quantity of a good exceeds the socially optimal quantity, reducing its production will increase total economic surplus. **Economic efficiency**, or **efficiency**, occurs when all goods and services in the economy are produced and consumed at their respective socially optimal levels.

Efficiency is an important social goal. Failure to achieve efficiency means that total economic surplus is smaller than it might have been. Movements toward efficiency make the total economic 'pie' larger, making it possible for everyone to have a larger slice. The importance of efficiency will be a recurring theme as we move forward, and we state it here as one of the core principles:

> **The Efficiency Principle**: Efficiency is an important social goal, because when the economic 'pie' grows larger, everyone can have a larger slice.

Is the market equilibrium quantity of a good efficient? That is, does it maximise the total economic surplus received by participants in the market for that good? When the private market for a given good is in equilibrium, we can say that the cost *to the seller* of producing an additional unit of the good is the same as the benefit *to the buyer* of having an additional unit. If all costs of producing the good are borne directly by sellers, and if all benefits from the good accrue directly to buyers, it follows that the market equilibrium quantity of the good will equate the marginal cost and marginal benefit of the good. And this means that the equilibrium quantity also *maximises total economic surplus*.

Sometimes the production of a good entails costs that fall on people *other than those who sell the good*. This will be true, for instance, for goods whose production generates significant levels of environmental pollution (a topic we shall explore in much greater detail in Chapter 11). As extra units of these goods are produced, the extra pollution harms other people besides sellers. In the market equilibrium for such goods, the benefit *to buyers* of the last good produced is, as before, equal to the cost incurred by sellers to produce that good. But since producing that good also imposed pollution costs on others, we know that the *full* marginal cost of the last unit produced – the seller's private marginal cost plus the marginal pollution cost borne by others – must be higher than the benefit of the last unit produced. So in this case the market equilibrium quantity of the good will be larger than the socially optimal quantity. Total economic surplus would be higher if output of the good were lower. Yet neither sellers nor buyers have any incentive to alter their behaviour.

Another possibility is that people *other than those who buy* a good may receive significant benefits from it. For instance, when someone purchases a vaccination against measles from her doctor, she not only protects herself against measles, but she also makes it less likely that others will catch this disease. From the perspective of society as a whole, we should keep increasing the number of vaccinations until their marginal cost equals their marginal benefit. The marginal benefit of a vaccination is the value of the protection it provides for the person vaccinated *plus* the value of the protection it provides for all others. Private consumers, however, will choose to be vaccinated only if the marginal benefit *to them* exceeds the price of the vaccination. In this case, then, the market equilibrium quantity of vaccinations will be smaller than the quantity that maximises total economic surplus. Again, however, individuals would have no incentive to alter their behaviour.

Situations like those just discussed provide examples of behaviours that we may call 'smart for one, dumb for all'. In each case, the individual actors are behaving rationally. They are pursuing their goals as best they can, and yet there remain unexploited opportunities for gain from the point of view of the whole society. The difficulty is that these opportunities cannot be exploited by individuals acting alone. In subsequent chapters we shall see how people can often *organise collectively* to exploit such opportunities. For now, we simply summarise this discussion in the form of the following core principle:

The Equilibrium Principle (also called the 'No-Cash-On-The-Table' Principle): A market in equilibrium leaves no unexploited opportunities *for individuals*, but may not exploit all gains achievable through *collective action*.

RECAP

Markets and social welfare

When the supply and demand curves for a good reflect all significant costs and benefits associated with the production and consumption of that good, the *market equilibrium price* will guide people to produce and consume the quantity of the good that results in the largest possible economic surplus.

WHAT MARKETS DELIVER 2: CENTRAL PLANNING VERSUS THE MARKET

No society – regardless of how it is organised – can escape the need to answer certain basic economic questions. For example, how much of our limited time and other resources should we devote to producing one product rather than another? What techniques should be used? Who should be assigned to each specific task? And how should the resulting goods and services be distributed among people?

In the many different societies for which records are available, issues such as these have been decided in essentially one of two ways. One approach is for all relevant economic decisions to be made *centrally*, by an individual or small number of individuals on behalf of a larger group. For example, in many agrarian societies throughout history, families or other small groups consumed only those goods and services that they produced for themselves, and a single clan or family leader made most important production and distribution decisions. On an immensely larger scale, the economic organisation of the former Soviet Union (and other communist countries) was also largely centralised. A centrally controlled bureaucratic structure established production targets for the country's farms and factories, based on an overall plan for achieving targets (including detailed instructions concerning who was to produce what) and set up guidelines for the distribution and use of the goods and services produced.

Neither form of centralised economic organisation is much in evidence today. When implemented on a small scale, as in a self-sufficient family enterprise, centralised decision making is certainly feasible. For the reasons discussed in Chapter 1, however, the jack-of-all-trades approach was doomed once it became clear how dramatically people could improve their living standards by specialisation – that is, by having each individual focus his or her efforts on a relatively narrow range of tasks. After the collapse of the Soviet Union between 1989 and 1991 and the overthrow of the Soviet-backed regimes in the East European countries that had been Soviet satellites since the late 1940s, there remain in 2008 only three countries worldwide that formally operate or claim to operate communist societies with **central planning**: Cuba, North Korea and China. The first two of these appear to be on their last legs, economically speaking, and China has by now largely abandoned any attempt to control production and distribution decisions from the centre. The major remaining examples of centralised allocation and control now reside in the bureaucratic agencies that administer programmes such as New York City's rent controls or Britain's NHS – programmes that are themselves becoming increasingly rare.

central planning the allocation of economic resources is determined by a political and administrative mechanism that gathers information as to technology, resource availability and end demands for goods and services

There are no *pure* free-market economies. Modern industrial countries are characterised by a mixture of structures that deliver goods and services to end users. Where markets do the job, they are commonly subject to various forms of regulation. In the case of some services, collective provision via state structures is common. Public transport is an obvious example. Hence, modern economies are more properly described as *mixed economies*, meaning that goods and services are allocated by a combination of free markets, regulation and other forms of collective control. Still, it makes sense to refer to such systems as free-market economies, or at least market economies, because people are for the most part free to start businesses, to shut them down or to sell them. And, within broad limits, the distribution of goods and services is determined by individual preferences backed by individual purchasing power.

In country after country, markets have replaced centralised control for the simple reason that they tend to assign production tasks and consumption benefits much more effectively. This has not been without controversy. For example, the UK experiment in privatising rail transport has been the subject of considerable criticism, and indeed has been effectively partially reversed. The fact that the process of extending the role of the market, including privatisation, has been far from problem-free and has resulted in some cynicism about economists and their ability to agree on policy measures. Nor has the operation of markets been without serious problems in all cases. The US 'sub-prime lending crisis' of 2007–8 that threw world financial markets into serious difficulties was an example of a market that failed to operate efficiently, because the true risk level involved in this lending was not clear to those who ended up financing it.

Despite these reservations, there is broad agreement among economists about markets, with the great majority accepting the superior performance of markets as means for *allocating* society's scarce resources.[11] In most cases, the experience of privatisation and reliance on markets has shown this belief to be correct. An obvious case in point is the passenger airline business, which from the 1930s to the 1980s was highly regulated,

---

[11] Substantial differences remain, of course, as to the distributional consequences of using markets to allocate resources, and these result in some economists in some circumstances opting for the use of regulated or collective provision of goods and services rather than relying on markets. In addition, as will become clear in Chapter 6 below, there is a significant class of economic activities where the market does not operate 'efficiently' as an allocation mechanism.

with severe restrictions on entry and competition between operators, and (in Europe and most of the world outside the US) was largely in the hands of state-owned operators with monopoly rights. No one seriously disputes the proposition that the privatisation and deregulation of the air traffic sector across Europe, long called for by transport economists, has revolutionised the choices and costs facing people who want to fly. Ryanair is the standing proof of markets working where state provision and restricted competition have failed.

To see why this is the case, we must explore how goods and services are allocated in private markets, and why intervention to restrict the operations of markets often does not produce the desired results.

SUMMARY: SUPPLY AND DEMAND ◆◆◆◆

- Focusing solely on differences in *costs of production* cannot adequately explain the difference in prices of goods or services. For example, this approach cannot explain why a conveniently located house sells for more than one that is less conveniently located. The same applies to focusing only on willingness to pay. This approach cannot explain why the price of a life-saving appendectomy is less than that of a surgical facelift.
- Alfred Marshall's model of supply and demand explains why, in order to explain variations in price, we must examine the *interaction of cost and willingness to pay*. Goods differ in price because of differences in their respective supply and demand curves.
- The demand curve is a downward-sloping line that tells what quantity buyers will demand at any given price. The supply curve is an upward-sloping line that tells what quantity sellers will offer at any given price. *Market* equilibrium occurs when the quantity buyers demand at the market price is exactly the same as the quantity that sellers offer. The equilibrium price–quantity pair is the one at which the demand and supply curves intersect. In equilibrium, market price measures both the value of the last unit sold to buyers and the cost of the resources required to produce it.
- When the price of a good lies above its equilibrium value, there is an *excess supply* of that good. This motivates sellers to cut their prices, and price continues to fall until the equilibrium price is reached. When price lies below its equilibrium value, there is *excess demand*. Frustrated buyers are motivated to offer higher prices, and the upward pressure on prices persists until equilibrium is reached.
- The market system, relying only on the tendency of people to respond in self-interested ways to market price signals, manages to coordinate the actions of literally billions of buyers and sellers worldwide. If prices and purchases are free to adjust, excess demand or supply tends to be small and temporary.
- The efficiency of markets in *allocating resources* does not eliminate social concerns about how goods and services are distributed among different people. Concern for the well-being of the poor has motivated many governments to intervene in a variety of ways to alter the outcomes of market forces. Sometimes these interventions take the form of laws that peg prices below their equilibrium levels. Such laws almost invariably generate harmful, if unintended, consequences, including shortages and black markets.
- If the difficulty is that the poor have too little money, the best solution is to discover ways of boosting their incomes directly.
- The basic *supply and demand model* is a primary tool of the economic naturalist. Changes in the equilibrium price of a good, and in the amount of it traded in the marketplace, can be predicted on the basis of shifts in its supply or demand curves. The following four rules hold for any good with a downward-sloping demand curve and an upward-sloping supply curve:

- An increase in demand will lead to an increase in equilibrium price and quantity.
- A reduction in demand will lead to a reduction in equilibrium price and quantity.
- An increase in supply will lead to a reduction in equilibrium price and an increase in equilibrium quantity.
- A decrease in supply will lead to an increase in equilibrium price and a reduction in equilibrium quantity.

- Incomes, tastes, population, expectations and the prices of substitutes and complements are among the factors that shift *demand schedules (curves). Supply schedules (curves)*, in turn, are primarily governed by such factors as technology, input prices, expectations, the number of sellers – and, especially for agricultural products – the weather.
- When (but only when) the supply and demand curves for a good reflect all significant costs and benefits associated with the production and consumption of that good, the market equilibrium price will guide people to produce and consume the quantity of the good that results in the largest possible economic surplus.

SUMMARY: ELASTICITY

- The price elasticity of demand is a measure of how strongly buyers respond to *changes in price*. It is the percentage change in quantity demanded that occurs in response to a 1 per cent change in price. The demand for a good is called 'elastic' with respect to price if its price elasticity is more than 1; 'inelastic' if its price elasticity is less than 1; and unit elastic if its price elasticity is equal to 1.
- Goods that occupy only a small share of the typical consumer's budget and have few or no good substitutes, tend to have low price elasticity of demand. Goods such as new cars of a particular make and model, which occupy large budget shares and have many attractive substitutes, tend to have high price elasticity of demand. Price elasticity of demand is higher in the long run than in the short run because people often need time to *adjust to price changes*.
- The *price elasticity of demand* at a point along a demand curve can also be expressed as the formula $\varepsilon = (\Delta Q/Q)/(\Delta P/P)$. Here, P and Q represent price and quantity at that point and ΔQ and ΔP represent small changes in price and quantity. For straight-line demand curves, this formula can also be expressed as $\varepsilon = (P/Q) \times (1/\text{slope})$. These formulations tell us that price elasticity *declines in absolute terms* as we move down a straight-line demand curve.
- A cut in price will increase total spending on a good if demand is elastic but reduce it if demand is inelastic. An increase in price will increase total spending on a good if demand is inelastic but reduce it if demand is elastic. *Total expenditure* on a good reaches a maximum when price elasticity of demand is equal to 1.
- Analogous formulae are used to define the elasticity of demand for a good with respect to *income* and the *prices of other goods*. In each case, elasticity is the percentage change in quantity demanded divided by the corresponding percentage change in income or price.
- *The price* elasticity *of supply* is defined as the percentage change in quantity supplied that occurs in response to a 1 per cent change in price. The mathematical formula for the price elasticity of supply at any point is $(\Delta Q/Q)/(\Delta P/P)$, where P and Q are the price and quantity at that point, ΔP is a small change in the initial price and ΔQ is the resulting change in quantity. This formula can also be expressed as $(P/Q) \times (1/\text{slope})$, where $(1/\text{slope})$ is the reciprocal of the slope of the supply curve.
- The price elasticity of supply of a good depends on how difficult or costly it is to acquire *additional units* of the inputs involved in producing that good. In general, the more easily additional units of these inputs can be acquired, the higher the

price elasticity of supply will be. It is easier to expand production of a product if the inputs used to produce that product are similar to the inputs used to produce other products, if inputs are relatively mobile, or if an acceptable substitute for existing inputs can be developed. And like the price elasticity of demand, the price elasticity of supply is greater in the long run than in the short run.

REVIEW QUESTIONS

1. Distinguish between the meaning of the expressions 'change in demand' and 'change in the quantity demanded'.
2. Last year a government official proposed that motor fuel price controls be imposed to protect the poor from rising motor fuel prices. What evidence could you consult to discover whether this proposal was enacted?
3. Explain the distinction between the horizontal and vertical interpretations of the demand curve.
4. Give an example of behaviour you have observed that could be described as 'smart for one, dumb for all'.
5. Why does a consumer's price elasticity of demand for a good depend on the fraction of the consumer's income spent on that good?
6. Why does the elasticity of demand for a good with respect to its own price decline as we move down along a straight-line demand curve?
7. Why do economists pay little attention to the algebraic sign of the elasticity of demand for a good with respect to its own price, yet pay careful attention to the algebraic sign of the elasticity of demand for a good with respect to another good's price?
8. Why is supply elasticity higher in the long run than in the short run?
9. Why is efficiency an important social goal?

PROBLEMS

connect

1. How would each of the following affect the EU market supply curve for wheat?
   a. A new and improved crop rotation technique is discovered.
   b. The price of fertiliser falls.
   c. The EU Commission offers new subsidies to farmers growing wheat.
   d. A tornado sweeps through northern France in July.

2. Indicate how you think each of the following would shift demand in the indicated market:
   a. Incomes of buyers in the market for Spanish sun holidays increase.
   b. Buyers in the market for pizza read a study linking hamburger consumption to heart disease.
   c. Buyers in the market for CDs learn of an increase in the price of audio cassettes.
   d. Buyers in the market for CDs learn of an increase in the price of CDs.

3. What will happen to the equilibrium price and quantity of olives in Italy if the wage paid to olive pickers rises?

4. How will an increase in immigration affect the equilibrium price of land?

5. What will happen to the equilibrium price and quantity of beef if the price of chicken-feed increases?

6. How will a new law mandating an increase in required levels of automobile insurance affect the equilibrium price and quantity in the market for new automobiles?

7. Suppose the current issue of the *Le Monde* reports an outbreak of mad cow disease in the Dordogne as well as the discovery of a new breed of chickens that gain more weight than existing breeds that consume the same amount of food. How will these developments affect the equilibrium price and quantity of chicken sold in the France?

8. What will happen to the equilibrium price and quantity of apples if apples are discovered to help prevent colds and a fungus kills 10 per cent of existing apple trees?

9. The schedule below shows daily purchases of bags of *pommes frites* bought in Leuven in Belgium, at a variety of prices.

Price of pommes frites (€/bag)	Number of bags purchased per day
6	0
5	3,000
4	6,000
3	9,000
2	12,000
1	15,000
0	18,000

   a. Graph the daily demand curve for bags of *pommes frites* in Leuven.
   b. Calculate the price elasticity of demand at the point on the demand curve at which the price is €3 .
   c. If all outlets increased the price from €3 to €4, what would happen to total sales revenues?

10. Is the demand for a particular brand of car, such as a Ford or a Volkswagen, likely to be more or less price elastic than the demand for all cars? Explain.

11. A 2 per cent increase in the price of milk causes a 4 per cent reduction in the quantity demanded of chocolate syrup. What is the cross-price elasticity of demand for milk with respect to the price of chocolate syrup? Are the two goods complements or substitutes?

12. What are the respective price elasticities of supply at *A* and *B* on the supply curve shown in the graph below?

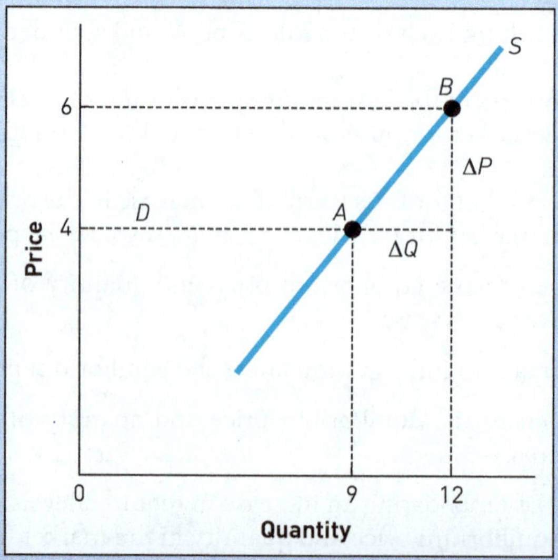

13. At point *A* on the demand curve shown below, by what percentage will a 1 per cent increase in the price of the product affect total expenditure on the product?

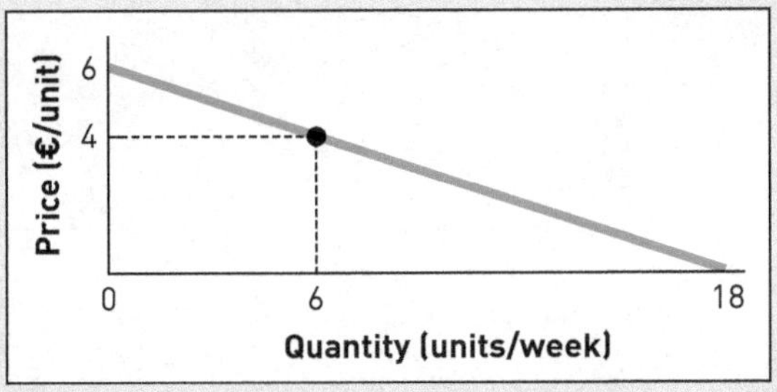

14. In an attempt to induce citizens to conserve energy, the government enacted regulations requiring that all air conditioners be more efficient in their use of electricity. After this regulation was implemented, government officials were then surprised to discover that people used even more electricity than before. Using the concept of price elasticity, explain how this happened.

REFERENCES

Elzinga, K. (1977) 'The Beer Industry', in W. Adams (ed.), *The Structure of American Industry*, 5th edn (New York, Macmillan).

Fisher, R. (1996) *State and Local Public Finance* (Chicago, Irwin).

Goodwin, P., J. Dargay and M. Hanly 'Elasticities of Road Traffic and Fuel Consumption With Respect to Price and Income: A Review', *Transport Reviews* (www.tandf.co.uk), Vol. 24, No. 3.

Houthakker, H. and L. Taylor (1970) *Consumer Demand in the United States: Analysis and Projections*, 2nd edn (Harvard U.P.).

Siciliani, L. and J. Hurst (2003) 'Explaining waiting time variations for elective surgery across OECD countries', *OECD Health Working Papers*, 2003/7.

Taylor, L. (1975) 'The Demand for Electricity: a Survey', *Bell Journal*, Spring, 1975, pp. 74–110.

Part 2

Competition and the 'Invisible Hand'

The basic core principles of economics described in Part 1 enable you to sharpen your understanding of how consumers and firms behave. In Part 2 we look at how things work in an idealised, perfectly competitive economy in which consumers are perfectly informed and no firm has market power.

We begin in Chapter 4 by looking at purchase decisions by consumers. To analyse this we consider what is the basis for rational choices by consumers, and how they should rationally respond to changes in prices, incomes or the types of goods available to them. This enables us to derive testable predictions about the impact of price, income and tastes on behaviour, and provides the theoretical underpinning for the downward-sloping demand curve already discussed in Part 1. In Chapter 5 our focus will shift to the seller's side of the market, where our task will be to see why upward-sloping supply curves are a consequence of production decisions taken by firms whose goal is to maximise profit.

Our agenda in Chapter 6 is to develop more carefully and fully the concept of economic surplus introduced in Part 1 and to investigate the conditions under which unregulated markets generate the largest possible economic surplus. We will also explore why attempts to interfere with market outcomes often lead to unintended and undesired consequences.

Finally, in Chapter 7 we will investigate the economic forces by which the invisible hand of the marketplace guides profit-seeking firms and satisfaction-seeking consumers in ways that, to a surprising degree, serve society's ends. These forces encourage aggressive cost cutting by firms, even though the resulting gains will eventually take the form of lower prices rather than higher profits. We also emphasise, and this sometimes offends public opinion, that in a competitive economy that seeks efficient resource allocation, firm closure (exiting a market) is something that cannot be avoided, and something of which it can be said that efforts to reduce or eliminate it negate the basic reasons for which market economies are said to be efficient. This helps us to see why misunderstanding of competitive forces often results in costly errors, both in everyday decision making and in government policy.

Chapter 4

Demand: the Benefit Side of the Market

Money doesn't make you happy. I now have $50 million but I was just as happy when I had $48 million.

Arnold Schwarzenegger

Learning Objectives

After studying this chapter you should be able to:

1. Understand that the demand curve, relating quantity demanded to price reflects the Cost–Benefit Principle;
2. Understand the concept of consumer equilibrium with respect to prices;
3. Explain how changes in the price of a good (and of other goods) affect the amount of that good purchased;
4. Use indifference curves to establish the downward sloping demand curve;
5. Understand income and substitution effects of a price change;
6. Understand and be able to apply the concept of consumer surplus.

Aldi and Lidl are two of Europe's largest cut-price supermarket chains. They offer consumers in many cases goods of similar quality to those available from higher-priced supermarket chains. They also offer goods that may well be less fancy (they would never accept that their goods are of lower quality) than those available in the more up-market outlets. How do the more expensive supermarkets survive? Indeed, going further, how do higher price and lower price 'traditional' (i.e., non-discount outlets) survive in the cohort of 'traditional' supermarkets?

Part of the answer is branding: in many cases you may not be able to buy 'national' or 'global' brand products in discount supermarkets. The latter stock mostly own-brand goods. Or some supermarkets may have exclusive contracts with suppliers for variants of products. However, more important factors are thought to be choice and convenience. The traditional supermarkets typically carry a broader range of products in any given category. They also often have locations that are more convenient or in better neighbourhoods. They will also usually have more checkout lines, and in some cases will offer a delivery service. They frequently operate boutique 'stores within stores', selling high-value and service-intensive goods.

Controlling for quality, the up-market outlets can compete with the discount stores because it is not only a simple money price paid for a good that determines where the good will be bought and in what quantities. The price paid for the good is only part of the cost of buying it. It may be possible to buy a good at a lower money price in another outlet, but a rational consumer may still prefer to buy in the more expensive outlet because the total cost of purchase is lower when the other aspects of the shopping decision are factored into the decision as to where to shop. Having to stand for 20 minutes in a checkout queue is a cost, no less so than having to part with some money.

Add this observation to a limited capacity to supply and you will understand why bars or restaurants do not go bankrupt by offering half-price drinks or 'early-bird' menus during a 5.30 to 7.00 pm happy hour.

While in many cases money prices alone perform the rationing function of allocating resources between competing users, in some cases other factors are substituted in whole or in part for money prices as a rationing device. The point being made here is that, although the demand curve is usually described as a relationship between the quantity demanded of a good and its monetary price, the relationship is really a much more general one. Fundamentally, the demand curve is a relationship between the quantity demanded and all costs – monetary and non-monetary – associated with acquiring a good.

In this chapter we will explore the demand side of the market in greater depth than was possible in Chapter 3. There we merely asked you to accept as an intuitively plausible claim that the quantity demanded of a good or service declines as its price in the broadest sense rises. This relationship is known as the 'law of demand', and we shall see how it emerges as a simple consequence of the assumption that people spend their limited incomes rationally. In the process, we shall see more clearly the dual roles of *income* and *substitution* as factors that account for the law of demand. We shall also see how to generate market demand curves by adding the demand curves for individual buyers horizontally. Finally, we shall see how to use the demand curve to generate a measure of the total benefit that buyers reap from their participation in a market.

We start by explaining the basic concepts lying behind the idea of the demand curve. These are then used to derive the proposition that demand curves in general will slope downwards based on logic rather than on simple (and sometimes misleading) notions of common sense. In this chapter this is done at two levels. We offer first a relatively non-technical explanation based on an assumption concerning consumer behaviour that is referred to as *'diminishing marginal utility'*. This approach suffices for most purposes, but depends on restrictive assumptions concerning people's preferences. Subsequently we offer a more rigorous and more general analysis of preferences to demonstrate the logical basis for the slope of demand curves. If you study this you will be introduced to a construct that is central to economics analysis after the introductory stage, the *'indifference curve'*. It is, however, possible to skip this section without losing the thread of the argument in the chapter, but we recommend that you do not take this option if you intend going on to further study in economics.

THE LAW OF DEMAND

Let us restate the *law of demand*:

> **Law of demand**: People do less of what they want to do as the cost of doing it rises.

Cost-Benefit Analysis

By stating the law of demand in this way, we can see it as a direct consequence of the *Cost–Benefit Principle* (Chapter 1), which says that an activity should be pursued if (and only if) its benefits are at least as great as its costs. Recall that we measure the benefit of an activity by the highest price we would be willing to pay to pursue it – namely, our *reservation price* for the activity. When the cost to us of an action rises, it is more likely to exceed our reservation price, and we are therefore less likely to take that action.

The law of demand applies to BMWs, cheap key rings and cut-price beer, not to mention compact discs, manicures, medical care and acid-free rain. It stresses that a 'cost' is the sum of *all* the sacrifices – monetary and non-monetary, implicit and explicit – we must make to engage in an activity.

THE ORIGINS OF DEMAND

How much are you willing to pay for the latest Adele CD? The answer will clearly depend on how you feel about her music. To Adele's diehard fans, buying the new release might seem absolutely essential; they'd pay a steep price indeed. But those who don't like Adele's music may be unwilling to buy it at any price.

Wants (also called 'preferences' or 'tastes') are clearly an important determinant of a consumer's reservation price for a good. Many tastes – such as the taste for water on a hot day or for a comfortable place to sleep at night – are largely biological in origin. But many others are heavily shaped by culture, and even basic cravings may be socially moulded. For example, people raised in southern India develop a taste for hot curry dishes, while those raised in England often prefer milder foods.

Tastes for some items may remain stable for many years, but tastes for others may be highly volatile. Although books about the *Titanic* disaster have been continuously available since the vessel sank in the spring of 1912, only with the appearance of James Cameron's blockbuster film did these books begin to sell in large quantities. In the spring of 1998, five of the fifteen books on the *New York Times* paperback bestseller list were about the *Titanic* itself or one of the actors in the film. Yet none of these books, or any other book about the *Titanic*, made the bestseller list in 1999. Still, echoes of the film continued to reverberate in the marketplace. In the years since its release, for example, demand for ocean cruises has grown sharply, and several American television networks have introduced shows set on cruise ships.

Peer influence provides another example of how social forces often influence demand. Indeed, it is often the single most important determinant of demand. For instance, to predict whether a young man will purchase an illegal recreational drug, knowledge of his income is not very helpful. Knowing the prices of whisky and other legal substitutes for illicit drugs also tells us little. They may influence purchase decisions, but by themselves they are weak predictors. However, the level of drug usage among most of his friends is a good predictor of whether he uses drugs.

Another important way in which social forces shape demand is in the relatively common desire to consume goods and services that are recognised as the best of their kind. Think about the brands of jeans and how their makers advertise them to encourage purchases.

Or think about buying a new suit to make a good impression at a job interview. At the very least, that means showing up in a suit that looks good. But 'looking good' is a relative concept. If everyone else shows up in a €200 suit, you'll look good if you show up in a €300 suit. But you won't look as good in that same €300 suit if everyone else shows up in suits costing €1,000. The amount you choose to spend on an interview suit, then, clearly depends on how much others in your circle are spending.

NEEDS VERSUS WANTS

In everyday language, we distinguish between goods and services people *need* and those they merely *want*. For example, we might say that someone wants a house with a view, but what he really needs is shelter from the elements. Likewise, since people need protein to survive, we might say that a severely malnourished person needs more protein. But it would strike us as odd to say that anyone – even a malnourished person – *needs* more prime fillet of beef, since health can be restored by consuming far less expensive sources of protein.

Economists like to emphasise that once we have achieved bare subsistence levels of consumption – the amount of food, shelter and clothing required to maintain our health – we can abandon all reference to needs and speak only in terms of wants. This linguistic distinction helps us to think more clearly about the true nature of our choices.

Think about the perennial political problems arising in southern California over the availability of water (much of which is supplied from aquifers in the distant Sierra Nevada mountains). A viewpoint that is often expressed in the media is: 'Californians don't have nearly as much water as they need.' Putting the problem this way suggests a different mind-set from that of a commentator who says 'Californians don't have nearly as much water as they want when the price of water is low.' The first person is likely to focus on regulations to prevent people from watering their lawns, or on projects to capture additional runoff from the Sierra Nevada mountains. The second person is more likely to focus on the low price of water in California. Whereas remedies of the first sort are often costly and extremely difficult to implement, raising the price of water is both simple and effective.

Scarcity

Cost-Benefit Analysis

Economic Naturalist 4.1
What happens when people do not have to pay for the water they use?

As most people know, it rains a lot in Ireland. So how is it that in recent years Ireland has seen significant episodes of water shortage, even when in the same season there has been flooding because of the rainfall? The problems arose because the water supply system, using supply infrastructure dating in many cases from the late nineteenth century, and controlled and operated by local municipal authorities, did not expand to meet growing demand. Worse, ageing cast-iron pipe systems were not maintained, and in the first decade of the twenty-first century it was estimated that more than 30 per cent of the water leaving the reservoirs that supplied Dublin leaked out into the ground through cracks and broken joints. The cause of this shortage in the presence of plenty was that households faced no charges for using water, and local authorities obtained no revenue from supplying water. Local authorities had little incentive to maintain, let alone expand, the basic water-supply infrastructure as demand rose. No political party was willing to make people pay for consuming water, so, inevitably with a zero price the availability of water to households demand exceeded supply. When people can have it for free, the predictable result is shortages.

TRANSLATING WANTS INTO DEMAND

It is a simple fact of life that although our resources are finite, our appetites for good things are boundless. Even if we had unlimited bank accounts, we'd quickly run out of the time and energy needed to do all the things we wanted to do. Our challenge is to use our *limited resources* to fulfil our desires to the greatest possible degree. And that leaves us with this practical question: 'How should we allocate our incomes among the various goods and services that are available?' To answer this question, it is helpful to begin by recognising that the goods and services we buy are not ends in themselves, but rather means for satisfying our desires.

MEASURING WANTS: THE CONCEPT OF UTILITY

Economists use the concept of *utility* to represent the satisfaction people derive from their consumption activities. The assumption is that people try to allocate their incomes so as to maximise their satisfaction, a goal that is referred to as *utility maximisation*.

Early economists imagined that the utility associated with different activities might some day be subject to precise measurement. The nineteenth-century British economist

Jeremy Bentham, for example, wrote of a 'utilometer', a device that could be used to measure the amount of utility provided by different consumption activities. Although no such device existed in Bentham's day, neuro-psychologists now have equipment that can measure satisfaction levels, if somewhat crudely.

For Bentham's intellectual enterprise, however, the absence of a real utilometer was of no practical significance. Even without such a machine, he could continue to envision the consumer as someone whose goal was to maximise the total utility he or she obtained from the goods consumed. Bentham's 'utility maximisation model', as we shall see, affords important insights about how rational consumers ought to spend their incomes. To explore the model, we begin with an unusually simple problem, that facing a consumer who reaches the front of the queue at a free ice cream stand. How many cones of ice cream should this person, Sarah, ask for? Table 4.1 shows the relationship between the total number of ice cream cones Sarah eats per hour and the total utility, measured in utils per hour, she derives from them. Note that the measurements in the table are stated in terms of cones per hour and utils per hour. Why 'per hour'? Because without an explicit time dimension we would have no idea whether a given quantity was a lot or a little. Five ice cream cones in a lifetime isn't much, but five in an hour would be more than most of us would care to eat.

Table 4.1 Sarah's Total Utility from Ice Cream Consumption

Cone quantity (cones/hour)	Total utility (utils/hour)
0	0
1	50
2	90
3	120
4	140
5	150
6	140

As the entries in Table 4.1 show, Sarah's total utility increases with each cone she eats, up to the fifth cone. Eating five cones per hour makes her happier than eating four, which makes her happier than eating three, and so on. But beyond five cones per hour, consuming more ice cream actually makes Sarah less happy as she feels bloated. Thus the sixth cone reduces her total utility from 150 utils per hour to 140 utils per hour.

We can display the utility information in Table 4.1 graphically, as in Fig. 4.1. Note in the graph that the more cones per hour Sarah eats, the more utils she gets – but again only up to the fifth cone. Once she moves beyond five, her total utility begins to decline. Sarah's happiness reaches a maximum of 150 utils when she eats five cones per hour. At that point she has no incentive to eat the sixth cone, even though it's absolutely free. Eating it would actually make her worse off.

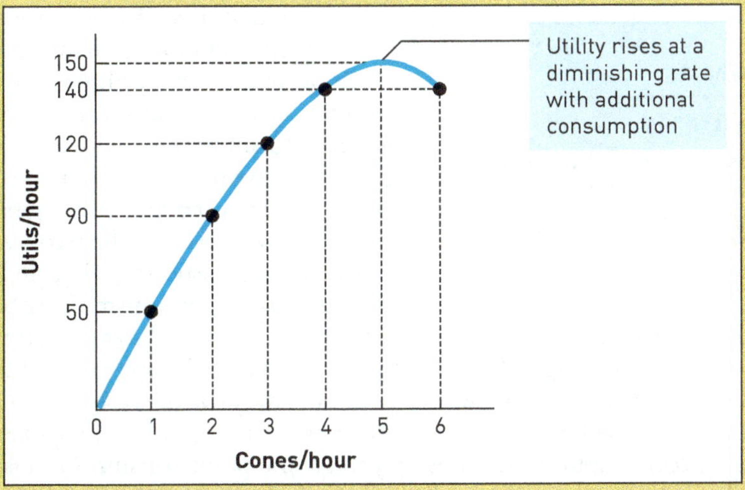

Figure 4.1 Sarah's Total Utility from Ice Cream Consumption

For most goods, utility rises at a diminishing rate with additional consumption.

Table 4.2 Sarah's Total and Marginal Utility from Ice Cream Consumption

Cone quantity (cones/hour) (1)	Total utility (utils/hour) (2)	Marginal utility (utils/cone) (3)	
0	0	–	
1	50		Marginal utility
		40	= Change in utility / Change in consumption
2	90		
		30	= (90 utils – 50 utils) / (2 cones – 1 cone)
3	120		
		20	= 40 utils/cone
4	140		
		10	
5	150		
		−10	
6	140		

Table 4.1 and Fig. 4.1 illustrate another important aspect of the relationship between utility and consumption: the additional utility from additional units of consumption declines as total consumption increases. Thus, whereas one cone per hour is a *lot* better – by 50 utils – than zero, five cones per hour is just a *little* better than four (just 10 utils' worth).

marginal utility the additional utility gained from consuming an additional unit of a good

The term **marginal utility** denotes the amount by which total utility changes when consumption changes by one unit. In Table 4.2, column (3) shows the marginal utility values that correspond to changes in Sarah's level of ice cream consumption. For example, the second entry in column (3) represents the increase in total utility (measured in utils per cone) when Sarah's consumption rises from one cone per hour to two. Note that the marginal utility entries in column (3) are placed midway between the rows of the preceding columns. We do this to indicate that marginal utility corresponds to the movement from one consumption quantity to the next. Thus we would say that the marginal utility of moving from one to two cones per hour is 40 utils per cone.

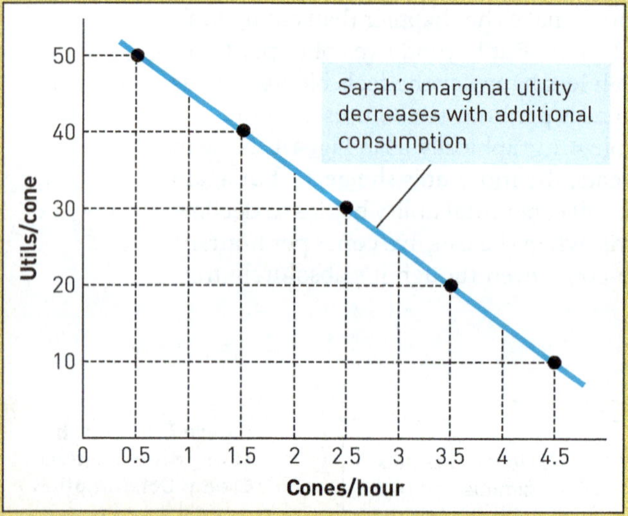

Figure 4.2 Diminishing Marginal Utility
The more cones Sarah consumes each hour, the smaller her marginal utility will be. For Sarah, consumption of ice cream cones reflects diminishing marginal utility.

Because marginal utility is the change in utility that occurs as we move from one quantity to another, when we graph marginal utility we normally adopt the convention of plotting each specific marginal utility value halfway between the two quantities to which it corresponds. Thus, in Fig. 4.2, we plot the marginal utility value of 40 utils per cone midway between one cone per hour and two cones per hour, and so on. (In this example, the marginal utility graph is a downward-sloping straight line for the region shown, but this need not always be the case.)

diminishing marginal utility the tendency for the additional utility gained from consuming an additional unit of a good to diminish as consumption increases beyond some point

In so far as there is a tendency for marginal utility to decline as consumption increases, beyond some point consumption is said to be subject to **diminishing marginal utility** (DMU). Observations suggest that this is a pervasive phenomenon, so pervasive that it is sometimes loosely – and wrongly – referred to as the 'law' of diminishing marginal utility. DMU certainly appears to apply not just for Sarah's consumption of ice cream here, but also for most other goods for most consumers. If we have one cake or one Ferrari, we're happier than we are with none; if we have two, we'll be even happier – but not twice as happy – and so on. However, pervasive as it is, it is not a law in the sense of holding true in general. Indeed, some consumption activities even seem to exhibit *increasing* marginal utility. For example, appreciation and enjoyment of an unfamiliar piece of music often increases when heard several times. Furthermore, your utility from consumption of a good or expenditure on a good or service may be affected by whether or not other people around you consume it and in what quantities. Cell phones, for example, offered more utility to existing users as more people bought cell phones. Nevertheless, diminishing marginal utility is a plausible description of the relationship between utility and consumption for many goods. Unless otherwise stated, we shall assume that it holds for the various goods we discuss.

Let's return to Sarah as she gets to the front of the queue. At that point, the opportunity cost of the time she spent waiting is a *sunk cost*, and is hence irrelevant to her decision about how many cones to order. And since there is no monetary charge for the cones, the cost of ordering an additional one is zero. According to the Cost–Benefit Principle, Sarah should therefore continue to order cones as long as the marginal benefit (here, the marginal utility she gets from an additional cone) is greater than or equal to zero. As we can see from the entries in Table 4.2, marginal utility is positive up to and including the fifth cone but becomes negative after five cones. Thus, as noted earlier, Sarah should order five cones.

Cost-Benefit Analysis

Incentives Matter

In this highly simplified example, Sarah's *utility-maximisation* problem is just like the one she would confront if she were deciding how much water to drink from a public fountain. (*Solution:* Keep drinking until the marginal utility of water declines to zero (see Economic naturalist 4.1, above)).

ALLOCATING A FIXED INCOME BETWEEN TWO GOODS

Most of us confront considerably more complex purchase decisions than the one Sarah faced. For one thing, we generally must make decisions not just about a single good but about many. Another complication is that the cost of consuming additional units of each good will rarely be zero.

To see how to proceed in more complex cases, suppose that Sarah must decide how to spend a fixed sum of money on two different goods, each with a positive price. Should she spend all of it on one of the goods, or part of it on each? The 'law' of diminishing marginal utility suggests that spending it all on a single good isn't a good strategy. Rather than devote more and more money to the purchase of a good we already consume in large quantities (and whose marginal utility is therefore relatively low), we generally do better to spend that money on other goods that we don't have much of, whose marginal utility will likely be higher.

The simplest way to illustrate how economists think about the spending decisions of a utility-maximising consumer is to work through a scenario like that in Example 4.1.

Is Sarah maximising her utility from consuming chocolate and vanilla ice cream (1)? **Example 4.1**

Chocolate ice cream sells for €2 per carton and vanilla sells for €1. Sarah has a budget of €400 per year to spend on ice cream, and her marginal utility from consuming each type varies with the amount consumed as shown in Fig. 4.3. If she is currently buying 200 cartons of vanilla and 100 cartons of chocolate each year, is she maximising her utility?

Figure 4.3 Marginal Utility Curves for Two Flavours of Ice Cream (1)

At Sarah's current consumption levels, her marginal utility of chocolate ice cream is 25 per cent higher than her marginal utility of vanilla. But chocolate is twice as expensive as vanilla.

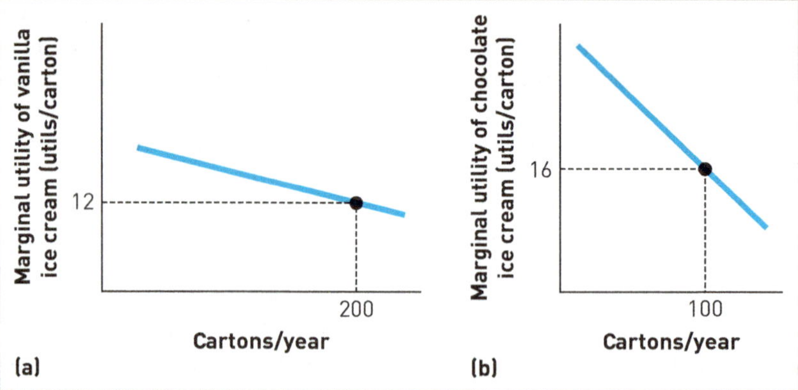

Note first that with 200 cartons per year of vanilla and 100 cartons of chocolate, Sarah spends €200 per year on each type of ice cream, for a total expenditure of €400 per year on ice cream, exactly the amount in her budget. By spending her money in this fashion, is she getting as much utility as possible? Note in Fig. 4.3(b) that her marginal utility from chocolate ice cream is 16 utils per carton. Since chocolate costs €2 per carton, her current spending on chocolate yields additional utility at the rate of (16 utils/carton)/(€2/carton) = 8 utils per euro. Similarly, note in Fig. 4.3(a) that Sarah's marginal utility for vanilla is 12 utils per carton. And since vanilla costs only €1 per carton, her current spending on vanilla yields (12 utils/carton)/ (€1/carton) = 12 utils per euro. In other words, at her current rates of consumption of the two flavours, her spending yields higher marginal utility per euro for vanilla than for chocolate. And this means that Sarah cannot possibly be maximising her total utility.

If she spent €2 less on chocolate (that is, if she bought one carton fewer than before), she would lose about 16 utils;[1] but with the same €2, she could buy two additional cartons of vanilla, which would boost her utility by about 24 utils,[2] a net gain of about 8 utils. So, under Sarah's current budget allocation, she spends too little on vanilla and too much on chocolate.

In Example 4.2, we shall see what happens if Sarah spends €100 per year less on chocolate and €100 per year more on vanilla.

Example 4.2 Is Sarah maximising her utility from consuming chocolate and vanilla ice cream (2)?

Sarah's total ice cream budget and the prices of the two flavours are the same as in Example 4.1. If her marginal utility from consuming each type varies with the amount consumed, as shown in Fig. 4.4, and if she is currently buying 300 cartons of vanilla and 50 cartons of chocolate each year, is she maximising her utility?

The way in which she rearranges her spending makes sense in the light of Example 4.1. She was spending too much on chocolate and too little on vanilla. Spending €100 less on chocolate ice cream causes her marginal utility from that flavour to rise from 16 to 24 utils per carton (Fig. 4.4(b)). Similarly, spending €100 more on vanilla ice cream causes her marginal utility from vanilla to fall from 12 to 8 utils per carton (Fig. 4.4(a)). Both movements are a simple consequence of diminishing marginal utility.

---

[1] The actual reduction would be slightly larger than 16 utils, because her marginal utility of chocolate rises slightly as she consumes less of it.

[2] The actual increase will be slightly smaller than 24 utils, because her marginal utility of vanilla falls slightly as she buys more of it.

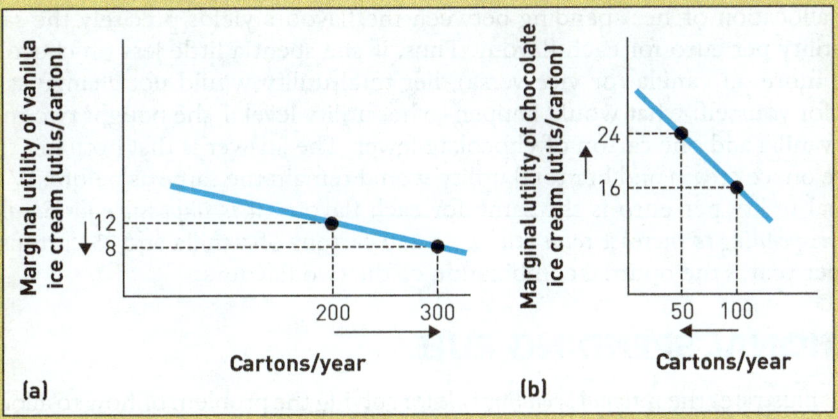

Figure 4.4 Marginal Utility Curves for Two Flavours of Ice Cream (2)

When Sarah increases her consumption of vanilla (a), her marginal utility of vanilla falls. Conversely, when she reduces her consumption of chocolate (b), her marginal utility of chocolate rises.

Since chocolate still costs €2 per carton, her spending on chocolate now yields additional utility at the rate of (24 utils/carton)/(€2/carton) = 12 utils per euro. Similarly, since vanilla still costs €1 per carton, her spending on vanilla now yields additional utility at the rate of only (8 utils/carton)/(€1/carton) = 8 utils per euro. So at her new rates of consumption of the two flavours, her spending yields higher marginal utility per euro for chocolate than for vanilla – precisely the opposite of the ordering we saw in Example 4.1.

Sarah has thus made too big an adjustment in her effort to remedy her original consumption imbalance. Starting from the new combination (300 cartons per year of vanilla and 50 cartons per year of chocolate), for example, if she then bought two fewer cartons of vanilla (which would reduce her utility by about 16 utils) and used the €2 she saved to buy an additional carton of chocolate (which would boost her utility by about 24 utils), she would experience a net gain of about 8 utils. So, again, her current combination of the two flavours fails to maximise her total utility. This time, she is spending too little on chocolate and too much on vanilla.

Exercise 4.1

Using the prices in Example 4.1, verify that the stated combination of flavours in Example 4.2 costs exactly the amount that Sarah has budgeted for ice cream.

What is Sarah's **optimal combination** of the two flavours? In other words, among all the combinations of vanilla and chocolate ice cream that Sarah can afford, which one provides the maximum possible total utility? Example 4.3 illustrates the condition that this optimal combination must satisfy.

optimal combination of goods the affordable combination that yields the highest total utility

Example 4.3

Is Sarah maximising her utility from consuming chocolate and vanilla ice cream (3)?

Sarah's total ice cream budget and the prices of the two flavours are again as in Examples 4.1 and 4.2. If her marginal utility from consuming each type varies with the amounts consumed as shown in Fig. 4.5, and if she is currently buying 250 cartons of vanilla and 75 cartons of chocolate each year, is she maximising her utility?

The combination of 250 cartons per year of vanilla and 75 cartons per year of chocolate again costs a total of €400, exactly the amount of Sarah's ice cream budget. Her marginal utility from chocolate is now 20 utils per carton (Fig. 4.5(b)), and since chocolate still costs €2 per carton, her spending on chocolate now yields additional utility at the rate of (20 utils/carton)/(€2/carton) = 10 utils per euro. Sarah's marginal utility for vanilla is now 10 utils per carton (Fig. 4.5(a)), and since vanilla still costs €1 per carton, her last euro spent on vanilla now also yields (10 utils/carton)/(€1/carton) = 10 utils per euro. This allocation of her spending between the flavours yields precisely the same marginal utility per euro for each flavour. Thus, if she spent a little less on chocolate and a little more on vanilla (or vice versa), her total utility would not change at all. Check this for yourself: what would happen to her utility level if she bought two more cartons of vanilla and one carton of chocolate fewer. The answer is that both her total expenditure on ice cream and her total utility would remain the same as before. When her marginal utility per euro is the same for each flavour, *it is impossible for Sarah to rearrange her spending to increase total utility*. So 250 cartons of vanilla and 75 cartons of chocolate per year is the optimal combination of the two flavours.

THE RATIONAL SPENDING RULE

Example 4.3 illustrates the *rational spending rule* for solving the problem of how to allocate a fixed budget across different goods. The optimal, or utility-maximising, combination must satisfy this rule.

> **Rational spending rule**: Spending should be allocated across goods so that the marginal utility per euro is the same for each good.

The rational spending rule can be expressed in the form of a simple formula. Use MU_C to denote marginal utility from chocolate ice cream consumption (again measured in utils per carton), and P_C to denote the price of chocolate (measured in euros, pounds, dollars . . . per carton). The ratio MU_C/P_C will represent the marginal utility per currency unit spent on chocolate, measured in utils per euro, etc. Similarly, if we use MU_V to denote the marginal utility from vanilla ice cream consumption and P_v to denote the price of vanilla, then MU_v/P_v will represent the marginal utility per euro spent on vanilla. The marginal utility per euro will be exactly the same for the two types – and hence total utility will be maximised – when the following simple equation for the rational spending rule for two goods is satisfied:

$$MU_C/P_C = MU_V/P_V$$

The rational spending rule is easily generalised to apply to spending decisions regarding large numbers of goods. In its most general form, it says that the ratio of marginal utility to price must be the same for each good the consumer buys. If the ratio were higher for one good than for another, the consumer could always increase her total utility by buying more of the first good and less of the second.

Figure 4.5 Marginal Utility Curves for Two Flavours of Ice Cream (3)

At Sarah's current consumption levels, marginal utility per euro is exactly the same for each flavour.

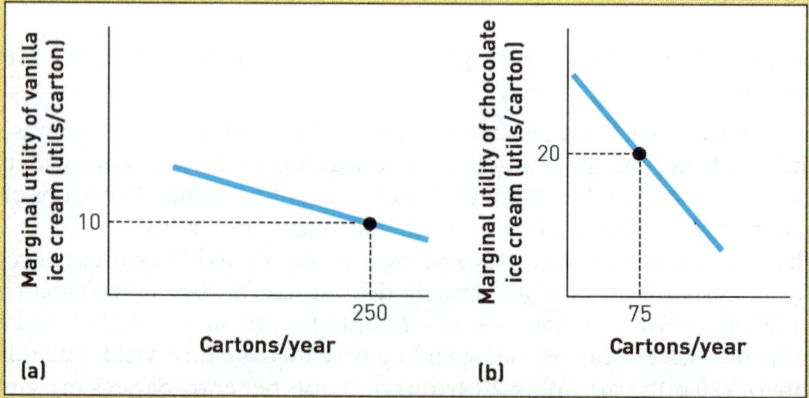

Strictly speaking, the rational spending rule applies to goods that are *perfectly divisible*, such as milk or petrol. Many other goods, such as cars and television sets, can be consumed only in whole-number amounts. In such cases, it may not be possible to satisfy the rational spending rule exactly. For example, when you buy one television set, your marginal utility per euro spent on televisions may be somewhat higher than the corresponding ratio for other goods, yet if you bought a second set the reverse might well be true. Your best alternative in such cases is to allocate each additional euro you spend to the good for which your marginal utility per euro is highest.[3]

The rational spending rule *follows directly from the Cost–Benefit Principle*. As such we don't list the rational spending rule as one of the core principles of economics, even though it is an important concept. As we noted earlier, there is considerable advantage in keeping the list of core principles as small as possible. (If we included 200 principles on this list, there's a good chance you wouldn't remember any of them a few years from now.)

Cost-Benefit Analysis

INCOME AND SUBSTITUTION EFFECTS REVISITED

In Chapter 3 we saw that the quantity of a good that consumers wish to purchase depends on its own price, the prices of substitutes and complements, and on consumer incomes. We also saw that when the price of a good changes, the quantity of it demanded changes for two reasons: the *substitution* effect and the *income* effect.

The *substitution* effect refers to the fact that when the price of a good goes up, substitutes for that good become relatively more attractive, causing some consumers to abandon the good for its substitutes. The *income* effect refers to the fact that a price change makes the consumer either poorer or richer in real terms. Consider, for instance, the effect of a change in the price of one of the ice cream flavours in Example 4.3. At the original prices (€2 per carton for chocolate, €1 per carton for vanilla), Sarah's €400 annual ice cream budget would have enabled her to buy at most 200 cartons per year of chocolate or 400 cartons per year of vanilla. If the price of vanilla rose to €2 per carton, that would reduce not only the maximum amount of vanilla she could afford (from 400 to 200 cartons per year) but also the maximum amount of chocolate she could afford in combination with any given amount of vanilla. For example, at the original price of €1 per carton for vanilla, Sarah could afford to buy 150 cartons of chocolate while buying 100 cartons of vanilla; but when the price of vanilla rises to €2, she can buy only 100 cartons of chocolate while buying 100 cartons of vanilla. As noted in Chapter 3, a reduction in real income shifts the demand curves for normal goods to the left.

The rational spending rule helps us see more clearly why a change in the price of one good affects demands for other goods. The rule requires that the *ratio of marginal utility to price* be the same for all goods. If the price of one good goes down, the ratio of its current marginal utility to its new price will be higher than for other goods. Consumers can then increase their total utility by devoting a larger proportion of their incomes to that good and smaller proportions to others.

How should Sarah respond to a reduction in the price of chocolate ice cream? **Example 4.4**

Sarah's ice cream budget is €400 per year and prices of the two flavours are €2 per carton for chocolate and €1 per carton for vanilla. Her marginal utility from consuming each type varies with the amounts consumed as shown in Fig. 4.5 above. She currently buys 250 cartons of vanilla and 75 cartons of chocolate each year, which is the optimal combination for her at these prices (see Example 4.3). How should she react if the price of chocolate ice cream falls to €1 per carton?

[3] See Problems 6 and 10 at the end of the chapter for examples.

Because the quantities shown in Fig. 4.5 constitute the optimal combination of the two flavours for Sarah at the original prices, they must exactly satisfy the rational spending rule:

$$MU_C/P_C = (20 \text{ utils/carton})/(\text{€}2/\text{carton}) = 10 \text{ utils/euro}$$
$$= MU_V/P_V = (10 \text{ utils/carton})/(\text{€}/\text{carton}) = 10 \text{ utils/euro}$$

When the price of chocolate falls to €1 per carton, the original quantities will no longer satisfy the rational spending rule. The marginal utility per euro for chocolate is now twice what it was before:

$$MU_C/P_C = (20 \text{ utils/carton})/(\text{€}1/\text{carton})$$
$$= 20 \text{ utils/euro} > MU_V/P_V = (10 \text{ utils/euro})$$

To redress this, Sarah must rearrange her spending on the two flavours in such a way as to increase the marginal utility per euro for vanilla relative to the marginal utility per euro for chocolate. And, as we see in Fig. 4.5, that will happen if she buys a larger quantity than before of chocolate and a smaller quantity than before of vanilla.

Exercise 4.2

John spends all his income on two goods: food and shelter. The price of food is €5 per kg and the price of shelter is €10 per m^2. At his current consumption levels, his marginal utilities for the two goods are 20 utils per kg and 30 utils per m^2, respectively. Is John maximising his utility? If not, how should he reallocate his spending?

In Chapter 1 we saw that people often make bad decisions because they fail to appreciate the distinction between average and marginal costs and benefits. As Example 4.5 illustrates, this pitfall also arises when people attempt to apply the economist's model of utility maximisation.

Example 4.5 Should Eric consume more apples?

Eric gets a total of 1,000 utils per week from his consumption of apples and a total of 400 utils per week from his consumption of oranges. The price of apples is €2 each, the price of oranges is €1 each, and he consumes 50 apples and 50 oranges each week. **True or false**: Eric should consume more apples and fewer oranges.

Eric spends €100 per week on apples and €50 on oranges. He thus averages (1,000 utils/week)/(€100/week) = 10 utils per euro from his consumption of apples and (400 utils/week)/(€50/week) = 8 utils per euro from his consumption of oranges. Many might be tempted to respond that because Eric's average utility per euro for apples is higher than for oranges, he should consume more apples. But knowing only his average utility per euro for each good simply does not enable us to say whether his current combination is optimal. To make that determination, we need to compare Eric's marginal utility per euro for each good. The information given simply doesn't permit us to make that comparison.

RECAP

Translating wants into demand

The Scarcity Principle (Chapter 1) challenges us to allocate our incomes among the various goods that are available so as to fulfil our desires to the greatest possible degree. The optimal combination of goods is the *affordable combination that yields the highest total utility*. For goods that are perfectly divisible, the rational spending rule tells us that the optimal combination is one for which the marginal utility per euro is the same for each good. If this condition were not satisfied, the consumer could increase utility by spending less on goods for which the marginal utility per euro was lower and more on goods for which the marginal utility per euro was higher.

APPLYING THE RATIONAL SPENDING RULE

The real payoff from learning the law of demand and the rational spending rule lies not in working through hypothetical examples, but in using these abstract concepts to make sense of the world around you. To encourage you in your efforts to become an economic naturalist, we turn now to a sequence of examples in this vein.

SUBSTITUTION AT WORK

In the first of these examples, we focus on the role of *substitution*. When the price of a good or service goes up, rational consumers generally turn to less expensive substitutes. Can't afford the monthly repayments for a new car? Then buy a used one, or rent a flat on a bus route or rail line. French cuisine restaurants are too expensive? Then go out for Chinese, or eat at home more often. Cup Final tickets cost too much? Watch the game on television, or read a book. Can't afford a book? Borrow one from your local library, or download some reading matter from the internet. Once you begin to see substitution at work, you will be amazed by the number and richness of the examples that confront you every day.

Economic Naturalist 4.2

Why do the people with the highest incomes in the wealthy countries today live in houses or apartments that are small fractions of the size of the accommodation of their equivalents before the First World War?

Most of the great country houses of England, the chateaux of the Loire and the palatial town houses of London and Paris are no longer the homes of the great families for whom they were built. Where they remain in the hands of families, they usually depend on paying visitors to keep them going. Instead they are hotels, offices or government buildings. The rich today, even the super-rich, choose to live in much more modest residences. The reason is precisely that France and Britain are much richer countries than they were a century ago, and this income is enjoyed by most people in both countries. That means that for most people incomes are multiples of what they could have earned a hundred years ago. However, higher incomes for most people mean that labour is more expensive: the relative price of labour has risen. The shift in the relative price of labour means that even the super-rich today consume less labour at home than they did then. At the same time, it is possible to live well with less labour, thanks to labour-saving technology. Great houses were large because (a) labour was cheap (average incomes were low) and (b) a high standard of living depended on using a lot of labour. Today high living standards can be maintained without direct consumption of labour, and enjoying the good life does not mean having to operate a house with grand salons and an army of retainers.

An especially vivid illustration of substitution occurred during the late 1970s, when fuel shortages brought on by interruptions in the supply of oil from the Middle East led to sharp increases in the price of petrol and other fuels. In a variety of ways – some straightforward, others remarkably ingenious – consumers changed their behaviour to economise on the use of energy. They formed car pools, switched to public transport, moved closer to work, took fewer trips, turned down their central heating thermostats, installed insulation, double glazing and solar heaters, and bought more efficient washing machines and similar appliances. In the United States, many people even moved south to the 'sunshine belt' states, especially Florida, to escape high winter heating bills.

Economic Naturalist 4.3 offers another example of how substitution changes consumption when prices change . . . and the need to treat rhetoric carefully!

Economic Naturalist 4.3
Do Irish drivers care more about stopping climate change than other Europeans?

Irish motorists, like others, were bombarded with messages about reducing fuel consumption because of climate-change issues. They would love to save the world, no doubt, and in 2010 and 2011 two-thirds of the new cars bought in Ireland were fuel-efficient, low-emission diesels, and most of the remainder had CO_2 emissions of less than 120 grams per kilometre. Up to then, a minority of cars bought in Ireland were diesels, and/or had petrol engines of less than 1.3 litre cubic capacity. Many commentators welcomed this as evidence of environmental consciousness.

Cynical economists might dismiss this preference for fuel-efficient cars as evidence of a willingness to change consumption patterns arising from a desire to save the planet, given that the Irish Government had decided to add to rising fuel prices by slapping a carbon tax on motor fuel while at the same time reducing VAT, registration tax and annual road tax on cars with low emissions and subsidising purchases of newer cars by paying people to scrap older ones. To this might be added that the fall in real incomes in Ireland between 2009 and 2011 would also have reduced demand for larger cars relative to that for smaller ones.

THE IMPORTANCE OF INCOME DIFFERENCES

The rich are different from you and me. F. Scott Fitzgerald
Yes, they have more money. Ernest Hemingway

The most obvious difference between the rich and the poor is that the rich have higher incomes. Scott Fitzgerald suggested that they have different preferences from those with lower incomes. Hemingway thought they simply could afford more and better things. To explain why the wealthy generally buy larger houses than the poor, we need not assume that the wealthy feel more strongly about housing than the poor. A much simpler explanation is that the total utility from housing, as with most other goods, increases with the amount that one consumes. As Economic Naturalist 4.4 illustrates, income influences the demand not only for housing and other goods, but also for quality of service.

Equilibrium

Economic Naturalist 4.4
Why can you get a Big Mac on demand in Paris, but usually have to book a table a week in advance at the Tour d'Argent, a restaurant said to be the *ne plus ultra* in gourmet cuisine in Paris?

You expect to have to queue longer at the checkout in discount supermarkets than in Harrods's Food hall, where prices are high and queues are unknown. Lower (higher) incomes mean lower (higher) opportunity cost of time. The rich will pay more for groceries to avoid queuing. So how do restaurants catering for the very rich get away with imposing what amounts to a form of queuing? Indeed, why do the restaurants choose to ration places by making people wait? Queuing, or waiting, is equivalent to paying a higher price to get what you want . . . but the higher willingness to pay is not captured by the vendor. So why does the restaurant not raise its prices even higher? A little excess demand can help control a restaurant's costs, but that is not a persuasive argument when price costs margins are already very high. A more plausible explanation lies in considering what such a restaurant is selling: a gourmet meal, yes, but a gourmet meal in very select company. The restaurant can always find a table at a moment's notice for a small number of diners, but what it has to preserve is exclusivity. To do this it must impose a barrier to exclude casual usage, so that it can to an extent choose its customers. Only then can it sell its joint product: a gourmet meal enjoyed among the 'right sort of people'!

RECAP

Applying the rational spending rule

Application of the rational spending rule highlights the important roles of *income* and *substitution* in explaining differences in consumption patterns – among individuals, among communities and across time. The rule also highlights the fact that *real*, as opposed to nominal, prices and income are what matter. The demand for a good falls when the real price of a substitute falls or the real price of a complement rises.

INDIFFERENCE CURVE ANALYSIS AND THE DEMAND CURVE

This section of the chapter is more technically demanding than the rest of the chapter. It can be skipped as it is not necessary to read it or master its content in order to continue the analysis of demand, but it introduces concepts that are fundamental to further study of economics. It also offers a rigorous basis for the proposition that demand curves slope downwards, and recasts rigorously the concept of consumer rationality.

So far, the analysis used to explain why demand curves slope down and the concept of consumer rationality has explicitly assumed that goods are subject to *diminishing marginal utility* (DMU) for a representative consumer. As a working hypothesis this is fine. There is plenty of evidence in the real world to support the proposition that DMU is a pervasive aspect of individual behaviour. It is also intuitively plausible.

However, as a general explanation of why demand curves slope downwards it suffers from two logical difficulties. The first is that it is easy to suggest examples of where it simply does not apply (but we still assume that demand curves for the goods or services concerned slope downwards). If they do slope downwards, then DMU is not in fact a universal aspect of consumer choice, and we can't rely on DMU as a general explanation for the slope of demand curves.

The second problem pertains to *measurement*. Earlier we made use of the assumption that we could measure satisfaction in objective units that we called 'utils'. This means that we can measure satisfaction levels 'cardinally'. This in turn permits us to add, subtract, multiply or divide people's levels of satisfaction. We did this as a pedagogic device, but in fact it is an assumption that is implicit in circumstances that are much more serious than demand theory in an introductory text. For example, we implicitly appeal to the concept when we argue that society is better off if we transfer wealth from the rich to the poor, because we reckon that the increase in the welfare of the recipients of the transfer exceeds the reduction in the welfare of those who are asked to pay. Philosophically, and empirically, it could obviously be true that the reverse was true.

Many would regard the idea that we can measure satisfaction cardinally as dubious, or even nonsensical. For example, you might be able to answer the question 'Are you happier today than yesterday?' and be quite unable to answer the question 'By how much are you happier today than yesterday?' But DMU implies being able to make that kind of evaluation.

These two considerations lead to the conclusion that a 'proof' of the downward-sloping demand curve and the rational-spending criterion that depends on DMU is at best a partial proof, and at worst may be no proof at all.

To deal with this, and also to introduce a tool of analysis that is widely used in economics, we drop any assumption of DMU, and start with a set of assumptions about rational choice.

First, we posit that an individual has a *preference ordering*. By that we mean that we have some means whereby we can in principle define an individual's preferences as to various bundles of goods or services he might consume. We make this as general and unrestrictive as possible.

- **Assumption 1:** The individual's preferences are **complete**. By this we mean that the individual can compare any two bundles of goods and services and say which is preferred or whether one is as good as the other. This is fundamental: the individual can *choose between bundles*.
- **Assumption 2:** The individual's preference ordering over bundles is **ordinal**, rather than **cardinal**. By this we mean that we only require a ranking, but don't require the individual to be able to answer the type of question given above about 'how much happier'. To do that the ranking has to be cardinal. The cardinal numbers are 1, 2, 3 . . . The ordinal numbers are 1st, 2nd, 3rd . . . A cardinal ordering enables us to say 'I am 50 per cent happier.' The ordinal ranking is a much less restrictive assumption or requirement.
- **Assumption 3:** The individual's preferences are **transitive**. By this we mean that if you say you prefer bundle *A* to bundle *B*, and bundle *B* to bundle *C*, you must prefer bundle *A* to bundle *C*.
- **Assumption 4:** The individual's satisfaction level is **monotonically increasing** with respect to any good. This is a technical way of saying that 'more of a good is better', so that, other things being equal, the individual is better off with more of any one good as long as she has the same amount as before of all other goods.
- **Assumption 5:** The individual's preferences are **continuous**. By this we mean that the individual can rank bundles that are very similar, for example containing a small amount more or less of any good or goods.
- **Assumption 6:** We then impose a further restriction on the consumer's preferences. We require them to display a **diminishing marginal rate of substitution**. This will be explained in context later on.

utility function the implication of these assumptions is that the preference ordering can be written as a utility function; this permits trade-offs

Assumptions 1–5 inclusive enable us to say that the individual's preferences over bundles of goods can be written as a **utility function**. By a utility function we mean that we can write an individual's preferences in the form

$$U_i = U_i\,(X, Y, \ldots, Z)$$

where U_i means the individual's utility, and the $X, Y, \ldots, Z$ are the bundles she is enjoying: her satisfaction is a function of the goods she consumes in the mathematical sense.

This approach to consumer choice means that the individual can trade off bundles in terms of their composition while maintaining a given level of satisfaction. While that may seem blindingly obvious, in fact it is not. Frequently, ethical or political choices are made between states of the world in a manner that does not permit trade-offs. An obvious case of this is the question of whether or not, and in what circumstances, abortion should be permitted. The same applies to capital punishment. Suppose both these are prohibited and the government proposes that they should be introduced in limited circumstances, resulting in a small number of cases of both in any year. Opponents of either are not likely to say 'We are against this being permitted, but if, say, everyone was given €1,000 a year more we would accept the proposal.' Instead, they rank states of the world on the basis that there is no compensation they would accept that would leave them as happy as before if either were allowed.

THE MODEL

The consumer has an income, Y, which is to be spent on two goods, A and B. The unit price of A is P_a and the unit price of B is P_b. Her income is exhausted on the two goods, and from this we derive her *budget constraint* (budget line):

$$Y = P_aA + P_bB$$

where A is the number of units of A consumed and B is the number of units of B consumed. She can consume Y/P_a units of A and Y/P_b units of B or any combination lying on the straight line between these points in Fig. 4.6. The line Y/P_a to Y/P_b is the budget constraint (budget line). Bundle 1 lies within the constraint: this bundle would not exhaust her income. Bundles 2 and 4 lie outside it: she hasn't enough income to buy either. Bundle 3 lies on the constraint. Only bundles on the constraint will exhaust her income. Given the assumptions above, she will never settle for a bundle lying within the constraint, because she can buy more of one or both and derive a higher level of utility.

If her income rises she can consume more, and bundle 4 becomes feasible (Fig. 4.7).

If the price of good A fell, her budget constraint would be shifted out on the A axis (Fig. 4.8).

The rational consumer will always be on her budget constraint . . . but where (Fig. 4.9)?

There is insufficient information so far to answer the question posed in Fig. 4.9. To do so, we have to go back to the *consumer's preferences*. In Fig. 4.10, for any points α, β, γ . . . the preference assumptions tell us that on a pair-wise comparison the individual

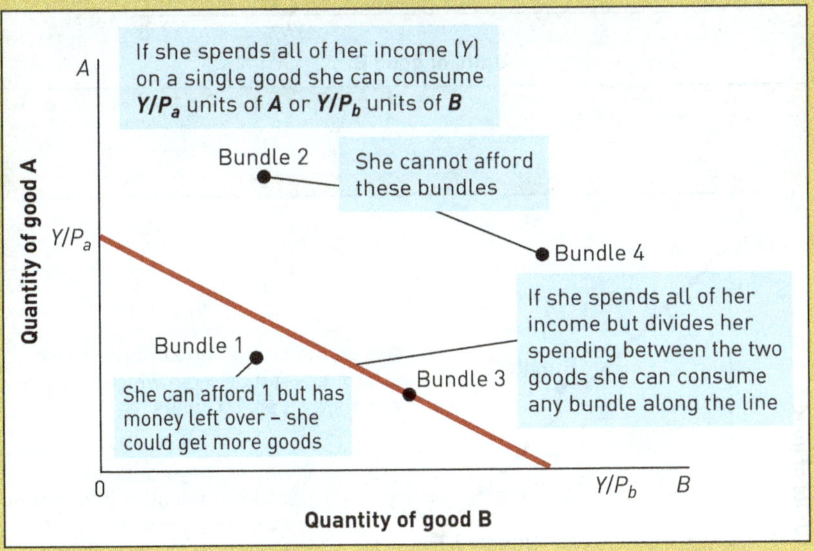

Figure 4.6 The Consumer's Budget

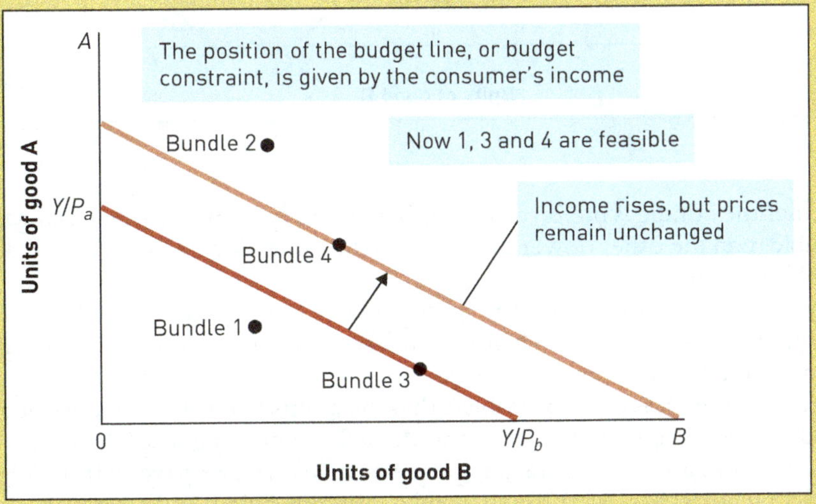

Figure 4.7 Consumer's Income Rises

Figure 4.8 Change in Price

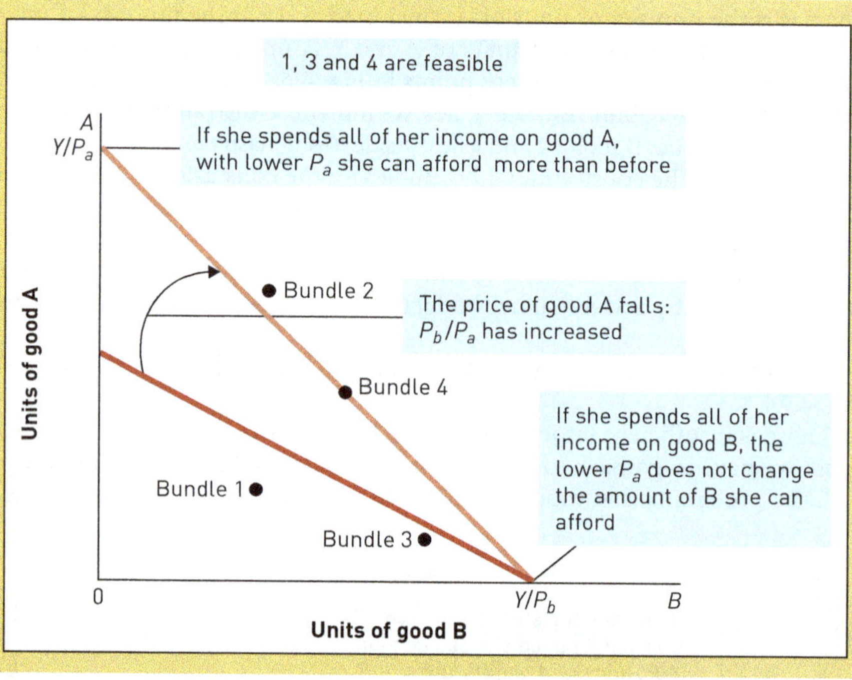

Figure 4.9 Where on the Budget Constraint?

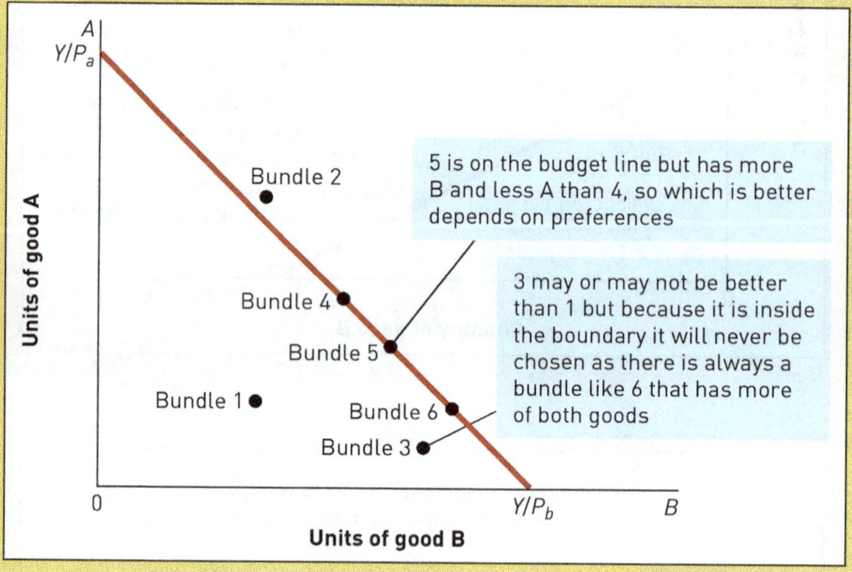

can say whether the bundle is preferred to (has higher utility than) the other, is regarded as less desirable than the other (lower utility), or is the same as the other (she is indifferent between the bundles).

Formally, for any points a and b in the space shown in Fig. 4.10a, either aPb or bPa or aIb, meaning either a is preferred to b or b is preferred to a or a and b are equally good (the individual is indifferent between them).

If we take any point, it is easy to establish that the points lying above and to the right are preferred, while those lying below and to the left are not as good. The points that are regarded as just as good as the starting point must lie on a line passing from left and above the starting point, passing through it and continuing below and right (Fig. 4.10b).

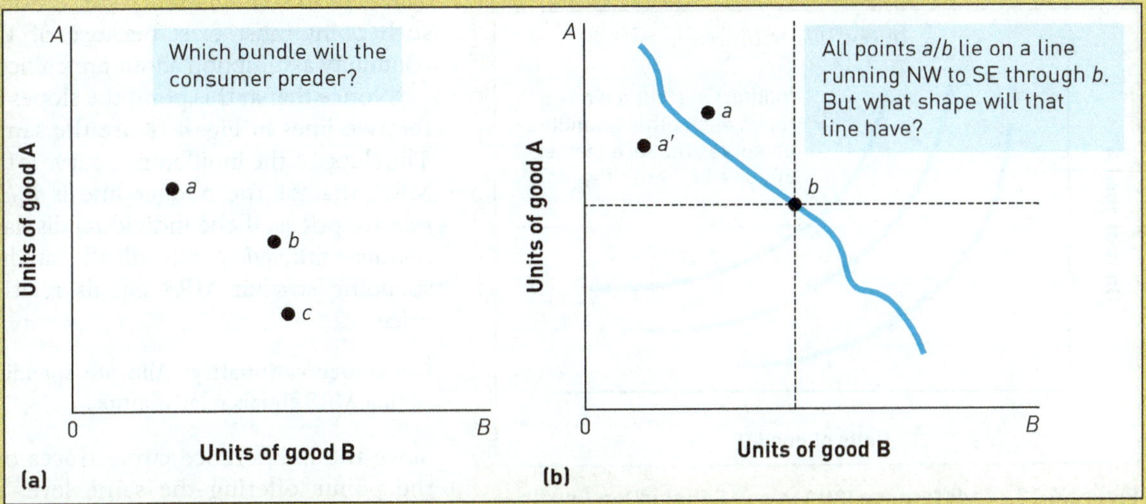

Figure 4.10 (a) Consumer's Preferences, (b) Indifference

This is where the final assumption concerning preferences comes in, that of a *diminishing marginal rate of substitution* (DMRS). It means that the less you have of good *A* the more *B* you will have to be given to make up for a further reduction in the quantity of *A*. If this holds true then the line joining points of indifference as in Fig. 4.10b will have to look as in Fig. 4.11. As you move along the indifference curve you trade units of *A* for *B* or vice versa while your utility is unchanged (hence you are indifferent). The slope of the **indifference curve** shows the marginal rate of substitution. DMRS implies that it is smoothly convex.

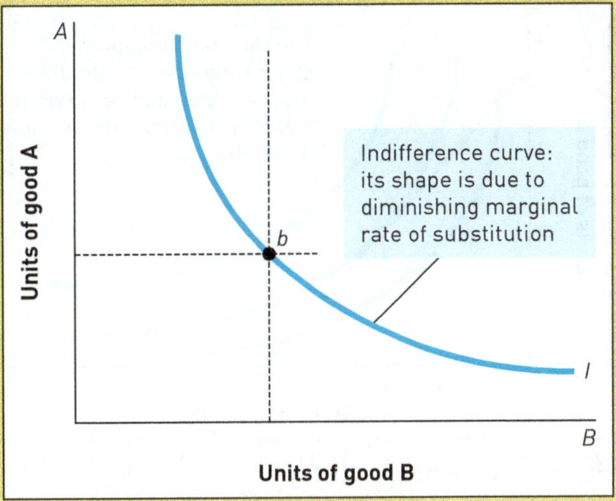

Figure 4.11 The Convex Indifference Curve

There is in principle an infinite number of indifference curves (Fig. 4.12), one for each level of satisfaction, and the further out the curve the higher the level of satisfaction to which it refers, since any point on it contains more of both goods than a point below and to the right. The more of both goods the consumer has, the higher is her satisfaction. Hence we can think of moving out from the origin on the graph as ascending a 'utility mountain', with the curves being contour lines on the map, just like contour lines on the physical map of a country. *Transitivity* implies that the curves cannot cross.

> **indifference curve** a smoothly convex curve; its slope is the consumer's marginal rate of substitution (MRS) between two goods

Exercise 4.3

To demonstrate this, draw two curves crossing and show why this is a contradiction in terms.

At this stage we bring the pieces together, the budget constraint and the indifference map. The consumer wants to maximise her utility but has to remain on her budget constraint. This happens (Fig. 4.13) when she is at a point on the constraint where it is

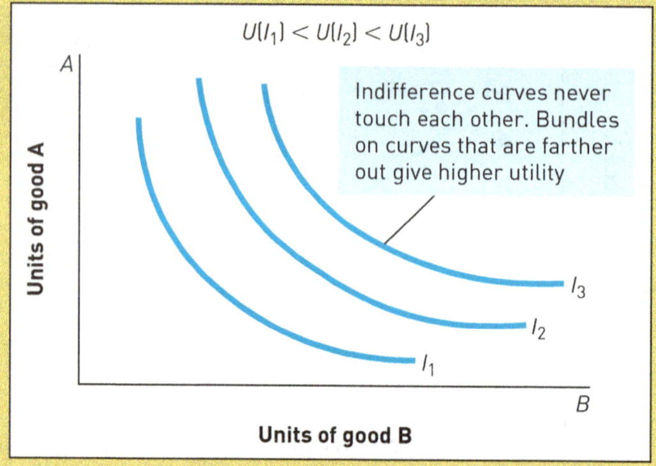

Figure 4.12 Indifference Curves and Satisfaction Levels
The further out an indifference curve is, the higher the consumer's utility from the bundles of *A* and *B* on the curve.

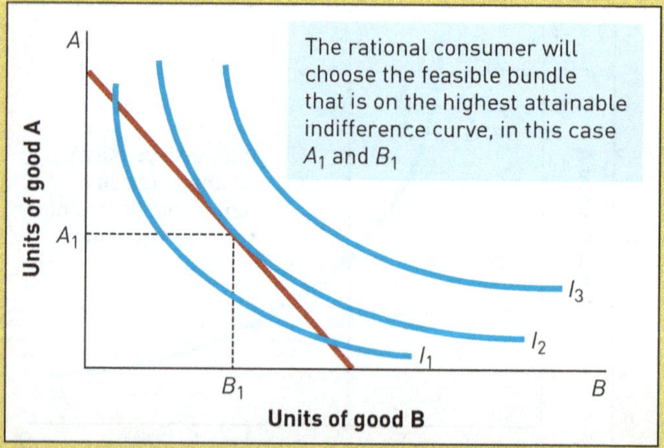

Figure 4.13 Rational Choice

a tangent to an indifference curve. Some such point must exist because of the continuity assumption about preferences.

Notice that at this point the slopes of the two lines in Fig. 4.13 are the same. The slope of the indifference curve is the MRS; that of the budget line is P_a/P_b, relative prices. If the individual displays *consumer rationality*, she will allocate her spending so that MRS equals relative price.

Consumer rationality: Allocate spending so that MRS equals relative price.

Since the indifference curve traces out the points offering the same level of utility, a move along it leaves utility unchanged. This can be written

$$\Delta U = (\mathrm{d}U/\mathrm{d}A)\,\Delta A + (\mathrm{d}U/\mathrm{d}B)\,\Delta B = 0$$

since an increase in *A* adds satisfaction that is offset by a reduction in *B*. This equation implies that

$$(\mathrm{d}U/\mathrm{d}A)\,\Delta A = -(\mathrm{d}U/\mathrm{d}B)\,\Delta B$$

If we gather terms, we get:

$$\Delta A/\Delta B = -(\mathrm{d}U/\mathrm{d}B)/(\mathrm{d}U/\mathrm{d}A)$$

The left-hand side is the slope of the indifference curve, the MRS; the right-hand side is the ratio of marginal utilities.

When the consumer is in equilibrium, maximising utility, the two curves are tangents, and the MRS equals the price ratio. That means that $P_a/P_b = (\mathrm{d}U/\mathrm{d}B)/(\mathrm{d}U/\mathrm{d}A)$ (we ignore the sign). That in turn implies that

$$(\mathrm{d}U/\mathrm{d}A)/P_a = (\mathrm{d}U/\mathrm{d}B)/P_b$$

which is the familiar *MU/P* rule we met earlier. So we get the same result without the restrictive assumptions lying behind the DMU assumption.

We can now use the indifference curve model to show that the consumption of a good will rise if its price falls and nothing else changes (i.e. that the demand curve slopes downwards). In Fig. 4.14 we allow the price of *B* to fall. The budget line swings around its anchor point on the *A* axis to let the consumer buy more *B* with the same money income.

When *B* becomes less expensive the new tangency point is at *y*, and consumption of *B* (measured on the horizontal axis) increases. A lower price results in more being demanded, or the demand curve slopes down.

Indifference curve analysis has, therefore, enabled us to conclude that if the price of a good falls, other things being equal, a rational consumer will purchase more of it.

This means that the consumer's demand curve slopes down from left to right, which was one of the things that we set out to prove without assuming either DMU or that utility could be measured cardinally.

This also demonstrates that the concept of consumer rationality that states that a consumer will allocate his or her budget between goods so that the ratio of marginal utility to price is the same across all goods is independent of any assumption that DMU applies.

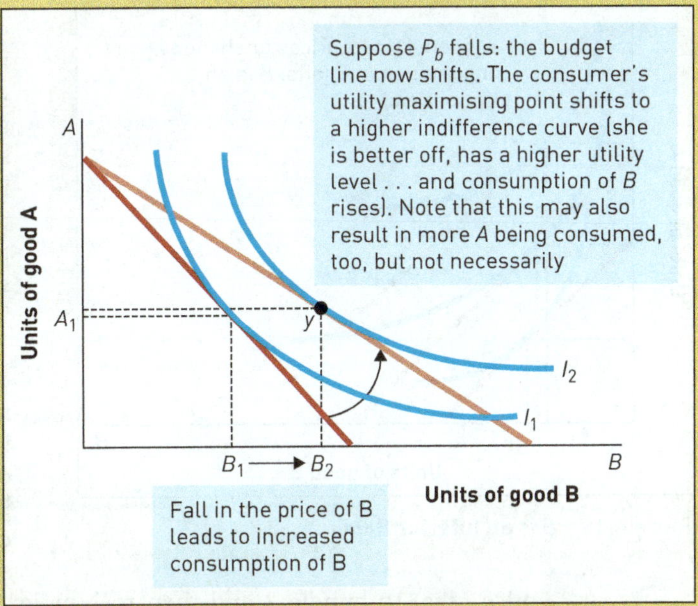

Figure 4.14 Rational Response to a Change in Price

The indifference curve approach has a further dividend. It makes clear the difference between the *income* and *substitution* effects of a price change. When the price of *B* fell the consumer's income permitted her to consume more of both goods than before. That fact alone means she is better off, and if she is, and if *B* is a normal good, she will consume more *B*. This is the *income* effect of the price change. But it also reduces the relative price of *B*, encouraging her to substitute some of the now cheaper good for some of what is now more expensive. This is the *substitution* effect of the price change.

INCOME EFFECTS

If a good is a 'normal' good, a rise in the consumer's income, prices unchanged, will result in the consumption of the good increases, and a fall in income reduces consumption. This is illustrated in Fig. 4.15. If, however, a rise in income results in a fall in consumption, the good is an inferior good, Fig. 4.16.

SUBSTITUTION EFFECTS

If the impact of a change in the price of a good is decomposed into the income effect (the consumer's real income has fallen because the quantity of goods he can buy from a given money income has fallen) and the substitution effect (the impact of relative prices on the consumer's allocation of his income over the goods bought), then we can isolate the substitution effect of a price change by subtracting the income effect. One way to do this is to perform the following thought experiment.

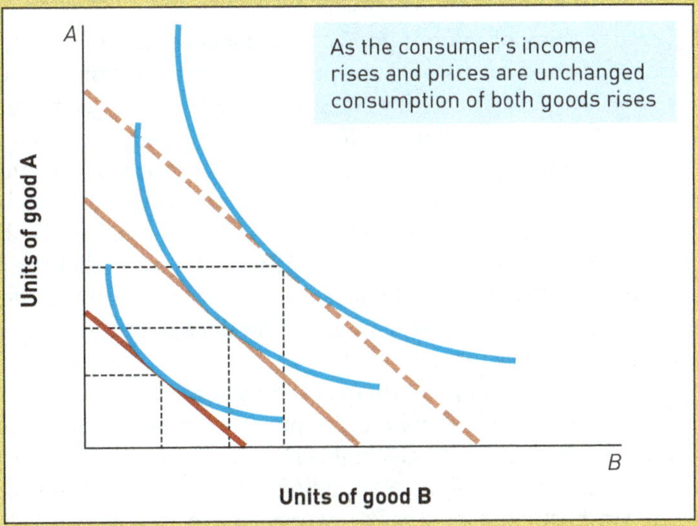

Figure 4.15 Both Goods are Normal Goods

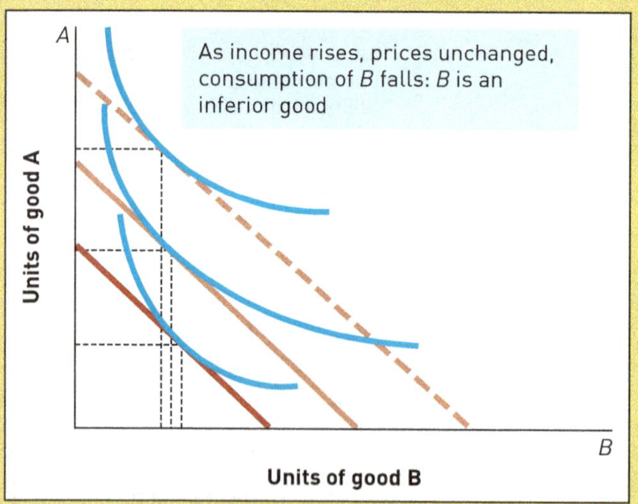

Figure 4.16 ***B* is an Inferior Good**

Suppose the consumer faces a significant price increase in an item that is an important component in his consumption basket. Suppose, further, that the government wanted to cushion the consumer's standard of living against the impact of the price change, and gave the consumer an extra weekly income that permitted him/her to achieve the same standard of living (utility level) as before. This is illustrated in Fig. 4.17.

The price of B has risen, and the consumer is less well off (is on a lower indifference curve). The government increases his money income by just enough to restore his real income (get him back on to the original indifference curve) (the red budget line). The consumer moves from bundle 1 (before the price hike) to bundle 2 and then to bundle 3 after his money income is increased. He does not move back to bundle 1. The income effect of the price change is the impact on his consumption of the fact that the price change has lowered his real income. It – the distance between the two indifference curves – has been compensated for by the government and is measured as the increase in money income necessary to compensate the consumer (the shift in the post-price-increase budget line). The substitution effect is the movement along the original indifference curve that reflects the fact that the price hike has altered the slope of the budget line. From the slope of the indifference curve it will always involve a move from the more expensive to the less expensive good(s).

Economic Naturalist 4.5
Lipstick is an inferior good?

It's easy to think of inferior goods: long-distance bus transport, generic as opposed to branded grocery goods, fast-food meals out (as opposed to serious dining) and so on. But lipstick? A colour piece in the *New York Times* of 1 May 2008 suggested that this is indeed the case. It quoted the CEO of Estée Lauder, Leonard Lauder, on lipstick sales. Against expectations he noted that in the economic downturn post-9/11 lipstick sales rose significantly. He explained buoyant lipstick sales as follows. He hypothesised that lipstick purchases are a way to gauge the economy. 'When it's shaky,' he said, 'sales increase as women boost their mood with inexpensive lipstick purchases instead of $500 sling-backs.' Before you start to consult lipstick sales to predict the behaviour of the economy, you should ask whether this story really does mean that lipstick is an inferior good. If it is, we should expect to see rich women buying less lip-gloss and lipstick (although perhaps spending more on quality) than poor women. Any takers?

It was a good story, but there could be another explanation. Suppose that lipstick sales are part of 'indulgence purchases', where the purchase may include a combination of low price (e.g. lipstick) goods and high price (e.g. slingbacks) goods purchased to make you feel good. A recession could well reduce total indulgence spending as incomes fall, but the proportion of the remaining spending going on lipstick (a relatively low-price item) could rise. This would not mean that lipstick is an inferior good in the sense that consumption falls as income rises.

GIFFEN GOODS

For normal goods income and substitution effects work in the same direction and reinforce each other. In the case of an inferior good the income effect works against the substitution effect since the change in real income from a price change pushes the consumer to purchase more (less) when the price rises (falls). In theory it is possible for the income effect of a price change in the case of an inferior good to swamp the substitution effect. This means that a rise in the price of a good will cause consumption of that good to rise. The impossible appears possible: demand curves could slope upwards.

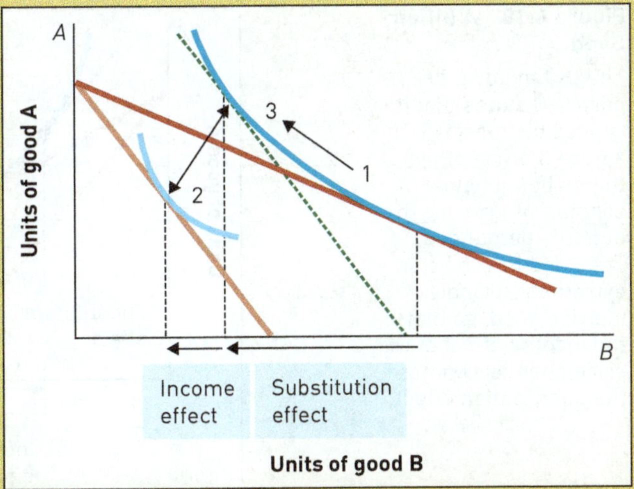

Figure 4.17 Income and Substitution Effect
Unlike the income effect of a price change, the substitution effect always pushes the consumer towards reduced purchases of the good the price of which has risen.

Fig. 4.18 shows a case of a Giffen good. The indifference curves are 'bunched' towards the *A* axis, indicating that *B* is an inferior good. This effect is so strong that it yields the result that when the price of *B* falls (rises) the consumption of *B* by a representative individual falls (rises). If this holds true for a sufficient number of consumers the implication is that, at least for a range of price changes, the observed demand curve will have a positive slope. Can this actually happen? (See Economic Naturalist 4.6.)

Economic Naturalist 4.6
Can demand curves slope upwards?

Until 2007 no convincing evidence of an example of a Giffen good had been found. It used to be said that potatoes in Ireland at the time of the Great Famine, 1845–49, were an example of a Giffen good. This was clearly not the case, since fewer, not more, potatoes were consumed by the starving peasantry, which is why a million of them died. Then, in 2007, two American economists, Robert Jensen and Nolan Miller, produced a paper* at the Harvard School of Government, based on analysis of consumption patterns among extremely poor peasants in China, especially in Hunan province. They found evidence that the peasants' dependence on noodles was such that when the price of noodles rose because demand for them in general rose, the quantity of noodles consumed by the peasants actually rose. This was because the higher price of noodles left them so little income to buy other more expensive foodstuffs that they spent the money on noodles. A rising price caused an increase in the quantity demanded among a defined population because the income effect swamped the substitution effect, and the demand curve consequently sloped upwards.

Unless this research is rebutted we must conclude that a Giffen good and an upward-sloping demand curve are both possible.

* Jensen, R. and N. Miller (2007) *Giffen Behaviour: Theory and Evidence* (Harvard School of Government, Faculty Research Working Paper RWP 03-030, December).

Exercise 4.4

Suppose good *B* is an inferior good. Draw an indifference curve diagram that has the effect that a rise in the consumer's money income leads to a fall in consumption of *B*.

Figure 4.18 A Giffen Good

The Giffen good, or paradox, states that it is possible for a fall in a good's price, other things being held constant, to reduce the quantity demanded. The good has to be an extremely strongly inferior good, so that the income effect of the price change swamps the substitution effect.

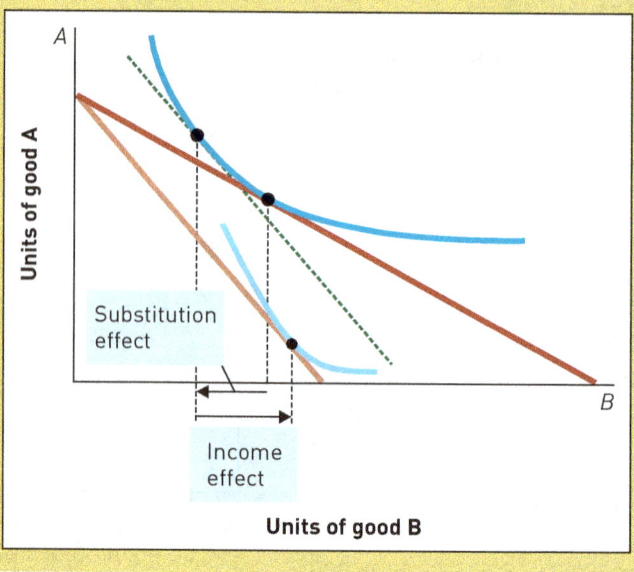

RECAP

Indifference curve analysis of rational choice

Instead of assuming DMU, we suppose that a consumer's preferences are such that we can say that she has a *utility function*. This enables us to analyse the consumer's behaviour as deriving the maximum utility from the budget at her disposal. Analytically this means choosing the 'best' point on the budget line. That happens when the budget line is tangent to an *indifference curve*, a contour of the utility function. Indifference curves are assumed to be smoothly convex. A change in the price of a good, other things remaining unchanged, means a change in the amount of that good the consumer can buy, and a corresponding change in the slope of the budget line. This gives an unambiguous prediction: a fall (rise) in the price for a good leads to an increase (reduction) in the amount the rational consumer will purchase, which gives us the individual's downward-sloping demand curve. The change in the amount bought can be decomposed into an income and a substitution effect of the price change.

INDIVIDUAL AND MARKET DEMAND CURVES

If we know what each individual's demand curve for a good looks like, how can we use that information to construct the market demand curve for the good? We must *add the individual demand curves together*, a process that is straightforward but requires care.

HORIZONTAL ADDITION

Suppose that there only two buyers – Smith and Jones – in the market for canned tuna, and that their demand curves are as shown in Fig. 4.19(a) and (b). To construct the market demand curve for canned tuna, we simply announce a sequence of prices and then add the quantity demanded by each buyer at each price. For example, at a price of €4 per can, Smith demands six cans per week (Fig. 4.19(a)) and Jones demands two cans per week (Fig. 4.19(b)), for a market demand of eight cans per week (Fig. 4.19(c)).

The process of adding individual demand curves in this way to get the market demand curve is known as *horizontal addition*, a term used to emphasise that we are adding *quantities*, which are measured on the horizontal axes of individual demand curves.[4]

[4] Strictly speaking, deriving market demand curves by this method requires that we assume that one individual's consumption of a good at a price is independent of other consumers' consumption of goods at that price.

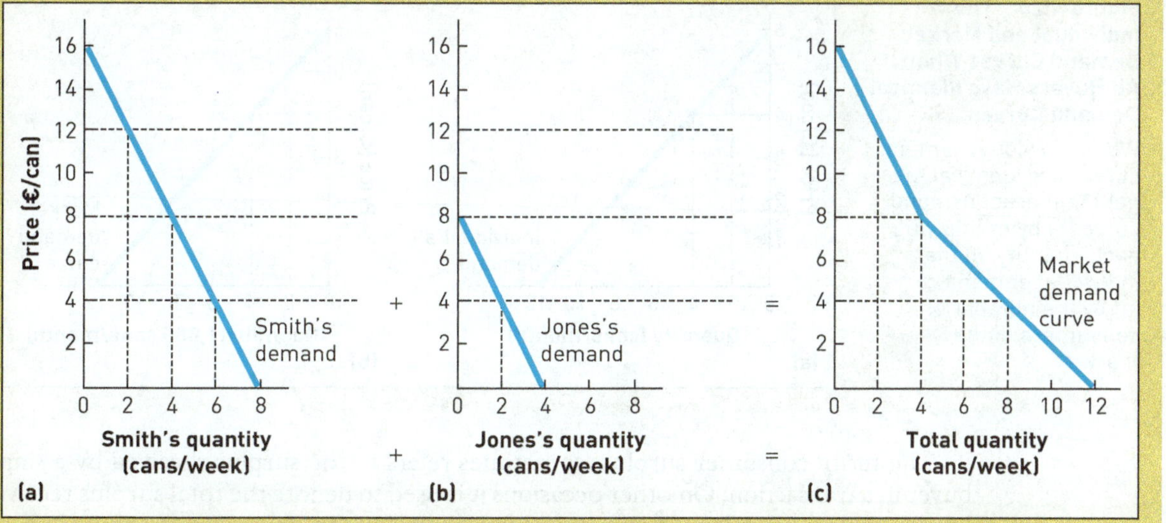

Figure 4.19 Individual and Market Demand Curves for Canned Tuna
The quantity demanded at any price on the market demand curve (c) is the sum of the individual quantities demanded at that price, (a) and (b).

Exercise 4.5

The buyers' side of the market for cinema tickets consists of two consumers whose demands are as shown in the diagram below. Graph the market demand curve for this market.

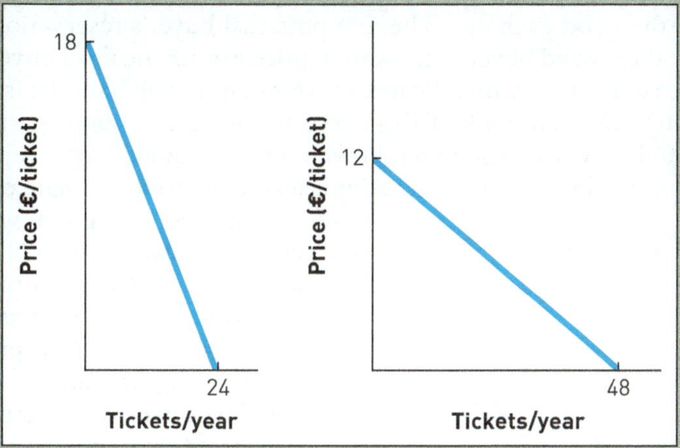

Figure 4.20 illustrates the special case in which each of 1,000 consumers in the market has the same demand curve (Fig. 4.20(a)). To get the market demand curve (Fig. 4.20(b)) in this case, we simply multiply each quantity on the representative individual demand curve by 1,000.

DEMAND AND CONSUMER SURPLUS

In Chapter 1 we first encountered the concept of economic surplus, which in a buyer's case is the difference between the most she would have been willing to pay for a product and the amount she actually pays for it. The economic surplus received by buyers is often referred to as **consumer surplus**.

consumer surplus the difference between a buyer's reservation price for a product and the price actually paid

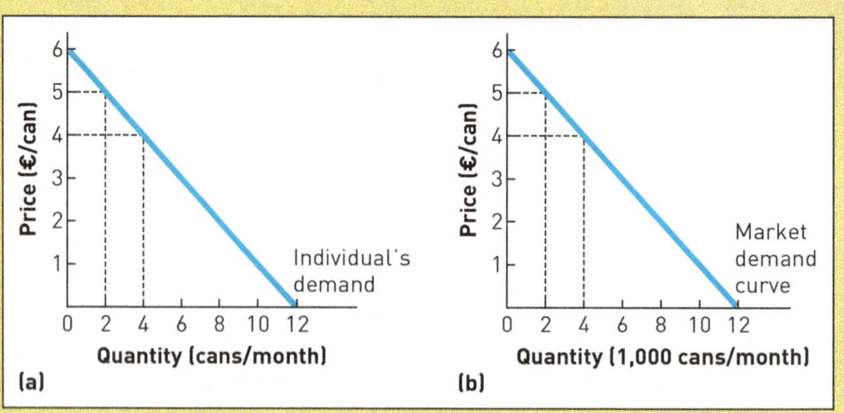

Figure 4.20 The Individual and Market Demand Curves When All Buyers Have Identical Demand Curves

When individual demand curves are identical, we get the market demand curve (b) by multiplying each quantity on the individual demand curve (a) by the number of consumers in the market.

The term 'consumer surplus' sometimes refers to the surplus received by a single buyer in a transaction. On other occasions it is used to denote the total surplus received by all buyers in a market or collection of markets.

CALCULATING ECONOMIC SURPLUS

For performing cost–benefit analysis it is often important to be able to measure the *total consumer surplus* received by all the buyers who participate in a given market. For example, a road linking a mountain village and a port city would create a new market for fresh fish in the mountain village; in deciding whether the road should be built, analysts would want to count as one of its benefits the gains that would be reaped by buyers in this new market.

To illustrate how economists actually measure consumer surplus, we shall consider a hypothetical market for a good with 11 potential buyers, each of whom can buy a maximum of one unit of the good each day. The first potential buyer's reservation price for the product is €11; the second buyer's reservation price is €10; the third buyer's reservation price is €9; and so on. The demand curve for this market will have the 'staircase' shape shown in Fig. 4.21. We can think of this curve as the digital counterpart of traditional analogue demand curves. (If the units shown on the horizontal axis were fine enough, this digital curve would be visually indistinguishable from its analogue counterparts.)

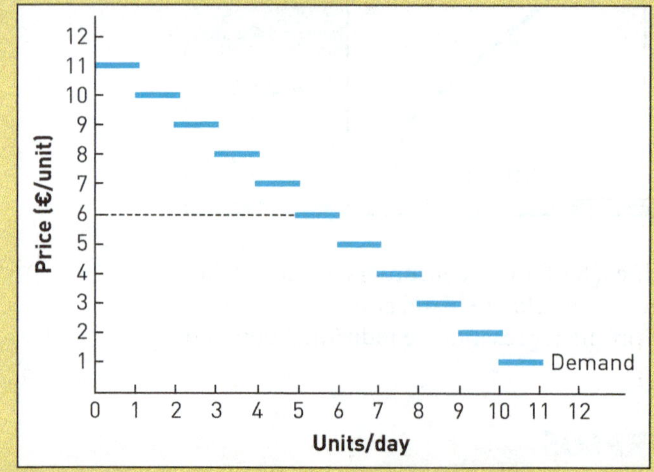

Figure 4.21 A Market with a 'Digital' Demand Curve

When a product can be sold only in whole-number amounts, its demand curve has the 'staircase' shape shown.

Suppose the good whose demand curve is shown in Fig. 4.21 were available at a price of €6 per unit. How much total consumer surplus would buyers in this market reap? At a price of €6, six units per day would be sold in this market. The buyer of the sixth unit would receive no economic surplus, since her reservation price for that unit was exactly €6, the same as its selling price. But the first five buyers would reap a surplus for their purchases. The buyer of the first unit, for example, would have been willing to pay as much as €11 for it, but since she would pay only €6, she would receive a surplus of exactly €5. The buyer of the second unit, who would have been willing to pay as much as €10, would receive a surplus of €4. The surplus would be €3 for the buyer of the third unit, €2 for the buyer of the fourth unit, and €1 for the buyer of the fifth unit.

If we add all the buyers' surpluses together, we get a total of €15 of consumer surplus each day. That surplus corresponds to the shaded area shown in Fig. 4.22.

Exercise 4.6

Calculate consumer surplus for a demand curve like the one just described except that the buyers' reservation prices for each unit are €2 higher than before.

Now, suppose we want to calculate consumer surplus in a market with a conventional straight-line demand curve. As Example 4.6 illustrates, this task is a simple extension of the method used for digital demand curves.

How much do buyers benefit from their participation in the market for milk? Example 4.6

Consider the market for milk whose demand and supply curves are shown in Fig. 4.23, which has an equilibrium price of €2 per litre and an equilibrium quantity of 4,000 litres per day. How much consumer surplus do the buyers in this market reap?

In Fig. 4.23, note first that, as in Fig. 4.20, the last unit exchanged each day generates no consumer surplus at all. Note also that for all milk sold up to 4,000 litres per day, buyers receive consumer surplus, just as in Fig. 4.23. For these buyers, consumer surplus is the cumulative difference between the most they would be willing to pay for milk (as measured on the demand curve) and the price they actually pay.

Total consumer surplus received by buyers in the milk market is thus the shaded triangle between the demand curve and the market price in Fig. 4.24. Note that this area is a right-angled triangle whose vertical arm is $h =$ €1/litre and whose horizontal arm is $b =$ 4,000 litres/day. And since the area of any triangle is equal to (1/2)(base × height), consumer surplus in this market is equal to

$$(1/2)(4{,}000 \text{ litres/day})(€1/\text{litre}) = €2{,}000/\text{day}$$

A useful way of thinking about consumer surplus is to ask what is the highest price consumers would pay, in the aggregate, for the right to continue participating in this milk market. The answer is €2,000 per day, since that is

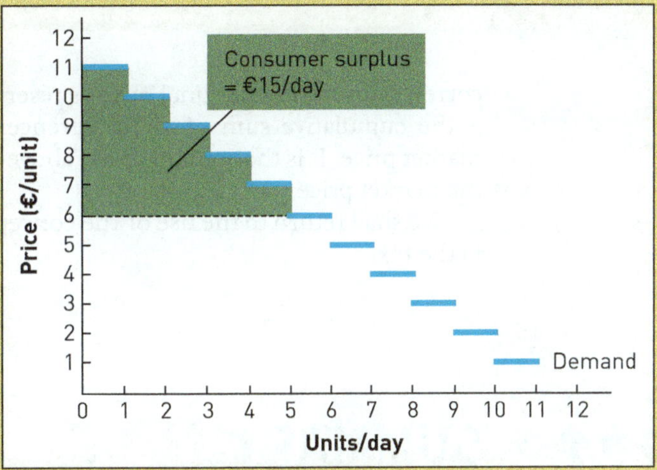

Figure 4.22 Consumer Surplus

Consumer surplus (shaded region) is the cumulative difference between the most that buyers are willing to pay for each unit and the price they actually pay.

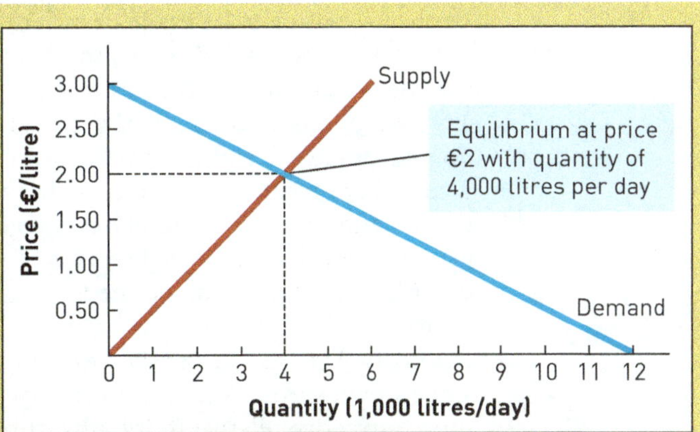

Figure 4.23 Supply and Demand in the Market for Milk

For the supply and demand curves shown, the equilibrium price of milk is €2 per litre and the equilibrium quantity is 4,000 litres per day.

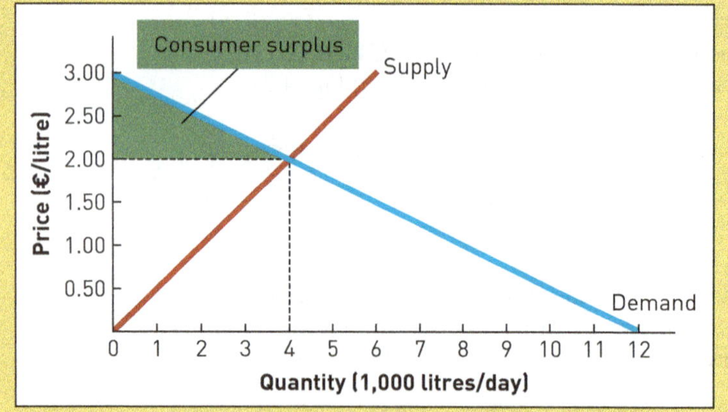

Figure 4.24 Consumer Surplus in the Market for Milk
Consumer surplus is the area of the shaded triangle (€2,000/day).

the amount by which their *combined benefits exceed their combined costs*.

As discussed in Chapter 3, the demand curve for a good can be interpreted either horizontally or vertically. The horizontal interpretation tells us, for each price, the total quantity that consumers wish to buy at that price. The vertical interpretation tells us, for each quantity, the most a buyer would be willing to pay for the good at that quantity. For the purpose of computing consumer surplus, we rely on the vertical interpretation of the demand curve. The value on the vertical axis that corresponds to each point along the demand curve corresponds to the marginal buyer's reservation price for the good. Consumer surplus is the cumulative sum of the differences between these reservation prices and the market price. It is the area bounded above by the demand curve and bounded below by the market price.

We shall return to the use of the concept of consumer surplus in Chapter 6 and later in the text.

◆◆◆◆ SUMMARY

- If diminishing marginal utility is assumed, the rational consumer allocates income among different goods so that the marginal utility gained from the last euro spent on each good is the same. This rational spending rule gives rise to the law of demand, which states that people do less of what they want to do as the cost of doing it rises. Here, 'cost' refers to the *sum of all monetary and non-monetary sacrifices* – explicit and implicit – that must be made in order to engage in the activity.
- *Indifference curve analysis* states that consumer rationality implies allocating expenditure between two goods so as to equate the marginal rate of substitution between any two goods to their relative price. This implies that demand curves will slope down from left to right, the basic law of demand.
- The ability to substitute one good for another is an important factor behind the law of demand. Because virtually every good or service has at least some substitutes, economists prefer to speak in terms of *wants* rather than needs. We face choices, and describing our demands as 'needs' is misleading because it suggests that we have no options.
- For normal goods, the *income effect* is a second important reason that demand curves slope downwards. When the price of such a good falls, not only does it become more attractive relative to its substitutes, but the consumer also acquires more real purchasing power, and this, too, augments the quantity demanded.
- The demand curve is a schedule that shows the amounts of a good *people want to buy at various prices*. Demand curves can be used to summarise the price–quantity relationship for a single individual, but more commonly we employ them to summarise that relationship for an entire market. At any quantity along a demand curve, the

corresponding price represents the amount by which the consumer (or consumers) would benefit from having an additional unit of the product. For this reason, the demand curve is sometimes described as a summary of the benefit side of the market.

- *Consumer surplus* is a quantitative measure of the amount by which buyers benefit as a result of their ability to purchase goods at the market price. It is the area between the demand curve and the market price.

REVIEW QUESTIONS

1. Why do economists prefer to speak of demands arising out of 'wants' rather than 'needs'?
2. Explain why economists consider the concept of utility useful, even if psychologists cannot measure it precisely.
3. Why does the law of diminishing marginal utility encourage people to spread their spending across many different types of goods?
4. Explain why a good or service that is offered at a monetary price of zero is unlikely to be a truly 'free' good from an economic perspective.
5. Give an example of a good that you have consumed for which your marginal utility increased with the amount of it you consumed.
6. Give examples of cardinal and ordinal measurements.
7. Show how the concept of consumer rationality is the same whether you use DMU or indifference curves to explain demand curves.
8. Show, using indifference curves, how a price rise for one good affects consumption of that good (a) by lowering the consumer's real income, and (b) by altering relative prices of the two goods.

PROBLEMS

connect

Problems marked with an asterisk (*) are more difficult.

1. In which type of restaurant do you expect the service to be more prompt and courteous: an expensive gourmet restaurant or an inexpensive diner? Explain.

2. You are having lunch at an all-you-can-eat buffet. If you are rational, what should be your marginal utility from the last morsel of food you swallow?

3. Martha's current marginal utility from consuming orange juice is 75 utils per centilitre and her marginal utility from consuming coffee is 50 utils per centilitre. If orange juice costs 25 cents per centilitre and coffee costs 20 cents per centilitre, is Martha maximising her total utility from the two beverages? If so, explain how you know. If not, how should she rearrange her spending?

4. Toby's current marginal utility from consuming peanuts is 100 utils per gram and his marginal utility from consuming cashews is 200 utils per gram. If peanuts cost 10 cents per gram and cashews cost 25 cents per gram, is Toby maximising his total utility from the two kinds of nuts? If so, explain how you know. If not, how should he rearrange his spending?

5. Sue gets a total of 20 utils per week from her consumption of pizza and a total of 40 utils per week from her consumption of yoghurt. The price of pizza is €1 per slice, the price of yoghurt is €1 per carton, and she consumes 10 slices of pizza and 20 cartons of yoghurt each week. **True or false:** Sue is consuming the optimal combination of pizza and yoghurt.

6. Anna Lucia lives in Cremona and commutes by train each day to her job in Milan (20 round trips per month). When the price of a round trip goes up from €10 to €20, she responds by consuming exactly the same number of trips as before, while spending €200 per month less on restaurant meals.
   a. Does the fact that her quantity of train travel is completely unresponsive to the price increase imply that Anna Lucia is not a rational consumer?
   b. Explain why an increase in train travel might affect the amount she spends on restaurant meals.

7. For the demand curve shown in the graph, find the total amount of consumer surplus that results in the petrol market if petrol sells for €2 per litre.

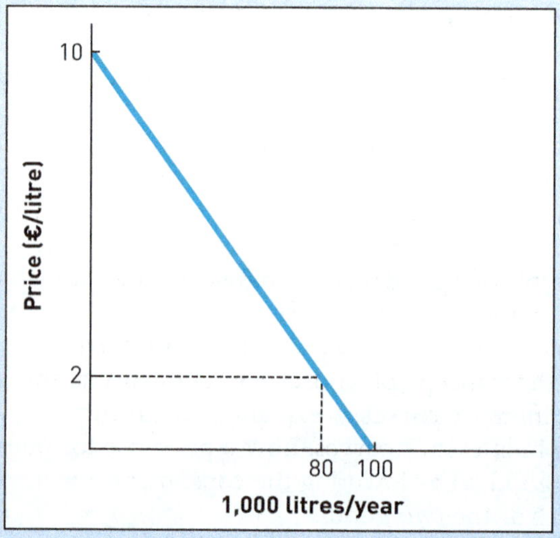

8. Tom has a weekly allowance of €24, all of which he spends on pizza and movie rentals, whose prices are €6 per slice and €3 per rental, respectively. If slices of pizza and movie rentals are available only in whole-number amounts, list all the possible combinations of the two goods that Tom can purchase each week with his allowance.

9.* Refer to Problem 8. Tom's total utility is the sum of the utility he derives from pizza and movie rentals. If these utilities vary with the amounts consumed as shown in the table below, and pizzas and movie rentals are again consumable only in whole number amounts, how many pizzas and how many movie rentals should Tom consume each week?

Pizzas/week	Utils/week from pizza	Movie rentals/week	Utils/week from rentals
0	0	0	0
1	20	1	40
2	38	2	46
3	54	3	50
4	68	4	54
5	80	5	56
6	90	6	57
7	98	7	57
8	104	8	57

10.* The buyers' side of the market for amusement park tickets consists of two consumers whose demands are as shown in the diagram below.
   a. Graph the market demand curve for this market.
   b. Calculate the total consumer surplus in the amusement park market if tickets sell for €12 each.

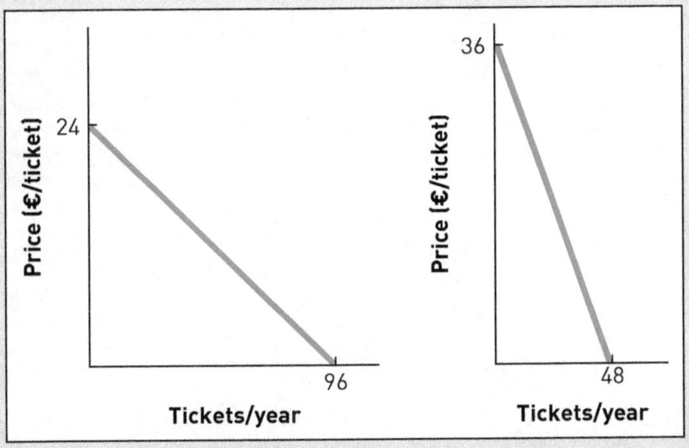

Chapter 5

Perfectly Competitive Supply: the Cost Side of the Market

It is not that pearls fetch a high price because men dived for them; but on the contrary, men dive for them because they fetch a high price.
Richard Whately

Learning Objectives

After studying this chapter you should be able to:

1. Understand why firms' short-run supply curves, based on marginal cost, can be modelled as upwards sloping;
2. Predict how changes in the prices of factors of production affect the technology firms use to produce goods;
3. Use and measure elasticity of supply;
4. Understand and explain how profit-seeking firms decide how much to produce;
5. Measure producer surplus.

Over the past 70 years output per man-hour in manufacturing has increased in the Western world at a rate unprecedented by historical standards. This is measured as the growth in labour productivity. In the past couple of decades a similar transformation (the IT revolution) has affected many marketed services (e.g., communications, banking, media) However, there are parts of the economies of all these countries where this change has been much less evident, if it happened at all. Haircuts take more or less the same amount of time and labour in 2010 that they took in 1930. You need the same number of musicians today as 75 or 100 years ago to perform a symphony by Brahms.

Given the spectacular growth in manufacturing workers' productivity, it is no surprise that their real wages rose more than fivefold during the twentieth century. But why have real wages for service workers risen by more or less the same increase as with manufacturing wages when productivity has changed little if at all?

Opportunity cost is part of the answer. If workers in service industries were not paid roughly as much as they could have earned in other occupations, many of them would not have been willing to work in service industries in the first place. So, the relative prices of haircuts or concert tickets have risen sharply over the last century.

There is an intimate link between the prices at which goods and services are offered for sale in the market and the opportunity cost of the resources required to produce them. In Chapter 4 we focused on the buyers' side of the market. Now our task is to gain insight into the factors that shape the supply curve, the schedule that tells how many units suppliers wish to sell at different prices.

Although the demand side and the supply side of the market are different in several ways, many of these differences are superficial. Indeed, the behaviour of both buyers and sellers is in an important sense fundamentally the same. After all, the two groups confront essentially similar questions: in the buyer's case, 'Should I buy another unit?' and, in the seller's, 'Should I sell another unit?' Each side of the market has the same basic motivation. A rational consumer will buy another unit if its benefit exceeds its cost; and a rational seller will sell another unit if the cost of making it is less than the extra revenue he can get from selling it (the familiar Cost–Benefit Principle again).

THINKING ABOUT SUPPLY: THE IMPORTANCE OF OPPORTUNITY COST

Many jurisdictions require bottles and drink cans to carry a deposit repayable when returned for recycling, directly or indirectly. Some people return their own containers to receive the deposit; others leave their used containers to be recycled by others, or simply get rid of them with other garbage. Returning containers is *supplying a service*, and obeys the same logic as the production of other goods and services. As with these, the supply curve for recycling is rooted in the individual's choice of whether to produce it.

Example 5.1 How much time should Harry spend recycling soft drink containers?

Harry has to divide his spare time between a job as a dishwasher in the student cafeteria at his university, which pays €6 an hour for as many hours as he chooses to work, and gathering soft drink containers around the college to redeem for the deposits, in which case his pay depends on both the deposit per container and the number of containers he finds. Earnings aside, Harry is indifferent between the two tasks, and the number of containers he will find depends, as shown in the table below, on the number of hours per day he searches.

Search time (hours/day) (1)	Total number of containers found (2)	Additional number of containers found (3)
0	0	
1	600	600
2	1,000	400
3	1,300	300
4	1,500	200
5	1,600	100

If the containers may be redeemed for 2 cents each, how many hours should Harry spend searching for containers?

An hour spent by Harry searching for containers costs him the €6 he could have earned as a dishwasher. This is his *hourly opportunity cost* of searching for soft drink containers. His benefit from each hour spent searching for containers is the number of additional containers he finds (shown in column (3) of the table) times the deposit he collects per container. Since he can redeem each container for 2 cents, his first hour spent collecting containers will yield earnings of 600(€0.02) = €12, or €6 more than he could have earned as a dishwasher.

By the Cost–Benefit Principle, then, Harry should spend his first spare-time each day searching for soft drink containers rather than washing dishes. A second hour searching for containers will yield 400 additional containers, for additional earnings of

€8, so it, too, satisfies the cost–benefit test. A third hour spent searching yields 300 additional containers, for 300(€0.02) = €6 of additional earnings, just what he would have earned as a dishwasher. He is indifferent between spending his third hour of work each day on one task or the other. For the sake of discussion, however, we shall assume that, when indifferent, he opts to search for containers, in which case he will spend three hours each day searching for containers.

Incentives Matter

What is the lowest deposit that would induce Harry to spend at least one hour per day recycling? Since he will find 600 containers in his first hour of search, a 1-cent deposit on each container would enable him to match his €6 per hour opportunity cost. Formally, if the redemption price is p, and another hour spent searching yields ΔQ additional containers, Harry's additional earnings from searching the additional hour will be $p(\Delta Q)$. This means that the smallest redemption price that will lead Harry to search another hour must satisfy the equation

$$p(\Delta Q) = €6 \tag{5.1}$$

How high would the deposit on containers have to be for Harry to search for a second hour? Since he can find $\Delta Q = 400$ additional containers if he searches for a second hour, the smallest redemption price that will lead him to do so must satisfy $p(400) = €6$, which solves for $p = 1.5$ cents.

Exercise 5.1

Referring to Example 5.1, calculate the smallest container deposit rate that will lead Harry to search for a third, fourth and fifth hour.

In Example 5.1, we saw that Harry's reservation prices for his third, fourth and fifth hours of container search are 2, 3 and 6 cents, respectively. Having calculated these reservation prices, we can now plot his supply curve of container-recycling services. This curve, which plots the redemption price per container on the vertical axis and the number of containers recycled each day on the horizontal axis, is shown in Fig. 5.1. It tells us the number of containers he is willing to recycle at various redemption prices.

Increasing Opportunity Cost

As in Chapter 3, the supply curve shown in Fig. 5.1 is upward-sloping. There are exceptions to this general rule, but sellers of most goods will offer higher quantities at higher prices than at lower prices.

The relationship between the individual and market supply curves for a product is analogous to the relationship between the individual and market demand curves. The market demand curve shows the sum of the quantities demanded at a given price by all individual buyers in the market. Likewise, the market supply curve tells us the sum of the quantities supplied at a given price by all individual sellers in the market.

Suppose, for example, that the supply side of the recycling services market

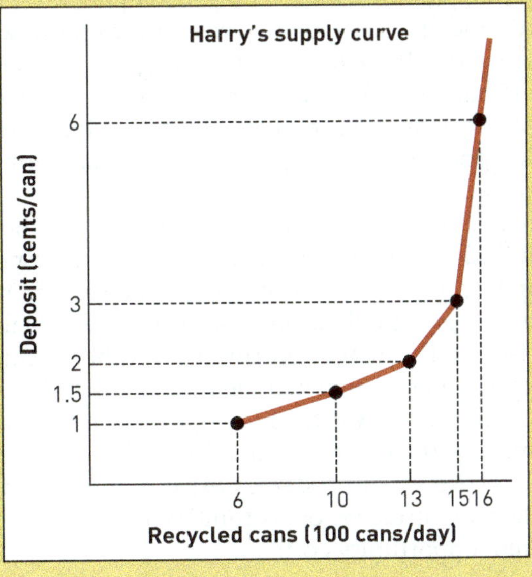

Figure 5.1 An Individual Supply Curve for Recycling Services

When the deposit price increases, it becomes attractive to abandon alternative pursuits to spend more time searching for soft drink containers.

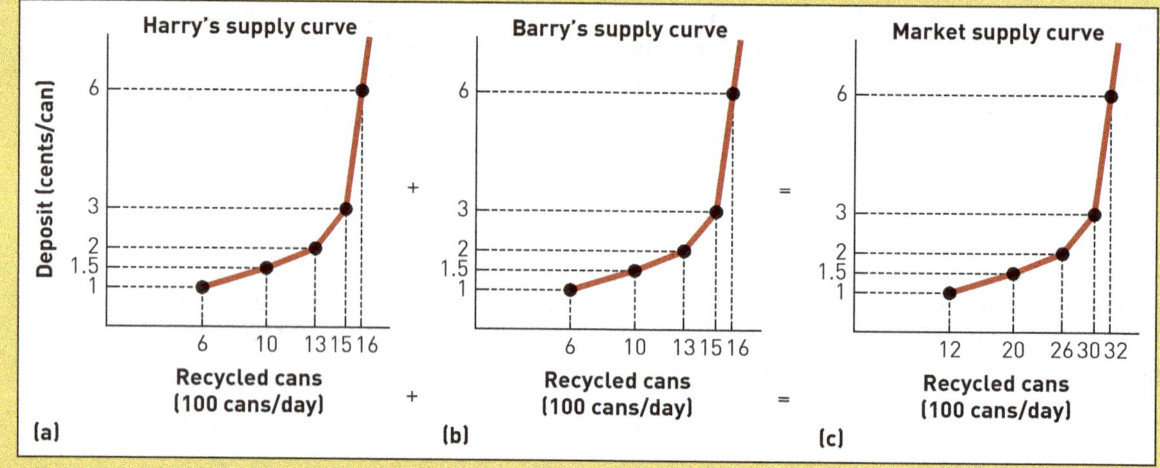

Figure 5.2 The Market Supply Curve for Recycling Services
To generate the market supply curve (c) from the individual supply curves (a) and (b), we add the individual supply curves horizontally.

consists only of Harry and his identical twin, Barry, whose individual supply curve is the same as Harry's. To generate the market supply curve, we first put the individual supply curves side by side, as shown in Fig. 5.2(a) and (b). We then announce a price, and for that price add the individual quantities supplied to obtain the total quantity supplied in the market. At a price of 3 cents per container, both Harry and Barry wish to recycle 1,500 cans per day, so the total market supply at that price is 3,000 cans per day. On this basis we generate the market supply curve for recycling services shown in Fig. 5.2(c). This is the same process of horizontal summation by which we generated market demand curves from individual demand curves in Chapter 4.

Alternatively, if there were n suppliers with individual supply curves identical to Harry's, we could generate the market supply curve by simply multiplying each quantity value on the individual supply curve by the number of suppliers, n. Figure 5.3 shows the supply curve for a market in which there are 1,000 suppliers with individual supply curves like Harry's. If all individuals have identical upward-sloping supply curves, the market supply curve will be upward-sloping as well.

Why do individual supply curves tend to be upward-sloping? One explanation is suggested by the Principle of Increasing Opportunity Cost, or Low-Hanging-Fruit Principle (Chapter 2). Container recyclers should always look first for the containers that are easiest to find – such as those in plain view in readily accessible locations. As the redemption price rises, it will pay to incur the additional cost of searching further from the beaten path.

But there is an important additional reason for the positive slope of market supply curves: individual suppliers generally differ with respect to their opportunity costs of supplying the product. (The Principle of Increasing Opportunity Cost applies not only to each individual searcher, but also *across* individuals.) Thus, whereas people facing unattractive employment opportunities in other occupations may be willing to recycle soft drink containers even when the redemption price is low, those with more attractive options will recycle only if the redemption price is relatively high.

In summary, then, the upward slope of the supply schedule reflects the fact that costs tend to rise when producers expand production, partly because each individual exploits the most attractive opportunities first, but also because different potential sellers face different opportunity costs.

PRODUCTION IN THE SHORT RUN

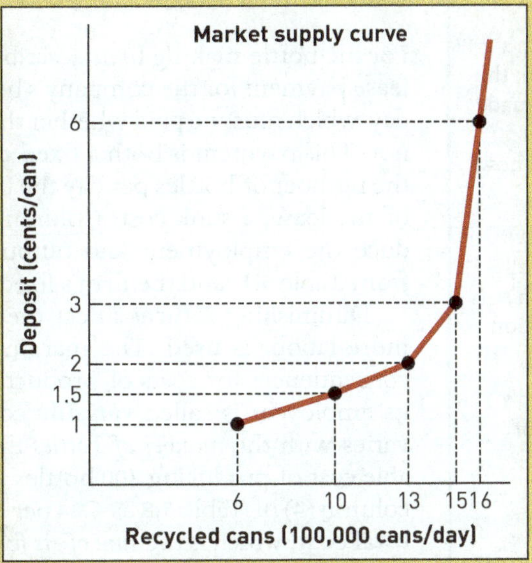

Figure 5.3 The Market Supply Curve with 1,000 Identical Sellers

To generate the market supply curve for a market with 1,000 identical sellers, we simply multiply each quantity value on the individual supply curve by 1,000.

To understand more fully the origins of the supply curve, consider a small firm confronting the decision of how much to produce. The firm in question is a company that makes glass bottles from silica, which for simplicity we will assume is available free of charge from a nearby desert deposit. Its electricity comes from solar panels. The only costs incurred by the firm are the wages of its employees and the lease payment on its bottle-making machine. The employees and the machine are the firm's only two **factors of production** – inputs used to produce goods and services. In more complex examples, factors of production might also include land, structures, entrepreneurship and possibly others, but for the moment we consider only labour and capital.

factor of production an input used in the production of a good or service

short run a period of time sufficiently short that at least some of the firm's factors of production are fixed

long run a period of time of sufficient length that all the firm's factors of production are variable

law of diminishing returns a property of the relationship between the amount of a good or service produced and the amount of a variable factor required to produce it; it says that when some factors of production are fixed, each extra unit of the good produced eventually requires ever larger increases in the variable factor

For our bottle maker, we will assume that the number of employees can be varied at short notice but that the capacity of its bottle-making machinery can be altered only with significant delay. The period of time for which in this example its machinery capacity is fixed is called the **short run**. By contrast, when we speak of the **long run**, we refer to a time period of sufficient length that all a firm's factors of production (in this case bottling machinery and labour) are variable.

Table 5.1 shows how the company's bottle production depends on the number of hours its employees work each day. It exhibits a pattern that is common to many such relationships. For every extra worker the firm employs, output grows; but beyond some point the additional output that results from each additional worker (more generally, unit of labour or man-hour) begins to diminish. Note in column (2), for example, that output gains begin to diminish with the third employee. Economists refer to this pattern as the **law of diminishing returns**, and it always refers to situations in which at least some factors of production are fixed, the short run. The law of diminishing returns says simply that successive increases in the labour input eventually yield smaller and smaller increments in bottle output. (Strictly speaking, the law ought to be called the law of *eventually* diminishing returns, because output may initially grow at an increasing rate with additional units of the variable factor.)

Typically, returns from additional units of the variable input eventually diminish because of some form of *congestion*. For instance, in an office with three secretaries and only a single desktop computer, we would not expect to get three times as many letters typed per hour as in an office with only one secretary, because only one person at a time can use the computer.

fixed cost the sum of all payments made to the firm's fixed factors of production; the payments that have to be made for the services of an input regardless of whether and how much production actually takes place

variable cost the sum of all payments made to the firm's variable factors of production

total cost the sum of all payments made to the firm's fixed and variable factors of production

marginal cost as output changes from one level to another, the change in total cost divided by the corresponding change in output; by definition it consists of variable costs

SOME IMPORTANT COST CONCEPTS

For the bottle-making firm described in Table 5.1, suppose that the lease payment for the company's bottle-making machine is €40 per day, which must be paid whether the company makes any bottles or not. This payment is both a **fixed cost** (since it does not depend on the number of bottles per day the firm makes) and, for the duration of the lease, a sunk cost. Columns (1) and (2) of Table 5.2 reproduce the employment and output entries (columns (1) and (2)) from Table 5.1, and the firm's fixed cost appears in column (3).

Diminishing returns affect the additional output of bottles as more labour is used. The marginal product of labour falls, with consequences for costs of production. The company's payment to its employees is called **variable cost** because, unlike fixed cost, it varies with the *number of bottles* the company produces. The variable cost of producing 200 bottles per day, for example, is shown in column (4) of Table 5.2 as €24 per day. Column (5) shows the firm's **total cost**, which is the *sum of its fixed and variable costs*. Column (6), finally, shows the firm's **marginal cost**, a measure of how its *total cost changes when its output changes*. Specifically, marginal cost is defined as the change in total cost divided by the corresponding change in output. Note, for example, that when the firm expands production from 80 to 200 bottles per day, its total cost goes up by €12, which gives rise to the marginal cost entry of (€12/day)/(120 bottles/day) = €0.10 per bottle. To emphasise that marginal cost refers to the change in total cost when quantity changes, we place the marginal cost entries between the corresponding quantity rows of Table 5.2.

Table 5.1 Employment and Output for a Glass Bottle Maker

Total number of employees per day (1)	Total number of bottles per day (2)
0	0
1	80
2	200
3	260
4	300
5	330
6	350
7	362

For our bottle-making firm, average variable cost and average total cost values are shown in columns (4) and (6) of Table 5.3. Using the entries in Table 5.3, we plot the firm's average total cost, average variable cost and marginal cost curves in Fig. 5.4. (Because marginal cost corresponds to the change in total cost as we move between two output levels, each marginal cost value in Table 5.3 is plotted at an output level midway between those in the adjacent rows.) Average costs are simply total cost divided by the number of units being produced.

Notice two features of the cost curves in Fig. 5.4. First, the upward-sloping portion of the marginal cost curve (*MC*) corresponds to the region of diminishing returns discussed earlier. Thus, as the firm moves beyond two employees per day (200 bottles per day), the increments to total output become smaller with each additional employee, which means that the cost of producing additional bottles (*MC*) must be increasing in this region.

Secondly, note that the definition of marginal cost implies that the marginal cost curve must intersect both the average variable cost curve (*AVC*) and the average total cost curve (*ATC*) at their respective minimum points. To see why, consider what happens to the average weight of children in an elementary school class when a new student joins the class. If the new (marginal) student is lighter than the previous average weight, average weight will fall, but if the new student is heavier than the previous average, average weight will rise. By the same token, when marginal cost is below average total cost or average variable cost, the corresponding **average cost** must be falling,

average cost total cost for any level of output divided by the number of units of output, often referred to as 'unit cost'; average total cost is the sum of average fixed cost plus average variable cost

Table 5.2 Fixed, Variable and Total Costs of Bottle Production

Employees per day (1)	Bottles per day (2)	Fixed cost (€/day) (3)	Variable cost (€/day) (4)	Total cost (€/day) (5)	Marginal cost (€/bottle) (6)
0	0	40	0	40	
1	80	40	12	52	0.15
2	200	40	24	64	0.10
3	260	40	36	76	0.20
4	300	40	48	88	0.33
5	330	40	60	100	0.40
6	350	40	72	112	0.60
7	362	40	84	124	1.00

Table 5.3 Average Variable Cost and Average Total Cost of Bottle Production

Employees per day (1)	Bottles per day (2)	Variable cost (€/day) (3)	Average variable cost (€/unit of output) (4)	Total cost (€/day) (5)	Average total cost (€/unit of output) (6)	Marginal cost (€/bottle) (7)
0	0	0		40		
1	80	12	0.15	52	0.65	0.15
2	200	24	0.12	64	0.32	0.10
3	260	36	0.138	76	0.292	0.20
4	300	48	0.16	88	0.293	0.33
5	330	60	0.182	100	0.303	0.40
6	350	72	0.206	112	0.32	0.60
7	362	84	0.232	124	0.343	1.00

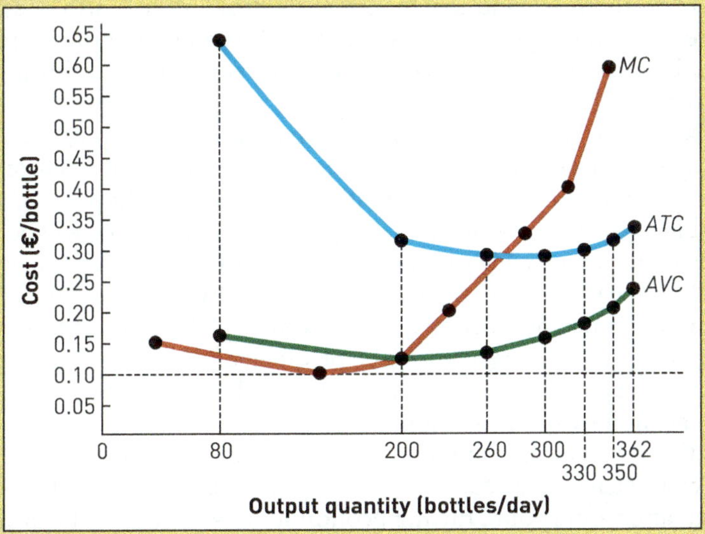

Figure 5.4 The Marginal, Average Variable and Average Total Cost Curves for a Bottle Manufacturer

The *MC* curve cuts both the *AVC* and *ATC* curves at their minimum points. The upward-sloping portion of the marginal cost curve corresponds to the region of diminishing returns.

and vice versa. And this ensures that the marginal cost curve must pass through the *minimum points* of both average cost curves.

Maths Box 5.1

Why a marginal cost curve must cut an average cost curve at its lowest point: a mathematical proof

Recall that average cost is total cost divided by the number of units being produced

$$AC = TC/Q$$

where Q is the number of units being produced.

Now consider the slope of average cost, dAC/dQ. Using the rules for differentiation in the maths appendix to Chapter 1 we have

$$\begin{aligned} dAC/dQ &= d(TC/Q)/dQ \\ &= [Q(dTC/dQ) - TC(dQ/dQ)]/Q^2 \\ &= dTC/dQ - TC/Q \end{aligned}$$

When AC is a minimum, $dAC/dQ = 0$, so $dTC/dQ - TC/Q = 0$

dTC/dQ is Marginal Cost, MC; TC/Q is Average Cost, AC.

Therefore $AC = MC$ at this point. Note that the slope of the AC curve is equal to the difference between AC and MC, so when, to the left of the bottom point, AC is falling MC < AC, and to the right MC > AC.

To the left the *AC* curve is falling (it has a negative slope) so *MC* must be less than *AC*; to the right of the bottom point it is rising (has a positive slope), so *MC* must be greater than *AC*. Therefore *MC* must cut the *AC* curve at the bottom point of the *AC* curve.

INPUT PRICES, PRODUCTION CAPACITY AND THE FIRM'S COST OF SUPPLY

In our glass bottle example, we specifically looked only at the short run, since we held the quantity of capital invested in machinery constant. Over the longer term it is possible for a firm to increase the plant and machinery at its disposal. It is also possible for it to take advantage of technological changes that permit changes in how it produces its output. This will be affected by the prices it faces for its inputs, and this in turn will affect its supply costs.

This means that (a) the law of diminishing returns may not be important in the long run, since both capital and labour employed can be expanded or contracted, and (b) that the firm can in principle choose to adopt new production technologies, including changes that enable it to lower its unit costs. Of particular importance will be an ability to change the proportions in which its production processes use labour and capital (in the form of machinery). Thus, in the short run, a rise in wage costs simply increases its unit costs of production in proportion to the amount of labour necessary to produce a unit of output. But, in the long run, it may be possible for the firm to invest in labour-saving additions to its capital employed, as it moves to a less labour-intensive and more capital-intensive technology of production.

Finally, firms that grow in size (in terms of capacity and output) may find that unit costs fall. In this case the firm is said to be benefiting from *economies of scale*. These may be limited, so that, after some point, further economies of scale cannot be obtained and diseconomies of scale may even set in.

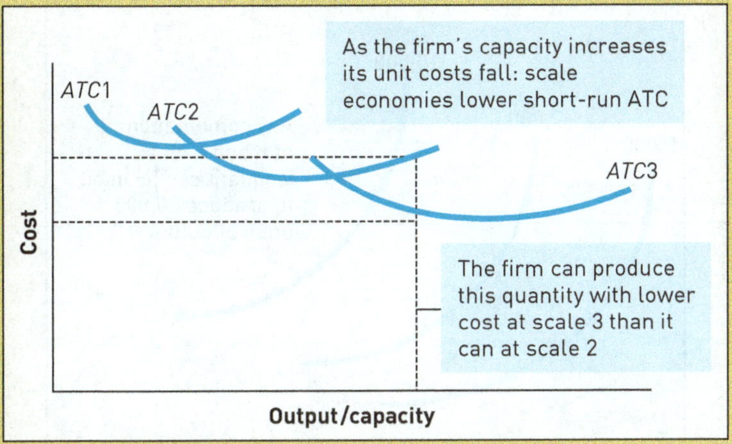

Figure 5.5 Long-run Average Cost and Scale Economies

The glass bottle company's ATC with one, two and three production lines: if it produces the quantity indicated with two production lines it is experiencing diminishing returns at scale 2. But if it can expand to three lines its unit costs will fall. It is taking advantage of scale economies and the diminishing returns problem at scale 2 have been avoided.

The first way, then, a firm may be able to reduce its costs in the long run is by *expanding capacity*. In the short run diminishing returns cause the firm's average total cost curve to turn upwards after some point when the advantages of spreading fixed costs over a larger output are offset by falling production efficiencies and rising wage costs arising from using more and more labour with a fixed machinery base. The important thing to note in this context is that the average cost curve reflects costs with a given fixed plant capacity. If, however, the capacity can be, and is, increased, a new ATC curve applies (or, if you like, the ATC is moved outwards) (Fig. 5.5).

Suppose the company can put in a second bottle production line: its ATC is now ATC2. A third line would mean the ATC moves to ATC3. In this case the larger plant (two or three production lines) will have lower unit costs (provided it is producing a larger output). Scale economies are lowering its costs. By expanding its scale of operations from scale 1 to scale 2 it can produce more without running into diminishing returns (although at scale 2 it faces diminishing returns if it expands production without expanding capacity to scale 3, and so on).

The second way to reduce its costs is by changing its production methods, or technology. By this we mean the processes used and the proportions in which inputs are used. The so-called IT revolution is a case in point where computer technology made possible a more capital-intensive approach to manufacturing using less labour per unit of output. Car assembly is a well-known example of this. A simple model explaining this is described in the following paragraphs.

(The following section is slightly more technical than what has come before. It can be ignored and you can proceed to the next section, which starts on page 158.) The other way in which a firm can alter its costs in the long run is by changing the technology of production. To illustrate this, we use the idea of a **production function**, which relates the firm's output to the inputs it uses. The glass bottle firm's technology choice concerns use of two factors of production, labour and capital (L and K), to process its energy and silica inputs to produce bottles. Its output, Q, then depends on its usage of labour and capital services, and can be represented as a function of the input usage:

> **production function** the technical relation between inputs in a production process and the outputs it produces

$$Q = f(K,L)$$

where K and L are the amounts of capital and labour employed in the firm to produce bottles. We will assume that the firm can smoothly substitute capital for labour or labour for capital, and that diminishing returns apply when you change the proportions

Figure 5.6 Production Isoquants for Three Levels of Output

From the firm's production function we can derive the different quantities of *K* and *L* that will produce a given output of bottles per week. The firm wants to produce 7,000, and has to choose a combination lying along the relevant isoquant.

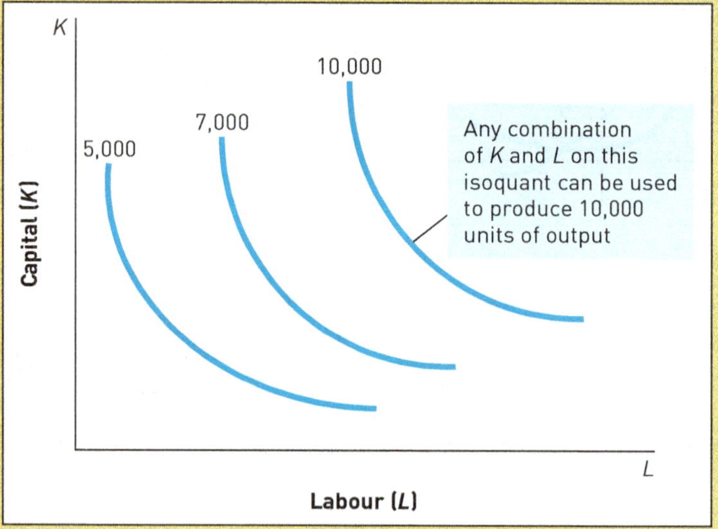

in which you use capital and labour. On this basis we can graph the combinations of capital and labour that the firm can use to produce a target output (Fig. 5.6). In this case we have a curve, called a *production isoquant*, for three levels of output per week, 5,000 bottles, 7,000 bottles and 10,000 bottles. The slope of the isoquant shows how many units of *K* are needed to replace a unit of *L* while maintaining output. This is given by the ratio of **marginal products** of *K* and *L* (the contribution of an extra unit of *K* or of *L* to output) at that point, *MPk*/*MPl*. If the firm wants to produce 7,000 bottles it can do so using any combination of *K* and *L* on the isoquant for 7,000. Other things being equal it will choose the lowest cost combination . . . but which is that?

> **marginal product** the change in total output from adding one more unit of a factor of production to the total employed while holding all other inputs constant

The cost of the inputs is $rK + wL$, where r is the hourly rental cost of capital and w is the wage rate for an hour of labour. The key to solving the problem is the relative cost of labour and capital, r/w. Suppose this is €6/€12. Then a line with a slope of 6/12 (or ½) shows all the combinations of labour and capital that can be bought with a given budget for purchasing inputs. In Fig. 5.7, three levels of spending on *K* and *L* are set down. Level 1 is too little to produce 7,000 units. Level 3 will do so . . . but is unnecessarily high. Level 2 is the minimum cost budget. The combination of *K* and *L* that minimises costs is at *A*. At this point the relative prices of the two factors are equal to the ratio of their marginal costs, or $MPk/r = MPl/w$. So to find the minimum cost level of factor usage we find that combination at which this equality holds.

Faced with a rise in the price of one factor (in this case, labour), the firm, given time, will produce any output with a more capital-intensive technique of production, increasing its investment in capital in order to economise on more expensive labour (move from A to B). This helps to offset the impact of higher labour costs on the firm's costs of supply. It also helps explain why we observe more capital-intensive production in richer countries and why labour-intensive production processes migrate to countries with lower incomes per head (and lower wages).

THE 'LAW' OF SUPPLY

The law of demand tells us that consumers buy less of a product when its price rises. If there were an analogous law of supply, it would say that producers offer more of a

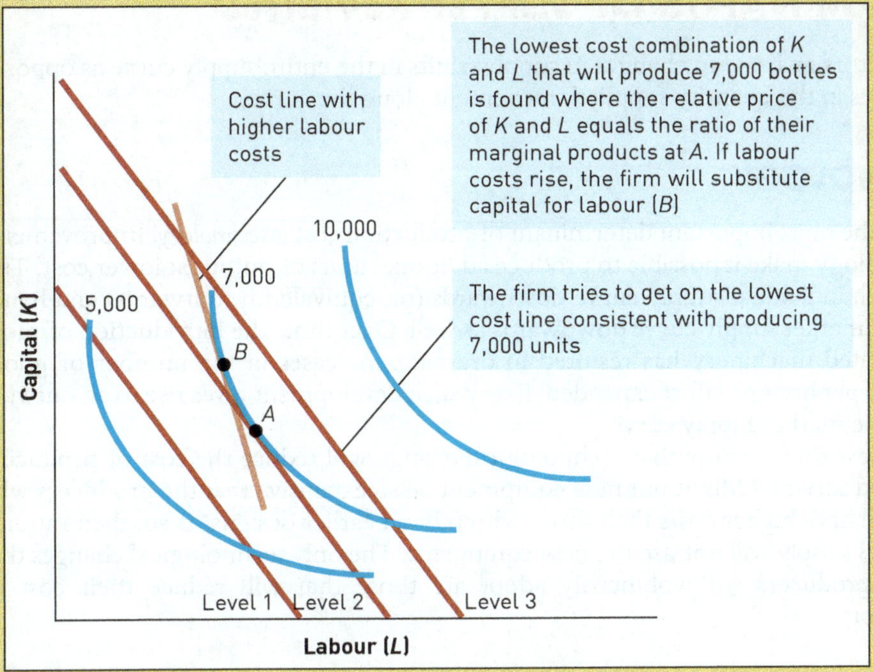

Figure 5.7 Efficient Factor Usage
The most efficient usage of factors is where relative factor costs equal the ratio of factor marginal products. A change in factor prices will induce a firm to alter the proportions in which it uses factors of production. Higher labour costs lead to the substitution of capital for labour.

product for sale when its price rises. Is there such a law? We know that supply curves are essentially *marginal cost curves*, and that because of the law of diminishing returns, marginal cost curves are upward-sloping in the short run. And so there is indeed a law of supply that applies in the short run.

In the long run, however, the law of diminishing returns does not apply. Because firms can vary the amounts of *all* factors of production they use in the long run, they can often double their production by simply doubling the amount of each input they use. In such cases costs would be exactly proportional to output, and the firm's marginal cost curve in the long run would be horizontal, not upward-sloping. So for now we shall say only that the 'law' of supply holds in the short run but not necessarily in the long run. For both the long run and the short run, however, for a firm in the type of market described in this chapter as perfectly competitive its supply curve is its *marginal cost curve*.[1]

Every quantity of output along the market supply curve represents the summation of all quantities individual sellers offer at the corresponding price. So the correspondence between price and marginal cost exists for the market supply curve as well as for the individual supply curves that lie behind it. That is, for every price–quantity pair along the market supply curve, *price will be equal to each seller's marginal cost of production*.

This is why we sometimes say that the supply curve represents the *cost side* of the market, whereas the demand curve represents the *benefit side* of the market. At every point along a market demand curve, price represents what buyers would be willing to pay for an additional unit of the product – and this, in turn, is how we measure the amount by which they would benefit by having an additional unit of the product. Likewise, at every point along a market supply curve, price measures what it would cost producers to expand production by one unit.

[1] Subject to the proviso that if price equals marginal cost the firm's total sales revenue has to be greater than its total variable cost, since otherwise it would be better not to produce at all.

DETERMINANTS OF SUPPLY REVISITED

What factors give rise to changes in supply (shifts in the entire supply curve as opposed to changes in the quantity supplied, movement along the curve)?

TECHNOLOGY

Perhaps the most important determinant of production cost is *technology*. Improvements in technology make it possible to produce additional units of output at lower cost. This shifts each individual supply curve downwards (or, equivalently, outwards) and hence shifts the market supply curve downwards as well. Over time, the introduction of more sophisticated machinery has resulted in dramatic increases in the number of goods produced per hour of effort expended. Every such development gives rise to an outward shift in the market supply curve.

But how do we know that technological change will reduce the cost of producing goods and services? Might not new equipment be so expensive that the producers who use it will have higher costs than those who rely on earlier designs? If so, then rational producers simply will not use the new equipment. The only technological changes that rational producers will voluntarily adopt are those that will reduce their cost of production.

INPUT PRICES

Whereas technological change generally (although not always) leads to gradual shifts in supply, changes in the prices of *important inputs* can give rise to large supply shifts literally overnight. For example, the price of crude oil, which is the most important input in the production of motor fuel, often fluctuates sharply, and the resulting shifts in supply cause fuel prices to exhibit corresponding fluctuations.

Similarly, when *wage rates* rise, the marginal cost of any business that employs labour also rises, shifting supply curves to the left (or, equivalently, upwards). When interest rates fall, the opportunity cost of capital equipment also falls, causing supply to shift to the right.

THE NUMBER OF SUPPLIERS

Just as demand curves shift to the right when population grows, supply curves also shift to the right as the number of *individual suppliers* grows. For example, if container recyclers die or retire at a higher rate than new recyclers enter the industry, the supply curve for recycling services will shift to the left. Conversely, if a rise in the unemployment rate leads more people to recycle soft drink containers (by reducing the opportunity cost of time spent recycling), the supply curve of recycling services will shift to the right.

EXPECTATIONS

Expectations about *future price movements* can affect how much sellers choose to offer in the current market. Suppose, for example, that recyclers expect the future price of aluminium to be much higher than the current price because of the growing use of aluminium components in cars. The rational recycler would then have an incentive to withhold aluminium from the market at today's lower price, in order to have more available to sell at the higher future price. Conversely, if recyclers expect next year's price of aluminium to be lower than this year's, their incentive would be to offer more aluminium for sale in today's market.

CHANGES IN PRICES OF OTHER PRODUCTS

Apart from technological change, perhaps the most important determinant of supply is variation in the prices of *other goods and services* that sellers might produce. Prospectors, for example, search for those precious metals for which the surplus of benefits over costs is greatest. When the price of silver rises, many stop looking for gold and start looking for silver. Conversely, when the price of platinum falls, many platinum prospectors shift their attention to gold.

REVENUES FROM SALES: PROFIT-MAXIMISING FIRMS IN COMPETITIVE MARKETS

So far, we have looked at the costs the firm faces. However, to determine how much it will produce, or even whether it will stay in production, we must relate costs to revenues from sales, out of which costs will have to be met. This means that, to explore the nature of the supply curve of a product more fully, we must say more about the *goals* of the organisations that supply the product, and the kind of economic environment in which they operate. In virtually every economy, goods and services are produced by a variety of organisations that pursue a host of different motives. Bureaucracies often behave as if trying to maximise their budgets and provide services accordingly. Voluntary organisations bring meals to the elderly because the members want to help people in need. Car wash employees are driven primarily by the hope of making some money to pay their living expenses.

PROFIT MAXIMISATION

Notwithstanding this rich variety of motives, *most* goods and services that are offered for sale in a market economy are sold by private firms whose main reason for existing is to earn **profit** for their owners. A firm's profit is the difference between the total revenue it receives from the sale of its product and all costs it incurs in producing it. We need to note in passing that this implies that the legal structure of the firm, the property rights it enjoys, and the contracts between the firm and its employees are such as to orientate the firm towards making profits. This is not always the case: in principle, a firm might be owned by the workers (a labour managed enterprise). Many state-owned enterprises across the world operate *de facto* as labour managed enterprises, and seek to maximise the interests of the employees rather than those of the owners (the taxpayers). Or the firm may in effect be owned by its customers rather than by conventional shareholders (mutuals), and behave like a customers' cooperative rather than a profit maximiser. However, most firms can plausibly be considered as aiming at maximising profits, and we will proceed on that assumption.

A **profit-maximising firm** is one whose primary goal is to maximise the amount of profit it earns. When economists use supply curves as discussed here they are tacitly assuming the market can plausibly be treated *as if* the goods or services concerned are sold by profit-maximising firms in **perfectly competitive markets**, where individual firms have no influence over the market prices of the products they sell, and so can be described as **price takers**. This does not mean that when economists use supply curves they are always strictly assuming that the markets concerned are actually perfectly competitive in this sense. For example, economists will frequently use supply and demand

> **profit** the total revenue a firm receives from the sale of its product minus all costs – explicit and implicit – incurred in producing it
>
> **profit-maximising firm** a firm whose primary goal is to maximise the difference between its total revenues and total costs
>
> **perfectly competitive market** a market in which no individual supplier has significant influence on the market price of the product
>
> **price taker** a firm that has no influence over the price at which it sells its product

curves to analyse what is happening in the oil market, even though the major crude oil producers do not display all the characteristics of perfectly competitive producers. In such circumstances the analysis is based on an assumption the level of competitive pressure is such that the outcome in the market is likely to be close to what would happen in a perfectly competitive market.

The following four conditions are often taken to be characteristic of markets that are perfectly competitive. Consider the market for glass bottles to be used to distribute beer or soft drinks.

1. **All firms sell the same standardised product** Although this condition is almost never literally satisfied, it holds as a rough approximation for many markets. Thus the markets for concrete building blocks of a given size, or for apples of a given variety, may be described in this way. This condition implies that buyers are willing to switch from one seller to another if by so doing they can obtain a lower price. In the current context a 33-centilitre bottle of a particular shape produced by one firm may be assumed to be viewed by a brewery as fully substitutable for a bottle produced by another bottle supplier.
2. **The market has many buyers and sellers, each of which buys or sells only a small fraction of the total quantity exchanged** This condition implies that individual buyers and sellers will be price takers, regarding the market price of the product as a fixed number beyond their control. For example, a single farmer's decision to plant fewer hectares of wheat would have no appreciable impact on the market price of wheat, just as an individual consumer's decision to become a vegetarian would have no perceptible effect on the price of beef. In the present case this means that we are looking at the production decision of one of a large number of firms producing virtually identical glass bottles.
3. **Productive resources are mobile** This condition implies that if a potential seller identifies a profitable business opportunity in a market, he or she will be able to obtain the labour, capital and other productive resources necessary to enter that market. By the same token, sellers who are dissatisfied with the opportunities they confront in a given market are free to leave that market and employ their resources elsewhere. There is free entry to and exit from the market. Labour and capital can move freely in and out of glass bottle production.
4. **Buyers and sellers are well informed** This condition implies that buyers and sellers are aware of the relevant opportunities available to them. If that were not so, buyers would be unable to seek out sellers who charge the lowest prices, and sellers would have no means of deploying their resources in the markets in which they would earn the most. All users know what is available and at what price from bottle producers.

In the real world the market for wheat closely approximates a perfectly competitive market. (The output of one wheat grower in northern France is (usually) indistinguishable from that of his neighbour.) The market for operating systems for desktop computers, however, does not. More than 90 per cent of desktop operating systems are sold by Microsoft, giving the company enough influence in that market to have significant control over the price it charges. For example, if it were to raise the price of its latest edition of Windows by, say, 20 per cent, some consumers might switch to Macintosh computers or install Linux if they own PCs, and others might postpone their next upgrade; but many – perhaps even most – would continue with their plans to buy.

By contrast, if an individual wheat farmer were to try to charge even just 10 cents more than the current market price for a tonne of wheat, he wouldn't be able to sell any of his wheat at all. And since he can sell as much wheat as he wishes at the market price, he has no motive to charge less.

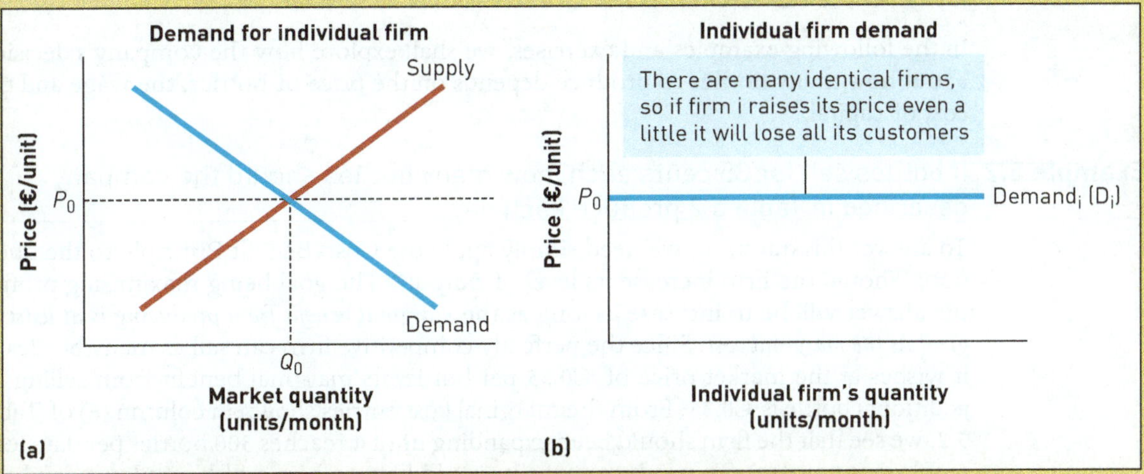

Figure 5.8 The Demand Curve Facing a Perfectly Competitive Firm
The market demand and supply curves intersect to determine the market price of the product (a). The individual firm's demand curve, D_i (b), is a horizontal line at the market price.

THE DEMAND CURVE FACING A PERFECTLY COMPETITIVE FIRM

From the perspective of an individual firm in a perfectly competitive market, what does the demand curve for its product look like? Since it can sell as much or as little as it wishes at the prevailing market price, the demand curve for its product is perfectly elastic at the market price. Figure 5.8(a) shows the market demand and supply curves intersecting to determine a market price of P_0. Figure 5.8(b) shows the product demand curve, D_i, as seen by any individual firm in this market: a horizontal line at the market price level P_0.

Many of the conclusions of the standard supply and demand model also hold for **imperfectly competitive firms** – those firms, like Microsoft, that have at least some ability to vary their own prices. But certain other conclusions do not, as we shall see when we examine the behaviour of such firms more closely in Chapter 8.

imperfectly competitive firm a firm that has at least some control over the market price of its product

Since a perfectly competitive firm has no control over the market price of its product, it needn't worry about choosing the level at which to set that price. As we have seen, the equilibrium market price in a competitive market comes from the intersection of the industry supply and demand curves. The challenge confronting the perfectly competitive firm is to choose its *output level* so that it makes as much profit as it can at that price. As we investigate how the competitive firm responds to this challenge, we shall see once again the pivotal role of our core principle that some costs are more important than others.

USING COSTS AND REVENUES TO DETERMINE HOW PROFITS ARE MAXIMISED

For our bottle-making firm, average variable cost and average total cost values are shown in columns (4) and (6) of Table 5.3 above. These were used to plot the firm's average total cost, average variable cost and marginal cost curves in Fig. 5.4.

CHOOSING OUTPUT TO MAXIMISE PROFIT

In the following examples and exercises, we shall explore how the company's decision about how many bottles to produce depends on the price of bottles, the wage and the cost of capital.

Example 5.2 If bottles sell for 35 cents each, how many bottles should the company described in Table 5.2 produce each day?

To answer this question, we need simply apply the Cost–Benefit Principle to the question: 'Should the firm increase its level of output?' The goal being maximising profits, the answer will be to increase as long as the *marginal benefit from producing is at least as great as the marginal cost*. Since the perfectly competitive firm can sell as many bottles as it wishes at the market price of €0.35 per bottle, its marginal benefit from selling an additional bottle is €0.35. From the marginal cost entries shown in column (6) of Table 5.2, we see that the firm should keep expanding until it reaches 300 bottles per day (four employees per day). To produce more it would have to hire a fifth employee, and the resulting marginal cost (€0.40 per bottle) would exceed the marginal benefit.

To confirm that the Cost–Benefit Principle thus applied identifies the profit-maximising number of bottles to produce, we can calculate profit levels directly, as in Table 5.4. Column (3) of Table 5.4 reports the firm's revenue from the sale of bottles, which is calculated as the product of the number of bottles produced per day and the price of €0.35 per bottle. Note, for example, that in the third row of column (3), total revenue is (200 bottles/day) (€0.35/bottle) = €70 per day. Column (5) reports the firm's total daily profit, which is just the difference between its total revenue (column (3)) and its total cost (column (4)). Note that the largest profit entry in column (5), €17 per day, occurs at an output of 300 bottles per day, just as suggested by our earlier application of the Cost–Benefit Principle.

As Exercise 5.2 demonstrates, an increase in the price of the product gives rise to an increase in the profit-maximising level of output.

Exercise 5.2 Same as Example 5.2, except now bottles sell for 62 cents each.

Exercise 5.3 illustrates that a fall in the wage rate leads to a decline in marginal cost, which also causes an increase in the profit-maximising level of output.

Exercise 5.3 Same as Example 5.2, except now employees receive a wage of €6 per day.

Table 5.4 Output, Revenue, Costs and Profit

Employees per day (1)	Output (bottles/day) (2)	Total revenue (€/day) (3)	Total cost (€/day) (4)	Profit (€/day) (5)
0	0	0	40	−40
1	80	28	52	−24
2	200	70	64	6
3	260	91	76	15
4	300	105	88	17
5	330	115.50	100	15.50
6	350	122.50	112	10.50
7	362	126.70	124	2.70

Suppose that in Example 5.2 the firm's fixed cost had been not €40 per day but €45 per day. How, if at all, would that have affected the firm's profit-maximising level of output? The answer is 'not at all': each entry in the profit column of Table 5.4 would have been €5 per day smaller than before, but the maximum profit entry still would have been 300 bottles per day.

The observation that the profit-maximising quantity does not depend on fixed costs is not an idiosyncrasy of this example. That it holds true in general is an immediate consequence of the Cost–Benefit Principle, which says that a firm should increase its output if, and only if, the *marginal* benefit exceeds the *marginal* cost. Neither the marginal benefit of expanding (which is the market price of bottles) nor the marginal cost of expanding is affected by a change in the firm's fixed cost.

When the law of diminishing returns applies (some costs are fixed) marginal cost rises as the firm expands production beyond some point. Under these circumstances, the firm's best option is to keep expanding output as long as *marginal cost is less than price*.

Note that in Example 5.2 if the company's fixed cost had been any more than €57 per day, it would have made a loss at *every* possible level of output. As long as it still had to pay its fixed cost, however, its best bet would have been to continue producing 300 bottles per day. It is better, after all, to experience a smaller loss than a larger one. If a firm in that situation expected conditions to remain the same, though, it would want to get out of the bottle business as soon as its equipment lease expired.

A NOTE ON THE FIRM'S SHUTDOWN CONDITION

It may seem that a firm that can sell as much output as it wishes at a constant market price would *always* do best in the short run by producing and selling the output level for which price equals marginal cost. But there are exceptions to this rule. Suppose, for example, that the market price of the firm's product falls so low that its revenue from sales is smaller than its variable cost at all possible levels of output. The firm should then cease production for the time being. By shutting down, it will suffer a loss equal to its fixed costs. But, by remaining open, it will suffer an even larger loss.

More formally, if P denotes the market price of the product and Q denotes the number of units produced and sold, then $P \times Q$ is the firm's total revenue from sales, and if we use VC to denote the firm's variable cost, the rule is that the firm should shut down in the short run if $P \times Q$ is less than VC for every level of Q:

Short-run shutdown condition: $P \times Q < VC$ for all levels of Q,

Exercise 5.4

In Example 5.2, suppose that bottles sold not for €0.35 but only €0.10. Calculate the profit corresponding to each level of output, as in Table 5.4, and verify that the firm's best option is to cease operations in the short run.

AVERAGE VARIABLE COST AND AVERAGE TOTAL COST

Suppose that the firm is unable to cover its variable cost at any level of output – that is, suppose that $P \times Q < VC$ for all levels of Q. It must then also be true that $P < VC/Q$ for all levels of Q, since we obtain the second inequality by simply dividing both sides of the first one by Q. VC/Q is the firm's **average variable cost (AVC)** – its variable cost divided by its output. The firm's short-run shutdown condition may thus be restated a second way: discontinue operations in the short run if the product price is less than the minimum value of its AVC. Thus:

average variable cost (AVC) variable cost divided by total output

Short-run shutdown condition (alternative version): $P <$ minimum value of AVC

As we shall see in the next section, this version of the shutdown condition often enables us to tell at a glance whether the firm should continue operations.

average total cost (ATC) total cost divided by total output

profitable firm a firm whose total revenue exceeds its total cost

A related cost concept that facilitates assessment of the firm's profitability is **average total cost (ATC)**, which is total cost (TC) divided by output (Q): $ATC = TC/Q$. The firm's profit, again, is the difference between its total revenue ($P \times Q$) and its total cost. And since total cost is equal to average total cost times quantity, the firm's profit is also equal to $(P \times Q) - (ATC \times Q)$. A firm is said to be **profitable** if its revenue ($P \times Q$) exceeds its total cost ($ATC \times Q$). A firm can thus be profitable only if the price of its product (P) exceeds its ATC for some level of output.

Keeping track of all these cost concepts may seem tedious. In the next section, however, we will see that the payoff from doing so is that it enables us to recast the profit-maximisation decision in a simple graphical framework.

Economic Naturalist 5.1
Loss-making airlines: is bankruptcy good for you?

Someone once said that the normal state of affairs for an American airline is to be in 'chapter 11'. This is a legal position whereby it can effectively suspend its creditors and carry on trading as long as it can persuade a court that, if the creditors are put on ice for a while, it will be able to trade out of its difficulties. A similar provision would be welcomed by many airlines in Europe. However, unlike their approach to the banking sector, European governments are more willing to contemplate bankruptcy for airlines. Swissair is a case in point. It went bankrupt in 2001 in the aftermath of 9/11 and had mountains of debt, and simply ceased to trade. It couldn't cover its total costs as passenger demand fell after 9/11. It closed down suddenly . . . and emerged as a new, smaller airline called, simply, Swiss, which continues to operate today, its assets having been sold as a going concern. Past debts represent sunk costs, and could not be serviced, so shareholders and creditors 'took a cold bath'. The problem with a chapter 11 regime, or having the state as an owner, as with another loss maker, Alitalia, is that it offers shelter to a loss-making firm rather than encouraging its assets to be reallocated to create economic surplus.

GRAPHICAL ANALYSIS OF THE MAXIMUM-PROFIT CONDITION

In Example 5.2 we implicitly assumed that the bottle maker could employ workers only in whole-number amounts. Under these conditions, we saw that the profit-maximising output level was one for which marginal cost was somewhat less than price (because adding yet another employee would have pushed marginal cost higher than price). In Example 5.3, we shall see that when output and employment can be varied continuously, the maximum-profit condition is that price be equal to marginal cost.

Example 5.3 For the bottle maker whose cost curves are as shown in fig. 5.9, find the profit-maximising output level if bottles sell for €0.20 each. How much profit will this firm earn? What is the lowest price at which this firm would continue to operate in the short run?

Cost-Benefit Analysis

The Cost–Benefit Principle tells us that this firm should continue to expand as long as price is at least as great as marginal cost. In Fig. 5.9 we see that if the firm follows this rule, it will produce 260 bottles per day, the quantity at which *price and marginal cost are equal*. To gain further confidence that 260 must be the profit-maximising quantity when the price is €0.20 per bottle, first suppose that the firm had sold some amount less than that – say, only 200 bottles per day. Its benefit from expanding output by one bottle would then be the bottle's market price, here 20 cents. The cost of expanding output by one bottle is equal (by definition) to the firm's marginal cost, which at 200 bottles per day is only 10 cents (see Fig. 5.9). So by selling the 201st bottle for 20 cents and producing it for an extra cost of only 10 cents, the firm will increase its profit by 20 – 10 = 10 cents per day. In a similar way, we can show that for *any* quantity less than the level at which price equals marginal cost, the seller can boost profit by expanding production.

Conversely, suppose that the firm was currently selling more than 260 bottles per day – say, 300 – at a price of 20 cents each. In Fig. 5.9 we see that marginal cost at an output of 300 is 33 cents per bottle. If the firm then contracted its output by one bottle per day, it would cut its costs by 33 cents while losing only 20 cents in revenue. As a result, its profit would grow by 13 cents per day. The same argument can be made regarding any quantity larger than 260, so if the firm is currently selling an output at which price is less than marginal cost, it can always do better by producing and selling fewer bottles.

Increasing Opportunity Cost

We have thus established that if the firm sold fewer than 260 bottles per day, it could earn more profit by expanding; and if it sold more than 260, it could earn more by contracting. It follows that at a market price of 20 cents per bottle, the seller maximises its profit by selling 260 units per week, the quantity for which price and marginal cost are exactly the same.

At that quantity the firm will collect total revenue of $P \times Q$ = (€0.20/bottle)(260 bottles/day) = €52 per day. Note in Fig. 5.9 that at 260 bottles per day the firm's average total cost is ATC = €0.12 per bottle, which means that its total cost is $ATC \times Q$ = (€0.12/bottle)(260 bottles/day) = €31.20 per day. The firm's profit is the difference between its *total revenue and its total cost*, or €20.80 per day. Note, finally, that the minimum value of the firm's *AVC* curve is €0.07. So if the price of bottles fell below 7 cents each, the firm would shut down in the short run.

Another attractive feature of the graphical method of finding the profit-maximising output level is that it permits us to calculate the firm's profit graphically. Thus, for the firm in Example 5.2, daily profit is simply the difference between price and *ATC* times the number of units sold: (€0.20/bottle – €0.12/bottle)(260 bottles/day) = €20.80 per day, which is the area of the shaded rectangle in Fig. 5.10.

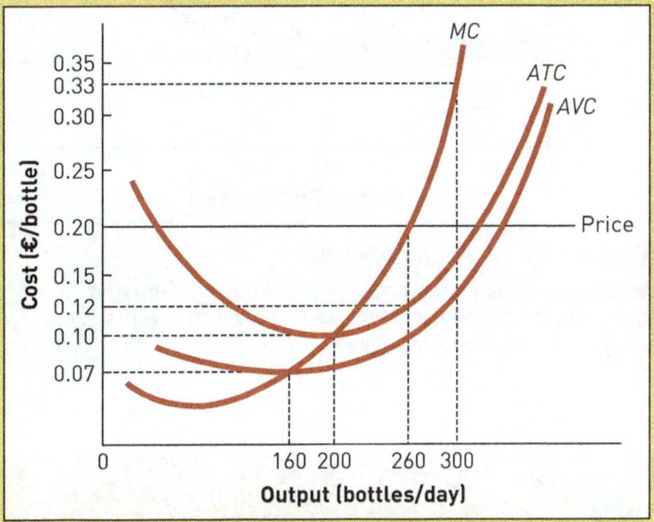

Figure 5.9 Price = Marginal Cost: the Perfectly Competitive Firm's Profit-maximising Supply Rule

If price is greater than marginal cost, the firm can increase its profit by expanding production and sales. If price is less than marginal cost, the firm can increase its profit by producing and selling less output.

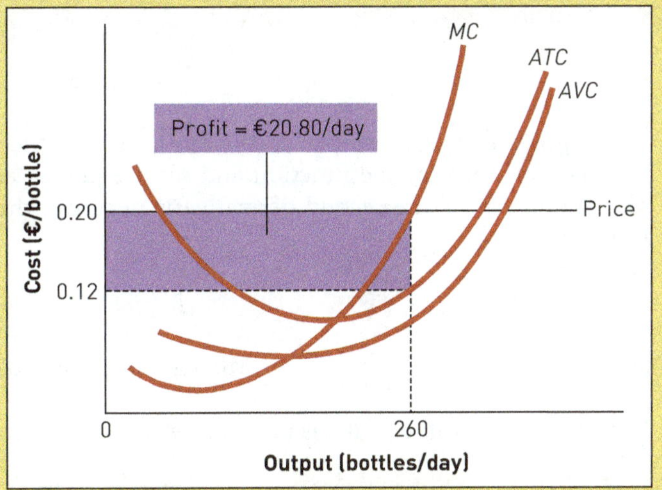

Figure 5.10 Measuring Profit Graphically

Profit is equal to $(P - ATC) \times Q$, which is equal to the area of the shaded rectangle.

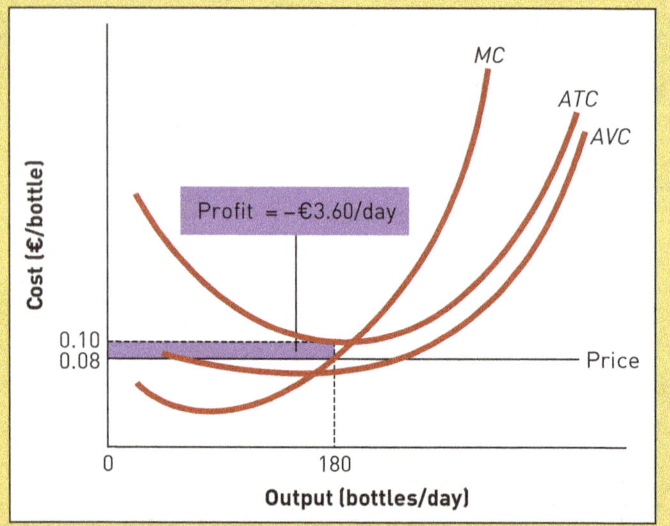

Figure 5.11 A 'Negative Profit'

When price is less than *ATC* as the profit-maximising quantity, the firm experiences a loss, which is equal to the area of the shaded rectangle.

Not all firms are as fortunate as the one shown in Fig. 5.10. Suppose, for example, that the price of bottles had been not 20 cents but only 8 cents. Since that price is greater than the minimum value of *AVC* (see Fig. 5.11), the firm should continue to operate in the short run by producing the level of output for which price equals marginal cost (180 bottles per day). But because price is less than *ATC* at that level of output, the firm will now experience a loss, or negative profit, on its operations. This profit is calculated as $(P - ATC) \times Q =$ (€0.08/bottle – €0.10/bottle) × (180 bottles/day) = –€3.60 per day, which is equal to the area of the shaded rectangle in Fig. 5.11.

In Chapter 7, we shall see how firms move resources in response to the incentives implicit in profits and losses. But such movements occur in the long run, and our focus here is on production decisions in the short run.

Maths Box 5.2
The mathematics of profit maximisation under perfect competition

The perfectly competitive firm is a *price taker*. The amount it sells has no effect on the price per unit sold it receives. Hence, total sales revenue is simply price (which is given) multiplied by the number of units sold.

Profits total sales revenue minus total costs incurred in production of the product sold. Let *B* be profit. It depends on the level of sales and of costs, both of which depend on the level of production. Hence, profits are a function of the level of production.

Formally,

$$B = B(q)$$

where q is the level of output of the firm. To find the maximum value of a function we obtain the first derivative of the function and set it equal to zero. At this value, it is either a maximum or a minimum. If the second derivative is negative, the value for q is that which maximises the function

$$B = TR(q) - TC(q)$$

and

$$\mathrm{d}B/\mathrm{d}q = \mathrm{d}TR/\mathrm{d}q - \mathrm{d}TC/\mathrm{d}q$$

For a maximum value of *B* it is necessary that this be equal to zero. That means

$$\mathrm{d}TR/\mathrm{d}q = \mathrm{d}TC/\mathrm{d}q$$

But $\mathrm{d}TR/\mathrm{d}q$ and $\mathrm{d}TC/\mathrm{d}q$ are (in the competitive case) simply price and marginal cost, respectively. Hence this necessary condition says that to maximise profits you produce the level of output that equates price to marginal cost. To be sure that this maximises rather than minimises profits we need to go further. It requires that the second derivative of the expression should be negative.

TC is the sum of fixed plus variable costs. Fixed costs are a constant, *a*. Variable costs, because of diminishing returns, have the form

$$TVC = b \times q + c \times q^2$$

meaning that average variable cost increases with *q* reflecting diminishing returns. Hence, the total cost function is

$$TC = a + b \times q + c \times q^2$$

So the profits function may be written

$$B = p \times q - (a + b \times q + c \times q^2)$$

Differentiating this gives

$$\mathrm{d}B/\mathrm{d}Q = p - (b + 2c \times q)$$

where p = price and $b + 2cq$ is marginal cost. Setting $\mathrm{d}B/\mathrm{d}Q = 0$ means price equals marginal cost. Differentiating again gives

$$\mathrm{d}^2B/\mathrm{d}q^2 = -2c < 0$$

so it is a maximum, and profits are maximised at this point.

RECAP

Determinants of supply

Among the relevant factors *causing supply curves to shift* are new technologies, changes in input prices, changes in the number of sellers, expectations of future price changes and changes in the prices of other products that firms might produce.

APPLYING THE THEORY OF SUPPLY

Whatever the activity, the same logic governs all supply decisions in perfectly competitive markets (and in any other setting in which sellers can sell as much as they wish to at a constant price): keep expanding output until marginal cost is equal to the price of the product. This logic helps us understand why recycling efforts are more intensive for some products than others, and why in some cases recycling simply doesn't work unless undertaken by public authorities.

In many countries beverage cans are recycled in large measure by private entities. This is particularly true of aluminium cans (for beer and soft drinks). They are light and easily compacted, and can be readily recycled into new aluminium products. Aluminium is costly to produce, so users will pay a good price for used aluminium. Glass bottles are heavy, troublesome to compact and contain colouring, while glass production costs are relatively low. Hence the cost of collecting and recycling is high relative to the price paid for the glass to be recycled. Paper is also recycled, but is bulky and hard to compact, while in most cases wood-pulp paper when recycled can be used only for low-value purposes. Collection costs are high and the value of recycled paper is low, so that the

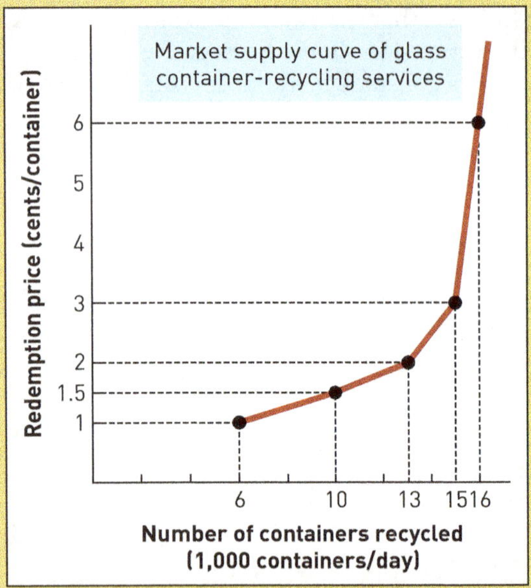

Figure 5.12 The Supply Curve of Container Recycling Services for Chinon, France

return to recycling is low, too. Not surprisingly, more effort is likely to be put into collecting cans than bottles while paper usually depends on garbage services choosing, or being obliged by regulation, to separate it for recycling purposes.

The acquisition of valuable raw materials is only one of two important benefits from recycling. The second is that, by removing litter, recycling makes the environment more pleasant for everyone. Supply-curve analysis not only explains differential efforts in dealing with the recycling problem by product, but also helps us understand an aspect of environmental policy on litter and recycling that is often badly misunderstood. That is the apparent decision to tolerate a significant level of environmental degradation through glass, beverage can and paper littering despite a commitment to eradication.

Suppose that there is an upward-sloping supply curve of collecting and recycling one of these litter items. That means that, as we achieve greater levels of recycling, the cost of further recycling (marginal cost) is rising. Now, suppose that we place a social value on eliminating litter from the environment, and that this is subject to diminishing marginal utility, so that at higher levels of recycling (lower levels of litter problems) we place lower value on further reductions in littering. If public authorities, whatever their rhetoric, are being economically rational they are unlikely to choose a level of recycling that reduces litter to zero. Unless the value of reducing litter at the margin exceeds the cost of doing so when the level of litter approaches zero it is not optimal to do further collection and recycling. We are better off with some litter not collected. Try, however, to convince environmental activists of this at your peril!

Cost-Benefit Analysis

Many people become upset when they first hear economists say that the socially optimal amount of litter is greater than zero. In the minds of these people, the optimal amount of litter is *exactly* zero. But this position completely ignores the scarcity principle. Granted, there would be benefits from reducing litter further, but there would also be costs. Spending more on litter removal therefore means spending less on other useful things.

Does that mean we can always and simply rely on market forces to reduce litter optimally? Unfortunately, no. For market forces to work efficiently, a necessary condition is that whoever bears the cost of an action also reaps the benefits. If litter has no or a very low re-use value, no one will have a sufficient (or perhaps any) incentive to collect it for disposal. Collective action to solve the problem is unavoidable . . . but will optimally still leave some litter uncollected. This may be mandatory recycling or mandatory high deposits (a tax on sales collected by those who return the containers) or public collection services. But some litter will still be uncollected.

Incentives Matter

Economic Naturalist 5.2
Are the laws of supply and demand suspended in California where litter is concerned?

Ireland introduced a tax on plastic bags distributed to shoppers in 2002. The object was to reduce drastically the problem of non-biodegradable litter. In the following year, the number of bags issued fell from 1.2 billion to 90 million. Prices really work. However, six years later it was noted that the number of bags distributed had increased by a third, so the government sharply increased the tax on the basis that the price effect was wearing off. They don't seem to have remembered that in the seven years after the tax was introduced GDP per head in Ireland rose by over 30 per cent (the years of the 'Celtic Tiger' boom). However, if this consequence of the income elasticity of demand was regrettable, it pales into significance compared with the reaction to the proposed introduction of a bag tax in San Jose, CA. The American Chemistry Council issued a statement early in 2011 to the effect that 'Banning recyclable plastic bags will not solve the litter problem or reduce the amount of waste in our sewers and landfills . . . Product bans often result in shifting one form of litter to another, and such measures only create new problems. *After all, there is no such thing as environmentally preferable litter* [our emphasis]. The few communities that have chosen to tax or ban the use of plastic grocery bags found that their efforts to help the environment actually had the opposite effect.' In Ireland, they claimed, plastic bag use by 2010 was 10 per cent higher than before the tax was introduced (totally untrue). We think they misplaced a zero. Another case of those damned dots.[2]

Exercise 5.5

If the supply curve of glass container-recycling services is as shown in Figure 5.12, and each of the city's 60,000 citizens would be willing to pay 0.00005 cents for each glass container removed from the landscape, at what level should the city government set the redemption price for glass containers, and how many will be recycled each day?

SUPPLY AND PRODUCER SURPLUS

The economic surplus received by a buyer is called *consumer surplus*. The analogous construct for a seller is **producer surplus**, the difference between the price a seller actually receives for the product and the lowest price for which she would have been willing to sell it (her reservation price, which in general will be her marginal cost).

producer surplus the amount by which price exceeds the seller's reservation price

As in the case of consumer surplus, the term 'producer surplus' sometimes refers to the surplus received by a single seller in a transaction, while on other occasions it describes the total surplus received by all sellers in a market or collection of markets.

CALCULATING PRODUCER SURPLUS

In Chapter 4 we saw that consumer surplus in a market is the area bounded above by the demand curve and bounded below by the market price. Producer surplus in a market is calculated in an analogous way. As Example 5.5 illustrates, it is the area bounded above by the market price and bounded below by the market supply curve (remember that the supply curve reflects marginal cost).

Example 5.5

How much do sellers benefit from their participation in the market for milk?

Consider the market for milk, whose demand and supply curves are shown in Fig. 5.13, which has an equilibrium price of €2 per litre and an equilibrium quantity of 4,000 litres per day. How much producer surplus do the sellers in this market reap?

---

[2] Randolph Churchill, a former British Chancellor and father of Prime Minister Winston Churchill, once remarked on the subject of decimals that he 'never could make out what those damned dots meant'.

Figure 5.13 Producer Surplus in the Market for Milk

Producer surplus is the area of the shaded triangle. its value is €4,000 per day.

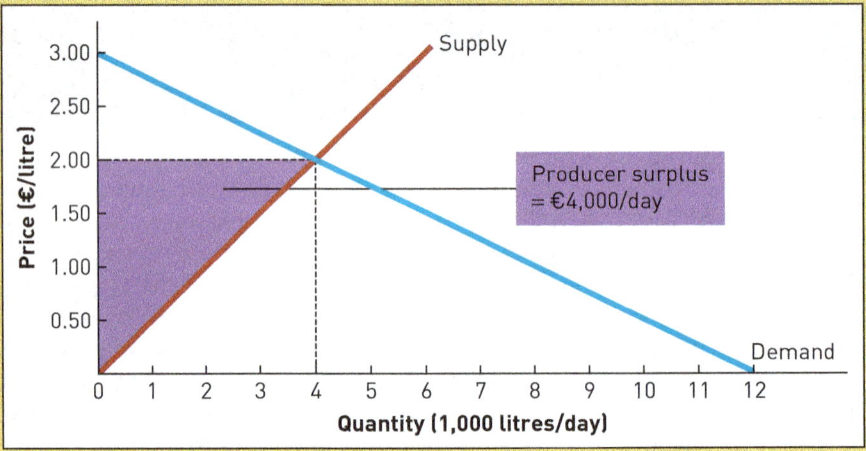

In Fig. 5.13 note first that for all milk sold up to 4,000 litres per day, sellers receive a surplus equal to the difference between the market price of €2 per litre and their reservation price as given by the supply curve. Total producer surplus received by buyers in the milk market is thus the shaded triangle between the supply curve and the market price in Fig. 5.13. Note that this area is a right-angled triangle whose vertical arm is $h = €2/\text{litre}$ and whose horizontal arm is $b = 4{,}000$ litres/day. And since the area of any triangle is equal to $(1/2)bh$, producer surplus in this market is equal to

$$(1/2)\ (4{,}000\ \text{litres/day})\ (€2/\text{litre}) = €4{,}000/\text{day}$$

Producer surplus in this example may be thought of as the highest price sellers would pay, in the aggregate, for the right to continue participating in the milk market. It is €4,000 per day, since that is the amount by which their *combined benefits exceed their combined costs*. It is the difference between what the producer expects to receive for that unit of output and the smallest amount the producer would be willing to accept for that unit of the good.

SUMMARY

- The supply curve for a good or service is a schedule that for any price tells us the *quantity that sellers wish to supply at that price*. The prices at which goods and services are offered for sale in the market depend, in turn, on the opportunity cost of the resources required to produce them.
- Supply curves tend to be upward-sloping, at least in the short run, in part because of the Low-Hanging-Fruit Principle. In general, rational producers will always take advantage of their best opportunities first, moving on to more difficult or costly opportunities only after their best ones have been exhausted. Reinforcing this tendency is the *law of diminishing returns*, which says that when some factors of production are held fixed, the amount of additional variable factors required to produce successive increments in output grows larger.
- For perfectly competitive markets – or, more generally, for markets in which individual sellers can sell whatever quantity they wish at constant price – the seller's best option is to sell that quantity of output for which *price equals marginal cost*, provided price exceeds the minimum value of average variable cost. The supply curve for the seller thus coincides with the portion of his marginal cost curve that exceeds average

variable cost. This is why we sometimes say that the supply curve represents the cost side of the market (in contrast to the demand curve, which represents the benefit side of the market).

- An important terminological distinction from the demand side of the market also applies on the supply side of the market. A 'change in supply' means a shift in the entire supply curve, whereas a 'change in the quantity supplied' means a movement along the supply curve. The factors that cause *supply curves to shift* include technology, input prices, the number of sellers, expectations of future price changes and the prices of other products that firms might produce.
- *Producer surplus* is a measure of the economic surplus reaped by a seller or sellers in a market. It is the cumulative sum of the differences between the market price and their reservation prices, which is the area bounded above by market price and bounded below by the supply curve.

REVIEW QUESTIONS

1. Explain why you would expect supply curves to slope upwards on the basis of the Principle of Increasing Opportunity Cost.
2. Which do you think is more likely to be a fixed factor of production for an ice cream producer during the next two months: its factory building or its workers who operate the machines? Explain.
3. Economists often stress that congestion helps account for the law of diminishing returns. With this in mind, explain why it would be impossible to feed all the people on Earth with food grown in a single flowerpot, even if unlimited water, labour, seed, fertiliser, sunlight and other inputs were available.
4. True or false? The perfectly competitive firm should always produce the output level for which price equals marginal cost.
5. Why do we use the vertical interpretation of the supply curve when we measure producer surplus?

PROBLEMS

connect

Problems marked with an asterisk (*) are more difficult.

1. Zoe is trying to decide how to divide her time between her job as a wedding photographer, which pays €27 per hour for as many hours as she chooses to work, and as a fossil collector, in which her pay depends both on the price of fossils and the number of them she finds. Earnings aside, Zoe is indifferent between the two tasks, and the number of fossils she can find depends on the number of hours a day she searches, as shown in the table below.

Hours per day (1)	Total fossils per day (2)
1	5
2	9
3	12
4	14
5	15

a. Derive a table with price in euro increments from €0 to €30 in column (1) and the quantity of fossils Zoe is willing to supply per day at that price in column (2).

b. Plot these points in a graph with price on the vertical axis and quantity per day on the horizontal. What is this curve called?

2. A price-taking firm makes air conditioners. The market price of one of its new air conditioners is €120. Its total cost information is given in the table below.

Air conditioners per day	Total cost (€ per day)
1	100
2	150
3	220
4	310
5	405
6	510
7	650
8	800

How many air conditioners should the firm produce per day if its goal is to maximise its profit?

3. The Paducah Slugger Company makes baseball bats out of lumber supplied to it by Acme Sporting Goods, which pays Paducah €10 for each finished bat. Paducah's only factors of production are lathe operators and a small building with a lathe. The number of bats per day it produces depends on the number of employee-hours per day, as shown in the table below.

a. If the wage is €15 per hour and Paducah's daily fixed cost for the lathe and building is €60, what is the profit-maximising quantity of bats?

b. What would be the profit-maximising number of bats if the firm's fixed cost were not €60 per day but only €30?

Number of bats per day	Number of employee-hours per day
0	0
5	1
10	2
15	4
20	7
25	11
30	16
35	22

4. In Question 3, how would Paducah's profit-maximising level of output be affected if the government imposed a tax of €10 per day on the company? (**Hint:** Think of this tax as equivalent to a €10 increase in fixed cost.) What would Paducah's profit-maximising level of output be if the government imposed a tax of €2 per bat? (**Hint:** Think of this tax as a €2 per bat increase in the firm's marginal cost.) Why do these two taxes have such different effects?

5. The supply curves for the only two firms in a competitive industry are given by $P = 2Q1$ and $P = 2 + Q2$, where $Q1$ is the output of firm 1 and $Q2$ is the output of firm 2. What is the market supply curve for this industry? (**Hint:** Graph the two curves side by side, then add their respective quantities at a sample of different prices.)

6. Calculate daily producer surplus for the market for pizza whose demand and supply curves are shown in the graph below.

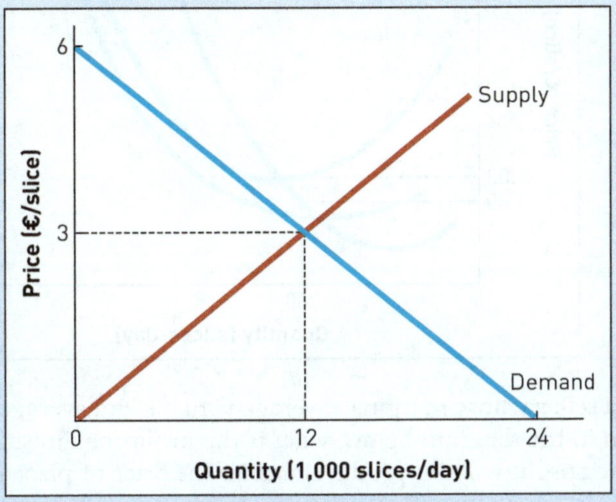

7. For the pizza seller whose marginal, average variable and average total cost curves are as shown in the diagram below, what is the profit-maximising level of output and how much profit will this producer earn if the price of pizza is €2.50 per slice?

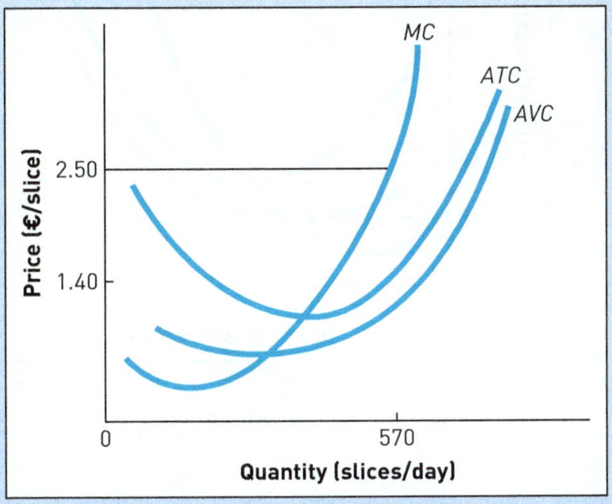

8. For the pizza seller whose marginal, average variable and average total cost curves are as shown in the diagram below, what is the profit-maximising level of output and how much profit will this producer earn if the price of pizza is €0.80 per slice?

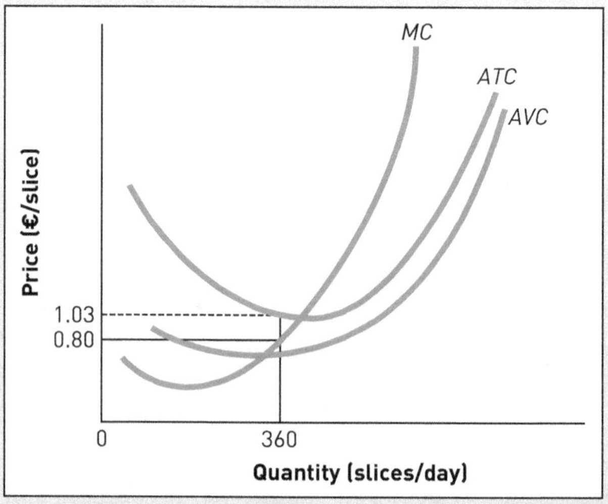

9.* For the pizza seller whose marginal, average variable and average total cost curves are as shown in the diagram below, what is the profit-maximising level of output and how much profit will this producer earn if the price of pizza is €0.50 per slice?

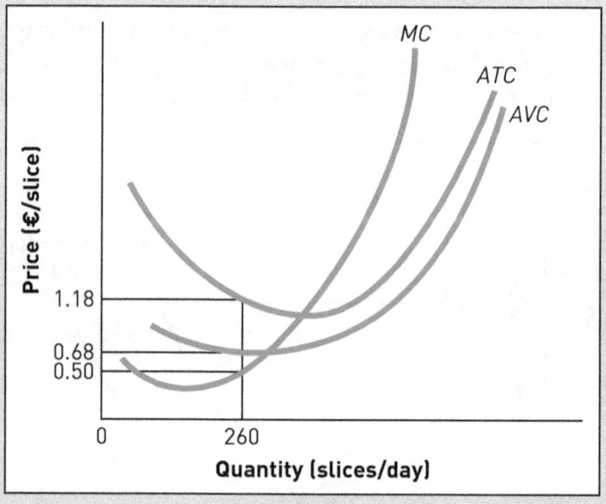

10.* For the pizza seller whose marginal, average variable and average total cost curves are as shown in the diagram below (the same seller as in Problem 9), what is the profit-maximising level of output and how much profit will this producer earn if the price of pizza is €1.18 per slice?

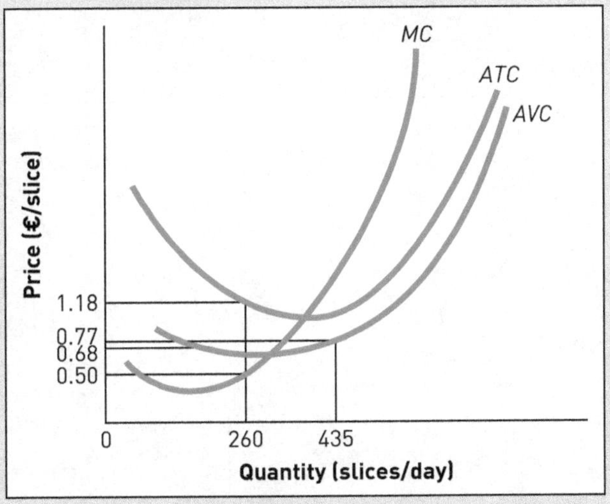

Chapter 6 Efficiency and Exchange

If you really need money, you can sell your kidney or even your car. — *Homer Simpson*

Learning Objectives

After studying this chapter you should be able to:

1. Explain economic efficiency of an economy in terms of generating surplus;
2. Demonstrate that, subject to certain well-defined conditions being met, a market economy is generally efficient;
3. Explain that efficiency is not the only criterion by which to evaluate an economic system, but that efficiency is a precondition for maximising economic welfare;
4. Understand how restrictions that prevent markets from clearing have economic efficiency implications;
5. Understand the importance of efficient design of pricing mechanisms affecting public sector production;
6. Understand how taxes affect market efficiency and consumer welfare.

The market economy based on free enterprise as a system of economic organisation has frequently been described in such glowing terms as 'the greatest engine of progress mankind has ever witnessed'. Its ability to deliver a high and rising standard of living to everyone (even if not equally to everyone) has been summed up in the saying: 'A rising tide lifts all boats.'

Even before the financial crisis that hit the world economy in 2007, not everyone would have agreed with this judgement. An immigrant worker from North Africa in one of the poorer areas of the Paris suburbs, plagued by urban violence, a drab and deteriorating environment, a long and expensive commute to a poorly paid job in the city centre might think otherwise. The same applies to an ex-coalminer, aged 60, unemployed after nearly 20 years in County Durham in England or a white-collar worker who has lost a job in Seattle because Boeing was losing market share to Airbus, and is unable to pay health insurance for an asthmatic child on the wages earned shelving goods in a supermarket. A degree of scepticism about the virtues of the system of free markets and private ownership of economic resources that we call 'free enterprise' would be entirely understandable.

Informed students of the market system understand that it could never be expected to avoid all these problems, and others like them, in the first place. In very broad domains markets are just as remarkable as their strongest proponents assert. Yet there are many problems they simply cannot be expected to solve. For example, private markets cannot by themselves guarantee an income distribution that most people regard as fair. Nor can they ensure clean air, uncongested roads or safe neighbourhoods for all. And unemployment can persist even in a booming economy. Most obviously, there are serious problems arising from the way in which financial markets operated in the first decade of the twenty-first century.

The types of problem just described point to an unavoidable conclusion. There are circumstances in which markets do not operate well and the outcome is less than acceptable. As a result, and even in the most successful free-market economies, markets are supplemented by active political coordination and collective provision of goods and services in at least some instances. It's important to understand why and where this is necessary. Equally, to organise economic life efficiently, it is important to know what tasks private markets can do well, and then allow them to perform those tasks.

The evidence that markets do not work efficiently in all circumstances has led some critics to conclude that markets are generally inefficient. This conclusion is misleading, and has prompted attempts to prevent markets from doing even those tasks which they do well. In this chapter we shall explore why many tasks are best left to the market. We shall explore the conditions under which unregulated markets generate the largest possible economic surplus. Market failure is a matter for later chapters.

MARKET EQUILIBRIUM AND EFFICIENCY

efficient (or **Pareto efficiency**) a situation is efficient if no change is possible that will help some people without harming others

We have already described, in Chapter 3, how markets coordinate the production of a large and complex list of goods and services. But economists make an even stronger claim – namely, that markets not only produce these goods, but also produce them as *efficiently* as possible.

The term **efficient**, as economists use it, has a narrow technical meaning. When we say that market equilibrium is efficient, we mean simply this: *if price and quantity take anything other than their equilibrium values, a transaction that will make at least some people better off without harming others can always be found.* This conception of efficiency is also known as **Pareto efficiency**, after Vilfredo Pareto, the nineteenth-century Italian economist who introduced it.

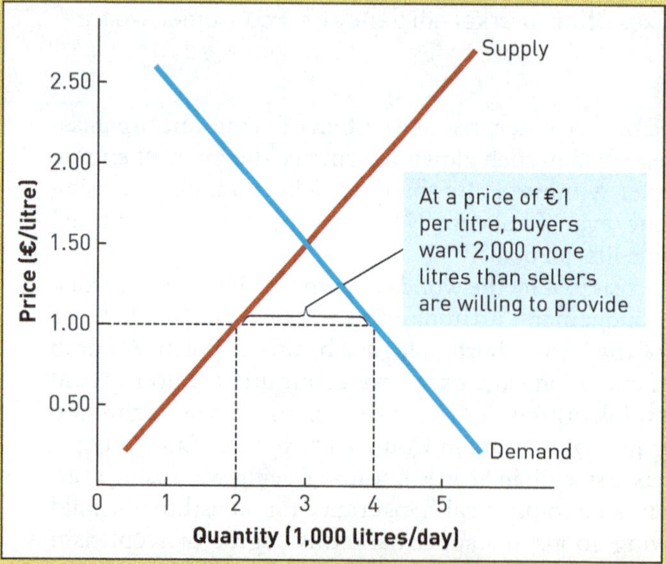

Figure 6.1 A Market in Which Price is Below the Equilibrium Level

In this market, milk is currently selling for €1 per litre, €0.50 below the equilibrium price of €1.50 per litre.

A market equilibrium is 'efficient' because, when a market is not in equilibrium, it is always possible to construct an exchange that helps some without harming others. In a sense, a 'free lunch' exists. Suppose, for example, that the supply and demand curves for milk are as shown in Fig. 6.1, and that the current price of milk is €1 per litre. At that price, sellers offer only 2,000 litres of milk a day. At that quantity, the marginal buyer values an extra litre of milk at €2. This is the price that corresponds to 2,000 litres a day on the demand

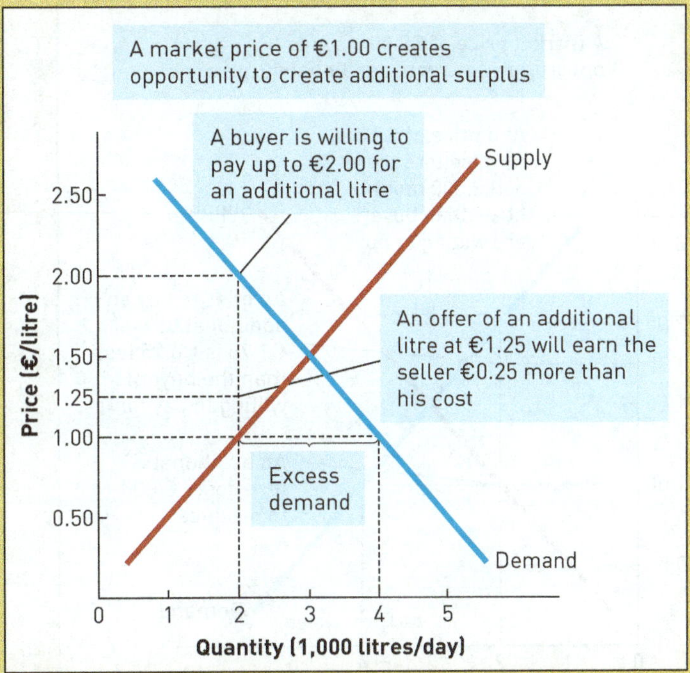

Figure 6.2 How Excess Demand Creates an Opportunity for a Surplus-enhancing Transaction

At a market price of €1 per litre, the most intensely dissatisfied buyer is willing to pay €2 for an additional litre, which a seller can produce at a cost of only €1. If this buyer pays the seller €1.25 for the extra litre, the buyer gains an economic surplus of €0.75 and the seller gains an economic surplus of €0.25.

curve, which represents what the marginal buyer is willing to pay for an additional litre (another application of the vertical interpretation of the demand curve). We also know that the cost of producing an extra litre of milk is only €1. This is the marginal cost, or supply price, of milk for a supply of 2,000 litres a day.

A price of €1 per litre leads to excess demand of 2,000 litres per day, which means that many frustrated buyers cannot buy as much milk as they want at the going price. Now, suppose a supplier sells an extra litre of milk to the most eager of these buyers for €1.25, as in Fig. 6.2. Since the extra litre cost only €1 to produce, the seller is €0.25 better off than before. And, since the most eager buyer values the extra litre at €2, that buyer is €0.75 better off than before. This transaction creates an extra €1 of economic surplus out of thin air!

Note that none of the other buyers or sellers is harmed by this transaction. Thus milk selling for only €1 per litre cannot be efficient. As Exercise 6.1 illustrates, there was nothing special about the price of €1 per litre. Indeed, if milk sells for *any* price below €1.50 per litre (the market equilibrium price), we can design a similar transaction, which means that selling milk for any price less than €1.50 per litre cannot be efficient.

Exercise 6.1

In Fig. 6.1, suppose that milk initially sells for 50 cents per litre. Describe a transaction that will create additional economic surplus for both buyer and seller without causing harm to anyone else.

If the price is above the equilibrium price a surplus-creating transaction can be described, too. Suppose, for example, that the current price is €2 per litre in the milk market shown in Fig. 6.1. At that price, we have excess supply of 2,000 litres per day (see Fig. 6.3). Suppose the most dissatisfied producer sells a litre of milk for €1.75 to the buyer who values it most highly. This buyer, who would have been willing to pay €2, will be €0.25 better off than before. Likewise the producer, who would have been willing to sell milk for as little as €1 per litre (the marginal cost of production at 2,000 litres per day), will be €0.75 better off than before. As when the price was €1 per litre, the new transaction creates €1 of additional economic surplus without harming any other buyer or seller. Since we could design a similar surplus-enhancing transaction at any price above the equilibrium level, selling milk for more than €1.50 per litre cannot be efficient.

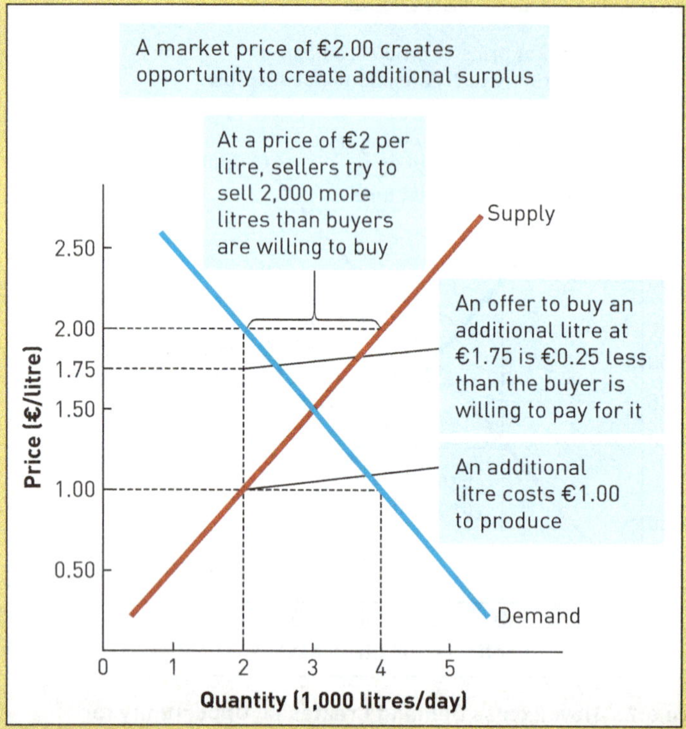

Figure 6.3 How Excess Supply Creates an Opportunity for a Surplus-enhancing Transaction

At a market price of €2 per litre, dissatisfied sellers can produce an additional litre of milk at a cost of only €1, which is €1 less than a buyer would be willing to pay for it. If the buyer pays the seller €1.75 for an extra litre, the buyer gains an economic surplus of €0.25 and the seller gains an economic surplus of €0.75.

The vertical interpretations of the supply and demand curves thus make it clear why only the equilibrium price in a market can be efficient. *When the price realised is either higher or lower than the equilibrium price, the quantity exchanged in the market will always be lower than the equilibrium quantity.*

If the price is below equilibrium, the quantity sold will be the amount that *sellers offer*. The market is supply constrained. If the price is above equilibrium, the quantity sold will be the amount that *buyers wish to buy*. The market is demand constrained. In either case, the value of an extra unit to buyers, must be larger than the marginal cost of producing that unit.

So the market equilibrium price is the only price at which buyers and sellers cannot design a surplus-enhancing transaction. The market equilibrium price leads, in other words, to the largest possible total economic surplus. In this specific, limited sense, free markets are said to produce and distribute goods and services efficiently.

Actually, to claim that the observed market equilibrium in terms of prices and quantities is always efficient even in this limited sense is an overstatement. The claim holds only if the following conditions are met.

1. **Buyers and sellers are well informed** If people do not know the quality of a good or service they may find it difficult to evaluate the price they are prepared to pay for it.
2. **Markets are perfectly competitive** A monopolist can use market power to drive a wedge between marginal cost and price, and hence between the cost of producing a good and what people are prepared to pay for it.
3. **The demand and supply curves satisfy certain other restrictions** For example, market equilibrium will not be efficient if the individual marginal cost curves that add up to the market supply curve fail to include all relevant costs of producing the product. Thus, as we saw in Chapter 3, the true cost of expanding output will be higher than indicated by the market supply curve if production generates pollution that harms others. The equilibrium output will then be inefficiently large and the equilibrium price inefficiently low. Likewise, market equilibrium will not be efficient if the individual demand curves that make up the market demand curve do not capture all the relevant benefits of buying additional units of the product. For instance, if a home owner's willingness to pay for ornamental shrubs is based only on the enjoyment she herself gains from them, and not on any benefits that may accrue to her neighbours, the market demand curve for shrubs will understate their value to the neighbourhood. The equilibrium quantity of ornamental shrubs will be inefficiently small, and the market price for shrubs will be inefficiently low.

4. **Transaction costs are low** For example, high tax costs on buying and selling houses can result in demand for existing housing space not being equal to supply; high travel costs can result in excess demand for labour in one part of a city and excess supply persisting in another.

We shall take up such market imperfections in greater detail in Chapters 8–11. For now, we shall confine our attention to perfectly competitive markets whose demand curves capture all relevant benefits and whose supply curves capture all relevant costs. For such goods, market equilibrium will always be efficient in the limited sense described earlier.

EFFICIENCY IS NOT THE ONLY GOAL

Markets, then, are efficient in so far as that they maximise economic surplus. However, 'efficient' does not mean the same thing as 'good'. For example, the market for milk may be in equilibrium at a price of €1.50 per litre, yet many poor families may be unable to afford milk for their children at that price.

Efficiency is a concept that is based on predetermined attributes of buyers and sellers – their incomes, tastes, abilities, knowledge, and so on. Through the combined effects of individual cost–benefit decisions, these attributes give rise to the supply and demand curves for each good produced in an economy. If we are concerned about inequality in the distribution of attributes such as income, we should not be surprised to discover that markets, while efficient, do not always yield the outcomes we like.

The claim that equilibrium in the market for milk is efficient means simply that, *taking people's incomes as given*, the resulting allocation of milk cannot be altered so as to help some people without at the same time harming others.

To this a critic of the market system might respond, 'So what?' Imposing costs on others may be justified if doing so will help those with sufficiently important unmet demands. For example, most people would prefer to provide some funding out of taxes to provide housing for the homeless rather than let the homeless freeze to death.

The trouble is that concern for the outcome for the poor can result in unnecessary costs of meeting their needs. For example, suppose the price of central heating oil was frozen by decree after a rise in the price of crude oil because of the implications of higher heating costs in winter for poor families. To non-economists, price controls might have been justified in the name of social justice.

But the economists' concept of market efficiency makes it clear that there *must* be a better alternative policy. Price controls on oil prevent the market from reaching equilibrium, and that means forgoing transactions that would benefit some people without harming others. It would have been more efficient to allow heating oil prices to rise, but to give those on low incomes money with which to buy it, rather than reduce prices for everyone and induce a shortage because demand exceeded supply (in which case there is no reason to believe that the oil would have gone to poorer families).

WHY EFFICIENCY SHOULD BE THE FIRST GOAL

Efficiency is important not because it is a desirable end in itself, but because it enables us to achieve all our other goals to the fullest possible extent. Whenever a market is out of equilibrium, it is always possible to generate additional economic surplus. To gain additional economic surplus is to gain more of the resources we need to do the things we want to do. Whenever any market is out of equilibrium, there is *waste*, and waste is always a bad thing.

RECAP

Equilibrium and efficiency

When a market is not in equilibrium the quantity exchanged on the market is always *less than the equilibrium level*. At such a quantity, a transaction can always be made in which both buyer and seller benefit from the exchange of an additional unit of output. A market in equilibrium is said to be efficient, or Pareto efficient, meaning that no reallocation is possible that will benefit some people without harming others. Total economic surplus in a market is maximised when exchange occurs at the equilibrium price. But the fact that equilibrium is 'efficient' in this sense does not mean that it is 'good'. All markets can be in equilibrium, yet many people may lack sufficient income to buy even basic goods and services. Still, permitting markets to reach equilibrium is important, because when economic surplus is maximised, it is possible to pursue every goal more fully.

THE COST OF PREVENTING PRICE ADJUSTMENTS

PRICE CEILINGS

The example above of the impact of a heating oil freeze reflects what actually happened in the US in 1979. Similar attempts to prevent oil markets from clearing efficiently occurred in many other countries at the same time. Example 6.1 illustrates graphically why imposing a price ceiling on heating oil, though well intended, was a bad idea.

Example 6.1 How much waste does a price ceiling on heating oil cause?

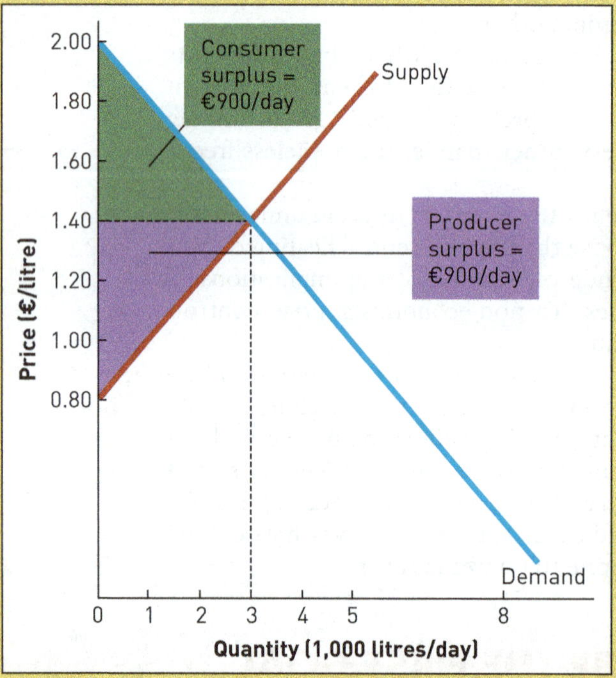

Figure 6.4 Economic Surplus in an Unregulated Market for Home Heating Oil

For the supply and demand curves shown, the equilibrium price of home heating oil is €1.40 per litre, and the equilibrium quantity is 3,000 litres per day. Consumer surplus is the area of the upper shaded triangle (€900 per day). Producer surplus is the area of the lower shaded triangle (also €900 per day).

Suppose the demand and supply curves for home heating oil are as shown in Fig. 6.4, in which the equilibrium price is €1.40 per litre. Legislators set the maximum price at €1 per litre. How much lost economic surplus does this policy cost society?

First, calculate total economic surplus without price controls. Without price control 3,000 litres per day will be sold at a price of €1.40 per litre. In Fig. 6.4, the economic surplus received by buyers is the area of the upper shaded triangle. Since the height of this triangle is €0.60 per litre, and its base is 3,000 litres per day, its area is equal to (1/2)(3,000 litres/day)(€0.60/litre) = €900 per day. The economic surplus received by producers is the area of the lower shaded triangle. Since this triangle also has an area of €900 per day, total economic surplus in this market will be €1,800 per day.

If the price of heating oil is fixed at €1 per litre, only 1,000 litres per day will be sold. The total economic surplus will be reduced by the area of the green triangle in Fig. 6.5. The base of this triangle is €0.80 per litre, and its height is 2,000 litres per day. Its area is (1/2)(2,000 litres/day)(€0.80/litre) = €800 per day. Producer surplus falls from €900 per day in the unregulated market to the area of the lower shaded triangle, or (1/2)(1,000 litres/day)(€0.20/litre) = €100 per day, a loss of €800 per day. With these demand and supply curves and this regulated price the loss in total economic surplus is equal to the loss in producer surplus, while consumer surplus is unchanged. The area of upper shaded area in Fig. 6.5 is again €900 per day. (**Hint:** To compute this area in Fig. 6.5, first split it into a rectangle and a triangle.)

In this example fixing the price at €1 wastes €800 of producer surplus per day without creating any additional surplus for consumers!

Exercise 6.2

In Example 6.1, by how much would total economic surplus have been reduced if the price ceiling had been set not at €1 but at €1.20 per litre?

Efficiency

In reality, the reduction in total economic surplus shown in Fig. 6.5 is likely to be an underestimate of the waste caused by attempts to hold price below its equilibrium level. First, the analysis assumes that each of the 1,000 litres per day that are sold in this market will end up in the hands of the consumers who value them most, those with reservation prices are above €1.80 per litre. But since all buyers with reservation prices above €1 per litre will queue to buy at the fixed price, much of the oil actually sold is likely to go to buyers whose reservation prices are below €1.80. Suppose a buyer whose reservation price was €1.50 per litre joins the queue to buy oil just ahead of a buyer whose reservation price was €1.90 per litre. If both have a 20-litre tank to fill, and if the first buyer got the last of the day's available oil, then total surplus would be smaller by €8 that day than if the oil had gone to the second buyer.

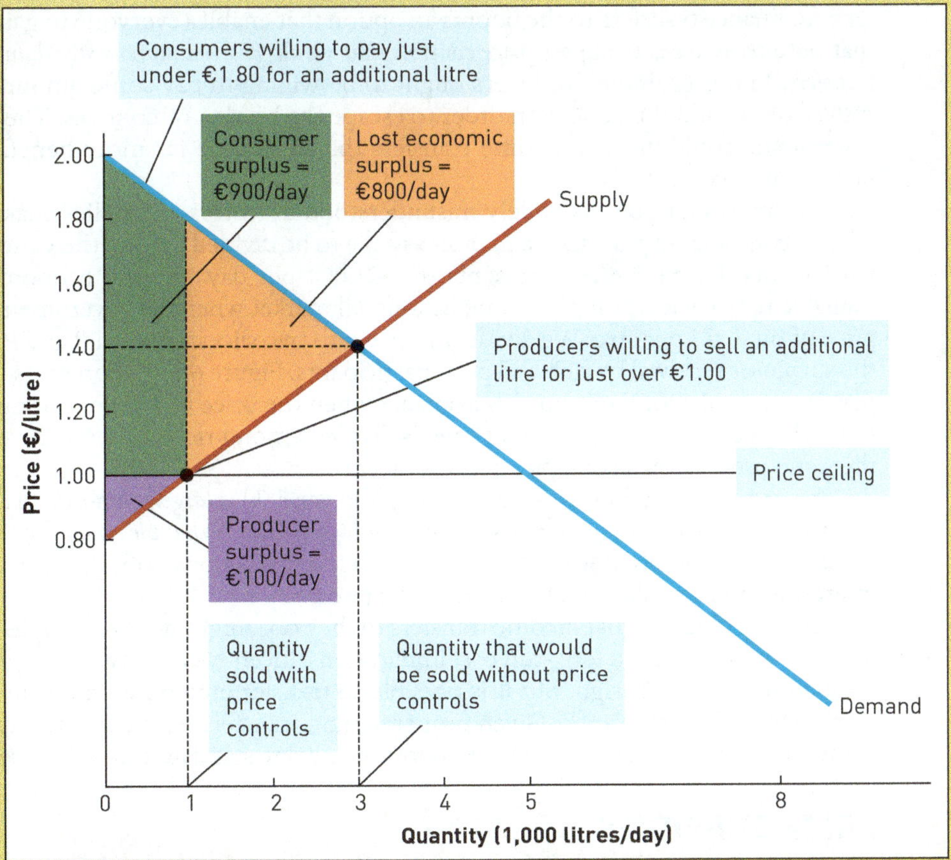

Figure 6.5 The Waste Caused by Price Controls

By limiting output in the home heating oil market to 1,000 litres per day, price controls cause a loss in economic surplus of €800 per day (area of the orange triangle).

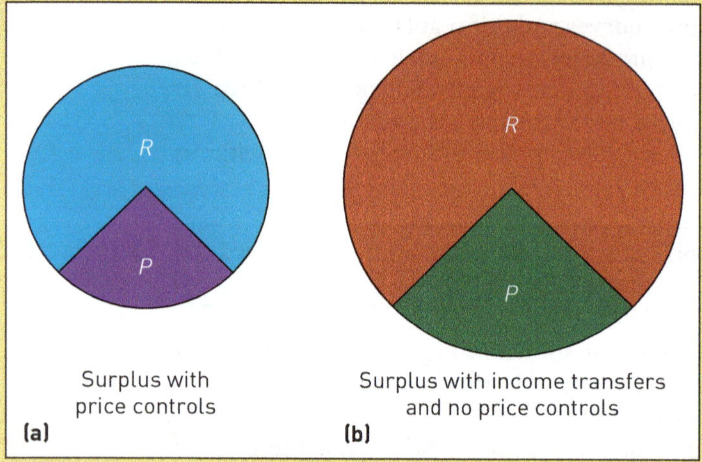

Figure 6.6 When the 'Pie' is Larger, Everyone Can Have a Bigger Slice

Any policy that reduces total economic surplus is a missed opportunity to make everyone better off.

A second reason that the reduction in surplus shown in Fig. 6.5 is likely to be an underestimate is that shortages typically prompt buyers to take costly actions to enhance their chances of being served. For example, if the heating oil distributor begins selling its available supplies at 6.00 am, many buyers may arrive several hours early to ensure a place near the front of the queue. Time in the queue is a cost to consumers that is wasted (not received by the seller).

Although price ceilings reduce total economic surplus, their defenders might argue that controls are justified because they enable at least *some* low-income families to buy heating oil at affordable prices. Yes, but the same objective could have been accomplished in a much less costly way – namely, by giving the poor more income with which to buy heating oil.

Given the cost (lost surplus) to producers and consumers, asking them to pay higher taxes to finance transfers to the poor is an option that enables everyone to gain provided that *the alternative is to impose price controls that would be even more costly than the income transfers*. In our example producers ought to be willing to pay some amount less than €800 a day in additional taxes in order to escape the burden of controls. The additional tax revenue could finance income transfers that would be far more beneficial to the poor than price controls.

This important point is widely misunderstood by voters and policy makers. Think of the economic surplus from a market as a pie to be divided among the various market participants. Figure 6.6(a) represents the €1,000 per day of total economic surplus available to participants in the home heating oil market when the government limits the price of oil to €1 per litre. We divide this 'pie' into two slices, labelled *R* and *P*, to denote the surpluses received by rich and poor participants. Figure 6.6(b) represents the €1,800 per day of total economic surplus available when the price of home heating oil is free to reach its equilibrium level. This 'pie' is divided among rich and poor participants in the same proportion as the 'pie' in the panel (a).

The important point is this: *because the pie in panel (b) is larger, both rich and poor participants in the home heating oil market can get a bigger slice of the 'pie' than they would have had under price controls*. Rather than tinker with the market price of oil, it is in everyone's interest to transfer additional income to the poor.

It may be objected that income transfers to the poor might weaken people's incentive to work, with significant long-run cost implications. Incentive issues are serious problems for income transfer design, but it is possible to transfer income without undermining work incentives significantly. Given proper design, transferring income to the poor will always be more efficient than trying to boost their living standard through price controls.

PRICE SUBSIDIES

Sometimes governments try to assist low-income consumers by subsidising the prices of 'essential' goods and services. Fuel and energy subsidies are fairly commonly used for this purpose, and in the past food subsidies were often used. Housing subsidies are found in nearly all countries. But as Example 6.2 illustrates, such subsidies are like price ceilings in that they reduce total economic surplus.

By how much do subsidies reduce total economic surplus in the market for oil and gas? **Example 6.2**

A small country produces hydrocarbons and can buy or sell the output at world prices. The price per tonne on world markets is €500. The domestic demand for hydrocarbons at world prices (100,000 tonnes per month) is less than total output (120,000 tonnes per month) and the country exports the balance (20,000 tonnes per month).

The government, concerned for its popular support among the less well off, introduces a 40 per cent subsidy to lower the price to domestic purchasers to €300 per tonne. What will be the impact of the subsidy on economic surplus?

In Figure 6.7 the cost of the subsidy in taxes is €26 million (€200 × 300,000). The subsidy reduces the price to domestic users from €500 to €300, and domestic consumer demand rises from 100,000 tonnes a month to 130,000 tonnes a month. The hydrocarbon producers divert product from exports to the domestic market, since they receive the world price of €500 either way. This supplies 20,000 tonnes to meet increased demand. The balance comes from imports, 10,000 tonnes per month. The marginal cost to the economy is €500 per tonne. This is what the hydrocarbons could fetch on world markets, and is the opportunity cost of every tonne of fuel produced domestically and consumed. It is also the cost of every tonne imported. The extra fuel consumed costs €30,000 × 500 or €15 million; the value to consumers of the extra fuel consumed is €(30,000 × 200) × 1/2 plus € (30,000 × 300), or €12 million in total. The difference between cost and benefit, €3 million, is the net loss, the loss of surplus. The mechanism for realising this loss is the change in the country's trade position. Its hydrocarbon exports of 20,000 tonnes per month have been diverted to domestic consumption, while it now also imports 10,000 tonnes per month. This means a trade deficit of €15 million per month.

Another way to see why the subsidy reduces total economic surplus by this amount is to note that total economic surplus is maximised at 100,000 tonnes per month, the quantity for which the marginal buyer's reservation price is equal to marginal cost, and that the subsidy induces additional consumption of 30,000 tonnes per month. Each additional tonne has a marginal cost of €500 but is worth less than that to the buyers (as indicated by the fact that the vertical coordinate of the demand curve lies below €500 for consumption beyond 100,000 tonnes). As monthly consumption expands from 100,000 tonnes to 130,000 tonnes per month, the cumulative difference between the marginal cost of oil and its value to buyers is the area of the orange triangle in Fig. 6.7, which is €3 million per month. This reduction in economic surplus constitutes pure waste – no different, from the perspective of participants in this market, from someone siphoning that much cash out of their bank account each month and throwing it into a bonfire.

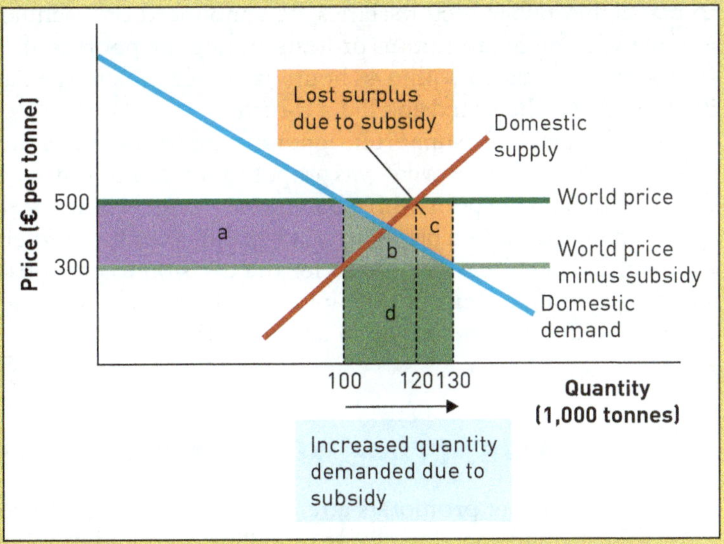

Figure 6.7 The impact on total surplus of a subsidy to domestic consumers

The total cost of the extra consumption is €15 million, while the value to consumers is only €12 million.

Exercise 6.3 How much total economic surplus would have been lost if the subsidy had been set at €100 per tonne instead of €200?

Compared with a subsidy, a much better policy would be to give low-income people some additional income and then let them purchase fuel on the open market. Subsidy advocates who complain that taxpayers would be unwilling to give low-income people income transfers must be asked to explain why people would be willing to tolerate subsidies, which are so much more costly than income transfers. Logically, if voters are willing to support subsidies, they should be even more eager to support income transfers to low-income persons.

This is not to say that the poor reap no benefit at all from subsidies. Since they get to buy fuel at lower prices and since the subsidy programme is financed by taxes collected primarily from middle- and upper-income families, poor families probably come out ahead on balance. *The point is that, for the same expense, we could do much more to help the poor.* Their problem is that they have too little income. The simplest and best solution is not to try to peg the prices of the goods they and others buy below equilibrium levels, but rather to give them some additional money.

Efficiency

Economic Naturalist 6.1

How does one of the world's poorest countries impoverish itself by subsidising fuel oil prices?

The example outlined above in which the consequences of subsidies are explained may seem far-fetched. However, an economic naturalist who reads the *Wall Street Journal* will not be surprised. Bolivia is one of the world's poorest countries, and in 2010 was heavily dependent on the regime in Venezuela, where President Hugo Chavez, an extreme left politician, was an ideological ally of the Bolivian President, Evo Morales. To bolster support among the poorer voters, Morales had introduced and maintained a 40 per cent-plus subsidy on fuel oil. The tax cost of this exercise (the areas $a + b + c$ in Fig. 6.7) was about 2 per cent of GDP. From being an exporter of hydrocarbons, Bolivia had become a fuel importer under the subsidy regime. Unable to meet this cost and at the same time to pay higher public sector salaries, he announced on 1 January 2011 that the subsidies were to be eliminated. This led to riotous protests among the poorest of Bolivia's population, and Morales had to reverse his decision within 48 hours as people took to the barricades. 'I pledge to govern by obeying the people', he stated and did a U-turn.

Were his erstwhile supporters ignorant and irrational, in the light of what we have learned about subsidies? Probably not: what was proposed was not to replace a wasteful and ineffective mechanism designed to help the poor with a better one along the lines we have suggested. Instead, a shortfall in tax revenues threatened his ability to keep public sector workers on side by increasing the public sector wage bill. This was the reason for the decision to cut subsidies. That is, the proposal was motivated by a desire to improve the lot of the better off by reducing subsidies, not a desire to use the money saved to do a better job in dealing with poverty.

Source: *WSJ Online edition*, 3 January 2011.

FIRST-COME, FIRST-SERVED POLICIES

Event promoters attempt to protect access by low-income purchasers to rock concerts and sporting events by selling a limited number of tickets below the market-clearing price on a first-come, first-served basis to people who are prepared to queue to get them.[1]

[1] That is certainly the stated reason. We shall see in Chapter 8, however, when dealing with pricing strategies of firms with market power, that this form of discounting may also be a discriminatory mechanism that may be expected to increase the sellers' revenues.

At one time the commercial airline industry used the first-come, first-served allocation method, to ration seats on overbooked flights. Flight overbooking is endemic to the industry. Many airlines have routinely accepted more reservations for their flights than there are seats on those flights. Most of the time, this practice causes no difficulty, because many reservation holders don't show up to claim their seats. Indeed, if airlines did not overbook their flights, most flights would take off with many more empty seats, forcing airlines to charge higher ticket prices to cover their costs.

The only real difficulty is that, every so often, more people actually do show up for a flight than there are seats on the plane. Until the late 1970s (i.e., before deregulation increased competition), US airlines dealt with this problem by boarding passengers on a first-come, first-served basis. For example, if 120 people showed up for a flight with 110 seats, the last 10 to arrive were 'bumped', or forced to wait for the next available flight.

The 'bumped' passengers often complained bitterly, and no wonder, since many of them ended up missing important business meetings or family events.

Economic Naturalist 6.2
How consumer protection damages markets: the EU Commission and overbooked flights

Despite being committed to a market economy, the European Union has a knack of intervening in markets to try to improve them, and ends up doing the opposite. Consider the announcement in 2004 of regulations requiring that airlines in Europe would have to pay fixed compensation amounts to passengers who were 'bumped' because the airlines had over-booked their flights. It sounds reasonable, but on reflection was unnecessary and tended to raise costs for passengers. Why?

Buying them back meant an increase in consumer surplus. The airlines were better off, too. They preferred to overbook by a small margin, because this enabled them to offer lower fares and fill their planes, which was revealed by the decision to do so to be more profitable, even after paying expected compensation, than flying with empty seats because of cancellations. So producer surplus was increased, too.

The Brussels bureaucrats knew better, of course. EU Transport Commissioner Loyola de Palacio introduced the payments as necessary to compensate the estimated 250,000 passengers bumped annually. 'Too many Europeans have a bad surprise when checking in for their flight. We want to protect passengers against cancellations of flights for which operators are responsible,' she announced in a statement. 'Strengthening the rights of passengers will help restore their confidence in air travel,' she said. So, fixed payments, based on the delay and length of the flight, were introduced, amounting at the top end to €1,500 euros. In the US, interestingly, airlines rarely found it necessary to offer over $200 to sort out the problem. It was a serious deterrent to overbooking, all right, but precisely because it was such a deterrent, airlines had to manage booking in such a way as to expect to fly with empty seats . . . or find another ploy, such as closing flights a longer time before departure to take advantage of people who had booked but had been delayed in getting to the airport . . . which well-known, low-fare airline has a 40-minute closing time before departure when the turnaround for the plane averages 25 minutes, and which is enforced even if the flight is delayed?

The first-come, first-served policy gives little weight to the interests of passengers with pressing reasons for arriving at their destination on time. Such passengers can sometimes avoid losing their seats by showing up early, but passengers coming in on connecting flights cannot control when they arrive. The cost of showing up early is likely to be highest for precisely those people who place the highest value on not missing a flight (such as business executives, whose opportunity cost of waiting in airports is high). This value is their willingness to pay to get on the overbooked flight.

Start with 37 ticket-holding passengers turning up for a flight on which there are 33 seats. One way or another, four people will not be accommodated on the flight. Bumping is a solution, but a very inefficient one, as we shall see. If Matthew, a wealthy banker trying to get home for a birthday party, would pay €100 to get on the flight while Stephanie, a penniless student who is not pressed for time, values getting on this flight at only €10, there is 'cash on the table'. If they can't trade and Stephanie, who arrived earlier, boards while Michael waits, there is a loss of consumer surplus of €90.

How costly is bumping? To establish this we could ask all the ticket holders, 'What is the most you would be willing to pay to fly now rather than wait?' Suppose that the person who is most willing to pay would pay up to €100 rather than miss the flight; that the person second-most willing to pay would pay up to €97; that the person third-most willing to pay would pay up to €94; and so on. With this information we can work out the average reservation price for the 37, say €50. Given the difficulty of controlling airport arrival times, the passengers who get 'bumped' under the first-come, first-served policy are not likely to differ systematically from others with respect to their reservation price for not missing the flight. On average, then, the total cost imposed on the four 'bumped' passengers would be four times the average reservation price of €50, or €200. As far as those four passengers are concerned, that total is a pure loss of consumer surplus.

If we could organise a 'market', it should be possible to arrange for the highest-value passengers to compensate the lowest-value passengers for agreeing to wait and take a later flight. In principle, it is obviously possible to identify the highest-value ticket holders and establish a market price for boarding that will equate the supply of seats to the demand for those seats, with the four highest-value people paying/compensating/bribing (whichever you like) the four lowest-value ticket holders to wait for the next flight. If this happens, surplus is maximised and there is no 'cash left on the table'. The trouble, of course, is that organising this market is time-consuming and costly, and we need a quick solution given that the plane will depart in ten minutes.

Organising the market is costly. So is bumping. Is there a simpler way that will deliver an efficient outcome? The answer is yes. All the airline has to do is to tell everyone the plane is overbooked and offer a price, say €11, for someone to wait: Stephanie will step forward. Maybe some else will, too, or maybe not. If four haven't volunteered, the airline then offers €12 and so on until it gets four takers. All four are paid the amount paid to the last accepting ticket holder. The problem is solved, and the 33 seats have been allocated to the 33 highest-value users. Surplus is maximised. That's what was adopted as a mechanism in the US . . . and was rejected by the EU Commission.

The airline loses, of course, because Michael does not pay Stephanie or one of the others for waiting. But since by definition all its customers are happy, it can now safely overbook (a bit, at least, since it has to expect some compensation payments when it does so) and fly with every seat filled, which enables it to be more cost competitive. Everyone wins. The compensation policy is more efficient than the first-come, first-served policy because it establishes a market for a scarce resource that would otherwise be allocated by non-market means.

Equilibrium

RECAP

The cost of blocking price adjustments

In an effort to increase the economic welfare of disadvantaged consumers, governments often implement policies that attempt to prevent markets from reaching equilibrium. Price ceilings and subsidies attempt to make housing and other basic goods more affordable for poor families. Private organisations also implement policies that prevent markets from reaching equilibrium, such as allocation on a first-come, first-served basis. Such policies always *reduce total economic surplus* relative to the alternative of letting prices seek their equilibrium levels. It is always possible to design alternative policies under which rich and poor alike fare better.

MARGINAL COST PRICING OF PUBLIC SERVICES

The largest possible total economic surplus is achieved in private markets when goods are exchanged at equilibrium prices, where the value of the last unit to the buyer is exactly equal to the seller's marginal cost of producing it. Suppose that the government has decided to become the provider of a good or service, such as water or electricity. If the government's goal is to maximise the resulting total economic surplus, how much should it charge its customers? The theory of *market exchange*, normally applied to perfectly competitive firms that can sell any quantity they choose at a constant market price, helps to answer this question. Prices should reflect marginal cost. The difficulty initially lies in identifying and measuring marginal cost of supplying electricity.

In this example, we assume that environmental costs have been correctly factored into generating costs (usually by using a carbon charge on electricity generation using fossil fuels).

What is the marginal cost of electricity?

Example 6.3

The answer to this question is: it depends on who is using it and when it is used as well as the cost of producing it. The reason for this is that for all practical purposes it is impossible (or extremely expensive, which, commercially, means impossible) to store electricity with today's technology. If it were as easy to store electricity commercially as it is to store cornflakes, the answer would be simple: set price equal to marginal cost, while using the generation technology that offers the lowest marginal cost.

The storage issue is critical to analysing marginal cost in the electricity market. Seasonally over the year, daily and weekly over the month, and hourly over the day the demand for electricity changes (see Fig. 6.8). It is very costly on the system as well as on users to ration power to users when demand exceeds supply capacity at peak times and to eliminate excess demand. It is also difficult or impossible to persuade users to ration themselves by refraining from using electricity when the value to the user exceeds the price to be paid. The outcome, at a single price equal to marginal cost with the lowest-cost technology, is that either the capacity has to suffice to meet peak demands (meaning excess capacity at other times) or unavoidable black-outs (or 'brown-outs', when

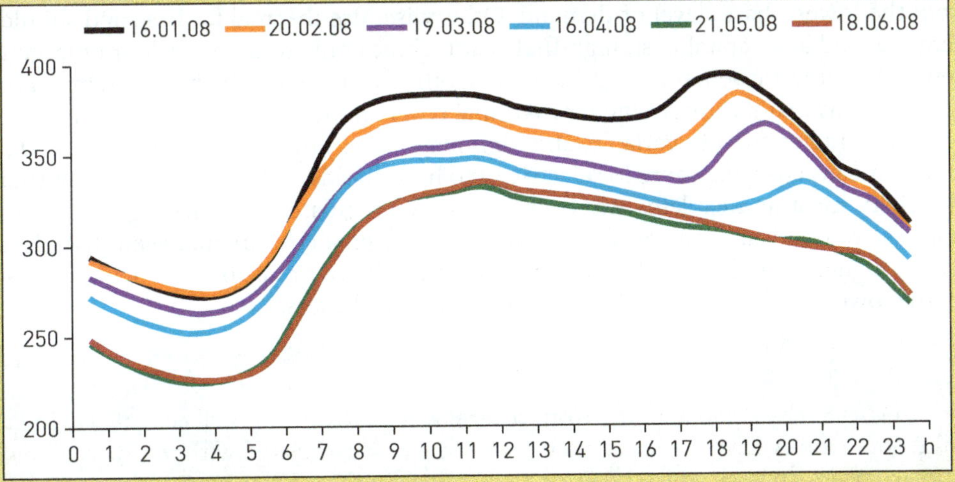

Figure 6.8 European Load Curves, January–June, 2008

Source: *ENTSOE Statistical Yearbook*, 2008. The curves show the loads across the European Network of Transmission Organisations for six days over a six month period. Output measured in GWH (million kwh). Note that this is after whatever load management instruments (pricing, rationing) were operational have had their effect on the actual consumption levels.

current is supplied, but at lower voltage than normal). That means either higher costs on average or rationing of supply to users, which raises costs relative to benefits for users, but somewhat unpredictably.

To see what the above implies for marginal cost, suppose all electricity in the country was generated from hydro-electric power stations. These are (a) very capital intensive, (b) fixed in number and capacity by the physical constraints of water flow, and (c) have marginal costs that are close to zero. How could the marginal cost rule be applied?

If the capacity installed is sufficient to meet demand on an annual basis in terms of units (kilowatt hours, kwh) while price equals marginal cost of producing power, there will be periods in the year in which excess demand is inevitable (and, of course, there is no money to meet capital costs!). So, let's look at marginal cost in another way, based on the idea of opportunity cost. In the case of cornflakes, a price covering marginal cost means that the consumer pays the cost to society of producing one more packet of cornflakes. That covers the resources used up to produce it, the value of which is the opportunity cost of those resources to society. But in this hydro-electric case the cost of my consuming a kwh of power at a point in time is the value of that kwh to another user. That is the opportunity cost of my consumption. This may be someone else at the same time, or me, or another user, at another time.[2] The logic of that is that the price I face should reflect the reservation price of the highest-value user for a unit of power, which may have little or nothing to do with the marginal cost of producing it as normally computed. Since reservation prices with a fixed capacity will be highest at times of peak demand, prices to users, too, should vary with what is called 'system load factor' (the percentage of installed capacity being used at any point of time). In principle if this is done properly actual usage can be kept within the capacity of the system to produce power.

The application of the marginal cost rule in electricity pricing is controversial because of what it implies for price structures. To show how this arises, suppose a bit more realistically that electricity can be generated from three technologies: nuclear power or coal-powered thermal generation or gas turbines. These have, respectively, lower capital costs per unit and higher marginal costs. Given the expected load curve it would be foolish to build sufficient nuclear or thermal capacity to meet peak demand. If nuclear marginal cost is lowest, but with very high capital costs, followed by thermal, with turbines the highest marginal cost technology, efficient generation implies installing nuclear capacity only as long as its total costs can be covered by the price available from the lowest (base) level of demand. Otherwise, use thermal for base and shoulder demand, and low-capital-cost, high-fuel-cost turbines only to meet peak or emergency demand. Domestic demand usage is normally the most variable by hour and by season, which means that it imposes higher marginal costs on the system. Hence, the marginal cost rule implies sharply variable, and high peak-time, prices for domestic users. That in turn means charging more for electricity to households at the times they want to use electricity most and explains why state-owned or regulated electricity generation, in response to political pressure, shies away from marginal cost pricing, even though this means higher overall costs of generation, with the higher price burden being imposed on the lower-marginal-cost industrial and commercial users.

RECAP

Marginal cost pricing of public services

When a good is provided by a public utility from several sources, the marginal cost of serving a customer is the opportunity cost of the product: that is, the cost associated with the *least efficient source in use* when more can be produced. When output is constrained by capacity, the opportunity cost will reflect the reservation price of the highest value user. A public utility should set price equal to marginal cost if its goal is to maximise economic surplus.

[2] The power station can hold water back in many circumstances if demand is low in order to release it when demand is high.

WHO PAYS A TAX IMPOSED ON SELLERS OF A GOOD?

Politicians seem to prefer to impose taxes on sellers (producers) than on buyers, (consumers) reflecting a feeling that (a) businesses can more easily afford to pay extra taxes, and (b) businesses don't vote. In terms of electoral behaviour, this may make sense, but in terms of economics it is less than rational. The burden of a tax collected from the sellers of a good need not fall exclusively on sellers. Suppose, for example, that a tax of €1 per kg is collected from potato farmers in the market whose demand and supply curves are shown as *D* and *S* in Fig. 6.9.

In this market the initial equilibrium price and quantity are €3 per kg and 3 million kg per month, respectively. To a farmer the imposition of a tax of €1 per kg is essentially the same as a €1 increase in the marginal cost of producing each kg of potatoes, and hence the tax results in an upward shift in the supply curve by €1 per kg.

The new equilibrium price (including the tax) will be €3.50, and the new equilibrium quantity will be 2.5 million kg per month. The net price per kg received by producers is one euro less than the price paid by the consumer, or €2.50. Even though the tax was collected entirely from potato sellers, the burden of the tax fell on both buyers and sellers – on buyers, because they pay €0.50 per kg more than before the tax, and on sellers because they receive €0.50 per kg less than before the tax.

The burden of the tax need not fall equally on buyers and sellers, as in the illustration just discussed. Indeed, a tax levied on sellers may end up being paid entirely by buyers.

Although the long-run supply curve shown in Fig. 6.10 is in one sense an extreme case (since its price elasticity is infinite), it is by no means an unrepresentative one. For, as we discussed in Chapter 3, the long-run supply curve will tend to be horizontal when it is possible to acquire more of all the necessary inputs at constant prices. As a first approximation, this can be accomplished for many – perhaps

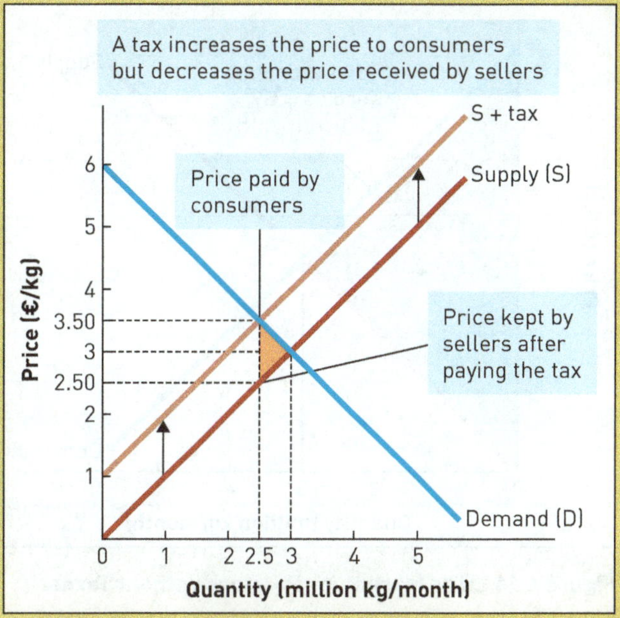

Figure 6.9 The Effect of a Tax on the Equilibrium Quantity and Price of Potatoes

With no tax, 3 million kg of potatoes are sold each month at a price of €3 per kg. With a tax of €1 per kg collected from sellers, consumers end up paying €3.50 per kg (including tax), while sellers receive only €2.50 per kg (net of tax). Equilibrium quantity falls from 3 million kg per month to 2.5 million.

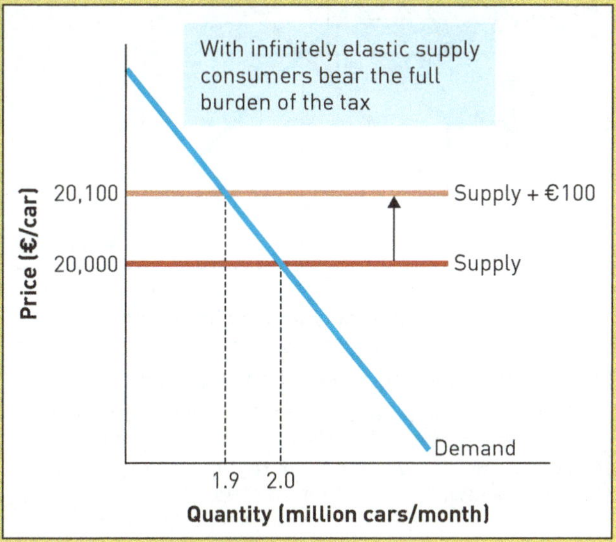

Figure 6.10 The Effect of a Tax on Sellers of a Good with Infinite Price Elasticity of Supply

When the supply curve for a good is perfectly elastic, the burden of a tax collected from sellers falls entirely on buyers.

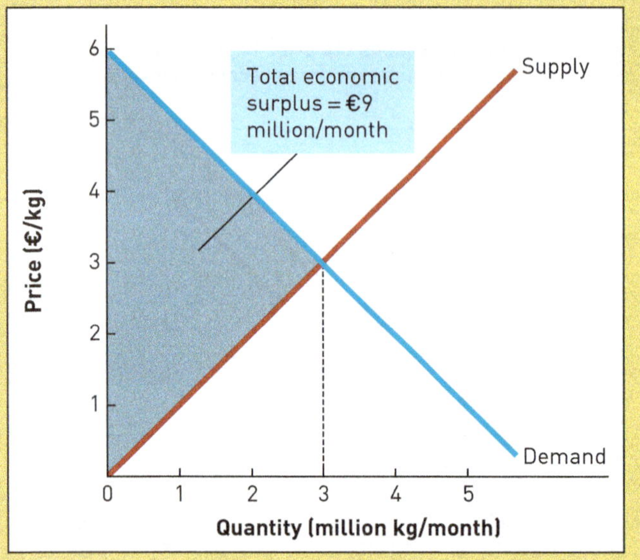

Figure 6.11 The Market for Potatoes without Taxes
Without taxes, total surplus in the potato market equals the area of the shaded triangle, €9 million per month.

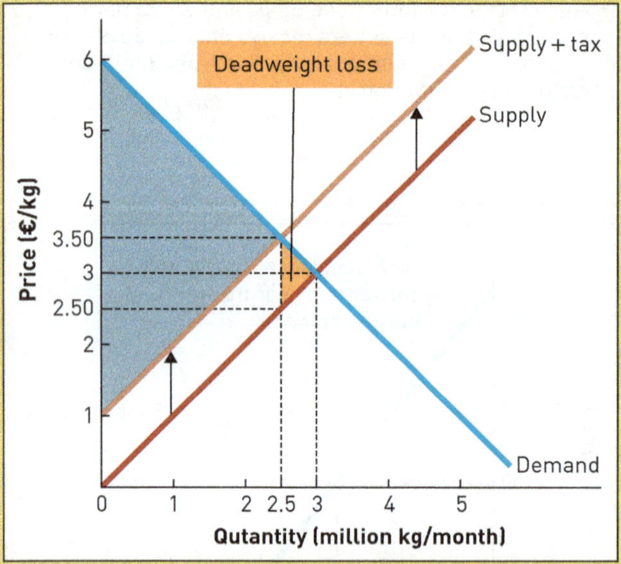

Figure 6.12 The Effect of a €1 per kg Tax on Potatoes
A €1 per kg tax on potatoes would cause an upward shift in the supply curve by €1. The sum of producer and consumer surplus would shrink to the area of the large shaded triangle, €6.25 million per month.

even most – goods and services in a typical economy.

For goods with perfectly elastic supply curves, the entire burden of any tax is borne by the buyer.[3] That is, the increase in the equilibrium price is exactly equal to the tax. For this empirically relevant case, then, there is a special irony in the common political practice of justifying taxes on business by saying that businesses have greater ability to pay than consumers. To the extent that supply curves are elastic, these taxes end up as higher prices to consumers.

HOW A TAX COLLECTED FROM A SELLER AFFECTS ECONOMIC SURPLUS

Perfectly competitive markets distribute goods and services efficiently if demand curves reflect all relevant benefits and supply curves reflect all relevant costs. Suppose a tax is imposed on sellers in such a market. What are the efficiency implications? The supply and demand curves of the potato market discussed in Fig. 6.9 are reproduced in Fig. 6.11. In the absence of a tax, 3 million kg of potatoes a month are sold in this market at a price of €3 per kg, and the resulting total economic surplus is €9 million per month (the area of the shaded triangle).

A tax of €1 per kg is imposed on potato sellers. At the new equilibrium the price of potatoes is €3.50 per kg (of which sellers receive €2.50, net of tax), and sales fall to 2.5 million kg of potatoes (see Fig. 6.12). The total economic surplus reaped by buyers and sellers in the potato market is the area of the shaded triangle shown in Fig. 6.12, which is €6.25 million or €2.75 million less than before.

This drop in surplus is a misleading measure of the economic cost because it fails to take account of the value of the *additional tax revenue collected*, which is equal to €2.5 million per month (€1 per kg on 2.5 million kg of potatoes). Suppose that the potato tax either replaces other tax revenues, or provides for services valued at €2.5 million per month. Then, although

[3] In the example given, the tax was collected from sellers. The same conclusions will apply when a tax is collected from buyers. It raises the supply price by the same amount.

buyers and sellers of potatoes lose €2.75 million per month in economic surplus, taxpayers as a whole enjoy a benefit of €2.5 million from lower taxes or from improved services. On balance, then, the net reduction in total economic surplus is only €0.25 million. This shown graphically as the small shaded triangle in Fig. 6.12. This loss in surplus is often described as the **deadweight loss** from the tax.

deadweight loss the reduction in total economic surplus that results from the adoption of a policy

Still, a loss in economic surplus, however small, is something that people would prefer to avoid, and taxes affecting work effort or goods or service prices cause deadweight loss and a net loss in output.

A tax reduces economic surplus because it distorts the basic cost–benefit calculation that would ordinarily guide efficient decisions about production and consumption. In the example just considered, the Cost–Benefit Principle tells us that we should expand potato production up to the point at which the benefit of the last kilogram of potatoes consumed (as measured by what buyers are willing to pay for it) equals the cost of producing it (as measured by the producers' marginal cost). That condition was satisfied in the potato market before the tax, but it is not satisfied once the tax is imposed. In Fig. 6.12, for example, note that when potato consumption is 2.5 million kg per month, the value of an additional kilogram of potatoes to consumers is €3.50, whereas the cost to producers is only €2.50, not including the tax. (The cost to producers, including the tax, is €3.50 per kg, but again we note that this tax is not a cost to society as a whole because it offsets other taxes that would otherwise have to be collected.)

Is a tax on potatoes necessarily 'bad'? (When economists say that a policy, such as a tax, is 'bad', they mean – or ought to mean – that it lowers total economic surplus.) To answer this question, we must first identify the *best alternative to taxing potatoes*. You may be tempted to say: 'Don't tax anything at all!' On a moment's reflection, however, you will realise that this is surely not the best option. No taxes means no public services! On balance, if taxing potatoes were the best way to avoid doing without highly valued public services, then a small deadweight loss in the potato market would be a small price indeed.

So the real question is whether there are other things we could tax that would be better than taxing potatoes. The problem with a tax on any activity is that if market incentives encourage people to pursue the 'right' amount of the activity (that is, the surplus-maximising amount), then a tax will encourage them to pursue too little of it. As economists have long recognised, this observation suggests that taxes will cause smaller deadweight losses if they are imposed on goods for which the equilibrium quantity is not highly sensitive to changes in production costs.

TAXES, ELASTICITY AND EFFICIENCY

Suppose that the government put a tax of 50 cents per kg on table salt. How would this affect the amount of salt you and others use? The demand for salt is highly inelastic with respect to price, because salt has few substitutes and occupies only a minuscule share in most family budgets. Because the imposition of a tax on table salt would not result in a significant reduction in the amount of it consumed, the deadweight loss from this tax would be relatively small. More generally, the deadweight loss from a per-unit tax imposed on the seller of a good will be smaller the smaller is the price elasticity of demand for the good.

Figure 6.13 illustrates how the deadweight loss from a tax declines as the demand for a good becomes less elastic with respect to price. In both Figures 6.13(a) and (b), the original supply and demand curves yield an equilibrium price of €2 per unit and an equilibrium quantity of 24 units per day. The deadweight loss from a tax of €1 per unit imposed on the good shown in Fig. 6.13(a) is the area of the shaded triangle in (a), which is €2.50 per day. The demand curve in Fig. 6.13(b), D_2, is less elastic at the

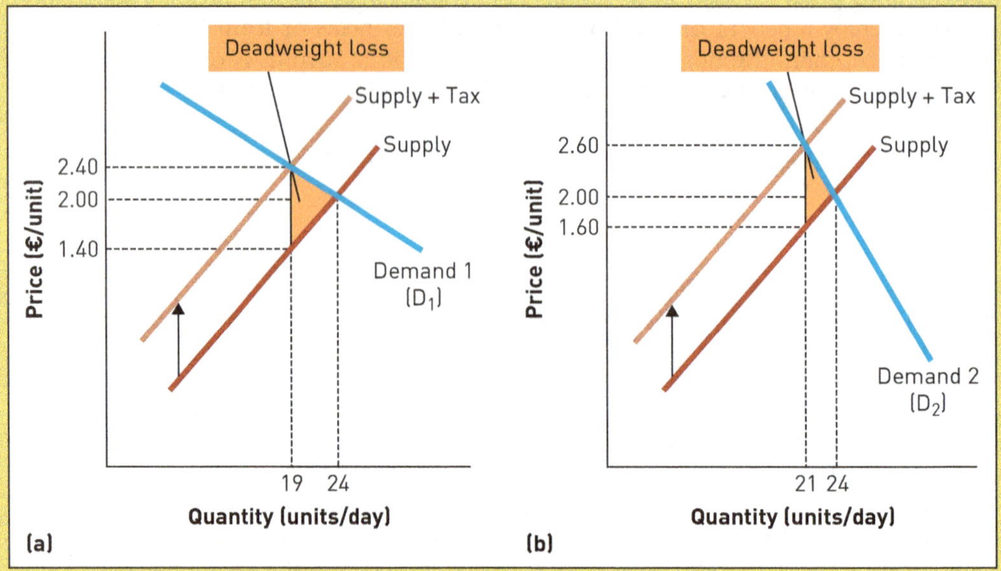

Figure 6.13 Elasticity of Demand and the Deadweight Loss from a Tax
At the equilibrium price and quantity, price elasticity of demand is smaller for the good shown in (b) than for the good shown in (a). The area of the deadweight loss triangle in (b), €1.50 per day, is smaller than the area of the deadweight loss triangle in (a), €2.50 per day.

equilibrium price of €2 than the demand curve in (a), D_1 (this follows from the fact that P/Q is the same in both cases, whereas 1/slope is smaller in (b)). The deadweight loss from the same €1 per unit tax imposed on the good in Fig. 6.13(b) is the area of the shaded triangle in (b), which is only €1.50 per day.

The reduction in equilibrium quantity that results from a tax on a good will also be smaller the smaller is the elasticity of supply of the good. In Fig. 6.14, for example, the original supply and demand curves for the markets portrayed in (a) and (b) yield an equilibrium price of €2 per unit and an equilibrium quantity of 72 units per day. The deadweight loss from a tax of €1 per unit imposed on the good shown in Fig. 6.14(a) is the area of the shaded triangle in (a), which is €6.50 per day. The supply curve in Fig. 6.14(b), S_2, is less elastic at the equilibrium price than the supply curve in (a), S_1 (again because P/Q is the same in both cases, whereas 1/slope is smaller in (b)). The deadweight loss from the same €1 per unit tax imposed on the good in Fig. 6.14(b) is the area of the shaded triangle in (b), which is only €4.50 per day.

The deadweight loss from a tax imposed on a good whose supply curve is perfectly inelastic will be zero. This explains why many economists continue to favour the tax advocated by Henry George in the nineteenth century. George proposed that all taxes on labour and goods be abolished and replaced by a *single tax on land*. Such a tax, he argued, would cause no significant loss in economic surplus because the supply of land is almost perfectly inelastic.

TAXES, EXTERNAL COSTS AND EFFICIENCY

Even more attractive than taxing land, from an efficiency standpoint, is taxing activities that people tend to *pursue to excess*. We have mentioned activities that generate environmental pollution as one example; in Chapter 11 we shall discuss others. Whereas a tax on land does not reduce economic surplus, a tax on pollution can actually increase total economic surplus. Taxes on activities that cause harm to others kill two birds with

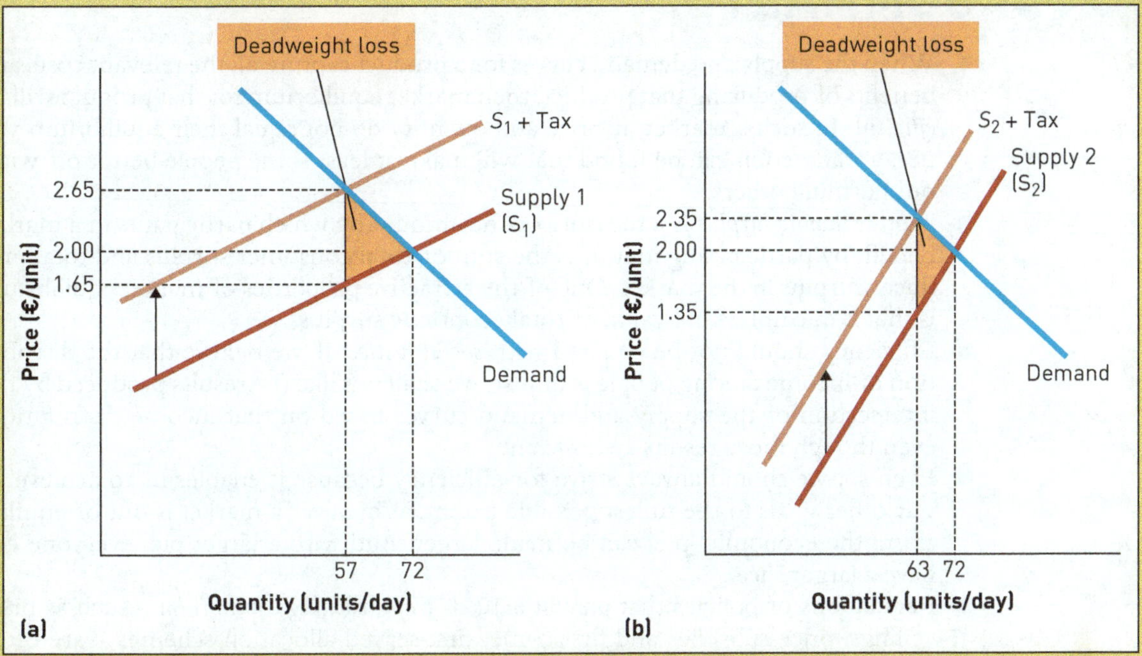

Figure 6.14 Elasticity of Supply and the Deadweight Loss from a Tax

At the equilibrium price and quantity, price elasticity of supply is smaller for the good shown in (b) than for the good shown in (a). The area of the deadweight loss triangle in (b), €4.50 per day, is smaller than the area of the deadweight loss triangle in (a), €6.50 per day.

one stone: they generate revenue to pay for useful public services and at the same time discourage people from pursuing the harmful activities. The notion that taxes always and everywhere constitute an obstacle to efficiency simply does not withstand careful scrutiny.

Efficiency

RECAP

Taxes and efficiency

A tax levied on the seller of a product has the same effect on equilibrium quantity and price as a rise in marginal cost equal to the amount of the tax. The burden of a tax imposed on sellers will generally be shared among both buyers and sellers. In the extreme case of a good whose elasticity of supply is infinite, the entire burden of the tax is borne by buyers.

A tax imposed on a product whose supply and demand curves embody all relevant costs and benefits associated with its production and use will result in a *deadweight loss* – a reduction in total economic surplus in the market for the taxed good. Such taxes may nonetheless be justified if the value of the public services financed by the tax outweighs this deadweight loss. In general, the deadweight loss from a tax on a good will be smaller the smaller are the good's price elasticities of supply and demand. Taxes on activities that generate harm to others may produce a net gain in economic surplus, even apart from the value of public services they finance.

SUMMARY

- When the supply and demand curves for a product capture all the relevant costs and benefits of producing that product, then market equilibrium for that product will be *efficient*. In such a market, if price and quantity do not equal their equilibrium values, a transaction can be found that will make at least some people better off without harming others.
- *Total economic surplus* is a measure of the amount by which participants in a market benefit by participating in it. It is the sum of total consumer surplus and total producer surplus in the market. One of the attractive properties of market equilibrium is that it maximises the value of total economic surplus.
- Efficiency should not be equated with *social justice*. If we believe that the distribution of income among people is unjust, we shall not like the results produced by the intersection of the supply and demand curves based on that income distribution, even though those results are efficient.
- Even so, we should always strive for efficiency because it enables us to achieve all our other goals to the fullest possible extent. Whenever a market is out of equilibrium, the economic 'pie' can be made larger. And with a larger pie, everyone can have a larger slice.
- Regulations or policies that *prevent markets from reaching equilibrium* – such as price ceilings, price subsidies and first-come, first-served allocation schemes – are often defended on the grounds that they help the poor. But such schemes reduce economic surplus, meaning that we can find alternatives under which both rich and poor would be better off. The main difficulty of the poor is that they have too little income. Rather than trying to control the prices of the goods they buy, we could do better by enacting policies that raise the incomes of the poor and then letting prices seek their equilibrium levels. Those who complain that the poor lack the political power to obtain such income transfers must explain why the poor have the power to impose regulations that are far more costly than income transfers.
- Even when a good is provided by a *public utility* rather than a private firm, the theory of competitive supply has important implications for how to provide the good most efficiently. The general rule is that a public utility maximises economic surplus by charging its customers the marginal cost of the goods it provides.
- Critics often complain that taxes make the economy less efficient. A tax will indeed reduce economic surplus if the supply and demand curves in the market for the taxed good reflect all the relevant costs and benefits of its production and consumption. But this decline in surplus may be more than offset by the increase in economic surplus made possible by public goods financed with the *proceeds of the tax*. The best taxes are imposed on activities that would otherwise be pursued to excess, such as activities that generate environmental pollution. Such taxes not only do not reduce economic surplus; they actually increase it.

REVIEW QUESTIONS

1. Why do economists emphasise efficiency as an important goal of public policy?
2. You are a politician considering how to vote on a policy that would increase the economic surplus of workers by €100 million per year but reduce the economic surplus of retirees by €1 million per year. What additional measure might you combine with the policy to ensure that the overall result is a better outcome for everyone?

3. Why does the loss in total economic surplus directly experienced by participants in the market for a good that is taxed overstate the overall loss in economic surplus that results from the tax?
4. Why is compensating volunteers to relinquish their seats on overbooked flights more efficient than a policy of first-come, first-served?
5. Why do price ceilings reduce economic surplus?

PROBLEMS

connect

Problems marked with an asterisk (*) are more difficult.

1. Suppose the weekly demand and supply curves for used DVDs in Brussels are as shown in the graph below. Calculate:
   a. the weekly consumer surplus
   b. the weekly producer surplus
   c. the maximum weekly amount that producers and consumers in Brussels would be willing to pay to be able to buy and sell used DVDs in any given week.

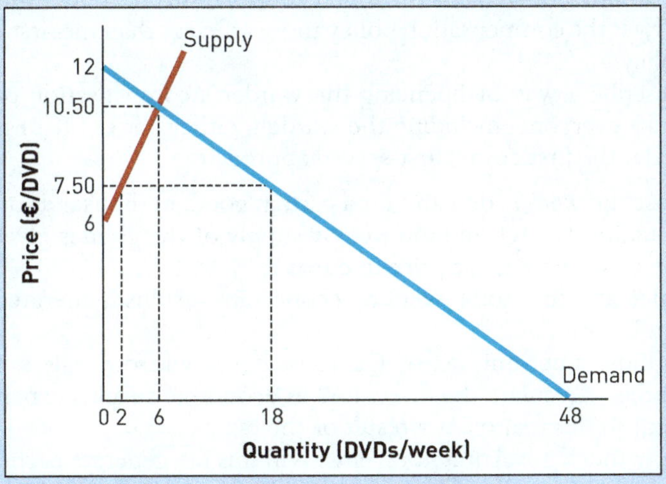

2. Refer to Problem 1. Suppose a coalition of students from a Brussels secondary school succeeds in persuading the local government to impose a price ceiling of €6.50 on used DVDs, on the grounds that local suppliers are taking advantage of teenagers by charging exorbitant prices.
   a. Calculate the weekly shortage of used DVDs that will result from this policy.
   b. Calculate the total economic surplus lost every week as a result of the price ceiling.
3. The Kubak crystal caves are renowned for their stalactites and stalagmites. The warden of the caves offers a tour each afternoon at 2 pm sharp. The caves can be shown to only four people per day without disturbing their fragile ecology. Occasionally, however, more than four people want to see the caves on the same day. The table below lists those who wanted to see the caves on 24 September 2005, together with their respective times of arrival and reservation prices for taking the tour that day.

	Arrival time	Reservation price (€)
Herman	1.48	20
Jon	1.50	14
Kate	1.53	30
Jack	1.56	15
Penny	1.57	40
Fran	1.59	12
Faith	2.00	17

a. If the tour is 'free' and the warden operates it on a first-come, first-served basis, what will the total consumer surplus be for the four people who get to go on the tour on that day?

b. Suppose the warden solicits volunteers to postpone their tour by offering increasing amounts of cash compensation until only four people still wish to see the caves that day. If he gives each volunteer the same compensation payment, how much money will he have to offer to generate the required number of volunteers? What is the total economic surplus under this policy?

c. Why is the compensation policy more efficient than the first-come, first-served policy?

d. Describe a way of financing the warden's compensation payments that will make everyone, including the warden, either better off or no worse off than under the first-come, first-served approach.

4. Suppose the weekly demand for a certain good, in thousands of units, is given by the equation $P = 8Q$, and the weekly supply of the good is given by the equation $P = 2 + Q$, where P is the price in euros.

a. Calculate the total weekly economic surplus generated at the market equilibrium.

b. Suppose a per-unit tax of €2, to be collected from sellers, is imposed in this market. Calculate the direct loss in economic surplus experienced by participants in this market as a result of the tax.

c. How much government revenue will this tax generate each week? If the revenue is used to offset other taxes paid by participants in this market, what will be their net reduction in total economic surplus?

5. Is a company's producer surplus the same as its profit? (**Hint:** A company's total cost is equal to the sum of all marginal costs incurred in producing its output, plus any fixed costs.)

6. In Dubrovnik, Croatia, citizens can get their electric power from two sources: a hydroelectric generator and a coal-fired steam generator. The hydroelectric generator can supply up to 100 units of power per day at a constant marginal cost of 1 cent per unit. The steam generator can supply any additional power that is needed at a constant marginal cost of 10 cents per unit. When electricity costs 10 cents per unit, residents of Dubrovnik demand 200 units per day.

a. Draw the marginal cost curve of electric power production in Dubrovnik.

b. How much should the city charge for electric power? Explain. Should it charge the same price for a family whose power comes from the hydroelectric generator as it does for a family whose power comes from the steam generator?

7. The municipal waterworks of Cortland draws water from two sources: an underground spring and a nearby lake. Water from the spring costs 2 cents per 100 litres to deliver, and the spring has a capacity of 1 million litres per day. Water from the lake costs 4 cents per 100 litres to deliver and is available in unlimited quantities. The demand for water in the summer months in Cortland is $P = 20\ 0.001Q$, where P is the price of water in cents per 100 litres, and Q is quantity demanded in hundreds of litres per day. The demand curve for water in the winter months is $P = 10\ 0.001Q$. If the waterworks wants to encourage efficient water use, how much should it charge for water in the summer months? In the winter months?

8.* Phil's demand curve for visits to a private-sector health clinic is given by $P = 48\ 8Q$, where P is the price per visit in euros and Q is the number of visits per season. The marginal cost of providing medical services at the clinic is €24 per visit. Phil has a choice between two health policies, *A* and *B*. Both policies cover all the costs of any serious illness from which Phil might suffer. Policy *A* also covers the cost of visits to the clinic, whereas policy *B* does not. Thus if Phil chooses policy *B*, he must pay €24 per visit to the clinic.

a. If the premiums the insurance company charges for policies *A* and *B* must cover their respective costs, by how much will the two premiums differ, and what will be the difference in Phil's total expenditure for medical care under the two policies?

b. Which policy will Phil choose?

c. What is the most Phil would be willing to pay for the right to continue buying that policy?

9.* The government of Islandia, a small island nation, imports heating oil at a price of €2 per litre and makes it available to citizens at a price of €1 per litre. If Islandians' demand curve for heating oil is given by $P = 6\ Q$, where P is the price per litre in euros and Q is the quantity in millions of litres per year, how much economic surplus is lost as a result of the government's policy?

10.* Refer to Problem 9. Suppose each of the 1 million Islandian households has the same demand curve for heating oil.

a. What is the household demand curve?

b. How much consumer surplus would each household lose if it had to pay €2 per litre instead of €1 per litre for heating oil, assuming that there were no other changes in the household budget?

c. With the money saved by not subsidising oil, by how much could the Islandian government afford to cut each family's annual taxes?

d. If the government abandoned its oil subsidy and implemented the tax cut, by how much would each family be better off?

e. How does the resulting total gain for the 1 million families compare with your calculation of the lost economic surplus in Problem 9?

Chapter 7

Profits, Entry and Exit: the Basis for the 'Invisible Hand'

I went into business for the money, and the art grew out of it. If people are disillusioned by that remark, I can't help it. It's the truth.
Charlie Chaplin

Learning objectives

After studying this chapter you should be able to:

1. Appreciate the role of profits, as the driving force for efficiency in a market economy, not a margin of exploitation;
2. Understand the difference between an economist's concept of profits and that of an accountant;
3. Explain the rationing as well as the allocative function of prices;
4. Understand how barriers to exit as well as to entry reduce economic efficiency;
5. Understand what is meant by the efficient markets hypothesis and its limitations.

Jobs, skills and services that were plentiful in big cities across Europe thirty or forty years ago have in many cases simply disappeared since then. Typing agencies and office printing firms are examples. So are hat shops and high street department stores in smaller towns. Employment has not fallen as these changes took effect. The reason is that other services and distribution methods have taken their place, from dog-walking to TM instruction, sushi bars to out-of-town shopping centres, either unknown or of little importance before the 1970s.

There has been an explosion in the choice of restaurants available in any big city, but the choice of bookshops has contracted sharply. Try to have your watch repaired today and you will find that watch-repair firms are few and far between. Similarly, it is hard in a modern European city to find a cobbler to mend shoes. In contrast, if you need immediate access to the internet for your laptop, Wi-Fi points abound.

The reasons for these changes are in some cases obvious. The PC has revolutionised document preparation, and electronic watches are cheap and disposable. Increased leisure and higher incomes have increased the demand for recreational services. Other changes, however, require deeper study to explain them.

However, what is of interest here is not the underlying cause of these changes, but what actually *happens to bring them about*. That is, the process whereby firms are set up, or disappear, or firms change what they do.

Driving these changes is the business owner's quest for profit. Businesses migrate to industries and locations in which profit opportunities abound, and desert those whose prospects appear bleak. In perhaps the most widely quoted passage from his landmark treatise, *The Wealth of Nations* (1776), Adam Smith wrote:

Incentives Matter

> It is not from the benevolence of the butcher, the brewer, or the baker that we expect our dinner, but from their regard of their own interest. We address ourselves not to their humanity, but to their self-love, and never talk to them of our necessities, but of their advantage.

Smith went on to argue that although the entrepreneur 'intends only his own gain', he is 'led by an invisible hand to promote an end which was no part of his intention'. As Smith saw it, even though self-interest is the prime mover of economic activity, the end result is an allocation of goods and services that serves society's collective interests remarkably well. If producers are offering 'too much' of one product and 'not enough' of another, profit opportunities immediately alert entrepreneurs to that fact and provide incentives for them to take remedial action. All the while, the system exerts relentless pressure on producers to hold the price of each good close to its cost of production – and, indeed, to reduce that cost in any ways possible.

The object of this chapter is to provide a deeper insight into the nature of the forces that guide the invisible hand. This involves confronting four questions.

1. What exactly does 'profit' mean, and how is it measured?
2. How does the pursuit of profit serve society's ends, as is asserted by economists who support the use of markets to allocate resources?
3. If competition holds price close to the cost of production, why do so many entrepreneurs become fabulously wealthy?
4. How does public policy affect economic welfare by limiting resource allocation changes?

THE CENTRAL ROLE OF ECONOMIC PROFIT

The economic theory of business behaviour is built on the assumption that the firm's goal is to *maximise its profit*. So we must be clear at the outset about what, exactly, 'profit' means.

THREE TYPES OF PROFIT

An economist has a different concept of profits from that of an accountant. The distinction between the two is important to understanding how the 'invisible hand' works.

Accountants define the annual profit of a business as the difference between the revenue it takes in and its **explicit costs** for the year, which are the actual payments the firm makes to its factors of production and other suppliers. Profit thus defined is called **accounting profit**:

> **explicit costs** the actual payments a firm makes to its factors of production and other suppliers
>
> **accounting profit** the difference between a firm's total revenue and its explicit costs
>
> **implicit costs** the opportunity costs of the resources supplied by the firm's owners

$$\text{Accounting profit} = \text{Total revenue} - \text{Explicit costs}$$

Accounting profit is the most familiar profit concept in everyday discourse. Companies use it when they provide statements about their profits in press releases or annual reports. Tax authorities use it to compute corporation tax liabilities.

Economists, by contrast, define profit as the difference between the firm's total revenue and its **implicit costs plus explicit costs**. Implicit costs refer to the resources supplied by the firm's owners even if no charge is made for them. They are the opportunity costs of all the resources used up by the firm's owners. Profit thus defined is called **economic profit**, in some cases **supernormal profit** or **excess profit**:

economic profit (or **supernormal profit** or **excess profit**) the difference between a firm's total revenue and the sum of its explicit and implicit costs

Economic profit = Total revenue − Explicit costs − Implicit costs

To illustrate the difference between accounting and economic profit, consider a firm with €400,000 in total annual revenue whose only explicit costs are workers' salaries of €250,000 per year. The owners of this firm have supplied machines and other capital equipment with a total resale value of €1 million. This firm's accounting profit, then, is the difference between its total revenue of €400,000 per year and its explicit costs of €250,000 per year, or €150,000 per year.

To calculate the firm's economic profit, we must first calculate the opportunity cost of the resources supplied by the firm's owners, *the equity capital of the firm*. Suppose that the current annual interest rate on savings accounts is 10 per cent. Instead of investing in capital equipment in the firm, they could have earned €100,000 per year interest by depositing their 1 million in a savings account. So the firm's economic profit is €400,000 per year − €250,000 per year − €100,000 per year = €50,000 per year.

Economic profit here is smaller than accounting profit by exactly the amount of the firm's *implicit costs* – the €100,000 per year opportunity cost of the resources supplied by the firm's owners. This difference between a business's accounting profit and its economic profit is called its **normal profit**. Normal profit is simply the opportunity cost of the resources supplied to a business by its owners.

normal profit the opportunity cost of the resources supplied by a firm's owners, equal to accounting profit minus economic profit

Figure 7.1 illustrates the difference between accounting and economic profit. Figure 7.1(a) represents a firm's total revenues, while Figs. 7.1(b) and (c) show how these revenues are apportioned among the various cost and profit categories.

In Example 7.1, we look at how these concepts are related.

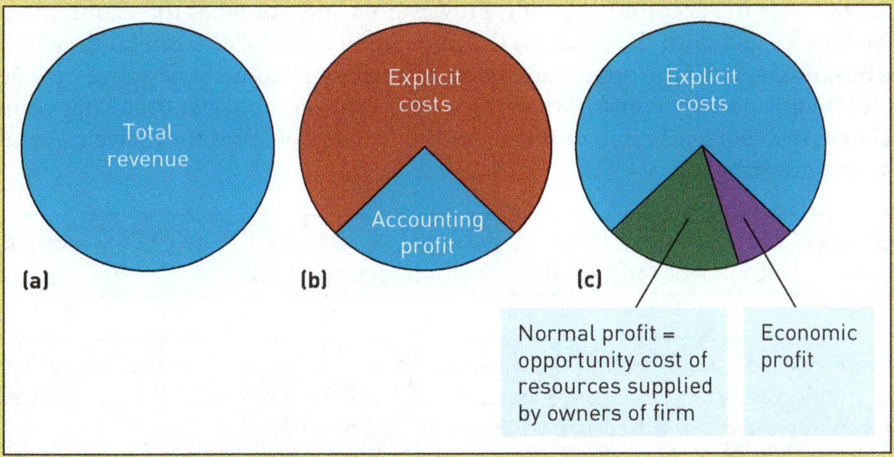

Figure 7.1 The Difference Between Accounting Profit and Economic Profit
Accounting profit (b) is the difference between total revenue (a) and explicit costs. Normal profit (c) is the opportunity cost of all resources supplied by firm's owners. Economic profit (c) is the difference between total revenue and all costs, explicit and implicit (also equal to the difference between accounting profit and normal profit).

Measuring profit

Example 7.1

James and Jeannette, two elementary school teachers, each earning €40,000, have won €500,000 in the national lottery. They decide to resign their jobs, and start a chicken- rearing business. This involves purchasing day-old chicks from breeders, raising them for three months and selling the mature chickens to a factory that supplies chicken meat to supermarkets. They purchase an existing business from its owner for €400,000. The balance they invest in a bank deposit yielding 5 per cent per annum. They hire an employee to help out. At the end of the year their accountant gives them the good news, that they have made a profit based on the following figures, and the bad news that they now owe €25,000 in profits tax to the government, the tax rate being 20 per cent.

J&J Chickens Annual Accounts	
Labour	€25,000
Cost of day-old chicks	€100,000
Feed costs	€50,000
Fuel, light, heat, phone etc	€25,000
Other production costs	€25,000
Repairs & maintenance	€10,000
Total costs	€235,000
Sale of three-month-old chickens	€350,000
Revenue from by-products	€10,000
Total Revenue	€360,000

To see the implications of all this, ask the following questions:

- What is their accounting profit?
- What is their economic profit?
- What is normal profit?
- Was it worth their while to change career?

The €125,000 is the accounting profit. However to find out what the economic profit was we have to add onto the costs (a) the opportunity cost of the capital they invested in the business, and (b) the opportunity cost of their own labour. They gave up €80,000 from teaching, and they could have earned 5 per cent on the €400,000. That comes to a total of €100,000. Economic profit, therefore, is €25,000. And they have to hand this over to the government.

Exercise 7.1 How would the position of James & Jeannette be affected if teachers' salaries fell by 10 per cent but interest rates on deposits increased to 7.5 per cent?

Exercise 7.2 Suppose that instead of buying the business, they rented it from the previous owner. How much could the owner have expected as rent? Would renting at this rent rather than buying make any difference to James and Jeannette?

RECAP

The central role of economic profit

A firm's accounting profit is the difference between its revenue and the sum of all explicit costs it incurs. Economic profit is the difference between the firm's revenue and all costs it incurs – both explicit and implicit. Normal profit is the opportunity cost of the resources supplied by the owners of the firm. When a firm's accounting profit is exactly equal to the opportunity cost of the inputs supplied by the firm's owners, the firm's economic profit is zero. For a firm to remain in business in the long run, it must earn an economic profit greater than or equal to zero.

THE 'INVISIBLE HAND' THEORY

TWO FUNCTIONS OF PRICE

In the free-enterprise system, market prices serve two important and distinct functions: rationing and allocation. The **rationing function of price** is to distribute scarce goods among potential claimants, ensuring that those who get them are the ones who value them most. Thus, if three people want the only antique clock for sale at an auction, the clock goes home with the person who bids the most for it.

The **allocative function of price** is to direct productive resources to different sectors of the economy. Resources leave markets in which price cannot cover the cost of production and enter those in which price exceeds the cost of production.

Both the allocative and rationing functions of price underlie Adam Smith's celebrated theory of the **'invisible hand'** of the market. Smith believed and taught that the market system channels the selfish interests of individual buyers and sellers so as to promote the greatest good for society. The carrot of economic profit and the stick of **economic loss**, he argued, were the only forces necessary to ensure not only that existing supplies in any market would be allocated efficiently, but also that resources would be allocated across markets to produce the most efficient possible mix of goods and services.

rationing function of price to distribute scarce goods to those consumers who value them most highly

allocative function of price to direct resources away from overcrowded markets and towards markets that are underserved

'invisible hand' theory Adam Smith's theory that the actions of independent, self-interested buyers and sellers will often result in the most efficient allocation of resources

economic loss an economic profit that is less than zero

Efficiency

RESPONSES TO PROFITS AND LOSSES

The response of firms to profit and loss is central to an understanding of how the invisible hand works. To remain in business in the long run a firm must cover all its costs, both explicit and implicit. A firm's normal profit should be treated as a cost of doing business. Hence, the owner of a firm that earns no more than a normal profit has managed only to recover the opportunity cost of the resources invested in the firm. By contrast, if a firm makes a positive economic profit, earning more than the opportunity cost of the invested resources, the owner earns more than a normal profit.

Markets in which firms are earning an economic profit tend to attract additional resources, whereas markets in which firms are experiencing economic losses tend to lose resources.

To see how this happens, we examine the workings of a hypothetical market for a product (in this case, wheat) whose short-run supply and demand curves are shown in Fig. 7.2(a). Figure 7.2(b) depicts the marginal and average total cost curves for a representative farm. The equilibrium price of €2 per tonne is determined by the supply–demand intersection in (a). The representative farm whose *MC* and *ATC* curves are shown in (b) then maximises its profit by producing the quantity for which price equals marginal cost, 130,000 tonnes of wheat per year.

From Chapter 5 we know that average total cost (*ATC*) at any output level is the sum of all costs, implicit and explicit, divided by output. The difference between price and *ATC* is thus equal to the average amount of economic profit earned per unit sold. In Fig. 7.2(b), that difference is €0.70 per unit. With 130,000 tonnes per year sold, the representative farm thus earns an economic profit of €104,000 per year.

The existence of positive economic profit in the wheat market means that producers in that market are earning more than their opportunity cost of farming. The opportunity cost of resources employed in producing wheat is the return to using them elsewhere. For simplicity, we assume that the inputs required to enter the wheat market – land, labour, equipment and the like – are available at constant prices and that anyone is free

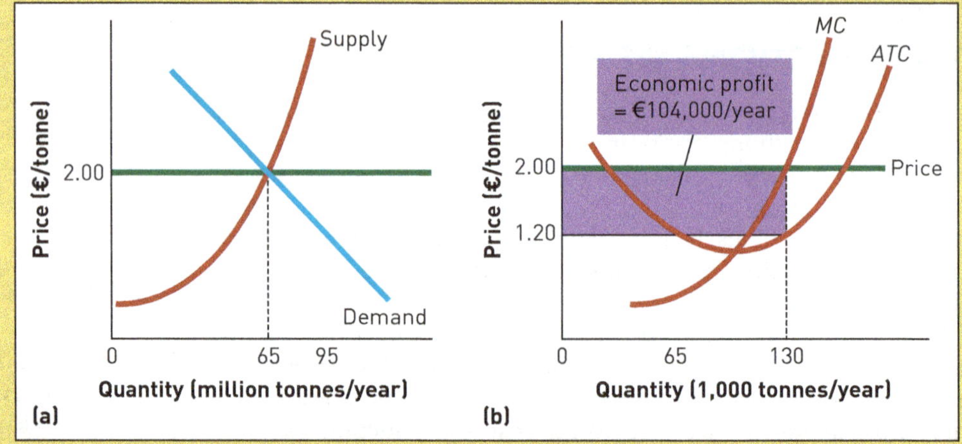

Figure 7.2 Economic Profit in the Short Run in the Wheat Market

At an equilibrium price of €2 per tonne (a), the typical farm earns an economic profit of €104,000 per year (b).

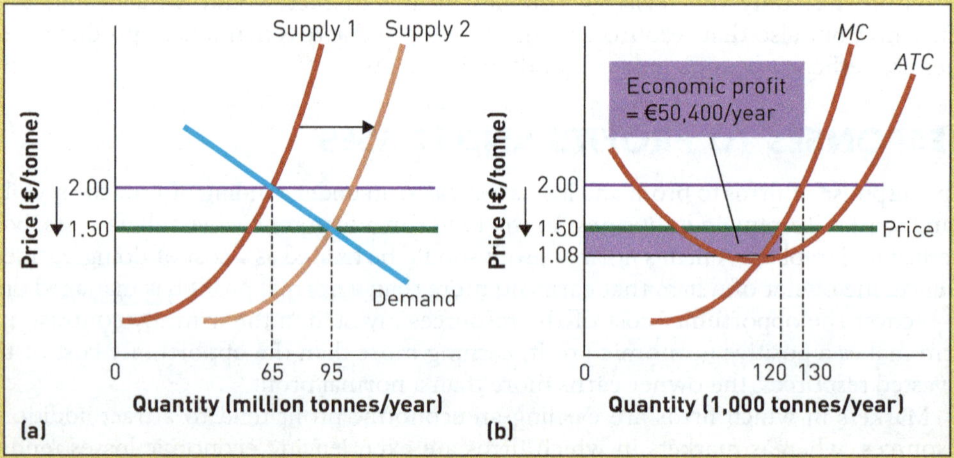

Figure 7.3 The Effect of Entry on Price and Economic Profit

At the original price of €2 per tonne, existing farmers earned economic profit, prompting new farmers to enter. With entry, supply shifts right (from *S* to *S'* in (a)) and equilibrium price falls, as does economic profit (b).

to enter this market if he or she chooses. The key point is that since price exceeds the opportunity cost of the resources required to enter the market, others *will* want to enter. As they add their wheat production to the amount already on offer, supply shifts to the right, causing the market equilibrium price to fall, as shown in Fig. 7.3(a). At the new price of €1.50 per tonne, the representative farm now earns much less economic profit than before, only €50,400 per year (Fig. 7.3(b)).

For simplicity, we assume that all farms employ the same standard production method (that is, the farmers are equally efficient, have access to the same technology and pay the same prices for their inputs), so that their *ATC* curves are identical. At any price higher than ATC economic profit would be positive. As long as price exceeds ATC entry would continue, driving price lower until it equals ATC. Recall from Chapter 5 that the short-run marginal cost curve intersects the *ATC* curve at the minimum point

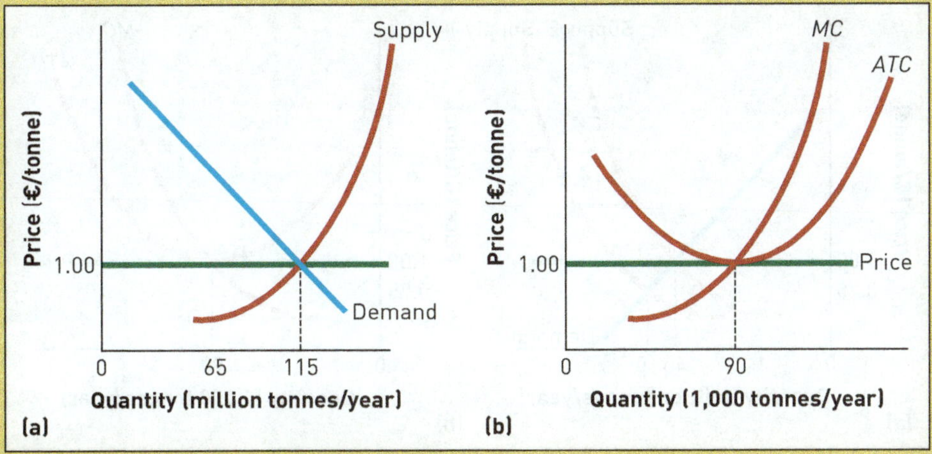

Figure 7.4 Equilibrium when Entry Ceases
Further entry ceases once price falls to the minimum value of *ATC*. At that point all farms earn a normal economic profit. Equivalently, each earns an economic profit of zero.

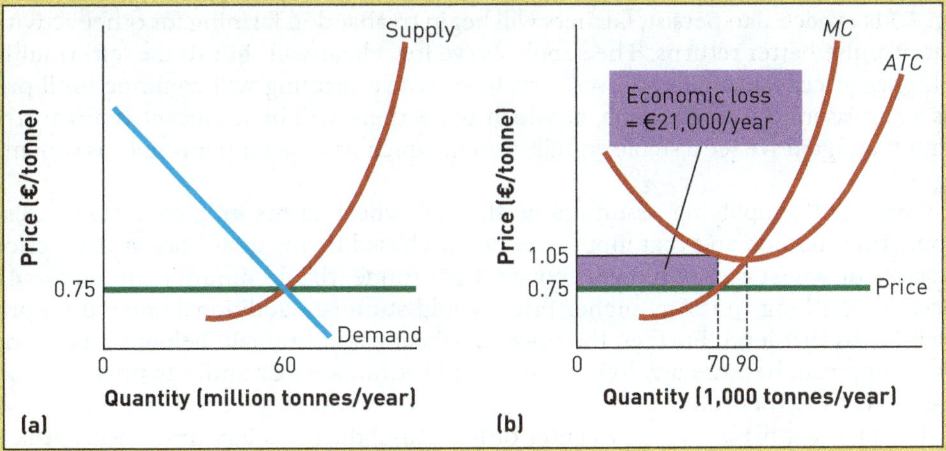

Figure 7.5 A Short-run Economic Loss in the Wheat Market
When price is below the minimum value of *ATC* (a), each farm sustains an economic loss (b).

of the *ATC* curve. This means that once price reaches the minimum value of *ATC*, the profit-maximising rule of setting price equal to marginal cost results in a quantity for which price and *ATC* are the same. And, when that happens, economic profit for the representative farm will be exactly zero, as shown in Fig. 7.4(b).

In the adjustment process just considered, the initial equilibrium price had been above the minimum value of *ATC*, giving rise to positive economic profits. Suppose instead that the market demand curve for wheat had intersected the short-run supply curve at a price below the minimum value of each farm's *ATC* curve, as shown in Fig. 7.5(b). As long as this price is above the minimum value of average variable cost, each farm will supply that quantity of wheat for which price equals marginal cost, shown as 70,000 tonnes per year in Fig. 7.5(b). Note, however, that at that quantity, the farm's average total cost is €1.05 per tonne, or €0.30 more than the price for which it sells each tonne. As shown in (b), the farm thus sustains an economic loss of €21,000 per year.

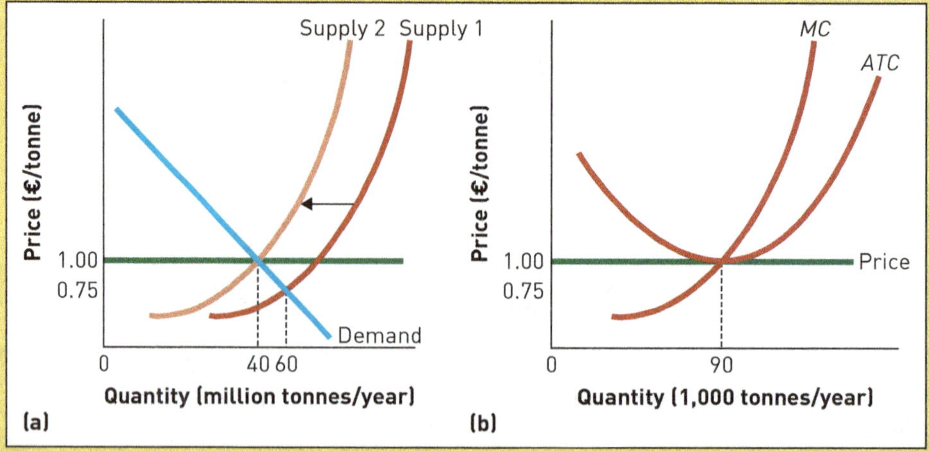

Figure 7.6 Equilibrium When Exit Ceases

Further exit ceases once price rises to the minimum value of *ATC*. At that point all farms earn a normal economic profit. Equivalently, each earns an economic profit of zero.

If the demand curve that led to the low price and resulting economic losses in Fig. 7.5 is expected to persist, farmers will begin to abandon farming for other activities that promise better returns. The supply curve for wheat will shift to the left, resulting in higher prices and smaller losses. Exit from wheat farming will continue until price has again risen to €1 per tonne, at which point there will be no incentive for further exit. Once again we see a stable equilibrium in which price is €1 per tonne, as shown in Fig. 7.6.

Given our simplifying assumptions that all wheat farms employ a standardised production method and that inputs can be purchased in any quantities at fixed prices, the price of wheat cannot remain above €1 per tonne (the minimum point on the *ATC* curve) in the long run. Any higher price would stimulate additional entry until price again fell to that level. Further, the price of wheat cannot remain below €1 per tonne in the long run, because any lower price would stimulate exit until the price of wheat again rose to €1 per tonne.

The fact that firms are free to enter or leave an industry at any time ensures that in the long run all firms in the industry will tend to earn zero economic profit. Their goal is not to earn zero profit. Rather, the zero-profit tendency is a consequence of the price movements associated with entry and exit. As the *Equilibrium Principle* – also called the No-Cash-on-the-Table Principle – predicts, when people confront an opportunity for gain, they are almost always quick to exploit it.

Equilibrium

What does the long-run supply curve look like in the wheat market just discussed? This question is equivalent to asking: 'What is the marginal cost of producing additional tonnes of wheat in the long run?' In general, adjustment in the long run may entail not just entry and exit of standardised firms, but also the ability of firms to alter the mix of capital equipment and other fixed inputs they employ. Explicit consideration of this additional step would complicate the analysis considerably but would not alter the basic logic of the simpler account we present here, which assumes that all firms operate with the same standard mix of fixed inputs in the short run. Under this assumption, the long-run adjustment process consists exclusively of the entry and exit of firms that use a single standardised production method.

The fact that a new firm could enter or leave this wheat market at any time means that wheat production can always be augmented or reduced in the long run at a cost of €1 per tonne. And this, in turn, means that the long-run supply curve of wheat will be

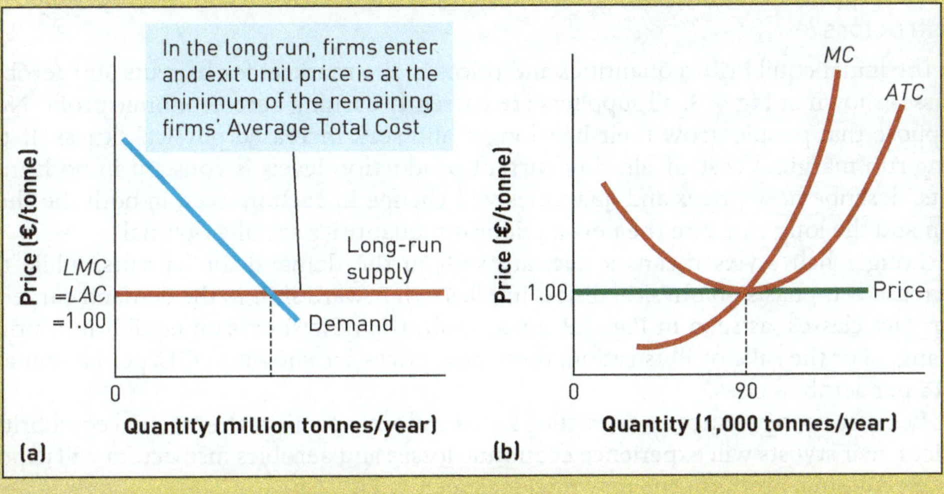

Figure 7.7 Long-run Equilibrium in a Wheat Market with Constant Long-run Average Cost

When each producer has the same *ATC* curve, the industry can supply as much or as little output as buyers wish to buy at a price equal to the minimum value of *ATC* (a). At that price, the representative producer (b) earns zero economic profit.

a horizontal line at a price equal to the minimum value of the *ATC* curve, €1 per tonne. Since the long-run marginal cost (*LMC*) of producing wheat is constant, so is the long-run average cost (*LAC*) and it, too, is €1 per tonne, as shown in Fig. 7.7(a). Figure 7.7(b) shows the *MC* and *ATC* curves of a representative wheat farm. At a price of €1 per tonne, this wheat market is said to be in *long-run equilibrium*. The representative farm produces 90,000 tonnes of wheat each year, the quantity for which price equals its marginal cost. And since price is exactly equal to *ATC*, this farm also earns an economic profit of zero.

These observations call attention to two attractive features of the invisible hand concept.

1. The first is that the *market outcome is efficient in the long run*. Note that when the wheat market is in long-run equilibrium, the value to buyers of the last unit of wheat sold is €1 per tonne, which is exactly the same as the long-run marginal cost of producing it. Thus, there is no possible rearrangement of resources that would make some participants in this market better off without causing harm to some others. If farmers were to expand production, for example, the added costs incurred would exceed the added benefits; and if they were to contract production, the cost savings would be less than the benefits forgone.
2. The second attractive feature of long-run competitive equilibrium is that the price buyers must pay is no higher than the cost incurred by suppliers. That cost includes a normal profit, the opportunity cost of the resources supplied by owners of the firm.

We must emphasise that Smith's 'invisible hand' does not mean that market allocation of resources is optimal in every way. It simply means that markets are 'efficient' in the limited technical sense discussed in Chapter 6. Thus, if the current allocation differs from the market equilibrium allocation, the 'invisible hand' theory implies that we can reallocate resources in a way that makes some people better off without harming others.

Example 7.3 affords additional insight into how Smith's 'invisible hand' works in practice.

Example 7.3 What happens in a city with 'too many' hair stylists and 'too few' aerobics instructors?

At the initial equilibrium quantities and prices in the markets for haircuts and aerobics classes shown in Fig. 7.8, all suppliers are currently earning zero economic profit. Now suppose that people grow their hair longer and seek increased physical fitness. If the long-run marginal cost of altering current production levels is constant in both markets, describe how prices and quantities will change in each market, in both the short run and the long run. Are the new equilibrium quantities socially optimal?

Longer hair styles means a leftward shift in the demand for haircuts, while the increased emphasis on physical fitness implies a rightward shift in the demand curve for aerobics classes, as seen in Fig. 7.9. As a result, the new short-run equilibrium prices change. For the sake of illustration, these new prices are shown as €12 per haircut and €15 per aerobics class.

Because each producer was earning zero economic profit at the original equilibrium prices, hair stylists will experience economic losses and aerobics instructors will experience economic profits at the new prices, as seen in Fig. 7.10.

Because the short-run equilibrium price of haircuts results in economic losses for hair stylists, some hair stylists will begin to leave that market in search of more favourable

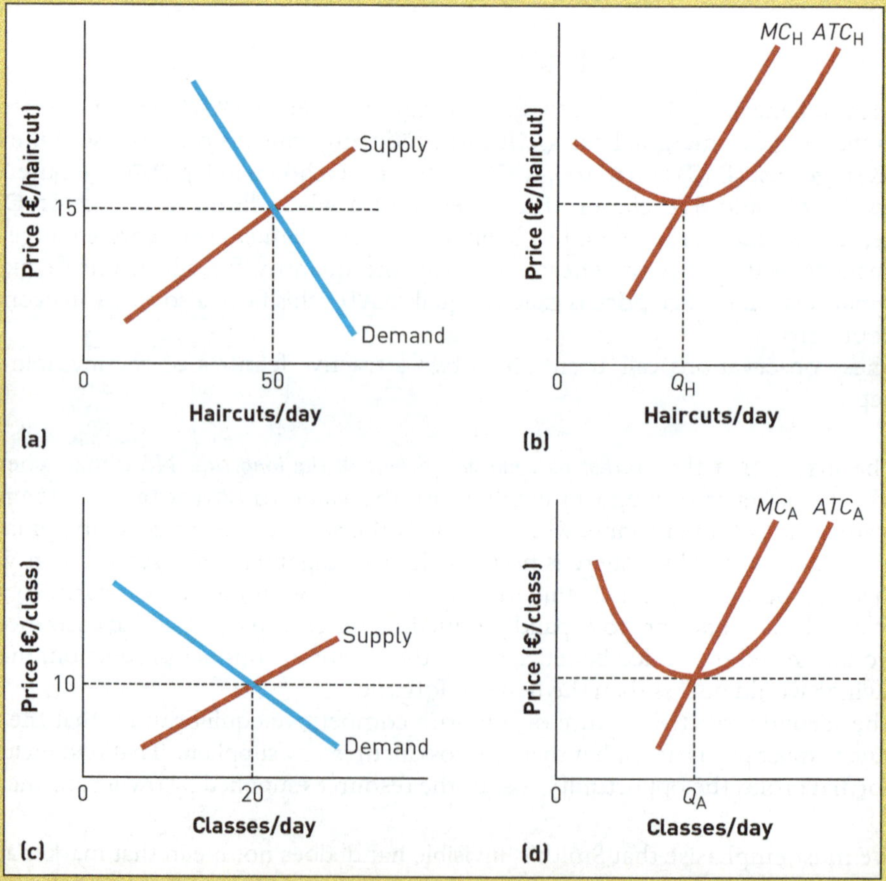

Figure 7.8 Initial Equilibrium in the Markets for (a) Haircuts and (b) Aerobics Classes

MC_H and ATC_H are the marginal cost and average total cost curves for a representative hair stylist, and MC_A and ATC_A are the marginal cost and average total cost curves for a representative aerobics instructor. Both markets are initially in long-run equilibrium, with sellers in each market earning zero economic profit.

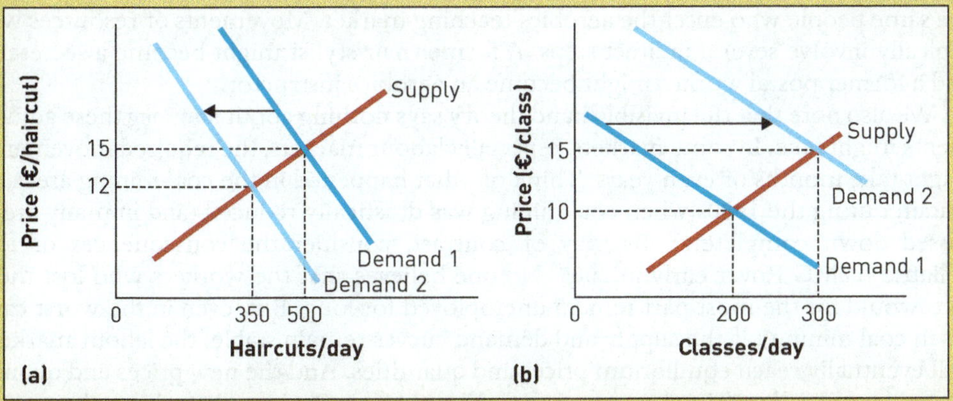

Figure 7.9 The Short-run Effect of Demand Shifts in Two Markets

The decline in demand for haircuts causes the price of haircuts to fall from €15 to €12 in the short run (a), while the increase in demand for aerobics classes causes the price of classes to rise from €10 to €15 in the short run (b).

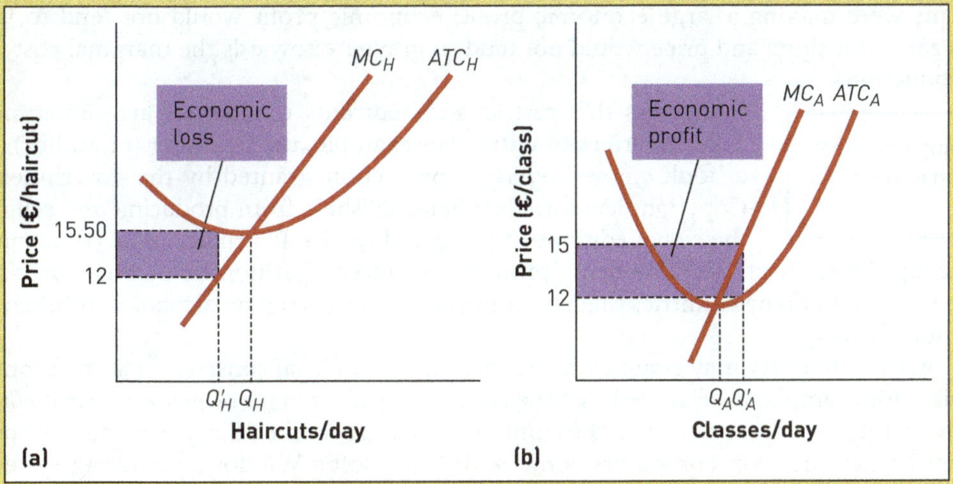

Figure 7.10 Economic Profit and Loss in the Short Run

The assumed demand shifts result in an economic loss for the representative hair stylist (a) and an economic profit for the representative aerobics instructor (b).

opportunities elsewhere. The short-run supply curve of haircuts will shift leftwards, resulting in a higher equilibrium price. Exit of hair stylists will continue until the price of haircuts rises sufficiently to cover the long-run opportunity cost of providing them, which by assumption is €15.

Similarly, because the short-run equilibrium price of aerobics classes results in economic profits for instructors, outsiders will begin to enter that market. The short-run supply curve of classes shifts rightwards. Entry will continue to enter until the price of classes falls to the long-run opportunity cost of providing them. By assumption, that cost is €10. Once all adjustments have taken place, there will be fewer hair stylists and more aerobics classes than before. But because marginal costs in both markets were assumed constant in the long run, the prices of the two goods will again be at their original levels.

Of course, those stylists who leave the hair-cutting market will not necessarily be the same people who enter the aerobics-teaching market. Movements of resources will typically involve several indirect steps. A former hair stylist might become a secretary, and a former postal worker might become an aerobics instructor.

We also note that the invisible hand theory says nothing about *how long* these adjustments might take. In some markets, especially labour markets, the required movements might take months or even years. Think of what happened in the coal-mining areas of Britain during the 1980s when coal mining was drastically reduced (and in many areas closed down completely). By way of contrast, consider the consequences of the collapse of MG Rover early in 2005. No one believes that the workers who lost their jobs would for the most part remain unemployed for long. But, even in the worst case (as in coal mining), if the supply and demand curves remain stable, the labour markets will eventually reach equilibrium prices and quantities. And the new prices and quantities will be socially optimal in the same sense as before. Because the value to buyers of the last unit sold will be the same as the marginal cost of producing it, no additional transactions will be possible that benefit some without harming others.

THE IMPORTANCE OF FREE ENTRY AND EXIT

The allocative function of price cannot operate unless firms can enter new markets and leave existing ones at will. If new firms could not enter a market in which existing firms were making a large economic profit, economic profit would not tend to fall to zero over time, and price would not tend to gravitate towards the marginal cost of production.

barrier to entry any force that prevents firms from entering a new market

Factors that restrict new entrants to markets are sometimes called **barriers to entry**. For example, the publisher (or author) of a book enjoys copyright protection granted by the government. Copyright law forbids other publishers from producing and selling their own editions of protected works. Pharmaceutical companies recoup the costs of R&D by being protected from competition by patents covering new drugs. In many countries the number of retail outlets selling alcohol or tobacco is limited by law.

Barriers to entry may result from practical as well as legal constraints. Some economists, for example, have argued that the compelling advantages of *product compatibility* have created barriers to entry in the computer software market. Since more than 90 per cent of new desktop computers come with Microsoft's Windows operating system (OS) software already installed, rival companies have difficulty selling other operating systems, as a different OS may make it difficult for users to exchange files with friends and colleagues. The bundling of MSWord with Windows, coupled to problems of importing documents prepared with other word-processing (WP) packages into MSWord, has undermined demand for other WP packages, especially WordPerfect. These compatibility problems, more than all other factors, are widely believed to explain Microsoft's spectacular profit history.

This last effect may be overstated. The emergence of the 'open architecture' freeware operating system, Linux, has threatened Microsoft's position in the OS market, something that would have been expected by economists of the Chicago School, who have always argued that markets tend to erode positions of market power.

Free exit is just as important as free entry. When the US domestic airline industry was regulated by the federal government, air carriers were often required to serve specific markets, even though they were losing money in them. Similar constraints continue to be imposed by national and EU regulation on a variety of utilities across Europe. They are termed 'universal service obligations' (USOs) in the literature on regulation, and they have the effect of increasing operating costs for suppliers subject to them. When firms discover that a market, once entered, is difficult or impossible to leave, they become reluctant to enter new markets. Like roads that are tolled, a payment when you leave is in effect a payment when you enter. Without reasonably free entry and exit, then, the implications of Adam Smith's 'invisible hand' theory cannot be expected to hold.

All things considered, however, producers enjoy a high degree of freedom of entry in most sectors of the market economies of the West. Recognition of the importance of ease of entry and exit has meant that even where, in countries or sectors, firms enjoy a lower degree of freedom, the consequences (arthritic economies) have led to pressure for change. Because free entry and exit is one of the defining characteristics of perfectly competitive markets, we shall, unless otherwise stated, assume its existence.

Economic Naturalist 7.1
What happens when you forget about maximising profits?

Some time after finishing the second edition of this textbook, we were intrigued by a story in the London *Daily Telegraph* (24 February 2008) about a gallant experiment undertaken by the owner of a restaurant near Poole, Dorset. The restaurant, the Penn Central at Sandbanks, introduced an 'anti-price' menu, which invited diners to pay whatever they thought the meal was worth on two nights a week, mid-week, to attract customers (food and water only, wine was not included). The owner told the paper that he believed people were basically fair, and that prices were within a couple of pounds of the normal prices. Apparently this innovation was greeted enthusiastically by patrons. The owner explained that he was inspired by the rock group, Radiohead, when they launched their album, *In Rainbows*, on the web in 2007 for downloading and asked fans to pay what it was worth to them.

When preparing this edition, we decided to call up the restaurant to see how the experiment had worked out. We were informed that the restaurant was now under new management, the previous owner having been bought out. The old pricing policy was no longer operative.

The problem was that when Radiohead did what they did, they had not launched an album for two years, a geological time period in the pop music industry. The offer was in effect a pre-launch one for a limited period to get publicity for the CD that followed, and the only cost to Radiohead was a limited number of sales that they might not have made anyway. The Penn Central, however, was cannibalising its revenues from sales to patrons at higher prices while incurring the same costs – a sure way to lose money. Somebody hadn't understood the idea of opportunity cost!

THE IMPORTANCE OF PUBLIC POLICY ON EXIT: THE 'GLOBALISATION' QUESTION

It is easy to see that serious consequences flow from policy measures that discourage or prohibit entry. When market demand for their output increases and existing firms face barriers to expanding capacity, or new firms face entry barriers, output cannot adequately expand to meet increased demand. Extra resources cannot be allocated to producing the goods for which demand has increased or inputs needed for their production. Prices for the goods for which demand has increased will rise, which means higher profits and wages in the sector. This explains why existing producers will always find reasons for calling for legislation to limit entry . . . in the public interest, of course.

Although the importance of free entry is widely accepted by public opinion and by policy makers in principle, the latter are prone to finding reasons to refuse to act accordingly from time to time. When, however, the question of exit arises, the situation, in terms of public opinion and policy response, is less receptive. What is different about exit?

When falling demand, or competition from new goods, or competition from foreign suppliers, reduces profits in an industry, firms, or at least some of them, start to experience losses. This frequently leads to pressure for government intervention to shore up the firms in the industry affected. This can take the form of subventions, restrictions on competition, or restrictions on entry to the relevant product market by new suppliers. Restrictions are imposed on imports from foreign suppliers who are often accused of 'dumping' (i.e. selling at below cost). In Britain, competitive pressure on the motor industry led to government intervention to restructure the British industry in the 1970s and 1980s, culminating in nationalising it. This support to prevent exit merely delayed the exit at huge expense of the entire 'British' industry, which was replaced by more efficient production of cars in Britain by 'foreign' producers. In the USA, competition, especially from Japanese car producers, led to a government bail-out of one firm (Chrysler) in 1980 and attempts to restrict imports from Japan by trade restrictions in order to preserve the business of the Detroit 'Big Three'. The policy failed. By the beginning of the twenty-first century 'American' production of cars had fallen from over 90 per cent of sales in the USA in the early 1970s to less than 50 per cent today, while direct imports and transplanted production of 'foreign' cars accounted for a 50 per cent plus, and growing, market share.

The political reason for the success of such calls for action is obvious: jobs are at stake and votes are up for grabs. It is easy to mobilise public support for measures, often described as temporary, to preserve the industry affected, especially if it is regionally concentrated. What is not understood is that measures that discourage exit effectively 'freeze' the allocation of resources in the economy just when long-term surplus maximisation requires that they move out of the affected sector, that the economy should move along its production possibility frontier, and the sector concerned should contract (or even disappear).

Efficiency

Put another way, measures that discourage exit have the same qualitative effect on economic efficiency as measures that discourage entry. Public perceptions, unfortunately, treat exits as a net cost to the economy (jobs lost, incomes reduced . . .) arising from increased competition and the public reacts accordingly. This is what underlies much of the rhetoric about the 'costs of globalisation' and the pressure to move away from freedom of exchange, trade and specialisation. There is a perception that opening markets in poorer countries to trade leads to a contraction in output, income and employment in sectors facing increased competition. The 'trade is better than aid' concept has growing support as a means of helping alleviate poverty in the Third World. People understand that restricting exports from poorer countries by barriers on imports in rich countries immiserises poorer countries. Economic growth in poor countries will be stunted, extending aid dependence. This has led to calls for asymmetric opening of trade: easier access for poor countries to rich-country markets, but restrictions on exports from rich countries to poorer countries (and even from poorer to richer countries) where these disrupt traditional production patterns. An example is the concern that some African countries are now successfully exporting vegetable products to the countries of the EU while production of foodstuffs for their domestic markets declines, making them more dependent on food imports. The fundamentally flawed basis to this is clear once we think about what increased exports means in the case of poorer countries: the movement of resources out of serving the local market and into serving markets in other countries, movement along the production possibility frontier to increase real income per head.

Comparative Advantage

Scarcity

Higher real incomes in poorer countries require replacing traditional production patterns. This is precisely how the richer countries in the world became richer in the first place, by permitting, even encouraging, exit from traditional occupations to permit expansion of new sectors in their economies. In a nutshell, this is what we mean by the concept of the Industrial Revolution of the eighteenth and nineteenth centuries, and the move in the OECD countries from manufacturing to services in the late twentieth and early twenty-first centuries.

RECAP

The 'invisible hand' theory

In market economies, the *allocative* and *rationing* functions of prices guide resources to their most highly valued uses. Firms enter markets and industries in which prices are sufficiently high to sustain an economic profit. This shifts industry supply to the right. They leave those in which low prices result in an economic loss, shifting industry supply to the left. In each case, the supply movements continue until economic profit reaches zero. In long-run equilibrium, the value of the last unit produced to buyers is equal to its marginal cost of production, leaving no possibility for additional mutually beneficial transactions.

ECONOMIC RENT VERSUS ECONOMIC PROFIT

The reason for the profitability of Microsoft, it is widely believed, is largely because the problem of compatibility prevents rival suppliers from competing effectively in the many software markets dominated by the company. This has led to regulatory and judicial confrontations on both sides of the Atlantic as anti-trust policy has been invoked to curb Microsoft's alleged abuses of its market position. Yet numerous people have become fabulously rich even in markets with no conspicuous barriers to entry. If market forces push economic profit towards zero, how can that happen?

The answer to this question hinges on the distinction between economic profit and **economic rent**. In everyday language the term 'rent' refers to the payment to a landlord for a flat, or to a car hire company for the use of a car. In economics, however, the term 'rent' has a different meaning, although it is connected to the everyday term in some cases. In economics *'economic rent'* (or simply, *rent*) is that portion of the payment for an input that is above the supplier's reservation price for that input, which is by definition the supply price of that input. Suppose, for example, that a landowner's reservation price for a hectare of land is €100 per year, reflecting its value to the landowner if he used it himself. He would be willing to lease it to a farmer as long as he received an annual payment of at least €100. If competition between would-be farmers resulted in one of them offering him an annual payment (in everyday usage, rents the land from the landowner) not of €100 but of €1,000, the landowner's *economic rent* from that payment would be €900 per year. If the land had no other use as far as the landowner was concerned, and he would be willing to let it for a very small sum, virtually the entire payment received would be an economic rent.

> **economic rent** that part of the payment for a factor of production that exceeds the owner's reservation price

If an economist working for a civil service department is paid €90,000 a year, and if the next highest salary available to someone with that skill set and experience in economics was in a university department at a salary of €80,000, €10,000 of the civil servant's salary would be an economic rent, assuming the jobs are equally (un)pleasant to a job holder.

In our economist's example, if it were easy for academic economists to leave universities and seek employment in the civil service, we would expect to see the economic rent element in civil service economists' earnings disappear. Economic profit is like economic rent in that it, too, may be seen as the difference between what someone is paid (the business owner's total revenue) and the reservation price for remaining in business (the sum of all costs, explicit and implicit). However, whereas competition pushes economic profit towards zero (by increasing supply and driving down price), it has no such effect on the economic rent for inputs if they cannot be replicated easily. For example, although the lease payments for land may remain substantially above the landowner's reservation price, year in and year out, new land cannot come onto the market to reduce or eliminate the economic rent through competition. There is, after all, only so much land to be had.

As Example 7.4 illustrates, economic rent can accrue to people as well as land.

Example 7.4 How much economic rent will a talented chef get?

France prides itself on the quality of its restaurants. There are thousands of them. Most are ordinary and unassuming (even if they might appear to be much better than run-of-the-mill eating establishments in less fortunate countries). And there is a small number of really outstandingly good restaurants, epitomised, perhaps, by La Tour d'Argent in Paris. The key to a restaurant's standing is the skill of the chef. In ordinary restaurants a chef might expect to be paid between €25,000 and €50,000 a year depending on experience and some modest differences in skills. But in establishments like La Tour d'Argent, the master chef could expect a significant multiple of that level of earnings.

Why? Because France takes gastronomy very seriously. French (and other) diners are prepared to pay through the nose to consume the creations of the most talented chefs in France. The restaurants that employ them can charge enormous prices. Consequently, restaurants compete fiercely for talented chefs, and their earnings reflect this competition for the small number of extraordinary *artistes de cuisine*. The bulk of chefs will be paid something like their supply price: what they could earn outside the industry. Their earnings contain little or no economic rent. Master chefs, on the other hand, earning sums of up to €200,000 and more, have the same supply price . . . and most of their earnings are rent, being derived from the fact they are few in number and supply cannot expand to meet demand.

Since the talented chef's opportunities outside the restaurant industry are no better than an ordinary chef's, why is it necessary to pay the talented chef so much? Suppose the employer were to pay him only €80,000, which they both would consider a generous salary, since it is twice what ordinary chefs earn. The employer would then earn a significant economic profit since his annual revenue would be an order of magnitude higher than that of ordinary restaurants, but his costs would be only €30,000 to €40,000 more.

But this economic profit would create an opportunity for the owner of some other restaurant to bid the talented chef away. For example, if the owner of a competing restaurant were to hire the talented chef at a salary of €90,000, the chef would be €10,000 per year better off, and the rival owner would earn an economic profit. Furthermore, if the talented chef is the sole reason that a restaurant earns a positive economic profit, the bidding for that chef should continue as long as any economic profit remains.

RECAP

Economic rent versus economic profit

Economic rent is the amount by which the payment to a factor of production exceeds the supplier's reservation price. Unlike economic profit, which is driven towards zero by competition, economic rent may persist for extended periods, especially in the case of factors with special talents that cannot easily be duplicated.

THE 'INVISIBLE HAND' IN ACTION

To help develop your intuition about how the invisible hand works, we will examine how it can help us gain insight into the patterns we observe in a wide variety of different contexts. In each case, the key idea we want you to focus on is that opportunities for private gain seldom remain unexploited for very long. Perhaps more than any other, this idea encapsulates the essence of that distinctive mind-set known as 'thinking like an economist'.

THE 'INVISIBLE HAND' AND COST-SAVING INNOVATIONS

When economists speak of perfectly competitive firms, they have in mind businesses whose contribution to total market output is too small to have a perceptible impact on market price. As explained in Chapter 5, such firms are often called *price takers*: they take the market price of their product as given and then produce that quantity of output for which marginal cost equals that price.

This characterisation of the competitive firm gives the impression that the firm is essentially a passive actor in the marketplace. Yet, for most firms, that is anything but the case. As Example 7.5 illustrates, even those firms that cannot hope to influence the market prices of their products have very powerful incentives to develop and introduce cost-saving innovations.

Example 7.5

How do cost-saving innovations affect economic profit in the short run? In the long run? And what have markets and incentives to do with this?

Consider the following scenario involving the dissemination of technology. Suppose 40 merchant marine companies operate supertankers that carry oil from the Middle East to Western Europe. The market is close to perfectly competitive. The cost per trip, including a normal profit, is €500,000. An engineer at one of these companies develops a more efficient propeller design that results in fuel savings of €20,000 per trip. How will this innovation affect the company's accounting and economic profits? Will these changes persist in the long run?

In the short run, the reduction in a single firm's costs will have no impact on the market price of transoceanic shipping services. The firm with the more efficient propeller will thus earn an economic profit of €20,000 per trip (since its total revenue will be the same as before, while its total cost will now be €20,000 per trip lower). As other firms learn about the new design, however, they will begin to adopt it, causing their individual supply curves to shift downwards (since the marginal cost per trip at these firms will drop by €20,000). The shift in these individual supply curves will cause the market supply curve to shift, which in turn will result in a lower market price for shipping and a decline in economic profit at the firm where the innovation originated. When all firms have adopted the new, efficient design, the long-run supply curve for the industry will have shifted downwards by €20,000 per trip, and each company will again be earning only a normal profit. At that point, any firm that did *not* adopt the new propeller design would suffer an economic loss of €20,000 per trip.

The importance of inter-firm competition and the profit motive is central to all this. The failure to disseminate technology in the former Soviet Union (USSR) was a major factor in explaining the failure of the Soviet economy in the long Cold War productivity competition with the West.[1] Despite major achievements in terms of advancing production technologies through research and development (R&D), the USSR's manufacturing capacity fell steadily behind that of the OECD countries in terms of productivity and product quality. One reason for this was that in the planned economy of the Soviet Union, the incentives for managers in state enterprises were related to meeting volume production targets. Innovation, quality and cost considerations were secondary. This reduced the incentive to respond to the possibilities of new technologies compared to those facing managers in Western firms.

The incentive to come up with cost-saving innovations in order to reap economic profit is one of the most powerful forces on the economic landscape. Its beauty, in terms of the invisible hand theory, is that competition among firms ensures that the resulting cost savings will be passed along to consumers in the long run.

THE 'INVISIBLE HAND' IN REGULATED MARKETS

The carrot of economic profit and the stick of economic loss guide resource movements in regulated markets no less than in unregulated ones. Consider the taxi industry, which many cities regulate by licensing taxi cabs and restricting their numbers. These

1 Iacopetta (2004).

licences are often referred to as 'plates' or 'medallions', because they are issued in the form of a metal disc that must be fixed to the cab, where enforcement officials can easily see it. Cities that regulate cabs in this fashion typically issue fewer medallions than the equilibrium number of taxi cabs in similar markets that are not regulated. Officials then allow the medallions to be bought and sold in the marketplace. As Economic Naturalist 7.2 demonstrates, the issuance of taxi medallions alters the equilibrium quantity of taxi cabs but does not change the fundamental rule that resources flow in response to profit and loss signals.

Economic Naturalist 7.2
The value and cost of restricting entry

The New York borough of Manhattan has a resident population of about 1.6 million. Only 8 per cent of households in Manhattan own a car. Every day about 1.2 million people commute into Manhattan to work. The work-day population is about 2.7 millions. Taxis (yellow cabs) must have a licence, and there are about 13,000 licensed taxis in Manhattan. They mainly supply service within Manhattan and between Manhattan and JFK airport. No other taxis or equivalent are allowed to ply for hire in Manhattan. Over the past 70 years only 400 new licences (plates) have been issued. To purchase a taxi plate in Manhattan in 2010 you could expect to pay anything up to $600,000. Over the past 60 years the dollar value of a taxi plate has risen by about 16 per cent per annum on average (the Dow Jones Industrial Average index of share prices on the NYSE increased by about 8 per cent per annum over the same period). To an economist the message is clear: there is, and has been, chronic excess demand for taxis in Manhattan, and this has resulted in substantial profits for the owners of plates despite the fact that fares are regulated. Or does it? If you have to pay $600,000 for a plate, this represents the capitalisation of the excess of revenue over the labour, maintenance, and capital cost of a taxi plus the expected capital gain from selling the plate in the future. This investment has to be serviced, so the profit is driven to zero for that person. The real gain is for those who have held plates for a long time in the past. If there were no restriction on numbers the number of taxis would increase until that margin was driven to zero, and the value of a plate would go to zero, too.

And the cost?

Restricting the number at a regulated price implies excess demand for taxi services. As with any price ceiling this implies a loss of surplus. Consumers lose because they cannot purchase the number of taxi-rides they would like to at the price. Producers and potential producers lose because they cannot expand the volume of service to clear the market. Look back at Figures 6.4 and 6.5 to check this.

Just theorising?

No: we have an example of what happens when the restriction is changed. In Dublin (pop. approx 1 million) restriction on entry to the taxi business was introduced in 1978, when there were about 1,800 licensed taxis. Over the following 23 years 150 new licences were issued so that by 2001 there were about 1,970 licences in existence. In 2001 taxi plates/medallions were worth about IRL£90,000 (€115,000). In that year the numerical restriction on entry was removed. Within two years there were 10,000 taxis operating, and the numbers have expanded since then, while the market price of a licence has dropped to zero.

Another regulated market in which the invisible hand was very much in evidence was the regulated commercial airline industry. In the United States, until late 1978, airlines were heavily regulated by the Civil Aeronautics Board (CAB), an agency of the federal government. In Europe it took strong pressure from the European Union from the early 1990s onwards to force national governments to liberalise the market, and the process is still not fully finished.

In Europe, national regulations not only determined who could fly on what route, and at what fares, but even how many flights they could put on a route. One of the declared objects of these regulatory regimes was to ensure an 'adequate' service on less popular routes. The standard practice was to set fares well above the cost of providing a service on most routes, and then require carriers to use some of the resulting economic profit to pay for service on sparsely travelled routes.

Ryanair has been the leader in taking advantage of deregulation (actually re-regulation on a more liberal basis) of the entire air transport sector. It has chosen a strategy of flying to secondary airports rather than the main airport of big-city destinations (in one case, Vienna, this involves landing in Slovakia!). Ryanair has been a severe critic of the behaviour of main airports as exploiters of market power by imposing high charges on users. Is this fair? Economic Naturalist 7.3 suggests this may not be the case all the time.

Economic Naturalist 7.3

Should British Airports Authority (which owns London Heathrow, Gatwick and Stansted) be obliged to lower its landing charges?

Ryanair does not use Heathrow but concentrates on London Stansted, where it has a main base and with which it has a contractual relationship. Table 7.1 gives the landing charges at London's three airports as of 2005. It's hardly surprising that Ryanair uses Stansted (and, to a lesser extent, Gatwick).

It's hard to believe that it costs BAA 50 per cent more (peak-time) or over 100 per cent more (off-peak) to handle a plane landing at Heathrow than at Gatwick. But Heathrow is far more in demand from both airlines and passengers than the others. So, it seems fair to say, BAA is using this in order to generate profits at the expense of the travelling public.

However, the fact is that there is excess demand for landing/takeoff time slots at Heathrow. They are a scarce resource. In 2003 British Airways paid Swiss £30 million for 8 slots. In 2008 Continental paid £100 million for 4 slots. Alitalia that year sold 25 per cent of its slots for €92 million. Slots have a capital value sufficiently high that airlines, faced with a use-it-or-lose it regime have from time to time flown empty planes to keep slots. From this perspective BAA's charges, if lowered, would increase the value of slots, a value that reflects passengers' preference for, and willingness to pay for, using Heathrow. The higher landing charges are simply an example of the price system operating as a device to allocate a scarce resource to highest-value users.

Table 7.1 London Airport Landing Charges

	Heathrow		Gatwick		Stansted	
Aircraft weight (tons)	Peak	Off-peak	Peak	Off-peak	Peak	Off-peak
MTOW ≤ 16	£590	£250	£385	£110	£95	£85
16 < MTOW ≤ 50	£590	£250	£385	£110	£142	£105
50 < MTOW ≤ 250	£590	£425	£385	£125	£231	£131
250 < MTOW	£590	£425	£385	£125	£400	£400

Notes:
1. Noise surcharges may apply to certain types of aircraft.
2. Peak, Heathrow: 07:00–09:59 and 17:00–18.59 GMT, April 1 – October 31.
3. Peak, Gatwick: 06:00–11:59 and 17:00–18.59 GMT, April 1 – October 31.
4. Peak, Stansted: April 1 – October 31.

Source: British Airports Authority website.

Exercise 7.4

Ryanair also led the way in 'unbundling prices' so that you pay separately for the seat, a meal, a drink, a checked-in suitcase and so on. Can you offer an efficiency argument to support the proposal to charge £1 to use the plane's WC?

THE 'INVISIBLE HAND' IN ANTI-POVERTY PROGRAMMES

As Example 7.6 shows, failure to understand the logic of the invisible hand can lead not only to inefficient government regulation, but also to anti-poverty programmes that are doomed to fail.

Example 7.6 How will an irrigation project affect the incomes of poor farmers?

The World Bank and other development agencies are always under pressure to increase spending on projects designed to increase the incomes of low-productivity farmers in some of the world's poorest countries. The impact on farm incomes frequently turns out to be disappointing. It is frequently said that either the World Bank is not using the funds effectively, or that the money is being siphoned off by corrupt officials in the recipient countries. Both of these may be correct in some cases. However, as the following example is designed to illustrate, part (most?) of the answer may lie in a failure to understand the workings of the invisible hand.

Consider a small country somewhere in southern Asia with a large population of tenant farmers growing rice, a staple of the local diet. Recently, Western investment has resulted in the establishment of a textile industry producing T-shirts, mostly for export to OECD countries. Suppose unskilled workers must choose between working in a textile factory, earning €4,000 per year and growing rice on a rented parcel of farmland. One worker can farm 8 ha of rice paddy, which costs €2,500 rent a year. Such holdings yield a crop that earns €8,000 per year in revenue, and the total non-labour costs of bringing the crop to market are €1,500 per year. The net incomes of rice farmers are thus €4,000 per year – the same as those of textile workers.

The small number of landowners, receive the rental income from the land, and have an income per head much larger than the tenant farmers. This inequitable distribution of income leads to calls for actions to support the incomes of the large numbers of poor farmers who are handing over a lot of money to the few and very rich landlords. As a result of political pressure, the World Bank announces that it will fund an irrigation project that doubles the output of rice on farms operated by tenant farmers. Rice being an internationally traded good, the level of output in this Third World country has no discernible effect on the price of rice. How will the project affect the absolute and relative incomes of tenant farmers in the long run?

The irrigation project succeeds in doubling rice yields, which means that each farmer will sell €16,000 worth of rice per year rather than €8,000. If nothing else changed, farmers' incomes would rise from €4,000 per year to €12,000 per year. But the No-Cash-on-the-Table principle tells us that this is unsustainable. The textile firms face given prices for T-shirts. But, to textile workers, there is cash on the table in farming. Seeing an opportunity to triple their incomes, many will want to switch to farming. But since the supply of land is fixed, farm rents will rise as textile workers begin bidding for them. They will continue to rise as long as farmers can earn more than textile workers. The long-run effect of the project, then, will be to raise the rent on rice farms, from €2,500 per year to €10,500 (since at the higher rent the incomes of rice farmers and textile workers will again be the same). Thus the irrigation project will increase the wealth of landowners but will have no long-run effect on the incomes of tenant farmers.

Exercise 7.5

Suppose the government imposes a rent freeze, so that existing farmers do not have to pay more to landlords, and cannot be evicted for not doing so. Can you explain why, after a few years, the World Bank is likely to find the rice still being grown by peasants earning a net €4,000 a year (assuming that nothing else has changed)?

THE 'INVISIBLE HAND' IN THE STOCK MARKET

The world's great stock markets (London, Frankfurt, New York and Tokyo are the most important), in which dealers trade in shares (stock) and bonds (fixed interest securities, debt of governments and firms) are among the most competitive markets in the world. Unfortunately, public understanding of how the invisible hand works in these markets is often no better than the state legislator's understanding of how the rice market works.

Calculating the value of a share of stock

A share of stock in a company is a claim to a share of the current and future accounting profits of that company. Thus, if you own 1 per cent of the total number of shares of a company's stock, you effectively own 1 per cent of the company's annual accounting profit, both now and in the future. The profit is either distributed as dividends or reinvested in the companies to increase future accounting profits and dividends which increases the value of the shares. The price of a share of stock depends not only on a company's accounting profit, however, but also on the market rate of interest, as Example 7.7 illustrates.

How much will a share of stock sell for?

Example 7.7

Suppose we know with certainty that a company's accounting profit will be €1 million this year and every year. If the company has issued a total of 200,000 shares of stock, and the annual interest rate is 5 per cent, at what price will each share sell?

Because there are 200,000 shares of stock, each share entitles its owner to 1/200,000 of the company's annual accounting profit, or €5 per year. Owning this stock is like having a bank deposit that earns €5 per year in interest. To calculate the economic value of the stock, therefore, we need only ask how much an investor would need to deposit in the bank at 5 per cent interest to generate an annual interest payment of €5. The answer is €100, and that is the price that each share will command in the stock market.

Maths Box 7.1

A technical digression: how to calculate present values of future costs and benefits

Earnings to be received in the future are less valuable than earnings received today. Consider a company whose only accounting profit, €14,400, will occur exactly two years from now. At all other times its accounting profit will be exactly zero. How much is ownership of this company worth?

To answer this question, we need to employ the concept of the **time value of money** – the fact that money deposited in an interest-bearing account today will *grow in value over time.*

Our goal is to compute what economists call the **present value** (*PV*) of a €14,400 payment to be received in two years. We can think of this present value as the amount that would have to be deposited in an interest-bearing bank account today to generate a balance of €14,400 two years from today. Let *PV* denote present value and *r* the market rate of interest, measured as a fraction. (For example, an annual interest rate of 10 per cent would correspond to $r = 0.10$.) If we put €100 in an account today at 10 per cent annual interest, we will have €100(1.10) = €110 in the account after one year. If we leave €100 in the same account for two years, we will have €100(1.10)(1.10) = €100$(1.10)^2$ = €121.

time value of money the fact that a given euro amount today is equivalent to a larger euro amount in the future, because the money can be invested in an interest-bearing account in the meantime; after *T* years: $PV - M/(1 - r)T$

present value for an annual interest rate *r*, the present value (*PV*) of a payment (*M*) to be received *T* years from now is the amount that would have to be deposited today at interest rate *r* to generate a balance of *M*

More generally, if we put PV in the bank today at the interest rate r, we will have $PV(1 + r)$ one year from now and $PV(1 + r)^2$ two years from now. So to find the present value of a €14,400 payment to be received two years from now we simply solve the equation €14,400 = $PV(1 + r)^2$ and get PV = €14,400/$(1 + r)^2$. If the interest rate is 20 per cent, then PV = €14,400/$(1.2)^2$ = €10,000. To verify this answer, note that €10,000 deposited at 20 per cent interest today would grow to €10,000(1 + 0.2) = €12,000 by the end of one year, and that amount left on deposit for a second year would grow to €12,000(1 + 0.2) = €14,400.

More generally, when the interest rate is r, the present value of a payment M to be received T years from now is given by the equation

$$PV = M/(1 + r)^T$$

Exercise 7.6 What is the present value of a payment of €1,728 to be received three years from now if the annual interest rate is 20 per cent?

THE EFFICIENT MARKETS HYPOTHESIS

The current price of a share will depend not on the actual amount of future profits, as yet unrealised, but on investors' estimates of them. These are based on available information about current profits, prospects for the company's industry, the state of the economy, demographic trends and a host of other factors. As this information changes, investors' estimates of future profits change with it, along with the prices of a share of stock.

efficient markets hypothesis the theory that the current price of stock in a company reflects all the relevant information about its current and future earnings prospects

Taking this to its logical conclusion leads us to what is called the **efficient markets hypothesis**. This states that the current price of any share incorporates all available information relevant to the company's future earnings. Consequently, if 'new' information arises the share price will adjust to reflect it more or less immediately. That means that the only way you can benefit from new information is if you obtain it before anyone else can, something that suggests 'insider trading'. The price adjusts because it changes what people are prepared to pay for a share and what other people would require to hold on to the share. Bids and offers will adjust the price smoothly and quickly to adjust for the new information.

The efficient market hypothesis implies that there is no point trying to predict share prices in the future by examining how they have behaved in the past (the basis of 'chart analysis'), which is rather like predictive seismology: using what preceded previous earth tremors to predict when/if a new tremor is likely. Nor can you expect to make a better return on your portfolio by time-consuming analysis of the 'fundamentals', market and firm related information already in the public domain. Finally, it says that you are wasting your time (and money) listening to investment analysts. The only way to earn a higher return than the average from a portfolio is to invest it in more risky shares.

The hypothesis does not exclude the possibility (even probability) that from time to time it is seen to have overpriced or underpriced some or all shares. The dotcom bubble of 2000 is a case in point. People can collectively interpret information incorrectly, but this will be corrected (the crash after the dotcom boom). It really boils down to saying that markets do not leave 'cash on the table' for long.

In practice, new information often takes time to interpret, and different investors may have different beliefs about exactly what it means. Early information may signal an impending change that is far from certain. As time passes, events may confirm or contradict the implications of the earlier information. The usual pattern is for information to emerge in bits and pieces, and for stock prices to adjust in small increments as each new bit of information emerges. But this does not mean that the price of a stock adjusts gradually to new information. Rather, it means that new information usually emerges gradually. And, as each piece of new information emerges, the market reacts almost instantly.

For example, in January 2011 the price of shares in the Apple Corporation fell by nearly 8 per cent on the Frankfurt market (US markets were closed for Martin Luther King Day) within minutes of an announcement in San Francisco that the entrepreneurial founder of Apple, Steve Jobs, was taking sick leave arising from his health problems associated with a liver transplant.

Despite such persuasive evidence in favour of the efficient markets hypothesis, many investors seem to believe that information about the next sure investment bonanza is as close as their stockbroker's latest newsletter. In most financial centres a large population of salespeople make a living telephoning potential investors to offer the latest tips on how to invest their money. The weekend quality newspapers across Europe have pages devoted to share analysis and advice on whether to buy, hold or sell various shares. The difficulty is that by the time you've read in the newspaper about a share worth buying the reason for buying it will be history.

The *Wall Street Journal* publishes a feature in which a group of leading investment advisers predict which stocks will increase most in price during the coming months. The *Journal* then compares the forecasts with the performance of a randomly selected set of stocks. The usual finding is that the randomly selected portfolios perform little differently from those chosen by the 'experts'. Some of the experts do better than average, others worse. This pattern is consistent with the economist's theory that the invisible hand moves with unusual speed to eliminate profit opportunities in financial markets.[2]

Economic Naturalist 7.4

Pension funds hold reviews on a regular basis of the performance of the fund management firms they retain to invest their clients' money. Does this make sense?

If it's true that a chimpanzee throwing darts at a share price page in the *Financial Times* (i.e., a random selection of shares) is expected to give the same return as a portfolio selected by professional fund managers, why bother reviewing the performance of funds? Why bother paying more for active management (selecting on a continuous basis shares to buy and shares to sell) rather than a passive 'buying the index' (i.e., buy a selection of shares held to be representative and hold onto them)?

The efficient markets hypothesis says the chimpanzee costs a few bananas, much less than a professional manager, and should get the job. On that basis, the City of London or Wall Street would look quite different! But (a) not everyone fully believes that financial markets are that efficient, so that (b) profitable opportunities, small, perhaps, to use information do occur, while (c) arbitraging is often profitable (taking advantage of prices that are out of line to bring them back into line). Lord Keynes didn't, and is regarded as one of the most successful investors of the twentieth century when Bursar of King's College, Cambridge. He was not a fan of broad portfolios, preferring to generate good information by careful study and then invest selectively. He once remarked that successful fund management required not forming an opinion on what market prices would be in the future, but an opinion as to what everyone else thought other people thought they would be . . . and taking an opposite position. Furthermore, whether active or passive, fund managers need to be kept on their toes (see the remote office game in Chapter 9) and the pension funds' customers need to know that their interests are being looked after. However, that *Fortune* article does indeed suggest that much professional investment advice is a waste of time and money.

---

[2] If this topic interests you, or you fancy yourself as a share punter, an accessible survey of the case for and against the hypothesis is contained in Malkiel (2003).

RECAP

The 'invisible hand' in action

Because individuals and firms are generally eager to improve their position, opportunities for gain seldom remain unexploited for long. Early adopters of *cost-saving innovations* enjoy temporary economic profits. But as additional firms adopt the innovations, the resulting downward supply shift causes price to fall. In the long run, economic profit returns to zero, and all cost savings are passed on to consumers.

The quest for advantage guides resources not only in perfectly competitive markets, but also in heavily regulated markets. Firms can almost always find ways to expand sales in markets in which the regulated price permits an economic profit or withdraw service from markets in which the regulated price results in an economic loss. An understanding of the invisible hand theory is also important for the design of anti-poverty programmes. An irrigation programme that makes land more productive, for example, will raise the incomes of tenant farmers only temporarily. In the long run, the gains from such projects tend to be captured as higher rents to landowners. The efficient markets hypothesis says that the price of a firm's stock at any moment reflects all available information that is relevant for predicting the firm's future earnings. This hypothesis identifies several common beliefs as false – among them that stocks in well-managed companies perform better than stocks in poorly managed ones and that ordinary investors can make large financial gains by trading stocks on the basis of information reported in the news media.

THE DISTINCTION BETWEEN AN EQUILIBRIUM AND A SOCIAL OPTIMUM

The Equilibrium, or No-Cash-on-the-Table, Principle tells us that when a market reaches equilibrium, no further opportunities for gain are available to individuals. This principle implies that the market prices of resources that people own will eventually reflect their *economic value*. (As we shall see in later chapters, the same cannot be said of resources that are not owned by anyone, such as fish in international waters.)

The No-Cash-on-the-Table Principle is sometimes misunderstood to mean that there are *never* any valuable opportunities to exploit. For example, the story is told of two American economists on their way to lunch when they spot what appears to be a $100 bill lying on the pavement. When the younger economist stoops to pick up the bill, his older colleague restrains him, saying: 'That can't be a genuine $100 dollar bill.' 'Why not?' asks the younger colleague. 'If it were, someone would have picked it up by now,' the older economist replies.

The No-Cash-on-the-Table Principle means not that there *never* are any unexploited opportunities, but that there are none when the market is *in equilibrium*. Occasionally a $100 bill does lie on the pavement, and the person who first spots it and picks it up gains a windfall. Likewise, when a company's earnings prospects improve, *somebody* must be the first to recognise the opportunity, and that person can make a lot of money by purchasing the stock quickly.

Equilibrium

Still, the No-Cash-on-the-Table Principle is important. It tells us, in effect, that there are only three ways to earn a big payoff: to work especially hard; to have some unusual skill, talent or training; or simply to be lucky. The person who finds a big bank note on the pavement is lucky, as are many of the investors whose stocks perform better than average. Other investors whose stocks do well achieve their gains through hard work or special talent. For example, the legendary investor Warren Buffett, whose portfolio has grown in value at almost three times the stock market average for the past 40 years, spends long hours studying annual financial reports and has a remarkably keen eye for the telling detail. Thousands of others work just as hard yet fail to beat the market averages.

It is important to stress, however, that a market being in equilibrium implies only that no additional opportunities are available *to individuals*. It does not imply that the resulting allocation is necessarily best from the point of view of society as a whole.

SMART FOR ONE, DUMB FOR ALL

Adam Smith's profound insight was that the individual pursuit of self-interest often promotes the broader interests of society. But unlike some of his modern disciples, Smith was under no illusion that this is *always* the case. Note, for example, Smith's elaboration on his description of the entrepreneur led by the invisible hand 'to promote an end which was no part of his intention':

> Nor is it *always* the worse for society that it was no part of it. By pursuing his own interest he *frequently* promotes that of society more effectively than when he really intends to promote it. (Smith, 1776, Book 4, Ch. 2).

As Smith was well aware, the individual pursuit of self-interest often does not coincide with society's interest. In Chapter 3 we cited activities that generate environmental pollution as an example of conflicting economic interests, noting that behaviour in those circumstances may be described as 'smart for one, dumb for all'.

In general, the efficacy of the invisible hand depends on the extent to which the individual costs and benefits of actions taken in the marketplace coincide with the respective costs and benefits of those actions to society. Exceptions notwithstanding, some of the most powerful forces at work in competitive markets clearly promote society's interests.

RECAP

Equilibrium versus social optimum

A market in *equilibrium* is one in which no additional opportunities for gain remain available to individual buyers or sellers. The No-Cash-on-the-Table Principle describes powerful forces that help push markets towards equilibrium. But even if all markets are in equilibrium, the resulting allocation of resources need not be socially optimal. Equilibrium will not be socially optimal when the costs or benefits to individual participants in the market differ from those experienced by society as a whole.

SUMMARY

- *Accounting* profit is the difference between a firm's revenue and its explicit expenses. *Economic* profit is the difference between revenue and the sum of the firm's explicit and implicit costs. *Normal* profit is the opportunity cost of the resources supplied to a business by its owners.
- The quest for economic profit is the 'invisible hand' that drives resource allocation in market economies. Markets in which businesses earn an economic profit tend to attract additional resources, whereas markets in which businesses experience an economic loss tend to lose resources. If new firms enter a market with economic profits, output rises, causing a reduction in the price of the product. Free entry means that prices will continue to fall until economic profits are eliminated. By contrast, the departure of firms from markets with economic losses causes output to contract, increasing the price of the product. Free exit will mean that prices will continue to rise until economic losses are eliminated. In the long run, market forces drive economic profits and losses towards zero.

- As long as firms' cost curves and market demand curves reflect the full underlying costs and benefits to society of the production of a good or service, the quest for economic profit ensures (a) that existing supplies are allocated efficiently among individual buyers, and (b) that resources are allocated across markets in the most efficient way possible. In any allocation other than the one generated by the market, resources could be rearranged to benefit some people without harming others.
- *Economic rent* is the portion of the payment for an input that exceeds the reservation price for that input. If a professional football player who is willing to play for as little as €100,000 per year is paid €15 million, he earns an economic rent of €14,900,000 per year. Whereas the invisible hand drives economic profit towards zero over the long run, economic rent can persist indefinitely, because replicating the services of players like Rio Ferdinand is impossible. Talented individuals who are responsible for the superior performance of a business will tend to capture the resulting financial gains as economic rents.
- Applying the concept of Adam Smith's invisible hand helps explain why regulation of markets can have unintended and wasteful consequences. For instance, when regulation prevents firms from lowering prices to capture business from rivals, firms generally find other ways in which to compete. Thus, if airline regulators set passenger fares above cost, air carriers will try to capture additional business by offering extra amenities and more frequent service. Likewise, many anti-poverty programmes have been compromised by failure to consider how incentives change people's behaviour.
- A share of stock in a company is a claim to a share of the current and future accounting profits of that company. The price of a share of stock depends not only on its accounting profits, but also on the market rate of interest, since the interest rate affects the present value of future costs and benefits. The total market value of the shares is the market estimate of the present value of the expected profits in the future. When the annual interest rate is r, the present value (PV) of a payment M to be received (or paid) T years from now is the amount that would have to be deposited in a bank account today at interest rate r to generate a balance of M after T years: $PV = M/(1+r)^T$.
- According to the efficient markets hypothesis, the market price of a stock incorporates all currently available information that is relevant to that company's future earnings. If this is not the case, people with superior information can consistently make profits in a more or less risk-free fashion.
- The No-Cash-on-the-Table Principle implies that if someone owns a valuable resource, full information and efficient markets mean that the market price of that resource will fully reflect its economic value. The implication of this principle is not that lucrative opportunities never exist, but rather that such opportunities cannot exist when markets are in equilibrium, and that prices will adjust to eliminate them.
- The benefit of an investment to an individual sometimes differs from its benefit to society as a whole. Such conflicting incentives may give rise to behaviour that is smart for one but dumb for all. Despite such exceptions, the invisible hand of the market works remarkably well much of the time. One of the market system's most important contributions to social well-being is the pressure it creates to adopt cost-saving innovations. Competition among firms ensures that the resulting cost savings get passed along to consumers in the long run.

REVIEW QUESTIONS

1. Why do most cities now have more radios but fewer radio repair shops than they did in 1960?
2. How can a business owner who earns 10 million per year from his business credibly claim to earn zero economic profit?

3. Why do market forces drive economic profit but not economic rent towards zero?
4. Why did airlines that once were regulated by government generally fail to earn an economic profit, even on routes with relatively high fares?
5. Why is a payment of 10,000 to be received one year from now more valuable than a payment of 10,000 to be received two years from now?

PROBLEMS

connect

1. Explain why the following statements are **true** or **false**.
   a. The economic maxim 'There's no cash on the table' means that there are never any unexploited economic opportunities.
   b. Firms in competitive environments make no accounting profit when the market is in long-run equilibrium.
   c. Firms that can introduce cost-saving innovations can make an economic profit in the short run.
2. Explain why new software firms that give away their software products at a short-run economic loss are nonetheless able to sell their stock at positive prices.
3. John Jones owns and manages a café whose annual revenue is €5,000. The annual expenses are as in the table below.

Expense	€
Labour	2,000
Food and drink	500
Electricity	100
Vehicle lease	150
Rent	500
Interest on loan for equipment	1,000

   a. Calculate John's annual accounting profit.
   b. John could earn €1,000 per year as a recycler of aluminium cans. However, he prefers to run the café. In fact, he would be willing to pay up to €275 per year to run the café rather than to recycle cans. Is the café making an economic profit? Should John stay in the business? Explain.
   c. Suppose the café's revenues and expenses remain the same, but recyclers' earnings rise to €1,100 per year. Is the café still making an economic profit? Explain.
   d. Suppose John had not had to get a €10,000 loan at an annual interest rate of 10 per cent to buy equipment, but instead had invested €10,000 of his own money in equipment. How would your answers to parts (a) and (b) change?
   e. If John can earn €1,000 a year as a recycler, and he likes recycling just as well as running the café, how much additional revenue would the café have to collect each year to earn a normal profit?
4. A city has 200 advertising companies, 199 of which employ designers of normal ability at a salary of €100,000 a year. Paying this salary, each of the 199 firms makes a normal profit on €500,000 in revenue. However, the 200th company employs Janus Jacobs, an unusually talented designer. This company collects €1,000,000 in revenues because of Jacobs' talent.
   a. How much will Jacobs earn? What proportion of his annual salary will be economic rent?
   b. Why will the advertising company for which Jacobs works not be able to earn an economic profit?

5. Explain carefully why, in the absence of a patent, a technical innovation invented and pioneered in one tofu factory will cause the supply curve for the entire tofu industry to shift to the right. What will finally halt the rightward shift?

6. The government of the Republic of Self-Reliance has decided to limit imports of machine tools, to encourage development of locally made machine tools. To do so, the government offers to sell a small number of machine-tool import licences. To operate a machine-tool import business costs €30,000, excluding the cost of the import licence. An importer of machine tools can expect to earn €50,000 per year. If the annual interest rate is 10 per cent, for how much will the government be able to auction the import licences? Will the owner of a licence earn an economic profit?

7. Unskilled workers in a poor cotton-growing region must choose between working in a factory for €6,000 a year or being a tenant cotton farmer. One farmer can work a 120-hectare farm, which rents for €10,000 a year. Such farms yield €20,000 worth of cotton each year. The total non-labour cost of producing and marketing the cotton is €4,000 a year. A local politician whose motto is 'Working people come first' has promised that, if he is elected, his administration will fund a fertiliser, irrigation and marketing scheme that will triple cotton yields on tenant farms at no charge to tenant farmers.
   a. If the market price of cotton would be unaffected by this policy and no new jobs would be created in the cotton-growing industry, how would the project affect the incomes of tenant farmers in the short run? In the long run?
   b. Who would reap the benefit of the scheme in the long run? How much would they gain each year?

8. You have a friend who is a potter. He holds a permanent patent on an indestructible teacup whose sale generates €30,000 a year more revenue than his production costs. If the annual interest rate is 20 per cent, what is the market value of his patent?

9. You have an opportunity to buy an apple orchard that produces €25,000 per year in total revenue. To run the orchard, you would have to give up your current job, which pays €10,000 per year. If you would find both jobs equally satisfying, and the annual interest rate is 10 per cent, what is the highest price you would be willing to pay for the orchard?

10. Ludovico, a renowned chef, owns one of the 1,000 spaghetti restaurants in Sicily. Each restaurant serves 100 plates of spaghetti a night at €5 per plate. Ludovico knows he can develop a new sauce at the same cost as the current sauce, which would be so tasty that all 100,000 spaghetti eaters would buy his spaghetti at €10 per plate. There are two problems: developing the new sauce would require some experimental cost; and the other spaghetti producers could figure out the recipe after one day.
    a. What is the highest experimental cost Ludovico would be willing to incur?
    b. How would your answer change if Ludovico could enforce a year-long patent on his new sauce? (Assume that the interest rate is zero.)

REFERENCES

Iacopetta, M. (2004) 'Dissemination of Technology in Planned and Market Economies', *Contributions to Macroeconomics*, 4(1).

Malkiel, B.G. (2003), 'The Efficient Market Hypothesis and its Critics', *Journal of Economic Perspectives*, vol. 17 no. 1, pp. 59–82.

Smith, A. (1776) *An Enquiry into the Nature and Causes of the Wealth of Nations*.

Part 3

Market Imperfections (1): Market Power

We now move away from the world implicitly, and to a lesser extent explicitly, assumed by Adam Smith. In that world, exchange is frictionless, parties to exchanges are fully informed and no one has significant market power. This means investigating what happens when people and firms interact in markets plagued by a variety of imperfections. Not surprisingly, the invisible hand that served society so well in the perfectly competitive world often goes astray in this new environment.

Our focus in Chapter 8 will be on how markets served by only one or a small number of firms differ from those served by perfectly competitive firms. We shall see that, although monopolies often escape the pressures that constrain the profits of their perfectly competitive counterparts, the two types of firm also have many important similarities.

In Chapter 9 we lay the foundation for understanding something of how firms operate in markets where there is neither monopoly nor a very large number of sellers. We do this by introducing the elements of decision making in circumstances where one person's decision affects the behaviour of others. (In perfect or monopolistic competition we look at situations where a firm can make a decision based on the assumption that it will not affect what other firms do.) The basic tool of analysis used here is what has become known as 'game theory'. In this chapter we use game theory in a variety of circumstances to show how it helps explain how decisions are made, and the consequences of those decisions, when the decision makers have to acknowledge interdependence affecting making choices.

In Chapter 10 we look at how firms make decisions in small-number markets where interdependence is the rule of the day. We develop the idea of a firm's reaction, or best response, function as a mechanism to explain what happens in such markets.

Chapter 8 Imperfect Competition and the Consequences of Market Power

The best of all monopoly profits is a quiet life. — *John Hicks*

Learning Objectives

After reading this chapter, you should be able to:

1. Understand the types of imperfectly competitive industries;
2. Define imperfect competition and how it differs in performance from the benchmark of perfect competition;
3. Appreciate that market power means being able to choose price, and the consequences for profit maximisation;
4. Understand price discrimination and its implications;
5. Recognise public policy to deal with market power.

People follow fashions, and none more so than teenagers. It is not sufficient to wear jeans: they must be Diesel, or Levi Strauss. The fact that perfectly serviceable jeans, often made in the same factory, and using the same cotton and thread, are available at a fraction of the price is irrelevant. The difference in price between the high-fashion brands and the more generic products can hardly be accounted for by differences in costs of production. It is reasonable to assume that the higher-priced fashion brands yield higher profits to the producers than the other brands.

As an economist, however, under these circumstances you might expect that producers of jeans would flood the market with imitations of the high-fashion brands. The reason this producer reaction is uncommon in the West is because producers have a *legally enforceable monopoly* on their brands – and, frequently, on the designs of their products. As a result, they can restrict output, safe from competition from replicas, and obtain a higher price for their products based on fashion. This particular legal ability to prevent imitations being produced is just one way in which producers of goods can *differentiate* their offerings from those of rivals. By doing so, they put themselves in a position to become **price setters** rather than price takers. They still have to compete for sales with producers of other variants of the good in question. Think about branded and own-brand products in supermarkets.

> **price setter** a firm with at least some latitude to set its own price
>
> **imperfectly competitive firms** firms that differentiate their products from those of their rivals, with whom they compete

When producers can, for whatever reason, differentiate their products from those of their rivals economists refer to the market concerned as being *imperfectly competitive*, and the firms as being **imperfectly competitive firms**. The key to this type of market is that the output of any producer is not perfectly substitutable for that of another producer. Hence, the purchaser of a unit of the product is not indifferent as to the identity of the producer.

This chapter considers the ways in which markets served by imperfectly competitive firms differ from those served by perfectly competitive firms. One salient difference is the imperfectly competitive firm's ability, under certain circumstances, to charge more than its cost of production. Nike can sell its latest trainers for €150 a pair (where production costs are perhaps €10). Nike and Diesel face competition from other products in their markets, but differentiation means that imperfectly competitive firms can earn an economic profit, even in the long run, and even without government protections such as copyright.

IMPERFECT COMPETITION

The concept of a perfectly competitive market should be thought of as an extreme or idealised version of competition. The actual markets we encounter in everyday life differ from the ideal in varying degrees. In analysing markets that are not perfectly competitive, economics texts usually distinguish among three types of imperfectly competitive market structure.

DIFFERENT FORMS OF IMPERFECT COMPETITION

pure monopoly the only supplier of a unique product with no close substitutes

Pure monopoly, a market in which a single firm is the lone seller of a unique product, is the polar opposite to perfect competition. A real-life example of a full-blown monopolist is not all that easy to find, unless the monopoly is created by law (e.g. a postal monopoly). Historically, creating monopolies was frequently used to raise revenues for the crown, and was common in feudal Europe where the local baron owned the only mill for grinding corn.

oligopolist a firm that produces a product for which only a few rival firms produce close substitutes

monopolistically competitive firm one of a large number of firms that produce slightly differentiated products that are reasonably close substitutes for one another

Oligopoly is a market structure in which only a few firms (**oligopolists**) sell a given product. Examples include the market for mobile (cellular) phone services, in which a handful of firms like Vodafone are the principal providers. In general, the large supermarket chains, of which there are in any country only a few, are accepted as being in a separate market from small convenience stores. As such, they form an oligopoly, a market in which most or all sales are in the hands of a small number of relatively large suppliers.

Closer still to perfect competition is the industry structure known as *monopolistic competition*, which typically consists of a relatively large number of firms that sell the same product with slight differentiations. Examples of **monopolistically competitive firms** include local petrol (gasoline) stations, which differ not so much in what they sell as in their physical locations; or medical services (where these are sold to users).

The essential characteristic that differentiates imperfectly competitive firms from perfectly competitive firms is the same in each of the three cases. So, for convenience, we shall use the term *monopolist* to refer to the price-setting ability of any of the three types of imperfectly competitive firms.

THE ESSENTIAL DIFFERENCE BETWEEN PERFECTLY AND IMPERFECTLY COMPETITIVE FIRMS

For our purposes in this text we will ignore more subtle classifications of markets favoured by advanced texts in order to focus on the single, common feature that differentiates all imperfectly competitive firms from their perfectly competitive counterparts. Whereas the perfectly competitive firm faces a perfectly elastic demand curve for its product, *the imperfectly competitive firm faces a downward-sloping demand curve*.

In the perfectly competitive market, the supply and demand curves intersect to determine an equilibrium market price. At that price, the perfectly competitive firm can sell as many units as it wishes. It can't charge more than the market price, because it won't sell anything if it does so. Nor does it have any incentive to charge less than the market price, because it can sell as many units as it wants to at the market price. The perfectly competitive firm's demand curve is thus a horizontal line at the market price, as we saw in Chapter 5.

By contrast, if a local petrol retailer or convenience store – an imperfect competitor – charges a little more than its rivals for some or all of what it sells, some of its customers may desert it. But others will remain, perhaps because they are willing to pay a little extra to continue shopping at their most convenient location. An imperfectly competitive firm thus faces a negatively sloped demand curve. Figure 8.1 summarises this contrast between the demand curves facing perfectly competitive and imperfectly competitive firms.

RECAP

Imperfect competition

Perfect competition is an ideal case, at best only approximated in actual industries. Economists study three other types of market structure that differ in varying degrees from perfect competition: *monopoly*, an industry with only one seller of a unique product; *oligopoly*, an industry with only a few sellers; and *monopolistic competition*, an industry in which many firms sell products that are close, but imperfect, substitutes for one another. The demand curve confronting a perfectly competitive firm is perfectly elastic at the market price, while the demand curve confronting an imperfectly competitive firm is downward-sloping.

FIVE SOURCES OF MARKET POWER

market power a firm's ability to raise the price of a good without losing all its sales

If firms face a downward-sloping demand curve for what they produce they are said to enjoy **market power**. By this is meant

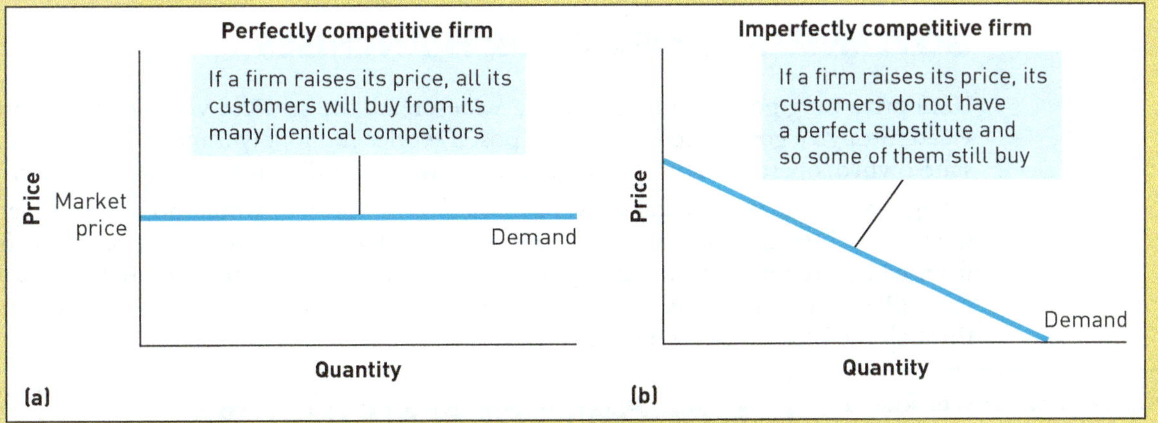

Figure 8.1 The Demand Curves Facing Perfectly and Imperfectly Competitive Firms
(a) The demand curve confronting a perfectly competitive firm is perfectly elastic at the market price. (b) The demand curve confronting an imperfectly competitive firm is downward-sloping.

that they can select a price at which they offer products to the market, or they can *set the prices* of their products. A common misconception is that a firm with market power can sell any quantity at any price it wishes. It cannot: all it can do is pick a price–quantity combination along its demand curve. If the firm chooses to raise its price, it must settle for reduced sales.

Why do some firms have market power while others do not? Since market power often carries with it the ability to charge a price above the cost of production, such power tends to arise from factors that limit competition. In practice, the following five factors often confer such power: exclusive control over important inputs; patents and copyrights; government licences or franchises; economies of scale; and network economies. In addition, of course, competing goods can be sold at different prices if their characteristics differ. But this is really a case of choosing the characteristics bundled into a good and selling the good at a competitive price, controlling for characteristics.

EXCLUSIVE CONTROL OVER IMPORTANT INPUTS

If a single firm controls an input *essential to the production* of a given product, that firm will have market power. Although there are other technical substitutes for Windows, in commercial terms this describes Microsoft's position in the market for PCs.

PATENTS AND COPYRIGHTS

Patents give the inventors or developers of new products the exclusive right to sell those products for a specified period of time. By insulating sellers from competition for an interval, patents enable innovators to charge higher prices to recoup their product's *development costs*. Pharmaceutical companies, for example, spend millions of euros on research in the hope of discovering new drug therapies for serious illnesses. The drugs they discover are insulated from competition for an interval by the granting of government patents. For the life of the patent, only the patent holder may legally sell that particular drug. This protection enables the patent holder to set a price above the marginal cost of production. The profits on the sales of the drug are expected to be sufficient (at least) to recoup the cost of the research on the drug. In the same way, copyrights protect the authors of movies, software, music, books and other published works.

GOVERNMENT LICENCES OR FRANCHISES

Until privatising postal services became widespread, the services were generally provided through a government grant of a postal service monopoly franchise to a (usually state-owned) operator. The goal of governments was for the most part the provision of a single-price universal postal delivery service. This, it is felt, would not be possible if the universal service operator faced competition in lucrative urban markets, the profits from which are said to be necessary to cross-subsidise loss-making operations in other parts of the country. Another goal was to facilitate international service agreements through the Universal Postal Union.

constant returns to scale a production process is said to have constant returns to scale if, when all inputs are changed by a given proportion, output changes by the same proportion

ECONOMIES OF SCALE (NATURAL MONOPOLIES)

If, when a firm doubles all its factors of production, output exactly doubles, the firm's production process is said to exhibit **constant returns to scale**. If output more than doubles, the production process is said to exhibit **increasing returns to scale**, or **economies of scale**. When production is subject to economies of scale, the average cost of production declines as the number of units produced increases. For example, in the generation of electricity, the use of larger generators lowers the unit cost of production. In some circumstances competition with increasing returns to scale leads to a single supplier emerging in a given market.

A monopoly that results from economies of scale is called a **natural monopoly**.

> **increasing returns to scale** a production process is said to have increasing returns to scale if, when all inputs are changed by a given proportion, output changes by more than that proportion; also called **economies of scale**
>
> **natural monopoly** a monopoly that results from economies of scale

A classic example of the impact of scale economies is the evolution of the structure of the passenger and military aircraft markets. In this case, the economies arise not just from the production process but from the enormous costs of designing and marketing new aircraft. In the United Kingdom, the main aircraft-producing country in Europe after the Second World War, there were in the early 1950s at least ten major firms producing military and commercial fixed-wing aircraft. By the early 1970s the industry had just two firms, resulting from mergers and exits: BAC and Hawker Siddeley. By the beginning of the twenty-first century no UK independent producer of large aircraft survived, and virtually the entire British industry (one firm, BAE Systems plc) had become part of a small number of larger multinational operations, being involved with EADS (the producer of Airbus) and Lockheed-Martin (the US producer of the next generation of STOVL strike fighters). For large commercial passenger planes, there were two European and three North American suppliers as recently as 1980. In 2008 only two remained, Airbus and Boeing, all the others having either merged or exited the industry.

Driving this process was the huge and rising costs of developing new aircraft. To recover these costs required increasing sales volumes for planes introduced to the market. Failure to achieve sufficient sales volumes would lead to company failure and amalgamations. The surviving firms grew larger relative to the market, while at the same time standardisation of airline fleets reduced costs for airlines (a scale economy for operators). The result is the structure of production and operators' fleets that we observe today.

NETWORK ECONOMIES

Many products become much more valuable to us as more people use them. In the 1980s a 'format war' erupted between Sony's Betamax system for tape-based recording of videos and the Philips/JVC-promoted VHS system. VHS, arguably a technically less advanced system, won simply because it managed through a lower retail price to gain a slight sales edge on the initial version of Betamax, which could not record programmes longer than one hour. Although Betamax later corrected this deficiency, the VHS lead proved insuperable, and this was reflected in the supply of material to rental agencies by the programme providers. This encouraged equipment purchasers to buy VHS format recorders. Once the fraction of consumers owning VHS passed a critical threshold, the reasons for choosing it became compelling – variety and availability of tape rental, access to repair facilities, the capability to exchange tapes with friends, and so on. Between 2005 and 2007 a similar 'format war' occurred between the Blu-ray (Sony) and HD-DVD (Toshiba) systems to replace standard DVD recordings. HD-DVD recordings and equipment cost less, but Blu-ray had a higher storage potential. Lowering the price was not a successful strategy for Toshiba when Sony adopted the strategy of persuading programme providers (major studios) and retailers (e.g. Wal-Mart in the USA) to supply Blu-ray technology products to end users. In 2007 sales of Blu-ray discs exceeded HD-DVD by about 200 per cent. The moving finger was writing. In February 2008, Toshiba announced it was pulling out of developing HD-DVD. The film industry ceased producing HD-DVD format releases and the format war was over.

In the format example one user's utility from purchasing a system depended on other users' purchases, and on compatibility with suppliers of complementary products.

Sometimes described as demand-side scale economies, this creates what is also known as *network effects*, or network economies, where increasing the number of users of a good or service increases its utility to any given user.

A similar network economy helped to account for the dominant position of Microsoft's Windows operating system, currently installed in more than 90 per cent of all personal computers. Microsoft's initial sales advantage from Windows over other DOS-type operating systems gave software developers a strong incentive to write for the Windows format. The inventory of available software in the Windows format is now much larger than that for any competing operating system even if, as many Apple users will say, and many others believe, Windows is inferior to Apple's system.

RECAP

Five sources of market power

A firm's power to raise its price without losing its entire market stems from exclusive control of important inputs, patents and copyrights, government licences, economies of scale or network economies. By far the most important and enduring of these are *economies of scale* and *network economies*.

ECONOMIES OF SCALE AND THE IMPORTANCE OF FIXED COSTS

As we saw in Chapter 5, variable costs are those that vary with the level of output produced, while fixed costs are independent of output. Strictly speaking, there are no fixed costs in the long run, because all inputs can be varied. But, as a practical matter, start-up costs often loom large for the duration of a product's useful life. Most of the costs involved in the production of computer software, for example, are fixed costs of this sort, one-time costs incurred in writing and testing the software. Once those tasks are done, additional copies of the software can be produced at a very low marginal cost. A good whose production entails large fixed costs and low variable costs, will be subject to significant economies of scale. Because, by definition, fixed costs don't increase as output increases, the average total cost of production for such goods will decline as output increases.

To illustrate, consider a production process for which total cost is given by the equation $TC = F + MQ$, where F is fixed cost, M is marginal cost (assumed constant in this illustration) and Q is the level of output produced. With this simple total cost function, variable cost is simply MQ, the product of marginal cost and quantity. Average total cost, TC/Q, is equal to $(F/Q) + M$. As Q increases, average cost declines, because the fixed costs are spread out over more and more units of output.

Figure 8.2 shows the total production cost (panel (a)) and average total cost (panel (b)) for a firm with the total cost curve $TC = F + MQ$ and the corresponding average total cost curve $ATC = (F/Q) + M$. The average total cost curve (panel (b)) shows the decline in per-unit cost as output grows. Though average total cost is always higher than marginal cost for this firm, the difference between the two diminishes as output grows. Average cost approaches marginal cost asymptotically.

As Examples 8.1 and 8.2 illustrate, the importance of economies of scale depends on how large *fixed cost* is in relation to *marginal cost*.

Example 8.1 Two video game producers, Nintendo and Playstation, each have fixed costs of €200,000 and marginal costs of €0.80 per game. If Nintendo produces 1 million units per year and Playstation produces 1.2 million, how much lower will Playstation's average total production cost be?

Table 8.1 summarises the relevant cost categories for the two firms. Note in the bottom row that PlayStation enjoys only a 3 cent average cost advantage over Nintendo. Even

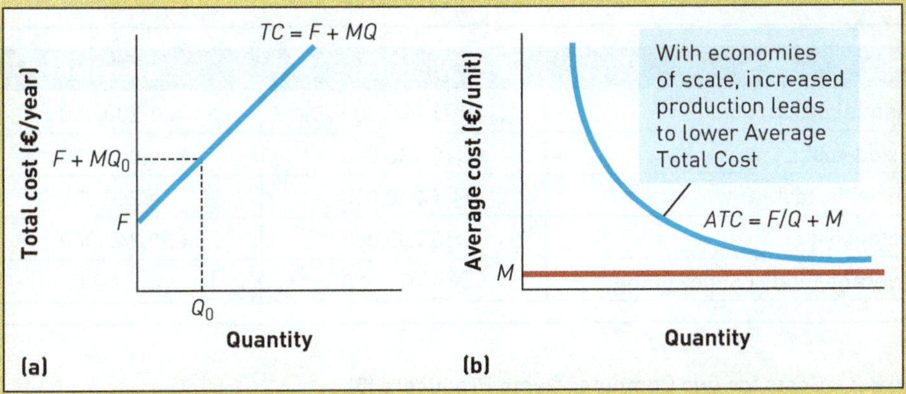

Figure 8.2 Total and Average Total Costs for a Production Process with Economies of Scale

For a firm whose total cost curve of producing Q units of output per year is $TC = F + MQ$, total cost (a) rises at a constant rate as output grows, while average total cost (b) declines. Average total cost is always higher than marginal cost for this firm, but the difference becomes less significant at high output levels.

Table 8.1 Costs for Two Computer Game Producers (1)

Cost	Nintendo	PlayStation
Annual production	1,000,000	1,200,000
Fixed cost	€200,000	€200,000
Variable cost	€800,000	€960,000
Total cost	€1,000,000	€1,160,000
Average total cost per game	€1.00	€0.97

though Nintendo produces 20 per cent fewer copies of its video game than PlayStation, it does not suffer a significant cost disadvantage because fixed cost is a relatively small part of total production cost.

But note how the picture changes when fixed cost looms large relative to marginal cost.

Example 8.2

Two video game producers, Nintendo and PlayStation, each have fixed costs of €10,000,000 and marginal costs of €0.20 per video game. If Nintendo produces 1 million units per year and PlayStation produces 1.2 million, how much lower will PlayStation's average total cost be?

The relevant cost categories for the two firms are now summarised in Table 8.2. The bottom row shows that PlayStation enjoys a €1.67 average total cost advantage over Nintendo, substantially larger than in Example 8.1.

Given high similarity between the two firms' products, the fact that PlayStation can charge significantly lower prices and still cover its costs should enable it to attract customers away from Nintendo. As more and more of the market goes to PlayStation, its cost advantage will become self-reinforcing. Table 8.3 shows how a shift of 500,000 units from Nintendo to PlayStation would cause Nintendo's average total cost to rise to €20.20 per unit, while PlayStation's average total cost would fall to €6.08 per unit. The fact that a firm could not long survive at such a severe disadvantage explains why the video game market is served now by only a small number of firms.

Table 8.2 Costs for Two Computer Game Producers (2)

Cost	Nintendo	PlayStation
Annual production	1,000,000	1,200,000
Fixed cost	€10,000,000	€10,000,000
Variable cost	€200,000	€240,000
Total cost	€10,200,000	€10,240,000
Average total cost per game	€10.20	€8.53

Table 8.3 Costs for Two Computer Game Producers (3)

Cost	Nintendo	PlayStation
Annual production	500,000	1,700,000
Fixed cost	€10,000,000	€10,000,000
Variable cost	€100,000	€340,000
Total cost	€10,100,000	€10,340,000
Average total cost per game	€20.20	€6.08

Exercise 8.1 How big will PlayStation's unit cost advantage be if it sells 2,000,000 units per year, while Nintendo sells only 300,000?

Over the last 40 years an increasing share of the value embodied in the goods and services we buy stems from *fixed investment in R&D*. For example, in 1984 some 80 per cent of the cost of a computer was in its hardware; the remaining 20 per cent was in its software. With the cost of memory and computing power roughly halving in real terms every couple of years, by 1999 these proportions were reversed. Hardware is cheap . . . but software, which is to an even greater degree than hardware the result of fixed investment in R&D, now accounts for most of the cost of a computer. Fixed costs account for about 85 per cent of total costs in the computer software industry, whose products are included in a growing share of ordinary manufactured goods.

Economic Naturalist 8.1
Why do some industry experts believe Intel's dominance of the chip market is bound to be eroded?

Intel's dominance of the CPU chip market rests on its history of R&D-led innovation. It has led the field, introducing new, more powerful CPU chips that it sells at initially higher prices to high-value users. Other chip-makers, such as AMD, follow with competing products, sometimes based on reverse engineering, and prices decline. Intel can recoup its R&D fixed costs from the high-value users sales, and then cover its variable costs from further sales, thus profitably sustaining market share, which is also supported by significant brand advertising. However, many industry sources are predicting a decline in the return to R&D in hardware development, including CPU development, as increased computing power from improved chip performance is running into diminishing returns. If this is correct, price considerations are likely to become relatively more important than newer chips as far as purchasers are concerned, and Intel's first-mover advantage will weaken or evaporate, and its market share will decline.

RECAP

Economies of scale and the importance of fixed costs

Research, design, engineering and other fixed costs account for an increasingly large share of all costs required to bring products successfully to market. For products with large fixed costs, marginal cost is lower, often substantially, than average total cost, and average total cost declines, often sharply, as output grows. This cost pattern explains why many industries are dominated by either a *single firm* or a *small number of firms*.

PROFIT-MAXIMISATION FOR THE MONOPOLIST

Given that, whether price takers or price setters, firms seek to maximise profits, the operational decision facing a firm is the same. Choose price or output to maximise the difference between total sales revenue and total costs. But there are some important differences in how the two types of firm carry out this decision.

For both types of firm, the marginal benefit of expanding output is the additional revenue the firm will receive if it sells one additional unit of output. This marginal benefit is called the firm's **marginal revenue**. For the perfectly competitive firm, marginal revenue is exactly equal to the market price of the product. The position for a price-setting firm is different. This is because the amount sold affects the price at which all units are sold.

marginal revenue the change in a firm's total revenue that results from a one-unit change in output

MARGINAL REVENUE FOR THE MONOPOLIST

The logic of profit-maximisation is precisely the same for the monopolist as for the perfectly competitive firm. The firm keeps expanding output as long as the benefit of doing so exceeds the cost. The calculation of marginal cost is also precisely the same for the monopolist as for the perfectly competitive firm. But for the monopolist, marginal revenue is not the same as price.

To a monopolist the marginal benefit of selling an additional unit is *strictly less than the market price*. The reason is that while the perfectly competitive firm can sell as many units as it wishes at the market price, the monopolist can sell an additional unit only if it accepts a fall in price (even if very small) for the units it is *currently selling*.

Suppose, for example, that a monopolist with the demand curve shown in Fig. 8.3 is currently selling 2 units of output at a price of €6 per unit. What would be its marginal revenue from selling an additional unit?

This monopolist's total revenue from the sale of 2 units per week is (€6 per unit) (2 units per week) = €12 per week. Its total revenue from the sale of 3 units per week would be €15 per week. The difference – €3 per week – is the marginal revenue from the sale of the third unit each week. Note that this amount is not only smaller than the original price (€6) but smaller than the new price (€5) as well.

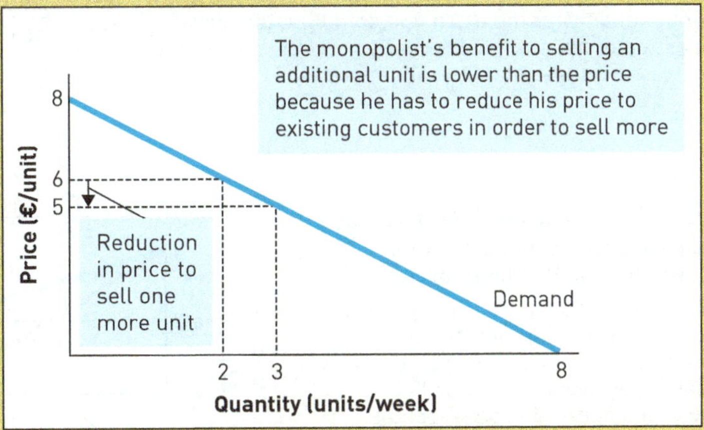

Figure 8.3 The Monopolist's Benefit from Selling an Additional Unit

The monopolist shown receives €12 per week in total revenue by selling 2 units per week at a price of €6 each. This monopolist could earn €15 per week by selling 3 units per week at a price of €5 each. In that case, the benefit from selling the third unit would be €15 – €12 = €3, less than its selling price of €5.

Exercise 8.2 Calculate marginal revenue for the monopolist in Fig. 8.3 as it expands output from 3 to 4 units per week, and then from 4 to 5 units per week.

Table 8.4 Marginal Revenue for a Monopolist (€ per unit)

Quantity	Marginal revenue
2	
	3
3	
	1
4	
	−1
5	

For the monopolist whose demand curve is shown in Fig. 8.3, a sequence of increases in output – from 2 to 3, from 3 to 4 and from 4 to 5 – will yield marginal revenue of €3, €1 and €1, respectively. We can display these results in tabular form, as in Table 8.4.

Note that in Table 8.4 the marginal revenue values are displayed between the two quantity figures to which they correspond. Strictly speaking, the marginal revenue corresponds to neither quantity but to the *movement between* those quantities, hence its placement in Table 8.4.

To graph marginal revenue as a function of quantity, we plot the marginal revenue for the movement from 2 to 3 units of output per week (€3) at a quantity value of 2.5, because 2.5 lies midway between 2 and 3. Similarly, we would plot the marginal revenue for the movement from 3 to 4 units per week (€1) at a quantity of 3.5 units per week, and the marginal revenue for the movement from 4 to 5 units per week (€1) at a quantity of 4.5. The resulting marginal revenue curve, *MR*, is shown in Fig. 8.4.

More generally, consider a monopolist with a straight-line demand curve whose vertical intercept is *a* and whose horizontal intercept is Q_0, as shown in Fig. 8.5. This monopolist's marginal revenue curve will also have a vertical intercept of *a*, and it will be twice as steep as the demand curve. Thus its horizontal intercept will be not Q_0, but $Q_0/2$, as shown in Fig. 8.5.

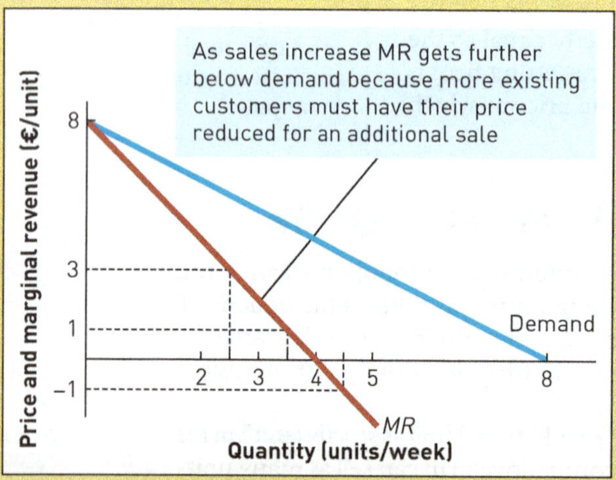

Figure 8.4 Marginal Revenue in Graphical Form
Because a monopolist must cut price to sell an extra unit, not only for the extra unit sold but also for all existing units, marginal revenue from the sale of the extra unit is less than its selling price.

Figure 8.5 The Marginal Revenue Curve for a Monopolist with a Straight-line Demand Curve
For a monopolist with the demand curve shown, the corresponding marginal revenue curve has the same vertical intercept as the demand curve, and a horizontal intercept only half as large as that of the demand curve.

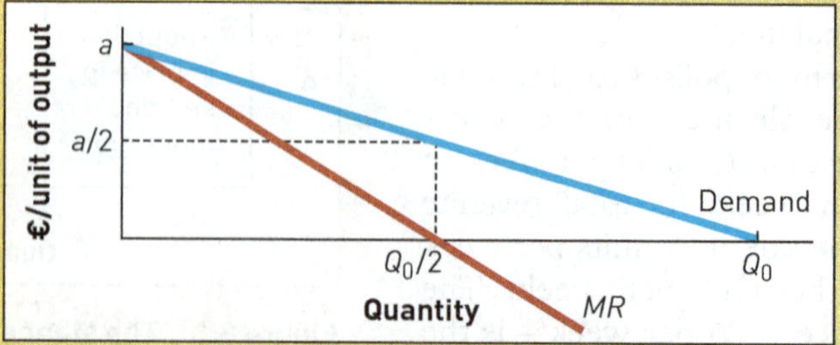

[1] Total revenue is average revenue (price) multiplied by *Q*. $TR = aQ - bQ^2$. Marginal revenue is dTR/dQ: $MR = a - 2bQ$.

Marginal revenue curves can also be expressed algebraically. If the formula for the monopolist's (inverse) demand curve is $P = a - bQ$, then the formula for its marginal revenue curve will be $MR = a - 2bQ$. This will be demonstrated in Maths box 8.1 below. If you have done calculus, this relationship is easy to derive,[1] but even without calculus you can verify it by working through a few numerical examples. First translate the formula for the demand curve into a diagram, and then construct the corresponding marginal revenue curve graphically. Reading from the graph, write the formula for that marginal revenue curve.

THE MONOPOLIST'S PROFIT-MAXIMISING DECISION RULE

Having derived the monopolist's marginal revenue curve, we can now describe how the monopolist chooses the output level that maximises profit. As in the case of the perfectly competitive firm, the Cost–Benefit Principle says that the monopolist should continue to expand output as long as the gain from doing so exceeds the cost. At the current level of output, the benefit from expanding output is the marginal revenue value that corresponds to that output level. The cost of expanding output is the marginal cost at that level of output. Whenever marginal revenue exceeds marginal cost, the firm should expand.

Conversely, whenever marginal revenue falls short of marginal cost, the firm should reduce its output. Profit is maximised at the level of output for which *marginal revenue precisely equals marginal cost.*

When the monopolist's profit-maximising rule is stated in this way, we can see that the perfectly competitive firm's rule is actually a special case of the monopolist's rule. When the perfectly competitive firm expands output by one unit, its marginal revenue exactly equals the product's market price (because the perfectly competitive firm can expand sales by a unit without having to cut the price of existing units). So when the perfectly competitive firm equates price with marginal cost, it is also equating marginal revenue with marginal cost.

In Figure 8.6, we begin by constructing the marginal revenue curve that corresponds to the monopolist's demand curve. It has the same vertical intercept as the demand curve, and its horizontal intercept is half as large. Note that the monopolist's marginal revenue at 12 units per week is zero, which is clearly less than its marginal cost of €3 per unit. This monopolist will therefore earn a higher profit by contracting production until marginal revenue equals marginal cost, which occurs at an output level of 8 units per week. At this profit-maximising output level the firm will charge €4 per unit, the price that corresponds to 8 units per week on the demand curve.

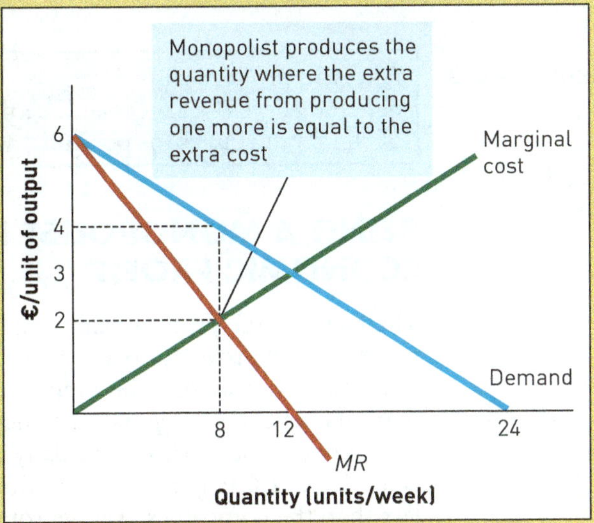

Figure 8.6 The Monopolist's Profit-maximising Output Level

This monopolist maximises profit by selling 8 units per week, the output level at which marginal revenue equals marginal cost. The profit-maximising price is €4 per unit, the price that corresponds to the profit-maximising quantity on the demand curve.

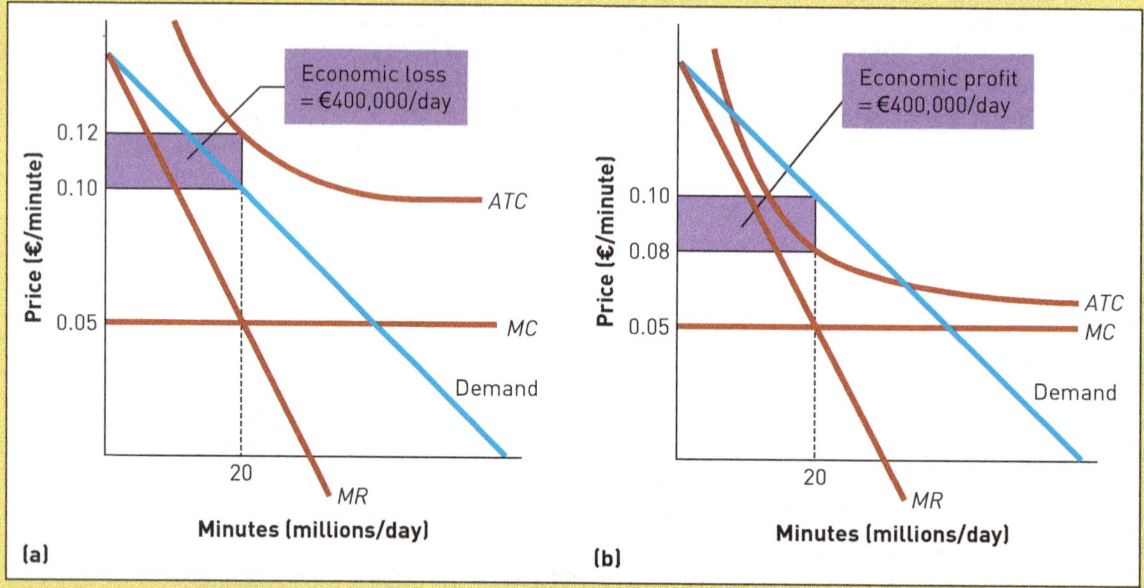

Figure 8.7 Even a Monopolist May Suffer an Economic Loss
The monopolist in (a) maximises its profit by selling 20 million minutes per day of calls but suffers an economic loss of €400,000 per day in the process. Because the profit-maximising price of the monopolist in (b) exceeds *ATC*, this monopolist earns an economic profit.

Exercise 8.3

Find the profit-maximising price and level of output for a monopolist with the demand curve $P = 12 - Q$ and the marginal cost curve $MC = 2Q$, where P is the price of the product in euros per unit and Q is output in units per week.

BEING A MONOPOLIST DOES NOT GUARANTEE AN ECONOMIC PROFIT

The fact that the profit-maximising price for a monopolist will always be greater than marginal cost provides no assurance that the monopolist will earn an economic profit. Consider, for example, the long-distance telephone service provider whose demand, marginal revenue, marginal cost and average total cost curves are shown in Fig. 8.7(a). This monopolist maximises its daily profit by selling 20 million minutes per day of calls at a price of €0.10 per minute. At that quantity, $MR = MC$, yet price is €0.02 per minute less than the company's average total cost of €0.12 per minute. As a result, the company sustains an economic loss of €0.02 per minute on all calls provided, or a total loss of (€0.02 per minute)(20,000,000 minutes per day) = €400,000 per day.

The loss occurred because its profit-maximising price was lower than its *ATC*. If the monopolist's profit-maximising price exceeds its average total cost, however, the company will of course earn an economic profit. Consider, for example, the long-distance provider shown in Fig. 8.7(b). This firm has the same demand, marginal revenue and marginal cost curves as the firm shown in Fig. 8.7(a). But because the firm in panel (b) has lower fixed costs, its *ATC* curve is lower at every level of output than the *ATC* curve in (a). At the profit-maximising price of €0.10 per minute, the firm in Fig. 8.7(b) earns an economic profit of €0.02 per minute, for a total economic profit of €400,000 per day.

Maths Box 8.1
Marginal revenue, marginal cost and profit maximisation when a firm has market power: the mathematical approach

This formal derivation of the $MC = MR$ rule for profit maximisation may be skipped without any loss of continuity.

Market power means that the firm can sell more . . . if it is prepared to let price drop. Consequently, when it sells more, the change in total revenue is not simply the extra sales multiplied by the price achieved for those sales, but must include the change in revenue arising from the previous volume of sales that are now being sold at a lower price, too. This can be expressed formally as follows.

The monopoly (market power) case

Market power (in the limiting case, monopoly) means that the price per unit the firm receives for the amount it puts on the market is a function of the amount being sold:

$$p = p(q)$$

in contrast with perfect competition, where the firm perceives price as given and independent of how much it chooses to sell.

The firm's total cost curve is

$$TC = a + b \cdot q + c \cdot q^2$$

and profits are $TR - TC$.

The firm's profits function is, therefore, written:

$$B = p(q) \cdot q - a - b \cdot q - c \cdot q^2$$

The first derivative is now

$$\mathrm{d}B/\mathrm{d}q = p + q(\mathrm{d}p/\mathrm{d}q) - b - 2c \cdot q$$

For profits to be maximised, it is necessary that $\mathrm{d}B/\mathrm{d}q = 0$, meaning that

$$p + q(\mathrm{d}p/\mathrm{d}q) = b + 2c \cdot q$$

The left-hand term is the value of $\mathrm{d}TR/\mathrm{d}q$ (MR) when $TR = p(q)q$. The right-hand side is marginal cost. The expression $q(\mathrm{d}p/\mathrm{d}q)$ is negative, since $\mathrm{d}p/\mathrm{d}q$ is the negative slope of the inverse demand curve. Therefore

$$p + q(\mathrm{d}p/\mathrm{d}q) < p$$

which means that $MR < P$.

Just as the slope of the total cost curve is marginal cost, the slope of the total revenue curve, $\mathrm{d}TR/\mathrm{d}Q$, is (by definition), marginal revenue. Hence, the condition for profit maximisation is setting $MR = MC$. The perfect competition case reflects the fact that under perfect competition, where firms have no market power, *price and marginal revenue are the same thing*. When a firm has market power it faces a downward-sloping demand curve. $TR = pq$, $AR = TR/q$; therefore p and AR are the same thing. Since p falls as q increases along the demand curve, AR is falling by definition. Since AR is falling we know that $MR < AR$. Hence, $MR < p$.

Note the implication that in the presence of market power the chosen level of output is one for which $p > MC$, implying loss of surplus relative to the perfectly competitive case.

Example 8.3 To show how this result can be used, take the following example. There is a type of doughnut sold in Germany known as a Berliner.[2] How many Berliners will be sold and at what price each week?

Suppose we know that the demand for Berliners in Berlin (and we suppose there is only one Berliner producer in Berlin) can be stated as:

$$€p = 20{,}000 - 6q$$

where q is thousands of doughnuts for sale in a week.

Suppose the weekly fixed cost is $€TC = 2{,}000q$. Then

$$TR = 20{,}000q - 6q_2;\ TC = 2{,}000q$$

$$MR = 20{,}000 - 12q;\ MC = 2{,}000;\ MR = MC \rightarrow 18{,}000 = 12q, \text{ or } q = 1{,}500$$

If $q = 1{,}500$, $p = 11{,}000$, and each doughnut sells for €1.10.

RECAP

Profit-maximisation for the monopolist

Both the perfectly competitive firm and the monopolist maximise profit by choosing the output level at which marginal revenue equals marginal cost. But whereas marginal revenue equals market price for the perfectly competitive firm, it is always less than market price for the monopolist. A monopolist will earn an economic profit only if price exceeds average total cost at the *profit-maximising level of output*.

WHY THE 'INVISIBLE HAND' BREAKS DOWN UNDER MONOPOLY

In our discussion of equilibrium in perfectly competitive markets in Chapters 6 and 7, we saw conditions under which the self-serving pursuits of consumers and firms were consistent with the broader interests of society as a whole. This was what was described as the workings of Adam Smith's 'invisible hand'.

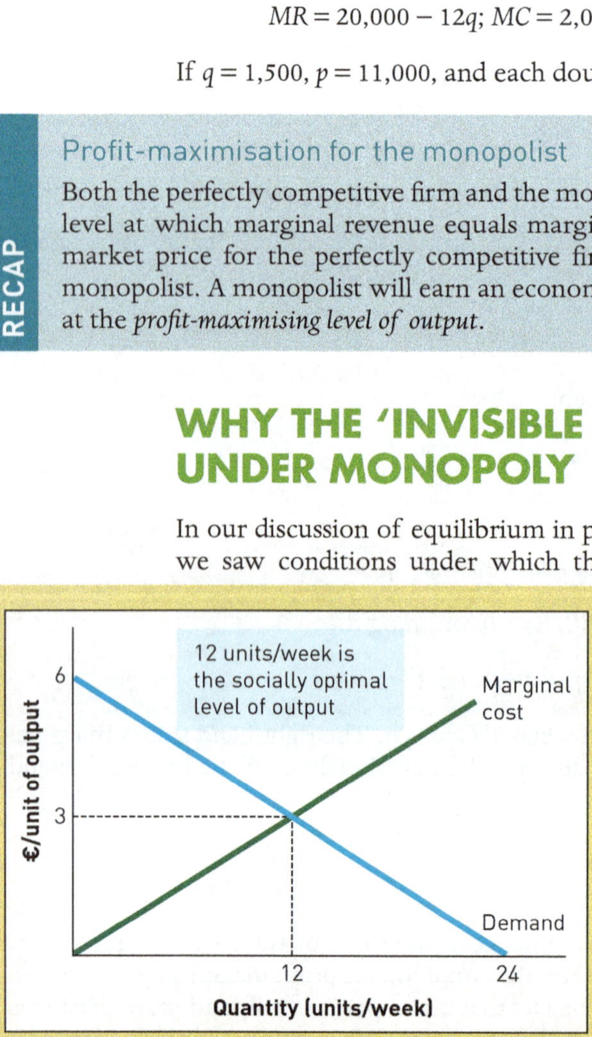

Figure 8.8 The Demand and Marginal Curves for a Monopolist

The socially optimal output level is 12 units per week, the quantity for which the marginal benefit *to the public* is exactly the same as marginal cost.

The material up to this point in this chapter raises a question: to what extent are Smith's conclusions regarding the invisible hand the same when we change assumptions about the market? Smith, after all, had in mind markets that were competitive and 'efficient' in the sense of earlier chapters in this text. To answer this question, we start with the case of monopoly.

Consider the monopolist in Figure 8.6. Is this firm's profit-maximising output level efficient from society's point of view? For any given level of output, the corresponding price on the demand curve indicates the amount that buyers would be willing to pay for an additional unit of output. When the

[2] This explains why there were a few chuckles when former US President John F. Kennedy in 1963 expressed his solidarity with the inhabitants of that city, after the Berlin Wall had divided it, in the lapidary phrase '*Ich bin ein Berliner.*'

monopolist is producing 8 units per week, the marginal benefit to society of an additional unit of output is thus €4. And since the marginal cost of an additional unit at that output level is only €2, society would gain a net benefit of €2 per unit if the monopolist were to expand production by one unit above the profit-maximising level. Because this economic surplus is not realised, the profit-maximising monopolist is *socially inefficient*.

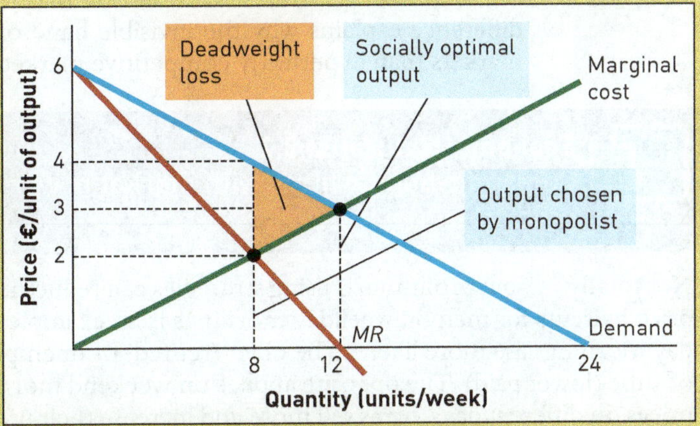

Figure 8.9 The Deadweight Loss from Monopoly

A loss in economic surplus results because the profit-maximising level of output (8 units per week) is less than the socially optimal level of output (12 units per week).

Recall that the existence of inefficiency means that the economic 'pie' is smaller than it might be. If that is so, why doesn't the monopolist simply expand production? The answer is that the monopolist would gladly do so if only there were some way to maintain the price of existing units and cut the price of only the extra units. As a practical matter, however, that is not always possible (but see Economic Naturalist 8.2).

Consider a monopolist whose demand and marginal cost curves are given in Fig. 8.9. For the market served by this monopolist, what is the socially efficient level of output?

Efficiency

Normally what the monopolist pays for the *resources* he uses represents the opportunity cost of the resources. It follows that, at any output level, the cost to society of an additional unit of output is the same as the cost to the monopolist, namely the amount shown on the monopolist's marginal cost curve. However, the marginal benefit to society from another unit being produced is not the same as the marginal benefit to the monopolist. The marginal benefit to *society* of an extra unit of output is simply the amount people are willing to pay for it, which can be measured on the monopolist's demand curve. To achieve social efficiency, the monopolist should expand production until the marginal benefit to society equals the marginal cost, which in this case occurs at a level of 12 units per week. Social efficiency is thus achieved at the output level at which the market demand curve intersects the monopolist's marginal cost curve.

The problem is that the marginal benefit to the monopolist is not what people would be willing to pay for another unit, but the change in his total sales revenues from selling one more unit, or marginal revenue. The value to society of an extra unit of output (its current price) is not equal to the value to the monopolist (its marginal revenue) from selling one more unit. The monopolist's demand curve slopes downwards meaning that to sell more he has to lower unit price. We already know that if any average (in this case price or average revenue) is declining, the marginal curve must lie below it. The marginal revenue curve for a monopolist must lie below the demand curve if he has to lower price for all units sold to increase sales.

Cost–Benefit Analysis

The fact that marginal revenue is less than price for the monopolist results in a *deadweight loss*. For the monopolist just discussed, the size of this deadweight loss is equal to the area of the shaded triangle in Fig. 8.9, which is (1/2)(€2 per unit)(4 units per week) = €4 per week. That is the amount by which total economic surplus is reduced because the monopolist produces too little.

For a monopolist, profit-maximisation occurs when marginal cost equals marginal revenue. Since the monopolist's marginal revenue is always less than price, the monopolist's profit-maximising output level is always below the socially efficient level. Under perfect competition, by contrast, profit-maximisation occurs when marginal cost equals the market price – the same criterion that must be satisfied for social efficiency. This difference explains why the invisible hand of the market is less evident in monopoly markets than in perfectly competitive markets.

Economic Naturalist 8.2
Can profit-hungry firms with market power overcome the social-inefficiency problem?

Not totally . . . but profit-maximising strategies can reduce it. Price discrimination is one way: lower-price haircuts for men on weekday mornings is an example. Men who have time to spare on week-day mornings are more likely to be older (retired) or unemployed or to have lower opportunity cost of time (lower paid). The opposite applies on weekend mornings. By offering the service at different prices on different days, firms sell more and increase their profits while selling the product at an average price closer to marginal cost. Another strategy is non-linear pricing: if you buy two suits we will sell you the third at a 50 per cent discount. This kind of offer has the same effect. Announcing in advance that there will be a sale on all goods after Christmas, selling airline tickets at a lower price if people book months in advance, frequent-flyer awards, all increase profits (otherwise they would not be offered) and also reduce price at the margin without cutting price intra-marginally.

Given that monopoly is socially inefficient, why not legislate it out of existence? A cynical response might well be that it would be ironic if parliaments that create monopolies (usually in the public sector) should decide that they are a bad thing in the first place. But it's not as simple as that. Monopolies can (if infrequently) evolve simply through the pressure of competition (which is accepted as a socially beneficial process). In this case, market forces produce concentration of production into a single firm, a natural monopoly, a firm that can produce the output at a lower average resource cost to society than if it were divided between two equally sized firms. Second, many economists believe that monopoly power is inherently transient, and contains within itself the seeds of its own destruction, as its profitability incites competition and innovation to break it down.

Although legal regimes do provide for breaking up monopolies (this is particularly true of the United States), for the most part they provide for its regulation. In part this probably reflects the acceptance that monopolies may derive their existence from scale economies, so that breaking them up would increase total costs of production. It also probably reflects a view that, while a monopoly may be a problem, deciding what exactly should replace it may not be a tractable problem for bureaucrats and legislators. Two firms? Three firms? Four firms? . . .

There are other reasons for reluctance to use the coercive power of the state to break monopoly power. Suppose, for example, that a monopoly results from a patent that prevents all but one firm from manufacturing some highly valued product. Would society be better off without patents? Probably not, because eliminating such protection would discourage innovation. Virtually all successful industrial nations grant some form of patent protection, which gives firms a chance to recover the R&D costs without which new products would seldom reach the market.

In short, we live in an imperfect world. Monopoly is socially inefficient and that, needless to say, is bad. But the alternatives to monopoly are not perfect, either.

RECAP

Why the monopolist produces 'too little' output

The monopolist maximises profit at the output level for which marginal revenue equals marginal cost. Because its profit-maximising price exceeds marginal revenue, and hence also marginal cost, the benefit to society of the last unit produced (the market price) must be greater than the cost of the last unit produced (the marginal cost). So the output level for an industry served by a profit-maximising monopolist is *smaller* than the socially optimal level of output.

MEASURING MARKET POWER

How pervasive is market power? How much market power does a firm enjoy? Will a merger or acquisition increase the market power of the new firm? To answer questions like these, which are important from a policy perspective, we need to be able to measure market power. A simple approach is to look at the number of firms in a market and to calculate an index of concentration. For example, we could ask what percentage of total sales is in the hands of the largest three or four firms. If they account for most sales in the market, the market is 'concentrated'. A more sophisticated approach is to use what is known as the Hirschman-Hefindahl Index (HHI). This is given by the sum of the squares of the shares of the firms in the market. It has a range of between 10,000 (100 squared) and close to zero. A value of over 2,000 would usually be held to indicate high concentration.

Both these approaches have serious data problems. The first is that we have to define the relevant product market. Is lager in a separate market from ales, or are both in the beer market? The second is that we have to define the relevant geographical market. Is there a French market for cement, or are sales in France merely a portion of sales in a single Europe-wide market? These can be handled, but they pose difficulties at a theoretical and practical level.

Another way to tackle the problem is to use what we have already learned about imperfect competition: it gives a firm market power. This means that the demand curve for its product slopes down. The firm will choose the output for which $MC = MR < P$.

Competition tends to drive price down towards cost. The existence of close substitutes means that a firm's sales will be significantly affected by any difference between its price and those of competing firms (the demand curve has a shallow slope) and *MR* is close to *P*.

It follows that an indicator of a firm's market power, and the market power of a group of firms in a market, is the relationship between marginal cost (or a proxy for *MC*) and price. This gives us the Lerner Index, defined as

$$L = \frac{(P - MC)}{P}$$

In perfect competition, $P = MR = MC$, and $L = 0$. As a firm's market power increases L increases, with a theoretical maximum value of 1 as $(P - MC) \rightarrow P$.

The Lerner Index has problems, too. First accurate measures of price and marginal cost may be difficult. Second, when the measurement is made the values could reflect temporary rather than permanent aspects of the observed margin, thus yielding misleading results. Third, high values for a firm's Lerner Index may result from offering a superior product, or using a more efficient production method which does not mean the market as a whole is uncompetitive, or that the firm does not face serious competition.[3]

CONTESTABILITY

The existing structure of a market, while important, may not be the only determinant of market power. Firms may face competitive constraints not only from existing suppliers, but also from potential competitors. If there are significant entry costs for new suppliers this will not be a problem. But if entry costs are low, high profits will attract entry, so that existing firms are constrained in their pricing policy by the threat of entry. Entry costs are costs incurred by an entrant that will not be recouped on exiting the market. As a sunk cost they constitute a sort of 'ticket price' facing a would-be entrant.

[3] If you want a more complete but understandable account of the problems involved in measuring market power, go to the US Federal Trade Commission website at www.ftc.gov/opp/jointvent/classic3.shtm.

When these costs are low (in the limiting case, when they are zero) so that a market is open to entry on a hit-and-run basis, it is said to be highly 'contestable'.

High contestability implies prices being driven down towards average cost. The concept of contestability has given rise to arguments about market power and intervention in markets that play down the issue of structure on the basis that, regardless of structure, it will be sufficient to rely on a high degree of contestability to ensure economic efficiency. When taken in conjunction with the Chicago School view that, in the long run, markets operate as if they are contestable (entry occurs, and/or competition from new products has the same effect as entry), the contestability approach has tended to reduce concern about concentrated market structures, and reduce support for policy measures designed to prevent increased market concentration (merger control regulation).

Perfect contestability requires some demanding assumptions. The following must be absent: legal or administrative barriers, problems in accessing customers of existing firms, costs advantages arising from being in the market already, an ability of incumbents to use pricing and other strategies to discourage customers from switching to an entrant or otherwise to impose costs on entrants. Only if these are absent will the market be vulnerable to hit-and-run entry, or perfectly contestable.[4]

While it has been established that some of the claims for the sufficiency of contestability to deliver economic efficiency have been overstated, this approach does contain more than a grain of truth. Low entry barriers and technical ease of entry do constrain incumbent firms in seeking to exploit concentrated market structures. The impact of low-cost airlines on the performance of the established carriers, and the repositioning of those carriers after deregulation, can be seen as a partial vindication of contestability theory. However, the unfortunate reality is that the conditions necessary for full contestability are extremely onerous. It is not plausible to argue for withdrawing policy intervention on the grounds that as an empirical matter most markets are sufficiently contestable to ensure economic efficiency regardless of changes in market structures. In addition, for contestability to be a realistic alternative to the standard approach to analysing markets would require treating markets as if they were devoid of uncertainty and the requirement for entrepreneurs to take risky decisions with imperfect information.[5]

PRICE DISCRIMINATION

The discussion earlier about social inefficiency and the material in Economic Naturalist 8.2 raise an interesting question, indeed two questions. The first is: why, for example, doesn't the monopolist from the earlier examples sell 8 units of output at a price of €4, and then once those buyers are out the door, cut the price for more price-sensitive buyers, a form of **price discrimination**? The second is: why do we punish price discrimination (see Economic Naturalist 8.4)?

price discrimination the practice of charging different buyers different prices for essentially the same good or service

To answer these questions we need to look at price discrimination more closely, starting by defining it. Price discrimination consists in charging different buyers different prices for the same good or service. Examples of price discrimination include senior citizens' and children's discounts on cinema tickets and price discounts on sales at certain times or days. In France and Italy, a standard practice is to offer access to art galleries and museums to the over-60s at a reduced rate. Something that is starting to be used in Europe but is widespread in the United States is the use of cut-out newspaper coupons entitling users to get discounts at supermarkets or other retail outlets (those who have a higher opportunity cost of time or lower marginal utility of income will not bother to cut out coupons and will pay more for their purchases).

Incentives Matter

[4] See Baumol *et al.* (1982).

[5] See Brätland (2004).

Price discrimination as exemplified in Economic Naturalist 8.2 may be profitable, and is more common than most people think (because they don't understand the basis for pricing strategies adopted by firms). It is not, however, universal when firms have market power. The obvious conclusion is that it may not be possible in some market situations. A little reflection indicates that two things are necessary: differences in demand between definable groups and absence of possibility of re-sale between purchasers. In many cases these may not exist.

Table 8.5 Family Reservation Prices

Family	Reservation price (€ per visit)
1	80
2	75
3	70
4	65
5	60
6	55
7	50
8	45
9	40
10	35

HOW PRICE DISCRIMINATION AFFECTS OUTPUT

As we pointed out earlier the use of price discrimination to extract more profits can have the counter-intuitive consequence of making society as a whole better off. The unexpected result of this reasoning arises from the fact that we (reasonably) assume that higher prices that produce higher profits involve less being offered for sale. But this is not necessarily the case. It's worth giving some attention to how and why this happens.

Suppose in a small village with a single doctor there are ten households. The doctor is a monopolist, and can set a single price at which he will maximise his profits as in Figure 8.9 above. Naturally, as economists, we pay no attention to what he says at village meetings about the ethics of public service. He is concerned to maximise his profits. Suppose that health regulations require that he has to post his prices for a month in advance, and sell his services to all at the posted price for a visit to his surgery.

Given good information as to the villagers' demand for healthcare, he will select the price and quantity of consultations the price that maximise his profits, setting $MC = MR$.

Suppose the ten families (reflecting their incomes, number of children and health status) have differing reservation prices for a weekly visit to the doctor. Rank them from the highest to the lowest, as in Table 8.5.

We could use this data to derive a village demand curve for a weekly visit (Fig. 8.10).

To make life easy, suppose that the doctor has a constant marginal cost of seeing a patient. Suppose his *MC* is 35.

The profit-maximising doctor will charge a price of €60 and see five families in the week. At this price, village welfare is not maximised. Maximisation of economic surplus would require seeing ten families (where $MC = P$).

The doctor's profits are €(5 × 25) = €125. Families 1–5 have a joint consumer surplus of €(20 + 15 + 10 + 5 + 0) = €50. Total surplus is, therefore, €175.

Now, suppose that the price regulation is removed, and he is allowed to charge

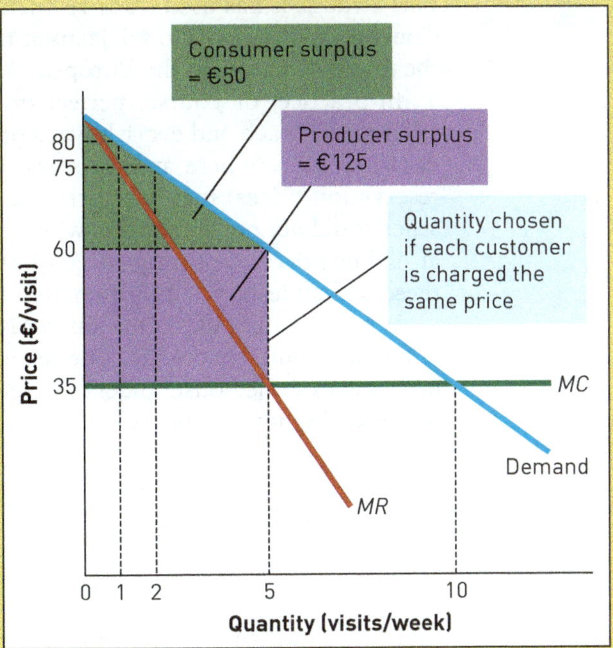

Figure 8.10 **Demand Curve for a Weekly Doctor's Visit**

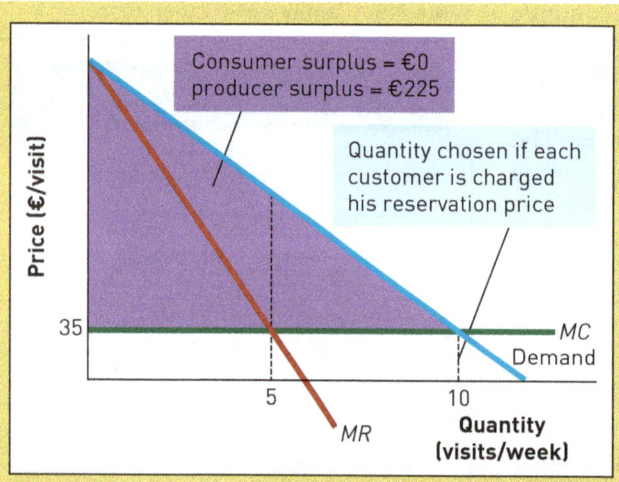

Figure 8.11 Perfect Discrimination Increases Output from 5 to 10 and Surplus to the Area Above the MC Line

each family its reservation price. He sells the visit to family 1 at €80, to family 2 at €75, and so on (Fig. 8.10). As long as a family is prepared to cover his marginal cost he has an incentive to see the family. He will see all the families, since the reservation price of family 10 is just equal to his *MC*. Each family pays its reservation price and so keeps no consumer surplus. The doctor has a profit of €(45 + 40 + 35 + 30 + 25 + 20 + 15 + 10 + 5 + 0) = €225. This is the total surplus. See Figure 8.11.

Total surplus is higher; more output is produced; the level of output is the efficient level ($P = MC$). Of course, from the point of view of families 1–5 this is a rough deal, but families 6–10 are better off (because they have chosen to purchase) even though they have no consumer surplus. The entire surplus has been appropriated by the doctor, who at the next village meeting is hailed as a latter-day Robin Hood because he appears to be charging more to the rich to finance supplying the poor.

perfectly discriminating monopolist a firm that charges each buyer exactly his or her reservation price

The doctor in this case is described as a **perfectly discriminating monopolist**. This is a monopolist who can sell each unit he produces at its reservation price. He is engaging in 'first-degree' price discrimination. A firm with market power that can discriminate between groups of purchasers in a market is said to be engaging in 'second-degree' price discrimination. An airline that sells tickets at different prices to different groups reflecting willingness to pay (business and tourist, off-peak and peak-time travel) is practising second-degree price discrimination. A firm that can segment whole markets is a third-degree price discriminator. An example is Levi-Strauss: it has used trade restrictions that have been sanctioned by the European Court of Justice (ECJ) to sell jeans at much lower prices in countries such as India than the prices it charges in the European Union.

In practice, of course, perfect price discrimination can never occur, because no seller knows each and every buyer's precise reservation price. But even imperfect price discrimination (where at least some goods are sold to customers for less than their reservation prices) may face practical difficulties. For example, in many markets the seller could not prevent buyers who bought at low prices from reselling to other buyers at higher prices, capturing some of the seller's business in the process. Despite such these difficulties, price discrimination is widespread, as we have seen.

Why is it unpopular? One answer is that it offends against what many people regard as fair and equitable pricing. The second is that, while in the doctor's case it is efficient, (a) it makes some householders worse of (numbers 1 to 5) while (b) allowing the doctor to pocket higher profits.

Economic Naturalist 8.3
Economies of scale have led to the concentration of production of cars into a small number of very large producers. Why, then, do they continue to produce so many different marques?

All over the world for the last 60 years car manufacturers have merged to create a decreasing number of larger firms each producing more cars in order to take advantage of a variety of scale economies. But the numbers of car types produced has only fallen by a few, meaning fewer cars per marque. Many manufacturers typically offer several different marques of what is basically the same car with different external appearances, some technical differences and differences in trim and accessories. VW sells its cars under four brands: VW, Audi, Skoda and Seat. In the United States, Ford operates the same strategy in differentiating between Ford and Mercury. General Motors has Chevrolet, Buick and Cadillac. In Italy, Fiat uses the Fiat, Alfa Romeo and Lancia brands. This reflects a strategy of designing and pricing cars to appeal to buyer groups with different tastes and reservation prices, which enables them to sell what are in many respects the same car at different prices, or engage in price discrimination, as prices differ between a firm's marques by more than production costs.

THE HURDLE METHOD OF PRICE DISCRIMINATION

Two primary obstacles prevent sellers from achieving maximum profits through discrimination. First, sellers don't know exactly how much each buyer is willing to pay. Second, they need some means of excluding those who are willing to pay a high price from buying at a low price. These are formidable problems, which no seller can hope to solve completely.

One common method by which sellers achieve a crude solution to both problems is to require buyers to overcome some obstacle to be eligible for a discount price. This method is called the **hurdle method of price discrimination**. For example, the seller might sell a product at a standard list price and offer a rebate to any buyer who takes the trouble to mail in a rebate coupon.

hurdle method of price discrimination the practice by which a seller offers a discount to all buyers who overcome some obstacle

The hurdle method solves both the seller's problems, provided that buyers with low reservation prices are more willing than others to jump the hurdle. Because the decision to jump the hurdle is subject to the cost–benefit test, such a link seems to exist. Buyers with low incomes are more likely than others to have low reservation prices. Because of the low opportunity cost of their time, they are more likely than others to take the trouble to send in rebate coupons. Rebate coupons thus target a discount towards those buyers whose reservation prices are low and who therefore might not otherwise buy the product.

A **perfect hurdle** is one that separates buyers precisely according to their reservation prices, and in the process imposes no cost on those who jump the hurdle. With a perfect hurdle, the highest reservation price among buyers who jump the hurdle will be lower than the lowest reservation price among buyers who choose not to jump the hurdle. In practice, perfect hurdles do not exist. Some buyers will always jump the hurdle even though their reservation prices are high. And hurdles will always exclude at least some buyers with low reservation prices. Even so, many commonly used hurdles do a remarkably good job of targeting discounts to buyers with low reservation prices.

perfect hurdle a threshold that completely segregates buyers whose reservation prices lie above it from others whose reservation prices lie below it, imposing no cost on those who jump the hurdle

IS PRICE DISCRIMINATION A BAD THING?

We are so conditioned to think of discrimination as 'bad' and 'unfair' that we may be tempted to conclude that price discrimination must run counter to the public interest.

Consider, however, the price coupon example. It is two weeks before Christmas. A supermarket advertises in a local paper, and states that anyone who cuts out and presents to the supermarket manager the coupon in the advertisement will receive a discount of 5 per cent on any oven-ready turkey in the week before Christmas.

On average, the supermarket believes that only those with low opportunity costs of time and a high marginal utility of money income (i.e. the less well-off) will take the trouble to jump the hurdle. Inevitably, some inveterate high-income bargain hunters will do so as well, but an astute supermarket chain will set the hurdle so as to ensure that most of those who jump it have a lower reservation price than those who don't.

By definition, the real income of those who jump the hurdle is improved by doing so: the cost is more than offset by the benefit from paying less for the turkey. Faced with the option of paying more and/or buying a smaller turkey, but not expending effort to jump the hurdle, or jumping, they jump. Their total surplus has increased. That of those who did not jump has not been reduced. The surplus of the supermarket operator must have increased as well . . . otherwise it would not have made the offer. The acid test is to ask whether a prohibition on coupons would have increased or reduced the total of consumer and producer surplus.

EXAMPLES OF PRICE DISCRIMINATION

Once you grasp the principle behind the hurdle method of price discrimination, you will begin to see examples of it all around you. Next time you visit a grocery, hardware store or electrical goods retail outlet, for instance, notice how many different product promotions include cash rebates. Temporary sales are another illustration of the hurdle method. Most of the time, stores sell most of their merchandise at the 'regular' price, but periodically they offer special sales at a significant discount. The hurdle in this instance is taking the trouble to find out when and where the sales will occur and then the cost of waiting before going to the store during that period. This technique works because buyers who care most about price (mainly those with low reservation prices) are more likely to monitor advertisements carefully and buy only during sale periods.

To give another example, book publishers typically launch a new book in hardcover form at a price from €20 to €30, and a year later they bring out a paperback edition priced between €5 and €15. People who are strongly concerned about price end up waiting for the paperback edition, while those with high reservation prices usually go for the hardback.

Consider the way in which major movies are released. The general rule is that they are released to cinemas first, then to terrestrial and satellite TV for pay-per-view, then to DVD or video for rental, and finally to free-to-air TV. Only movies that are not believed to have initial high reservation prices from a significant number of potential viewers appear in rental outlets first. The hurdle is willingness to wait to see the movie.

Commercial airlines have perfected the hurdle method to an extent matched by almost no other seller. To be eligible for deep discounts on standard fares, travellers must purchase their tickets a long time in advance, and their journey may have to include a Saturday-night stopover. Vacation travellers can more easily satisfy these restrictions than business travellers. Business travellers' reservation price tends to be much higher than the vacation traveller's. Airlines can vary prices continuously over time, and even between purchases at any point in time (if you ask for four tickets from London to Paris you may be quoted a different price from that which would be charged for two tickets).

Recall that the efficiency loss from single-price monopoly occurs because, to the monopolist, the benefit of expanding output is smaller than the benefit to society as a whole. The hurdle method of price discrimination reduces this loss by giving the monopolist a practical means of cutting prices for price-sensitive buyers only. In general, the more finely the monopolist can partition a market using the hurdle method, the smaller the efficiency loss. Hurdles are not perfect, however, and some degree of efficiency will inevitably be lost.

Economic Naturalist 8.4

If price discrimination can improve economic efficiency and consumer welfare, why does European competition policy (sometimes) punish it?

To a casual observer, European competition law appears to face two ways at once. In 2002 the European Court found that Levi-Strauss were not offending against competition policy by prohibiting re-export from non-EU countries to the UK of Levi-Strauss jeans that it sold elsewhere at a fraction of the price at which it sold them in Europe (which is third-degree price discrimination, and certainly damages consumer welfare in Europe). Then in 2003 the EU Commission imposed a fine of €149 million on Nintendo, and a further €9 million on its distributors, for operating a scheme whereby Nintendo games could not be sold across borders within the EU to take advantage of the substantial difference in prices at which Nintendo sold the goods in the different states. The fine was upheld by the Court of First Instance and the ECJ. The reasoning was that in the jeans case Levi-Strauss was not 'distorting competition' within the EU by segmenting the EU market, while Nintendo's policy had the effect of creating several markets within the EU. The offence lay not in price discrimination *per se*, but in price discrimination on a geographical basis within Europe. Interesting!

RECAP

Using discounts to expand the market

A price-discriminating monopolist is one who charges different prices to different buyers for essentially the same good or service. A common method of price discrimination is the hurdle method, which involves granting a discount to buyers who jump over a hurdle, such as mailing a rebate coupon. An *effective hurdle* is one that is more easily cleared by buyers with low reservation prices than by buyers with high reservation prices. Such a hurdle enables the monopolist to expand output and thereby reduce the deadweight loss from monopoly pricing.

PUBLIC POLICY TOWARDS MONOPOLIES

Monopoly is seen as a problem because (a) there is a loss in efficiency associated with restricted output, and (b) because the monopolist earns an economic profit at the buyer's expense. For these reasons many governments have adopted policies aimed at controlling firms enjoying substantial market power, including natural monopolies.

In the case of natural monopolies, where competition is not commercially feasible, there are several options. A government may assume ownership and control of a natural monopoly, or it may merely attempt to regulate the prices it charges. Government can solicit competitive bids from private firms to produce natural monopoly services. Governments may decide to dissolve natural monopolies into smaller entities that compete with one another. But, as always, there are costs associated with implementing policy. The practical challenge is to come up with the solution that yields the greatest surplus of benefits over costs. Natural monopoly may be inefficient (see Fig. 8.12) and unfair but, as noted earlier, the alternatives to it are far from perfect.

The need to achieve social control of natural monopolies was the generally accepted rationale that led to virtually all the network industries in Europe coming into state ownership: railways, postal services, telephone systems, airlines. This is easy to understand,

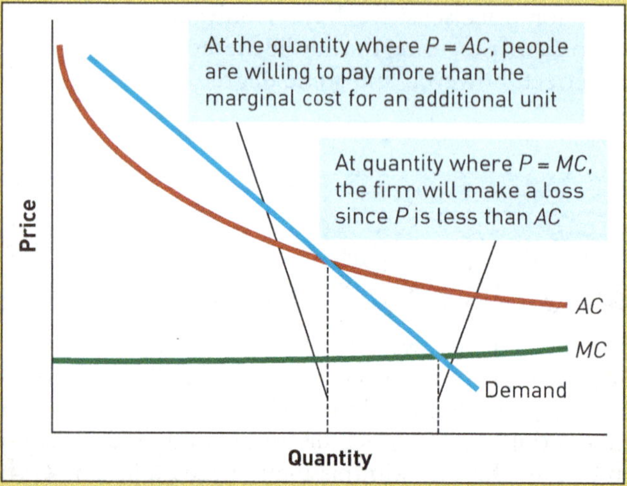

Figure 8.12 Natural Monopolies are Inefficient

If the firm produces the output where price just covers average cost, price must be greater than marginal cost, and if price is set equal to marginal cost the firm makes a loss.

but may be based on a misunderstanding! Easy to understand: think about fixed-line telephone systems. They (mostly) depend on copper-wire or fibre-optic local loop connectivity (the line from the customer to the nearest exchange). Imagine the average cost of local connectivity if three or four competing firms all had to put in local loops in any neighbourhood. Misunderstanding? In many cases the question of whether or not the cost structure of the sector concerned actually had the technical character of a natural monopoly was never rigorously examined. Indeed, there was a sort of circularity of argument in many cases: the state set up state-owned firms, or nationalised private firms and amalgamated them, giving them monopoly rights and justified continuing public ownership on natural monopoly grounds. Postal services are often analysed on this basis.

STATE OWNERSHIP AND MANAGEMENT

Monopoly, including natural monopoly, is inefficient because the monopolist's profit-maximising price is greater than its marginal cost. But even if the natural monopolist *wanted* to set price equal to marginal cost, it could not do so and hope to remain in business. After all, the defining feature of a natural monopoly is *economies of scale in production*, which means that marginal cost will always be less than average total cost. Setting price equal to marginal cost would fail to cover average total cost, which implies an economic loss.

Consider the case of a local cable television company. Once an area has been wired for cable television, the marginal cost of adding an additional subscriber is very low. Efficiency dictates a price equal to MC, but such a price would not cover the sunk fixed costs, so, if imposed, it would make investment in the system impossible. This same applies not just to cable television companies but to all other natural monopolies.

One way to attack the efficiency and fairness problems is for the government to take over the industry, set price equal to marginal cost and then absorb the resulting losses out of general tax revenues. This approach was followed with good results in the state-owned electricity utility industry in France, Electricité de France, whose efficient pricing methods have set the standard for electricity pricing worldwide.

But state ownership and efficient management do not always go hand in hand. A state-owned natural monopoly may choose to charge marginal cost, but privately owned natural monopolies are expected to engage in more cost containment than their government-owned counterparts. When the private monopolist figures out a way to cut €1 from the cost of production, its profit goes up by €1. But when the government manager of a state-owned monopoly cuts €1 from the cost of production, the government typically cuts the monopoly's budget by €1.

X-inefficiency where market power results in inefficient production rather than higher profits

This is an example of what economists call **X-inefficiency**, whereby monopoly power results in higher costs being incurred as a means of absorbing the inherent profitability of the monopoly enterprise. It is a much more serious problem in the public sector because, in the private sector, shareholders can (and do) fire inefficient managers so as to realise profits, while, in the public sector, governments have weak incentives to act decisively to contain costs, and have poor information on which to act. Whether the efficiency that is gained by being able to set price equal to marginal cost outweighs the inefficiency that results from a weakened incentive to cut costs is an empirical question.

STATE REGULATION OF PRIVATE MONOPOLIES

Dissatisfaction with public ownership has led to widespread divestment of state enterprise across Europe and Australasia. However, the consequences have frequently been the creation of privately owned suppliers with substantial market power, bordering on monopoly. As a result, privatisation has been accompanied by increased emphasis on regulation: legal and administrative structures that are entitled to lay down operational requirements and controls (pricing, availability, quality, and so on) for the firms concerned. While this is relatively new in Europe (dating for the most part from the 1980s), it has been the standard US procedure for dealing with natural monopolies and similar circumstances for a very long time. The basic objective of the regulatory regime is to ensure that a privately owned natural monopoly cannot use its monopoly power to generate monopoly profits. In addition, regulation is often used to ensure that low revenue (or even loss generating) customers are supplied. This involves pricing regulation to permit cross-subsidisation between customers.

The most common US method of curbing monopoly profits is for government merely to regulate the natural monopoly rather than own it. Most US states, for example, take this approach with electricity utilities, natural gas providers, local telephone companies and cable television companies. The standard procedure in these cases is called **cost-plus regulation**: government regulators gather data on the monopolist's explicit costs of production and then permit the monopolist to set prices that cover those costs, plus a mark-up to assure a normal return on the firm's investment.

> **cost-plus regulation** a method of regulation under which the regulated firm is permitted to charge a price equal to its explicit costs of production plus a mark-up to cover the opportunity cost of resources provided by the firm's owners

Cost-plus regulation has several pitfalls. First, it generates costly administrative proceedings in which regulators and firms quarrel over which of the firm's expenditures can properly be included in the costs it is allowed to recover. This question is difficult to answer even in theory. Consider a firm such as Pacific Telesis, originally the Californian telecommunications operator, but now a communications conglomerate. Its local telephone service is subject to cost-plus regulation but other products and services are unregulated. Many Pacific Telesis employees, from the president down, are involved in both regulated and unregulated activities. How should their salaries be allocated between the two? The company has a strong incentive to argue for greater allocation to the regulated activities, which allows it to capture more revenue from captive customers in the local telephone market.

A second problem with cost-plus regulation is that it reduces incentives to adopt cost-saving innovations, as lower costs invite cuts in regulated prices. Investment in cost saving presumes retaining at least a substantial proportion of the ensuing savings into the future. Worse, in some circumstances a cost-plus approach to regulating price can give a firm an incentive to raise its costs so as to retain profits. The term 'gold-plating' of costs applies here, referring to the fact that the regulated monopolist may earn a higher profit by installing gold-plated water taps in the company rest rooms.

Finally, cost-plus regulation does not solve the natural monopolist's basic problem: the inability to set price equal to marginal cost without losing money. Although these are all serious problems, governments seem to be in no hurry to abandon cost-plus regulation.

Another mechanism frequently used is *rate of return* regulation. This lays down the maximum profits a supplier may earn by reference to the capital employed. For example, it could be obliged to set prices on the basis that they permit a 15 per cent return to capital employed. If profits exceed this amount they are either taken away from the firm or it is obliged to reduce prices. *X-inefficiency* is a problem here, too, since a firm can allow other costs to increase since it will lose the profits anyway. More seriously, it can lead to firms investing in capital assets not on the basis of their contribution to net output but simply to permit retention of profits.

For these reasons, recent developments in European regulation have emphasised using *price rules* to sweat productivity out of regulated industries. A classic example of this is the RPI-X approach of the UK regulator in the electricity sector, Ofelec. RPI stands for retail price index, the main UK measure for inflation. The RPI-X approach sets a rule: your price may rise only at *X* per cent less than the inflation rate. *X* is set at a level designed to oblige the firm to implement cost-saving technology as it becomes available, and to rely on productivity gains rather than higher price–cost margins to generate profits.

Such a rule also has its problems, because it can lead to cost cutting at the expense of consumer safety (alleged in the United Kingdom in the case of Railtrack, the entity that was vested with the ownership of the railway infrastructure). It requires the regulator to have accurate knowledge of the potential for cost savings from new technology and productivity improvements that may in fact be difficult to know at all, or knowledge that is in effect confined to the firms being regulated.

EXCLUSIVE CONTRACTING FOR NATURAL MONOPOLY

One of the most promising methods for dealing with natural monopoly is for the government to invite private firms to bid for the natural monopolist's market. The government specifies in detail the service it wants and firms submit bids describing how much they will charge for the service. The lowest bidder wins the contract.

The incentive to cut costs under such an arrangement is every bit as powerful as that facing ordinary competitive firms. Competition among bidders should also eliminate any concerns about the fairness of monopoly profits. And if the government is willing to provide a cash subsidy to the winning bidder, exclusive contracting even allows the monopolist to set price equal to marginal cost.

Contracting has been employed with good results in municipal fire protection and refuse collection. US communities that employ private companies to provide these services often spend only half as much as adjacent communities served by municipal fire and sanitation departments.

Unfortunately, exclusive contracting is not without problems, especially when the service to be provided is complex or requires a large fixed investment in capital equipment. In such cases, contract specifications may be so detailed and complicated that they become tantamount to regulating the firm directly. And in cases involving a large fixed investment – electricity generation and distribution, for example – officials face the question of how to transfer the assets if a new firm wins the contract. The winning firm naturally wants to acquire the assets as cheaply as possible, but the retiring firm is entitled to a fair price for them. What, in such cases, is a 'fair price'? Fire protection and refuse collection are simple enough, so the cost of contracting out these functions is not prohibitive. But, in other cases, such costs might easily outweigh any savings made possible by exclusive contracting.

This approach is becoming very common in Europe. The highest bridge in Europe, opened in 2004 in Tarn in France, was built by a private-sector firm that won the contract to build the bridge and charge a toll. A significant proportion of London bus transport is carried out by franchised private operators. In New Zealand, although it remains in state ownership, the postal service is operated by New Zealand Post under a franchise contract with the government.

NATURAL MONOPOLY: DO NOTHING?

A final possibility is simply to ignore the problem of natural monopoly: to let the monopolist choose the quantity to produce and sell it at whatever price the market will bear. The obvious objections to this policy are the two we began with – namely, that a natural monopoly is not only inefficient but also unfair. But just as the hurdle method of price discrimination mitigates efficiency losses, it also lessens the concern about taking unfair advantage of buyers.

Consider first the source of the natural monopolist's economic profit. This firm, recall, is one with economies of scale, which means that its average production cost declines as output increases. Efficiency requires that price be set at marginal cost, but because the natural monopolist's marginal cost is lower than its average cost, it cannot charge all buyers the marginal cost without suffering an economic loss.

The depth and prevalence of discount pricing suggests that whatever economic profit a natural monopolist earns will generally not come out of the discount buyer's pocket. Although discount prices are higher than the monopolist's marginal cost of production, in most cases they are lower than the average cost. Thus the monopolist's economic profit, if any, must come from buyers who pay the list price. And since those buyers have the option, in most cases, of jumping a hurdle and paying a discount price, their contribution, if not completely voluntary, is at least not strongly coerced.

So much for the source of the monopolist's economic profit. What about its disposition? Who gets it? A large chunk goes to government via a corporation tax. The remainder is paid out to shareholders, some of whom are wealthy and some of whom are not. However, when we realise that over 80 per cent of shares are held by 'institutions', mostly pension funds, the redistributive consequences of monopoly power become much less clear.

Both the source of the monopolist's economic profit (the list-price buyer) and the disposition of that profit (largely, to fund public services) cast doubt on the claim that monopoly profit constitutes a social injustice on any grand scale. Nevertheless, the hurdle method of differential pricing cannot completely eliminate the fairness and efficiency problems that result from monopoly pricing. In the end, then, we are left with a choice among imperfect alternatives. As the Cost–Benefit Principle emphasises, the best choice is the one for which the balance of benefits over costs is largest. But which choice that is will depend on the circumstances at hand.

SORTING OUT MONOPOLY POWER: ANTI-TRUST REGULATION

The later nineteenth century witnessed the accumulation of massive private fortunes, particularly in the protected industrial sector of the booming US economy. Public sentiment ran high against the so-called 'robber barons' of the period – the Carnegies, Mellons, Rockefellers and others. In 1890 US Congress passed the Sherman Act, which declared illegal any conspiracy 'to monopolise, or attempt to monopolise . . . any part of the trade or commerce among the several States'. In 1914, Congress passed the Clayton Act, whose aim was to prevent corporations from acquiring shares in a competitor if the transaction would 'substantially lessen competition or create a monopoly'.

Since the Second World War, but mostly since the requirements of EU membership began to take effect, European countries and the Union have followed the US example by legislation and regulation affecting market concentration and the behaviour of firms with substantial market power. These are built into the grounding treaty provisions of the Union treaties.

Generically, these measures are described as 'anti-trust laws', recognising their origin in the United States. Anti-trust laws have helped to prevent the formation of *cartels*, or coalitions of firms that collude to raise prices above competitive levels. An early European example of this was the action of the EEC (as it was then) to punish

United Brands, the largest banana supplier in Europe, for third-degree price discrimination by segmenting the EEC markets of the six states in the 1960s. More recently, the French authorities and the Union imposed heavy fines on the cement producers of Europe, which were found to be operating a cartel. The motor trade in Europe was radically changed in the early 2000s by EU anti-trust actions designed to outlaw vertical distribution agreements operated by manufacturers and retailers that reduced intra-brand and inter-brand competition in the sector.

But such activities have also caused some harm. For example, US federal anti-trust officials spent more than a decade trying to break up the IBM Corporation in the belief that it had achieved an unhealthy dominance in the computer industry. That view was proved comically wrong by IBM's subsequent failure to foresee and profit from the rise of the personal computer. By breaking up large companies and discouraging mergers between companies in the same industry, anti-trust laws may help to promote competition, but they may also prevent companies from achieving *economies of scale*. Similarly, the US and EU cases against Microsoft have been criticised in some quarters as a waste of time, as they assumed that Microsoft's position, undoubtedly bolstered by some dubious practices in 'bundling' and in generating artificial incompatibilities, needed legal action to remedy the situation. And then along comes Linux . . .

RECAP

Public policy towards monopoly

A monopolist, including a natural monopoly firm, sets price above marginal cost, resulting in too little output from society's point of view (the *efficiency* problem). The monopolist may also earn an economic profit at buyers' expense (the *fairness* problem). Policies for dealing with the efficiency and fairness problems include state ownership and management, state regulation, exclusive contracting and vigorous enforcement of anti-trust laws. Each of these remedies entails problems of its own.

SUMMARY

- Our concern in this chapter was the conduct and performance of the *imperfectly competitive firm*, a firm that has at least some latitude to set its own price. Economists often distinguish among three different types of imperfectly competitive firms: the pure monopolist, the lone seller of a product in a given market; the oligopolist, one of only a few sellers of a given product; and the monopolistic competitor, one of a relatively large number of firms that sell similar though slightly differentiated products.
- Although advanced courses in economics devote much attention to differences in behaviour among these three types of firm, our focus was on the common feature that differentiates them from perfectly competitive firms. Whereas the perfectly competitive firm faces an infinitely elastic demand curve for its product, the imperfectly competitive firm faces a *downward-sloping demand curve*. For convenience, we use the term *monopolistic* to refer to any of the three types of imperfectly competitive firm.
- Monopolists are sometimes said to enjoy *market power*, a term that refers to their power to set the price of their product. Market power stems from exclusive control over important inputs, from economies of scale, from patents and government licences or franchises, and from network economies. The most important and enduring of these five sources of market power are economies of scale and network economies.
- Unlike the perfectly competitive firm, for which marginal revenue exactly equals market price, the monopolist realises a *marginal revenue that is always less than its price*. This shortfall reflects the fact that, to sell more output, the monopolist must cut the price not only to additional buyers but to existing buyers as well. For the

monopolist with a straight-line demand curve, the marginal revenue curve has the same vertical intercept and a horizontal intercept that is half as large as the intercept for the demand curve.

- Whereas the perfectly competitive firm maximises profit by producing at the level at which marginal cost equals the market price, the monopolist maximises profit by equating marginal cost with marginal revenue, which is significantly lower than the market price. The result is an output level that is best for the monopolist but smaller than the level that would be best for society as a whole. At the *profit-maximising* level of output, the benefit of an extra unit of output (the market price) is greater than its cost (the marginal cost). At the *socially efficient* level of output, where the monopolist's marginal cost curve intersects the demand curve, the benefit and cost of an extra unit are the same.
- Market power is reduced to the extent that a market is contestable, meaning that it is open to competition from firms currently not supplying the market. Perfect contestability, involving easy hit-and-run entry, tends to drive price down to cost.
- Both the monopolist and its potential customers can do better if the monopolist can grant discounts to price-sensitive buyers. The extreme example is the *perfectly discriminating monopolist*, who charges each buyer exactly his or her reservation price. Such producers are socially efficient, because they sell to every buyer whose reservation price is at least as high as the marginal cost.
- One common method of targeting discounts towards price-sensitive buyers is the *hurdle method* of price discrimination, in which the buyer becomes eligible for a discount only after overcoming some obstacle, such as mailing in a rebate coupon. This technique works well because those buyers who care most about price are more likely than others to jump the hurdle. While the hurdle method reduces the efficiency loss associated with single-price monopoly, it does not completely eliminate it.
- The various policies that governments employ to mitigate concerns about fairness and efficiency losses arising from natural monopoly include state ownership and management of natural monopolies, state regulation, private contracting and vigorous enforcement of anti-trust laws. Each of these remedies entails costs as well as benefits. In some cases, a *combination* of policies will produce a better outcome than simply allowing natural monopolists to do as they please. But in other cases, a *hands-off* policy may be the best available option.

REVIEW QUESTIONS

1. What important characteristic do all three types of imperfectly competitive firm share?
2. True or false: A firm with market power can sell whatever quantity it wishes at whatever price it chooses.
3. Why do most successful industrial societies offer patents and copyright protection, even though these protections enable sellers to charge higher prices?
4. Why is marginal revenue always less than price for a monopolist but equal to price for a perfectly competitive firm?
5. True or false: Because a natural monopolist charges a price greater than marginal cost, it necessarily earns a positive economic profit.

PROBLEMS

connect

1. Two car manufacturers, Saab and Volvo, have fixed costs of €1 billion and marginal costs of €10,000 per car. If Saab produces 50,000 cars per year and Volvo produces 200,000, calculate the average production cost for each company. On the basis of these costs, which company's market share do you think will grow in relative terms?

In Problems 2–4, state whether the statements are **true or false**, and explain why.

2. **a.** In a perfectly competitive industry the industry demand curve is horizontal, whereas for a monopoly it is downward-sloping.
b. Perfectly competitive firms have no control over the price they charge for their product.
c. For a natural monopoly, average cost declines as the number of units produced increases over the relevant output range.

3. A single-price profit-maximising monopolist:
a. causes excess demand, or shortages, by selling too few units of a good or service
b. chooses the output level at which marginal revenue begins to increase
c. always charges a price above the marginal cost of production
d. also maximises marginal revenue.
e. None of the above statements is true.

4. If a monopolist could perfectly price discriminate:
a. the marginal revenue curve and the demand curve would coincide
b. the marginal revenue curve and the marginal cost curve would coincide
c. every consumer would pay a different price
d. marginal revenue would become negative at some output level
e. the resulting pattern of exchange would still be socially inefficient.

5. Explain why price discrimination and the existence of slightly different variants of the same product tend to go hand in hand. Give an example from your own experience.

6. What is the socially desirable price for a natural monopoly to charge? Why will a natural monopoly that attempts to charge the socially desirable price invariably suffer an economic loss?

7. TotsPoses, a profit-maximising business, is the only photography business in town that specialises in portraits of small children. George, who owns and runs TotsPoses, expects to encounter an average of eight customers per day, each with a reservation price as shown in the table below.

Customer	Reservation price (€ per photo)
A	50
B	46
C	42
D	38
E	34
F	30
G	26
H	22

a. If the total cost of each photo portrait is €12, how much should George charge if he must charge a single price to all customers? At this price, how many portraits will George produce each day? What will be his economic profit?
b. How much consumer surplus is generated each day at this price?
c. What is the socially efficient number of portraits?
d. George is very experienced in the business and knows the reservation price of each of his customers. If he is allowed to charge any price he likes to any consumer, how many portraits will he produce each day, and what will his economic profit be?

e. In this case, how much consumer surplus is generated each day?
f. Suppose that George is permitted to charge two prices. He knows that customers with a reservation price above \$30 never bother with coupons, whereas those with a reservation price of €30 or less always use them. At what level should George set the list price of a portrait? At what level should he set the discount price? How many photo portraits will he sell at each price?
g. In this case, what is George's economic profit, and how much consumer surplus is generated each day?

8. Suppose that a university student cinema is a local monopoly whose demand curve for adult tickets on Saturday night is $P = 12 - 2Q$, where P is the price of a ticket in euros and Q is the number of tickets sold in hundreds. The demand for children's tickets on Sunday afternoon is $P = 8 - 3Q$, and for adult tickets on Sunday afternoon, $P = 10 - 4Q$. On both Saturday night and Sunday afternoon, the marginal cost of an additional patron, child or adult, is €2.
a. What is the marginal revenue curve in each of the three sub-markets?
b. What price should the cinema charge in each of the three sub-markets if its goal is to maximise profit?

9. Suppose you are a monopolist in the market for a specific video game. Your demand curve is given by $P = 80 - Q/2$, and your marginal cost curve is $MC = Q$. Your fixed costs equal €400.
a. Graph the demand and marginal cost curve.
b. Derive and graph the marginal revenue curve.
c. Calculate and indicate on the graph the equilibrium price and quantity.
d. What is your profit?
e. What is the level of consumer surplus?

10. Beth is an eight-year-old who old sells homemade lemonade on a street corner in a suburban neighbourhood. Each paper cup of lemonade costs Beth 20 cents to produce; she has no fixed costs. The reservation prices for the ten people who walk by Beth's lemonade stand each day are as listed in the table below.

Person	A	B	C	D	E	F	G	H	I	j
Reservation price (€)	1.00	0.90	0.80	0.70	0.60	0.50	0.40	0.30	0.20	0.10

Beth knows the distribution of reservation prices (that is, she knows that one person is willing to pay €1, another €0.90, and so on), but she does not know any specific individual's reservation price.
a. Calculate the marginal revenue of selling an additional cup of lemonade. (Start by figuring out the price Beth would charge if she produced only one cup of lemonade, and calculate the total revenue; then find the price Beth would charge if she sold two cups of lemonade; and so on.)
b. What is Beth's profit-maximising price?
c. At that price, what are Beth's economic profit and total consumer surplus?
d. What price should Beth charge if she wants to maximise total economic surplus?

Now suppose that Beth can tell the reservation price of each person. What price would she charge each person if she wanted to maximise profit? Compare her profit to the total surplus calculated in part (c).

REFERENCES

Baumol, W., J.C. Panzar and R.D. Willig (1982) *Contestable Markets and the Theory of Industry Structure* (New York: Harcourt Brace Jovanovich).

Brätland, J. (2004) 'Contestable markets theory as a regulatory framework: an Austrian post-mortem', *Quarterly Journal of Austrian Economics*, vol. 7, no. 3, pp. 3–28.

Chapter 9

Thinking Strategically (1): Interdependence, Decision Making and the Theory of Games

Never keep up with the Joneses. Drag them down to your level. It's cheaper.

Quentin Crisp

Learning Objectives

After reading this chapter, you should be able to:

1. Understand the basic elements of games and their application to economics;
2. Recognise the importance of interdependence to analysing how firms and individuals make decisions;
3. Understand the concept of an outcome as an equilibrium solution to a game problem;
4. Appreciate that cooperation/collusion is not always in the general interest;
5. Understand the importance of factors affecting timing commitment and uncertainty in economic and other relations.

Often when we make decisions about actions we propose to take, the 'payoff' to the decision depends not only on what we decide to do, but on what other people decide to do as well. Often, but not always: if I decide to buy a new car, I don't have to worry about whether someone else is going to buy one or not. The car's price and its value to me are independent of what other potential purchasers decide to do. But suppose the car manufacturer is thinking about replacing (expensively) a popular car with a new one. The payoff will be affected by what other manufacturers will do. Hence, the decision to go ahead or not depends on his views as to rivals' reactions.

Then, there is the question of timing. It can matter greatly whether you can (or must) act (make a decision) before someone else, or can (or must) wait until after the other person's decision. Consider the story in Economic Naturalist 9.1.

The payoff to many actions depends not only on the actions themselves but also on when they are taken and how they relate to actions taken by others. In Chapters 5–8, economic decision makers confronted an environment that was essentially fixed. This chapter will focus on cases in which people and especially firms must consider the effect of their behaviour on others. For example, an imperfectly competitive firm will in many circumstances want to weigh the likely responses of rivals when deciding whether to cut prices or to increase marketing expenditure. *Interdependencies* of this sort are the rule rather than the

Economic Naturalist 9.1
Why did Warner have to pay Tony Bennett $200,000 to sing a song in a film when he probably would have been happy to do it for $15,000?[1]

The answer is timing. The film was the Warner comedy, *Analyze This*, featuring Robert De Niro as a mobster who was a great fan of Bennett, an important element in the story line. Before making the film, De Niro asked Bennett at a party if he would be willing to sing 'Got the World on a String' in the final scene, to which he assented, and the matter rested there. When the film was completed except for the song scene, Warner phoned Bennett's agent, but unfortunately let him know that the song was the last piece of the whole jigsaw. Not surprisingly, the agent (Bennett's son), knowing he had them over a barrel, was not prepared to sign up for a 'normal' fee of $15,000, but extracted $200,000 from Warner because otherwise a large chunk of the film would have to have been remade with an altered script and final scene.

exception in much of economic and social life. To make sense of the world we live in, then, we must take these interdependencies into account.

To analyse this type of problem we use '*game theory*'. Its origins may be found in a book published in 1944, written by John von Neumann and Oskar Morgenstern, *The Theory of Games and Economic Behavior*.[2] They started from the proposition that much economic behaviour can be analysed as a choice of a *strategy* in situations where people's interests clash, so that *conflict between decision makers* is inevitable. In the early 1950s, John Nash,[3] a mathematician at Princeton, produced a couple of path-breaking papers dealing with the concept of an *equilibrium in a game* – meaning, loosely, an outcome that is stable and predictable, given the motives of, and constraints facing, the players. Modern game theory has been built on these foundations, and Nash was subsequently awarded the Nobel Prize in Economics in 1994.

THE THEORY OF GAMES

In tennis, or any other game, your payoff from a given move depends on *what your opponent does in response*. In choosing your move, therefore, you must anticipate your opponent's responses, how you might respond and what further moves your own response might elicit.

Take the following as an economics example of a game. You have decided to open a small supermarket in your home-town neighbourhood, where there is already an established store belonging to a major national chain. You do so because you believe that you can offer a better value-for-money service, so that you can profitably attract a sufficient number of customers from the incumbent. Undercutting the prices of the incumbent is one option. Another is to offer a different choice of goods. So is offering a level of service that will attract a sufficient number of higher-income shoppers from the one-size-fits-all offerings of the established chain. But will it work? That depends on how the incumbent firm reacts.

It could decide to hold its market share by lowering prices. It could decide that there is room in the market for both of you, and it might be happy to leave the upper end of the market (with all the problems of dealing with picky purchasers) to you. It could

[1] *New York Times*, 2 May 1999.

[2] Von Neumann and Morgenstern (1944).

[3] Nash's sad life (he was diagnosed paranoid schizophrenic) was the subject of the movie *A Beautiful Mind*. For an economist, unfortunately, the movie is marred by its failure to make clear the significance, simple elegance and enormous analytical implications of his exposition of what is now known as the concept of a Nash equilibrium (see p. 281).

decide to discourage any potential entrants in other local markets, threatening the financial viability of its operations as a whole, and so launch a price war to force you out. A corpse hanging from a gibbet deters imitation.

Whether or not you enter the market, and the strategy you adopt in the market, will reflect what you think the incumbent will do in response to your decision. It's not at all clear that it makes sense to enter just because you see a profitable opportunity in the form of 'cash on the table'. In order to analyse and to predict outcomes in such situations, where payoffs to actors depend on opponents' responses, economists and other behavioural scientists have devised the mathematical theory of games.

In this chapter we will first introduce the basic elements of game theory, and use them in a variety of hypothetical situations in order to explain some aspects of how people and firms behave. In the next chapter we will use the insights and tools developed here to look at competition in markets where the number of firms competing with each other is small, and in which, therefore, decision-making has to recognise the pervasive effects of interdependency.

THE THREE ELEMENTS OF A GAME

Any game has three **basic elements**: the *players*, the list of possible actions (or *strategies*) for each player and the *payoffs* the players receive for each combination of strategies. How these elements combine to form the basis of a theory of behaviour will become clear in the context of Examples 9.1–9.3.

basic elements of a game the players, the strategies available to each player and the payoffs each player receives for each possible combination of strategies

Should Lufthansa spend more money on advertising?

Example 9.1

Suppose that Lufthansa and Alitalia, the only air carriers serving the Frankfurt–Milan route, each currently earns an economic profit of €6,000 per flight. If Lufthansa increases its advertising spending in this market by €1,000 per flight and Alitalia leaves its advertising spending unchanged, Lufthansa's profit will rise to €8,000 per flight and Alitalia's will fall to €2,000. If both spend €1,000 more on advertising, each will earn an economic profit of €5,500 per flight as, although the advertising by each will offset the impact of the other's advertising, higher advertising spending by both increases market demand. These payoffs are symmetric, so if Lufthansa stands still while Alitalia increases its spending by €1,000, Lufthansa's economic profit will fall to €2,000 per flight and Alitalia's will rise to €8,000. Each must decide independently whether to increase spending on advertising. What should Lufthansa do?

This is a game with the airlines as players. Each must choose between raising spending by €1,000 and leaving it the same. The payoffs are the economic profits that correspond to the four possible scenarios resulting from their choices. We summarise the relevant information about this game by displaying the players, strategies and payoffs in the form of a simple table called a **payoff matrix** (see Figure 9.1).

payoff matrix a table that describes the payoffs in a game for each possible combination of strategies

The essence of strategic thinking is to begin by looking at the situation from the other party's point of view. Suppose Alitalia assumes that Lufthansa will raise its spending on advertising (the top row in Figure 9.1). In that case, Alitalia's best bet would be to follow suit (the left column in Figure 9.1). Why? Because Alitalia's economic profits, given in the upper-left cell of Figure 9.1, will be €5,500 as compared with only €2,000 if it keeps spending level (see the upper-right cell).

Alternatively, suppose Alitalia assumes that Lufthansa will keep spending unchanged (that is, Lufthansa will choose the bottom row in Figure 9.1). In that case, Alitalia would still do better to increase spending, because it would earn €8,000 (the lower-left cell) as compared with only €6,000 if it keeps spending level (the lower-right cell). So, no matter what Lufthansa decides, Alitalia will earn a higher economic profit by increasing

Figure 9.1
The Payoff Matrix for an Advertising Game

Lufthansa's choice	Alitalia's choice: Raise ad spending	Alitalia's choice: Leave ad spending the same
Raise ad spending	Alitalia gets €5,500; Lufthansa gets €5,500	Alitalia gets €2,000; Lufthansa gets €8,000
Leave ad spending the same	Alitalia gets €8,000; Lufthansa gets €2,000	Alitalia gets €6,000; Lufthansa gets €6,000

its spending. And since this game is perfectly symmetric, a similar conclusion holds for Lufthansa: no matter which strategy Alitalia chooses, Lufthansa will do better by increasing its spending on ads.

When one player has a strategy that yields a higher payoff no matter which choice the other player makes, that player is said to have a **dominant strategy**. Not all games involve dominant strategies, but both players in this game have one, and that is to increase spending on ads. For both players, to leave ad spending the same is a **dominated strategy** – one that leads to a lower payoff than an alternative choice, regardless of the other player's choice.

dominant strategy one that yields a higher payoff no matter what the other players in a game choose

dominated strategy a strategy available to a player that yields a lower payoff than some other strategy

Notice, however, that when each player chooses the dominant strategy, the resulting payoffs are smaller than if each had left spending unchanged. Lufthansa and Alitalia each earns only €5,500 in economic profits as compared with the €6,000 each would have earned without the increase.

NASH EQUILIBRIUM

A game is said to be in equilibrium if each player's strategy is the best he or she can choose, given the other players' chosen strategies. This definition of equilibrium is sometimes called a **Nash equilibrium**, after John Nash. At an equilibrium outcome in a game, no player has any incentive to deviate from his or her current strategy.

Nash equilibrium any combination of strategies in which each player's strategy is his or her best choice, given the other players' strategies

If each player in a game has a dominant strategy, as in Example 9.1, equilibrium occurs when each player follows that strategy. But even in games in which not every player has a dominant strategy, we can often identify an equilibrium outcome. Consider, for instance, the following variation on the advertising game in Example 9.1.

Example 9.2 Should Alitalia or Lufthansa spend more money on advertising?

Once again, suppose that Lufthansa and Alitalia are the only carriers serving the Frankfurt–Milan route, and that the payoffs are as in Figure 9.2. Has Lufthansa a dominant strategy? Has Alitalia? If each firm does the best it can, given the incentives facing the other, what will be the outcome of this game?

Lufthansa's choice	Alitalia's choice: Raise ad spending	Alitalia's choice: Leave ad spending the same
Raise ad spending	Alitalia gets €4,000; Lufthansa gets €3,000	Alitalia gets €3,000; Lufthansa gets €8,000
Leave ad spending the same	Alitalia gets €5,000; Lufthansa gets €4,000	Alitalia gets €2,000; Lufthansa gets €5,000

Figure 9.2 Equilibrium When One Player Lacks a Dominant Strategy

In this game, with these payoffs, no matter what Lufthansa does, Alitalia will do better to raise its ad spending, so raising the advertising budget is a dominant strategy for Alitalia. Lufthansa, however, has no dominant strategy. If Alitalia raises its spending, Lufthansa will do better to stand still; if Alitalia stands still, however, Lufthansa will do better to spend more. But even though Lufthansa hasn't a dominant strategy, we can still predict what is likely to happen in this game. Lufthansa's managers know what the payoff matrix is, so they can predict that Alitalia will spend more on ads (since that is Alitalia's dominant strategy). Thus the best strategy for Lufthansa, given the prediction that Alitalia will spend more on ads, is to keep its own spending unchanged. This game will end in the lower-left cell of the payoff matrix in Figure 9.2: Alitalia will raise its spending on ads and Lufthansa will not. When both players are positioned in the lower-left cell, neither has any incentive to change its strategy. Therefore the choices corresponding to the lower-left cell in Figure 9.2 satisfy the definition of a Nash equilibrium, a combination of strategies for which each player's choice is the best available option, given the choice made by the other player.

Equilibrium

RECAP

The theory of games

The three elements of any game are the players, the list of strategies from which they can choose and the payoffs to each combination of strategies. Players in some games have a *dominant strategy*, one that yields a higher payoff regardless of the strategies.

Equilibrium in a game occurs when each player's strategy choice yields the highest payoff available, given the strategies of other players. Such a combination of strategies is called a *Nash equilibrium*.

THE PRISONER'S DILEMMA

The game in Example 9.1 belongs to an important class of games called the **prisoner's dilemma**. In the prisoner's dilemma, when each player chooses his dominant strategy, the result is unattractive to the group of players as a whole.

prisoner's dilemma a game in which each player has a dominant strategy and, when each plays it, the resulting payoffs are smaller for each than if each had played a dominated strategy

Figure 9.3 The Payoff Matrix for a Prisoner's Dilemma

Horace's choice	Jasper's choice: Confess	Jasper's choice: Remain silent
Confess	Jasper gets 5 years; Horace gets 5 years	Jasper gets 20 years; Horace gets 0 years
Remain silent	Jasper gets 0 years; Horace gets 20 years	Jasper gets 1 year; Horace gets 1 year

THE ORIGINAL PRISONER'S DILEMMA

Example 9.3 recounts the original scenario from which the prisoner's dilemma drew its name.

Example 9.3 Should the prisoners confess?

There is a classic example of the prisoner's dilemma at work (well, at least Hollywood fashion) in the film, *Murder by Numbers*. Two suspects are interviewed separately, and given to understand that whoever is convicted of the murder in question will be executed or be imprisoned for life without parole. The police know that without a confession they cannot get a conviction. The first to give up his accomplice is offered leniency.[4]

A stylised version of the *Murder by Numbers* story is set down in Figure 9.3, but with a less drastic choice of outcomes. The cells contain the payoffs for the two prisoner players. Have they a dominant strategy? If so, what is it?

They have a dominant strategy. It is for each prisoner to confess. No matter what Jasper does, Horace will get a lighter sentence by speaking out. If Jasper confesses, Horace will get five years (upper-left cell in Figure 9.3) instead of 20 (lower-left cell). If Jasper remains silent, Horace will go free (upper-right cell) instead of spending a year in jail (lower-right cell). Because the payoffs are perfectly symmetrical, Jasper will also do better to confess, no matter what Horace does. When each follows his dominant strategy and confesses, both will do worse than if each had said nothing. Hence, the name of this game: the prisoner's dilemma (or, indeed, prisoners' dilemma). And in the movie clip we see one suspect start to cut a deal.

Equilibrium

PRISONER'S DILEMMAS IN EVERYDAY LIFE

The prisoner's dilemma is one of the most powerful metaphors in all of human behavioural science. Countless social and economic interactions have payoff structures analogous to the one confronted by the two prisoners. Some of those interactions occur between only two players, as in the examples just discussed; many others involve larger groups. But regardless of the number of players involved, the common thread is

[4] Check this out in the movie clip at *www.gametheory.net/educators.html*. The movie clip tells the story.

one of conflict between the narrow self-interest of individuals and the broader interests of larger communities. In Economic Naturalist 9.2 we look at the apparently irrational behaviour of fans at some sports games.[5]

Economic Naturalist 9.2

Why do people at rugby games stand up on one side in all-seater stadiums and obscure each other's view at critical moments in the game, while soccer fans seem to remain seated when a score is imminent?

The answer lies in how points are scored, but also reflects a prisoner's dilemma in the case of rugby. For those who do not follow the code, which is played with 15 players on each side and an oval ball, the highest points are scored by touching the ball down over the opponent's goal line and this can take place at the edge of the field. In the case of soccer, of course, it's just a case of booting the ball into the goal in the centre of each end line. When players in rugby look like scoring at the edge of the field, the fans on that side all jump to their feet. As a result no one sees any better what is happening near the score line than if they had remained seated, but it's always in someone's interest to stand, so all stand.

The prisoner's dilemma concept will help you understand and answer some questions that seem to suggest that people behave irrationally. Consider Exercise 9.2.

Exercise 9.2

Use the prisoner's dilemma model to explain the following three scenarios.

1. A fire breaks out in the orchestra pit in a theatre during the performance of a play. The next day newspapers comment on the numbers killed and injured in the rush to leave the auditorium, and the numbers who died from smoke inhalation because the doors were jammed by those rushing out, and castigate the audience for panicking and behaving irrationally, when they could all have left the building safely if they had done so row by row.
2. You are invited to a party and return home afterwards with laryngitis developed by having to shout for two hours to make yourself heard. Many other guests suffer similarly.
3. It was reported at the end of 2004 that the use of mobile phones on planes does not pose a safety hazard. In 2008 the EU Commission decided to amend European regulations to permit the use of mobile phones under certain conditions in aircraft. How likely is it that all airlines will completely lift the restriction even if it is no longer legally binding on them to impose it?

TIT-FOR-TAT AND THE REPEATED PRISONER'S DILEMMA

When all players cooperate in a prisoner's dilemma, each gets a higher payoff than when all defect. So people who confront a prisoner's dilemma will be on the lookout for ways to create incentives for mutual cooperation. What they need is some way to *penalise* players who defect. When players interact with one another only once, this turns out to be difficult to achieve. But when they expect to interact repeatedly, new possibilities emerge.

repeated prisoner's dilemma a standard prisoner's dilemma that confronts the same players repeatedly

A **repeated prisoner's dilemma** is a standard prisoner's dilemma that confronts the same players not just once but many times.

[5] A reviewer of an earlier draft of this chapter suggested that this example should be dropped because some readers on the European continent would not understand the point as they had never been at a rugby game. We understand that the EU Sports Commissioner is to ensure that this instance of cultural deprivation will be rectified by subsidising rugby in Mitteleuropa, but in the meantime we hope that a redraft will make the point clearer.

tit-for-tat a strategy for the repeated prisoner's dilemma in which players cooperate on the first move, then mimic their partner's last move on each successive move

Incentives Matter

Experimental research on repeated prisoner's dilemmas in the 1960s identified a simple strategy that proves remarkably effective at limiting defection. The strategy is called **tit-for-tat**, and here is how it works. The first time you interact with someone, you cooperate. In each subsequent interaction you simply do what that person did in the previous interaction. Thus, if your partner defected on your first interaction, you would then defect on your next interaction with her. If she then cooperates, your move next time will be to cooperate as well.

The success of tit-for-tat requires a reasonably stable set of players, each of whom can remember what other players have done in previous interactions. It also requires that players have a significant stake in what happens in the future, for it is the fear of *retaliation* that deters people from defecting.

RECAP

The prisoner's dilemma

The *prisoner's dilemma* is a game in which each player has a dominant strategy. The payoff to each player when each chooses that strategy is smaller than if each had chosen a dominated strategy. Incentives analogous to those found in the prisoner's dilemmas help to explain a broad range of behaviour in business and everyday life – among them, excessive spending on advertising, cartel instability, standing at concerts and shouting at parties. Cooperation in repeated prisoner's dilemmas can often be sustained by the *tit-for-tat* strategy, in which players cooperate on the first move and mimic their partner's previous move thereafter.

GAMES IN WHICH TIMING MATTERS

In the games discussed so far, players were assumed to choose their strategies simultaneously, and which player moved first didn't particularly matter. But in other situations, such as that described in Economic Naturalist 9.1, timing is of the essence.

When players move simultaneously (or can be modelled as doing so) the approach to the game and its outcome based on a simple payoff matrix is inadequate, and what is described as an *extensive form* of the game becomes necessary. In graphic terms, the payoff matrix is replaced by a decision tree.

THE ULTIMATUM BARGAINING GAME

To illustrate this, we use a simple example of timing in a game at the level of individual behaviour: the so-called 'ultimatum game'.

Example 9.4 Should Michael accept Tom's offer?

Tom and Michael are subjects in an experiment. The experimenter begins by giving €100 to Tom, who must then propose how to divide the money between himself and Michael. Tom can propose any division he chooses, provided the proposed amounts are whole euros and he offers Michael at least €1. Suppose Tom proposes €X for himself and €$(100 - X)$ for Michael, where X is a whole number no larger than 99. Michael must then say whether he accepts the proposal. If he does, each will get the proposed amount. But if Michael rejects the proposal, each player will get zero, and the €100 will revert to the experimenter. If Tom and Michael know they will play this game only once, and each wants to make as much money for himself as possible, what should Tom propose?

A payoff matrix is not a useful way to summarise the information in this game, because it says nothing about the timing of each player's move. For games in which

Figure 9.4 Tom's Best Strategy in an Ultimatum Bargaining Game

Because Tom can predict that Michael will accept any positive offer, Tom's income-maximising strategy at *A* is to offer Michael the smallest positive amount possible, €1.

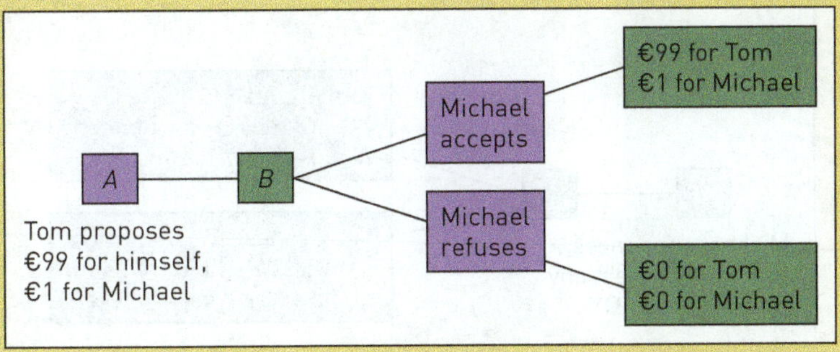

timing matters, a **decision tree (or game tree)** is more useful. This is called an 'extended' form of the game. This type of diagram describes the possible moves in the sequence in which they may occur, and lists the final payoffs for each possible combination of moves.

decision tree (or game tree) a diagram that describes the possible moves in a game in sequence and lists the payoffs that correspond to each possible combination of moves

The decision tree for such a game in Example 9.4 is shown in Fig. 9.4. At *A*, Tom begins the game by making his proposal. At *B*, Michael responds to Tom's proposal. If he accepts (the top branch of the tree), Tom will get €*X* and Michael will get €(100 – *X*). If he refuses (the bottom branch of the tree), both will get nothing.

The key for Tom is to put himself in Michael's shoes and imagine how he might react to various proposals. This reflects '*interdependence*' affecting the player's choice of move. Because he knows that Michael's goal is to make as much money as possible, Tom knows that Michael will accept his offer no matter how small, because the alternative is to reject it and get nothing. For instance, suppose that Tom proposes €99 for himself and only €1 for Michael. At *B*, Michael's best option is to accept the offer. This is a Nash equilibrium, because neither player has any incentive to deviate from the strategy he chose.

This type of game has been called the **ultimatum bargaining game**,[6] because of the power of the first player to confront the second player with a take-it-or-leave-it offer. Michael could refuse a one-sided offer from Tom, but doing so would make him worse off than if he accepted it.

ultimatum bargaining game one in which the first player has the power to confront the second player with a take-it-or-leave-it offer

Example 9.4 illustrates the importance of the *timing of moves* in determining the outcome of the ultimatum bargaining game.

What should Michael's acceptance threshold be?

Example 9.5

Suppose we change the rules of the ultimatum bargaining game slightly so that Michael has the right to specify *in advance* the smallest offer he will accept. This means that Michael, rather than Tom, moves first. If Tom's task is again to propose a division of the €100, what amount should Michael specify?

This seemingly minor change in the rules completely alters the game. Once Michael announces that €*Y* is the smallest offer he will accept, his active role in the game is over. If *Y* is €60 and Tom proposes €*X* for himself and €(100 – *X*) for Michael, his offer will be rejected automatically if *X* exceeds 40. The decision tree for this game is shown in Fig. 9.5.

6 Experiments with the ultimatum game have uncovered something that may not surprise you. When classroom experiments are played using sociology students, literature students and similar groups as test populations, the offers that are made are usually much closer to a 50/50 split than when they are carried out using economics students. In our experience applying this game in class, economics and business students have more 70/30 or 90/10 outcomes than other students. Figure that out! Does economics make you 'rational', or do more 'rational' people take economics?

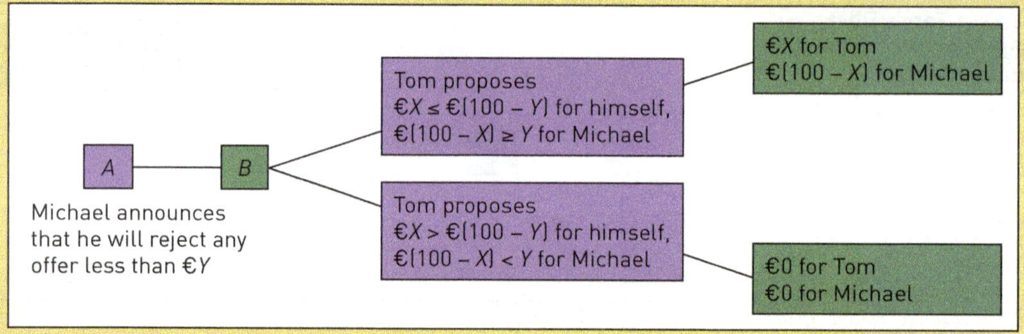

Figure 9.5 The Ultimatum Bargaining Game with an Acceptance Threshold

If Michael can commit himself to a minimum acceptable offer threshold at A, he will fare dramatically better than in the standard ultimatum bargaining game.

When Michael announces that €*Y* is the smallest offer he will accept, the best Tom can do is to propose €(100 – *Y*) for himself and €*Y* for Michael. If he proposes any amount less than €*Y* for Michael, both will get nothing at all. Since this reasoning holds for any value of *Y* less than 100, Michael's best bet is to announce an acceptance threshold of €99 – the largest whole number that is less than €100. The equilibrium outcome of the game will then be €99 for Michael and only €1 for Tom, exactly the opposite of the outcome when Tom had the first move.

CREDIBLE THREATS AND PROMISES

Why couldn't Michael have threatened to refuse a one-sided offer in the original version of the game? While nothing prevented him from doing so, such a threat would not have been credible. In the language of game theory, a **credible threat** is one that is in the threatener's interest to carry out when the time comes to act. The problem in the original version of the game is that Michael would have no reason to carry out his threat to reject a one-sided offer in the event that he actually received one. To do so would make him worse off than if he accepted the offer. Refusing it would not pass the cost–benefit test.

> **credible threat** a threat to take an action that is in the threatener's interest to carry out

In Economic Naturalist 9.1, Warner could not credibly threaten Bennett's agent that they would go ahead without Bennett. At that point adapting the film to another singer would have been prohibitively costly. In contrast, a similar threat made before production of the movie had begun would have been credible. A credible threat must also be received and understood as such by the other side. In the satirical comedy, *Dr Strangelove*, the world is destroyed because the Soviet President, who loved surprises, didn't tell the US that the USSR had built the Doomsday Bomb, controlled irreversibly by a computer so as to wipe out the northern hemisphere if the US attacked the USSR.

> **credible promise** a promise that is in the interests of the promisor to keep when the time comes to act

Just as in some games credible threats are impossible to make, in others **credible promises** are impossible.

Example 9.6 Should the business owner open a remote office?

The owner of a thriving business wants to start up an office in a distant city. If she hires someone to manage the new office, she can afford to pay a weekly salary of €1,000 – a premium of €500 over what the manager would otherwise be able to earn – and still earn a weekly economic profit of €1,000 for herself. The owner's concern is that she will not be able to monitor the manager's behaviour. The owner knows that by managing

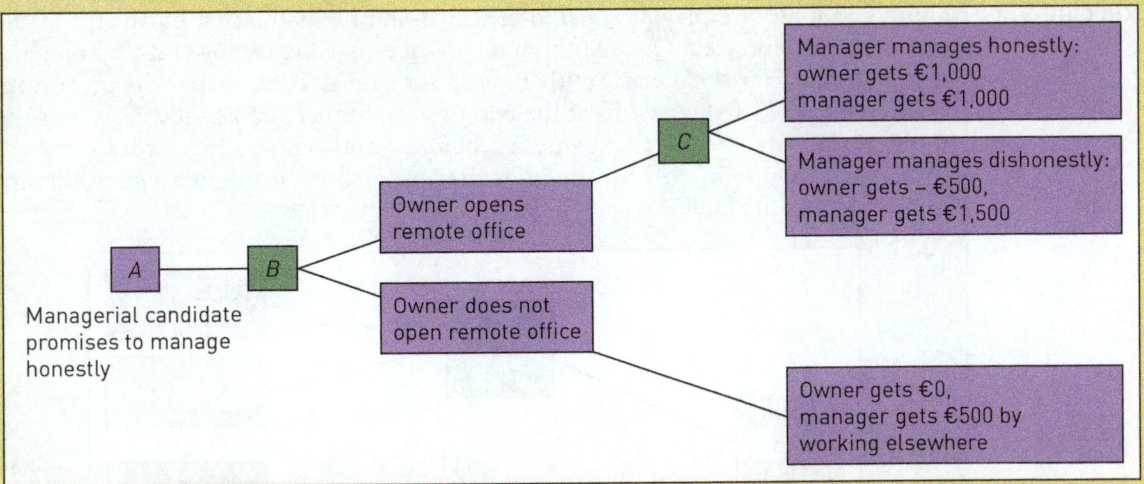

Figure 9.6 Decision Tree for the Remote Office Game

The best outcome is for the owner to open the office at *B* and for the manager to manage the office honestly at *C*. But if the manager is purely self-interested and the owner knows it, this path will not be an equilibrium outcome.

the remote office dishonestly, the manager can boost his take-home pay to €1,500 while causing the owner an economic loss of €500 per week. If the owner believes that all managers are selfish income maximisers, will she open the new office?

The decision tree for the remote office game is shown in Fig. 9.6. At *A*, the managerial candidate promises to manage honestly, which brings the owner to *B*, where she must decide whether to open the new office. If she opens it, they reach *C*, where the manager must decide whether to manage honestly. If the manager's only goal is to make as much money as he can, he will manage dishonestly (bottom branch at *C*), since that way he will earn €500 more than by managing honestly (top branch at *C*).

So, if the owner opens the new office, she will end up with an economic loss of €500. If she had not opened the office (bottom branch at *B*), she would have realised an economic profit of zero. Since zero is better than –€500, the owner will choose not to open the remote office. In the end, the opportunity cost of the manager's inability to make a credible promise is €1,500: the manager's forgone €500 salary premium and the owner's forgone €1,000 return.

The commitment problem here is that a potential manager of the distant office can promise to behave correctly . . . but lacks any mechanism to make the promise credible, since it will pay the candidate for the job to behave opportunistically.

COMMITMENT PROBLEMS

> **commitment problem** a situation in which people cannot achieve their goals because of an inability to make credible threats or promises

Games like those in Exercise 9.3 (below), as well as the prisoner's dilemma, the ultimatum bargaining game and the remote office game, confront players with a **commitment problem**, a situation in which they have difficulty achieving the desired outcome because they cannot make credible threats or promises. If both players in the prisoner's dilemma (Example 9.3) could make a binding promise to remain silent, both would be assured of a shorter sentence; hence the logic of the underworld code of *omertà*, under which the family of anyone who provides evidence against a fellow mob member is killed. A similar logic explains the adoption of military arms- control agreements, in which opponents sign an enforceable pledge to curtail weapons spending.

Exercise 9.3

Smith and Jones are playing a game in which Smith has the first move at *A* in the following decision tree. Once Smith has chosen either the top or bottom branch at *A* Jones, who can see what Smith has chosen, must choose the top or bottom branch at *B* or *C*. If the payoffs at the end of each branch are as shown, what is the equilibrium outcome of this game? If, before Smith chose, Jones could make a credible commitment to choose either the top or bottom branch when his turn came, what would he do?

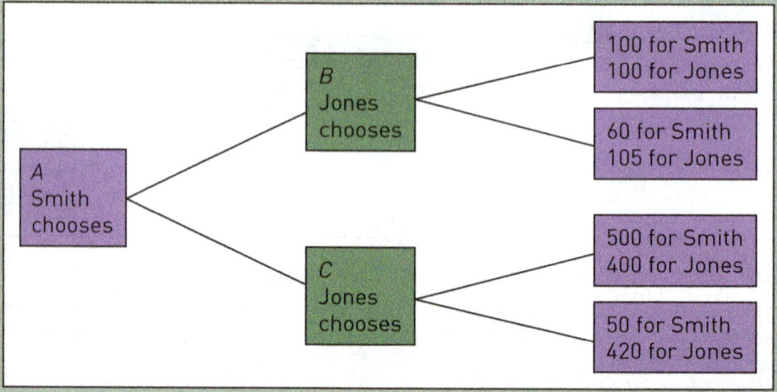

The commitment problem in a game can be solved if the potential beneficiary can find some way of committing himself to a course of action in the future. For example, suppose firm *A* wants to discourage firm *B* from price cutting, and knows that to do so involves acting in a way that makes *B* confident that *A* will not overtly or tacitly engage in price cutting itself. It could sell firm *B* a 'put' option, whereby firm *B* could oblige firm *A* to buy specified quantities of its output at some critical price below today's price. If the two firms have a price of 100, and B has the right to sell a large amount to A at, say, a price of 98, then if A lowers its price to, say, 95, it will have to buy product from B at 98 and sell it on at 95, incurring a loss. Hence, the put option is in effect a guarantee that A will not lower price below 98. A tacit promise not to cut prices would be made credible by this **commitment device**.

commitment device a way of changing incentives so as to make otherwise empty threats or promises credible

Business owners seem well aware of commitment problems in the workplace and have adopted a variety of commitment devices to solve them. Consider, for example, the problem confronting the owner of a restaurant. She wants her table staff to provide good service so that customers will enjoy their meals and come back in the future. And since good service is valuable to her, she would be willing to pay waiters extra for it. For their part, waiters would be willing to provide good service in return for the extra pay. The problem is that the owner cannot always monitor whether the waiters do provide good service. Her concern is that, having been paid extra for it, the waiters may slack off when she isn't looking. Unless the owner can find some way to solve this problem, she will not pay extra, the waiters will not provide good service, and she, they and the diners will suffer. A better outcome for all concerned would be for the waiters to find some way to commit themselves to good service.

Restaurateurs in many countries have tried to solve this commitment problem by encouraging diners to leave tips at the end of their meals. The attraction of this solution is that the diner is *always* in a good position to monitor service quality. The diner should be happy to reward good service with a generous tip, since doing so will help to ensure good service in the future. And the waiter has a strong incentive to provide good service, because he knows that the size of his tip may depend on it.

The various commitment devices just discussed – the underworld code of *omertà*, the tip for the waiter – all work because they change the material incentives facing the decision makers. But, as Example 9.7 illustrates, sometimes this simple calculus of incentives is not a complete explanation.

Will Federico leave a tip when dining on the road?

Example 9.7

Federico has just finished a €30 dinner at Ristorante Stendhal, just off the Milan–Ancona autostrada near Parma, some 300 km from home. The meal was superb, and the waiter provided good service. If Federico cares only about himself, will he leave a tip?

Once the waiter has provided good service, there is no way for him to take it back if the diner fails to leave a tip. In restaurants patronised by local diners, failure to tip is not a problem, because the waiter can simply provide poor service the next time a non-tipper comes in. And no one wants to appear mean in front of people who might care. But the waiter lacks that leverage with out-of-town diners eating alone. Having already received good service, Federico must choose between paying €30 or €35 for his meal. If he is an essentially selfish person, the former choice may be a compelling one. But if you know that the waiter depends for much of his living on tips you are likely to tip anyway, even if not overly generously, for the same reason as most people do not engage in shoplifting even when they know they would get away with it: our moral sense overrides our instinct for self-advancement.

Economic Naturalist 9.3
The IMF arrives in town: a loss of independence, or just dealing with a commitment problem?

In the autumn of 2010 it became clear that, on top of a fiscal deficit, Ireland was facing an enormous debt problem arising from a previous decision in 2008 to guarantee its insolvent banks' liabilities that in turn arose from the collapse of the property boom that peaked in 2007. Funding of the country's borrowing requirement over the following few years became impossible, as money markets became convinced that, if they made the necessary loans to Ireland, they would see these being defaulted as the burden of servicing them became too heavy to support. When the IMF and the EU Commission came up with a package of loans with some harsh conditionality in October 2010, it was a mantra of press and opposition that the Irish government had effectively handed over the country's sovereignty, a charge which contributed to the electoral wipe-out of the ruling coalition parties in the election that followed in February 2011.

An economic naturalist, with a smattering of game theory might have suggested another, less cataclysmic way of interpreting what happened. A loan applicant can put his house as collateral. If the borrower defaults on the loan, the bank can claim the house. But can a sovereign state credibly commit to repayment of its loans? How can Ireland put potential creditors at ease? Can Ireland use the beautiful County Kerry as collateral? If Greece doesn't repay its debts, can Germany take a few of the Aegean Islands? The lack of a commitment device can make it very difficult for sovereign states to borrow in private markets.

The IMF is as concerned about the repayment of the loan as any private creditor. Because the IMF is a single large lender it is in a better position than small lenders to put conditions on its loans. Since sovereign states cannot put down collateral on the loan, the IMF closely monitors the economic policies of the sovereign state to make sure that the IMF policy recommendations are followed. These recommendations are made to ensure that the country is able to repay its debt and typically involve reducing budget deficits and real wages. However, often governments wish to spend the IMF funds for political gains, frequently in the form of increased social spending before elections. Hence, the IMF makes conditional loans and releases tranches of credit in small instalments. In effect, by doing this, the IMF supplies the commitment mechanism. We'll see!

RECAP

Games in which timing matters

The outcomes in many games depend on the *timing* of each player's move. For such games, the payoffs are best summarised by a *decision tree* rather than a payoff matrix.

The inability to make credible threats and promises often prevents people from achieving desired outcomes in many games. Games with this property are said to confront players with *commitment problems*. Such problems can sometimes be solved by employing *commitment devices* – ways of changing incentives to facilitate making credible threats or promises.

THE STRATEGIC ROLE OF PREFERENCES

In all the games we have discussed so far, players were assumed to care only about obtaining the best possible outcome for themselves. Thus, each player's goal was to get the highest monetary payoff, the shortest jail sentence, the best chance of survival, and so on. The irony, in most of these games, is that players do not attain the best outcomes. Better outcomes can sometimes be achieved by altering the material incentives selfish players face, but not always.

If altering the relevant material incentives is not possible, commitment problems can sometimes be solved by altering people's psychological incentives. In a society in which people are strongly conditioned to develop moral sentiments – feelings of guilt when they harm others, feelings of sympathy for their trading partners, feelings of outrage when they are treated unjustly – commitment problems arise less often than in more narrowly self-interested societies.

Exercise 9.4

In a moral society, will the business owner open a remote office?

Consider again the owner of the thriving business who is trying to decide whether to open an office in a distant city. Suppose the society in which she lives is one in which all citizens have been strongly conditioned to behave honestly. Will she open the remote office?

ARE PEOPLE FUNDAMENTALLY SELFISH?

The assumption that people are 'self-interested' in the narrow sense of the term does not always capture the full range of motives that govern choice in strategic settings. Researchers have found that tipping rates in restaurants patronised mostly by out-of-town diners are essentially the same as in restaurants patronised mostly by local diners.

Reflect also on how you would behave in some of the other games we have discussed. In the ultimatum bargaining game, what would you do if your partner proposed €99 for himself and only €1 for you? Would you reject the offer? If so, you are not alone. Two findings of extensive laboratory studies of the ultimatum bargaining game challenge the assumption that most players are narrowly self-interested. First, the most common proposal by the first player in this game is not a 99/1 split, but a 50/50 split. And, second, on the few occasions when the first player does propose a highly one-sided split, the second player typically rejects it. Subjects who reject the offer often mention the satisfaction they experienced at having penalised the first player for an 'unfair' offer.

Indeed, there are many exceptions to the outcomes predicted on the basis of the assumption that people are self-interested in the most narrow sense of the term. People who have been treated unjustly often seek 'revenge' even at ruinous cost to themselves. Every day people walk away from profitable transactions whose terms they believe to be 'unfair'.

Incentives Matter

In 1982 Argentina, pursuing a claim of sovereignty over the islands, mounted a surprise invasion of the British crown colony of the Falklands Islands (aka the Malvinas). The Argentine junta, in common with many other observers, were surprised by the British decision to spend vast sums, lose lives and risk the core of the Royal Navy's surface fleet to recover the desolate colony. After all, as the Argentine writer Jorge Luis Borges observed, the Falkland War made about as much sense as two bald men fighting over a comb.[7] It looked like a case of other values taking precedence over narrow self-interest. Possibly true: Mrs Thatcher was no ordinary Prime Minister, and rejoiced in the nickname of the 'Iron Lady'. However, at the time, Spain was putting pressure on Britain over Gibraltar (British since 1713), and Britain was facing difficult negotiations with China over the future administration of Hong Kong after its inevitable cession to China. And the UK government was facing internal opposition from the unionised coal miners who were threatening general strikes if the industry was rationalised. In these circumstances, does it seem so economically irrational to demonstrate that you will not be trampled on?

THE FALKLANDS WAR: ANOTHER EXPLANATION

Suppose we think about the war another way. When Argentina contemplated invading the Falklands, assuming they had good intelligence of British capabilities, they should have known that Britain was capable of ejecting them. In that case it was irrational to invade, provided the outcome was known with certainty. But suppose (as was surely the case) that it was not certain how Britain would respond, so that the Junta could choose Invade / Don't Invade, but the British response was a matter of probability. In that case, in game theory terms the British had a probability of fighting, x, and a probability of not fighting, (1 – x). Britain, in game theory terms, operated a 'mixed' strategy: x per cent of invasions would be resisted, (100 – x)per cent would be accommodated. That changes the game greatly, because the percentages had to be guessed by the Junta, given that Mrs Thatcher's pronouncements could be bluff, and there was little to go by in terms of past experience.

PREFERENCES AS SOLUTIONS TO COMMITMENT PROBLEMS

Economists tend to view preferences as ends in themselves. Taking them as given, they calculate what actions will best serve those preferences. This approach to the study of behaviour is widely used by other social scientists and by game theorists, military strategists, philosophers and others. In its standard form, it assumes purely self-interested preferences for present and future consumption goods of various sorts, leisure pursuits and so on. Concerns about fairness, guilt, honour, sympathy and the like typically play no role.

Preferences clearly affect the choices people make in strategic interactions. Sympathy for one's trading partner can make a businessperson trustworthy even when material incentives favour cheating. A sense of justice can prompt a person to incur the costs of retaliation, even when incurring those costs will not undo the original injury. It can also induce people to reject one-sided offers, even when their wealth would be increased by accepting them.

Note, however, that although preferences can clearly shape behaviour in these ways, that alone does not solve commitment problems. The solution to such problems requires not only that a person *have* certain preferences, but also that others have some way of *discerning* them. Unless the business owner can identify the trustworthy

---

[7] Quoted in Barnstone (1993).

employee, that employee cannot land a job whose pay is predicated on trust. Unless the predator can identify a potential victim whose character will motivate retaliation, that person is likely to become a victim. And unless a person's potential trading partners can identify him as someone predisposed to reject one-sided offers, he will not be able to deter such offers.

From among those with whom we might engage in ventures requiring trust, can we identify reliable partners? If people could make *perfectly* accurate character judgements, they could always steer clear of dishonest persons. That people continue to be victimised, at least occasionally, by dishonest persons suggests that perfectly reliable character judgements are either impossible to make or prohibitively expensive.

Vigilance in the choice of trading partners is an essential element in solving (or avoiding) commitment problems, for if there is an advantage in being honest and being perceived as such, there is an even greater advantage in only *appearing* to be honest. After all, a liar who appears trustworthy will have better opportunities than one who glances about furtively, sweats profusely and has difficulty making eye contact. Indeed, the liar will have the same opportunities as an honest person but will get higher payoffs because the liar will exploit them to the full.

In the end, the question of whether people can make reasonably accurate character judgements is an empirical one. Experimental studies have shown that, even on the basis of brief encounters involving strangers, subjects are adept at predicting who will cooperate and who will defect in prisoner's dilemma games. For example, in one experiment in which only 26 per cent of subjects defected, the accuracy rate of predicted defections was more than 56 per cent. One might expect that predictions regarding those we know well would be even more accurate.

Do you know someone who would return an envelope containing €1,000 in cash to you if you lost it at a crowded concert? If so, then you accept the claim that personal character can help people to solve commitment problems. As long as honest individuals can identify at least some others who are honest and can interact selectively with them, honest individuals can prosper in a competitive environment.

RECAP

The strategic role of preferences

Most applications of the theory of games assume that players are 'self-interested' in the narrow sense of the term. In practice, however, many choices, such as leaving tips in out-of-town restaurants, appear inconsistent with this assumption.

The fact that people seem driven by a more complex range of motives makes behaviour more difficult to predict but also creates new ways of solving commitment problems. *Psychological incentives* can often serve as commitment devices when changing players' material incentives is impractical. For example, people who are able to identify honest trading partners and interact selectively with them are able to solve commitment problems that arise from lack of trust.

SUMMARY

- Economists use the mathematical theory of games to analyse situations in which the payoffs of one's actions depend on the actions *taken by others*. Games have three basic elements: the *players*; the list of *possible actions*, or *strategies*, from which each player can choose; and the *payoffs* the players receive for those strategies. The *payoff matrix* is the most useful way to summarise this information in games in which the timing of the players' moves is not decisive. In games in which the timing of moves does matter, a *decision tree* summarises the information in a much more useful format.
- A *dominant strategy* is one that yields a higher payoff regardless of the strategy chosen by the other player. In some games, such as the prisoner's dilemma, each player has a dominant strategy. The equilibrium occurs in such games when each player chooses his or her dominant strategy. In other games, not all players have a dominant strategy.
- Although the equilibrium outcome of any game is any combination of choices in which each player does the best he can, given the choices made by others, the result is often unattractive from the perspective of players as group. The prisoner's dilemma has this feature. The *incentive structure* of this game helps explain such disparate social dilemmas as excessive advertising, military arms races and failure to reap the potential benefits of interactions requiring trust.
- Individuals can often resolve these dilemmas if they can make *binding commitments* to behave in certain ways. Some commitments, such as those involved in military arms control agreements, are achieved by altering the material incentives confronting the players. Other commitments can be achieved by relying on psychological incentives to counteract material payoffs. Moral sentiments such as guilt, sympathy and a sense of justice often foster better outcomes than can be achieved by narrowly self-interested players. For this type of commitment to work, the relevant moral sentiments must be discernible by one's potential trading partners.
- Building on the idea of payoffs and games enables economists to construct models that indicate the importance of such things as beliefs and modes of competition in understanding how *smallnumber markets operate*.
- These models yield interesting and plausible conclusions that explain some features of *market behaviour* that are not explained by the simple models of perfect competition or monopolistic competition.

REVIEW QUESTIONS

1. Explain why a military arms race is an example of a prisoner's dilemma.
2. Why did Warner Brothers make a mistake by waiting until the filming of *Analyze This* was almost finished before negotiating with Tony Bennett to perform in the final scene?
3. Suppose General Motors is trying to hire a small firm to manufacture the door handles for Opel and Holden saloon cars. The task requires an investment in expensive capital equipment that cannot be used for any other purpose. Why might the CEO of the small firm refuse to undertake this venture without a long-term contract fixing the price of the door handles?
4. Would you be irrational to refuse a one-sided offer in an ultimatum bargaining game if you knew that you would be playing that game many times with the same partner?
5. Describe the commitment problem that narrowly self-interested diners and waiters confront at restaurants located on interstate highways. Given that in such restaurants tipping does seem to assure reasonably good service, do you think people are always selfish in the narrowest sense?

PROBLEMS

Problems marked with an asterisk (*) are more difficult.

1. In studying for his economics final, Sam is concerned about only two things: his grade and the amount of time he spends studying. A good grade will give him a benefit of 20; an average grade, a benefit of 5; and a poor grade, a benefit of 0. By studying a lot, Sam will incur a cost of 10; by studying a little, a cost of 6. Moreover, if Sam studies a lot and all other students study a little, he will get a good grade and they will get poor ones. But if they study a lot and he studies a little, they will get good grades and he will get a poor one. Finally, if he and all other students study for the same amount of time, everyone will get average grades. Other students share Sam's preferences regarding grades and study time.
   a. Model this situation as a two-person prisoner's dilemma in which the strategies are to study a little and to study a lot, and the players are Sam and all other students. Include the payoffs in the matrix.
   b. What is the equilibrium outcome in this game? From the students' perspective, is it the best outcome?

2. Consider the following 'dating game', which has two players, *A* and *B*, and two strategies, to buy a cinema ticket or a football ticket. The payoffs, given in points, are as shown in the matrix below. Note that the highest payoffs occur when both *A* and *B* attend the same event.

B \ A	Buy cinema ticket	Buy football ticket
Buy cinema ticket	2 for A; 3 for B	0 for A; 0 for B
Buy football ticket	1 for A; 1 for B	3 for A; 2 for B

   Assume that players *A* and *B* buy their tickets separately and simultaneously. Each must decide what to do knowing the available choices and payoffs but not what the other has actually chosen. Each player believes the other to be rational and self-interested.
   a. Does either player have a dominant strategy?
   b. How many potential equilibria are there? (**Hint:** To see whether a given combination of strategies is an equilibrium, ask whether either player could get a higher payoff by changing his or her strategy.)
   c. Is this game a prisoner's dilemma? Explain.
   d. Suppose player *A* gets to buy her ticket first. Player *B* does not observe *A*'s choice but knows that *A* chose first. Player *A* knows that player *B* knows she chose first. What is the equilibrium outcome?
   e. Suppose the situation is similar to part (d), except that player *B* chooses first. What is the equilibrium outcome?

3. Blackadder and Baldrick are rational, self-interested criminals imprisoned in separate cells in a dark medieval dungeon. They face the prisoner's dilemma displayed in the matrix below.

Baldrick \ Blackadder	Confess	Deny
Confess	5 years for Blackadder; 5 years for Baldrick	20 years for Blackadder; 0 years for Baldrick
Deny	0 years for Blackadder; 20 years for Baldrick	1 year for Blackadder; 1 year for Baldrick

Assume that Blackadder is willing to pay 1,000 ducats for each year by which he can reduce his sentence below 20 years. A corrupt jailer tells Blackadder that before he decides whether to confess or deny the crime, he can tell him Baldrick's decision. How much is this information worth to Blackadder?

4. What should Lufthansa and Alitalia do if the payoff matrix in Example 9.2 is modified as follows?

Lufthansa's choice \ Alitalia's choice	Raise ad spending	Leave ad spending the same
Raise ad spending	Alitalia gets €2,000; Lufthansa gets €3,000	Alitalia gets €2,000; Lufthansa gets €4,000
Leave ad spending the same	Alitalia gets €3,000; Lufthansa gets €2,000	Alitalia gets €4,000; Lufthansa gets €3,000

5. The owner of a thriving business wants hire someone who will manage a new office in a distant city honestly. He can afford to pay a weekly salary of €2,000 (€1,000 more than the manager would be able to earn elsewhere) and still earn an economic profit of €800. He fears that he will not be able to monitor the behaviour of the manager, who will therefore be in a position to embezzle money from the business. The owner knows that if the remote office is managed dishonestly, the manager can 'earn' €3,100 while causing the owner an economic loss of €600 per week.

   a. If the owner believes that all managers are narrowly self-interested income-maximisers, will he open the new office?

b. Suppose the owner knows that a managerial candidate is a devoutly religious person who condemns dishonest behaviour and who would be willing to pay up to €15,000 to avoid the guilt she would feel if she were dishonest. Will the owner open the remote office?

6. You are sitting in your car in a university car park that is currently full, waiting for a place to become free. Just as one becomes free a driver who has just arrived overtakes you in order to park in the vacated spot before you can. Suppose this driver would be willing to pay up to €10 to park in that spot and up to €30 to avoid getting into an argument with you At the same time the other driver guesses, accurately, that you too would be willing to pay up to €30 to avoid a confrontation and up to €10 to park in the vacant spot.
   a. Model this situation as a two-stage decision tree in which the other driver's bid to take the space is the opening move and your strategies are (1) to protest and (2) not to protest. If you protest (initiate an argument), the rules of the game specify that the other driver has to let you take the space. Show the payoffs at the end of each branch of the tree.
   b. What is the equilibrium outcome?

7. Newfoundland's fishing industry has declined sharply due to over-fishing, even though fishing companies were supposedly bound by a quota agreement. If all fishing companies had abided by the agreement, yields could have been maintained at high levels.
   a. Model this situation as a prisoner's dilemma with players Company *A* and Company *B*, and the strategies are to keep the quota and break the quota. Include appropriate payoffs in the matrix. Explain why over-fishing is inevitable in the absence of effective enforcement of the quota agreement.
   b. In many potential prisoner's dilemmas, a way out for a would-be cooperator is to make reliable character judgements about the trustworthiness of potential partners. Explain why this solution is not available in many situations involving degradation of the environment.

8. You are playing a game of 'matching pennies' with a friend. Each of you has a penny hidden in your hand, facing either heads up or tails up (you know which way the one in your hand is facing). On the count of 'three' you simultaneously show your pennies to each other. If the face-up side of your coin matches the face-up side of your friend's coin, you get to keep the two pennies. If the faces do not match, your friend gets to keep the pennies.
   a. Who are the players in this game? What are each player's strategies? Construct a payoff matrix for the game.
   b. Is there a dominant strategy? If so, what?
   c. Is there an equilibrium? If so, what?

9. Harry has four 2 euro pieces. He can offer Sally from one to four of them. If she accepts his offer, she keeps the coins Harry offered her and Harry keeps the others. If Sally declines Harry's offer, they both get nothing. They play the game only once, and each cares only about the amount of money he or she ends up with.
   a. Who are the players? What are each player's strategies? Construct a decision tree for this ultimatum bargaining game.
   b. Given their goal, what is the optimal choice for each player?

10.* Jill and Jack both have two pails that they must use to carry water down a hill. Each makes only one trip down the hill, and each pail of water can be sold for €5. Both the children would be willing to pay €2 each to avoid carrying one bucket down the hill and an additional €3 to avoid carrying a second bucket down the hill.
   a. Given market prices, how many pails of water will each child fetch from the top of the hill?

b. Their parents are worried that the two children don't cooperate enough with one another. They make Jill and Jack share their revenues from selling the water equally. Given that both are self-interested, construct the payoff matrix for the decisions Jill and Jack face regarding the number of pails of water each should carry. What is the equilibrium outcome?

REFERENCES

Barnstone, W. (1993) *With Borges on an Ordinary Evening in Buenos Aires* (Champaign, IL: University of Illinois Press).

Von Neumann, J. and O. Morgenstern (1944) *The Theory of Games and Economic Behavior* (Princeton, NJ: Princeton University Press).

Chapter 10

Thinking Strategically (2): Competition Among the Few

Competition is a sin. — *John D. Rockefeller*

Learning objectives

After reading this chapter, you should be able to:

1. Understand how game theory explains interactions in oligopoly markets;
2. Apply the prisoner's dilemma game to pricing, investment and research decisions;
3. Understand the cartel problem;
4. Apply the elements of game theory in a case-study environment of product development;
5. Use backward induction;
6. Understand Cournot and Bertrand explanations of oligopoly.

COMPETITION AMONG THE FEW: INTERDEPENDENCE AND FIRM BEHAVIOUR

In this chapter we will use the concepts discussed in Chapter 9 to analyse how firms behave in markets in which there are relatively few players. In these circumstances a firm's actions (e.g., prices to charge) will be taken in the knowledge that its competitors' behaviour will reflect the decisions it takes. This is described as 'interdependence' of decision making. We start by looking at the use of the concept of the prisoner's dilemma as an explanatory model of firm behaviour in interdependent markets.

Should Schering Plough or Novartis develop a new tumour-retarding drug?

Example 10.1

Suppose two pharmaceutical companies both produce a drug that slows down and may reverse the growth of malignant soft-tissue tumours. In each case the success rate is around 70 per cent. Each firm believes that modifying the molecular structure of the active compound in its drug could increase the success rate to around 80 per cent. However, refining the compound and testing it is an expensive process. Each firm currently earns €200 millions in profits a year from sales of its drug. The first to introduce an improved drug, having passed the testing process, will have an unassailable lead over the other in terms of capturing market share and profits. The loser in this race will see its profits decline as its existing

Novartis	Schering Plough: Don't invest	Schering Plough: Invest
Don't invest	200 for Schering; 200 for Novartis	300 for Schering; 25 for Novartis
Invest	25 for Schering; 300 for Novartis	150 for Schering; 150 for Novartis

Figure 10.1 A Prisoner's Dilemma in an R&D Game

The dominant strategy in this game is for both to invest, even though each firm's expected profits would be higher if neither invested.

drug loses market share. If a firm does not invest in improving its product (while the other firm does invest) profits decline from their present (no investment) level of €200 million to €25 million. Each has a 50 per cent chance of winning the race. Profits from an improved drug, after allowing for development costs, will be €300 million per annum, so the expected profit for each is 0.5 (€300) million, or €150 million if they invest in developing the new drug.

The payoffs to the firms from investing in the required R&D or not investing are laid out in Fig. 10.1.

This game is an example of the prisoner's dilemma game introduced in the last chapter. It casts an interesting light on the behaviour of high-tech firms where R&D is concerned: to maintain profits firms may feel they have to spend competitively on R&D even if to do so reduces profits. If we extend the story to cover the costs of R&D to each firm, a potentially disturbing aspect of this game emerges. The costs will be incurred by both firms, but will be recouped only by the winner of the race to develop the new drug. Suppose R&D costs are the same for both, and amount to €350 million each. Total resources spent to develop the drug are, therefore, €700 million. If the value to society is approximated by the total of the cost of developing the winning drug plus the winning firm's profits from selling it, the total value of the resources spent on drug development (€700 million) exceeds the value to society of the new drug (€650 million). This of course does not happen all the time, but it points to the possibility of 'too much' money being spent on R&D.

Exercise 10.1

GM and Chrysler must both decide whether to invest in a new assembly system for cars. Games 1 and 2 show how their profits depend on the decisions they might make. Which of these games is a prisoner's dilemma?

Game 1

GM's choice	Chrysler's choice: Don't invest	Chrysler's choice: Invest
Don't invest	10 for Chrysler; 10 for GM	12 for Chrysler; 4 for GM
Invest	4 for Chrysler; 12 for GM	5 for Chrysler; 5 for GM

Game 2

GM's choice	Chrysler's choice: Don't invest	Chrysler's choice: Invest
Don't invest	12 for Chrysler; 4 for GM	5 for Chrysler; 5 for GM
Invest	10 for Chrysler; 10 for GM	4 for Chrysler; 12 for GM

PRISONER'S DILEMMAS CONFRONTING IMPERFECTLY COMPETITIVE FIRMS

A cartel is any coalition of firms or producers that conspires to restrict production for the purpose of earning an economic profit by increasing price relative to cost. The world's best-known (and for some reason widely tolerated) cartel is OPEC, the Organization of Petroleum Exporting Countries, formed in 1960 to control oil production. Its members account for a very large share of the world's oil production. Historically it exhibited the usual cartel problem: cutting production to raise prices created incentives for members to cheat. In recent years, however, cheating has become less of a problem. In part this may reflect the fact that market conditions have resulted in higher prices without cartel actions, but it is plausible that members have learned from the past, so that the one-off game solution (cheat) no longer dominates cooperation to maintain higher prices in a repeated game. The prisoner's dilemma model explains the historic weakness and instability of cartels as we shall see in Economic Naturalist 10.1, while the repeated game model imparts stability.

cartel a coalition of firms that agrees to restrict output for the purpose of earning an economic profit

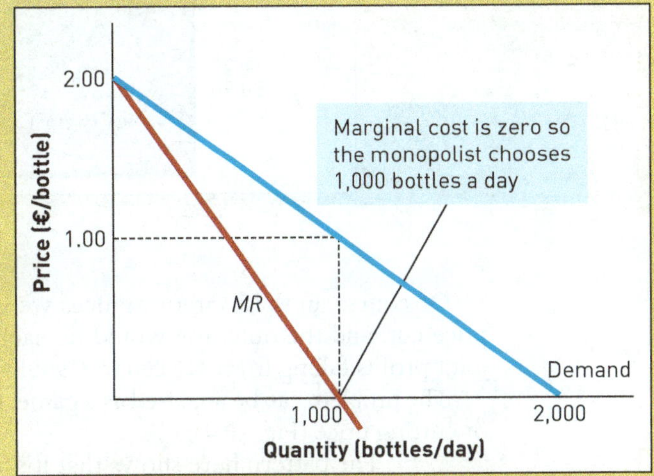

Figure 10.2 The Market Demand for Mineral Water

Faced with the demand curve shown, a monopolist with zero marginal cost would produce 1,000 bottles per day (the quantity at which marginal revenue equals zero) and sell them at a price of €1.00 per bottle.

WHY ARE CARTEL AGREEMENTS NOTORIOUSLY UNSTABLE?

Start by looking at the situation described in Fig. 10.2. It shows the potential profit of a monopolist in a table water market. Suppose, however, there are two similar producers, Mineral Spring and Aquapure, selling water into this market. If they agree to act in concert, and charge the monopoly price while sharing the profits between them they can make the profits of a potential monopolist, but to do so they have to agree to restrict output to what a real monopolist would put on the market.

In this example we assume that costs are zero, so all revenue is profit. If the firms agree to share the market equally, and stick to this agreement, each will earn profits of €500 per day. Unfortunately, each knows that, since the products are very similar, if it undercuts its 'partner' it can scoop the market. For example, if Aquapure decides to drop its price to €0.90 total sales will rise to 1,100 bottles a day, all produced by Aquapure (Fig. 10.3).

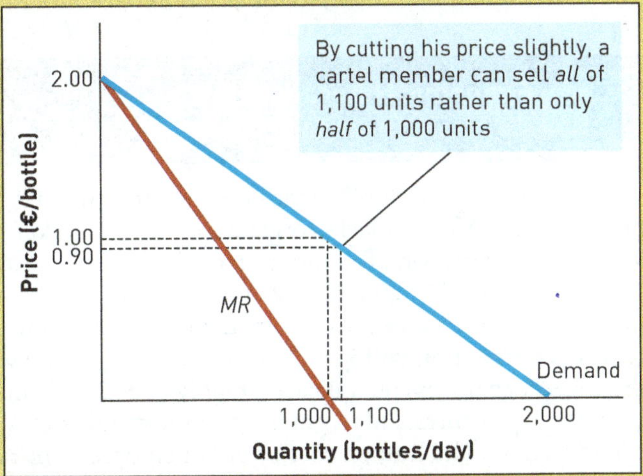

Figure 10.3 The Temptation to Violate a Cartel Agreement

By cutting its price from €1 per bottle to €0.90 per bottle, Aquapure can sell the entire market quantity demanded at that price, 1,100 bottles per day, rather than half the monopoly quantity of 1,000 bottles per day.

Figure 10.4 The Payoff Matrix for a Cartel Agreement

Aquapure's choice	Mountain Spring's choice: Charge €1	Mountain Spring's choice: Charge €0.90
Charge €1	€500/day for Mountain Spring; €500/day for Aquapure	€990/day for Mountain Spring; €0/day for Aquapure
Charge €0.90	€0/day for Mountain Spring; €990/day for Aquapure	€495/day for Mountain Spring; €495/day for Aquapure

Of course, in these circumstances we would expect Mountain Spring to match the price cut, and the outcome would be each firm now selling 550 bottles at €0.90, and joint profits falling from €1,000 to €990: €495 each.

The problem can be analysed as a game. Let's do so by setting up the payoffs to holding or cutting price (Fig. 10.4).

Incentives Matter

The pattern here shows that it's a prisoner's dilemma game once again. Each player has an incentive to choose the lower price. Furthermore, you should by now be able to see why this is not the end of the story: at a price of €0.90, each player will have an incentive to choose a lower price, which will drive price down towards zero.

This is why cartels are unstable: once they are in place they create a strong incentive to cheat, and to last will require members to have an efficient mechanism to police each other's behaviour and enforce observation of the cartel agreement.

Economic Naturalist 10.1
So how do cartels actually survive?

The *ancien regime* in South Africa deregulated the taxi business in 1987. This offered a chance for poorer South African blacks to get a foot on the ladder to prosperity by entering the taxi industry, and a rapid expansion of numbers in the business ensued. Competition was fierce, and, to quote the *New York Times* (17 September 2006), after the end of apartheid in 1994 'taxi owners banded into groups, and the groups mushroomed into cartels, using gangland tactics to expand their turf'. Thus, to limit competition within groups and to carve up the wider market without price competition, the organised taxi drivers put in place a highly effective, if unpleasant, mechanism to enforce observation of cartel procedures and to punish deviation and competition from non-members (i.e. members of other cartels). The human cost of cartel enforcement ran into a couple of thousand fatalities. The success of this mechanism was demonstrated by the fact that organised crime mobs subsequently decided to muscle into the taxi market.

This leads to an interesting question from the economics analysis of crime: why do 'turf wars' so frequently and murderously, and costly to the participants, break out arising from sale of illegal drugs? Think of drug gangs that (informally) share a given metropolitan market for drugs. To keep prices up, the market has to be shared and competition for sales restricted. The price–cost margin is an incentive to any single gang to increase sales by encroaching on another's territory. The credible threat of a violent reaction is a deterrent, but an imperfect one because it is so costly to both sides. A better solution may be the emergence of a crime lord who enforces shares, at a price. In the US an alternative was the arrangement whereby mafia 'families' agreed to the decisions of a Capo di Capi (the Godfather of Hollywood myth) to police the behaviour of the families.

Economic Naturalist 10.2
How can lenient regulatory treatment of cartel activity member reduce cartel strength?

A standard weapon used by government agencies with responsibility for implementing competition law is what is called a 'leniency programme'. An agency starts an investigation of a suspected price fixing agreement and makes a public announcement of its investigation. At the same time it draws attention to the provision whereby a 'whistle-blower', a firm that decides to break ranks and give evidence of the cartel's activities, will be treated 'leniently' (it may avoid any financial or criminal penalty). That creates a prisoner's dilemma for the members of the cartel. If they all keep silent the agency may be unable to secure a conviction and life will continue profitably . . . but this is uncertain, so there is some probability of being convicted of price fixing, with attendant costs. On the other hand, the first firm that cooperates with the agency will get off lightly. The dilemma model clearly applies. Does it work?

According to the OECD it certainly does. In the US alone, between 2000 and 2002 30 convictions for price fixing were secured and over $1 billion in fines levied on the basis of evidence derived from the leniency programme (OECD Observer no. 234, October, 2002). Leniency programmes have been introduced or strengthened in many countries as a result of observing their success. Without cooperation from a cartel member, it is hard to get the evidence necessary to secure a conviction, but the dominant strategy, it seems, is not to take a chance on someone else giving what they want to the authorities first!

TIT-FOR-TAT AND THE CARTEL STABILITY PROBLEM

In Chapter 9 we considered a 'tit-for-tat' strategy as a solution to the prisoner's dilemma problem when a game is repeated frequently. We saw that the problem is to create an incentive not to defect from a strategy that maximises their joint interests. What is needed is some way to *penalise* players who defect.

Since rival firms in the same industry interact with one another repeatedly, it might seem that the tit-for-tat strategy would ensure widespread collusion to raise prices. One difficulty is that tit-for-tat's effectiveness is greatly weakened if there are more than two players in the game. In competitive and monopolistically competitive industries there are generally many firms, and even in oligopolies there are often several. When there are more than two firms, and one defects now, how do the cooperators selectively punish the defector later? By cutting price? That will penalise everyone, not just the defector. Even if there are only two firms in an industry, these firms realise that other firms may enter their industry. So the would-be cartel members have to worry not only about each other, but also about the entire list of firms that might decide to compete with them. Each firm may see this as an impossible task and decide to defect now, hoping to reap at least some economic profit in the short run. What seems clear, in any event, is that the practical problems involved in implementing tit-for-tat have made it difficult to hold cartel agreements together for long.

STABILITY-ENHANCING ARRANGEMENTS

Cartel stability can be reinforced by arrangements that provide for the sharing of markets, or costs of abiding by the cartel agreement or sharing profits derived from higher prices. In the European Union the competition authorities imposed substantial fines on firms in the cement industry in 1995 after investigation of complaints of price-fixing conspiracies. Central to the operation of the illegal arrangements were devices to create geographical markets for each player.[1] Economic Naturalist 10.3 offers an example of how a cartel can be supported by a side arrangement between player.

Economic Naturalist 10.3
Why did South African milk producers get into hot water by selling milk to each other?

At the end of 2006 the South African Competition Commission took legal action against the country's eight major milk processors for price fixing through cartel agreements. Four of the largest among them had an arrangement whereby each could sell any 'surplus' milk to the others, who had to take it at agreed prices. There was also a network of other agreements on supply and marketing covering the eight players.

The surplus (and other) arrangements had the effect of reducing the incentive to supply milk 'under the counter' to increase any one player's profits, but undermining the cartel's pricing structure. If any one of the four major players found itself unable to sell milk at the cartel price, the surplus supply agreement meant that the major players would share the cost of taking it off the market. The arrangement meant that the cost to one firm of not selling at below the cartel price was shared between the participating firms. This was held by the SACC to reduce the incentive to cheat, and consequently was a mechanism that assisted price fixing.

RECAP

In small-number markets where firms' decision-making must take into account responses by rivals we can analyse firm behaviour by using the tools of game theory. Powerful concepts like dominant strategies and the prisoner's dilemma can help us understand how decisions are made. They help explain why collusion is profitable, but tends to break down in the absence of mechanisms to detect and punish breaking agreements.

TIMING AND COMMITMENT PROBLEMS IN OLIGOPOLISTIC MARKETS

In concentrated markets the same issues arise as in simple games at the individual level, which we looked at in Chapter 9. In particular, timing may matter greatly when firms make decisions concerning the dimensions of competition between them. This covers capacity expansion, R&D and product innovation. To illustrate this, and the importance of recognising timing and commitment issues, we look at a real-world example of a major competitive decision in a global industry in which interdependence is a major factor.

Example 10.2 A case study: How did Airbus end up as the only producer of a super-jumbo airliner?

This example uses a stylised presentation of the main elements of the strategic interaction between the world's two largest aircraft producers when consideration was

[1] The text of the decision and the facts and reasoning behind it are published as 94/815/EC, 30/11/1994, available on the EU website or in the EU *Official Journal*, OJ L33/1 1995.

being given to producing a plane that would carry 50 per cent more passengers than the then largest passenger plane, the B747 jumbo.[2] In the mid-1990s decision makers at Boeing (in Seattle) and Airbus (in Toulouse) were considering whether or not to develop a 'super-jumbo'. The options for Boeing were to develop a new plane or to build a 'stretch' version of the B747. Airbus had a wide-bodied plane (the A300/330/340 series) that competed with Boeing's B767 and B777, but had no plane that competed with the B747 and could be stretched. For Airbus, therefore, a super-jumbo meant a wholly new plane.

Boeing believed that, because the likely development of the long-distance travel market would need a greater number of smaller planes rather than fewer but larger planes, the market for super-jumbos was considerably smaller than Airbus expected. On this basis it was not clear that Boeing should produce a super-jumbo even if Airbus did not. For Airbus, the complication was that, whether its more optimistic view of the market was correct or not, the established airline preference for using one supplier's planes meant that the demand for Airbus offerings was constrained by its inability to offer a jumbo-type plane.

From Boeing's perspective there was no point in developing a stretch version of the B747 . . . unless Airbus went ahead with its own super-jumbo. If, however, Airbus did go ahead, it would have a monopoly of super-jumbos. The fact that airlines prefer to use one supplier in many cases, and that the super-jumbo would reduce demand for B747s, meant that Boeing could find itself losing profitable sales across the range of planes it produced. If, however, Boeing did challenge Airbus in the super-jumbo segment it believed it would (a) lose money directly because neither maker could break even on Boeing's estimate of the likely size of the market, and (b) super-jumbo sales by Boeing could lose the company sales of the existing B747. Boeing's total profits would be badly hit.

Even on Airbus's optimistic view of the size of the market, an entry by Boeing would make it doubtful that either could make a profit from sales of the super-jumbos (unless, of course, they colluded, which was (a) illegal and (b) impossible to police). The best outcome from Boeing's point of view would be for neither to enter the super-jumbo segment of the market. Therefore, if it could persuade Airbus that it would follow Airbus in the event of a launch by Airbus it could deter Airbus from launching, which would maximise Boeing's profits.

Finally, each firm knew the other's opinions of likely market size and market shares and, therefore, had a good idea of what the other side would expect in terms of the impact of the decisions taken on expected profits.

APPLYING THE TOOLS OF GAME THEORY

This scenario enables us to show how (a) moving from simultaneous decision-making to sequential decision-making helps explain how a game plays out, and (b) the importance of credible commitment in influencing players' actions.

We start with a standard presentation of the payoffs to the various moves in the form presented earlier when we looked at the airline advertising game. Each player has a choice between launching a new plane and not launching (Y and N, respectively). The payoffs are not supposed to be the actual expected values, but represent the relative returns to the different outcomes.

The payoffs are presented in Fig. 10.5 in the familiar two-by-two matrix form that is appropriate when two players are modelled as moving simultaneously. Viewed as a

[2] The presentation we use here is a simplified version of part of an analysis of the issues by two researchers at the Harvard Business School: B. Esty and P. Ghemawat (2002).

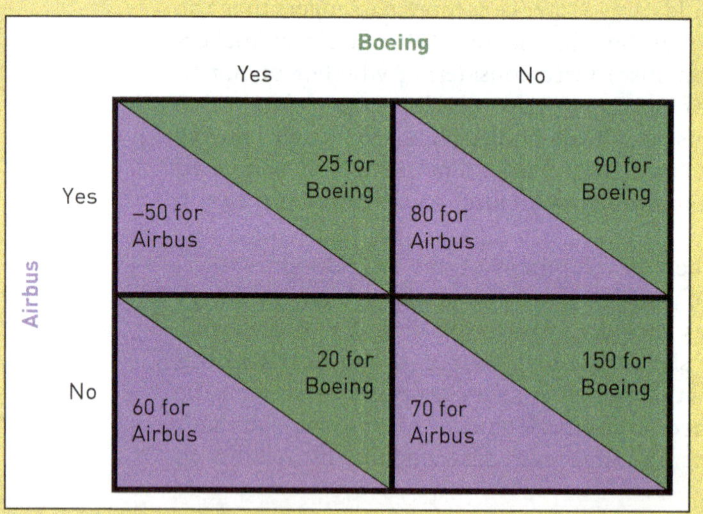

Figure 10.5 The Payoffs to the Players in the Super-jumbo Launch Game

simultaneous movement game the outcome is obvious. In our presentation the structure of payoffs represents that expected for the players by Boeing, and constitute a worst-case scenario for Airbus, which was more optimistic about possible absolute levels of profits, but would accept the relative returns in the different cells.

Boeing has a dominant strategy: do not launch. Airbus knows this although it has no dominant strategy. Consequently, Airbus can confidently choose to launch. Neither side has an incentive to alter its behaviour, given what the other chooses to do. This is a Nash equilibrium. All very simple: this 'normal' form of the game tells us what should (and did) happen. However, real life is a bit more complicated. Airbus chose to launch the A380, and Boeing (in the end) chose to leave the super-jumbo segment of the market to Airbus, and subsequently developed the B787 'Dreamliner'. But it all took some time, and the episode was characterised by uncertainty (at least in terms of public information) as to what Boeing would do. To understand why, we have to look at the game as a game in which timing mattered, and in which Boeing's decision on what it would do depended on what Airbus decided to do, and was committed to doing.

Boeing's moves depend on what Airbus has decided. This in fact puts Boeing in the position where it has to decide what to do (a) if Airbus launches, and (b) if Airbus does not launch. It has to have a strategy (choice of moves) covering both possibilities. A strategy is a complete plan of action for playing the game that sets down what to do at each point of the game. Boeing has a choice between four strategies:

1. build a super-jumbo ('yes') regardless of what Airbus has decided ('yes' or 'no'); call this strategy (Yes, Yes)
2. don't build a super-jumbo in either case; call this strategy (No, No)
3. build the plane if Airbus builds, and don't build if Airbus does not; call this strategy (Yes, No)
4. build only if Airbus does not build; call this strategy (No, Yes).

So, while Airbus has a choice between two moves (Yes, build; No, don't build), Boeing has in principle four options, depending on its choice of strategy. The table of payoffs in Fig. 10.5 has to be extended as in Fig. 10.6.

The Airbus decision depends on its information as to what strategy Boeing has adopted. Although Airbus decides first as to whether to build, this decision will depend on what strategy it believes Boeing has adopted (how it will respond to any move by Airbus). This in turn can reflect what Boeing says and does before Airbus decides. If Boeing can persuade Airbus that it will do what Airbus does (has a Yes, No strategy) Airbus will choose not to build. So a threat to follow Airbus will result in no super-jumbo being built, and Boeing's profits are maximised. As we will see, such a threat can be interpreted from Boeing's actions . . . but Airbus went ahead. Why?

Airbus \ Boeing	Yes, Yes	Yes, No	No, Yes	No, No
Yes	25 for Boeing; −50 for Aibus	25 for Boeing; −50 for Aibus	***90 for Boeing***; ***80 for Aibus***	***90 for Boeing***; ***80 for Aibus***
No	70 for Boeing; 60 for Aibus	***150 for Boeing***; ***70 for Aibus***	70 for Boeing; 60 for Aibus	150 for Boeing; 70 for Aibus

Figure 10.6 Different Strategies Result in Different Nash Equilibria

Boeing's payoffs depend on which of the four strategies it decided on before Airbus moves. There are three Nash equilibria (the cells with bold and italic payoffs).

To help answer this question, we use the extended form of the game, the decision tree, developed in Chapter 9. It has two stages. In the first stage, Airbus chooses between launch and do not launch. In the second stage, Boeing decides on its reaction. We establish what is the best strategy for Boeing given that Airbus has moved. We use this information to determine how Airbus will move. This is known as *backward induction*: establishing second stage (or later stage) outcomes in order to see how the first stage will work out.

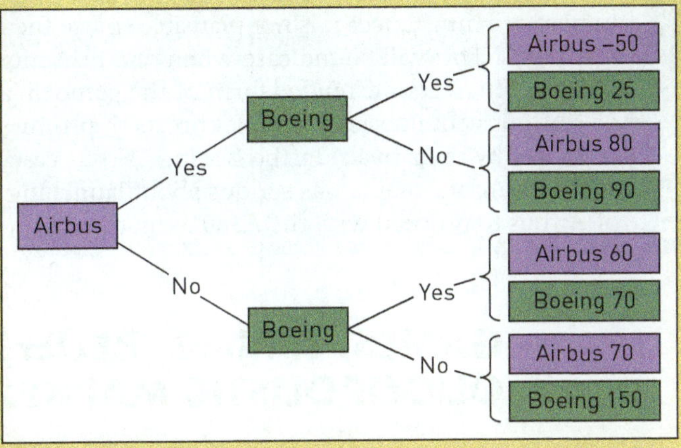

Figure 10.7 The Extensive Form of the Game, with Airbus as First Mover

This is the basis for the extensive form of the game illustrated in Fig. 10.7. On these payoffs Boeing's interest lies in not launching whether or not Airbus launches. Hence Airbus, in reaching its decision, can safely ignore the payoffs that would flow from an outcome in which Boeing chooses to launch, which means that not all the strategies that Boeing could adopt are actually serious possibilities. Airbus can, therefore, ignore them in making its decision.

Airbus can choose between don't launch (in which case Boeing will not launch either) with the payoffs indicated (Airbus 70, Boeing 150) and launch (and Boeing does not launch) with payoffs of Airbus 80, Boeing 90. The latter will be selected.

The first key to the outcome is the fact that the game is one in which one player, Boeing, will have to choose only after the other, Airbus, has chosen. The second concerns Boeing's behaviour during Airbus's decision making and its implications for the other possible strategies that Boeing might adopt.

CREDIBLE THREATS

During this time, Boeing began to plan for a stretched 747. Its engineers did preliminary design work. Its assembly works began to prepare for construction. Boeing started to negotiate with potential airline customers on the configuration of a stretched B747. In short, Boeing's activity was consistent with a corporate decision to go ahead with its challenger. If Airbus believed this, and accepted the payoff structure, its rational response would be to abandon the A380 project, since it would lose money (Airbus – 50). Boeing was making a threat. Although stated that it believed that it was not likely that the market could support profitable sales of two super-jumbos, and possibly even one, it would for various reasons be willing to enter the fray if Airbus proceeded with the A380. This was supported by a view that if Airbus launched, Boeing would launch at relatively low cost by developing an existing model, the B747, rather than introducing a wholly new plane. The object was to ensure that Airbus did not launch, in which case Boeing's profits would be maximised at (Boeing 150).

The problem here is that, on these payoffs, which by assumption were common knowledge, the threat was not credible. No matter what Airbus decided to do, it would never be better for Boeing to launch. This can be seen from the decision tree (extended form) model. Hence, the threat was not credible.

It remains to be seen whether the Airbus decision to go ahead will in fact turn out to be profitable, but the point is that (a) at the time it looked profitable, and (b) it was profitable only because Boeing could not credibly threaten to enter if Airbus moved and Airbus could move first.[3]

RECAP

In many circumstances it is not plausible to use the normal presentation of a game as a matrix of payoffs. This will be the case when one firm moves before the other(s). In this case we use the decision tree, or extended form of the game. In analysing games in this context the concept of commitment merges. Credible threats or promises will have an effect on how firms respond to moves by their rivals. In the Boeing–Airbus case the low credibility of Boeing's attempt to convince Airbus that it was serious about launching a rival to the A380 resulted in the decision of Airbus to proceed with the A380 as first mover.

GAMES, TIMING, BELIEFS AND BEHAVIOUR: OLIGOPOLISTIC MARKETS

The concepts developed in Chapter 9 and the discussion up to this point in this chapter can help explain and predict the behaviour of firms in markets where a small number of large firms determine product characteristics, prices and output levels. The menu of possible outcomes in such markets is long and varied, reflecting permutations and combinations of firm strategies and beliefs, modes of competition, and numbers and sizes of firms. In this section, we shall look at some basic models that help explain how differences in market structure, firms' beliefs, and the manner in which firms compete can affect prices and outputs in those markets.

- **Structure** By 'market structure' we mean the degree of *similarity or difference between* firms (players, in game theory terms) and the *number of firms*. For example, in most parts of Britain or France the everyday grocery trade is shared by a small number of similar-sized large firms (small convenience stores abound, especially in Britain, but they largely sell into another market). On the other hand, retail sales of clothing is divided between a small number of large chain stores (Marks & Spencer, C&A, Debenhams, Galeries Lafayette . . .) and a very large number of much smaller outlets.
- **Beliefs** In the prisoner's dilemma, the outcome reflected the *knowledge and beliefs of each of the players about the other*. The outcome depends on the idea that each expects

[3] Over 10 years later, in early 2011, Boeing announced that it was producing a stretched B747 after all, the B747-8, capable of carrying 460 passengers, six years after the A380 was unveiled. Initial orders were a bit disappointing: two airlines and 33 planes. In early 2011 A380 orders stood at around 250 from 19 airlines.

the other to behave independently in a one-off situation to maximise his own utility subject to no external influence or concern about the future. This may (or may not) be plausible in terms of suspects in police custody, but a wider set of beliefs, etc. is plausible in the case of firms interacting in markets.

- **Competition** Firms also differ as to how they *compete*, usually reflecting the products they are engaged in producing. For example, car producers can plausibly be modelled as deciding on a volume of output of a particular type of car, for which they tool up (commit themselves to produce, hoping to be able to sell them). Quantity is the decision competition variable: the firm lets market demand determine how much it realises for a given volume of production, or average revenue, meaning unit price. If firms compete by setting quantities, competition between firms is called 'Cournot competition' (see p. 292). A life assurance producer is best thought of as developing a financial product range, pricing it and waiting to see how many units of the product it can sell. Price is the decision variable, with market demand determining the amount sold. If firms compete by setting prices, competition is called 'Bertrand competition' (see p. 296).

THE OLIGOPOLIST'S 'REACTION FUNCTION'

To explain how strongly interdependent firms interact in a market, we must be able to predict what each will wish to do given the actions of the other or others. This means being able to establish each firm's *best response function*, or *reaction function*. This tells us what A will do in any set of circumstances that reflect what B (or B and C) choose to do.

In the case of the airline advertising game we looked at in Example 9.1 in the previous chapter, the problem is as follows: what is the best thing Alitalia can do, given an action of Lufthansa, and what is the best thing Lufthansa can do, given an action by Alitalia?

Here the choice is simple: increase or do not increase spending. But suppose both firms could choose between 50 levels of advertising. This is where a reaction function is needed in order to determine (if this is possible) what the outcome would be. This means identifying the best that each player can do for any value chosen by the other for advertising spending.

In the simple game theory examples used earlier there were two possible actions by each player, and payoffs derived from these produced a single-equilibrium outcome. It described the best choice of action contingent on what the other player might do. However, where pricing or output decisions are concerned there is a theoretical infinity of choices a firm can make, with related payoffs. Hence we have a range of *best values* for one firm depending on the choices of the other. This leads us to develop the concept of a **reaction function**, or a 'reaction curve'. This will show the preferred action of a given firm as a function of the action of the other firm(s).

> **reaction function** shows the preferred response of a firm in terms of a decision variable as a response to a value of that variable chosen by the other firm(s)

MODELS OF OLIGOPOLY

In analysing competition among the few firms in an oligopoly market two basic models are widely used. The difference between them reflects how firms compete. This will reflect the type of goods that they produce and the technology of production. It can also reflect the time period over which the analysis is undertaken (long-run or short-run analysis). The first model, and arguably the most important, is referred to as the 'Cournot model'. It assumes firms compete by determining how much to produce (or, perhaps, the capacity they will install in cases such as road or air transport). It dates from pioneering work in the area by the French economist, Augustin Cournot, in the early part of the nineteenth century. Firms are thought of as deciding how much they will supply to the market given what other firms in the market supply or could supply. Demand then determines prices realised. Examples of oligopolistic Cournot markets would include cement production, plate-glass production and car production.

The second model is called the 'Bertrand model', developed by Joseph Bertrand (also French). It assumes firms compete on price. Firms decide on the price at which they will sell, and the quantity sold is determined by demand. Examples include insurance services, restaurants and supermarkets (at least in the short run).

These models enable us to analyse competition, and the consequences of competition and collusion in markets in which all (or most) production is undertaken by a small number of large firms, and in which the incumbents are unconcerned about possible entry. The menu of possible variants in this analysis is very long. For example, firms may have different costs of production, or scale. The goods may be differentiated by producer, or be highly substitutable. Firms may be independent decision makers, or be price or output followers. These will affect the outcome in terms of levels of production/sales, prices and numbers of producers. However, simple models making some basic assumptions actually yield some interesting and robust conclusions concerning the strength of competition in oligopolistic industries.

In this presentation we will look at the smallest number of firms short of a monopoly, a duopoly, meaning two firms in the market, because it is easier to use graphical analysis with two firms. However, much of what these simple models predict can be extended to markets with more than two firms. The material that follows is aimed at giving the results in a non-technical fashion. The formal derivation of the basic results can be found in the technical appendix to this chapter, but it is fairly demanding, and can be skipped.

THE COURNOT MODEL

Consider two equally sized producers with similar costs of production, supplying highly substitutable goods to a market. Each firm knows what market demand is, and has to decide on its profit maximising level of production. This will depend on what the other firm is producing. For example, if the first firm happens to be producing whatever level of production would be offered were the market perfectly competitive there is simply no room for any output by the second firm, since it would by definition lose money by producing, as more output would lower market price below average variable cost. If, on the other hand, for some reason the first firm produced nothing at all, the profit-maximising output for the second firm would be the monopoly output.

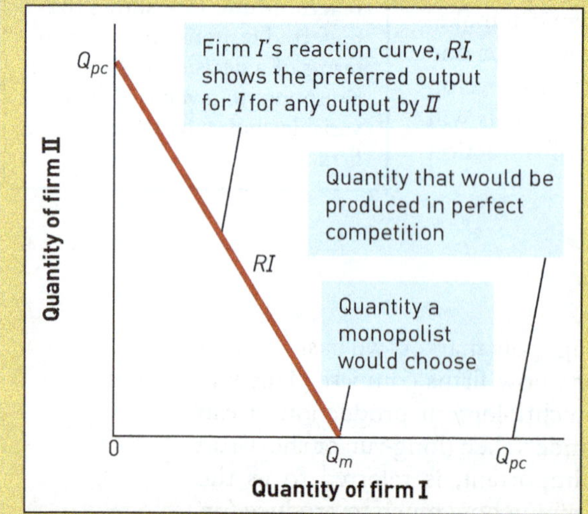

Figure 10.8 Firm *I*'s Reaction Curve, *RI*

Since the firms face similar demand and have similar costs, this is symmetrical. Consequently, we know that the output that maximises either firm's profits given the output of the other lies between zero (the other is producing the competitive output) and the monopoly output (the other is producing nothing). For simplicity we will assume that the market demand curve is a straight line, and the firms have constant unit costs.

On this basis we can determine the profit-maximising output for Firm *I* in a duopoly for any output by Firm *II*. In Fig. 10.8 Firm *I*'s output is measured on the horizontal axis, from zero at the origin on the left through the monopoly output Q_m to the perfectly competitive output, Q_{pc} where price equals average cost on the right. Firm *II*'s output is similarly indicated on the vertical axis from zero through Q_m to Q_{pc}.

The best output for Firm *I* given any output produced by Firm *II* is given by Firm *I*'s Reaction Curve (RC I). Reading over from Firm *II*'s output on the vertical axis to the RC I and down to Firm *I*'s axis, we get the best (profit-maximising) output for Firm *I* given the output for Firm *II*. the RC. Thus, if Firm *II* produced the perfectly competitive output (Q_{pc}), with price equal to average cost, and no profits, Firm *I*'s best choice is to produce nothing as it would not pay Firm *I* to produce any output. If Firm *II* chose to produce nothing, leaving the entire market to Firm *I*, the best output for Firm *I* is the monopoly output.

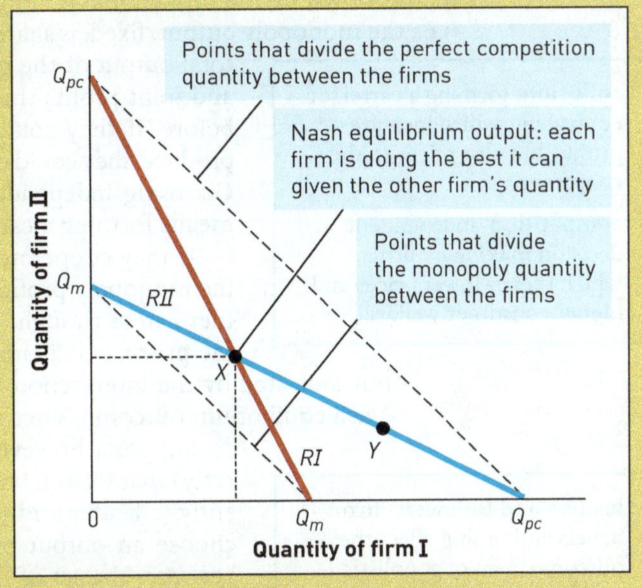

Figure 10.9 Both Players Choose their Outputs Independently

With the assumptions just made about demand curves and cost curves, the reaction curve for Firm *I* will be a straight line, as drawn in Fig. 10.8. It runs from the monopoly output on Firm *I*'s axis to the competitive output on Firm *II*'s axis. It shows the profit-maximising output for Firm *I* for any output by Firm *II*. The further out a firm is on its reaction curve the lower are its profits. For either firm, the closer its output is to the monopoly output on its own axis the higher are its profits.

In Figure 10.9 we show the reaction curves for both firms. Where they intersect the output for both firms is that which maximises their profits given what the other firm is producing. Neither has an incentive to change its output given how the other would react to any change. If either chooses an output other than that given by point *X* the response by the other will be such that it will increase the first's profits to reverse its decision.

Suppose *II* decided to increase its output above the level indicated by X, the reaction curves' intersection point, moving towards the monopoly output on its own axis. For this to be profitable for *II* Firm *I* would have to accommodate *II* by reducing its own output by an amount indicated by *II*'s RC. Otherwise *II*'s profits would not increase as it increased its output. But if we look at the diagram, we see from *I*'s RC what it would do if *II* increased production: it would indeed lower production, but by less than what would be required for *II* to increase his profits by raising his production, so *II*'s profits would fall, giving him an incentive to reverse the decision.

Remember the definition of a Nash equilibrium. At the level of output for each indicated by point *X* in Fig. 10.9, neither has any incentive to alter its output. Hence *X* is a Nash equilibrium in quantities, and, in these circumstances, it is a stable equilibrium.

Notice also the broken lines joining Q_{pc} on each axis and Q_m on each axis. These represent the competitive output and monopoly output divided between the two firms in proportion to the shares indicated by any point on the line. They also, therefore, represent the competitive level of profits (zero) and the monopoly level similarly divided between them. The firm outputs given by the intersection of the two reaction curves involve a level of profits below the monopoly level and above the competitive level shared equally.

It follows that this Nash equilibrium is not the best possible outcome for the two players. The best possible outcome is the monopoly output and profit shared between them, shown by the broken line joining the monopoly output levels on the two axes (i.e., the monopoly output, fixed, is shared between the two players). It involves a lower total output of the good they produce, which, means higher prices and joint profits than at the Nash equilibrium. We have met this before. If they could **collude** and decide jointly on how much to produce, they could do better. This, therefore, is a prisoner's dilemma. Choosing independently means, in effect, **competing**. Colluding means forming a cartel or equivalent.

collusion forming a cartel, or equivalent, which increases profits, but also prices to the consumer

competition independent decision making by firms, which means lower prices and higher consumer welfare

If they cooperate (collude rather than compete) they can share the monopoly profits. If they choose independently what to do and they can be thought of as deciding what to do simultaneously (as in the prisoner's dilemma), neither can do better than select the output indicated by the intersection of the two reaction curves. The outcome is a Nash equilibrium outcome, since neither firm has an incentive to depart from it.

Incentives Matter

Suppose, however, that Firm *I* moves first, and believes (correctly) that Firm *II* will follow its move, rather than move independently (a **leader and follower** game). Firm *I* knows that Firm *II* will choose an output on the basis of its reaction curve. That curve becomes the set of outputs for the two firms among which Firm *I* has to choose. The Nash equilibrium is a feasible choice for Firm *I*, but an output level and share that is preferable for Firm *I* exists. It is at a point like *Y* in Fig. 10.9. Total output is higher, and price and industry profits are lower than at the Nash equilibrium. This is shown by the fact that a line drawn through *Y* parallel to the line joining the competitive output on both axes (the total output shared between the two firms as indicated by point *X*) lies nearer to the competitive output line (the competitive output shared between them) than the Nash equilibrium output line, meaning an output level that is higher and industry profits that are lower than at the Nash equilibrium output. There exists some point like *Y* such that Firm *I*'s output share is sufficiently large to give Firm *I* a higher level of profit despite lower prices than at the Nash equilibrium, meaning of course that Firm *II* does much worse. This is called a 'Stackelberg equilibrium point'.

leaders and followers firms' beliefs and timing affect the outcome in an oligopolistic market

By changing our assumptions about how firms react to each other, and the timing of moves, we change the predicted outcome.

The Cournot duopoly model indicates that even when there is no collusion between firms a market such as that just looked at, with a small (two) number of large players, will produce an output that is lower than the competitive output, other things being equal. The implication is that consumer welfare is reduced by a high degree of concentration of production into a small number of firms. Two questions arise at this stage.

1. In a Cournot market, does increased (reduced) concentration on its own generally decrease (increase) consumer welfare? Put another way, is the Nash equilibrium output of the firms affected by the degree of concentration? Intuition suggests that this is the case. For once, intuition is supported by theoretical reasoning. Although proof of this proposition requires some mathematical manipulation of the firms' reaction functions, its conclusion is as follows. If N is the number of equal-sized firms supplying a market where demand and cost conditions are as assumed here, the Nash equilibrium level of market output will be given as

$$Q = \left\{\frac{N}{(N+1)}\right\} Q_{pc}$$

where Q_{pc} is the output level associated with perfect competition. As N rises, oligopolistic market output, Q, tends to Q_{pc}. The derivation of this equation is fully explained in the appendix on Cournot & Bertrand models at the end of this chapter. Notice that as N becomes very large (as in perfect competition), the industry output approaches the perfectly competitive output as $N/(N+1)$ approaches 1.

2. Does a fall in the number of firms affect the plausibility of assuming independence of decision-making? Independence does not mean assuming that competitors will not react to decisions, although this is the case under perfect competition. It means here not engaging in actions that will result in an output level below the Nash equilibrium, or tacit or overt collusion.[4] There is no simple answer to this question, meaning that a case-by-case approach to the consequences of increased concentration is indicated.

These last two points may be seen as being reflected in the way in which EU competition policy looks at mergers in terms of their effects on economic welfare. This approach is now widely observed outside the EU, and was itself based on the US approach. Mergers are considered in terms of whether they result in a 'significant lessening of competition' (SLC). SLC in turn is seen as being derived from 'unilateral effects' and 'coordinated effects'. The first of these considers whether the merged entity has the power to raise prices profitably simply because it is now bigger relative to the market. A market with a smaller number of larger firms will produce less output and prices will rise as a consequence. The second concerns the impact of the merger on firms' assumptions as to other firms' behaviour and the effect of a firm's decisions on other firms' decisions. As the number of players falls, interdependence of decision making becomes more important, and the potential for coordinated actions that lead to higher prices increases.

Economic Naturalist 10.4
Is bottled water different from other goods? Or is it just that France is different?

The market for sparkling water in France in the early 1990s was dominated by three players, Nestlé (16–18 per cent share), BSN (21–24 per cent) and Perrier (34–38 per cent). The balance was supplied by a large number of smaller producers on a regional basis. In 1991, after an Italian firm tried to enter the French market by acquiring Perrier, Nestlé made an agreed bid to buy Perrier, but, to keep the EU Commission on side, agreed to sell a Perrier product, Volvic, to BSN. This would have increased BSN's share to around 38 per cent, while the Nestlé + Perrier – Volvic share would have been about 38 per cent as well. The EU Commission would not agree to this, on the grounds that the result would be a market with two firms having 76 per cent of the market, which would make collusion much more likely. However, it was allowed to go through after some further capacity from Perrier was sold off. Was this sensible? Many economists think not.

The reaction to the Italian bid smacked of a response to a threat of entry into a market where tacit collusion was in place. If so, the outcome, even with a further transfer of capacity to a third party, would not change the incentive or ability to collude. Curiously, the original proposal with no transfer of Volvic could have lessened the probability of collusion, as the incentive to compete aggressively for the third firm would in all probability have been stronger because the firms were so different in market share. Collusion is more likely, *ceteris paribus*, when the players are similar in size.

[4] This is a controversial point. Tacit collusion is sometimes used to describe the consequence of the recognition of interdependence. However, from a competition policy and law perspective any concentrated market will then exhibit 'tacit collusion', even if all firms act fully independently, which is meaningless in terms of regulation to redress the problem. A more restrictive definition of tacit collusion that is meaningful in terms of legal and regulatory control is that given here: conduct that results in output (price) that is lower (higher) than indicated by a Nash equilibrium.

RECAP

When a firm has to choose a value for price or quantity that is best for it given any value chosen by its rival(s) the value it selects will be given by its 'best response function' or 'reaction function'. This indicates the best choice for a firm given any choice of the rival(s). Where the reaction curves derived from these functions intersect the outcome is a Nash equilibrium. Hence, given these functions, the outcome of the game is determined, and the firms' outputs or prices are such that neither wishes to change. In this case the firms choose independently, or simultaneously. In the case of Cournot (quantity) competition the reaction curves have a negative slope, and indicate the values for output levels. When one firm can move first, and the other is a follower the result is a Stackelberg equilibrium. In these markets the quantity produced is less than the competitive output but more than the monopoly output.

THE BERTRAND MODEL

Suppose, now, that firms compete on *price*. This possibility was analysed by another French mathematician and economist, Joseph Bertrand, who argued in 1883 that the Cournot solution did not generally hold and derived an alternative result where firms decided on prices rather than output levels – this is **Bertrand competition**.

Bertrand competition firms choose a price and accept that quantity sold depends on demand at that price

In the Cournot game discussed above the outcome was a level of output between the competitive and the monopoly levels. In game theory terms, the players' strategies involved setting quantities to produce. Now suppose we think about markets in which firms choose prices rather than quantities, so that the players' strategies involve choosing prices. In the simplest case we look at a firm setting a price when its product is identical to that of the other firm, and they each have the same costs. Each firm knows that for any price it chooses that is higher than marginal cost the best response of the other firm is to set a price that is a little lower. If it sets the same price it shares industry profits equally, since it will sell the same amount as the competitor. But a slightly lower price will give it the whole market and all the profits.

You can try this as a problem, but a little thought will result in the following conclusion. Each firm will choose a price at which profits are zero. Price will be set equal to marginal cost, and with constant costs this means zero profits. A price equal to marginal cost constitutes a Nash equilibrium (check back to the definition of Nash equilibrium to see that this is so).

This leads to what has been called the '*Bertrand Paradox*'. As long as there are at least two similar firms supplying the market each firm has an incentive to set price lower than that of its rival(s) in order to capture sales profitably, which means that price will be driven down to cost, at which point undercutting no longer makes sense. Increasing the number beyond two, or reducing the number as long as there are at least two has no effect: the game results in a zero price cost margin. Industry structure has no apparent effect on price.

This result points to different conclusions depending on whether firms can best be treated as competing on quantity or price.

But, if we look around, we can see that there are cases where firms can plausibly be treated as competing in terms of setting *prices* (Bertrand as opposed to Cournot competitors), and profits are not zero. The first serious attempt to tackle the Bertrand Paradox conclusion was what is known as the *Edgeworth critique*. The Irish economist and statistician, Francis Ysidro Edgeworth (1845–1926), demonstrated that if the firms face rising marginal costs, or, in the limit, a capacity constraint such that neither can supply the entire market at competitive prices then price will not be driven down to average cost, and firm prices can differ.

We can also see examples of higher prices and profit margins in Bertrand markets when there are fewer competitors. Petrol retailing in local markets is an obvious example of both these market characteristics.

How do we square this with the Bertrand model just described?

There are two bases on which to suggest that the Bertrand Paradox outcome is not consistent with what we observe in real-world oligopolies with Bertrand competition. First, the products of the firms may not be *perfectly substitutable*, so that the products will not have to be sold at the same price (think of toothpaste on supermarket shelves). When this is the case, it is possible to look at a firm's pricing decision in the same way as we looked at the output decision in the basic Cournot model. We construct a reaction curve for each firm, showing its preferred price given any price set by the competitor (Fig. 10.10).

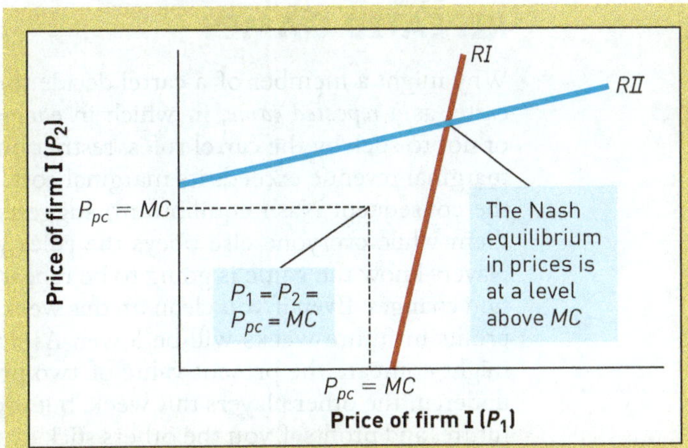

Figure 10.10 The Nash Equilibrium in Prices

In this case, R_1 shows Firm *I*'s preferred price for its own product given (as a function of) Firm *II*'s price. R_2 is Firm *II*'s reaction curve. Neither will set a price below marginal cost. Assuming constant unit cost and price elasticity of demand symmetry the reaction curves will be straight lines, and a Nash equilibrium in prices is where they intersect. Once again, this price, and the joint profits of the firms, will be lower than if they colluded to set the monopoly price and shared the market. However, the point is that the Nash equilibrium does not mean that prices are set equal to marginal cost. Positive profits can be earned in equilibrium without collusion. Furthermore, if there are more firms/products on offer, meaning that each firm/product faces closer substitutes, a firm's reaction curve becomes steeper, and the Nash equilibrium approaches the perfectly competitive price ($P = MC$). In the absence of cooperative behaviour, the more petrol stations there are in a town the lower we would expect prices to be.

There is a second, and even more important, reason for not expecting prices to fall to marginal cost under Bertrand competition, even if the products of each firm are very similar to those of others. The analysis so far treats the pricing decision as if it were taken just once, and never changed. In fact, of course, firms have to make decisions on price frequently through time. As supply costs move, and/or as demand conditions change, the 'correct' price for a firm to set changes too. We must assume that firms have memories. We must also assume that firms know how to signal how they will respond to price cutting, and how to indicate by their pricing behaviour whether or not they intend competing aggressively or adopting a 'live and let live' approach. Put another way, pricing decisions involve choosing not just a set of prices for your products, but deciding on a *pricing strategy*, or adopting a rule on setting prices as circumstances change.

The consequences of this approach to pricing include a high degree of 'price stickiness' in small-number markets where players can easily observe their competitors' prices accurately. It makes sense to analyse the pricing behaviour of firms in these markets in terms of repeated games, pricing rules, signalling and tacit collusion. This approach is also useful because it helps us understand when and why this *tacitly coordinated behaviour* breaks down, and we see price wars breaking out.

REPEATED GAMES

Why might a member of a cartel decide to break ranks? One answer is to analyse the cartel as a *repeated game*, in which in each period any player has to choose whether or not to stick by the cartel rules, restrict output and sell at a price at which the firm's marginal revenue exceeds its marginal cost. The single-period dominant strategy (and the consequent Nash equilibrium) suggests breaking the rules, because by breaking them while everyone else obeys the rules you stand to clean up. However, if all the players know the game is going to be repeated indefinitely into the future, the calculation changes. Even if you clean up this week, by undermining the cartel you know that profits in future weeks will be lower. As a result, it is reasonable to believe that you might compare the present value of two profit streams into the future: profits if you undercut the other players this week, but everyone sells at a much lower price into the future, and profits if you the others stick by the rules.

Of course, a small player, that doesn't lower prices by too much might believe that a little cheating will go unnoticed or be ignored. Suppose, however, that either by experience, or by some explicit and credible threat, it was clear that cheating would not be tolerated, and price cuts targeted on the cheater's customers by large competitors were the expected response to cheating. For example, suppose trade magazines published frequent, reliable and detailed information on who was charging what prices for which goods. Cheating would be much less likely.

Difficulty in observing the quality-adjusted price because the product as sold differs among customers makes price fixing less likely. Uncertainty as to future market conditions, and therefore as to future profits, makes cheating more likely. Higher interest rates reduce the present value of future profits relative to present profits, and encourage cheating.

Explicit pricing agreements are prohibited under competition law everywhere. Participation not only results in being liable to substantial financial penalties, but in some circumstances can result in a prison sentence. However, and especially in small-number situations, firms can decide to operate a pricing policy that is based on a recognition that how they behave affects others' behaviour, and vice versa. Recognition of *interdependence of decisions* leads to a situation in which the observed behaviour resembles what might flow from an explicit agreement not to compete aggressively on price. For this reason this behaviour is frequently described as **tacit collusion**.

> **tacit collusion** firms behaving in a manner that resembles what might emerge from a collusive agreement because they recognise their interdependence

Tacit collusion in oligopolistic and imperfectly competitive industries is frequently supported by *pricing* and *signalling* strategies designed to discourage competition and reinforce cooperative behaviour. One common device, which to an uninformed observer looks like aggressive competition on price, is a commitment to match or beat any price by guaranteeing to be the lowest-price seller. This is very widespread as a promotional device but, on closer examination, may in fact operate to support existing prices rather than ensure that buyers face the lowest possible prices. When a large white-goods retailer makes such a promise, he is signalling credibly to competitors small and large that if they lower prices he will lower his.

Conditions facilitating tacit collusion do not always exist, even where there are few firms and they recognise the fact that their behaviour affects that of the others. First of all, firms may face different cost structures. This can result in significant differences between them in terms of what pricing structure and behaviour maximise profits when demand conditions change. For example, the lower a firm's variable costs relative to its fixed costs, the more likely it is to prefer to cut price rather than to cut output if demand weakens.

Economic Naturalist 10.5
Why was Statoil forced to abandon a rebate scheme that would have helped petrol retailers cut their prices?

In 2002 the Competition Authority in Dublin, Ireland, threatened legal action against a major oil company, Statoil, as a result of an arrangement it had entered into with its retailers in a country town in Ireland.[5] Statoil's scheme involved (a) fixing a maximum price at which petrol could be sold, and (b) offering a rebate to its dealers to enable them to cut their prices if other petrol outlets cut their prices below a marker price. While the first might have been part of a campaign to persuade people that Statoil petrol was a good buy (people notoriously appear not to pay much attention to actual prices per litre), the second element meant that other dealers knew that there was no point reducing price below the marker price since Statoil dealers could costlessly follow them down. This would clearly dampen price competition. Statoil withdrew the scheme.

Pricing may not be transparent, with each unit being sold at a price negotiated with the purchaser on a confidential basis. Tacit collusion on pricing becomes meaningless. This factor on its own is probably the main reason why we see cut-throat competition between Boeing and Airbus.

Differences in product characteristics may mean that firms face different price elasticities of demand. This means they differ in terms of how they view the consequences of a change in prices.

As a result, we do not observe high prices supported by tacit collusion as inevitably following an observation of a small number of large producers in a market. And, even when it does occur, it is frequently undermined by repeated episodes of price wars.

RECAP

Bertrand competition describes markets in which firms compete by choosing a price rather than deciding on how much to produce. In this case a firm will choose a higher (lower) price if its rival(s)'s price is higher (lower). Nash equilibrium occurs where the curves intersect. The Bertrand paradox is resolved if we assume that firms have memories and can predict other firms' behaviour.

WHEN DO PRICE WARS BREAK OUT, AND HOW DO THEY END?

In mid-2004 the Chinese Ministry of Information announced that it was stepping up its regulatory supervision of pricing in the telecoms sector in China in order to avoid price wars. Until earlier in the year mobile telephony charges had been set by the Ministry, which was also the regulator. In order to encourage the development of the sector, these price controls were relaxed. As elsewhere in the world, mobile telephony in China was dominated by a small number of players, all large. As soon as price controls were relaxed, a price war broke out, as firms slashed prices to increase market share in what was seen as an expanding market. The government, however, wanted the companies to maintain high profit margins and use them to finance qualitative upgrading of the mobile network. When the government intervened to restrict price cutting, of course, the industry greeted this warmly.[6] Regulation produced higher profits.

[5] The Competition Authority has described the confrontation and its outcome in Decision E/03/002, which is available on its website: www.TCA.ie.

[6] The story can be found in the English-language *China Daily*, on its website at www.chinadaily.cn/English/doc/2004-07/03/content_345216.htm.

One possibility here is that under a tight regulatory regime firms had not been able to learn how others would react to price changes, nor been able to estimate demand elasticities correctly. This would interpret the price war as flowing from poor information as to demand conditions and the degree of interdependence of pricing. Another possibility is that, even with good information, tacit collusion and weak price, competition was unlikely under deregulation because of the extraordinary degree of non-transparency of pricing: mobile phone pricing packages are numerous, complex and difficult to compare.

The impact of poor information is a useful starting point. Suppose a firm sees its sales falling, and has poor information as to market conditions. Three possible reasons will arise. The first is that market demand has weakened, and it is sharing the pain with other firms.

The second is that for some reason it has lost competitiveness. The third is that supply has increased as a competitor has increased production. Unfortunately, the firm is not able with any degree of certainty to establish what exactly is going on.

If it had been content not to compete aggressively on price up to this point, it now faces a problem. Suppose its best guess is that there has been a fall in demand. It must choose between (a) tacit collusion on the basis that this is a temporary blip in demand, everyone is in the same boat and price cutting will achieve nothing as it will be imitated; (b) price cutting anyway because the demand reduction may be permanent so that even if everyone is similarly affected there are fewer seats in the boat than potential passengers, and the last to cut prices exits the market. Suppose, however, it suspects that it has lost competitiveness. The options are not to do anything and accept a lower volume of sales (and possibly further falls) or reduce price to make its products more attractive. Finally, it might suspect that the problem is not its own offerings, or demand in the market, but a competitor increasing production. If it does nothing, it accepts a lower market share. If it wishes to protect its market share and signal its intention to do so to anyone who wants to raise theirs, it will respond by reducing price.

What will happen? In all three scenarios, cutting price looks a better bet, even if a case can be made for not cutting price. Betting against a price cut under uncertainty as to what is going on looks unwise. Hence, it is easy to understand why price wars can be triggered by falling demand or by an overestimate of market demand.

Notice, too, that the scenarios point to a further reason for price wars: market disciplining and market 'restructuring'. Responding to price cuts by one supermarket operator by a 'race to the bottom' may not seem to make much sense until you reflect that the expectation that this will happen in future will be reinforced by an aggressive response. It can also be a mechanism to secure a shake-up in an industry, leading to a consolidation among players.

Finally, of course, an episode of price cutting can arise as a consequence of changes on the supply side. New entrants to a market can disturb a collusive equilibrium. Even with tacit collusion, a fall in input costs can result in the collusive equilibrium level of prices falling. Alternatively, a significant fall in one firm's costs that is not enjoyed by other firms can lead to the lower-cost firm seeking to increase share on the back of lower costs.

SUMMARY

- Analysing competition between firms in small-number markets requires that we accept that the firms, or players, recognise their interdependence. Consequently, decisions on price, output levels, advertising, R&D and other dimensions of competition must reflect an understanding of how other firms will respond.
- This means that, in addition to such factors as costs of production and market demand, decisions will reflect strategic considerations.
- Game theory, as introduced in Chapter 9, provides a basis for analysing strategic decisions by firms in such circumstances. Many competition problems have the features of prisoner's dilemma games.
- Building on the elements of game theory enables us to build models that help us to understand how things like beliefs and modes of competition have an influence on how firms actually behave in *small-number markets*.
- These models yield interesting and plausible conclusions that explain some features of *market behaviour* that are not explained by the simple models of perfect competition or monopolistic competition.
- Timing and the order in which players move are important in understanding what happens, as in the Boeing Airbus game. This means using the decision-tree approach to describing a game. In these circumstances, promises, threats and other commitment devices are important elements in predicting outcomes.
- The analysis of competition and industry structures in these circumstances will also reflect how best to model how players compete, namely as Cournot or Bertrand competitors. In general, Cournot-type markets will be more predictably affected by the number of players than Bertrand-type markets.

REVIEW QUESTIONS

1. Can you explain why cartels offer an example of a prisoner's dilemma problem, and suggest how (ignoring legalities) the problem could be solved for the members of the cartel?
2. Suppose Boeing had entered into a contract with a large airline to produce a stretched B747. How would this have affected Airbus's decision?
3. What differences in firms' cost structures would lead you to treat them as Cournot or Bertrand competitors?
4. Can you show where (approximately) prices would settle if Firm *I* were a leader and Firm *II* a follower in the price-setting game in Fig. 10.10 (the equivalent to point *Y* in the quantity setting game in Fig. 10.9)?
5. Explain why advertising campaigns announcing that 'we will not beaten on price, and will refund twice the difference . . .' can be a mechanism to reduce rather than intensify price competition.

PROBLEMS

connect

1. Two aeroplane manufacturers are considering the production of a new product, a 550-passenger jet. Both are deciding whether to enter the market and produce the new plane. The payoff matrix is as shown below (payoff values are in million euros).

		Boeing: Produce	Boeing: Don't produce
Airbus	Produce	−5 for Boeing −5 for Airbus	100 for Boeing 0 for Airbus
	Don't produce	0 for Boeing 100 for Airbus	0 for Boeing 0 for Airbus

The implication of these payoffs is that the market demand is large enough to support only one manufacturer. If both firms enter, both will sustain a loss.

a. Identify two possible equilibrium outcomes in this game.

b. Consider the effect of a subsidy. Suppose the European Union decides to subsidise the European producer, Airbus, with a subsidy of €25 million if it enters the market. Revise the payoff matrix to account for this subsidy. What is the new equilibrium outcome?

c. Compare the two outcomes (pre- and post-subsidy). What qualitative effect does the subsidy have?

2. Can you explain why a competition authority might be more concerned at the emergence of leader–follower behaviour in a market with Bertrand competition than in one with Cournot competition?

3. An incumbent firm can choose between fighting an entrant and accommodating an entrant by yielding some market share to the entrant. Can you create a 2 × 2 table of payoffs such that the dominant strategy for the incumbent is to accommodate?

4. Suppose the entrant decides that he wishes to signal to the incumbent that he doesn't want a price war. Suppose he believes that a price war would not be in their interests, and also that a small share of a profitable market would be preferable to a large share of a market where prices dropped substantially. To illustrate this, he decides to commit himself to a small scale of entry. Assuming that the entrant moves first, can you create a decision tree that reflects these beliefs?

5. Why might subsidies to R&D by governments reduce economic welfare?

6. In Economic Naturalist 10.4 the prospect of a duopoly leading to reduced competition and higher prices is considered. Contrast this with the situation in the aircraft market, where most observers believe there is very strong competition between the two producers. What features of the aircraft market make competition in a duopoly more likely than in the case of bottled water?

7. Why would an economics naturalist expect that a system in which students are graded by reference to a distribution rather than by an absolute ranking (i.e., the top 5 per cent get an A, the next 10 per cent get a B, the next 30 per cent get a C, the next 40 per cent get a D and the bottom 15 per cent get F) should lead to less cheating in exams but more thefts from the library?

8. How could it be profit enhancing for firms in an industry with a few large producers to maintain significant volumes of unused capacity?

9. During the First World War it was observed that, despite the fact that soldiers on each side were trying to kill each other, and to do so it was useful to prevent supplies from reaching the enemy's trenches, frequently they didn't shell their opponents' supply lines between 12.00 pm and 1.00 pm (at which time food was being brought up for the main meal). Use a 2 × 2 matrix to analyse this so as to explain once-off as opposed to repeated games, and relate it to firms' pricing strategies.

10. (Refer to the mathematical appendix to this chapter.) The demand for widgets in a given market is given by $P = 150 - 2Q$, where P is the price of a widget in dollars, euros or whatever and Q is the quantity of widgets offered to the market. Two firms supply widgets to the market, and face a constant production cost of 30 euros per widget. What will be total output supplied to the market, the market price, the sales of each of the two firms and the profits each of the two firms? What would total output and price be if the widgets were supplied as under perfect competition?

REFERENCES

Esty, B. and P. Ghemawat (2002) *Airbus v Boeing in Super Jumbos: a Case of Failed Pre-emption* (Harvard Business School, Strategy Working Paper, 02-061, February 2002).

Appendix

COURNOT AND BERTRAND MODELS

In this appendix we show how the Cournot and Bertrand market equilibria are reached in worked out examples. We start with some basic expressions derived from earlier chapters. We assume two firms, firm 1 and firm 2, producing identical products. For simplicity we assume they face the same constant unit costs,

$TC = c \cdot q$ for each firm where q is the level of output of the firm.

1. We have the relationship between price and quantity demanded in the market, again a simple one, $P = a - b \cdot Q$ where $Q = (q_1 + q_2)$.
2. We know that $Q = (a - c)/b$ is the competitive output in the market, where price equals average and marginal cost.
3. We use π to mean profit, the difference between total cost and total revenue.

Cournot market: *each firm chooses a level of output.*

The profit function for firm 1 indicates how profits behave as its output varies:

$$\pi_1 = q_1 \cdot P - c \cdot q_1 = q_1 \cdot (a - b \cdot Q) - c \cdot q_1 = q_1 \cdot (a - b \cdot q_1 - b \cdot q_2) - c \cdot q_1$$

The profit maximum value of q_1 is found by differentiating with respect to q_1 and solving for q_1.

$$\delta\pi_1 / \delta q_1 = a - 2b \cdot q_1 - b \cdot q_2 - c = 0 \text{ for a maximum, from which}$$

$$q_1 = (a - c)/2b - q_2/2.$$

This firm 1's best response function, giving it the highest profit output given firm 2's output. Graphed, it traces out firm 1's reaction curve. If firm 2 produces the competitive output, firm 1's best option is to produce nothing. If firm 2 produces nothing firm 1 will produce the monopoly output (half the competitive output in this model).

Given the same cost functions and market demand, firm 2's best response function is

$$q_2 = (a - c)/2b - q_1/2.$$

If the market is to be in equilibrium we need to find the value of each firm's output that simultaneously satisfies the two best response functions. We do this by substituting the value of one firm's function into the other's.

$$q_2 = (a - c)/2b - \{(a - c)/2b - q_2/2\}/2.$$

This gives us

$$q_1 = q_2 = 1/3(a - c)/b \text{ and } Q = 2/3(a - c)/b$$

To get a numerical value, just insert the numerical values for unit cost, (c) and the intercept (a) and the slope (b) of the demand curve in this last expression.

BERTRAND MARKET (WITH PRODUCT DIFFERENTIATION): *EACH FIRM SELECTS A PRICE*

We use the demand curve, not the inverse as in the Cournot case, because the firm is choosing price. We allow the firms' products to be differentiated (the basis for choosing a price is that your product is not the same as anyone else's). This means that relative prices affect sales.

The demand curve for firm 1 now is

$$q_1 = a - \beta \cdot p_1 + \alpha \cdot p_2$$

where α is the effect of firm 2's price on firm 1's sales, which is positive and vice versa. The profit function is

$$\pi_1 = p_1 \cdot (a - \beta \cdot p_1 + \alpha \cdot p_2) - c \cdot (a - \beta \cdot p_1 + \alpha \cdot p_2)$$

The profit maximizing price for firm 1 is given by

$$\delta\pi_1 / \delta p_1 = a - 2\,\beta \cdot p_1 + \alpha \cdot p_2 + c \cdot \beta = 0$$

and the best response (reaction function) is given by

$$p_1 = (a + \alpha \cdot p_2 + c \cdot \beta)/2\beta$$

The reaction function is now upward sloping since $dp_1/dp_2 = \alpha/2\beta > 0$.

As before we solve for market equilibrium by substituting for p_2 in the expression for p_1.

This gives us a solution

$$p_1 = p_2 = (a + c \cdot \beta)/(2b - \alpha)$$

Part 4

Market Imperfections (2): Externalities, Information, Distribution and the Role of the Government in a Market Economy

The current preoccupation with the issues involved in global warming can be thought of as a concern over the failure of a market economic system to 'protect the environment'. Some of the issues underlying the climate question have been central to mainstream economics for over 70 years. Policy on the climate problem is in many respects grounded in this area of economics analysis. In Chapter 11 we seek to examine how markets are inefficient when activities generate costs or benefits accruing to people not directly involved in those activities, and the self-interested actions of individuals usually will not lead to economically efficient outcomes.

The invisible hand theory assumes that buyers and sellers are well informed about all relevant options. This is not always the case. In Chapter 12 we explore how basic economic principles can help imperfectly informed individuals and firms make the best use of the limited information they possess.

Why is income and wealth unequally distributed? In today's world many see this question is seen as being as important as climate change. Our aim in Chapter 13 will be to apply simple economic principles in an attempt to answer this question. Differences in people's characteristics, inherited or acquired, and referred to as human capital, are only part of the story. Factors considered include labour unions, winner-take-all markets, discrimination and the effect of non-wage conditions of employment. In this chapter we shall also explore whether income inequality is something society should be concerned about and, if so, whether practical remedies exist for it.

Chapter 14 looks at two further aspects of government action in a market economy. The first is the function of government as 'regulator': taking legal and administrative steps to change the way in which firms or households behave. The second is the role of the government as producer of goods and services. In most Western economies, governments produce goods and services that could easily be (and in many cases are) produced by firms through markets. Why? There are, however, some activities of government as producer that cannot easily be replicated through markets. Why?

Chapter 11 Externalities and Property Rights

Upon the sacredness of property civilization itself depends – the right of the laborer to his hundred dollars in the savings bank, and equally the legal right of the millionaire to his millions.
Andrew Carnegie

Learning objectives

After reading this chapter you should be able to:

1. Understand how positive and negative externalities make markets less efficient;
2. Understand the importance of the Coase theorem;
3. Analyse policy responses to externalities;
4. Appreciate the role of property rights in the efficient functioning of markets;
5. Understand positional externalities and their efficiency implications.

MARKET EFFICIENCY: A REMINDER

We have stressed in several chapters that for markets to be an efficient mechanism to allocate a society's economic resources they must (a) exist and (b) be efficient. Efficiency requires that on both sides of the market prices reflect the value of goods and services to purchasers and the opportunity cost of resources used up in producing them. When markets are not competitive (for example, when a supplier has substantial market power) markets are inefficient because prices in equilibrium diverge from marginal and average cost. Now we look at another source of market inefficiency. Even when prices are established by the usual forces of supply and demand, some costs or benefits may not reflected in the prices facing consumers or producers.

Efficiency

external cost (or **negative externality**) a cost of an activity that falls on people other than those who pursue the activity

external benefit (or **positive externality**) a benefit of an activity received by people other than those who pursue the activity

externality an external cost or benefit of an activity

EXTERNAL COSTS AND BENEFITS

Many activities generate costs or benefits that accrue to people not directly involved in those activities. These effects are generally unintended. They are called **external costs** and **benefits** – **externalities**, for short. Disease control provides an introductory example.

Vaccination (inoculation) helps control and eradicate infectious diseases by providing immunity against the infective agent. It has wiped out smallpox. The 1950s epidemic of poliomyelitis in North America and Europe resulted in the use of the Salk vaccine that has almost eradicated polio since then. In general, the success of vaccination relies initially on private decisions to seek protection, usually for children. In recent years, and a matter of controversy, the classic case here was the MMR vaccine that protected against measles, mumps and rubella (German measles). Parents decide to accept the small but inevitable risk associated with vaccination (a cost) in order to inoculate a newborn child against a variety of infectious diseases to protect that child (a benefit). When the child is inoculated, however, this confers benefits on other, unidentified parents and children, because it also reduces the probability of someone else being infected, as it eliminates part of the transmission vector for the infection. It is reasonable to assume that the parents' decision is not normally based on the benefits to others flowing from their decision. If the inoculation were expensive, it is equally reasonable to assume that fewer children would be inoculated, with the consequence that the incidence of rubella among pregnant women would increase. Hence we have subsidised or free (and even compulsory) vaccination programmes to takeaccount of this beneficial spillover effect from decisions to vaccinate.

Cost-Benefit Analysis

The point here is that the *private decision* to take the action reflects the *private calculus of private costs and benefits*. These are *'internalised'* into the decision-making process. What are not internalised are *the costs and benefits to others* of the decision. These are described as *'external effects'* (spillover effects) of the actions they take. These effects are described in economics as *'externalities'*.

Inoculation involves a positive externality: it confers benefits on others at no cost to the decision maker, benefits that do not increase the welfare of the decision maker. Other actions involve negative externalities, imposing costs on others at no cost to the person undertaking the action. An example is a decision to use a car in an urban area during the rush hour. The driver computes into his decision the costs and benefits to him or her of using the car to make a journey at that time. What does not enter into the calculation is that on the journey the driver may delay a large number of motorists, each by a small amount, because the road is already congested.

In general, where there are positive externalities private decision making tends to result in a less than socially optimal (marginal cost = marginal benefit) level of the activity concerned. This is because the resource allocation reflects *marginal private costs* and *marginal private benefits*. Positive externalities mean that marginal private benefits are not the same as marginal social benefits. Put another way, the decision maker does not capture all the benefits of his decision. Similarly, negative externalities imply that 'too much' of the activity occurs, as the decision maker does not pay all the costs. This chapter first focuses on how externalities affect the allocation of resources. Adam Smith's theory of the 'invisible hand' (Chapter 7) applies to an ideal marketplace in which externalities do not exist. In such situations, Smith argued, the self-interested actions of individuals would lead to socially efficient outcomes. We shall see that when the parties affected by externalities can easily negotiate with one another, the 'invisible hand' will still produce an efficient outcome. A corollary of this is that we can think usefully about externalities in terms of the absence of, or poorly defined, tradable property rights.

But, in many cases, such as in the cases of rush-hour traffic and inoculation, negotiation is impractical. In those cases, the self-serving actions of individuals simply will not lead to efficient outcomes. Because externalities are widespread, the attempt to forge solutions to the problems they cause is one of the most important rationales not only for the existence of government but for a variety of other forms of collective action as well.

HOW EXTERNALITIES AFFECT RESOURCE ALLOCATION

The way in which externalities distort the allocation of resources can be seen clearly in Examples 11.1 and 11.2, and Economic Naturalist 11.1.

Does the honeybee keeper face the right incentives?

Example 11.1

Phoebe earns her living as a keeper of honeybees. Her neighbours on all sides grow apples. Because bees pollinate apple trees as they forage for nectar, the more hives Phoebe keeps, the larger the harvests will be in the surrounding orchards. If Phoebe takes only her own costs and benefits into account in deciding how many hives to keep, will she keep the socially optimal number of hives?

For the orchard owners, Phoebe's hives constitute an external benefit, or a *positive* externality. If she takes only her own personal costs and benefits into account, she will add hives only until the added revenue she gets from the last hive just equals the cost of adding it. But since the orchard owners also benefit from additional hives, the total benefit of adding another hive at that point will be greater than its cost. Phoebe, then, will keep too few hives (but see Economic Naturalist 11.1: in reality we don't believe this is a serious example of a positive externality!).

Based on this, can you see how there might be 'too many' beehives if they were located near a school or a nursing home?

Economic Naturalist 11.1
Why are positive production externalities hard to find?

Most discussions of externalities concentrate on negative externalities, such as pollution of the environment by industry. Positive externalities exist: vaccination is an example, but further examples of positive production externalities are much more difficult to find. Why?

First of all, think of a negative externality as not paying a cost associated with an activity while enjoying the benefits, and of a positive externality as supplying a benefit, perhaps at a cost, to another person but not being reimbursed for so doing. Businesses are good at spotting external beneficiaries of their activities and figuring out ways of making them pay for their pleasures. When they succeed, the external effect is internalised into decision making. The positive externality disappears.

Positive externalities, however, do exist. Consider the following. How would you feel as a retailer of up-market clothing on a high street if some one opened a sex shop next door? That's an example of a negative externality, and explains why businesses are strong supporters of zoning restrictions affecting that sort of business. Then, think of the fact that some retailers tend to cluster together in large cities – jewellers' or clothing shops, for example. Why? Jewellery and certain items of clothing, such as jeans or a smart dress, tend to be what are called 'search goods'. People spend time looking and comparing before buying. Given that retailers in the business have differentiated offerings available, an increased number of retailers increases the 'footfall' of potential customers, which benefits all. You will see the same phenomenon in car dealerships and antiques stores. Can you see why small convenience grocery stores do not tend to cluster?

Every activity involves *costs* and *benefits*. When all the relevant costs and benefits of an activity accrue directly to the person who carries it the level of the activity that is best for the individual will be best for society as a whole. But when an activity generates externalities individual self-interest does not produce the best allocation of resources. Individuals who consider only their own costs and benefits will tend to engage too much in activities that generate negative externalities and too little in activities that generate positive externalities.

Cost–Benefit Analysis

Efficiency

THE GRAPHICAL PORTRAYAL OF EXTERNALITIES

The effects of externalities on resource allocation can be portrayed graphically. Consider first the case of negative externalities. Figure 11.1(a) depicts the supply (Private *MC*) and demand curves for electricity from a hydro-electric generator whose production involves no external costs or benefits. The resulting equilibrium price and quantity in the market for this product will then be socially optimal, for the reasons discussed in Chapters 3 and 6: the value to buyers of the last unit of the product consumed will be exactly equal to the marginal cost of producing it (€1,300 per Mwh in each case), leaving no further possible gains from exchange.

Suppose instead that electricity production relies on coal-burning generators (Figure 11.1(b)). Now each Mwh of output produced is accompanied by an external pollution cost of $XC =$ €1,000, as shown in Fig. 11.1(b). Since the external pollution cost falls not on producers but on others who live downwind from the power stations, Private *MC* is again the supply curve for this product, and its demand curve is again as before, so that the equilibrium price and quantity will be exactly the same as in Fig. 11.1(a), as determined by the intersection of the demand curve (*D*) and the supply curve (Private *MC*). But this time the private market equilibrium is not socially optimal. To see why, note that at $Q_{pvt} = 12{,}000$ Mwhs per year, the value to consumers of the last unit of output produced was only €1,300 per Mwhs, while the cost of producing that last unit (including the external cost) was €2,300 per Mwhs. This means that society could gain additional economic surplus by producing fewer units of the product. The 'correct' level of production is 8,000 Mwhs per year, the output level at which the demand curve intersects Social *MC*. Social *MC*, the socially optimal supply curve of the product, is the result of adding the external cost, *XC*, to every value along Private *MC*. exchange. For a good whose production generates external costs, the market equilibrium quantity will be higher than the socially optimal quantity.

Suppose production generates external benefits? In Fig. 11.2, Private demand is the demand curve for a product whose production generates an external benefit of *XB* per

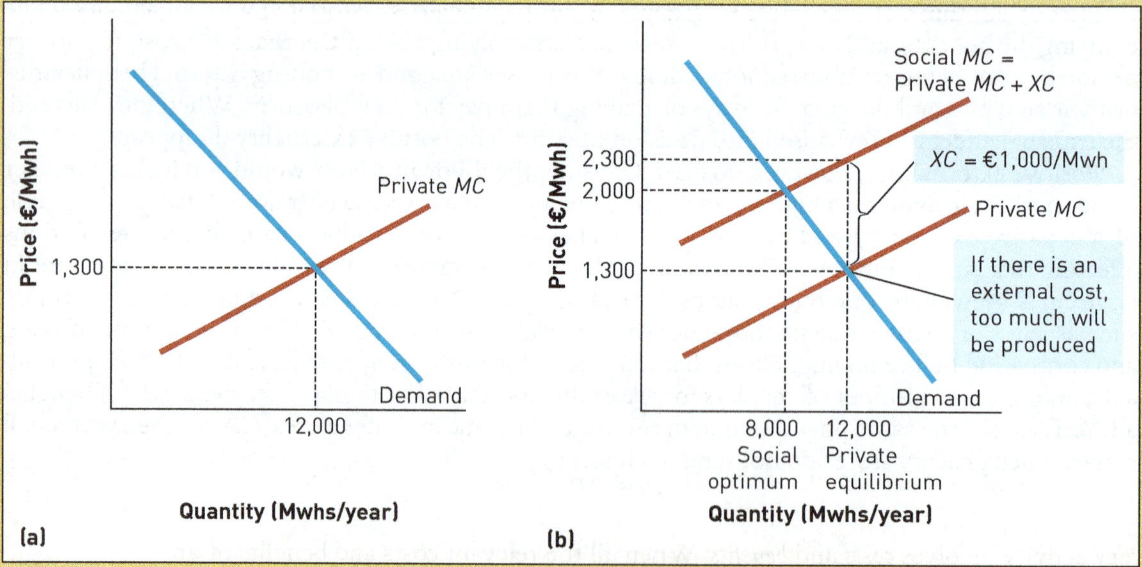

Figure 11.1 How External Costs Affect Resource Allocation
When a market has no external costs or benefits (a), the resulting equilibrium quantity and price are socially optimal. By contrast, when production of a good is accompanied by an external cost (b), the market equilibrium price (€1,300 per Mwh) is too low, and the market equilibrium quantity (12,000 Mwhs per year) is too high.

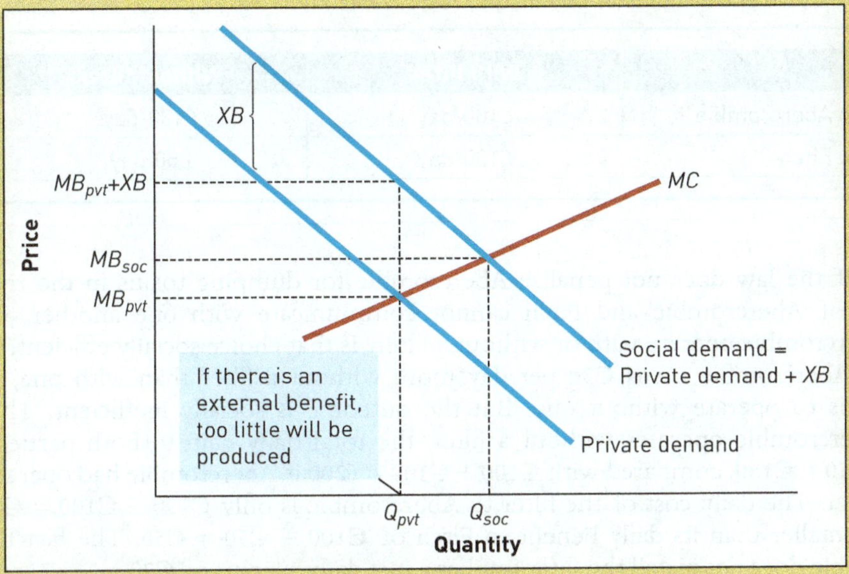

Figure 11.2 A Good Whose Production Generates a Positive Externality for Consumers

The market equilibrium quantity, Q_{pvt}, is smaller than the socially optimal quantity, Q_{soc}, because individual buyers are willing to pay only for the benefits they reap from directly consuming the product.

unit. The market equilibrium quantity of this good Q_{pvt}, is the output level at which Private demand intersects the supply curve of the product (*MC*). This time, market equilibrium quantity is smaller than the socially optimal level, denoted Q_{soc}. Q_{soc} is the output level at which *MC* intersects the socially optimal demand curve (Social demand), which is obtained by adding the external benefit, *XB*, to every value along Private demand. Note that in Fig. 11.2 in the case of positive externalities the private market equilibrium again fails to exhaust all possible gains from exchange. Thus at Q_{pvt} the marginal cost of producing an additional unit of output is only MB_{pvt}, which is smaller than the marginal benefit of an additional unit by the amount *XB*. For a good whose production generates external benefits, the market equilibrium quantity will be smaller than the socially optimal quantity.

No matter whether externalities are positive or negative, they *distort the allocation of resources* in otherwise efficient markets. When externalities are present, the individual pursuit of self-interest will not result in the largest possible economic surplus. And when it does not, the outcome is by definition inefficient.

THE COASE THEOREM

To say that a situation is 'inefficient' means that it can be rearranged in a way that would make at least some people better off without harming others. The existence of inefficiency means that there is 'cash on the table' (Chapter 3), which provides an incentive to capture it. For example, we saw that because monopoly pricing results in an inefficiently low output level, the potential for gain gave monopolists an incentive to make discounts available to price-sensitive buyers. As Examples 11.2 and 11.3 illustrate, the inefficiencies that result from externalities create similar incentives for remedial action.

Will Abercrombie dump toxins in the river (1)?

Example 11.2

An industrialist named Abercrombie has built a textile factory beside a river. The water supplies power, but is also used in the production process. The process produces a toxic waste by-product from the dyes used. If Abercrombie releases untreated water back into the river the toxins cause damage to Fitch, a commercial fisherman located downstream. At a cost, Abercrombie can filter out the toxins, in which case Fitch will suffer no damage at all. The relevant gains and losses for the two individuals are listed in Table 11.1.

Table 11.1 Costs and Benefits of Eliminating Toxic Waste (1)

	With filter	Without filter
Gains to Abercrombie	£100/day	£130/day
Gains to Fitch	£100/day	£50/day

Efficiency

If the law does not penalise Abercrombie for dumping toxins in the river, and if Abercrombie and Fitch cannot communicate with one another, will Abercrombie operate with or without a filter? Is that choice socially efficient?

Since Abercrombie earns €30 per day more without a filter than with one, his incentive is to operate without one. But the outcome is socially inefficient. Thus, when Abercrombie operates without a filter, the total daily gain to both parties is €130 + €50 = €180, compared with €100 + €100 = £200 if Abercrombie had operated with a filter. The daily cost of the filter to Abercrombie is only €130 − €100 = €30, which is smaller than its daily benefit to Fitch of €100 − €50 = €50. The fact that Abercrombie does not install the filter implies a lost daily surplus of €20.

Example 11.3 Will Abercrombie dump toxins in the river (2)?

Suppose now that Abercrombie and Fitch can now communicate with one another at no cost. Even though the law does not require him to do so, will Abercrombie use a filter?

This time, Abercrombie will use a filter. Recall from Chapter 7 the observation that when the economic 'pie' grows larger, everyone can have a larger slice (the efficiency principle). Because a filter would result in the largest possible economic surplus, it would enable both Abercrombie and Fitch to have a larger net gain than before. Fitch has an incentive to *pay* Abercrombie to use a filter. Suppose Fitch offers Abercrombie €40 per day to compensate him for operating with a filter. Both Abercrombie and Fitch will then be exactly €10 per day better off than before, for a total daily net gain of €20.

Because we now assume that they can bargain and enter into some form of contract (requiring well-defined tradable property rights) the externality problem is solved.

Exercise 11.1 In Example 11.3, what is the largest amount, to the nearest euro, by which Fitch could compensate Abercrombie for operating with a filter and still be better off than before?

Ronald Coase, a professor at the University of Chicago Law School, who was born in England and worked there as a professional economist before the Second World War, was the first to see clearly that if people can negotiate with one another at no cost over the right to perform activities that cause externalities, they will always arrive at an efficient solution. This insight, which is often called the **Coase theorem**, is a profoundly important idea, for which Coase was awarded the 1991 Nobel Prize in Economics.[1]

Coase theorem if at no cost people can negotiate the purchase and sale of the right to perform activities that cause externalities, they can always arrive at efficient solutions to the problems caused by externalities

Why should Fitch pay Abercrombie to filter out toxins that would not be there in the first place if it were not for Abercrombie's factory? Coase points out that externalities are *reciprocal* in nature. The toxins harm Fitch, but preventing Abercrombie from emitting them would penalise Abercrombie, by exactly €30 per day. Why should Fitch have the right to harm Abercrombie?

[1] Coase's highly readable paper (and one of the most influential of the twentieth century), which enunciated what is now referred to as the Coase theorem, appeared in 1960 (Coase 1960).

Table 11.2 Costs and Benefits of Eliminating Toxic Waste (3)

	With filter	Without filter
Gains to Abercrombie	€100/day	€150/day
Gains to Fitch	€100/day	€70/day

Will Abercrombie dump toxins in the river (3)?

Example 11.4

Suppose the law says that Abercrombie may *not* dump toxins in the river unless he has Fitch's permission. If the relevant costs and benefits of filtering the toxins are as shown in Table 11.2, and if Abercrombie and Fitch can negotiate with one another at no cost, will Abercrombie filter the toxins?

Note that now the most efficient outcome is for Abercrombie to operate without a filter, for the total daily surplus in that case will be €220 compared with only €200 with a filter. Legally, however, Fitch has the right to insist that Abercrombie use a filter. We might expect him to exercise that right, since his own gain would rise from €70 to €100 per day if he did so. But this outcome would be socially inefficient, implying that each party can do better.

Suppose, for example, that Abercrombie gives Fitch €40 per day in return for Fitch's permission to operate without a filter. Each would then have a net daily gain of €110, which is €10 better for each of them than if Fitch had insisted that Abercrombie use a filter. Abercrombie's pollution harms Fitch, but failure to allow the pollution would have caused even greater harm to Abercrombie.

The implication of the Coase theorem is that whoever is held liable for damages, the affected parties will achieve *efficient* solutions to externalities if they can negotiate costlessly with one another. But note that this does not imply that affected parties will be indifferent as to who is liable for damages. If polluters are liable, they will end up with lower incomes and those who are injured by pollutants will end up with higher incomes than if the law does not hold polluters liable – even though the same efficient production methods are adopted in each case. If polluters are liable, they must remove the pollution at their own expense; otherwise those who are injured by pollution must pay polluters to cut back.

Externalities are hardly rare and isolated occurrences. On the contrary, finding examples of actions that are altogether free of them is difficult, and because externalities can distort the allocation of resources, it is important to recognise them and deal intelligently with them. Consider Example 11.5, an externality that arises because of shared living arrangements.

Will Ann and Betty share an apartment?

Example 11.5

Ann and Betty can live together in a two-bedroom one bathroom apartment at a rent of €600 per month, or separately in two one-bedroom apartments, for €400 per month each. If the rent paid were the same for both alternatives, the two women would be indifferent between living together or separately, except for one problem: Ann spends an inordinate time in the bathroom every morning. Ann values this use of the bathroom at €250 per month. Betty would pay up to €150 per month to have better access to the bathroom. Should they live together or separately?

Ann and Betty should live together only if the benefit of doing so exceeds the cost. The benefit of living together is the reduced rent, €200 per month. Their cost of living together is the least costly arrangement they can make to deal with Ann's bathroom dependence. Since Ann would be willing to pay up to €250 per month to avoid changing her behaviour, the €200 rent saving is too small to persuade her to change. But Betty is willing to put up with Ann's behaviour for a compensation payment of only €150 per

Table 11.3 The Gain in Surplus from Shared Living Arrangements

Benefits of shared living		
Total cost of separate apartments	**Total cost of shared apartment**	**Rent savings from sharing**
(2)(€400/month) = £800/month	€600/month	€200/month

Costs of shared living			
Problem	**Ann's cost of solving problem**	**Betty's cost of solving problem**	**Least costly solution to the problem**
Ann's bathroom usage	Curtailed usage: €250/month	Tolerate usage: €150/month	Betty tolerates Ann's usage: €150/month

Gain in surplus from shared living				
Rent savings (€200/month)	–	Least costly accommodation to shared living problems (€150/month)	=	Gain in surplus: €50/month

month. Since that amount is smaller than the total saving in rent, the least costly solution to the problem is for Betty to live with Ann and simply put up with her behaviour.

Table 11.3 summarises the relevant costs and benefits of this shared living arrangement. The Cost–Benefit Principle tells us that Ann and Betty should live together if and only if the benefit of living together exceeds the cost. The cost of the shared living arrangement is not the sum of all possible costs but the least costly accommodation to the problem (or problems) of shared living. Since the €200 per month saving in rent exceeds the least costly accommodation to the bathroom problem, Ann and Betty can reap a total gain in economic surplus of €50 per month by sharing an apartment.

Initially you might think that Ann and Betty should not live together, because the rent is shared equally, Betty will pay €300 per month – which when added to the €150 cost of putting up with Ann's bathroom usage comes to €50 more than the cost of living alone. Persuasive as this may be, it is mistaken. The source of the error, as Example 11.6 makes clear, is the assumption that the two must share the rent equally.

Example 11.6 What is the highest rent Betty would be willing to pay for the two-bedroom apartment?

In Example 11.5, what is the highest rent Betty would be willing to pay to share an apartment with Ann? Betty's alternative is to live alone, which would mean paying €400 per month, her reservation price for a living arrangement with no bathroom problem. Since the most she would be willing to pay to avoid the bathroom problem is €150 per month, the highest monthly rent she would be willing to pay for the shared apartment is €400 – €150 = €250. If she pays that amount, Ann will have to pay the difference, namely, €350 per month, which is clearly a better alternative for Ann than paying €400 to live alone.

LEGAL REMEDIES FOR EXTERNALITIES

Efficient solutions to externalities can be found whenever the affected parties can negotiate with one another at no cost. But negotiation is not always practical. A motorist with a noisy exhaust silencer, for example, imposes costs on others, yet they cannot realistically flag him down and offer to pay him to fix it. In recognition of this difficulty, most governments simply require that cars have working silencers. Indeed, the explicit or implicit purpose of such laws is to solve problems caused by externalities. The object is to help people achieve the outcome they might have reached had they been able to negotiate with one another.

When negotiation is costless, the task of adjustment generally falls on the party who can accomplish it at the lowest cost. For instance, in Example 11.5, Betty put up with Ann's annoying habits because doing so was less costly than asking Ann to change her habits. Many municipal noise abatement orders also place the burden of adjustment on those who can accomplish it at lowest cost. Consider a municipal proposal to restrict severely loud music at parties during the working week, but less severely at weekends. This pattern reflects both the fact that the gains from loud music tend to be larger at weekends (more people want to party at weekends) and the fact that the disturbance costs of such music are likely to be higher on weeknights (people cannot have a lie-in the next morning). The abatement regime would place the burden on party-goers during the week and on sleepers during the weekend.

Exercise 11.2

Coase's 1960 paper referred to a case heard in the Chancery Division of the High Court in London in 1879.[2] The facts were as follows. A confectioner (Bridgeman) had for years operated a business from his premises on a London street that involved using mortars and pestles to grind and mix ingredients. A doctor, Sturges, who had a practice in an adjoining premises, built a consultation room up against the wall of Bridgeman's premises. The vibrations from the confectionery business interfered with the doctor's ability to listen to people's chests. He sued the confectioner for 'nuisance', a common law tort (an injury to a person or property). What would you have decided in this case (a) if you had never heard of the Coase theorem, and (b) if you were fully aware of the Coase theorem?

Exercise 11.3

Use the idea of externality resolution to explain why there exist the following legal interventions to influence individual behaviour:

(a) Why is it frequently mandatory for motorists to have, and use, snow chains in mountainous regions when there is snow on the ground?
(b) Why are strongly enforced zoning restrictions on occupations and building types in most urban areas?
(c) Why do governments frequently use taxpayers' money to subsidise non-commercial research by university academics?

THE OPTIMAL AMOUNT OF NEGATIVE EXTERNALITIES IS NOT ZERO

The Cost–Benefit Principle developed in Chapter 5 applies to public policy in relation to externalities. Curbing negative externalities entails both costs and benefits. The best policy is to curtail pollution, for example, until the cost of further abatement (marginal cost) just equals the marginal benefit. In general, the marginal cost of abatement rises with the amount of pollution eliminated. If diminishing marginal utility applies to environmental action, it suggests that, beyond some point, the marginal benefit of pollution reduction tends to fall as more pollution is removed. As a result, the marginal cost and marginal benefit curves almost always intersect well before pollution is reduced to zero.

The intersection of the two curves marks the *socially optimal level of pollution reduction*. If pollution is reduced by less, society will gain more than it will lose by further reduction.

---

[2] Sturges v Bridgeman, 11 Chancery Division, 852, 1879.

But reduction beyond the point at which the marginal cost and benefit curves intersect, means incurring costs that exceed the benefits. The existence of a *socially optimal level of pollution reduction* implies the existence of a socially optimal level of pollution, and that level will almost always be greater than zero.

Cost–Benefit Analysis

This point, obvious to a trained economist, is one that the public at large are not comfortable with. It implies that there is an acceptable level of something that people regard as intrinsically unacceptable. How often have you heard the statement that there is no acceptable level of death on the roads? Life is priceless (?). Actually, it is easy to show that we do put a price on life, even our own. And we do not in reality behave individually as if no road death is tolerable, even our own. However, because people have been conditioned to think of pollution as bad, many cringe when they hear the phrase 'socially optimal level of pollution'. But the concept of a socially optimal level of pollution does not mean that *pollution is good*. It is merely to recognise that society has an interest in cleaning up the environment, but only up to a certain point. The underlying idea is no different from the idea of an optimal level of dirt in a flat. After all, even if you spent the whole day, every day, vacuuming your flat, there would be *some* dirt left in it. And because you have better things to do than vacuum all day, you probably tolerate substantially more than the minimal amount of dirt. A dirty apartment is not good, nor is pollution in the air you breathe. But in both cases, the clean-up effort should be expanded only until the marginal benefit equals the marginal cost.

RECAP

External costs and benefits

Externalities occur when the costs or benefits of an activity accrue to people other than those directly involved in the activity. The *Coase theorem* says that when affected parties can negotiate with one another without cost, activities will be pursued at efficient levels, even in the presence of positive or negative externalities. But when negotiation is prohibitively costly, inefficient behaviour generally results. Activities that generate negative externalities are pursued to excess, while those that generate positive externalities are pursued too little. Laws and regulations are often adopted in an effort to alter inefficient behaviour that results from externalities.

PROPERTY RIGHTS AND THE 'TRAGEDY OF THE COMMONS'

In the advanced economies we tend to take the institution of private property for granted, accepting that people have the right to own any property they acquire by lawful means and to use it much as they see fit. In reality, however, property laws are considerably more complex in terms of the rights they confer and the obligations they impose. Moreover, the set of property rights created and enforced at law has significant implications in terms of the efficiency with which resources are used.

In 1968 an article was published in *Science* that gave the debate on economic policy a memorable phrase that is now a commonplace term in the analysis of property rights and their implications.[3] This was the **'tragedy of the commons'**. The 'tragedy' is that when valuable assets are held in common, the end result is usually that the assets are overexploited and wasted. Common ownership has the same consequences as *no ownership at all*.

'tragedy of the commons' the tendency for a resource that has no price to be used until its marginal benefit falls to zero

A well-known paper, published by two economists from the University of Delaware in 1975, demonstrated this point and its consequences.[4] They provided persuasive evidence of the effects of common ownership as opposed to private ownership of oyster fisheries on the US eastern

[3] Hardin (1968).

[4] Agnello and Donnelly (1975).

seaboard. Common ownership resulted in lower output per head because the oyster beds were overexploited. Anyone who refrained from harvesting a kilogram of oysters was investing the income forgone in maintaining production potential. Under common ownership there was insufficient investment in maintaining the productive potential of the beds. If someone left a kilo unharvested, not only could he not benefit from the increased production in the future resulting from his actions, but he was conferring a 'free lunch' on all the others who were entitled to harvest the oysters. The inevitable consequence was overexploitation of the biomass.

Example 11.7

The Tragedy of the Commons and EU fisheries policy.

After fish stocks in north-west European waters collapsed in the 1990s, the EU Commission proposed drastic reductions in fishing quotas in 2004. The collapse was a consequence of the exacerbation of a tragedy of the commons by the EU's Common Fisheries Policy (CFP). Under the CFP the deep-sea fishery waters of all EU states must be open to fishing boats from any member state. The problem existed to a lesser extent before the CFP was introduced. Member state governments had to face the problem of over-fishing of national waters by their own fishing fleets. For example, even before full liberalisation of access, Irish drift-net fishing in Irish coastal waters reduced Atlantic salmon stocks in Irish rivers to close to extinction. Irish waters, some of the richest in fish stocks in Europe, were opened by the CFP to boats from other states. The result has been a fish-stock crash, and the current attempt to reverse it through drastic curbs on catches.

Incentives Matter

Economic Naturalist 11.2
Are the issues of externalities, property rights, resource use and economic efficiency just a passing obsession?

Not so: take the example of smoke abatement in Britain. The London 'Great Fog' of December 1952 is now slipping out of folk memory in Britain, but its consequences led to clean-air legislation that revolutionised urban living in Britain. The combination of adverse weather system developments and high levels of coal burning and the introduction of thousands of diesel-powered buses to replace electric trams and trolley buses led to the Great Fog. The results included semi-paralysis of surface transport in London and severe direct pollution of buildings and other structures. In one opera house the performance had to be abandoned because the audience couldn't see the stage. More serious was a sharp increase in mortality. Ten days of fog caused an estimated 12,000 deaths. To put this in context, London civilian deaths during the 1940–41 Luftwaffe 'blitz' were about 20,000 over nine months. What is surprising is how long it took for the authorities to react to what had become a chronic problem. As early as 1661 a tract by a proto-environmentalist[5] identified coal-burning as the cause of the curse of London fog and called for restrictions on burning sea coal.

THE PROBLEM OF UNPRICED RESOURCES

The tragedy of the commons is part of a more general problem that arises when scarce resources are not priced or underpriced to users. To understand the laws that govern the use of property, we must begin by asking why societies created the institution of private property in the first place. Examples 11.7 and 11.8, which show what happens to property that nobody owns, suggest an answer.

Example 11.8

How many cattle will villagers graze on the commons?

A village has five households, each of which has accumulated savings of €100. The village has a commonly owned tract of grazing land. Each villager can use the money

[5] Evelyn, John (1661).

Table 11.4 The Relationship between Herd Size and Steer Price

Number of steers on the commons	Price per two-year-old steer (€)	Income per steer (€/year)
1	126	26
2	119	19
3	116	16
4	113	13
5	111	11

to buy a government bond that pays 13 per cent interest per year or to buy a year-old bullock, send it on to the commons to graze, and sell it after one year. The price the villager will get for the two-year-old animal depends on the amount of weight it gains while grazing on the commons, which in turn depends on the number of steers sent on to the commons, as shown in Table 11.4.

The price of a two-year-old steer declines with the number of cattle grazing on the commons, because the more cattle, the less grass available to each. The villagers make their investment decisions one at a time, and the results are public. If each villager decides how to invest individually, how many cattle will be sent on to the commons and what will be the village's total income?

If a villager buys a €100 government bond, he will earn €13 interest income at the end of one year. Thus he should buy and graze a bullock on the commons if and only if the animal will command a price of at least €113 as a two year old. When each villager chooses in this self-interested way, we can expect four households to send a steer on to the commons. (Actually, the fourth villager would be indifferent between investing in a steer or buying a bond, since he would earn €13 either way. For the sake of discussion, we shall assume that, in the case of a tie, people choose to be cattle grazers.) The fifth householder, seeing that he would earn only €11 by sending a fifth steer on to the commons, will choose instead to buy a government bond. As a result of these decisions, the total village income will be €65 per year – €13 for the one bondholder and 4 × (€13) = €52 for the four cattle grazers.

Has Adam Smith's invisible hand produced the most efficient allocation of these villagers' resources? We can tell at a glance that it has not, since their total village income is only €65 – precisely the same as it would have been had the possibility of cattle raising not existed. The source of the difficulty will become evident in Example 11.9.

Example 11.9 What is the socially optimal number of cattle to graze on the commons?

Suppose the five households in Example 11.8 confront the same investment opportunities as before, except that this time they are free to make their decisions as a group rather than individually. How many bullocks will they send on to the commons, and what will be their total village income?

This time, the villagers' goal is to maximise the income received by the group as a whole. When decisions are made from this perspective, the criterion is to send a steer on to the commons only if its marginal contribution to village income is at least €13, the amount that could be earned from a government bond. As the entries in column (5) of Table 11.5 indicate, the first bullock clearly meets this criterion, since it contributes €26 to total village income. But the second does not. Sending it on to the commons raises the village's income from cattle raising from €26 to €38, a gain of just €12. The €100 required to buy the second bullock would thus have been better invested in a government bond. Worse, the collective return from grazing a third animal is only €10; from a fourth, only €4; and, from a fifth, only €3.

Table 11.5 Marginal Income and the Socially Optimal Herd Size

Number of steers on the commons (1)	Price per two-year-old steer (€) (2)	Income per steer (€/year) (3)	Total cattle income (€/year) (4)	Marginal income (€/year) (5)
1	126	26	26	26
2	119	19	38	12
3	116	16	48	10
4	113	13	52	4
5	111	11	55	3

In sum, when investment decisions are made with the goal of *maximising total village income*, the best choice is to buy four government bonds and send only a single bullock on to the commons. The resulting village income will be €78: €26 from grazing the single animal and €52 from the four government bonds. That amount is €3 more than the total income that resulted when villagers made their investment decisions individually. Once again, the reward from moving from an inefficient allocation to an efficient one is that the economic 'pie' grows larger. And when the 'pie' grows larger, everyone can get a larger slice. For instance, if the villagers agree to pool their income and share it equally, each will get €15.60, or €2.60 more than before.

Efficiency

Exercise 11.4

How would your answers to Examples 11.8 and 11.9 differ if the interest rate were not 13 per cent but 11 per cent per year?

Why do the villagers in Examples 11.8 and 11.9 do better when they make their investment decisions collectively? The answer is that when individuals decide alone, they ignore the fact that sending another steer on to the commons will cause existing steers to gain less weight. Their failure to consider this effect makes the return from sending another steer seem misleadingly high to them.

The grazing land on the commons is a valuable *economic resource*. When no one owns it, no one has any incentive to take the opportunity cost of using it into account. And, when that happens, people will tend to use it until its marginal benefit is zero. This problem, and others similar to it, are examples of the tragedy of the commons. The essential cause of the tragedy of the commons is the fact that one person's use of commonly held property imposes an *external cost* on others by making the property less valuable. The tragedy of the commons also provides a vivid illustration of the Equilibrium Principle (see Chapter 3). Each individual villager behaves rationally by sending an additional steer on to the commons, yet the overall outcome falls far short of the attainable ideal.

THE EFFECT OF PRIVATE OWNERSHIP

As Example 11.9 illustrates, one solution to the tragedy of the commons is to place the village grazing land under private ownership.

Example 11.10

How much will the right to control the village commons sell for?

Suppose the five households face the same investment opportunities as before, except that this time they decide to auction off the right to use the commons to the highest bidder. Assuming that the villagers can borrow as well as lend at an annual interest rate of 13 per cent, what price will the right to use the commons fetch? How will the owner of that property right use it, and what will be the resulting village income?

To answer these questions, simply ask yourself what you would do if you had complete control over how the grazing land were used. As we saw in Example 11.9, the most profitable way to use this land is to send only a single steer to graze on it. If you do so, you will earn a total of €26 per year. Since the opportunity cost of the €100 you spent on the single yearling steer is the €13 in interest you could have earned from a bond, your economic profit from sending a single steer on to the commons will be €13 per year, provided you can use the land for free. But you cannot; to finance your purchase of the property right, you must borrow money (since you used your €100 savings to buy a year-old bullock).

What is the most you would be willing to pay for the right to use the commons? Since its use generates an income of €26 per year, or €13 more than the opportunity cost of your investment in the bullock, the most you would pay is €100 (because that amount used to purchase a bond that pays 13 per cent interest would also generate income of €13 per year). If the land were sold at auction, €100 is precisely the amount you would have to pay. Your annual earnings from the land would be exactly enough to pay the €13 interest on your loan and cover the opportunity cost of not having put your savings into a bond.

Note that when the right to use the land is auctioned to the highest bidder, the village achieves a more efficient allocation of its resources, because the owner has a strong incentive to take the opportunity cost of more intensive grazing fully into account. Total village income in this case will again be €78. If the annual interest on the €100 proceeds from selling the land rights is shared equally among the five villagers, each will again have an annual investment income of €15.60.

The logic of *economic surplus maximisation* helps to explain why the most economically successful nations have all been ones with well-developed private property laws. Property that belongs to everyone belongs, in effect, to no one. Not only is its potential economic value never fully realised, it usually ends up being of no value at all.

Bear in mind, however, that in most countries the owners of private property are not free to do *precisely* as they wish with it. For example, local planning regulations or zoning laws may give the owner of a plot of residential building land the right to build a three-storey house but not a six-storey house. Here, too, the logic of economic surplus maximisation applies, for a fully informed and rational legislature would define property rights so as to create the largest possible total economic surplus. In practice, of course, such ideal legislatures never really exist. Yet one view of the essence of politics is the creation of arrangements that make people better off. If a legislator could propose a change in the planning regime affecting his constituency that would enlarge the total economic surplus for the people in that constituency, he could also propose a scheme that would give each constituent a larger income by sharing out the gain, thus enhancing his chances of re-election.

As an economic naturalist, challenge yourself to use this framework when thinking about the various restrictions you encounter in private property laws: zoning laws that constrain what you can build and what types of activities you can conduct on your land; traffic laws that constrain what you can do with your car; employment and environmental laws that constrain how you can operate your business. Your understanding of these and countless other laws will be enhanced by the insight that everyone can gain when the private property laws are defined so as to create the largest total economic surplus.

WHEN PRIVATE OWNERSHIP IS IMPRACTICAL

Do not be misled into thinking that the law provides an *ideal* resolution of all problems associated with externalities and the tragedy of the commons. Defining and enforcing efficient property rights entails costs, after all, and sometimes the costs outweigh the gains.

Economic Naturalist 11.3
Is there any evidence to back up the story of villagers and cattle?

Although it had been occurring slowly and haphazardly since the late Middle Ages, the enclosure movement did most of its work transforming British agriculture between 1700 and 1850. Enclosure meant abolishing the manorial system of land tenure that, *inter alia*, involved peasants renting and cultivating land in small packets (strips) in 'open fields' separated from each other on the landlord's land, and relations between tenants and between tenants and landlords being very dependent on customary law. Enclosure meant the landlord by consent or by legislation being enabled to consolidate the land and use it himself or rent it out in contiguous parcels to tenants. Economic historians agree that a consequence of enclosure was to increase the productivity of agricultural land, although there are disagreements as to the sources and levels of the improved productivity. However, enclosure undoubtedly meant, in the context of our example, an ability to take decisions based more closely on the marginal calculus, so increasing the aggregate income from the land. This begs a question suggested by the Coase theorem: if there were such gains to be made: why did the tenants not negotiate a better system for using the land? In some cases in a sense they did, since there were many enclosures by consent. But in a majority of cases, it seems, compulsion was involved. It also suggests that perhaps there were 'good' reasons for the scattered holdings that escaped the attention of some investigators. Interested? Have a look at two easily read papers by D. McCloskey.[6] As a final note, consider the Zimbabwe land grab by Mugabe and his supporters as a massive dis-enclosure: it helps explain how the economy collapsed as agricultural productivity fell.

Here are some further examples of the tragedy of the commons.

Harvesting timber on remote public land

If remote forest land is publicly owned, enforcing restrictions on permitted tree felling may be impractical. Everyone knows that a tree not harvested this year will be bigger, and hence more valuable, next year. But if he doesn't cut the tree down this year, someone else will. In contrast, private companies that own the land have no incentive to harvest timber prematurely and a strong incentive to prevent outsiders from doing so.

Whaling

Each whaler knows that killing an extra whale reduces the breeding population, and hence the size of the future whale population. But the whaler also knows that any whale that is not harvested today will be taken by some other whaler. The oceans are vast, and the behaviour of whalers is hard to monitor. And even if their behaviour could be monitored, the concept of national sovereignty would make the international enforcement of property rights problematic.

Absence of enforcement of private ownership rights coupled to commercial value is a threat to a species, survival. Contrast the whale conservation problem with the probable survival of domestic cattle. No one worries that Colonel Sanders might threaten the extinction of chickens. It suggests that allowing people to harvest ivory legally from herds that they own may be the best way to protect elephants from poachers in sub-Saharan Africa, and ecotourism is the best hope for the survival of the South-east Asian tiger population.

[6] McCloskey (1972 and 1991).

Controlling multinational environmental pollution

If the environment is common property into which all are free to dump, there is a powerful incentive to pollute. If all polluters live under the jurisdiction of a single government, enforcing laws and regulations restricting pollution may be practical. But if polluters come from many different countries, solutions are much more difficult to implement. Thus the Mediterranean Sea has long suffered serious pollution. The many nations that border it lack an adequate economic incentive to consider the effects of its discharges on other countries. The smaller number of countries involved (and the fact that almost all were members of the then EEC) permitted agreements to be reached to control and reduce the pollution of the River Rhine, which suffered on a similar basis to that of the Mediterranean.

RECAP

Property rights and the tragedy of the commons

When a valuable resource has a price of zero, people will continue to exploit it as long as its marginal benefit remains positive. The tragedy of the commons describes situations in which valuable resources are squandered because users are not charged for them. In many cases, an efficient remedy for such waste is to define and enforce rights to the use of valuable property. But this solution is difficult to implement for resources such as the oceans and the atmosphere, because no single government has the authority to *enforce property rights* for these resources.

POSITIONAL EXTERNALITIES

PAYOFFS THAT DEPEND ON RELATIVE PERFORMANCE

In professional tennis and many other competitive situations, the rewards received depend not only on how individuals' absolute performance but on their performance relative to rivals. David Beckham in soccer, Brian O'Driscoll in rugby, were similar to Maria Sharapova in tennis. Competitors have an incentive to take actions that will increase their odds of winning. Hence the demand for personal fitness trainers and sports psychologists to travel with them on the tour. It is why the Olympics are plagued by the performance-enhancing drugs problem. Yet a little thought tells us that the sum of all expected individual payoffs from such investments will be larger than the collective payoff. In any tennis match, for example, each player's performance payoff (absolute) from money spent on trainers and psychologists is significant, yet each match will have exactly one winner and one loser, no matter how much players spend. The overall gain to tennis spectators is likely to be small, and the overall gain to players as a group must be zero. To the extent that each contestant's financial payoff depends on his or her relative performance, then, the incentive to undertake such investments will be excessive, from a collective point of view.

POSITIONAL ARMS RACES

positional externality occurs when an increase in one person's performance reduces the expected reward of another in situations in which reward depends on relative performance

A **positional externality** means that, whenever the payoffs to one contestant depend at least in part on performance relative to a rival's, any step that improves one side's relative position must necessarily worsen the other's. Just as the invisible hand of the market is weakened by the presence of standard externalities, it is also weakened by positional externalities.

Economic Naturalist 11.4
Why do political parties so often vote for restrictions on campaign spending?

There is a widespread belief that spending during election campaigns affects the expected outcome, so parties that can amass large war-chests can expect a dividend in the form of more seats won. Whether and to what extent this is, in fact, backed up by statistical analysis of campaign spending and electoral outcomes is a matter of uncertainty, given the results of much analysis of (especially) electoral patterns in the US. Despite this, the effort parties put into fund-raising where permitted in order to finance campaigns certainly supports the hypothesis that the parties consider that spending affects outcomes. It is not surprising when parties that find fund-raising difficult strongly support spending restrictions. However, support for restrictions among successful fund-raisers is another matter. Partly, this may reflect bending to accommodate public opinion. But there are rational explanations for a genuine preference for spending restrictions even from successful fund-raisers.

One possibility is that incumbent politicians may have non-monetary advantages over challengers such as name recognition or the power of their office. In order to overcome these advantages a challenger might need to outspend his rival. So incumbents may prefer spending limits in order to limit challengers' ability to do so.

However, if we apply the idea of positional externalities, another possible rationale becomes clear. Fund-raising is costly resource for political parties. If outcomes are affected primarily by relative spending rather than absolute spending, then agreeing and enforcing limits will leave the relative positions of incumbent parties that are successful fund-raisers where they were while maintaining as incumbents an advantage over entrants. At the same time it will release resources, including parliamentarians' time and effort, for other functions.

When positional externalities often lead contestants to engage in an escalating series of mutually offsetting investments to secure a prize, we call such spending patterns **positional arms races**.

positional arms race a series of mutually offsetting investments in performance enhancement that is stimulated by a positional externality

positional arms control agreement an agreement in which contestants attempt to limit mutually offsetting investments in performance enhancement

POSITIONAL ARMS CONTROL AGREEMENTS

Because positional arms races produce inefficient outcomes, people have an incentive to curtail them. Steps taken to reduce positional arms races, such as rules against anabolic steroids, may therefore be thought of as **positional arms control agreements**.

Once you become aware of positional arms races, you will begin to see examples of them almost everywhere. You can hone your skills as an economic naturalist by asking these questions about every competitive situation you observe. What form do the investments in performance enhancement take? What steps have contestants taken to limit these investments? Sometimes positional arms control agreements are achieved by the imposition of formal rules or by the signing of legal contracts. We shall now consider two examples of this type of agreement.

Arbitration agreements

In the business world, contracting parties often sign a binding agreement that commits them to arbitration in the event of a dispute. By doing so, they sacrifice the option of pursuing their interests as fully as they might wish to later, but they also insulate themselves from costly legal battles. In the United Kingdom and Ireland, what is called 'case management' is required by judges in many High Court civil cases. This means obliging the parties to exchange reports and have expert witnesses remove from consideration by the court matters on which there is no dispute, thus avoiding costly court time hearing testimony on which there is agreement between the parties.

Mandatory starting dates for school

A child who is a year or so older than most of her elementary (primary) classmates is likely to perform better, in relative terms, than if she had entered school with children her own age. And since most parents are aware that admission to universities and eligibility for top jobs upon graduation depend largely on *relative* academic performance, many are tempted to keep their children out of kindergarten a year longer than necessary. Yet there is no social advantage in holding *all* children back an extra year, since their relative performance will essentially be unaffected. In many jurisdictions, therefore, the law requires children who reach a determined age by a given date in a year to start school in that year. However, this needs qualification. The use of the feminine pronoun in this case is deliberate, not simply politically correct. Most developmental psychologists will agree that, on average, between the ages of 12 and 18 boys develop mentally more slowly than girls (which is part of the reason teenage girls give boys in their classes such a hard time socially). It follows that if boys and girls take terminal exams and leave school at the same age, girls will do better than boys . . . and better than if they were ranked at the same mental age. Requiring boys to start schooling at the same age as girls, then, is equivalent to giving girls as a group a slight edge in competitive exams at 18. Unfortunately, in today's political climate it looks rather unlikely that any government will pick up that hot potato.

SOCIAL NORMS AS POSITIONAL ARMS CONTROL AGREEMENTS

In some cases, *social norms* may take the place of formal agreements to curtail positional arms races. Here are two familiar examples.

Nerd norms

When students care only about grades (rather than learning!) and are graded on a curve – that is, on the basis of their performance relative to other students – a positional arms race ensues, because if all students were to double the amount of time they studied, the distribution of grades would remain essentially the same. Students who find themselves in this situation are often quick to embrace 'nerd norms', which brand as social misfits those who 'study too hard'.

Norms against vanity

Cosmetic and reconstructive surgery has produced dramatic benefits for many people, enabling badly disfigured accident victims to recover a more normal appearance. It has also eliminated the extreme self-consciousness felt by people born with strikingly unusual features. Such surgery, however, is by no means confined to the conspicuously disfigured. Increasingly, 'normal' people are seeking surgical improvements to their appearance. Demand has continued to grow steadily. Once a carefully guarded secret, these procedures are now sometimes offered as prizes in charity raffles.

In individual cases, cosmetic surgery may be just as beneficial as reconstructive surgery is for accident victims. Buoyed by the confidence of having a straight nose or a wrinkle-free complexion, patients sometimes go on to achieve much more than they ever thought possible. But the growing use of cosmetic surgery has also had an unintended side effect: it has altered the standards of normal appearance. A nose that once would have seemed only slightly larger than average may now seem jarringly big. The same person who once would have looked like an average 55 year old may now look nearly 70. And someone who once would have tolerated slightly thinning hair or an average amount of cellulite may now feel compelled to undergo hair transplantation or liposuction. Because such procedures shift people's frame of reference, their payoffs to individuals are misleadingly large. From a social perspective, therefore, reliance on them is likely to be excessive. Legal sanctions against cosmetic surgery are difficult to imagine. But some communities have embraced powerful social norms against cosmetic surgery, heaping scorn and ridicule on the consumers of facelifts and tummy tucks. In individual cases, such norms may seem cruel. Yet without them, many more people might feel compelled to bear the risk and expense of cosmetic surgery.

SUMMARY

- *Externalities* are the costs and benefits of activities that accrue to people who are not directly involved in those activities. When all parties affected by externalities can negotiate with one another at no cost, the invisible hand of the market will produce an efficient allocation of resources. According to the *Coase theorem*, the allocation of resources is efficient in such cases because the parties affected by externalities can compensate others for taking remedial action.
- Negotiation over externalities is often impractical, however. In these cases, the self-serving actions of individuals typically will not lead to an efficient outcome. The attempt to forge solutions to the problems caused by externalities is one of the most important rationales for *collective action*. Sometimes collective action takes the form of laws and government regulations that alter the incentives facing those who generate, or are affected by, externalities. Such remedies work best when they place the burden of accommodation on the parties who can accomplish it at the lowest cost. Traffic laws, zoning laws, environmental protection laws and free speech laws are examples.
- Curbing pollution and other negative externalities entails *costs* as well as *benefits*. The optimal amount of pollution reduction is the amount for which the marginal benefit of further reduction just equals the marginal cost. In general, this formula implies that the socially optimal level of pollution, or of any other negative externality, is greater than zero.
- When grazing land and other valuable resources are owned in common, no one has an incentive to take into account the opportunity cost of using those resources. This problem is known as the *tragedy of the commons*. Defining and enforcing private rights governing the use of valuable resources is often an effective solution. Not surprisingly, most economically successful nations have well-developed institutions of private property. Property that belongs to everyone belongs, in effect, to no one. Not only is its potential economic value never fully realised, it usually ends up having no value at all.
- The difficulty of *enforcing* property rights in certain situations explains a variety of inefficient outcomes, such as the excessive harvest of whales in international waters and the premature harvest of timber on remote public lands. The excessive pollution of seas that are bordered by many countries also results from a lack of enforceable property rights.
- Situations in which people's rewards depend on how well they perform in relation to their rivals give rise to *positional externalities*. In these situations, any step that improves one side's relative position necessarily worsens the other's. Positional externalities tend to spawn positional arms races – escalating patterns of mutually offsetting investments in performance enhancement. Collective measures to curb positional arms races are known as *positional arms control agreements*. These collective actions may take the form of formal regulations or rules, such as rules against anabolic steroids in sports, campaign spending limits, and binding arbitration agreements.

REVIEW QUESTIONS

1. What incentive problem explains why the freeways in cities such as Los Angeles suffer from excessive congestion?
2. How would you explain to a friend why the optimal amount of freeway congestion is not zero?
3. If a country's government could declare any activity that imposes external costs on others illegal, would such legislation be advisable?
4. Why does the Great Salt Lake, which is located wholly within the state of Utah, suffer lower levels of pollution than Lake Erie, which is bordered by several states and Canada?

PROBLEMS

connect

Problems marked with an asterisk (*) are more difficult.

1. Determine whether the following statements are **true or false**, and briefly explain why.
   a. A given total emission reduction in a polluting industry will be achieved at the lowest possible total cost when the cost of the last unit of pollution curbed is equal for each firm in the industry.
   b. In an attempt to lower their costs of production, firms sometimes succeed merely in shifting costs to outsiders.
2. Phoebe keeps a bee farm next door to an apple orchard. She chooses her optimal number of beehives by selecting the honey output level at which her private marginal benefit from beekeeping equals her private marginal cost.
   a. Assume that Phoebe's private marginal benefit and marginal cost curves from beekeeping are normally shaped. Draw a diagram of them.
   b. Phoebe's bees help to pollinate the blossoms in the apple orchard, increasing the fruit yield. Show the social marginal benefit from Phoebe's beekeeping in your diagram.
   c. Phoebe's bees are Africanised killer bees that aggressively sting anyone who steps into their flight path. Phoebe, fortunately, is naturally immune to the bees' venom. Show the social marginal cost curve from Phoebe's beekeeping in your diagram.
   d. Indicate the socially optimal quantity of beehives on your diagram. Is it higher or lower than the privately optimal quantity? Explain.
3. Suppose the supply curve of boom box rentals at a holiday resort in the Mediterranean is given by $P = 5 + 0.1Q$, where P is the daily rent per unit in euros and Q is the volume of units rented in hundreds per day. The demand curve for boom boxes is $20 - 0.2Q$. If each boom box imposes €3 per day in noise costs on others, by how much will the equilibrium number of boom boxes rented exceed the socially optimal number?
4. Refer to Problem 3. How would the imposition of a tax of €3 per unit on each daily boom box rental affect efficiency in this market?
5. Suppose the law says that Jones may *not* emit smoke from his factory unless he gets permission from Smith, who lives downwind. If the relevant costs and benefits of filtering the smoke from Jones' production process are as shown in the table below, and if Jones and Smith can negotiate with one another at no cost, will Jones emit smoke?

	Jones emits smoke (€)	Jones does not emit smoke (€)
Surplus for Jones	200	160
Surplus for smith	400	420

6. John and Karl can live together in a two-bedroom flat for €500 per month, or each can rent a single-bedroom flat for €350 per month. Aside from the rent, the two would be indifferent between living together and living separately, except for one problem: John leaves dirty dishes in the sink every night. Karl would be willing to pay up to €175 per month to avoid John's dirty dishes. John, for his part, would be willing to pay up to €225 to be able to continue his sloppiness. Should John and Karl live together? If they do, will there be dirty dishes in the sink? Explain.
7. How, if at all, would your answer to Problem 6 differ if John would be willing to pay up to €30 per month to avoid giving up his privacy by sharing quarters with Karl?
8. Barton and Statler are neighbours in an apartment complex in London's Canary Wharf. Barton is a concert pianist and Statler is a poet working on an epic poem. Barton rehearses his concert pieces on the baby grand piano in his front room, which is directly above Statler's study. The matrix below shows the monthly payoffs to Barton and Statler when Barton's front room is and is not soundproofed. The soundproofing will be effective only if it is installed in Barton's apartment.

	Soundproofed	Not soundproofed
Gains to Barton	£100/month	£150/month
Gains to Statler	£120/month	£80/month

   a. If Barton has the legal right to make any amount of noise he wants and he and Statler can negotiate with one another at no cost, will Barton install and maintain soundproofing? Explain. Is his choice socially efficient?
   b. If Statler has the legal right to peace and quiet and can negotiate with Barton at no cost, will Barton install and maintain soundproofing? Explain. Is his choice socially efficient?
   c. Does the attainment of an efficient outcome depend on whether Barton has the legal right to make noise, or Statler the legal right to peace and quiet?
9. Refer to Problem 8. Barton decides to buy a full-sized grand piano. The new payoff matrix is as follows.

	Soundproofed	Not soundproofed
Gains to Barton	£100/month	£150/month
Gains to Statler	£120/month	£60/month

   a. If Statler has the legal right to peace and quiet and Barton and Statler can negotiate at no cost, will Barton install and maintain soundproofing? Explain. Is this outcome socially efficient?
   b. Suppose that Barton has the legal right to make as much noise as he likes and that negotiating an agreement with Barton costs £15 per month. Will Barton install and maintain soundproofing? Explain. Is this outcome socially efficient?

c. Suppose Statler has the legal right to peace and quiet, and it costs £15 per month for Statler and Barton to negotiate any agreement. (Compensation for noise damage can be paid without incurring negotiation cost.) Will Barton install and maintain soundproofing? Is this outcome socially efficient?

d. Why does the attainment of a socially efficient outcome now depend on whether Barton has the legal right to make noise?

10.* A village has six residents, each of whom has accumulated savings of €100. Each villager can use this money either to buy a government bond that pays 15 per cent interest per year or to buy a year-old llama, send it on to the commons to graze, and sell it after one year. The price the villager gets for the two-year-old llama depends on the quality of the fleece it grows while grazing on the commons. That in turn depends on the animal's access to grazing, which depends on the number of llamas sent to the commons, as shown in the table below. The villagers make their investment decisions one after another, and their decisions are public.

Number of llamas on the commons	Price per two-year-old llama (€)
1	122
2	118
3	116
4	114
5	112
6	109

a. If each villager decides individually how to invest, how many llamas will be sent on to the commons, and what will be the resulting net village income?

b. What is the socially optimal number of llamas for this village? Why is that different from the actual number? What would net village income be if the socially optimal number of llamas were sent on to the commons?

c. The village committee votes to auction the right to graze llamas on the commons to the highest bidder. Assuming villagers can both borrow and lend at 15 per cent annual interest, how much will the right sell for at auction? How will the new owner use the right, and what will be the resulting village income?

REFERENCES

Agnello, R.J. and L. Donnelly (1975) 'Property rights and efficiency in the oyster industry', *Journal of Law and Economics*, 18.

Coase, R. (1960) 'The problem of social cost', *Journal of Law and Economics*, 4.

Evelyn, J. (1661) *Fumifugium, or the Inconvenience of Aer and Smoak of London Dissipated, Together with Some Remedies Humbly Proposed.*

Hardin, G. (1968) 'The tragedy of the commons', *Science*, 162.

McCloskey, D. (1972) 'The Enclosure of Open Fields: Preface to the Study of its Implications on the Efficiency of English Agriculture in the 18th Century', *Journal of Economic History*, 32.

— (1991) 'The Prudent Peasant: New Findings on Open Fields', *Journal of Economic History*, 51.

Chapter 12 The Economics of Information

Half the money I spend on advertising is wasted; the trouble is I don't know which half.
James Wannamaker

Learning Objectives

After reading this chapter, you should be able to:

1. Appreciate the importance of information in creating efficient exchange;
2. Understand the role of middlemen in market systems;
3. Analyse the value, demand and supply side of markets for information;
4. Understand the uncertainty aspect of information in markets;
5. Understand signalling, credibility and adverse selection in markets.

Cities in the Near and Middle East are famous for their bazaars. Unlike large stores in the West, in the bazaar it is expected that purchaser and seller will bargain before any deal is done. No one, other, perhaps, than a naive tourist, would agree to pay the seller's initial asking price, which is by custom a considerable amount greater than the seller's reservation price. So what will a rational purchaser offer for the brass ornament or silk scarf or whatever? Obviously not more than his/her own reservation price. Typically therefore, the would-be purchaser will make an offer below his/her reservation price. After prolonged haggling either a deal is done or it is not done. We know that it will not be done if the buyer's reservation price is below the seller's. But can we be sure it will be done if the buyer's reservation price exceeds the seller's?

Before saying it will of course be done, reflect for a moment. What in fact drives your reservation price in this one-on-one bargaining situation? If we think of it simply as the money value you place on the object then the deal will be done. But suppose you believe that another seller in the bazaar might be prepared to accept less than your reservation price – would you agree to hand that amount over to the first seller?

In this second case your willingness to pay reflects other people's valuations. There is nothing unusual about this. If you walk into an antiques shop and see an eighteenth-century Hogarth print that you would like at the price, but a friend whispers to you that an identical print was sold at auction three weeks ago for 50 per cent of the dealer's price, would you pay the asking price?

Was the auction price an outlier (no one interested in Hogarth prints attended)? Or is that all you would normally expect to pay? Before deciding to pay the price or not you need more information. Your willingness to pay will, therefore, in some circumstances reflect your own relevant knowledge, and may reflect your beliefs about other people's willingness to pay. Both factors may be summed up as 'information'. You may be well or poorly informed when contemplating a decision to buy or sell. This has significant implications for how markets work.

Adam Smith's invisible hand theory presumes that buyers are fully informed about the myriad ways in which they might spend their money: what goods and services are available, what prices they sell for, how long they last, how frequently they break down, and so on. But of course no one is ever really *fully* informed about anything. And sometimes people are completely ignorant of even the most basic information. Still, life goes on, and most people muddle through somehow.

There are many ways in which consumers acquire information: reading *Which?* magazine, talking to people, visiting stores, kicking the tyres on used cars, and so on. But one of the most important aspects of choosing intelligently without having complete information is having at least some idea of the extent of one's ignorance. Someone once said that there are two kinds of consumers in the world: those who don't know what they're doing and those who don't know that they don't know what they're doing. The latter are the ones who are most likely to choose foolishly. Auctioneers (and used-car salesmen) just love them. They frequently walk away with the prize, but only because they were prepared to pay, and did pay, more than anyone else would pay, and did so because they were unable accurately to estimate its true value. With better information about the object they would have paid less or not bought at all.

In this chapter, we will explore how basic economics principles tell us about how much information to acquire and how to make the best use of limited information.

HOW THE MIDDLEMAN ADDS VALUE

One of the most common problems consumers confront is the need to choose among different versions of a product whose many complex features they do not fully understand. As Example 12.1 illustrates, in such cases consumers can sometimes rely on the knowledge of others.

Example 12.1 How should a consumer decide which pair of skis to buy?

On a ski holiday you decide to buy a new pair of skis, but you don't know which of the current brands and models would be best for you. The big ski goods shop beside the main gondola lift has the largest selection, so you go there and ask for advice. The salesperson appears to be well informed; after asking about your experience level and how aggressively you ski, he recommends the Salomon X-Scream 9. You buy a pair for €600, then head back to your chalet and show them to your roommate, who helpfully tells you that you could have bought them on the internet for only €400. How do you feel about your purchase?

Internet retailers can sell for less because their costs are so much lower than those of full-service retail stores. Those stores, after all, must hire knowledgeable salespeople, put their merchandise on display, rent expensive retailing space, and so on. Internet retailers and mail-order houses, by contrast, typically employ unskilled telephone clerks, and they store their merchandise in cheap warehouses. But if you are a consumer who doesn't know which is the right product for you, the extra expense of shopping at a speciality retailer is likely to be a good investment. Spending €600 on the right skis is smarter than spending €400 on the wrong ones.

Many people believe that wholesalers, retailers and other agents who assist manufacturers in the sale of their products play a fundamentally different economic role from the one played by those who actually make the products. The production worker is seen by some as the ultimate source of economic value added. Sales agents are often disparaged as mere middlemen, parasites on the efforts of others who do the real work.

Superficially, this view might seem to be supported by the fact that many people go to great lengths to avoid paying for the services of sales agents. Many manufacturers cater to them by offering consumers a chance to 'buy direct' and sidestep the middleman's commission. But, on closer examination, we can see that the economic role of sales agents is essentially the same as that of production workers. Consider Example 12.2.

How does better information affect economic surplus?

Example 12.2

You have decided to sell, a pair of nineteenth-century silver candlesticks, and your reservation price is €300. How do you go about it? In your small home town there is no (trustworthy) antiques dealer. You realise that as an alternative to putting an advertisement in the local newspaper, offering them to the highest bidder, you could decide to auction them on eBay. The cost of the advertisement would be €20; the commission payable to eBay is 5 per cent of the amount paid by the winning bidder. In each case this represents the costs of providing the service.

Using eBay, you can reach a much higher number of potential buyers than by advertising locally. This means increasing the probability that potential buyers with the highest reservation prices will be aware of the objects for sale. Now suppose that the local highest reservation price is €400, while in the much larger population of potential bidders on eBay there are two people with reservation prices of €800 and €900 respectively, who bid accordingly. eBay uses a second price auction. The object is sold to the highest bidder, but at the second highest bidder's highest offer.[1]

Using eBay rather than the local newspaper will increase economic surplus. You will receive (net) €760: €460 more than your reservation price. The purchaser will receive surplus of €100 (why?). The total surplus is €560. Had you used the newspaper the total surplus would be (€400 − 300 − 20) or €80. If you sold at €400, the surplus is yours; at a price below €400 it is divided between you and the local bidder. But the total, no matter at what price you sell it, is €80.

eBay in this example is providing a service by making information available to people who can make good use of it. A real increase in economic surplus results when an item ends up in the hands of someone who values it more highly than the person who otherwise would have bought it. That increase is just as real and valuable as the increase in surplus that results from manufacturing cars, growing corn, or any other productive activity.

RECAP

How the middleman adds value

In a world of incomplete information, sales agents and other middlemen add genuine economic value by increasing the extent to which goods and services find their way to the consumers who value them most. When a sales agent causes a good to be purchased by a person who values it by €20,000 more than the person who would have bought it in the absence of a sales agent, that agent augments total economic surplus by €20,000, an achievement on a par with the production of a €20,000 car.

[1] Why does eBay use the rarer second price auction? Obviously, because it thinks that this way it will earn higher commissions, which means that on average it expects higher payments by winning bidders. In some circumstances a rational strategy for a bidder will be to 'shade' his bid (offer less than his reservation price) in the hope of obtaining a higher surplus if he wins the auction. If this applies, the expected highest bid will be reduced. Then using a second price auction changes the optimal strategy for a bidder, since if he wins by revealing his reservation price he will be asked to pay something less than that. When circumstances (the number of bidders, the mechanism, the type of object being sold) are such as to make shading likely, using a second price auction tends to induce bidders to offer their reservation prices.

Second price auctions are not common, but they have been used more widely than many economists think. In particular they have been widely used for well over a century in philately (stamp collecting). If you are interested, see a very readable paper: Lucking-Reiley (2000).

THE OPTIMAL AMOUNT OF INFORMATION

Having more information is better than having less. But information is generally costly to acquire. In most situations, the value of additional information will decline beyond some point. Typically the marginal benefit of information will decline, and its marginal cost will rise, as the amount of information gathered increases. The Low-Hanging-Fruit Principle tell us that people tend to gather information from the cheapest sources first before turning to more costly ones.

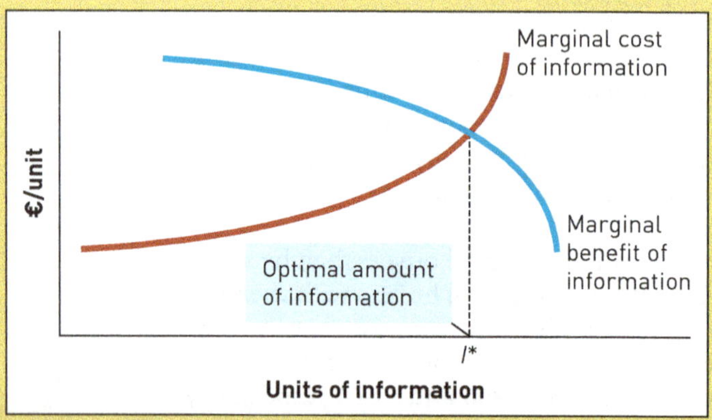

Figure 12.1 The Optimal Amount of Information

Beyond the optimal amount of information, information costs more to acquire than it is worth.

THE COST–BENEFIT TEST

As with any other activity, the Cost–Benefit Principle tells us that a rational consumer will continue to gather information as long as its marginal benefit exceeds its marginal cost. Suppose we have devised a scale that permits us to measure units of information, as on the horizontal axis of Figure 12.1. If the relevant marginal cost and marginal benefit curves are as shown in the diagram, a rational consumer will acquire I^* units of information, at which the marginal benefit of information equals its marginal cost.

Cost-Benefit Analysis

Alternatively, Figure 12.1 shows the optimal level of ignorance. When the cost of acquiring more information exceeds the gain in value from the decision it will facilitate, people are better off to remain ignorant.

THE FREE-RIDER PROBLEM

Does the invisible hand assure that the optimal amount of advice will be made available to consumers in the marketplace? The next example suggests one reason that it might not.

Economic Naturalist 12.1
Are online bookstores free riding?

Online sellers like Amazon unquestionably reduce the prices paid by customers for new books. That should mean higher sales, which should delight publishers. True, Amazon can drive hard bargains with publishers, but so can large conventional retailers like W.H. Smith, Waterstones, or Barnes & Noble, and these, too, can sell books at below the recommended retail price suggested by publishers.

However, online sellers don't face high retailing costs, and this has caused a contraction in the conventional retail book sector. This a problem for publishers as well as for retailers. Why? Visit any large retail bookstore and watch how people browse before purchasing. They are acquiring information directly on available books (instead of being restricted to the outpourings of reviewers or online extracts). Conventional retailers worry that people are acquiring information at their stores and then making their purchases online. Since online stores do not have to rent expensive retail space or hire knowledgeable sales people, they can offer the books at lower prices. The claim is that the online stores are free riding on the information provided by conventional retailers.

It is certainly true that competition from online stores has decreased the number of traditional sellers. However, in the long run this retreat from the market by conventional bookstores may make acquiring information by customers more difficult. This could lead to reduce demand for books, if the information provision service which in the past was provided by retailers is not taken up by either the online retailers or the publishers themselves.

Exercise 12.1

How is increased access to the internet likely to affect total economic surplus?

TWO GUIDELINES FOR RATIONAL SEARCH

In practice, of course, the exact value of additional information is difficult to know, so the amount of time and effort one should invest in acquiring it is not always obvious. But as Examples 12.3 and 12.4 suggest, the Cost–Benefit Principle provides a strong conceptual framework for thinking about this problem.

Example 12.3

How much time should you spend looking for an apartment?

There are two aspects of acquiring information involved here. The first is the likely return to searching. If apartments where you are thinking of living are relatively inexpensive the return to acquiring information is lower than if you are going to live in London's Mayfair, or Paris' seventh arondissement, or close to the Via Veneto in Rome. The second is the cost of making a bad decision because you didn't search enough. Suppose you know that, controlling for price, apartments vary greatly in quality, so that you can't estimate quality simply by looking at the price. Then, given your budget, your aim is to get an idea of what quality apartments are available in your price range before making a choice. This requires that you search until you form an estimate of the quality distribution, and only then proceed to choose an apartment. The higher the variability of quality at any price the greater the risk of making a decision based on viewing a small number of apartments.

Example 12.4

Who should expect to search longer for a good apartment?

Two students are looking for an apartment in Sydney. One has an aunt in Sydney who will give her a bed while she looks. The other is moving from London, knows no one and has to stay in a hostel while searching. The answer is obvious, but the point being made is that higher search costs indicate doing less searching for information, even if it means not getting the best result possible.

THE GAMBLE INHERENT IN SEARCH

In Examples 12.3 and 12.4 there is a common thread: uncertainty arising from the cost and availability of information. Making a choice under uncertainty is risky, and has the characteristics of a gamble. In deciding about an apartment in either example you are incurring known costs in order to obtain an unknown benefit, just as if you pop down to a bookie and put some money on a horse. At the margin, your search decision is in effect a gamble.

In thinking rationally about any gamble, the first step is to compute its **expected value** – the average amount you would win (or lose) if you played that gamble an infinite number of times. To calculate the expected value of a gamble with more than one outcome, we first multiply each outcome by its corresponding

expected value of a gamble the sum of the possible outcomes of the gamble weighted by their probability of occurrence

fair gamble a gamble whose expected value is zero

better-than-fair gamble one whose expected value is positive

risk-neutral person someone who would be willing to accept any fair gamble (or better than fair gamble)

risk-averse person someone who would refuse any fair gamble

probability of occurring, and then add. For example, suppose you win €1 if a coin flip comes up heads and lose €1 if it comes up tails. Since 1/2 is the probability of heads (and also the probability of tails), the expected value of this gamble is (1/2)(€1) + (1/2)(–€1) = 0. A gamble with an expected value of zero is called a **fair gamble**. If you played this gamble a large number of times, you wouldn't expect to make money, but you also wouldn't expect to lose money.

A **better-than-fair gamble** is one with a positive expected value. (For example, a coin flip in which you win €2 for heads and lose €1 for tails is a better-than-fair gamble.) A **risk-neutral person** is someone who would accept any gamble that is fair or better. A **risk-averse person** is someone who would refuse to take any fair gamble.

Exercise 12.2 Consider a gamble in which you win €4 if you flip a coin and it comes up heads and lose €2 if it comes up tails. What is the expected value of this gamble? Would a risk-neutral person accept it?

In Example 12.5 we apply these concepts to the decision of whether to search further for an apartment.

Example 12.5 Should you search further for an apartment?

You have arrived in San Francisco for a semester at San Francisco State University and are searching for a one-bedroom apartment. You learn at the student union that 80 per cent of landlords in the area detest SFSU students; 20 per cent love them. Apartments of the type you are looking for cost $400 if owned by one of the 80 per cent, but $360 if owned by one of the 20 per cent, The only way you can find out the price is by visiting the apartment. Suppose bus fares and shoe leather mean that it costs $6 each visit. Suppose the first suitable apartment you looked at turns out to be a $400 apartment. Should you search further?

If you visit one more apartment, you have a 20 per cent chance of it being one that rents for $360 and an 80 per cent chance of it being one that rents for $400. Since the cost of a visit is $6, visiting another apartment is a gamble with a 20 per cent chance to win $40 – $6 = $34 and an 80 per cent chance of losing $6 (which means 'winning' – $6). The expected value of this gamble is thus (0.20)($34) + (0.80)(–$6) = $2. Visiting another apartment is a better-than-fair gamble, and if you are risk-neutral you should take it.

Exercise 12.3 Refer to Example 12.5. Suppose you visit another apartment and discover that it, too, is one that rents for $400. If you are risk-neutral, should you visit a third apartment?

THE COMMITMENT PROBLEM WHEN SEARCH IS COSTLY

Most tenants, and landlords, prefer longer- to shorter-term rental agreements. Similarly, few people accept a full-time job in their chosen field unless they expect to hold the job for several years. Firms, too, generally prefer employees who will stay for extended periods. Finally, when most people search for mates, they are looking for someone with whom to settle down.

Because in all these cases search is costly, examining every possible option will never make sense. Whether seeking or renting an apartment, seeking employment or an employee, or finding a suitable long-term relationship, search costs mean that rational individuals will limit their searches. They will end their searches, even though they know a more attractive option may well, or even surely, exist out there somewhere.

But then, what happens when, by chance, a more attractive option comes along after the search has ceased? Would you rent an apartment if you thought the landlord could kick you out the moment another tenant came along who was willing to pay a couple of euros more a month? As a landlord, would you be happy to rent to a tenant if she could move out the moment she discovers a cheaper apartment? Employers, job seekers and people who are looking for mates would have similar reservations about entering relationships that could be terminated by the other side once a better option happened to come along.

In a world of perfect information this potential difficulty in maintaining stable matches between partners in ongoing relationships would not arise. Everyone would end up in the best possible relationship, so no one would be tempted to renege. But when information is costly and the search must be limited, there will always be the potential for existing relationships to dissolve.

In most contexts, people solve this problem not by conducting an exhaustive search (which is usually impossible, in any event) but by committing themselves to remain in a relationship once a mutual agreement has been reached to terminate the search. Landlords and tenants sign a lease that binds them to one another for a specified period, usually six months or a year. Employees and firms enter into employment contracts, either formal or informal, under which each promises to honour his obligations to the other, except under extreme circumstances. In most countries a marriage contract penalises those who abandon their spouses. Entering into such commitments limits the freedom to pursue one's own interests. Yet most people freely accept such restrictions, because they know the alternative is failure to solve the search problem.

Incentives Matter

RECAP

The optimal amount of information

Additional information creates value, but it is also costly to acquire. A rational consumer will continue to acquire information until its marginal benefit equals its marginal cost. Beyond that point, it is rational to remain uninformed.

Markets for information do not always function perfectly. Free-rider problems often hinder retailers' efforts to provide information to consumers.

Search inevitably entails an element of risk, because costs must be incurred without any assurance that search will prove fruitful. A rational consumer can minimise this risk by concentrating search efforts on goods for which the variation in price or quality is relatively high and on those for which the cost of search is relatively low.

ASYMMETRIC INFORMATION

One of the most common information problems occurs when the participants in a potential exchange are not equally well informed about the product or service that is offered for sale. For instance, the owner of a used car may know that the car is in excellent mechanical condition, but potential buyers cannot know that merely by inspecting it or taking it for a test drive. Economists use the term **asymmetric information** to describe situations in which buyers and sellers are not equally well informed about the characteristics of products or services. Although sellers are typically much better informed than buyers, sometimes the reverse will be true.

asymmetric information where buyers and sellers are not equally informed about the characteristics of products or services

As Example 12.6 illustrates, the problem of asymmetric information can easily prevent exchanges that would benefit both parties.

Selling your car privately

Example 12.6

You own and would consider selling a Ford Fiesta, four years old, with 100,000 kilometres (60,000 miles) on the clock. Driven carefully, serviced regularly, never damaged in an accident. The car is in excellent condition. The going price for four-year-old Fiestas is €6,000. You price yours in a newspaper advertisement at €7,500.

Someone who sees your advertisement in the local paper wants to buy a good four-year-old Fiesta, for which he would pay €8,000 if it is in excellent condition (like yours), but only €6,000 if it is in average condition for that age. All he has to go on is your description and a bunch of receipts, unless he incurs the cost of hiring a mechanic to examine the car, which is expensive, and even if he does many problems cannot be detected even by a mechanic. Will he buy your car?

Because your car looks the same as other four-year-old Fiestas, he is unlikely to be willing to pay €7,500 for it. For only €6,000, he can buy some other car that is in just as good condition, as far as he can tell. The probability is that he will buy another Fiesta. He therefore will buy someone else's car, and yours will go unsold. This outcome is not efficient.

THE 'LEMONS' MODEL

Example 12.6 serves as a useful introduction to what is called the problem of the 'market for lemons'. In colloquial American usage in the late 1960s and early 1970s a 'lemon' was a car that was, or might be, in poor condition in a way that would be unknowable to a buyer.

The problem lies in the economic incentives created by asymmetric information. These suggest that the selection of used cars of any given age being offered for sale will be of lower quality than the average in the total population of used cars of that age. One reason is that people who mistreat their cars, or whose cars were never very good to begin with, are more likely than others to want to sell them. Buyers know from experience that cars for sale on the used car market are more likely to be 'lemons' than cars that are not for sale. This realisation causes them to lower their reservation prices for a used car.

But that's not the end of the story. Once used car market prices have fallen, the owners of cars that are in good condition have an even stronger incentive to hold on to them. Your Fiesta is 'worth' €8,000, but all you will get for it is €6,000, so you are unlikely to sell. This causes the average quality of the cars offered for sale on the used car market to decline still further. It helps explain why new cars depreciate so much once they have been bought. University of California at Berkeley economist George Akerlof, a Nobel laureate, was the first to explain the logic behind this downward spiral.[2] Economists use the term **lemons model** to describe Akerlof's explanation of how asymmetric information affects the average quality of the used goods offered for sale.

lemons model George Akerlof's explanation of how asymmetric information tends to reduce the average quality of goods offered for sale

Bringing together the lemon concept and the gamble involved in making a decision under uncertainty enables us to see how information problems are connected to observed prices. The observation that is of interest is the dramatic drop in the re-sale value of new cars once they have been sold.

Akerlof's lemons model tells us that cars for sale in the used car market will be of lower average quality cars of the same vintage that are not for sale. To see why and how, consider the following example.

Suppose there are only two kinds of car: good ones and lemons. An owner knows with certainty which type of car she has, but potential buyers cannot distinguish between the two types. Suppose 10 per cent of all new cars produced are lemons. Good used cars are worth €10,000 to their owners, but lemons are worth only €6,000. If used one-year-old cars are a random selection of new cars sold a year ago, only 10 per cent will be lemons. Consider a naive consumer who believes this and who is risk-neutral, How much would he be willing to pay for a used car? The answer is 0.90 (€10,000) + 0.10 (€6,000), or €9,600 (see Example 12.7 below). Result: owners of good cars would

[2] Akerlof (1970).

be unwilling to sell, while owners of lemons would love to sell. Hence, the actual population of used cars for sale will be of a lower average quality than the average quality of the original population of new cars and of the average of cars of the same vintage that are not for sale. That goes a long way to explain why new cars often lose 20 per cent of their value once they are driven home.

The lemons model has important practical implications for consumer choice. Here is an example. You will often hear that you should never buy a car from a close friend or a member of your family. The reasoning is that if things go wrong with the car the impact on relationships can be serious. But if you trust the vendor to tell the truth about the car and if the price asked is the average for cars of that model, condition and age, then if you can get the car for the average price for such a car the lemons model suggests you are getting a good buy.

Examples 12.7 and 12.8 articulate aspects of the consequences of the Akerlof model.

How much will a naive buyer pay for a used car?

Example 12.7

Buying a car of unknown quality is a gamble. If the buyer can't tell the difference between a good car and a lemon, the probability that he will end up with a lemon is simply the proportion of lemons among the cars from which he chooses. Suppose the buyer is aware that he has a 90 per cent chance of getting a good car and a 10 per cent chance of getting a lemon. Given the prices of €10,000 for a good car and €6,000 for a lemon we have already used, his expected value of the car he buys will thus be 0.90(€10,000) + 0.10(€6,000) = €9,600. If he is risk-neutral, that is his reservation price for a used car.

Who will sell a used car for what the naive buyer is willing to pay?

Example 12.8

Refer to Example 12.7. If you were the owner of a good used car, what would it be worth to you? Would you sell it to a naive buyer? What if you owned a lemon?

Since you know your car is good, it is worth €10,000 to you, by assumption. But since a naive buyer would be willing to pay only €9,600, neither you nor any other owner of a good car would be willing to sell to that buyer. If you had a lemon, of course, you would be happy to sell it to a naive buyer, since the €9,600 the buyer is willing to pay is €3,600 more than the lemon would be worth to you. So the only used cars for sale will be lemons. In time, buyers will revise their naively optimistic beliefs about the quality of the cars for sale on the used car market. In the end, all used cars will sell for a price of €6,000, and all will be lemons.

Economic Naturalist 12.2
Are used car sales people always liars?

On the basis of the lemons model we should conclude that all used cars offered for sale are lemons, and we know that this is not what you will be told by the sales staff in a used car sales lot. The answer is that the lemons model explains why lemons are expected to be disproportionately more likely in the population of used cars for sale, and explains why relatively new used cars sell at a significant discount to new cars. However, it is also the case that cars will be offered for sale independently of lemons problems. For example, rental fleets are sold off usually after two years. And there is a significant number of car owners that simply want to own a new car, and change cars every one to two years, and are prepared to trade them in at a significant discount to their original prices. The account of the lemons model just discussed doesn't take factors such as these into account. There may be a good number of Pinocchios on used car lots . . . but there are also good cars among the offerings. The trick is to know the difference between honest and dishonest sales people and good and bad cars. Any time you pay the 'blue book' price for a used car that is for sale for some reason unrelated to its condition, you are beating the market.

THE CREDIBILITY PROBLEM IN TRADING

Buyers' and sellers' interests tend to conflict. Sellers of used cars, for example, have an economic incentive to overstate the quality of their products. Buyers, for their part, have an incentive to understate the amount they are willing to pay for used cars and other products (in the hope of bargaining for a lower price). Job seekers may be tempted to overstate their qualifications. And as for people searching for mates . . .

Most people may not *consciously* misrepresent the truth in communicating with their potential trading partners. But information is usually presented in such a way as to support the presenter's interests, and may be ambiguous. Thus, 92 per cent of factory employees surveyed in one study rated themselves as more productive than the average factory worker.[3]

Consequently, the parties to a potential exchange can often gain if they can find some means to communicate their knowledge truthfully. In general, however, mere statements of relevant information will not suffice. But, as the next example illustrates, though communication between potential adversaries may be difficult, it is not impossible.

Example 12.9 How can a used car seller signal high-quality credibly?

The answer lies in providing *reliable* information. What kind of signal about the car's quality would the purchaser find credible?

Instead of relying on mere statements about the car's quality, the seller could offer a warranty to remedy any defects the car develops over the next six months. If the vendor knows that the car is unlikely to need expensive repairs, it is to that extent not a costly commitment. If he knows otherwise, the warranty will cost the vendor a packet. Hence, assuming the warranty is enforceable, the purchaser can believe assertions of good quality if backed by a potentially costly warranty. The warranty is a credible signal that the car is in good condition. It enables the purchaser to buy the car with confidence, to both his and the seller's benefit.

THE COSTLY-TO-FAKE PRINCIPLE

costly-to-fake principle to communicate information credibly to a potential rival, a signal must be costly or difficult to fake

The preceding examples illustrate the **costly-to-fake principle**: if parties whose interests potentially conflict are to communicate credibly with one another, the signals they send must be costly or difficult to fake. If the seller of a defective car could offer an extensive warranty just as easily as the seller of a good car, a warranty offer would communicate nothing about the car's quality.

Incentives Matter

Sellers have an incentive to portray a product in the most flattering light possible. Their interests conflict with those of buyers, who want the most accurate assessment of product quality possible. Note that in the following example, the costly-to-fake principle applies to a producer's statement about the quality of a product.

[3] Some psychologists call this phenomenon the 'Lake Wobegon effect', after Garrison Keillor's mythical Minnesota town, where 'all the children are above average'.

Economic Naturalist 12.3
Why would Renault spend a pile of money on a TV ad campaign that shows a Mirage 2000 fighter accelerating down the runway faster than a Renault Clio?

A quick answer might be that it just goes to show that consumers aren't rational, and/or that they don't actually value information. However, if we believe that information is valuable, and that consumers are rational, then much expensive advertising needs some explanation. Clearly it must promote sales, as otherwise such glossy advertising would not be undertaken. A persuasive explanation is as follows. A product's quality, in a general sense, can be estimated from the willingness of the producer to spend money to get you to buy it. Start with the proposition that ads cannot persuade buyers that a bad product is a good one. If people are misled as to quality, two things happen. They are not likely to make a repeat purchase, and they are not likely to encourage others to buy it. The misleading ad campaign identifies the product as one not to buy again. If this is true, a company that spends millions of euros advertising a bad product is wasting its money. This suggests that a firm will only spend a large amount of money on advertising its product the producer *thinks* its product is a good one. The only way it can get its money back is through increased future sales. By spending a large sum of money it is signalling that it believes that satisfied consumers will reimburse it through increased purchases. The signal as to quality is the willingness to spend, not the provision of information on quality in the message. But, of course, consumers must be aware of this spending to promote the product . . . so the ad messages have to be interesting and attention catching.

CONSPICUOUS CONSUMPTION AS A SIGNAL OF ABILITY

There are some people like Virgin CEO Richard Branson and Michael O'Leary of Ryanair who dress in jeans and open-neck shirts. But most successful business and professional people tend to buy expensive clothes and drive expensive cars. In competitive markets the people with the most ability tend to receive the highest salaries. The more someone earns, the more he or she is likely to spend on high-quality goods and services. As a result, these tendencies often lead us to infer a person's ability from the amount and quality of the goods he consumes and is seen to consume.

There is a problem with this: if any management consultant can signal superior quality by buying a Jaguar F-type and wearing €1,000 suits, why should we infer superior ability when we see him so accoutred? If his current car is discouraging potential clients from hiring him, buying a better one may simply be a prudent investment.

The things people consume continue to convey relevant information about their respective ability levels because of the costly-to-fake principle: the Jaguar F-type is an effective quality signal precisely because the consultant of low ability cannot afford one. Buying one won't help if he doesn't generate enough business to afford it. If his ability is weak (as with misleading advertising), that will not happen. As they say, you're only as good as your last piece of work. We see less conspicuous consumption to indicate quality where alternative information channels are available. In smaller towns, where people tend to know one another well, an accountant who tries to impress people by conspicuous spending is likely to succeed only in demonstrating how foolish she is. Thus, the wardrobe a professional person 'needs' in towns like Inverness or Perugia costs less than the wardrobe the same person would need in Edinburgh or Rome.

STATISTICAL DISCRIMINATION

In a competitive market with perfect information, the buyer of a service would pay the seller's cost of providing the service. In many markets, however – the market for fire insurance is one example – the seller does not know the exact cost of serving each individual buyer.

In such cases, the missing information has an economic value. If the seller can come up with even a rough estimate of the missing information, she can improve her position. As Economic Naturalist 12.4 illustrates, firms often do so by imputing characteristics to individuals on the basis of the groups to which they belong.

Economic Naturalist 12.4
What happens when firms are forbidden to use information in reaching pricing decisions?

In early 2011 the European Court of Justice, persuaded by a court Advocate General, ruled that equality directives from the EU Commission required that life and non-life insurance companies could no longer 'discriminate' by offering insurance products at different prices to males and females. This was held to be discriminating by gender, not by risk.

Males, especially young males, are notoriously more prone to crash cars than females, even young females. That is, the probability of an accident on the road involving a male driver, controlling for the number of males and females who drive, is much greater than that of involving a female driver. While there are some very safe male drivers, and some quite lunatic female ones, the fact is than each is a very small, and very difficult to identify *ex ante*, group of male and female drivers. By prohibiting 'discrimination' the ECJ is imposing a single price structure, the immediate consequence of which is to oblige female drivers to subsidise male drivers as a group. This, to most observers, is a rather unusual way to promote gender equality. It also has startling implications for road safety.

Less well publicised, but at least as serious in terms of its consequences, was the requirement that retirement pensions should not distinguish between genders. Life expectancy for females at age 65 is 3–4 years higher than for males in most EU countries. Hence, a given retirement fund will buy a lower annual pension (have a lower annuity rate per cent) for a female than for a male, since the money has to provide the pension for a longer period because the recipient is likely to live longer. The Advocate General, in her wisdom, held, and the ECJ accepted, that this constituted 'discrimination', and should be prohibited. In this case a single rate for both sexes implied less for men and more for women, the reverse direction for the cross-subsidisation. Henceforth men will have to save more over their working lives, and women less, to obtain a given pension.

What has not generally been understood is that, not only does the decision involve cross-subsidisation as between groups, but it must raise insurance costs overall. The 'discrimination' in competitive insurance markets reflected the costs of insurance by group. Obliging insurance companies to price differently means obliging them to use a pricing mechanism that was always open to them, but was not adopted because it would increase the overall costs of insuring the two groups. One reason for this is adverse selection, discussed in the next section. However, in general, any binding constraint imposes net costs on the constrained parties.

statistical discrimination the practice of making judgements about the quality of people, goods or services based on the characteristics of the groups to which they belong

The insurance industry's policy of charging high rates to young male drivers is an example of **statistical discrimination**. The same applies to house insurance as between urban and rural locations. It also applies to the common practice of paying higher salaries to people with college degrees than to people without them. Statistical discrimination occurs whenever people or products are judged on the basis of the groups to which they belong.

Even though everyone *knows* that the characteristics of specific individuals can differ markedly from those of the group to which they belong, competition promotes statistical discrimination. For example, insurance companies know perfectly well that *some* young males are careful and competent drivers. But unless they can identify *which* males are the better drivers, competitive pressure forces them to act on their knowledge that, as a group, young males are more likely than others to generate insurance claims.

Similarly, employers know that many people with only a secondary education are more productive than the average university graduate; but because employers usually cannot tell in advance who those people are, competitive pressure leads them to offer higher wages to graduates, who are more productive, on average, than those with only a secondary education.

Statistical discrimination is the *result* of observable differences in group characteristics, not the cause of those differences. Young males, for example, do not generate more insurance claims because of statistical discrimination. Rather, statistical discrimination occurs because insurance companies know that young males generate more claims. Nor does statistical discrimination cause young males to pay insurance rates that are high in relation to the claims they generate. Among any group of young male drivers, some are careful and competent, and others are not. Statistical discrimination means the more able males will pay high rates relative to the volume of claims they generate, but it also means the less able male drivers will pay low rates relative to the claims they generate. On average, the group's rates will be appropriate to the claims its members generate.

Still, these observations do little to ease the frustration of the young male who knows himself to be a careful and competent driver, or the high-school graduate who knows herself to be a highly productive employee. Competitive forces provide firms with an incentive to identify such individuals and treat them more favourably whenever practical. Insurance companies in Ireland and elsewhere are now introducing programmes to help identify 'careful' drivers from among the young male population. These include voluntary limitations on time of driving (most fatalities occur between 11.00 pm and 5.00 am), drinking and speed, as well as taking advanced driving courses.

ADVERSE SELECTION

Although insurance companies routinely practise statistical discrimination, each individual within a group pays the same rate, even though individuals within the group often differ sharply in terms of their likelihood of filing claims. Within each group, buying insurance is thus most attractive to those individuals with the highest likelihood of filing claims. As a result, high-risk individuals are more likely to buy insurance than low-risk individuals, a pattern known as **adverse selection**. Adverse selection forces insurance companies to raise their premiums, which makes buying insurance even less attractive to low-risk individuals, which raises still further the average risk level of those who remain insured. In some cases, only those individuals faced with extreme risks may continue to find insurance an attractive purchase.

adverse selection the pattern in which insurance tends to be purchased disproportionately by those who are most costly for companies to insure

MORAL HAZARD

Moral hazard is the tendency for people to take greater risk when they are protected from the full consequences when the risk turns out badly. Despite its name, it is not a 'moral' issue but simply a matter of incentives. Suppose that you go to Monte Carlo and bet all of your money on black (taking a large risk). If you are lucky you

moral hazard the tendency of people to take greater risks when they are protected from the full consequences when the risk turns out badly will be rich. However if you are unlucky you will lose everything. The fear of losing everything is what keeps most of us from placing this bet. However, suppose that the government stepped in and said that, if you won you could keep your winnings but if you were unlucky, it would pay the casino. With this government 'gambling insurance' people would be protected from the negative side of gambling and so they would place more bets – that is, they would take on more risk. Moral hazard is simply this tendency to engage in riskier behaviour when you are protected from the downside of risk. While, fortunately, we do not usually see governments offering this kind of gambling insurance, the same incentives arise in many markets. Not usually, but consider the appetite for risk among entrepreneurs or established companies when governments attract them into a country by offering non-refundable investment subsidies or offsets against existing tax liabilities in the country.

For example, in late 2007 the UK bank Northern Rock was in severe financial difficulties and the government and the Bank of England had to decide whether to step in and bail out the bank. The argument in favour of bailing out Northern Rock was that the failure of this bank would cause a ripple effect and potentially bring down other banks and lead to a recession. In Chapter 23 we will discuss how the banking system works and how this could happen. The main argument against bailing out Northern Rock was that it would create a moral hazard problem. Banks operate by taking money in as deposits at low interest rates and then loaning that money out at higher interest rates, pocketing the difference. The riskier the loans a bank makes, the larger its profits if the loans do get paid back. However, in normal operation a bank will balance this against the possibility that the risky loans might not be paid back and it would be forced out of business. This is what keeps it from taking on too much risk. However, if the government starts bailing out banks that get into trouble, the downside of taking on risk is much less. If the loans don't get paid back, the government will step in and solve the problem. So, the concern was that by bailing out Northern Rock the government would increase the incentives for other banks to engage in risky lending. Nevertheless, in early 2008 the UK government nationalised Northern Rock. Although their exact methods differ, since 2007 most governments have also bailed out their distressed banks, with the notable exception of Iceland. Only time will tell whether the resulting moral hazard problem leads to a less stable banking system in the future.

Performance bonuses, like those received by equity fund managers, also create a moral hazard problem. An equity fund manager decides how to invest the fund's backers' money. A typical manager is paid a salary, but the bulk of his or her income comes from performance bonuses based on how much profit the fund earns. Consider a manager whose contract specified a 2 per cent bonus. If the fund earns €50 million, the manager would get a €2 million bonus. However, if the fund loses money the manager still gets his or her salary. This type of contract, which is quite common, creates a moral hazard problem since the manager benefits when the fund performs well but does not lose when the fund loses money. Hence, the manager will tend to engage in risky investments which maximise the possible profits without adequate concern for the size of the potential loses.

Moral hazard also arises in insurance markets. Some people take fewer precautions when they know they are insured. Someone whose car is insured, for example, may take less care to prevent it from being damaged or stolen. Driving cautiously and searching for safe parking spaces require effort, after all, and if the losses from failing to engage in these precautions are covered by insurance, some people will become less vigilant. Because people take less care when they are insured, the costs to insurance companies rise and therefore so do premiums.

By offering policies with deductible provisions (excesses), insurance companies help many of their potential clients soften the consequences of problems like moral hazard and adverse selection. Under the terms of an automobile collision insurance policy with, say, a €1,000 excess provision, the insurance company covers only those collision repair costs in excess of €1,000. For example, if you have an accident in which €3,000 in damage occurs to your car, the insurance company covers only €2,000, and you pay the remaining €1,000.

An excess means that the insured is sharing part of the risk with the insurer. For this reason this is sometimes referred to as an example of 'co-insurance'. Carrying more of the risk makes the insured party take more precautions. A system of no-claims bonuses operates in the same way: if you make a claim your costs will increase when the time comes to renew the policy. This reduces the incentive to make a claim rather than carry the full cost of an accident yourself.

How does the availability of such policies mitigate the negative effects of adverse selection and moral hazard? Since the policies are cheaper for insurance companies to provide, they sell for lower prices. The lower prices represent a much better bargain, however, for those drivers who are least likely to file insurance claims, since those drivers are least likely to incur any uncovered repair costs. Policies with deductible provisions also confront careless drivers with more of the extra costs for which they are responsible, giving them additional incentives to take precautions.

These policies benefit insurance buyers in another way. Because the holder of a policy with an excess provision will not file a claim at all if the damage to his car in an accident is less than the deductible threshold, insurance companies require fewer resources to process and investigate claims, savings that get passed along in the form of lower premiums.

RECAP

Asymmetric information

Asymmetric information describes situations in which not all parties to a potential exchange are equally well informed. In the typical case, the seller of a product will know more about its quality than the potential buyers. Such asymmetries often stand in the way of mutually beneficial exchange in the markets for high-quality goods, because buyers' inability to identify high quality makes them unwilling to pay a commensurate price.

Information asymmetries and other communication problems between potential exchange partners can often be solved through the use of signals that are costly or difficult to fake. Product warranties are such a signal, because the seller of a low-quality product would find them too costly to offer.

Buyers and sellers also respond to asymmetric information by attempting to judge the qualities of products and people on the basis of the groups to which they belong. A young male may know he is a good driver, but auto insurance companies must nonetheless charge him high rates because they know only that he is a member of a group that is frequently involved in accidents.

SUMMARY

- Virtually every market exchange takes place on the basis of *less than complete information*. More information is beneficial both to buyers and to sellers, but information is costly to acquire. The rational individual therefore acquires information only up to the point at which its marginal benefit equals its marginal cost. Beyond that point one is rational to remain ignorant.
- Retailers and other sales agents are important sources of information. To the extent that they enable consumers to find the right products and services, they add economic value. In that sense they are no less productive than the workers who manufacture goods or perform services directly. Unfortunately, the *free-rider problem* often prevents firms from offering useful product information.

- Several principles govern the *rational search for information*. Searching more intensively makes sense when the cost of a search is low, when quality is highly variable or when prices vary widely. Further search is always a gamble. A risk-neutral person will search whenever the expected gains outweigh the expected costs. A rational search will always terminate before all possible options have been investigated. Thus in a search for a partner in an ongoing bilateral relationship, there is always the possibility that a better partner will turn up after the search is over. In most contexts, people deal with this problem by entering into contracts that commit them to their partners once they have mutually agreed to terminate the search.
- Many potentially beneficial transactions are prevented from taking place by *asymmetric information* – the fact that one party lacks information that the other has. For example, the owner of a used car knows whether it is in good condition, but potential buyers do not. Even though a buyer may be willing to pay more for a good car than the owner of such a car would require, the fact that the buyer cannot be sure he is getting a good car often discourages the sale. More generally, asymmetric information often prevents sellers from supplying the same quality level that consumers would be willing to pay for.
- Both buyers and sellers can often gain by finding ways of communicating what they know to one another. But because of the potential conflict between the interests of buyers and sellers, mere statements about the relevant information may not be credible. For a signal between potential trading partners to be credible, it must be *costly to fake*. For instance, the owner of a high-quality used car can credibly signal the car's quality by offering a warranty – an offer that the seller of a low-quality car could not afford to make.
- Firms and consumers often try to estimate missing information by making use of what they know about the *groups to which people or things belong*. For example, insurance firms estimate the risk of insuring individual young male drivers on the basis of the accident rates for young males as a group. This practice is known as *statistical discrimination*. Other examples include paying college graduates more than high-school graduates and charging higher life insurance rates to 60 year olds than to 20 year olds. Statistical discrimination helps to explain the phenomenon of disappearing political discourse, which occurs when opponents of a practice such as the death penalty remain silent when the issue is discussed publicly.

REVIEW QUESTIONS

1. Can it be rational for a consumer to buy a Toyota without having first taken test drives in competing models built by Ford, VW, Renault, Honda and others?
2. Explain why a gallery owner who sells a painting might actually create more economic surplus than the artist who painted it.
3. Explain why used cars offered for sale are different, on average, from used cars not offered for sale.
4. Explain why the used car market would be likely to function more efficiently in a community in which moral norms of honesty are strong than in a community in which such norms are weak.
5. Why might leasing a new Porsche be a good investment for an aspiring Hollywood film producer, even though he can't easily afford the monthly payments?

PROBLEMS

connect

1. State whether the following are **true or false**, and briefly explain why.
   a. Companies spend billions of dollars advertising their products on network TV primarily because the texts of their advertisements persuade consumers that the advertised products are of high quality.
   b. You may not get the optimal level of advice from a retail shop when you go in to buy a lamp for your bike, because of the free-rider problem.
   c. If you need a lawyer, and all your legal expenses are covered by insurance, you should *always* choose the best-dressed lawyer with the most expensive car and the most ostentatiously furnished office.
   d. The benefit of searching for a spouse is affected by the size of the community you live in.
2. Consumers know that some fraction x of all new cars produced and sold in the market are defective. The defective ones cannot be identified except by those who own them. Cars do not depreciate with use. Consumers are risk-neutral and value non-defective cars at €10,000 each. New cars sell for €5,000 and used ones for €2,500. What is the fraction x?
3. Carlos is risk-neutral and has an ancient farmhouse with great character for sale in Slaterville Springs, Montana. His reservation price for the house is €130,000. The only possible local buyer is Whitney, whose reservation price for the house is €150,000. The only other houses on the market are modern ranch houses that sell for €125,000, which is exactly equal to each potential buyer's reservation price for such a house. Suppose that if Carlos does not hire a real estate agent, Whitney will learn from her neighbour that Carlos's house is for sale and will buy it for €140,000. However, if Carlos hires a real estate agent, he knows that the agent will put him in touch with an enthusiast for old farmhouses who is willing to pay up to €300,000 for the house. Carlos also knows that if he and this person negotiate, they will agree on a price of €250,000. If agents charge a commission of 5 per cent of the selling price and all agents have opportunity costs of €2,000 for negotiating a sale, will Carlos hire an agent? If so, how will total economic surplus be affected?
4. Ann and Barbara are computer programmers in Nashville, Tennessee, who are planning to move to Portland, Oregon. Each owns a house that has just been appraised for €100,000. But whereas Ann's house is one of hundreds of highly similar houses in a large, well-known suburban development, Barbara's is the only one that was built from her architect's design. Who will benefit more by hiring an estate agent to assist in selling her house, Ann or Barbara?
5. For each pair of occupations listed, identify the one for which the kind of car a person drives is more likely to be a good indication of how good she is at her job:
   a. primary school teacher; estate agent
   b. dentist; municipal government administrator
   c. engineer in the private sector; engineer in the military.
6. Brokers who sell stocks over the internet can serve many more customers than those who transact business by mail or over the phone. How will the expansion of internet access affect the average incomes of stockbrokers who continue to do business in the traditional way?
7. Whose income do you predict will be more affected by the expansion of internet access:
   a. stockbrokers or lawyers?
   b. doctors or pharmacists?
   c. book-shop owners or the owners of galleries that sell original oil paintings?

8. How will growing internet access affect the number of film actors and musicians who have active fan clubs?

9. Fred, a retired accountant, and Jim, a senior civil servant, are 63-year-old identical twins who collect antique pottery. Each has an annual income of €100,000 (Fred's from a pension, Jim's from salary). One buys most of his pottery at local auctions and the other buys most of his from a local dealer. Which brother is more likely to buy at an auction, and does he pay more or less than his brother who buys from the local dealer?

REFERENCES

Akerlof, G. (1970) 'The market for lemons', *Quarterly Journal of Economics*, 84.

Lucking-Reiley, D. (2000) 'Vickrey auctions in practice: from nineteenth-century philately to twenty-first century e-commerce', *Journal of Economic Perspectives*, 14, 3, pp. 183–92.

Chapter 13

Labour Markets, Income Distribution, Wealth and Poverty

In spite of the cost of living, it's still popular. — Laurence J. Peter

Learning Objectives

After reading this chapter you should be able to:

1. Understand the relationship between productivity, skills and the demand for factor services;
2. Understand how different types of labour market work, and the impact of technology on incomes;
3. Distinguish the various factors that cause earnings to vary between individuals and groups;
4. Explain the impact of unions and regulation in labour markets;
5. Understand income distribution measurement;
6. Understand how policy measures to alter income distribution affect outcomes.

Differences in incomes are sometimes hard to rationalise in terms of differences in the abilities of the people concerned. An Olympic gold medal winner can expect to earn substantial sums afterwards from advertising and endorsement contracts. The margin between the gold and silver medal winners' abilities and performances is frequently tiny, but a silver medal winner will be lucky to earn a small fraction of the income of the gold medal winner.

People with similar abilities in different countries or in different sectors of the same country frequently earn very different incomes, controlling for the amount of work they undertake. For example, nurses in southern and eastern Asia earn much less that nurses with similar skills in western Europe; economists working in government departments typically earn lower salaries than equally competent analysts working in the financial sector or in consultancy firms.

How do we explain these differences in earnings? Few questions in economics have stimulated as much interest and discussion. It's not just a reflection of differences in measures of wealth as between countries: living in America does not guarantee a person a higher income than that earned by someone living in Italy. Many of the wealthiest people in the world come from extremely poor countries, and many Americans are homeless and malnourished.

In this chapter simple economic principles are used to help explain why incomes differ as between people, and, indeed, countries. We shall discuss the human capital model, which emphasises the importance of differences in personal characteristics. That, however, does not explain why people with similar personal characteristics often earn sharply different incomes. Other explanatory factors to be considered include trades unions, discrimination, the effect of non-wage conditions of employment, and winner-take-all markets. Do differences in incomes matter? Is *income inequality* something society should be concerned about? If so, do practical remedies for it exist. Because government programmes to redistribute income have costs as well as benefits, policy makers must compare an imperfect status quo with the practical consequences of imperfect government remedies.

We use the tried and tested technique of applying the analysis of markets to the problem, on the basis that a person's earnings from labour can be thought of as reflecting the price received for an hour of work and the number of hours worked (i.e. sold by the worker and bought by the employer). The same applies to incomes earned from the ownership of productive assets.

THE ECONOMIC VALUE OF WORK

In some respects, the sale of human labour differs profoundly from the sale of other goods and services. For example, although someone may legally relinquish all future rights to the use of her TV set by selling it, in societies with Western legal systems the law no longer permits people formally to sell themselves into slavery or to trade in people in the sense of selling and buying an absolute right of disposal of a person's services. The law does, however, permit employers to 'rent' our services. This rental market for labour services functions much like the market for most other goods and services. Each specific category of labour has a *demand curve* and a *supply curve*. These curves intersect to determine both the *equilibrium wage* and the *equilibrium quantity of employment* for each category of labour.

Shifts in the relevant demand and supply curves produce changes analogous to those produced by shifts in the demand and supply curves for other goods and services. For instance, an increase in the demand for a specific category of labour will generally increase both the equilibrium wage and the equilibrium quantity of employment in that category. By the same token, an increase in the supply of labour to a given occupation will tend to increase the level of employment and lower the wage rate in that occupation.

As in our discussions of other markets, our strategy for investigating how the labour market works will be to go through a series of examples that shed light on different parts of the picture. In Economic Naturalist 13.1, we focus on how the equilibrium principle can help us to understand how wages will differ among workers with different levels of productive ability.

Economic Naturalist 13.1

Given that slavery and indentured labour are prohibited, how do football and other professional sports clubs purchase players?

The answer is that they don't. What they do is to pay another club to tear up the contract by which it has a right to a player's services for an agreed period of time at an agreed rate of pay, an employment contract. Labour contracts frequently have a *time dimension* to them and these impose restrictions on one or both sides in terms of freedom to end the relationship. These are the consequences of explicit contract negotiations between the parties and/or legal requirements imposed by labour law. The player simply changes employer. No one has bought him. But someone did buy out his *contractual obligations*.

How much will the potters earn?

Example 13.1

Glazed earthenware pots sold in garden centres and DIY stores are mostly made in China and nearby countries in the Far East. In many cases, the pots are made unglazed and then sold to firms that apply the glazing. It is at this stage that the pots become distinctive. As originally produced, the output of one pottery producer is more or less the same as that of any other producer. It is something close to what we would describe as a perfectly competitive industry. Suppose that Peking Pottery Works (PPW) is one of numerous identical companies in China that hire potters who make standard clay pots. The going price for such pots is 1.20 yuan each. A finishing company glazes and fires them, and then sells them in the retail marketplace. Clay and water, both available free of charge in unlimited quantities, are the only inputs used by the potters. The wheels and ovens are owned by the proprietor of PPW, who charges the potters 0.10 yuan per pot to cover his costs and allow him some income. Currently only two potters work for PPW, whose only cost other than potters' salaries is a 0.10 yuan handling cost for each pot it delivers to the finisher. Potter Han delivers 100 pots per week and potter Lee delivers 120. If the labour market for potters is perfectly competitive, how much will each be paid?

We begin with the assumption that Han and Lee have decided to work full time as potters, so our focus is not on how much they will work but on how much they will be paid. After taking handling costs and the equipment charge into account, the value of the pots that Han delivers is 100 yuan per week, and that is the amount PPW will pay him. To pay him less would risk having him bid away by a competitor. For example, if PPW paid Han only 90 yuan per week, the company would then enjoy an economic profit of 10 yuan per week as a result of hiring him. Seeing this cash on the table (Chapter 3), a rival firm could then offer Han 91 yuan, thus earning an additional economic profit of 9 yuan per week by bidding him away from PPW. So under the bidding pressure from rival employers, PPW will have difficulty keeping Han if it pays him less than 100 yuan per week. And the company would suffer an economic loss if it pays him more than 100 yuan per week. Similarly, the value of the pots delivered each week by Lee is 120 yuan, and this will be her competitive equilibrium wage.

In Example 13.1, the number of pots each potter delivered each week was that potter's **marginal physical product** (or **marginal product** (**MP** for short) **of labour**. More generally, a worker's marginal product is the extra output the firm gets as a result of hiring that worker. When we multiply a worker's marginal product by the net price for which each unit of the product sells, we get that worker's **value of marginal product**, or **VMP of labour**. (In Example 13.1, the 'net price' of each pot was 1.00 yuan – the difference between the 1.20 sale price and the 0.20 handling and equipment charge.) The general rule in competitive labour markets is that a worker's pay in long-run equilibrium will be *equal to her VMP, which is the net contribution she makes to the employer's revenue.* Employers might like to pay workers less than their respective VMPs, but if labour markets are truly competitive they cannot get away with doing so for long.

> **marginal physical product, or marginal product of labour (MP)** the additional output a firm gets by employing one additional unit of labour
>
> **value of marginal product of labour (VMP)** the money value of the additional output a firm gets by employing one additional unit of labour

In Example 13.1, each worker's VMP was independent of the number of other workers employed by the firm. In such cases, we cannot predict how many workers a firm will hire. PPW could break even with two potters, with ten, or even with 1,000 or more. In many other situations, however, we can predict exactly how many workers a firm will hire. Consider Example 13.2.

> Cost-Benefit Analysis

How many workers should WTK AG hire?

Example 13.2

Wilhelm Tell Kunstfabrik AG (WTK), located in Zurich, hires workers in a competitive labour market at a wage of Sfr350 per week to make cuckoo clock cases from scrap wood that is available free of charge. If the cases sell for Sfr20 each and the company's

Table 13.1 Employment and Productivity in WTK (When Clock Cases Sell for Sfr20 Each)

Number of workers (1)	Total number of clock cases/week (2)	MP (extra clock cases/week) (3)	VMP (Sfr/week) (4)
0	0		
1	30	30	600
2	55	25	500
3	76	21	420
4	94	18	360
5	108	14	280

weekly output varies with the number of workers hired, as shown in Table 13.1, how many workers should WTK hire?

In Example 13.1 our focus was on wage differences for employees whose productive abilities differed. In contrast, we assume here that all workers are equally productive and the firm faces a fixed market wage for each. The fact that the marginal product of labour declines with the number of workers hired is a consequence of the *law of diminishing returns*. (As discussed in Chapter 5, this law says that with fixed values for a firm's capital or other productive inputs in the short run, adding workers beyond some point results in ever smaller increases in output.) Column (3) of Table 13.1 reports the marginal product for each additional worker, and column (4) reports the value of each successive worker's marginal product – the number of clock cases he or she adds times the selling price of Sfr20. WTK should keep hiring as long as the next worker's VMP is at least Sfr350 per week (the market wage). The first four workers have VMPs larger than Sfr350, so WTK should hire them. But since hiring the fifth worker would add only Sfr280 to weekly revenue, WTK should not hire that worker.

The perfectly competitive firm's decision on the number of workers to hire is similar to the firm's output decision we considered in Chapter 5. When labour is the only variable factor of production, the two decisions are essentially the same; the unique correspondence between total output and the total number of workers hired means that, deciding how many workers to hire is the same as deciding *how much output to supply*.

The worker's attractiveness to the employer depends not only on how many clock cases she produces, but also on the price of clock cases and on the wage rate. For example, because higher prices raise VMP, an increase in product price will lead employers to increase employment. Employers will also increase hiring when the wage rate falls.

Exercise 13.1 In Example 13.2, how many workers should WTK hire if the price of clock cases rises to Sfr26?

Exercise 13.2 How many workers should WTK hire if the wage rate falls to Sfr275 per week?

RECAP

The economic value of work

In competitive labour markets, employers face pressure to pay each worker the value of his or her marginal product. When a firm can hire as many workers as it wishes at a given market wage, it should expand employment as long as the value of *marginal product of labour exceeds the market wage*.

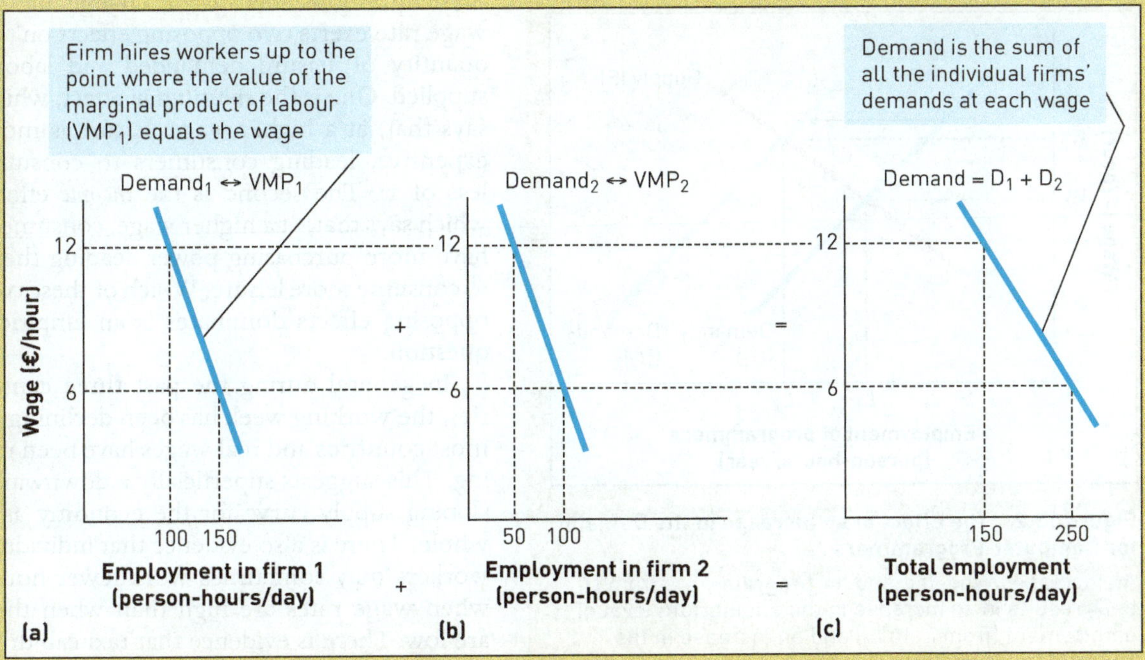

Figure 13.1 The Occupational Demand for Labour

If firm 1 and firm 2 are the only firms that employ labour in a given occupation, we generate the demand curve for labour in that occupation by adding the individual demand curves horizontally.

THE EQUILIBRIUM WAGE AND EMPLOYMENT LEVELS

As we saw in Chapter 3, the equilibrium price and quantity in any competitive market occur at the intersection of the relevant supply and demand curves. The same is true in competitive markets for labour.

THE DEMAND FOR LABOUR

An employer's reservation price for a worker is the most the employer could pay without suffering a decline in profit. This reservation price for the employer in a perfectly competitive labour market is simply VMP, the value of the worker's marginal product. The law of diminishing returns implies that the marginal product of labour, and hence VMP, declines in the short run as the quantity of labour rises. The individual employer's demand curve for labour in any particular occupation may thus be shown, as in Fig. 13.1(a), as a downward-sloping function of the wage rate. Suppose firm 1 (panel (a)) and firm 2 (panel (b)) are the only two firms that employ computer programmers in a given community. The demand for programmers in that community will then be the horizontal sum of the individual firm demands (panel (c)).

THE SUPPLY CURVE OF LABOUR

Does the supply curve of labour for a specific occupation slope upwards, meaning that more labour be offered at high wage rates than at low wage rates? If more work means less leisure, will individuals wish to consume *less leisure* at high wage rates than at low wage rates. Economic theory does not provide a simple and unambiguous answer to

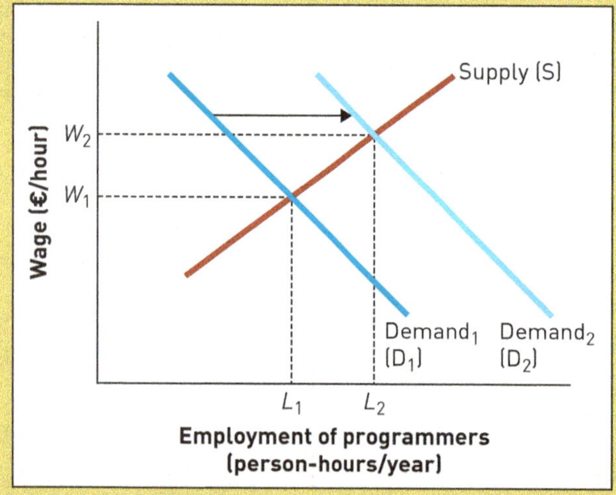

Figure 13.2 The Effect of an Increase in the Demand for Computer Programmers

An increase in the demand for programmers from D_1 to D_2 results in an increase in the equilibrium level of employment (from L_1 to L_2) and an increase in the equilibrium wage (from W_1 to W_2).

these questions, because a change in the wage rate exerts two opposing effects on the quantity of leisure demanded and labour supplied. One is the *substitution* effect, which says that, at a higher wage, leisure is more expensive, leading consumers to consume less of it. The second is the *income* effect, which says that, at a higher wage, consumers have more purchasing power, leading them to consume more leisure. Which of these two opposing effects dominates is an empirical question.

In general during the past three centuries, the working week has been declining in most countries and real wages have been rising. This suggests superficially a downward-sloping supply curve for the economy as a whole. There is also evidence that individual workers may sometimes work fewer hours when wage rates are high than when they are low. There is evidence that taxi cab drivers in New York City quit earlier on rainy days (when the effective wage is high because of high demand for cab rides) than on sunny days (when the effective wage is lower).[1] The same effect was observed in Dublin after the taxi market was liberalised in 2001. More taxis on the streets meant that the expected number of fares per hour (and, therefore, the expected hourly income of a representative taxi driver) fell. Previously, with chronic excess demand, taxi drivers could expect their cars to be full any time they chose to take them on to the streets. Now drivers had to go looking for fares. The fall in expected hourly income resulted in more hours being worked.

Whether any individual's labour supply curve is upward-sloping depends on income and substitution effects. When we move to groups of workers this can still be the case, provided that they are shielded from competition from new entrants. These observations notwithstanding, with easy entry to an occupation the supply of labour *to any particular occupation* is almost surely upward-sloping, because wage differences among occupations influence occupational choice. It is no accident, for example, that many more people are choosing jobs as computer programmers now than in 1970. Wages of programmers have risen sharply since the 1970s, which has led many people to forsake other career paths in favour of programming. Curve S in Fig. 13.2 represents the supply curve of computer programmers. Its positive slope is typical of the supply curves for most individual occupations.

MARKET SHIFTS

As more tasks have become computerised since the 1980s, the demand for programmers has grown, as shown by the shift from D_1 to D_2 in Fig. 13.2. Equilibrium in the market for computer programmers occurs at the intersection of the relevant supply and demand curves. The increase in demand has led to an increase in the equilibrium level of programmers from L_1 to L_2 and a rise in the equilibrium wage from W_1 to W_2.

As discussed in Chapter 8, the market for stocks and other financial assets reaches equilibrium very quickly in the wake of shifts in the underlying supply and demand curves. Labour markets, by contrast, are often much slower to adjust. When the demand

[1] Babcock et al., 1997.

for workers in a given profession increases, shortages may remain for months, or even years, depending on how long it takes people to acquire the skills and training needed to enter the profession.

> RECAP
>
> **Equilibrium in the labour market**
>
> The demand for labour in a perfectly competitive labour market is the horizontal sum of each employer's VMP curve. The supply curve of labour for an individual labour market is upward-sloping, even though the supply curve of labour for the economy as a whole may be vertical or even downward-sloping. In each labour market the demand and supply curves intersect to determine the *equilibrium wage and level of employment*.

EXPLAINING DIFFERENCES IN EARNINGS

The theory of competitive labour markets tells us that differences in pay reflect differences in the corresponding VMPs. Thus, in Example 13.1, Lee earned 20 per cent more than Han because she made 20 per cent more pots each week than he did. Why was Lee able to (and/or chose to) produce more pots than Han? Note that if it simply represented a decision by Han to work less hard there is nothing that really needs explaining. Otherwise, we need to explain why Lee was more productive than Han in order to explain the difference in their incomes. It could simply be talent: Lee is naturally more dexterous than Han. Or it could be that Lee has been working at the job longer than Han and has improved skill levels arising from this experience. Or it could be that Lee took a course in pot throwing at the local technological institute, and Han did not.

But even if people appear equally talented and hard-working, we may observe differences in their incomes. Why, for example, do some lawyers earn so much more than those plumbers who are just as smart as they are and work just as hard? And why do surgeons usually earn so much more than general practitioners? The No-Cash-on-the-Table Principle suggests that we should expect that if plumbers could earn more by becoming lawyers, they would just switch occupations. Similarly, if general practitioners could boost their incomes by becoming surgeons, why didn't they become surgeons in the first place?

THE HUMAN CAPITAL EXPLANATION

Human capital theory suggests some answers. The theory holds that an individual's VMP is proportional to his or her stock of **human capital** – an amalgam of factors such as education, experience, training, intelligence, energy, work habits, trustworthiness and initiative. According to this theory, some occupations pay better than others because they require larger stocks of human capital. For example, a general practitioner could become a surgeon, but only by undertaking formal training for several more years. An even larger investment in additional education is required for a plumber to become a lawyer.

> **human capital theory** a theory of pay determination that says a worker's wage will be proportional to his or her stock of human capital
>
> **human capital** an amalgam of factors such as education, training, experience, intelligence, energy, work habits, trustworthiness and initiative that affect the value of a worker's marginal product

Other things being equal, the more human capital you possess the higher will be your earnings, because human capital increases your VMP. However, because human capital is in most cases costly to acquire (money costs of training, time and opportunity costs of earnings forgone) it is relatively scarce and commands a high price. The payment received by owners of human capital is the *supply price* of that capital, the social benefit of which is increased labour productivity – and, therefore, income per head – in society as a whole.

Differences in demand can result in some kinds of human capital being more valuable than others. Consider two occupations: tax accountants and computer programmers. Both occupations require demanding technical training. Since the 1970s there has been a steady increase in the demand for skilled programmers in virtually all advanced Western economies. During that period, the demand for the services of US tax accountants has fallen as more and more American taxpayers have used tax-preparation software in lieu of hiring accountants to help them with their taxes. This is less evident in Europe, where online tax returns are a fairly recent development, and where the combination of complex tax codes and high marginal tax rates have supported the use of tax accountants and equivalent professionals in dealing with the tax authorities. In the United States incomes of computer programmers have risen relative to the incomes of people employed as tax accountants because the training of programmers (the human capital of programmers) now yields a higher return in the labour market.

TRADES UNIONS

> **labour union** a group of workers who bargain collectively with employers for better wages and working conditions

Two workers with the same amount of human capital may earn different wages if one of them belongs to a **labour union** and the other does not. A labour (or trade) union is an organisation through which workers attempt to bargain collectively with employers for better wages and working conditions.

The impact of trades unions in labour markets is something about which there is considerable controversy in economics. This is reflected in a wider political and social debate about the role of unions and the legal immunity and protection they receive. Many people, including some economists, believe that unions can ensure levels of real income and working conditions to employees as a whole in excess of those that would be enjoyed in the absence of unions and their immunities. Obviously, this view is widely held by members of trades unions and their professional advisers. Others, including economists, believe that whatever value unions may have had a hundred years ago in protecting disorganised workers from exploitation by capitalist employers with market power in the labour market has largely disappeared. Instead, they regard unions as affecting labour markets in much the same way that cartels affect product markets.

To illustrate, consider a simple economy with two labour markets, neither of which is unionised initially. Suppose the total supply of labour to the two markets is fixed at $S_0 = 200$ workers per day, and that the demand curves are as shown by *VMP*1 and *VMP*2 in Fig. 13.3(a) and (b). The sum of the two demand curves, *VMP*1 + *VMP*2 (panel (c)), intersects the supply curve to determine an equilibrium wage of €9 per hour. At that wage, firms in market 1 hire 125 workers per day (panel (a)), and firms in market 2 hire 75 (panel (b)).

Now suppose that workers in market 1 form a union and refuse to work for less than €12 per hour. Because demand curves for labour are downward-sloping, employers of unionised workers reduce employment from 125 workers per day to 100 (Fig. 13.4(a)). The 25 displaced workers in the unionised market would of course be delighted to find other jobs in that market at €12 per hour. But they cannot, and so they are forced to seek employment in the non-unionised market. The result is an excess supply of 25 workers in the non-union market at the original wage of €9 per hour. In time, wages in that market decline to $W_N = €6$ per hour, the level at which 100 workers can find jobs in the non-unionised market (Fig. 13.4(b)).

It might seem that the gains of the unionised workers are exactly offset by the losses of non-unionised workers. On closer inspection, however, we see that pegging the union wage above the equilibrium level actually *reduces* the value of total output. If labour were allocated efficiently between the two markets, its VMP would have to be the same in each. Otherwise, the total value of output could be increased by moving workers from the low-VMP market to the high-VMP market. With the wage set

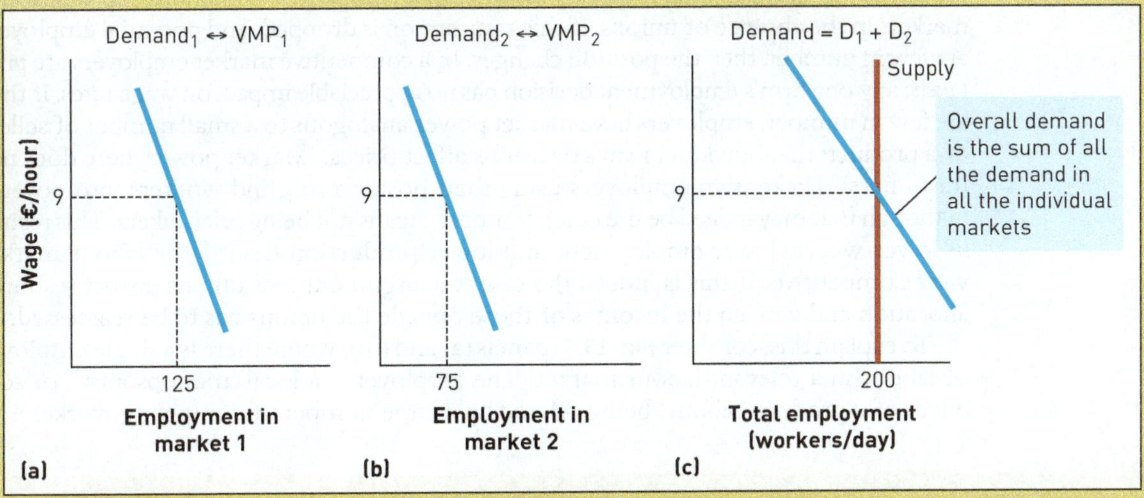

Figure 13.3 An Economy with Two Non-unionised Labour Markets

Supply and demand intersect to determine a market wage of €9 per hour (c). At that wage, employers in market 1 hire 125 workers per day and employers in market 2 hire 75 workers per day. The VMP is €9 in each market.

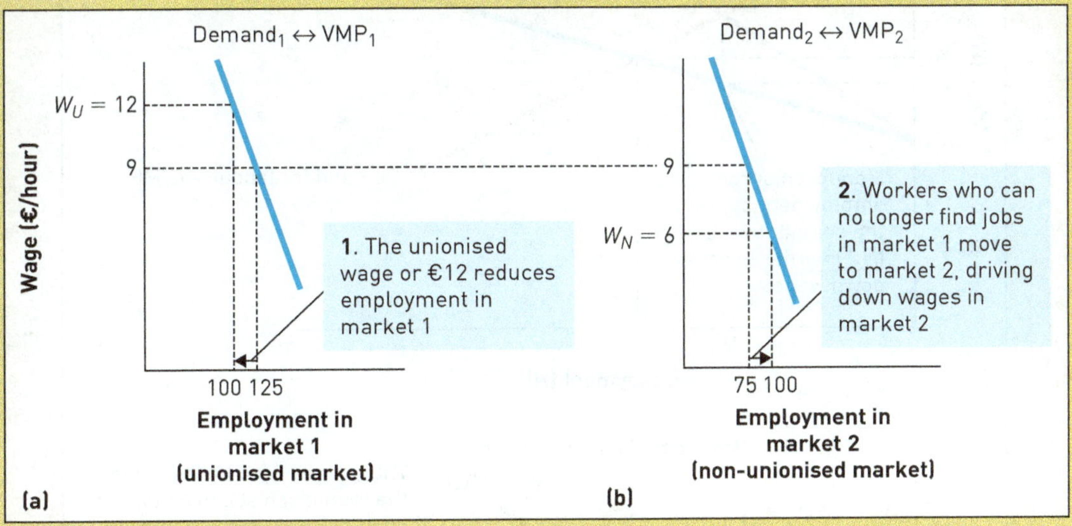

Figure 13.4 The Effect of a Union Wage Above the Equilibrium Wage

When the unionised wage is pegged at W_u = €12/hour (a), 25 workers are discharged. When these workers seek employment in the non-unionised market, the wage in that market falls to W_N = €6/hour (b).

initially at €9 per hour in both markets, the condition for efficient allocation was met, because labour's VMP was €9 per hour in both markets. But because the collective bargaining process drives wages (and hence VMPs) in the two markets apart, the value of total output is no longer maximised. To verify this claim, note that if a worker is taken out of the non-unionised market, the reduction in the value of output there will be only €6 per hour, which is less than the €12 per hour gain in the value of output when that same worker is added to the unionised market.

Equilibrium

Exercise 13.3

In Fig. 13.4, by how much would the total value of output be increased if the wage rate were €9 per hour in each market?

However, the above analysis implicitly assumes that competitive conditions apply in labour markets in the absence of unions. If this assumption is dropped, and potential employers are few in number, then the position changes. In a competitive market employers are *price takers*: any one firm's employment decision has no appreciable impact on wage rates. If they are few in number, employers have market power analogous to a small number of sellers of a product: the individual firm's decisions affect prices. 'Market power' here does not mean harsh Dickensian employers using their position to grind workers into poverty (although that may indeed be the case). It simply means not being price takers. This results in lower wages, lower employment and lower production than if the labour market were competitive. If this is indeed the case, the argument that unions distort resource allocation and worsen the incomes of those outside the unions has to be reassessed.

To explain this, consider Fig. 13.5 (panels (a) and (b)), where there is a single employer of labour in a relevant labour market. The employer is a local 'monopsonist', or sole buyer of a product (labour) being offered by a large number of competing workers.

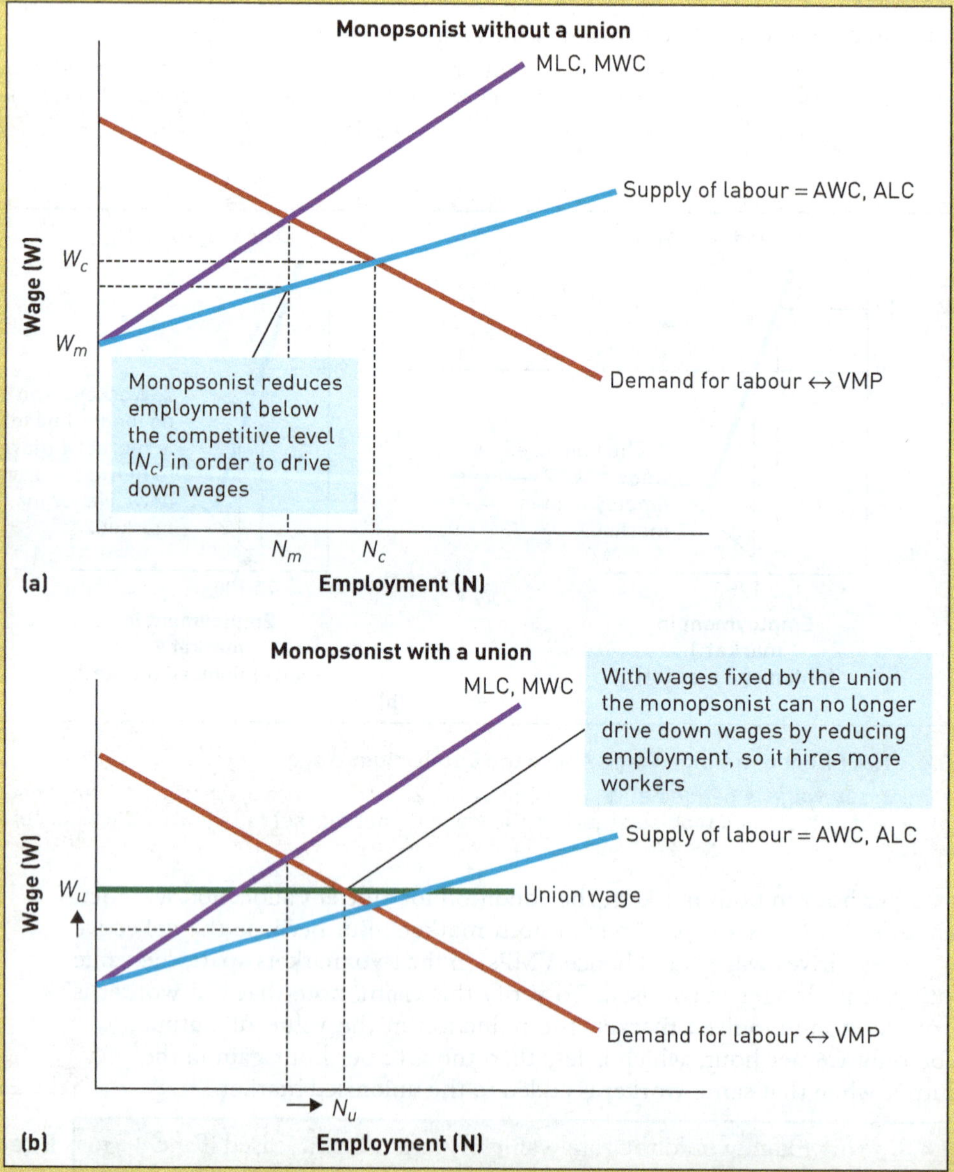

Figure 13.5 How a Union Can Increase Employment when the Employer Has Market Power

The employer's demand curve for labour (the *VMP* curve) is, as usual, downward-sloping. He faces an upward-sloping supply curve of labour. The more labour he demands the higher the price (wages) he will have to pay. If the market had been competitive the level of employment and the level of wages would be determined by the intersection of the supply curve and the demand curve (W_c and N_c) (panel (a)). But, if the monopsonist employer wishes to maximise profits this will not happen. Why?

The supply curve of labour represents the *average cost of labour to the employer* (because total labour cost is simply the rectangle formed by the level of employment and the corresponding point on the labour supply curve). For this reason, it is also labelled *ALC*. As the employer purchases more labour wages rise (he is not a price taker in the labour market). To maximise profits the employer will hire that quantity of labour for which the *marginal* cost of labour, not the average cost of labour, equals the value marginal product. Since *AWC* is upward-sloping, the marginal cost of labour must lie above it: the *MLC* line. That intersects the *VMP* curve to the left of the hypothetical competitive level of employment. The monopsonistic employer will purchase less labour than in the case of a competitive market, N_m. Nor is that the end of the matter: if he seeks only that amount of labour, the market-clearing wage rate is W_m, from the labour supply curve (*ALC*). He not only purchases less labour, but will pay a lower wage than if the market were competitive.

Now, suppose a union appears and organises the workers. The union demands a wage increase to $W_u > W_m$, and enters into an agreement with the employer (formal or informal) that he may hire as much or as little labour as he likes provided he pays W_u. Now the employer now faces a fixed *ALC* curve (and when an average is constant, the marginal equals the average). Hence his *MLC* is now a horizontal line from W_u, and, to maximise profits, he will purchase the quantity of labour for which *MLC* = *VMP*. The consequence of the arrival of the union is higher wages *and* higher employment. Total surplus in the economy is increased because, other things being equal, more labour hired means more goods being produced and lower product prices.

So there is a valid theoretical reason for concluding that the picture in Figure 13.4 may not represent the consequence of union activity in labour markets after all. Is this just another example of two-handed economics resulting in no conclusions? On balance, we think not. Although the second approach is useful in explaining some aspects of the labour market (for example, the role of unions in the public sector in mixed economies, where the employer is protected from competition and is the only employer), the assumption of weak competition among employers (market power) is less plausible when a longer-term view of labour markets in modern circumstances is adopted. In these circumstances, an assumption that markets are more rather than less competitive is in most circumstances more plausible. This reflects the observation that (especially given sufficient time) markets for final goods and markets for labour are subject to relatively free entry and exit.

Ease of entry into the final goods market reduces the market power of incumbent firms as purchasers of labour: they are likely to find themselves competing for labour more intensively and having to pay 'the going rate'. The monopsonistic market model has an implicit assumption that an employer is the only person to whom the workers can sell their labour. But labour mobility between jobs and between locations makes this hard to sustain as mobility forces employers to compete, and cannot exploit market power to pay wages that are below competitive levels. This, of course, reduces the incentive to join a union in the first place. The evidence of declining union membership across the developed world is the strongest argument for the competitive model's basic plausibility in the context of a modern capitalist economy.

Wages paid to workers in a unionised firm are sometimes 50 per cent or more above the wages paid to their non-unionised counterparts. This begs a question: how do firms with unionised workforces survive in a competitive environment? For example, consider the airline business: Ryanair has become the largest airline in the European market, and is non-unionised, but unionised airlines (some at least) have been able to continue to operate profitably. One answer is product differentiation: flying to more convenient airports, or offering superior service, in the case of airlines. More generally, unionised firms may be in a stronger position to select better applicants for jobs. Unionised workers who stay with a firm because of the higher wages may acquire firm-specific human capital. Job security can improve labour-force flexibility. Dispute settling may be easier. Labour turnover (and hiring and firing costs) may be reduced.

Unionisation is a more plausible explanation of wage differentials in Europe than in the United States. In the United States, unionisation now involves about 14 per cent of the workforce (down from 20 per cent in the early 1980s and 35 per cent in 1954). Furthermore, while the average is around 14 per cent, when public-sector employment is ignored, the average falls to 10 per cent (about 40 per cent of US public-sector employees are in a union). Because the union wage premium is small and applies to only a small fraction of the labour force, US union membership is probably not an important explanation for why workers with similar qualifications often earn sharply different incomes.

In Western Europe the average union density is higher although, in most countries, falling. In the EU15, in 2001, unionisation was about 30 per cent (measured as 'union density', the percentage of the dependent employed workforce belonging to a union). Within this average there was enormous variation: Sweden and Denmark had density levels around 80 per cent in 2004, while Spain's was about 16 per cent. Germany, France, Italy, the United Kingdom and the Netherlands were all within about 5 per cent of the average (not surprising, since they account for most of the EU15's employment). The pattern in Europe resembles that in the United States in that union density is much higher in the public sector. The larger size of public sectors in Europe boosts overall union density. In the United Kingdom, 60 per cent of public-sector employees are in unions. Only 20 per cent of private-sector employees are in a union, and this percentage is falling steadily. Union membership across the EU and in the US is higher among older than among younger workers, where it is falling significantly.

Unionisation helps to explain differences in pay and conditions between public and private sector employees in some European countries. Public-sector employment is less volatile, while pension entitlements are much greater. The impact of union power is stronger in the case of public-sector employment in parts of economies that are sheltered from competition. However, under EU liberalisation programmes, this is likely to be a diminishing influence on relative wages as between public- and private-sector employees.

Union influence on wage levels is also likely to be reduced by increased globalisation, especially reflecting the growing importance of foreign direct investment (FDI) in Europe. One reason is the increasing resistance of new employers to union recognition. The Irish experience points this out dramatically. Ireland has received a proportionately much greater share of non-EU FDI into the Union since the 1980s than any other EU15 country. The largest component of this *inward investment* came from US companies. But, while 80 per cent of FDI set-ups from other EU countries in Ireland between 1987 and 1997 involved union recognition (and 20 per cent did not), in the case of US-sourced FDI in Ireland the percentages were 90 per cent non-recognition and 10 per cent recognition.[2]

COMPENSATING WAGE DIFFERENTIALS

If people are paid the value of what they produce, why do panel beaters in a car repair shop earn more than lifeguards on a crowded summer beach? If your central heating unit breaks down. the hourly rate at which the repair technician is paid is likely to be higher than the hourly rate for an intensive-care unit staff nurse. In both examples most people would say the more important work is paid the lower wage.

---

[2] Gunnigle and O'Sullivan, 2003.

Economic Naturalist 13.2
Should workers on oil rigs, where risks to life and limb are significantly higher than in other occupations, welcome health and safety regulations that reduce job hazards?

It sounds like a no-brainer, but maybe they wouldn't. High-risk jobs carry higher rewards, and those who seek them have lower risk aversion than workers in general. This is a classic case of compensating wage differentials. Suppose the government imposes regulations that greatly reduce the job-related risks on oil rigs. The first consequence is that operating costs are increased. That will reduce the demand for labour on rigs. It will also reduce the need to pay workers to take on more risk. On the supply side, however, lower risk means more people with higher risk aversion will consider employment on rigs. Increased labour supply and weaker labour demand will put downward pressure on wages, and reduce the welfare of the low risk aversion current workers. So, now do you think they will they support the new regulations?

However, the amount paid to someone is not simply a matter of the value of what that person does, but, as Example 13.3 illustrates, the wage for a particular job depends not only on the value of what workers produce in that job, but also on how attractive they find the *working conditions* associated with the job.

Why do some public relations (PR) personnel earn more than others? **Example 13.3**

Suppose that on graduation you were offered a choice of two jobs, (a) working in a firm that specialises in dealing with the problems of organisations such as Oxfam and Médecins Sans Frontières, or (b) joining a firm that represents the interests of Imperial Tobacco, British American Tobacco and a couple of the oil majors. Except for the subject matter, working conditions are identical in the two jobs, and each pays €30,000 per year and offers the same prospects for advancement, which would you choose? When a similar question was recently posed to a sample of final-year undergraduate students at Cornell University, almost 90 per cent of them chose the first type of job. When asked how much more they would have to be paid to induce them to switch to the second type of job, their median response was a premium of $15,000 per year.

Other things being equal, we expect, then, that jobs with attractive working conditions will pay less than jobs with poor conditions. Wage differences associated with differences in working conditions are known as **compensating wage differentials**. Economists have identified compensating differentials for a host of different specific working conditions. Recent work on the UK labour market has shown a significant effect on wages from whether the firms concerned issued pollutants that posed a risk to health. When wages in 'clean industries' were compared with those in dirty industries. This was even more marked within 'dirty industries', where wages tended to be higher in the dirtier parts of industries.[3] Similarly, in the US empirical work has provided evidence of a positive correlation between risk to life among workers and wage rates (but with significantly different impacts as between workers from different racial backgrounds).[4] Studies have also found that wages vary in accordance with the attractiveness of the work schedule.

compensating wage differential a difference in the wage rate – negative or positive – that reflects the attractiveness of a job's working conditions

[3] Cole, Elliott and Lindley, 2009.

[4] Leeth and Ruser, 2003.

DISCRIMINATION IN THE LABOUR MARKET

Some of the claims about discrimination against women in labour markets can be dismissed as being based on incorrect use of labour-market statistics. For example, an extreme version asserts there is discrimination because taking all workers and comparing the average pay rates or earnings for males and females shows that male rates/earnings exceed female rates/earnings. Demonstrating that this proves nothing is easy. However, there are reasons for considering whether, how and why discrimination can still affect earnings. There is strong evidence in some areas that women and minorities continue to receive lower wage rates, on average, than white males with similar measures of human capital. If this can be shown to happen, it poses a profound challenge to standard theories of competitive labour markets, which hold that competitive pressures will eliminate wage differentials not based on differences in productivity. The standard defence of orthodoxy is to seek explanations by reference to unmeasured differences in human capital, and/or to preferences on the part of different categories of workers, and/or to differences in non-wage costs of employment across different groups of workers. This does not fully convince every critic, and the issue of assumptions of fully competitive markets may be unwarranted, in which case, as we shall see, discrimination is quite possible.

DISCRIMINATION BY EMPLOYERS

employer discrimination an arbitrary preference by an employer for one group of workers over another

Employer discrimination refers to wage differentials reflecting an arbitrary preference by an employer for one group of workers over another. It means that if two labour force groups, such as males and females, are on average equally productive yet an employer prefers hiring males and is willing to pay higher wages to do so. Similar considerations apply to career prospects and promotions, summed up in the case of gender differentials in the concept of the 'glass ceiling', the invisible barrier that reduces career advancement prospects for women.

Most consumers in most circumstances neither know nor care about the gender of workers producing a good, and are unwilling to pay more to reflect a gender preference. The implication is that, if many firms pay men more than women for comparable work, their profits will be smaller the more males it employs, because males cost more yet are no more productive. So female wages are less than male wages. This creates a profitable opportunity for any gender blind firm. The initial wage differential provides an opportunity for employers who hire mostly females to grow at the expense of their rivals. But as profit-seeking, non-discriminating firms continue to pursue a strategy of seeking women workers, female wage rates will start to rise. At the same time, lost market share by discriminating firms will reduce the demand for male labour. The process will continue until the wage of females reaches parity with the wage of males. The wage for both males and females will thus settle at the common value of their VMP.

The critical point to understand here is that the no free-lunch principle applies. Discrimination is costly to the discriminator. Giving preference in hiring or promotion to lower VMP workers rather than higher VMP workers must increase total costs. If he faces competition in the market into which he is selling the product of the firm, he will be undercut by firms that do not discriminate. Eventually he must cease discrimination or go out of business. Discrimination is feasible only as long as there are potential profits to be absorbed by the costs of discrimination. Competition from other firms eliminates that source of funds to finance discrimination.

Equilibrium

The only way to survive and discriminate is for the owners of such firms to be protected from the consequences of their actions either by government or by the absence of competitive pressure. Successful discrimination relies on absence of, or weak, competition and/or regulatory or legislative intervention that has the effect of supporting discrimination

DISCRIMINATION BY OTHERS

customer discrimination the willingness of consumers to pay more for a product produced by members of a favoured group, even if the quality of the product is unaffected

If employer discrimination is not the primary explanation of the wage gap in competitive markets, what is? In some instances, **customer discrimination** may provide a plausible explanation. If this sounds unlikely, think about Fair Trade coffee. Exactly who benefits and by how much from the marketing of Fair Trade coffee is a matter of some dispute, but what is clear is that consumers are prepared to pay more for a product produced by one group of producers than if produced by other workers. Or remember the reaction in the US to French opposition to the 2003 Gulf War: there was a consumer boycott of French wine for about six months, and wine sales fell, it is estimated, by about 13 per cent over the period (being down 27 per cent at the peak of the boycott).[5] If people believe that juries and clients are less likely to take female or minority ethnic group lawyers seriously, members of these groups will face a reduced incentive to attend law school, and law firms will face a reduced incentive to hire those who do.

Economic Naturalist 13.3
Why was Kavanagh a QC?

The status of Queen's (or King's) Counsel is something that barristers in Britain work hard to get. As senior counsel, they earn higher incomes, because they get cases that offer higher fees. Of course, being a senior barrister doesn't improve your ability, or your marginal product, relative to the day before you were 'called to the Inner Bar' . . . but your earnings increase (you hope . . . if the juicy briefs don't arrive you can't fall back on the day-to-day work of a junior barrister). The TV series, *Kavanagh QC*, was built around the eponymous senior counsel. The point is that the status is awarded only to those who are deemed to have demonstrated their ability. In effect, it's a quality approval mark. Acquiring it means signalling your superior ability. In 2003 the Lord Chancellor of England proposed to abolish the distinction on the basis of a view that somehow the status led to higher costs because QCs charged higher fees. The reality was that superior barristers could command higher fees with or without the quality mark, but the status of senior counsel enabled purchasers of the services to choose horses for courses. The proposal was dropped, to some extent because minority lawyers felt they would be disadvantaged by not being allowed to apply for a quality mark, and would suffer accordingly.

OTHER SOURCES OF THE WAGE GAP

Part of the wage gap may be explained by compensating wage differentials that spring from differences in preferences for other non-wage elements of the compensation package (see Economic Naturalist 13.2). Jobs that involve exposure to physical risk, for example, command higher wages, and if men are relatively more willing to accept such risks than women, they will earn more than females with otherwise identical stocks of human capital. (The same difference would result if employers felt constrained by social norms not to assign female employees to risky jobs.)

Elements of human capital that are difficult to measure may also help to explain earnings differentials. For example, productivity is influenced not only by the quantity of education an individual has, which is easy to measure, but also by its *quality*, which is much harder to measure. Part of the observed aggregate black–white differential in US wages may thus be due to the fact that schools in black neighbourhoods have not been as good, on average, as those in white neighbourhoods.

[5] Chavis and Leslie, 2008.

Differences in the courses at university or other third-level institutions appear to have similar implications for differences in productivity. For instance, students in maths, engineering or business – both male and female – tend to earn significantly higher salaries than those who study the humanities but do not acquire other professional training after graduating. If males are disproportionately represented in the former group, the result is a male wage premium unrelated to employer discrimination.

As economists have grown more sophisticated in their efforts to measure human capital and other factors that influence individual wage rates, unexplained wage differentials by sex and race have grown steadily smaller,[6] and have even disappeared altogether in some studies. Some work, however, continues to find significant unexplained differentials by race and sex.

WINNER-TAKE-ALL MARKETS

Differences in human capital do much to explain observed differences in earnings. Yet earnings differentials have also grown sharply in many occupations within which the distribution of human capital among workers seems essentially unchanged. Consider Economic Naturalist 13.4.

Economic Naturalist 13.4
Why did Tiger Woods at the peak of his career earn a multiple of the earnings of golfers of slightly lesser ability?

By 2007 Woods had earned about $770 millions in his professional career. Of this about $100 m was prize money, and about $670 m was from 'endorsements'. It was predicted he would have earned over $1 billion by 2010. In fact he hit that target in 2009. At his peak he earned about $128 million in 2009, while his nearest rival, Phil Mickelson, earned a mere (?) $62 millions. Alas, Woods' domestic problems then intervened: in the ensuing two years his earnings fell by 30 per cent. Other players earn what most people would regard as seriously high incomes, but which are still fractions of the top players' earnings. Why is this earnings differential so large?

The answer lies in a fundamental change in the way in which we follow sport compared with 50 years ago. This reflects the technology of communication. Today you can watch the US Open in real time and in colour from anywhere in the world. This has resulted in huge broadcasting revenues that feed through to prize money. People want to watch the best players, and they pocket the lion's share of the revenues. They get this by being better than others, not just for being good players. Off the course, the same applies: the best are paid to endorse products. That applies in all sports, but golf has enormous followings. To this should be added what can be earned by being involved in designing and upgrading courses . . . again, the best, not just the very good, get the contracts.

winner-take-all labour market one in which small differences in human capital translate into large differences in pay

The market for golf professionals is an example of a **winner-take-all labour market**, one in which small differences in ability or other dimensions of human capital translate into large differences in pay. Such markets have long been familiar in entertainment and professional sports. But as technology has enabled the most talented individuals to serve broader markets, the winner-take-all reward structure has become an increasingly important feature of modern economic life, permeating such diverse fields as law, journalism, consulting, medicine, investment banking, corporate management, publishing, design, fashion and even universities.

Contrary to what the name seems to imply, a winner-take-all market does not mean a market with literally only one winner. Indeed, hundreds of professional musicians

[6] Polackek and Kim, 1994.

earn multimillion-euro annual salaries. However, tens of thousands of others, many of them nearly as good, struggle to pay their bills.

The fact that small differences in human capital often give rise to extremely large differences in pay might seem to contradict human-capital theory. Note, however, that the winner-take-all reward pattern is completely consistent with the competitive labour market theory's claim that individuals are paid in accordance with the contributions they make to the *employer's net revenue*. The leverage of technology often amplifies small performance differentials into very large ones.

RECAP

Explaining differences in earnings among people

Earnings differ among people in part because of differences in their *human capital*, an amalgam of personal characteristics that affects productivity. But pay often differs substantially between two people with the same amount of human capital. This can happen for many reasons: one person may belong to a labour union while the other does not; one may work in a job with less pleasant conditions; one may be the victim of discrimination; or one may work in an arena in which technology or other factors provide greater leverage to human capital.

TRENDS IN INEQUALITY

In most market economies most citizens receive most of their income from the sale of their own labour. An attractive feature of the free-market system is that it rewards initiative, effort and risk taking: the harder, longer and more effectively a person works, the more he or she will be paid.

Yet relying on the market to distribute income also implies an important drawback: some people earn vastly more money than they can spend, while others often cannot afford even basic goods and services. The fact that there are people in Europe and the US who go to bed hungry at night, and that some are homeless has led to philosophical assertions that such poverty in the midst of plenty is impossible to justify on moral grounds. It is thus troubling that income inequality has been growing rapidly since the 1970s. The data in Table 13.2 offer an indication of the extent of this problem in the US context.

The US economy grew steadily at around 3 per cent from the end of the Second World War until the early 1970s. This growth in living standards affected most household, rich and poor, alike. In the ensuing years, however, the pattern of income growth has been dramatically different.

In the first column of Table 13.2, for example, notice that families in the bottom 20 per cent of the income distribution saw their share of (an admittedly growing) national income decline from 4.1 to 3.4 per cent, while the last column shows that

Table 13.2 Shares of Households in Total Household Income, US 1970–2008 by Income Quintile

	Lowest	2nd	3rd	4th	Highest
1970	4.1	10.8	17.4	24.5	43.5
1980	4.2	10.2	16.8	24.7	44.1
1990	3.8	9.6	15.9	24.0	46.6
2000	3.6	8.9	14.8	23.0	49.8
2008	3.4	8.6	14.6	23.2	50.3

Source: US Census Bureau.

the share of the top 20 per cent of households grew from 43.5 to 50.3 per cent. The share of the lower 60 per cent of households in total income declined from 32.3 to 26.6 per cent.

There can be little argument with the proposition that, whatever has happened to absolute incomes of households, in terms of shares in the total there has been a significant shift from the less well off to those at the top of the distribution. That said, it is important to emphasise that being near the bottom of the income distribution in one year does not necessarily mean being stranded there for ever. Many chief executive officers (CEOs) now earning multimillion-dollar pay cheques, for example, were struggling young graduate students in 1980, and were classified in the bottom 20 per cent of the income distribution for that year. We must bear in mind, too, that not all economic mobility is *upward*. Many US blue-collar workers, for instance, had higher real incomes in 1980 than they do today.

A NOTE ON POVERTY

Many aspects of government intervention in economic life are based on a policy aimed at reducing poverty. A simple and tautological definition of poverty is that it means being poor. However, that begs further questions. The first is how we decide what is 'poor'. We could argue that 'poor' means not being able to enjoy a defined level of consumption of goods and services. This means defining an 'absolute poverty line': those who cannot afford the defined bundle of purchases are in poverty. However this approach leads to a position in which, when a society's real income rises, and average standards of living rise, a family that could enjoy an average standard of living ten years ago, and was not treated as 'poor' could find itself at the bottom of the income distribution today and still not be poor. In other words, it ignores the relative income aspect of poverty: it is your standard of living relative to others' standards of living that determines to some extent whether we consider you to be poor.

Hence, measuring poverty, and the effectiveness of poverty policy, must first deal with the philosophical problem of absolute versus relative poverty lines. The former uses an ability to purchase a bundle of goods; the latter uses the position on the income distribution. Using an absolute definition can lead to absurd results. So, unfortunately can using a purely relative definition. A common way to compromise on this is to define poverty in terms of having a given percentage of the average or median income.

Then there is the issue of persistence. If, for example everyone had the same lifetime income, but it varied over the life cycle, we would still observe statistically, on absolute and relative bases, that there were 'rich' and 'poor' households. The question can be asked: is being poor today statistically correlated with being poor at some date in the future? Going further, we might ask whether a person's probability of being rich or poor reflects the income level of his/her parents? Is there intergenerational persistence of poverty?

This field of study in economics is large and extremely interesting, as well as statistically complex. We have touched only on a few better-known problems. Here all we can do is to alert the student of economics to the complexity of the questions involved.

MEASURING THE DISTRIBUTION OF INCOME OR WEALTH

Just as important as data such as those for the US in Table 13.2 is a means of measuring differences in distributions. Such a measure enables us to track how distributions change over time, or differ between countries. In addition, such a measure will help determine how fiscal or other interventions affect distributions. To do these things, we must have an *agreed and objective measure of income distribution*. Of the several measures available but the one that is most widely used and easiest to both understand and compute is what is known as the **Gini coefficient**. It does not, note, 'explain' the level or change in any distribution; it does not evaluate distributions (that in country *X* is worse or better than that in country *Y*); it merely provides a basis for *comparing distributions* on an objective numerical basis.

Gini coefficient a measure of equality of distribution that compares the actual distribution with a benchmark of absolute equality

The measure was developed by the Italian statistician, Corrado Gini (1884–1965), in a monograph published in 1912.[7] It measures the degree to which an observed distribution differs from a hypothetical perfectly equal distribution. It is demonstrated in graph form in Fig. 13.6.

On the vertical axis are the percentiles of the income distribution being measured from 0 to 100 per cent. On the horizontal axis are the percentiles of the population over which the distribution is being measured. If the income of the population was perfectly equally distributed, then any 1 per cent of the population would earn 1 per cent of total population income, and any 10 per cent or 20 per cent would earn 10 per cent or 20 per cent of the total. Starting, then, with an arbitrary 1 per cent of the population, then 2 per cent, then 3 per cent, and so on, and graphing the percentage of the total income they account for, we would get the 45° straight line in Fig. 13.6. Then, taking the actual distribution, we start with the poorest 1 per cent on the horizontal axis and plot their share of total income, then that of the bottom 2 per cent and continue until we have accounted for the entire population. The graph we get is called the **Lorenz curve**.[8]

Lorenz curve the graph of the cumulative distribution of income or wealth by percentages of households or individuals from poorest to richest

The Gini coefficient is the ratio of the area between the Lorenz curve and the 45° line (*A*) to the total area under the 45° line (*A* + *B*). It has a value somewhere between 0 (perfect equality) and 1 (one person has all the income, perfect inequality). The higher the value, the less equal is the distribution.

Table 13.3 contains data on Gini coefficients for a number of countries. The Gini coefficient is widely used, but it is not the only measure that is relevant to the measurement of income distribution. For example, instead of being concerned with a measure of equality over the entire range of incomes, we might be more interested in whether or not there is a wide disparity between those at the top of the distribution and those at the bottom. So in Table 13.3 we also include another statistic: the ratio of the average income among the top 10 per cent of incomes to that in the bottom 10 per cent, the UN 10 per cent Rich/Poor statistic. Notice that there is a far from perfect rank correlation between the two. This illustrates the potential to use and abuse statistics in debates about income inequality. The data refer to years between 2005 and 2008.

Table 13.4 shows values for several countries in years between 1993 and 2005. The values for the Gini coefficients in this table suggest that, broadly speaking, there has not been much change in the rankings across countries, and that there is some evidence of a trend towards greater equality in the countries with more unequal distributions.

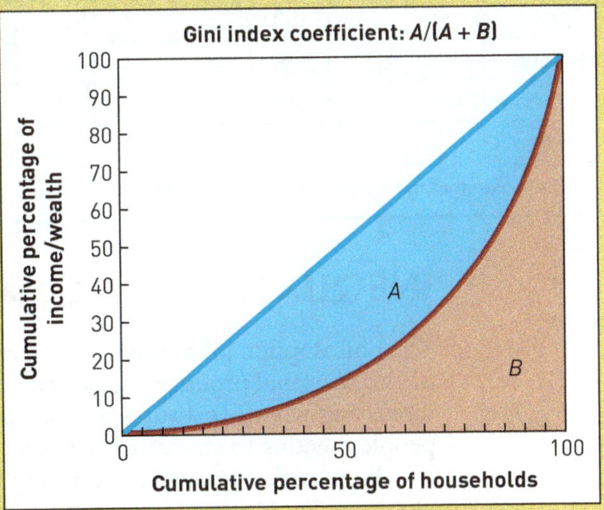

Figure 13.6 Gini Index: a Measure of Distribution

[7] Gini, 1912.

[8] Lorenz, 1905.

Table 13.3 Inequality Coefficients by Country

	UN R/P 10	Gini		UN R/P 10	Gini
Finland	5.6	.30	Italy	11.6	.32
Ukraine	5.9	.31	Kenya	13.6	.43
Norway	6.1	.25	UK	13.8	.34
Sweden	6.2	.25	Georgia	15.4	.41
Austria	6.9	.26	US	15.9	.45
Denmark	8.1	.29	China	21.6	.42
Belgium	8.2	.28	S. Africa	33.1	.65
India	8.6	.37	Argentina	40.9	.45
France	9.1	.33	Venezuela	48.3	.41
Ireland	9.4	.31	Brazil	51.3	

Source: R/P 10: UN, *Human Development Report* (2007/8); Gini: CIA World Factbook, 2008.

Table 13.4 Gini Coefficients by Country Over Time

	1993	1994	1995	1996	1997	1998	1999	2000	2001	2002	2003	2004	2005
Neth'ld		.257					.231						
Norway		.238						.251					
Sweden		.221						.252					.237
Swtzld								.280		.224			
Italy	.339		.338			.346		.333					
UK		.339	.344			.343							.345
USA	.355				.372			.368				.372	
Spain			.353					.336					
Poland			.318				.313						
Russia			.447					.434					
Mexico		.495		.477		.492		.491				.458	

Source: Luxembourg Income Study, based on OECD estimates.

INEQUALITY: A MORAL PROBLEM?

The philosopher, John Rawls of Harvard University, has constructed an ethical critique of the marginal productivity system based on the economic theory of choice itself.[9] In discussing what constitutes a 'just distribution of income', Rawls asks us to imagine people meeting to choose the rules for distributing income behind a 'veil of ignorance', which conceals from participants any knowledge of what talents and abilities each has. Not knowing his abilities relative to others, a person can't know what rules of distribution would work to his own advantage. Rawls argues that the rules people would choose in such a state of ignorance would necessarily be fair; and, if the rules are fair, the income distribution to which they give rise will also be fair.

[9] Rawls, 1971.

Rawls argues that in these circumstances, and if the national income were a fixed amount, most people support equal shares for all. That scenario is likely, Rawls argues, because most people are strongly risk averse. Since an unequal income distribution would involve not only a chance of doing well but a chance of doing poorly, most people would prefer to eliminate the risk by choosing an equal distribution. If diminishing marginal utility applies to wealth, a given chance of a given gain over the average income is less valuable than avoiding the same chance of the same loss relative to the average. Most of us, most of the time, behave in a risk-averse fashion. The logical extreme of the Rawlsian thought experiment is that people would choose a fully egalitarian outcome if they could not choose (or influence) their position in society. Given this, an egalitarian distribution is ethically superior to an unequal one.

Rawls' logic is appealing . . . but is not necessarily convincing, at least in its extreme version. It depends first of all on an assumption that a person's economic welfare depends on his income alone, and that no benefits are derived by anyone from the activities of those who are better off: no pop stars; no patrons of the arts. It also expressly assumes that the size of the cake is independent of the way it is sliced. This is fine for real cakes, but not for the 'cake' of gross national product (GNP). While there are several dissenting voices, most economists would support the proposition that a successful market economy cannot function properly without incentives that imply some *inequality of outcome*. If either or both of these factors is built into Rawls' thought experiment it is not at all obvious that a risk-averse individual would choose a highly equal distribution from behind a veil of ignorance.

The problem is that the attraction of a commitment to a high degree of equality is far from absolute when we consider its impact in the real world. For many, the goal of absolute equality is quickly trumped by other concerns when we set about making the rules for distributing wealth in modern market economies. If each person were guaranteed an equal amount of income, few would invest in education or the development of special talents; and the incentive to work would be sharply reduced. In a country without rewards for hard work and risk taking, national income would be dramatically smaller than in a country with such rewards. Material rewards for effort and risk taking necessarily lead to inequality.

Efficiency

Rawls accepts, to be fair, that people would be willing to accept a certain degree of inequality as long as these rewards produced a sufficiently large increase in the total amount of output available for distribution. But how much inequality would people accept? Much less than the amount produced by untrammelled competition, Rawls argues. The idea is that, behind the veil of ignorance, each person would fear ending up in a disadvantaged position, so each would choose rules that would produce a more equal distribution of income than exists under the marginal productivity system. Hence, Rawls argues, fairness requires at least some attempt to reduce the inequality produced by the market system. Most people would agree with this weaker Rawls proposition. After all, most people voluntarily redistribute income through gifts and donations to the poor or disaster relief: look at the global, non-governmental response to the tsunami catastrophe of Christmas 2004 in South-east Asia.

RECAP

Why is income inequality a moral problem?

John Rawls argues that the degree of inequality typical of unregulated market systems is unfair because people would favour substantially less inequality if they chose distributional rules from *behind a veil of ignorance*.

METHODS OF INCOME REDISTRIBUTION

A political consensus that the existing distribution of income is less than optimal leads to policies by government designed to improve the distribution. These take two basic forms. The first is to do something to change the *underlying factors* that produce the observed distribution. The second is to compensate for the *outcome observed*. An example of the first would be to improve the ability of children from poor families to obtain third-level education. An example of the second would be direct payments to households with incomes below some threshold value.

Although societies assert an interest in limiting income inequality, redistribution programmes are often fraught with practical difficulties. It is difficult to raise the incomes of those who cannot fend for themselves without at the same time undermining their incentive to work, and without using scarce resources to subsidise those who are not poor. Then there is the problem that taxes to finance redistribution may reduce the *global income* from which the funds are raised.

Of course, some people simply cannot work, or cannot find work that pays enough to live on. In a world of perfect information, the government could make generous cash payments to those people, and withhold support from those who can fend for themselves. In practice, however, the two groups are often hard to distinguish. So we must choose among imperfect alternative measures.

Redistribution takes place through one or both of two channels. The first is designing the *tax structure*, which produces the revenues to finance government spending, in such a way that those with greater resources pay more for the services provided to all, or to some. If this is the case the incidence of taxation is 'progressive' (as opposed to 'regressive', when the incidence is heavier on those with fewer resources). The second is a bias in the *composition of public spending* towards providing income or services to those with fewer resources. The net redistributive impact of the government reflects the balance of the effects of policies on taxation and spending. Hence it can be misleading to judge a particular tax or spending item without looking at the overall impact of all taxes and spending structures in order to judge the effectiveness of the government in terms of income redistribution.

WELFARE PAYMENTS AND IN-KIND TRANSFERS

In all advanced countries the government tries to alter the distribution of income and wealth by creating entitlements to money payments and by providing goods and services free of charge or at a price that is below the cost of provision. Economists have long argued the merits of these two approaches. The balance of conclusions is that *money payments* are preferable to provision of what are really benefits in kind.

in-kind transfer a payment made not in the form of cash, but in the form of a good or service

In-kind transfers are direct transfers of goods or services to low-income individuals or families. This includes both free-of-charge provision and provision at below cost. Examples are subsidised public housing, subsidised school meals, education without fees and 'free' medical care. In many European jurisdictions they also include some more dubious features such as benefits to defined groups of people: for example, the elderly benefit from such things as free public transport, exemption from refuse collection charges, and reductions in the price of electricity. Economists criticise these on two grounds. The first is that (unless you do not trust those on low incomes to spend wisely) it is axiomatically true that it is welfare enhancing for the poor to give them money to spend as they wish rather than to constrain them to consume a predetermined bundle of goods of equal cost. The second is that in-kind transfers tend not to be accurately related to the means of those receiving them. Why should we think that all those over 65 (the elderly) are poor? This approach benefits the rich and poor alike. The motivation is to help the poor; the effect is to transfer real resources to recipients regardless of their means.

Monetary transfers consist of cash (or equivalent) payments to recipients who are designated by some standard as entitled to the payment. Non-contributory old age pensions are an example of this kind of payment. Children's allowances are another.

The single most important element in this structure is *unemployment relief*: people who are unable to find work are entitled to a replacement of their earnings by a sum paid by the state. In the United States such payments are severely limited in terms of the duration of any period of receipt of payments. European countries are mostly much more liberal. Obviously, unemployment is the most important proximate cause of poverty, so entitling the unemployed to cash income support tackles poverty head on. Unfortunately, it can have perverse incentive effects, since it can discourage people from accepting employment. This is why there is growing pressure in Europe to follow the US model and make it limited in duration – and, where it is already limited, to reduce the period further.

UNIVERSALITY AND MEANS TESTING

In the United States there is a strong bias towards a system of cash or in-kind benefits based on objective means testing. To qualify for Medicaid, households have to demonstrate a level of income that is sufficiently low to qualify for the health cost benefit. The Aid to Families with Dependent Children (AFDC) programme is **means-tested** on a sliding scale. In Europe there is a stronger emphasis on universalist provision. The UK's universal National Health Service (NHS) is a classic example. Child-support payments, a common feature of European social support structures in one form or another, are a further example.

> **means-tested** a benefit programme whose benefit level declines as the recipient earns additional income

It appears wasteful and illogical to raise taxes in order to make payments to the very people from whom the tax is raised rather than raise less taxation and deliver the funds to those who are less well off. There are, however, two strong counter-arguments supporting a universalist approach. The first is an administrative one, and one that also has an element of social sensitivity in it. This is the argument that (a) it is significantly more costly to devise, administer and modify a social spending programme that is based on establishing recipients' qualifications to receive transfers, and (b) it is kinder and more effective to support people in need without requiring them to devote time and resources to proving that they meet the legal requirements of an entitlement. The second argument concerns what is known as the *poverty trap*. If a family that is entitled to, say, a rent subsidy manages to increase its income but in so doing ceases to be eligible for the subsidy, the loss of the subsidy is in effect a tax on the extra income the family has earned. Unemployment benefit implies a tax on taking up a job offer. Programmes of support to single mothers frequently mean that if the father co-habits with the mother and helps support the family, the support is withdrawn. That does not exactly encourage two-parent families. This kind of thing can lead to a position in which poorer families face an extremely high *effective marginal tax rate* if they take steps that will reduce their poverty and, as a result, have a very weak incentive to take those steps, thus creating for them the 'poverty trap'.

INCOME TAX AND REDISTRIBUTION

One obvious way of dealing with the issues just discussed is to apply income tax to any universal social-support programme receipts. This has the effect of (a) ensuring that the benefits flow preponderantly to those on lower incomes, and (b) the level of payment can be increased without increasing taxes generally. The potential to use the tax system as the engine for redistribution that this raises has been the subject of debate among both economists and social workers. It has been suggested that it might be possible to replace the whole panoply of income-support programmes by a reform of the tax code. The central element in this proposal is what is called **negative income tax (NIT)**.

> **negative income tax (NIT)** a system under which the government would grant every citizen a cash payment each year, financed by an additional tax on earned income

There are several variants of this concept, but they have in common the idea that income tax takes away a proportion of the payer's income over some threshold, and that the threshold could be used as a basis for paying money to people whose incomes are below that threshold. For example, suppose there is a 25 per cent income tax on family incomes above, say, €10,000 per annum. This would be replaced by a tax of 25 per cent of (income – €10,000). A household with an income of €8,000 would face a tax bill of €0.25(8,000 – 10,000) = –€500. A negative tax bill is, of course, a receipt. The family would receive a cheque for €500, an NIT payment. In this case everyone, regardless of income, faces the same effective tax rate. If a family with €15,000 earns an extra €1,000, it retains €750 (75 per cent) and pays €250 (25 per cent) in tax. A family with €8,000 that earns an extra €1,000 keeps the whole €1,000, but receives €250 rather than €500. The extra €1,000 leaves it with a net increase of €750 (75 per cent) as it loses the €250 (25 per cent) NIT payment.

The big problem with this type of proposal is the incentive difficulty. Note that in the last example a household with no income at all would receive €2,500. Suppose (rather unrealistically) that this constituted what the government considered to be the **poverty threshold**, the level of income below which a family is 'poor' – i.e. has insufficient income to sustain an acceptable lifestyle. At a marginal effective tax rate of 25 per cent, no one would pay any tax to the Exchequer until they had an income four times the poverty level. A widely used poverty threshold is 40 per cent of the average industrial wage. On that basis no one earning less than 160 per cent of the average industrial wage would pay any income tax. In most Western economies that would mean about 60 per cent of households paying no income tax. It would be very difficult to finance current government spending programmes if only 40 per cent of people paid any income taxes, and then only at 25 per cent for some time after hitting the threshold, unless taxes on the rest were confiscatory, something that would have very serious incentive effects on work effort and risk taking.

> **poverty threshold** the level of income below which a family is 'poor'

Exercise 13.4 Using the data above, what would the tax rate have to be if everyone below and those just above the tax threshold (€10,000) were to face the same effective tax rate while the poverty threshold is set at half the tax threshold?

Finally, the higher the basic payment (the poverty threshold) relative to the income tax threshold, the lower is the incentive to work at all, since work does, you will remember, have an *opportunity cost*: what you can do with the time you spend working if you don't work.

MINIMUM WAGES

Very many, but not all, industrialised countries have sought to increase the standard of living of low-wage workers by enacting general minimum wage legislation – laws that prohibit all employers from paying workers less than a specified hourly wage. Of those that haven't, the majority have sectoral or industrial minimum wage provisions, affecting significant numbers of employees. The general minimum wage rate varies from country to country. Figure 13.7 shows the structure of minimum wages as of early 2011 in the EU, candidate countries and EFTA countries in Europe. Several countries without a statutory minimum wage have sectoral wage floors covering a significant part of the economy based on collective bargaining mechanisms. Outside Europe, in 2008, while there were widespread sectorally binding minimum rates in force in both countries, neither South Africa nor Australia had a generally applicable minimum wage rate. In the US the Federal rate was set at $7.25 per hour in 2009. This sets a minimum value for minimum wages for covered workers in all states. Many states have higher

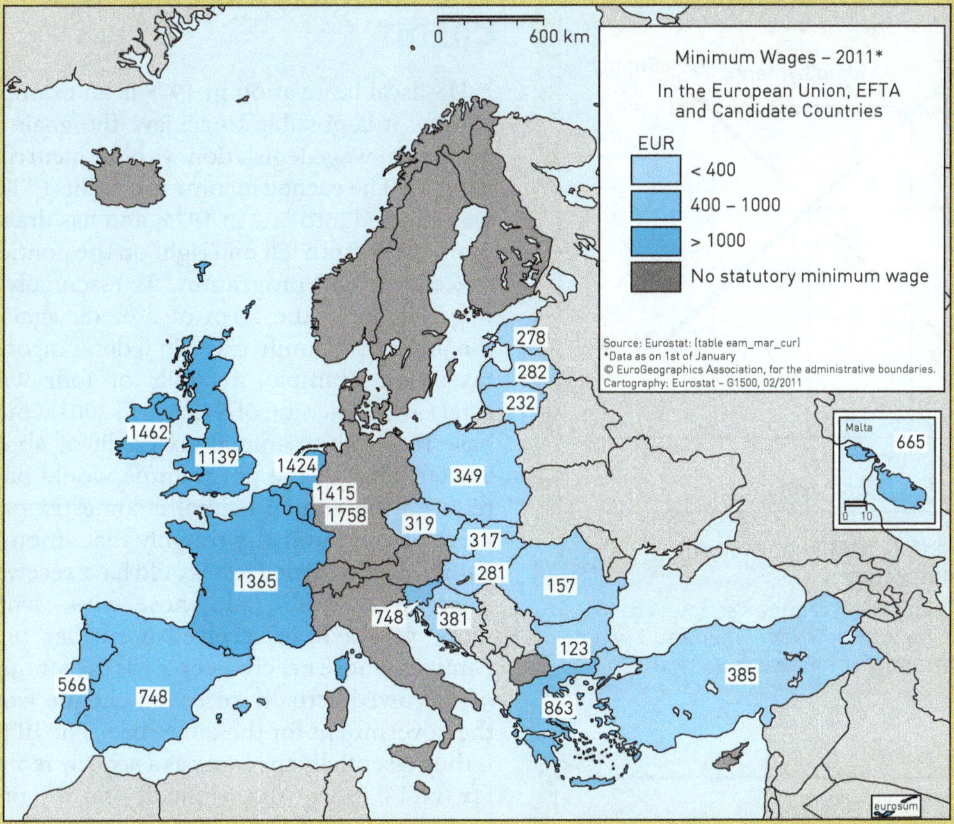

Figure 13.7 Minimum Wages in the EU, Candidate and EFTA Countries
Source: *Eurostat*, January, 2011.

minimum wages than the Federal rate, and some have lower minimum wages for workers not covered by the Federal rate. In New Zealand it was NZ$13 per hour from April, 2011. In Australia it is Aus $569.90 per month from 2010. South Africa has different sectoral minimum wages covering several sectors of the economy.

Economists as a whole tend to be critical of minimum wage legislation on the grounds that elementary theory suggests that such interventions in labour markets damage employment prospects and hurt those not covered by the minimum wage. Some economists have now questioned this blanket opposition to minimum wage laws, citing studies that have failed to show significant reductions in employment following increases in minimum wage levels. These studies may well imply that, as a group, low-income workers are better off with minimum wage laws than without them. But as we saw in Chapter 6, any policy that prevents a market from reaching equilibrium causes a reduction in *total economic surplus* – which means society ought in principle to be able to find a more effective policy for helping low-wage workers.

Efficiency

How does a minimum wage affect the market for low-wage labour? In Fig. 13.8, note that when the law prevents employers from paying less than W_{min}, employers hire fewer workers (a decline from L_0 to L_1). Unemployment results. The L_1 workers who keep their jobs earn more than before, but the $L_0 - L_1$ workers who lose their jobs earn nothing. Whether workers together earn more or less than before thus depends on the *elasticity of demand for labour*. If elasticity of demand is less than 1, workers as a group will earn more than before. If it is more than 1, workers as a group will earn less.

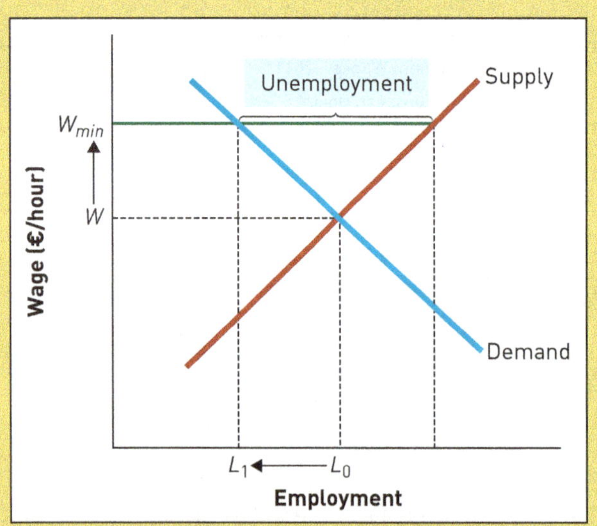

Figure 13.8 The Effect of Minimum Wage Legislation on Employment

If minimum wage legislation requires employers to pay more than the equilibrium wage, the result will be a decline in employment for low-wage workers.

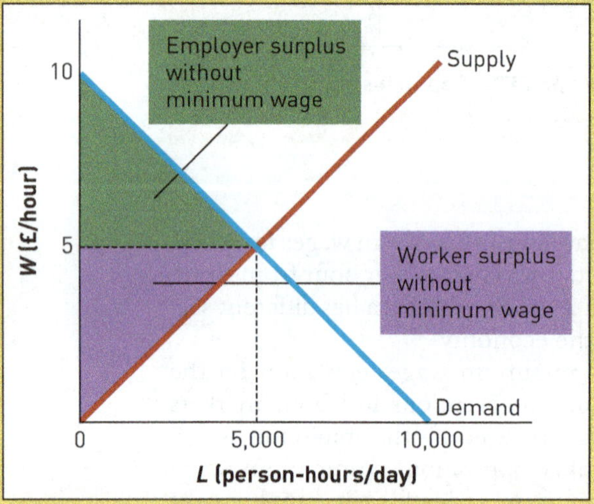

Figure 13.9 Worker and Employer Surplus in an Unregulated Labour Market

For the demand and supply curves shown, worker surplus is the area of the lower shaded triangle, £12,500 per day, the same as employer surplus (upper shaded triangle).

THE EARNED INCOME TAX CREDIT

A US fiscal innovation in 1975 is an example of how it is possible to achieve the goals of minimum wage legislation without incurring its costs. The earned income tax credit (EITC) was enacted into law in 1975, and has drawn praise from both left and right on the political spectrum. The programme is essentially a *wage subsidy* in the form of a credit against the amount a family owes in federal income taxes. For example, a family of four with total earned income of $13,000 in 2001 would have received an annual tax credit of about $4,000. That is, the programme would have reduced the annual federal income tax payment of this family by roughly that amount. Families who earned less would have received a larger tax credit, and those who earned more would have received a smaller one. Families whose tax credit exceeds the amount of tax owed actually receive a cheque from the government for the difference. The EITC is thus essentially the same as a *negative income tax* (NIT), except that eligibility for the programme is confined to people who work. Like both the NIT and the minimum wage, the EITC puts extra income into the hands of workers who are employed at low wage levels. But unlike the minimum wage, the EITC creates no incentive for employers to lay off low-wage workers.

In contrast to the EITC, we can think of the minimum wage as an *off-budget tax* on employers of low-wage workers, the proceeds of which are transferred to the employee rather than to the government. Unless minimum wage recipients are exempt from income tax and social security contributions, minimum wage systems have the bizarre implication that they tax the employment of low-skill labour by employers (reducing the demand for such labour) and then tax the tax in the hands of the recipient.

Example 13.4 By how much will a minimum wage reduce total economic surplus?

Suppose the demand and supply curves for unskilled labour in the Birmingham labour market are as shown in Fig. 13.9. By how much will the imposition of a minimum wage at £7 per hour reduce total economic surplus? By how much do worker surplus and employer surplus change as a result of adopting the minimum wage?

In the absence of a minimum wage, the equilibrium unskilled wage for Birmingham would be £5 per hour, and employment would be 5,000 person-hours per day. Both employers and workers would enjoy economic surplus equal to the area of the shaded triangles in Fig. 13.9: £12,500 per day.

With a minimum wage set at £7 per hour, employer surplus is the area of the upper shaded triangle in Fig. 13.10, £4,500 per day, and worker surplus is the area of the lower-left shaded area, £16,500 per day. The minimum wage thus reduces employer surplus by £8,000 per day and increases worker surplus by £4,000 per day. The net reduction in surplus is the area of the right-hand shaded triangle shown in Fig. 13.10: £4,000 per day.

Exercise 13.5

In Example 13.4, by how much would total economic surplus have been reduced by the £7 minimum wage if labour demand in Birmingham had been perfectly inelastic at 5,000 person-hours per day?

Example 13.5 illustrates the central message of the efficiency principle, which is that if the economic 'pie' can be made larger, everyone can have a larger slice.

Example 13.5

Refer to Example 13.4. How much would it cost the government each day to provide EITC under which workers as a group receive the same economic surplus as they do under the £7 per hour minimum wage? (Assume for simplicity that the EITC has no effect on labour supply.)

With an EITC in lieu of a minimum wage, employment will be 5,000 person-hours per day at £5 per hour, just as in the unregulated market. Since worker surplus in the unregulated market was £4,000 per day less than under the minimum wage, the government would have to offer a tax credit worth £0.80 per hour for each of the 5,000 person-hours of employment to restore worker surplus to the level obtained under the £7 minimum wage. With an EITC of that amount in effect, worker surplus would be the same as under the £7 minimum wage.

Equilibrium

If the EITC were financed by a £4,000 tax on employers, employer surplus would be £4,000 greater than under the £7 minimum wage.

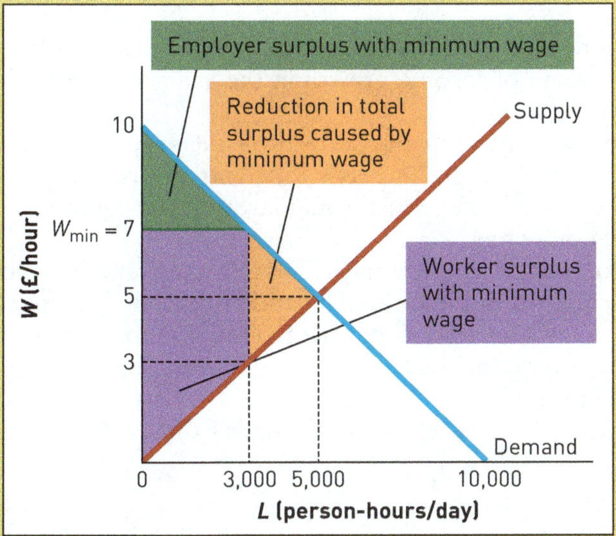

Figure 13.10 The Effect of a Minimum Wage on Economic Surplus

A minimum wage of £7 per hour reduces employment in this market by 2,000 person-hours per day, for a reduction in total economic surplus of £4,000 per day (area of the right-hand shaded triangle). Employer surplus falls to £4,500 per day (area of upper shaded triangle), while worker surplus rises to £16,500 per day (lower-left shaded area).

We stress that our point is not that the minimum wage produces no gains for low-income workers, but rather that it is possible to provide even larger gains for these workers if we avoid policies that try to prevent labour markets from reaching equilibrium.

SUMMARY

- A worker's long-run equilibrium pay in a competitive labour market will be equal to the value of her marginal product (VMP) – the market value of whatever goods and services she produces for her employer. The law of diminishing returns says that when a firm's capital and other productive inputs are held fixed in the short run, adding workers beyond some point results in ever-smaller increases in output. Firms that purchase labour in competitive labour markets face a constant wage, and they will hire labour up to the point at which VMP equals the *market wage*.
- *Human capital theory* says that an individual's VMP is proportional to his stock of human capital – an amalgam of education, experience, training, intelligence and other factors that influence productivity. According to this theory, some occupations pay better than others simply because they require larger stocks of human capital.
- Wages often differ between individuals whose stocks of human capital appear nearly the same, as when one belongs to a labour union and the other does not. Compensating *wage differentials* – wage differences associated with differences in working conditions – are another important explanation for why individuals with similar human capital might earn different salaries. They help to explain why refuse collectors earn more than lifeguards and, more generally, why individuals with a given stock of human capital tend to earn more in jobs that have less attractive working conditions.
- Many firms pay members of certain groups – notably minority groups and women – less than they pay other people who seem to have similar employment characteristics. If such *wage gaps* are the result of employer discrimination, their existence implies profit opportunities for firms that do not discriminate. Several other factors, including discrimination by customers and institutions other than firms, may explain at least part of the observed wage gaps.
- Technologies that allow the most productive individuals to serve broader markets can translate even small differences in human capital into enormous differences in pay. Such technologies give rise to *winner-take-all* markets, which have long been common in sports and entertainment, and which are now becoming common in other professions.
- Although incomes grew at almost 3 per cent a year for all income classes from the 1950s to the 1980s, the lion's share of income growth in the years since has been concentrated among the *top earners*.
- Philosophers have argued that at least some *income redistribution* is justified in the name of fairness, because if people chose society's distributional rules without knowing their own personal circumstances, most would favour less inequality than would be produced by market outcomes.
- Policies and programmes for *reducing poverty* include minimum-wage laws, the EITC, food and housing vouchers, subsidised school lunches, free healthcare, public housing and income supplements. Of these, all but the EITC fail to maximise total economic surplus, either by interfering with work incentives or by preventing markets from reaching equilibrium.
- The NIT works much like the EITC, except that it includes those who are not employed.

REVIEW QUESTIONS

1. Why is the supply curve of labour for any specific occupation likely to be upward-sloping, even if, for the economy as a whole, people work fewer hours when wage rates increase?
2. True or false: If the human capital possessed by two workers is nearly the same, their wage rates will be nearly the same. Explain.
3. How might recent changes in income inequality be related to the proliferation of technologies that enable the most productive individuals to serve broader markets?
4. Give two self-interested reasons that a top earner might favour policies to redistribute income.
5. Why is exclusive reliance on the negative income tax unlikely to constitute a long-term solution to the poverty problem?

PROBLEMS

Problems marked with an asterisk (*) are more difficult.

connect

1. H2Oclean Ltd supplies domestic kitchen water filters to the retail market in Essex and hires workers to assemble the components. An air filter sells for €26, and H2Oclean can buy the components for each filter for €1. Kevin and Sharon are two workers for H2Oclean Ltd. Sharon can assemble 60 air filters per month, and Kevin can assemble 70. If the labour market is perfectly competitive, how much will each be paid?
2. Stone, Inc. owns a clothing factory, hiring workers in a competitive market to cut denim to make jeans. The fabric costs €5 per pair. The company's weekly output varies with labour usage, as shown in the table below.

Number of workers	Jeans (pairs/week)
0	0
1	25
2	45
3	60
4	72
5	80
6	85

   a. If the jeans sell for €35 a pair, and the competitive market wage is €250 per week, how many workers should Stone hire? How many pairs of jeans will the company produce each week?
   b. Suppose the Clothing Workers Union now sets a weekly minimum acceptable wage of €230 per week. All the workers Stone hires belong to the union. How does the minimum wage affect Stone's decision about how many workers to hire?
   c. If the minimum wage set by the union had been €400 per week, how would the minimum wage affect Stone's decision about how many workers to hire?
   d. If Stone again faces a market wage of €250 per week but the price of jeans rises to €45, how many workers will the company now hire?

3. Reacteurs de France, SA (RdF), supplier of engines for France's space exploration programme, hires workers to assemble the components. An engine sells for €30,000, and RdF can buy the components for each engine for €25,000. Belmondo and Halliday are two workers for RdF. Belmondo can assemble 1/5 of an engine per month, and Halliday can assemble 1/10. If the labour market is perfectly competitive and components are RdF's only other cost, how much will each be paid?

4. Carolyn owns a soda factory and hires workers in a competitive labour market to bottle the soda. Her company's weekly output of bottled soda varies with the number of workers hired, as shown in the table below.

Number of workers	Cases/week
0	0
1	200
2	360
3	480
4	560
5	600

   a. If each case sells for €10 more than the cost of the materials used in producing it and the competitive market wage is €1,000 per week, how many workers should Carolyn hire? How many cases will be produced per week?
   b. Suppose the Soda Bottlers Union now sets a weekly minimum acceptable wage of €1,500 per week. All the workers Carolyn hires belong to the union. How does the minimum wage affect Carolyn's decision about how many workers to hire?
   c. If the wage is again €1,000 per week but the price of soda rises to €15 per case, how many workers will Carolyn now hire?

5. Suppose the equilibrium wage for unskilled workers in New Jersey is $7 per hour. How will the wages and employment of unskilled workers in New Jersey change if the state legislature raises the minimum wage from $5.15 per hour to $6 per hour?

6. Jones, who is currently unemployed, is a participant in three means-tested welfare programmes: food vouchers, rent vouchers and day care vouchers. Each programme grants him €150 per month in vouchers, which can be used like cash to purchase the good or service they cover.
   a. If benefits in each programme are reduced by 40 cents for each additional euro Jones earns in the labour market, how will Jones' economic position change if he accepts a job paying €120 per week?
   b. In the light of your answer to part (a), explain why means testing for welfare recipients has undesirable effects on work incentives.

7. Sue is offered a job re-shelving books in the University of Limerick library from noon until 1 pm each Friday. Her reservation wage for this task is €10 per hour.
   a. If the library director offers Sue €100 per hour, how much economic surplus will she enjoy as a result of accepting the job?
   b. Now suppose the library director announces that the earnings from the job will be divided equally among the 400 students who live in Sue's residence. Will Sue still accept?
   c. Explain how your answers to parts (a) and (b) illustrate one of the incentive problems inherent in income redistribution programmes.

8. Can you explain why professional golfers earn more from endorsements than professional snooker player?

9.* Suppose the demand and supply curves for unskilled labour in the Bremen labour market are as shown in the graph below. By how much will the imposition of a minimum wage of €12 per hour reduce total economic surplus? Calculate the amounts by which employer surplus and worker surplus change as a result of the minimum wage.

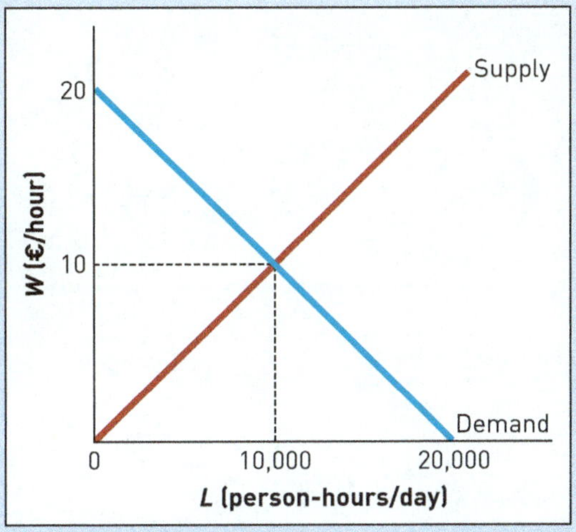

10.* Refer to Problem 8. How much would it cost the government each day to provide an EITC under which workers as a group receive the same economic surplus as they do under the €12 per hour minimum wage? (Assume for simplicity that the EITC has no effect on labour supply.)

REFERENCES

Babcock, L., C. Camerer, G. Loewenstein and R. Thaler 'Labor supply of New York City cab drivers: one day at a time', *Quarterly Journal of Economics*, vol. 111.

Chavis, L. and P. Leslie 'Consumer Boycotts: The impact of the Iraq war on French wine sales in the US', *Quantitative Marketing and Economics*, vol. 7.

Cole, M.A., R.J.R. Elliott and J.K. Lindley 'Dirty Money: Is there a premium for working in a pollution intensive industry?' *Journal of Risk and Uncertainty*, vol. 39.

Gini, C. *Variabilità e mutabilità: contributo allo studio delle distribuzioni e delle relazioni statistiche* (Bologna: Tipografi a di Paolo Cuppin).

Gunnigle, P. and M. O'Sullivan 'Organized labour in the Celtic tiger: trends in trade union penetration in the Republic of Ireland', 13th Congress of the International Industrial Relations Association, Berlin.

Leeth, J.D. and J. Ruser 'Compensating Wage Differentials For fatal and Non-fatal Injuries by Gender and Race', *Journal of Risk and Uncertainty*, vol. 27.

Lorenz, M.O. 'Methods of measuring the concentration of wealth', *Publications of the American Statistical Association*, vol. 9.

Polackek, S. and M. Kim 'Panel estimates of the male–female earnings functions', *Journal of Human Resources*, vol. 29.

Rawls, J. (1971) *A Theory of Justice* (Cambridge, MA: Harvard University Press).

Chapter 14

Government in the Market Economy: Public Sector Production and Regulation

Business ethics is to ethics as Monopoly money is to money. — *Harold Hendersen*

Learning Objectives

After reading this chapter, you should be able to:

1. Understand the difference between public and private goods;
2. Define efficiency in public goods production;
3. Recognise the rationale for market and non-market production of public goods;
4. Appreciate regulation as a remedy for market failure;
5. Understand regulatory mechanisms;
6. Appreciate the possibility and consequences of regulatory failure;
7. Understand the micro foundations of the Financial Crisis.

In this chapter we look at the role of government in the market economy under two headings. The first of these is where government acts directly to organise production of goods and services. In the main this involves what are known as *public goods* and *merit goods*. The second is the role of government as regulator of how markets work.

GOVERNMENT IN THE ECONOMY: PRODUCING PUBLIC GOODS

In most economies the government has a significant role as a producer of goods and services that are either consumed or are inputs into further production. To see this, just think of the size of the public sector and the functions and products for which it is responsible. Economists usually consider such activities under two headings: **public goods** and **merit goods**.

The term 'public goods' is used to describe certain outputs that for technical reasons simply cannot be produced efficiently if production is left to the interaction of supply and demand in a market. By 'efficiently' is meant the quantity being produced being that for which marginal benefits equal marginal costs.

public good a good or service that, to at least some degree, is both non-rival and non-excludable

merit goods goods produced under non-market conditions by the state for political reasons

Merit goods are goods that can be efficiently produced in markets, but for political reasons are produced under non-market conditions by the state. Obvious examples are health services, education and housing. All these can be, and are, produced in markets in nearly all countries . . . but are also produced by (or for) the state to allocate on a basis other than conventional demand expressed in terms of willingness to pay.

The involvement of the state in the provision of merit goods is pervasive, but in the end reflects political rather than economic pressures. Public goods provision, on the other hand, is the consequence of purely economic factors affecting the potential for market provision of certain types of output. As we shall see, the provision of public goods requires collective decisions on whether to produce them, how much to produce and finding the money to pay for provision.

PUBLIC GOODS VERSUS PRIVATE GOODS

Government spending in OECD countries is equivalent to 30–50 per cent of GNP, varying between countries. Much of this is, of course, *redistribution*. But, typically, half or more represents the cost of government direct provision of goods and services (the justice system, for example, or defence forces' salaries). Another tranche represents purchases of the output of private-sector firms (for example, when public housing, roads, hospitals or ground attack fighters are produced). Then there are state-owned enterprises that sell goods or services to firms or consumers (for example, state-owned energy producers).

In many cases these are 'merit' goods. In the other cases the spending is on 'public' goods. In this treatment of the government as an *economic agent* concentrate on considering the issue of public goods provision.

A 'public good' is one that is, **non-rival** and **non-excludable**. A non-rival good is one whose consumption by one person does not diminish its availability for others. For example, if the armed forces prevent a hostile nation from invading your city, your enjoyment of that protection does not diminish its value to your neighbours. A good is non-excludable if it is difficult to exclude non-payers from consuming it. For instance, even if your neighbours don't pay their share of the cost of maintaining an army, they will still enjoy its protection.

> **non-rival good** a good whose consumption by one person does not diminish its availability for others
>
> **non-excludable good** a good that it is difficult, or costly, to exclude non-payers from consuming

Another example of a non-rival and non-excludable good is a terrestrial (i.e. not via cable or satellite) TV broadcast. The fact that you tune in one evening does not make the programme any less available to others, and once the broadcast has been broadcast 'to air' (you may ask why it is called 'terrestrial'!) anyone can receive it. Similarly, when the millennium celebrations in many cities across the world involved magnificent fireworks displays, the municipal authorities concerned couldn't charge people for watching, given that the display was (and had to be) visible over a wide area, although private individuals could charge viewers if they owned or provided a limited amount of superior viewing facilities.

In contrast, the typical *private* good is diminished one-for-one by any individual's consumption of it. For instance, when you eat a sandwich, it is no longer available for anyone else, while people can easily be prevented from consuming sandwiches if they don't pay.

Exercise 14.1

Which of the following, if any, is non-rival?

a. The website of the EU Commission at 3 am.
b. The World Cup soccer championship game watched in person.
c. The World Cup soccer championship game watched on TV.

Goods that are both highly non-excludable and non-rival are often called **pure public goods**. Two reasons favour government provision of such goods. First, for-profit private companies would have obvious difficulty recovering their cost of production. Many people might be willing to pay enough to cover the cost of producing the good, but if it is non-excludable, the company cannot easily charge for it (the free-rider problem). And, second, if the marginal cost of serving additional users is zero once the good has been produced, then charging for the good would be inefficient, even if there were some practical way to do so.

pure public good a good or service that, to a high degree, is both non-rival and nonexcludable

collective good a good or service that, to at least some degree, is non-rival but excludable

This inefficiency often characterises the provision of **collective goods** – non-rival goods for which it is possible to exclude non-payers. Pay-per-view cable television is an example. People who don't subscribe to Sky TV may be unable to view some programmes as soon as subscribers can. This explains the controversy over restricting broadcasting rights to football games to pay-TV channels. Since the marginal cost to society of those excluded from viewing is literally zero, excluding these viewers is wasteful.

A **pure private good** is one from which non-payers can easily be excluded and for which one person's consumption creates a one-for-one reduction in the good's availability for others. The theory of perfectly competitive supply developed in Chapter 5 applies to pure private goods.

A **pure commons good** is a rival good that is also non-excludable, so called because goods with this combination of properties almost always result in a tragedy of the commons (see Chapter 11). Fish stocks in ocean waters are an example.

pure private good one for which non-payers can easily be excluded and for which each unit consumed by one person means one unit fewer available for others

pure commons good one for which non-payers cannot easily be excluded and for which each unit consumed by one person means one unit fewer available for others

The classification scheme defined by the non-rival and non-excludable properties is summarised in Table 14.1. The columns of indicate the extent to which one person's consumption of a good fails to diminish its availability for others. Goods in the right-hand column are non-rival, and those in the left-hand column are not. The rows indicate the difficulty of excluding non-payers from consuming the good. Goods in the top row are non-excludable, those in the bottom row, excludable. Private goods (lower-left cell) are rival and excludable. Public goods (upper-right cell) are non-rival and non-excludable. The two hybrid categories are commons goods (upper-left cell), which are rival but non-excludable, and collective goods (lower-right cell), which are excludable but non-rival.

Collective goods are provided sometimes by government, sometimes by private companies. Most pure public goods are provided by government, but even private companies can sometimes find profitable ways of producing goods that are both non-rival *and* non-excludable. An example is broadcast radio and TV, which covers its costs by selling airtime to advertisers.

Table 14.1 Private, Public and Hybrid Goods

		Non-rival	
		Low	High
Non-excludable	High	Commons good (fish in the ocean)	Public good (national defence)
	Low	Private good (wheat)	Collective good (pay-per-view TV)

This broadcasting example shows us that the mere fact that a good is a pure public good does not necessarily mean that government ought to provide it or that only a government can provide it. First of all, economics suggests that the only public goods the government should even *consider* providing are those whose benefits exceed their costs. The cost of a public good is simply the sum of all the explicit and implicit costs incurred to provide it. The benefit of a public good is measured by asking how much people would be willing to pay for it. Although that sounds similar to the way we measure the benefit of a private good, an important distinction exists. The benefit of an additional unit of a private good, such as a cheeseburger, is the highest sum that any individual buyer would be willing to pay for it. In contrast, the benefit of an additional unit of a public good, such as an additional broadcast episode of *Sesame Street*, is the sum of the reservation prices of all people who will watch that episode.

Even if the amount that all beneficiaries of a public good would be willing to pay exceeds its cost, government provision of that good makes sense only if there is no other less costly way of providing it. For example, while city governments often pay for fireworks displays, they almost invariably hire private companies to put on these events.

PAYING FOR PUBLIC GOODS

Not everyone benefits equally from the provision of a given public good. For example, some people find fireworks displays highly entertaining, but others simply don't care about them and still others actively dislike them. Ideally, it might seem that the most equitable method of financing a given public good would be to tax people in proportion to their willingness to pay for the good. To illustrate this approach, suppose Jones values a public good at €100, Smith values the same good at €200 and the cost of the good is €240. Jones would then be taxed €80, and Smith would be taxed €160. The good would be provided, and each taxpayer in this example would reap a surplus equal to 25 per cent of his tax payment: €20 for Jones, €40 for Smith.

In practice, however, government officials usually lack the information they would need to tax people in proportion to their willingness to pay for specific public goods. People are unlikely to answer truthfully if asked to reveal willingness to pay. Examples 14.1–14.3 illustrate some of the problems that arise in financing public goods, and suggest possible solutions to these problems.

Example 14.1 Will rural roads in Tuscany be upgraded?

One of the picturesque features of countryside in central Italy is the number of 'white' (i.e. unpaved) roads that wander between fields, vineyards and olive groves to small groups of houses. Unfortunately, although picturesque, they wreck car suspensions, and in the winter are frequently impassable. So why are they not upgraded to tarmac by the households using them?

Two families, the Camerons and the Sarkozys, have holiday villas in Le Marche, side by side at the end of a 2 km white road some distance up the hills. Being unable to use the villas during the ski season, they are considering the question of upgrading the road. A local construction firm has quoted a price of €10,000 to do the job. Both families favour upgrading the road, but because the Sarkozys earn twice what the Camerons earn they differ as to willingness to pay. For the Sarkozys it is worth €8,000. To the Camerons it is worth only €4,000. Would either family be willing to foot the bill individually? Is it efficient for them to share the cost?

Neither would pay the full cost because each has a reservation price that is *below its cost*. But because the two together value the upgrading of the road at €12,000, sharing the cost would be socially efficient. Total economic surplus would be increased by €2,000. Cost sharing being efficient, we might expect that the families would quickly reach agreement to finance the project. Unfortunately, however, the joint purchase and sharing of facilities is often more easily proposed than accomplished. One hurdle is that people must incur costs merely to get together to discuss joint purchases. With only two people involved, those costs might not be significant. But if hundreds or thousands of people were involved, communication costs could be prohibitive.

With large numbers of people, there is a major free-rider problem. Each potential beneficiary knows that the project will either succeed or fail independently of his contribution to it. Everyone has an incentive to withhold contributions – or get a free ride – in the hope that others will contribute.

Finally, even with only a few people involved, reaching agreement on a fair sharing of the total expense may be difficult. For example, the Sarkozys and the Camerons might be reluctant to disclose their true reservation prices to one another.

A solution could be to ask the construction firm to get the local administration to do the job. Unfortunately, the Comune is likely to argue that if the road is upgraded at the taxpayers' expense the two families will capture all the benefits while paying only a tiny fraction of the costs. The Comune might reasonably enough say that it was a matter for the two families, not the Comune.

These practical concerns may lead us to empower government to buy public goods on our behalf and then tax us. But, as Example 14.2 makes clear, this approach does not eliminate the need to reach political agreement on how public purchases are to be financed.

Will the Comune get consent to upgrade the road if it is financed by an 'equal tax' rule? — Example 14.2

Suppose the two families ask the Comune to help broker the road upgrading. Suppose that it is obliged by law not to charge one beneficiary more than another, while the good will be provided only if a majority of citizens agree. What will happen?

A tax that collects the same amount from every citizen is called a **poll tax**. A poll tax is a **regressive tax** (the tax paid declines as a proportion of a taxpayer's income as the taxpayer's income rises). If the Comune must rely on a poll tax, it must raise €5,000 from each family. But since the upgrading is worth only €4,000 to the Camerons, they will vote against the project, thus denying it a majority.

This is a general problem with poll tax finance, leaving aside considerations of fairness. Whenever people have significantly different incomes, they are likely to place significantly different valuations on public goods. An equal-tax rule under these circumstances will often rule out the provision of many worthwhile public goods.

> **poll tax** a tax that collects the same amount from every taxpayer
>
> **regressive tax** a tax under which the proportion of income paid in taxes declines as income rises

As Example 14.3 suggests, one solution to this problem is to allow taxes to vary by income.

Incentives Matter

Will the road be upgraded if the Comune can levy a proportional tax on income? — Example 14.3

Suppose that the Camerons propose that the revenue be raised by imposing a proportional tax on income. Will the Sarkozys agree?

A **proportional income tax** is one under which all taxpayers pay the same percentage of their incomes in taxes. Under the proportional tax on income, the Camerons would contribute €3,333 towards the €10,000 cost of the road and the Sarkozys would contribute €6,667. The road would be upgraded, resulting in additional surpluses of €667 for the Camerons and €1,333 for the Sarkozys.

> **proportional income tax** one under which all taxpayers pay the same proportion of their incomes in taxes

Economic Naturalist 14.1 makes the point that just as equal contributions are often a poor way to pay for public goods, they are also often a poor way to share expenses within the household.

Economic Naturalist 14.1
Should a couple who believe in equality between the sexes agree to pay equal shares of expenses when they set up house together?

An economic naturalist will answer, no, if they want the union to last unless they have the same income and general tastes. Why? Because expenditure patterns depend on tastes, while equal shares make possible 'exporting' costs to the other party. The poorer person might prefer jug wine when the richer party wanted to buy Chateau Petrus 1998. Equal payments would mean ruling out Chateau Petrus. The poorer party might object to being asked to pay 50 per cent of a holiday in Bermuda rather than in a French campsite. The richer party might object to paying for the upkeep of an organic vegetable garden rather than consuming exotic greens from Harrod's Food Hall. It's not hard to see why a rule revision might be the only way to avoid a messy split. Alternatively, don't live with someone with different tastes and income!

Public goods and jointly consumed private goods are different from individually consumed private goods in the following important way: different individuals are free to consume whatever quantity and quality of most private goods they choose to buy, but *jointly consumed goods must be provided in the same quantity and quality for all persons.*

As with most private goods, people's willingness to pay for public goods is generally an increasing function of income. Suppose wealthy individuals value public goods more than low-income people do, not just because the wealthy have different tastes but because they have more money. A poll tax (head tax) would result in high-income persons getting smaller amounts of public goods than they want. By increasing the total economic surplus available for all to share, a tax system that assigns a larger share of the tax burden to people with higher incomes would provide a better outcome for both rich and poor alike. Ignoring income redistribution, this points towards countries adopting at least mildly **progressive tax** systems, which means that the proportion of income paid in taxes rises with a family's income.

> **progressive tax** one in which the proportion of income paid in taxes rises as income rises

Studies have shown that the income elasticity of demand for public goods such as parks and recreation facilities, clean air and water, public safety, uncongested roads and aesthetically pleasing public spaces is substantially greater than 1. Exclusive reliance on poll taxes, or even proportional taxes, would curtail the provision of public goods and services that are of greatest value to high-income families, and result in under-provision of such public goods and services.

We turn now from payment methods to questions about what *level* and *quality* of a public good to provide.

THE DEMAND CURVE FOR A PUBLIC GOOD

To calculate the socially optimal quantity of a public good, we must first construct the *demand curve* for that public good. The process for doing so differs in an important way from the one used to generate the market demand curve for a private good.

For a *private* good, all buyers face the same price and each chooses the quantity to purchase at that price. The market demand curve reflects the lateral summation of the quantities demanded by individuals consumers at any and all prices. In Figure 14.1 we add the individual demand curves for a private good, D_1 and D_2 (panels (a) and (b)), horizontally to obtain the market demand curve for the good D (panel (c)).

For a *public* good, all buyers necessarily consume the same quantity, although each may differ in terms of willingness to pay for additional units of the good. Constructing the demand curve for a public good entails *vertical* rather than horizontal summation of

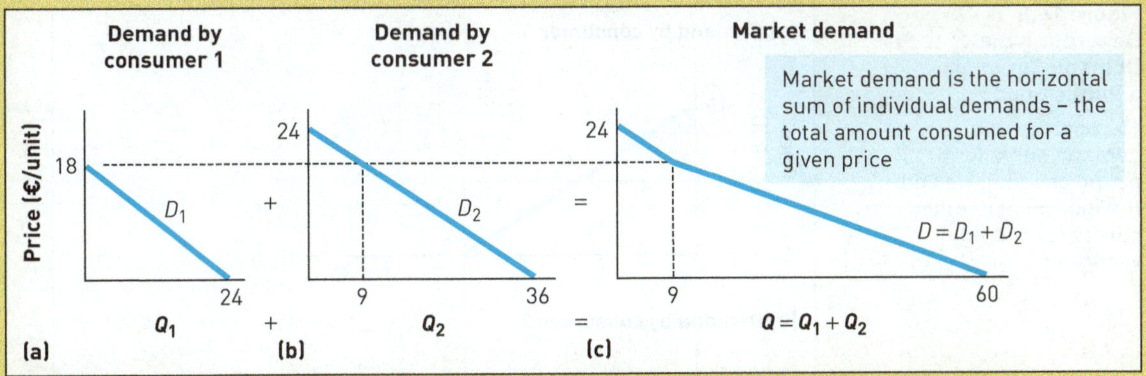

Figure 14.1 Generating the Market Demand Curve for a Private Good
To construct the market demand curve for a private good (c), we add the individual demand curves (a) and (b) horizontally.

the individual demand. That is, for each of a series of quantity values, we must add the prices that individuals are willing to pay for an additional unit of the good. The curves D_1 and D_2 in Fig. 14.2(a) and (b) show individual demand curves for a public good by two different people. At each quantity, these curves tell how much the individual would be willing to pay for an additional unit of the public good. If we add D_1 and D_2 vertically, we obtain the total demand curve D for the public good (panel (c)).

Exercise 14.2

Bill and Tom are the only demanders of a public good. If Bill's demand curve is $P_B = 6 - 0.5Q$ and Tom's is $P_T = 1 - 2Q$, construct the demand curve for this public good.

In Example 14.4, we see how the demand curve for a public good might be used in conjunction with information about costs to determine the optimal level of public park provision in a city.

Example 14.4

What is the optimal quantity of urban park space?

The city government of a new, planned community must decide how much parkland to provide. The marginal cost curve and the public demand curve for urban parkland are as shown in Fig. 14.3. Why is the marginal cost curve upward-sloping and the demand curve downward-sloping? Given these curves, what is the optimal quantity of parkland?

The marginal cost schedule for urban parkland is upward-sloping because of the Low-Hanging-Fruit Principle (Chapter 2): the city acquires the cheapest parcels of land first, and only then turns to more expensive parcels. The marginal willingness-to-pay (WTP) curve is downward-sloping reflecting diminishing marginal utility: people are willing to pay less for the 101st ha of parkland than for the 100th ha. Given these curves, A^* is the optimal quantity of parkland. For any quantity less than A^*, the benefit of additional parkland exceeds its cost, which means that total economic surplus can be made larger by expanding the amount of parkland. For example, at A_0, the community would be willing to pay €200,000 for an additional hectare of urban parkland, but its cost is only €80,000. Similarly, for any quantity of parkland in excess of A^*, the community would gain more than it would lose by selling off some parkland.

PRIVATE PROVISION OF PUBLIC GOODS

One advantage of using the government to provide public goods is that once a tax collection agency has been established to finance a single public good, it can be expanded at

Figure 14.2 Generating the Demand Curve for a Public Good

To construct the demand curve for a public good (c), we add the individual demand curves (a) and (b) vertically.

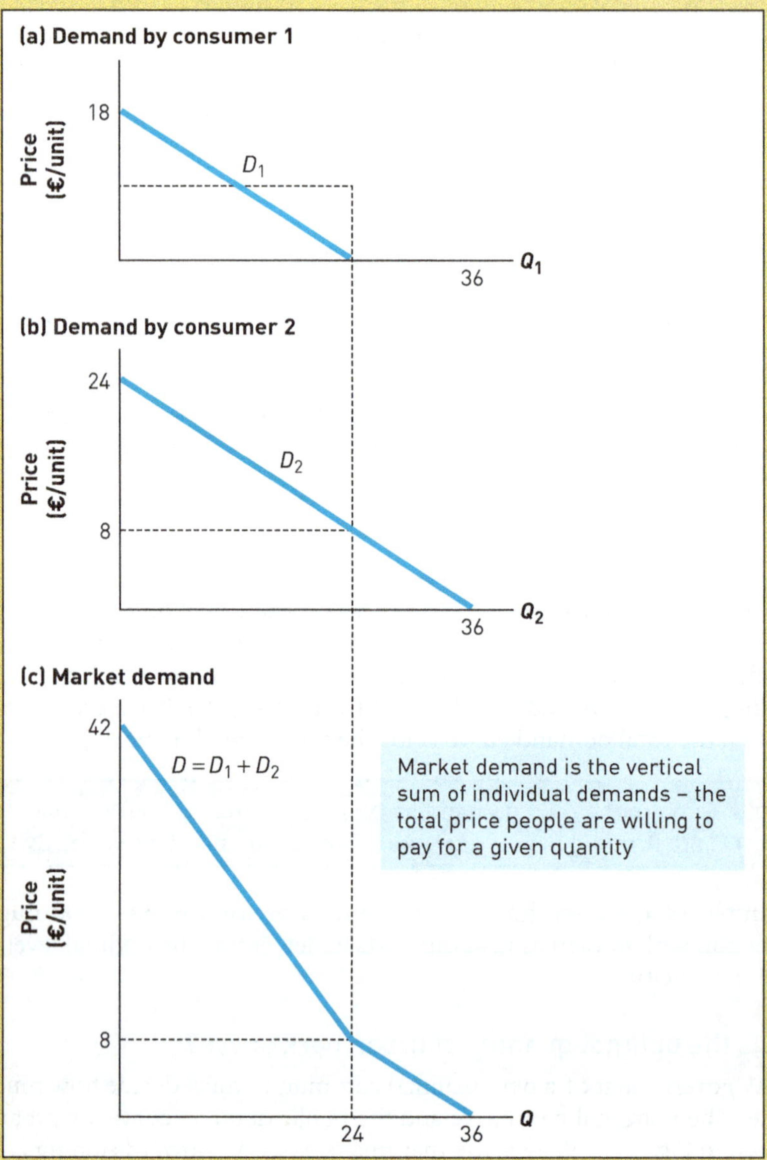

relatively low cost to generate revenue for additional public goods. Another advantage is that because government has the power to tax, it can summarily assign responsibility for the cost of a public good without endless haggling over who bears what share of the burden. And in the case of goods for which non-payers cannot be excluded, the government may be the only feasible provider.

Exclusive reliance on government also entails disadvantages, however. Most fundamentally, the government's one-size-fits all approach invariably requires many people to pay for public goods they don't want, while others end up having to do without public goods they want desperately. For example, many people vehemently oppose the provision of *any* sex education in schools, while others fervently believe that far more such instruction should be provided than is currently offered in most school curricula. In addition, mandatory taxation strikes many people as coercive, even if they approve of the particular public goods being provided.

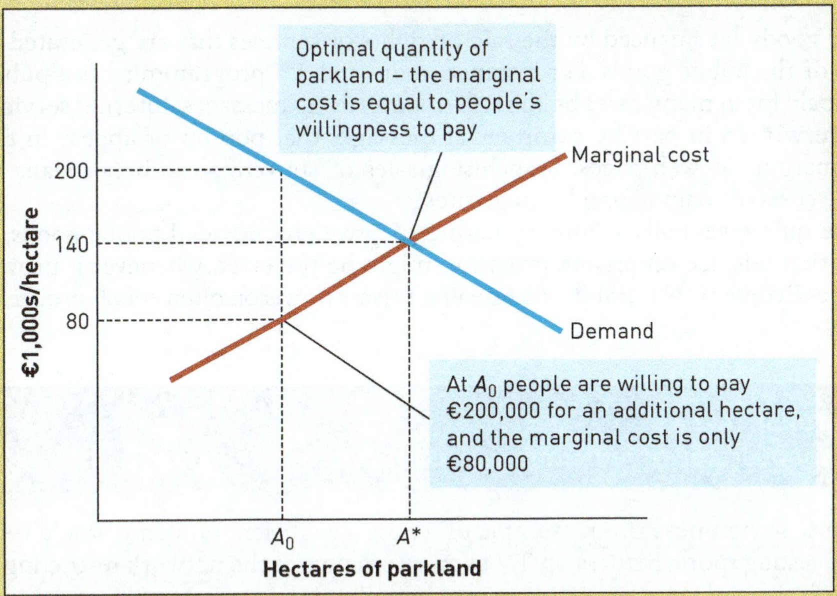

Figure 14.3 The Optimal Quantity of Parkland

The optimal number of hectares of urban parkland is A^*, the quantity at which the public's willingness to pay for additional parkland is equal to the marginal cost of parkland.

It is no surprise, then, that governments are not the exclusive providers of public goods in any society. Indeed, many public goods are routinely provided through private channels. The challenge, in each case, is to devise a scheme for raising the required revenues.

Funding by donation

Two well-known mechanisms that result in private provision of public goods are philanthropy and volunteer work effort; a third is commercial sponsorship. In the United States, and to a lesser extent in Europe, there is a strong tradition of endowment of research and the arts by wealthy individuals. In most countries, ordinary individuals offer their time on a voluntary basis to help such organisations as Oxfam and get involved in political life through political parties. Commercial sponsorship may be motivated by the payback to the sponsor from good publicity, but such sponsorship frequently takes the form of provision of local public goods – as, for example, when a firm pays for improvements in a children's playground.

Development of new means to exclude non-payers

New electronic technology makes it possible to exclude non-payers from many goods that in the past could not be thus restricted. For instance, TV stations now have the ability to scramble their signals, making them available only to those consumers who purchase descrambling devices.

Private contracting

More than 8 million Americans now live in gated private communities. They are increasingly the rule in middle-class areas in South Africa, and are starting to become common in parts of Europe. Many of these associations provide landscaping, maintenance, security services, schools and fire protection and in other ways function much like ordinary local governments. The associations usually bill home owners for those services directly, a form of tax. Many of the rules imposed by these associations are even more restrictive than those imposed by local governments, a distinction that is defended on the grounds that people are always free to choose some other neighbourhood if they don't like the rule. Many people would be reluctant to tolerate a municipal ordinance that prevents people from painting their houses purple, yet such restrictions are common in the by-laws of housing associations.

Sale of by-products

Many public goods are financed by the sale of rights or services that are generated as by-products of the public goods. For instance, radio and TV programming is a public good that is paid for in many cases by the sale of advertising messages. Internet services are also underwritten in part by commercial messages that pop up or appear in the headers or margins of web pages. Franchising sales of souvenirs can be a means of financing the costs of maintaining heritage sites.

Given the quintessentially voluntary nature of privately provided public goods, it might seem that reliance on private provision might be preferred whenever it proved feasible. But, as Economic Naturalist 14.2 explains, private provision often entails problems of its own.

Economic Naturalist 14.2
Is commercial sponsorship an efficient way to produce public goods?

The answer is, sometimes yes, sometimes no. An example of a possible efficient outcome would be when a firm sponsors broadcasting sports fixtures on TV as an alternative to the network restricting access on a pay-per-view basis. By and large we would expect hypothetical aggregate willingness to pay to be closely correlated to the numbers who would view a fixture if it were 'free to air'. Pay per view would exclude viewers, while allowing commercial sponsorship would enable a network to 'sell' a greater number of viewers to advertisers. On that basis, the greater the number of potential viewers, the greater the total value to viewers and the greater the TV revenues from commercial advertising or sponsorship. Allocating scarce peak viewing time between sports fixtures time by competition between sponsors could then be efficient.

However, consider whether a given hour is to be used to broadcast a live performance of *Rigoletto* at La Scala or a film-length programme of highlights from past episodes of *Desperate Housewives* or *Coronation Street*. The number of opera fans is likely to be much lower than the number of *Coronation Street* enthusiasts, but the aggregate willingness of the opera lovers to pay might well exceed that of the soap viewers. A commercial sponsorship allocation could be inefficient in these circumstances. Is there any evidence to support this? Yes: cinemas can make money showing live performances at the New York Metropolitan Opera House, but we are not aware of cinemas seeking to attract patrons by running four-hour programmes of re-runs of old TV soaps. It follows that reliance on advertising and other indirect mechanisms for financing public goods provides no assurance that the result will maximise economic surplus.

Example 14.5 By how much is economic surplus reduced by a pay-per-view charge?

If a recently released movie is available on a pay-per-view channel on Thursdays at 10 pm, the demand curve for each episode is given by $P = 20 - Q$, where P is the price per household in euros and Q is the number of households who choose to watch the programme (in millions). If the regulated pay-per-view charge is €10 per household, by how much would economic surplus rise if the same episode were shown instead on 'free' network TV?

With a fee of €10 per episode, 10 million households will watch (see Fig. 14.4). But if the same episode were shown on network TV, 20 million households would watch. The additional economic surplus reaped by the extra 10 million households is the area of the shaded triangle, €50 million. The marginal cost of permitting these additional households to watch is zero, so the total gain in surplus is €50 million. In general, charging a positive price for a good whose marginal cost is zero will result in a loss in surplus. As we saw in Chapter 7, the size of the loss that results when price is set above marginal cost depends on the *price elasticity of demand*. When demand is more elastic, the loss in surplus is greater. Exercise 14.3 provides an opportunity to see that principle at work.

Exercise 14.3

How would your answer to Example 14.5 have been different if the demand curve had been given instead by $P = 15 - 2Q$?

GOVERNMENT IN THE ECONOMY: REGULATION

In the course of Chapter 8, where we looked at the performance of firms that enjoy substantial market power we saw that market power results in a reduction in economic efficiency. Such firms normally do not choose outputs and prices that equate price to marginal cost. They exploit market power to extract profits by restricting output, something that transfers real income from consumers to producers. It is just one instance of market failure, by which is meant that markets do not deliver economically efficient outcomes.

To respond to this and other problems of market failure we rely on governmental (or, indeed, supranational) intervention in the form of **regulation**. This takes the form of restrictions on how firms operate, and on the structures of markets. Where market power is a problem, it is the basis for regulation in the form of competition policy, and mergers and acquisitions (M&A) policy. It is also the basis for policy to deal with other sources of market failure, such as environmental problems.

regulation legal intervention in markets to alter the way in which firms or consumers behave

GOVERNMENT AND REGULATION

The efficiency consequences of monopoly power are just one instance of *market failure*. Economists see the use of regulation is seen by economists as a means of correcting market failure. However, in order to do this correctly, governments or agencies that regulate economic activity need to understand the economics foundations of regulatory intervention. When they don't understand why, when, how and where regulation works well they can end up pursuing irrational or counter-productive policies: instead of market failure we have *regulatory failure*.

THE REGULATORY FRAMEWORK

First, let us look at how regulation is implemented. It starts with some form of legislative intervention to modify individuals' or firms' behaviour by changing the legal framework of property rights and contract law that underpins the workings of markets. Efficient markets depend on an adequate legal framework. Changes to that framework change how firms and individuals behave in terms of market transactions.

That is not to say there are no markets without the legal institutions provided by a state as we know it. Somalia has had no effective government for 30 years. There are,

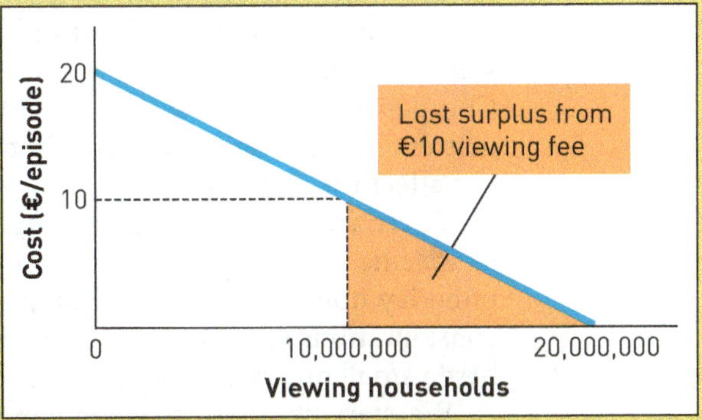

Figure 14.4 The Loss in Surplus from a Pay-per-view Fee

Twice as many households would watch the programme if its price were zero instead of €10. The additional economic surplus is the area of the shaded triangle, or €50 million.

however, burgeoning markets in most goods and many relatively technologically complex services in a territory that has no functioning government making and enforcing laws. Local warlords provide a set of enforced property rights, and enforce contracts where necessary . . . and take a cut of the action (a sort of informal tax system).[1]

Markets can function outside the law. The narcotics market is an obvious example. However, transactions in these markets are very costly compared with transactions in markets that can rely on the legal establishment and enforcement of property rights and contractual relations. The violence associated with these illegal markets is an inevitable social cost of contract and property rights enforcement.

In legally supported markets the legal framework lays down the ground rules for *market exchange*. Changes in that framework are the first form of regulation to be considered. Labour markets all over the world are heavily regulated. Governments legislate for certain workers' rights that supersede simple contracts between employers and employees (pay rates, statutory notice periods, statutory holiday entitlements, entitlements to redundancy payments, working time restrictions, and so on). Germany was notorious for legal restrictions on opening hours for retail establishments that made German cities and towns commercial dead zones at weekends. In Italy shops must close for a weekly rest period. In France only a very small number of outlets ('*tabacs*') may sell tobacco. In most countries you cannot practise medicine unless you possess a set of qualifications laid down by law. In some EU countries it is prohibited to sell a range of goods at less than the price on the invoice covering their purchase by a retailer.

These are examples of *direct legislative regulation*. The law defines the permissible range of activities, and the normal procedures for law enforcement are used to make sure the restrictions are respected.

In addition to examining direct regulation and its consequences, much attention has been paid by economists to *delegated regulation*. The legislature sets up an agency to regulate an industry or market along prescribed lines. The agency in turn issues legally binding regulations and decisions affecting the structure and/or performance of the entities covered in its remit.

Some agencies exist to moderate particular aspects of behaviour across all sectors of the economy. In the US the Department of Justice and the Federal Trade Commission act to regulate market behaviour by firms to counter abuse of market power. Under EU law all member states must have a 'competition authority' (although not necessarily using exactly that title: in the United Kingdom it has been the Competition Commission since 2000; in France it is the *Conseil de Concurrence*, or Competition Council). Competition agency guidelines are set down under national and EU law. The agency is responsible for the implementation of competition policy within the member states. It polices markets in general to deal with problems such as collusive fixing of prices, and can stop or modify mergers/acquisitions that are larger than a defined threshold size. The Competition Directorate of the EU Commission concerns itself with competition matters having a wider dimension than the member state. Its findings are binding and can affect the decisions of national governments.

There are also sector-specific regulatory agencies. These supervise the performance of specific industries. Typically they determine what prices may be charged. They also often lay down conditions of supply. It is most frequent in industries where technical considerations suggest that there will be only one (a natural monopoly) supplier or at best a small number of suppliers (reflecting substantial economies of scale).

We start by looking at regulatory intervention in markets under three headings in order to demonstrate how and why regulation occurs and some problems facing regulators. These are (i) regulation to deal with environmental degradation; (ii) regulation of public utilities (in this case, electricity production and sale); (iii) health and safety regulation affecting household and labour market behaviour.

---

[1] Cockburn, 2002.

In this we are focusing on two issues. The first is *regulatory design and practice*. Regulation is supposed to correct market failure. Its success (or failure) depends on how it is designed and how it functions. The second is why poor regulation occurs, given the reasons for which it is introduced.

THREE CASE STUDIES

1. Regulation to protect the environment from industrial pollution: using price incentives in environmental regulation

Goods whose production generates negative externalities, such as atmospheric pollution, tend to be overproduced whenever negotiation among private parties is costly. Suppose we decide as a society that there should be 50 per cent lower CO_2 emissions than would occur under completely unregulated conditions. In that case, how should the clean-up effort be distributed among those firms that currently discharging CO_2 ?

The most efficient distribution of effort is the one for which *each polluter's marginal cost of abatement is exactly the same*. To see why, imagine that under current arrangements the cost to one firm of removing a tonne of pollutant from the air is larger than the cost to another firm. Society could then achieve the same total reduction in pollution at lower cost by having the first firm discharge 1 tonne more into the air and the second firm 1 tonne less.

Unfortunately, government regulators seldom have detailed information on how the cost of reducing pollution varies between firms. Traditionally, many control regimes therefore require all polluters simply to cut back their emissions by the same proportion or to meet the same absolute emissions standards. In general this approach is not efficient as different polluters have different marginal costs of pollution abatement. That is now changing, thanks to increased interest in using market devices to improve regulatory control of emissions.

Taxing pollution

Alternative policies can distribute the clean-up more efficiently, even if the government lacks detailed information about abatement costs across firms. One method is to tax pollution and allow firms to decide for themselves how much pollutant to emit. Example 14.6 illustrates the logic of this approach.

What is the least costly way to cut pollution by half?

Example 14.6

Each of two firms, Sludge Oil and Northwest Lumber, has access to five production processes, each having a different cost and creating a different amount of pollution. The daily costs of the processes and the number of tonnes of smoke emitted are shown in Table 14.3. We assume no regulation and an impossibility of negotiation along Coase theorem lines. Each firm uses process A, the least costly. Each firm emits 4 tonnes of pollutant per day, for a total of 8 tonnes of pollutant per day.

Cost-Benefit Analysis

The government wishes to reduce total emissions by half. It could legislate to force each firm to curtail its emissions by half. Alternatively, it could impose a tax of €T per tonne of smoke emitted each day. How large must T be to curtail emissions by half? What would be the total cost to society under each alternative?

If obliged to cut pollution by half, both firms must switch from process A to process C. The result will be 2 tonnes per day of pollution for each firm. The cost to Sludge Oil will be €600 per day − €100 per day = €500 per day. The cost to Northwest Lumber will be €380 per day − €300 per day = €80 per day, for a total cost of €580 per day.

Suppose instead each firm faced a tax of €T per tonne of pollutant. A reduction by 1 tonne per day will save €T per day in tax payments. Whenever the cost of cutting

Table 14.3 Costs and Emissions for Different Production Processes

Process (smoke)	A (4 tonnes/day)	B (3 tonnes/day)	C (2 tonnes/day)	D (1 tonne/day)	E (0 tonnes/day)
Cost to Sludge (€/day)	100	200	600	1,300	2,300
Incremental cost	–	100	400	700	1,000
Cost to Northwest (€/day)	300	320	380	480	700
Incremental cost	–	20	60	100	220

a tonne of pollutant is less than €*T*, then each firm has an incentive to switch to a cleaner process. If the tax were set at €40 per tonne, Sludge Oil would stick with process A, because switching to process B would cost €100 per day extra but would save only €40 per day in taxes. Northwest Lumber, however, would switch to process B, because the €40 saving in taxes would be more than enough to cover the €20 cost of switching.

A €40 per tonne per day tax results in a reduction of only 1 tonne per day, 3 short of the 4 tonne target. If the tax is increased to €101 per tonne Sludge Oil would then adopt process B, because the €100 extra daily cost of doing so would be less than the €101 saved in taxes. Northwest Lumber would adopt process D, because for every process up to and including C, the cost of switching to the next process would be less than the resulting tax saving.

Incentives Matter

The tax of €101 per tonne would result in the desired pollution reduction of 4 tonnes per day. The total cost of the reduction, €280 per day (€100 per day for Sludge Oil and €180 per day for Northwest Lumber), would be €300 per day less than the firms were each required to cut pollution by half. (The taxes paid by the firms do not constitute a cost of pollution reduction, because the money raised can be used to reduce other taxes).

Exercise 14.11 In Example 14.6, if the tax were €61 per tonne of pollutant emitted each day, which production processes would the two firms adopt?

The advantage of the tax approach is that it concentrates emissions abatement in the hands of the firms that can accomplish it *at least cost*. Requiring identical or proportional cuts from all firms ignores the fact that some firms can reduce pollution much more cheaply than others. Adopting a tax-based approach implies that the cost of the last tonne of smoke removed is the same for all firms, so the efficiency condition is satisfied.

Efficiency

The tax approach is not without problems. To work properly the government must have detailed knowledge about each firm's cost of reducing pollution. A low tax may result in too much pollution, while a high tax may result in too little. The government could start by setting a low tax rate and gradually increasing the rate until it achieves the target. But if firms incur substantial *sunk costs* when they switch from one process to another, that approach might be even more wasteful than requiring all firms to cut their emissions by the same proportion.

Auctioning pollution permits

Another alternative is to establish a target level for emissions and then auction off permits to emit. The virtues of this approach are illustrated in Example 14.7.

How much will pollution permits sell for?

Example 14.7

Two firms, Sludge Oil and Northwest Lumber, again have access to the production processes described in Table 14.3. The government's goal is still to cut emissions, 8 tonnes per day, by half. To do so, the government auctions off four permits, each of which entitles the bearer to emit 1 tonne of smoke per day. Emissions without a permit are prohibited. What price will the pollution permits fetch at auction, how many permits will each firm buy and what will be the total cost of the resulting pollution reduction?

If Sludge Oil has no permits, it must use process E, which costs €2,300 per day to operate. If it had one permit, it could use process D, which would save it €1,000 per day.

The most Sludge Oil would be willing to pay for a single 1 tonne pollution permit is €1,000 per day. With a second permit, Sludge Oil could switch to process C and save another €700 per day; with a third permit, it could switch to process B and save another €400; and with a fourth permit, it could switch to process A and save another €100. Using similar reasoning, we can see that Northwest Lumber would pay up to €220 for one permit, up to €100 for a second, up to €60 for a third and up to €20 for a fourth.

Suppose the government starts the auction at a price of €90. Sludge Oil will then demand four permits and Northwest Lumber will demand two, a total demand for six permits. Since the government wishes to sell only four permits, it will keep raising the price until the two firms together demand a total of only four permits. Once the price reaches €101, Sludge Oil will demand three permits and Northwest Lumber will demand only one, a total quantity demanded for four permits. Compared to the unregulated alternative, in which each firm used process A, the daily cost of the auction solution is €280: Sludge Oil spends €100 switching from process A to process B, and Northwest Lumber spends €180 switching from A to D. This total is €300 less than the cost of requiring each firm to reduce its emissions by half. (Again, the permit fees paid by the firms are not a cost as the money can be used to reduce taxes that would otherwise have to be collected.)

Equilibrium

The auction method has the same virtue as the tax method: it concentrates pollution reduction in the hands of those firms that can accomplish it *at the lowest cost*. But the auction method has other attractive features that the tax approach does not have. First, it does not induce firms to commit themselves to costly investments that they will have to abandon if the clean-up falls short of the target level. Secondly, compared with the tax, the Government doesn't need to know the costs facing the two firms. Thirdly, it allows private citizens a direct voice in determining where the emission level will be set. For example, any group that believes the pollution target is too lenient could raise money to buy permits at auction. By keeping those permits locked away in a safe, the group could ensure that they will not be used to emit pollution.

Since economists first proposed the auctioning of pollution permits, or **emissions trading**, there has been a considerable level of opposition, especially from 'green' environmentalists. A typical objection is that the proposal permits rich firms to pollute to their heart's content. This betrays a total misunderstanding of the forces that generate pollution. Firms pollute not because they *want* to pollute, but because dirty production processes are cheaper than clean ones. Society's only real interest is in keeping the *total amount of pollution* from becoming excessive, not in who actually does the

emissions trading a system whereby firms can trade emission reductions, with the result that any given level of emissions reduction is undertaken by those with the lowest costs of achieving reductions polluting. The firms that do most of the polluting under an auction system will not be rich firms, but those for whom pollution reduction is least costly.

Comparative Advantage

Economists have argued patiently against these misinformed objections to the auction system, and their efforts have borne fruit. The sale of pollution permits is now common in several parts of the United States, and there is growing interest in other countries in such an approach.

Economic Naturalist 14.3
How can the EU reduce CO_2 emissions by permitting them?

The EU operates a scheme whereby heavy energy users face charges, but are allocated what amount to CO_2 emission permits that can be traded, and therefore have an opportunity cost if used to avoid emissions reductions by the holders. It is also possible to offset reduced emissions within the EU by verified emissions reductions outside the EU undertaken by, or paid for by, EU firms. Firms given allowances must hold sufficient allowances to cover their emissions at the end of the year. Any shortfall involves a financial penalty unless they purchase allowances from other firms at the end of the year. This creates a market for emissions permits. A firm with a permit can choose to use it to avoid a penalty or sell it to another firm. A price per tonne of CO_2 results from supply and demand, reflecting a price to be paid for emissions at the margin. This price gives firms an incentive: reductions are rewarded, and increased emissions are penalised.

RECAP

Using price incentives in environmental regulation

An efficient programme for reducing pollution is one for which the *marginal cost of abatement* is the same for all polluters. Taxing pollution has this desirable property, as does the auction of pollution permits. The auction method also has the advantage that regulators can achieve a desired abatement target without having detailed knowledge of the abatement technologies available to polluters.

2. Using regulation to counteract the exploitation of market power: energy transmission systems

Until the early 1990s the norm in Europe was for state-owned, monopoly, electricity-supply systems to operate in each country or region. Generation, transmission and distribution of electricity were in general vertically integrated into a single state-controlled entity being responsible for the three functions: producing power, transmitting current to the user and selling the power to the user. Regulation was seen as unimportant, since the suppliers were in public ownership, and as such were presumed not to be motivated by profits so as to exploit market power. Monopoly was believed to be unavoidable because it was generally accepted that electricity was a natural monopoly.

In the United States, in contrast, the norm was for privately owned, and vertically integrated, firms to produce and sell electricity. Because they were privately owned, it was felt necessary to subject them to regulatory control, in order to ensure that they could not abuse their monopoly position and pricing power to generate huge profits at the expense of end users. So, regulation has been a feature of the US energy sector for much longer than in Europe.

The economics analysis of the electricity supply industry, and the view that private-sector production is generally more efficient than production by publicly owned firms led to the move to privatise power production and distribution, which can be seen as an extreme form of deregulation because it permits, even obliges, firms to operate on a profit-maximising basis. This is why, in a sense, deregulation has increased the need for regulation. Since the early 1990s power generation and sales were opened to competition and for-profit firms entered the market, while monopoly access to end users by the state supplier was reduced. What became clear was that the natural monopoly assumed to apply to the whole business was seen to be confined in reality to transmission systems and, possibly, local distribution. This meant that the benefits of competition at the generation level, and at the retail sales level, could be thwarted by a monopoly owner of the transmission system, while, if the latter owned generation capacity as well, it could use control of transmission to protect its own generators. The focus of attention was now the need for regulation because of the network features of the market, as with some other network markets (gas and telecommunications being other cases). The management of the transmission system so as to allow competitive entry by power suppliers to the system and purchase of power from the system by power retailers came to be seen as dependent on the creation of an effective regulatory regime that aligned the behaviour of the grid operator with market efficiency upstream and downstream.

3. Regulation and health and safety: remedying defective incentives

Workplace safety regulations

Most industrialised countries have laws that attempt to limit the extent to which workers are exposed to health and safety risks on the job. These laws are usually justified as necessary to protect workers against exploitation. Given working conditions in the early stages of the Industrial Revolution, the idea that such exploitation pervades unregulated private markets has intuitive appeal.

The miserable conditions of factory workers, juxtaposed with the often opulent lifestyle enjoyed by factory owners, seemed to confirm the idea that owners were exploiting workers. But if conditions in the factories were in fact too dangerous, how much safer should they have been?

Consider the question of whether to install a specific safety device – say, a guard rail on a lathe. Many people are reluctant to employ the Cost–Benefit Principle to answer such a question. To them, safety is an absolute priority, so the guard rail should be installed regardless of its cost. Yet most of us do not make personal decisions about our own health and safety that way. No one gets the brakes on his car checked every day, even though doing so would reduce the likelihood of being killed in an accident. We do not regard the reduction in risk as worth the cost.

The same logic can be applied to installing a guard rail on a lathe. If the amount one is willing to pay to reduce the likelihood of an accident exceeds the cost of the guard rail, it should be installed; otherwise, it should not be. And no matter how highly we value reducing the odds of an accident, we will almost surely settle for less than perfect safety. After all, to reduce the risk of an accident to nearly zero, one would have to enclose the lathe in a thick Plexiglas case and operate it with remote-controlled mechanical arms. Faced with the prohibitive cost of such an alternative, most of us would decide that the best approach is to add safety equipment the benefit from which exceeds its cost and then exercise caution while operating the machine.

But will unregulated employers offer the level of workplace safety suggested by the Cost–Benefit Principle? Most nations appear to have decided that they will not. Virtually every industrial country now has comprehensive legislation governing safety standards in the workplace. These are usually described as safeguards against the exploitation of workers.

Yet the exploitation argument raises troubling questions. An economist might suggest that competition for workers encourages firms to provide the socially optimal level of amenities. For example, if an amenity – say, a guard rail on a lathe – costs €50 per month to install and maintain, and workers value it at €100 per month, then the firm must install the device or risk losing workers to a competitor. If a competing firm were to pay workers €60 per month less than they currently earn, it could cover the cost of the device with €10 to spare, while providing a compensation package that is €40 per month more attractive than the first employer's.

Critics respond to this by saying that there is very little competition in the labour market: incomplete information, worker immobility and other difficulties mean that workers have little choice but to accept whatever conditions employers offer. Alternatively, they argue that workers are unable to make 'rational' decisions in relation to health and safety. Finally, there is an argument to the effect that people will take more risks if someone else pays the costs. If society is committed to paying for medical treatment or to replacing earnings in the case of workplace injuries, this introduces 'moral hazard' and a higher level of injury than if workers and employers had to meet these costs.

The first of these arguments has the following weakness: even if a firm were the only employer in the market, it would still have an incentive to install a €50 safety device that is worth €100 to the worker. Failure to do so would be to leave cash on the table.

The argument about inability to decide rationally, too, is troubling, because competing firms would have a strong incentive to call the devices to the workers' attention.

If the problem is that workers can't move to the competing firm's location, then the firm can set up a branch near the exploited workers. Collusive agreements to restrain such competition should prove difficult to maintain, because each firm can increase its profit by cheating on the agreement.

In fact, worker mobility between firms is high, as is entry by new firms into existing markets; and, as noted in Chapter 10, cartel agreements have always been notoriously unstable. Information may not be perfect, but if a new employer in town is offering a better deal, sooner or later word gets around.

Finally, if, despite these checks, some firms still manage to exploit their workers, we should expect those firms to earn a relatively high profit. But in fact we observe just the opposite. Year in and year out, firms that pay the *highest* wages are the most profitable. And so we are left with a puzzle. The fear of exploitation by employers with market power has led governments to adopt sweeping and costly safety regulations; yet the evidence suggests that exploitation cannot be a major problem. As Example 14.8 suggests, however, safety regulation might prove useful even in a perfectly competitive environment with complete information.

The strongest argument is the third one: regulation is designed to shelter taxpayers from the costs of accidents. There is, however, another interesting argument in favour of regulation, derived from the tools of game theory we developed in Chapter 10.

Example 14.8 Will Don and Michael choose the optimal amount of safety?

Suppose Don and Michael are the only two members of a hypothetical community. They get satisfaction from three things – their income, safety on the job and their position on the economic ladder. Suppose Don and Michael must both choose between two jobs, a safe job that pays €50 per week and a risky job that pays €80 per week. The value of safety to each is €40 per week. Having more income than one's neighbour is worth €40 per week to each; having less income than one's neighbour means a €40 per week reduction in satisfaction. Will Don and Michael make the best job choices possible in this situation?

Viewed in isolation, each person's decision should be to take the safe job. It pays €30 per week less than the risky job, but the extra safety it offers is worth €40 per week. So, relative income apart, the value of the safe job is €90 per week (its €50 salary plus €40 worth of safety), or €10 per week more than the risky job.

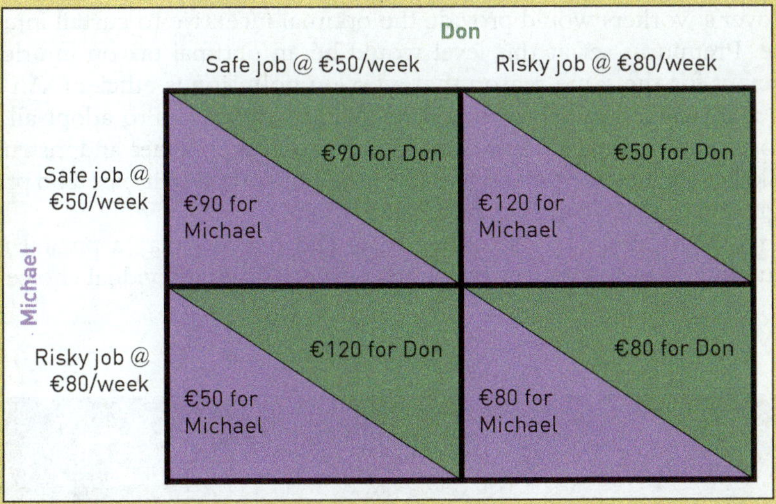

Figure 14.5 The Effect of Concern about Relative Income on Worker Choices Regarding Safety

Satisfaction from relative income, however, changes the decision logic in a fundamental way. Now the attractiveness of each job depends on the job chosen by the other. The four possible combinations of choices and their corresponding levels of satisfaction are shown in Figure 14.5. If each chooses a safe job, he will get €50 of income, €40 worth of satisfaction from safety and zero satisfaction from relative income. When each chooses the safe job, each gets a total of €90 worth of satisfaction. If, instead, each chooses the risky job, each gets €80 of income, zero satisfaction from safety, and because each has the same income as the other, zero satisfaction from relative income. If we compare the upper-left cell of Figure 14.5 with the lower-right cell, then, we can say unequivocally that Don and Michael would be happier if each took a safe job at lower income than if each chose a risky job with more income.

Refer back to the discussion in Chapter 9 to confirm the following conclusion: choosing the risky job is a dominant strategy for both men. This is yet another Prisoner's Dilemma game. No matter which job Michael chooses, Don will get more satisfaction by choosing the risky job. Likewise, no matter which job Don chooses, Michael will do better by choosing the risky job. Each ends up with only €80 per week of satisfaction —€10 less than if each had chosen the safe job.

Exercise 14.12

How would your answer to the question posed in Example 14.8 have differed if the value of safety had been not €40 per week, but €20?

Example 14.8 suggests an alternative explanation for safety regulation from protecting workers from exploitation. If Don and Michael could choose collectively, they would pick the safe job and maximise their combined satisfaction. Thus each might support legislation that establishes safety standards in the workplace.

Regulation, however, does not always improve matters. The labour market may not be perfect, but government regulators aren't perfect either.

The issue is not that there is no role for regulation, but that it is not clear that the regulations imposed are not more onerous than are necessary to correct the market failure, whatever that is. Many economists argue for increasing employers' financial incentives to reduce workplace injuries. Injury compensation insurance provides a mechanism to achieve this. If insurance premiums reflect the experience and safety record of the firm, poor-risk employers will face higher premiums, and have an incentive to increase workplace safety.

Revising insurance premiums to reflect the full social cost of the injuries sustained by each employer's workers would provide the optimal incentive to curtail injuries in the workplace. Premiums set at this level would be an optimal tax on injuries, and would be efficient for the same reason that a tax on pollution is efficient. An injury tax set at the *marginal cost of injury* would encourage employers to adopt all safety measures whose benefits exceed their costs. Choices among policies and instruments are far more likely to achieve optimal safety levels in the workplace if based on practical cost–benefit grounds rather than slogans about markets.

As Economic Naturalist 14.4 illustrates, costs and benefits play a pivotal role in decisions about whether the government chooses to constrain individual choice in the safety domain, and, if so, how.

Economic Naturalist 14.4

Why does the government require safety seats for infants who travel by road, but not for infants who travel by air?

To drive with a 6-month-old infant to a nearby grocery shop not strapped into a government-approved safety seat earns points on your licence. But no restraint at all is required for the baby on a flight from London to Rome. Why this difference?

In case of an accident in a car or a plane an infant who is strapped into a safety seat is more likely to escape injury or death than one who is unrestrained. But the probability of being involved in a serious car accident is hundreds of times higher than a serious accident than when travelling by air, so the benefit of having safety seats is greater for trips made by car. Using safety seats on plane trips is also far more costly. Most cars have room for a safety seat, but you would need to purchase an extra ticket to use one on a plane. Most parents appear unwilling to pay more per trip for a small increment in safety, for either themselves or their children.

PUBLIC HEALTH AND SAFETY

Because public health regulation is designed to protect our health, political leaders are often reluctant to discuss public health spending in cost–benefit terms. But because we live in a world of scarcity, we cannot escape the fact that spending more in these areas means spending less on other things of value. The same applies to regulation designed to promote safety.

We tend (correctly) to think of accidents as costly, and, therefore reductions in accidents as benefits. We rarely think about the fact that prevention of accidents is costly, and that economics logic implies that there is some optimal level of accident incidence and an optimal level of injury or death in excess of zero unless the marginal cost of reducing accidents is zero. Road safety is, probably, the most obvious case in point. At what point do you think a politician could say 'It is not worth while spending more money, or imposing further restrictions on road users, or increasing penalties, to reduce road deaths'?[2] Yet, traffic law enforcement, road reconstruction, restrictions on road usage, regulation of vehicle standards, all involve economic costs.

[2] In Sweden in 1996 it was decided that the ultimate objective of road safety policy was the total elimination of death and serious injury on the roads, on the basis that this was the only ethically tenable position. This was incorporated in the Vision Zero policy document of the Kommunikationsdepartementet. At face value this implies something approaching an infinite value on human life, something that on a daily basis rational people going about their normal business clearly do not accept, whatever the rhetoric with which they feel comfortable.

Economic Naturalist 14.5

Many governments encourage, even enforce, universal vaccination against MMR; they discourage and try to eliminate completely tobacco usage. These measures are adopted to reduce morbidity and mortality from related diseases. Why, then, do they frequently restrict access by women to subsidised mammography to detect early-stage breast cancer?

The arguments for regulation to reduce smoking and to increase vaccination are based not only on the reduced costs of treating smokers or people infected by diseases, or costs to the victims themselves, but on externality issues. It is not only smokers who are affected by tobacco smoke, and infected individuals can infect others. In the case of breast cancer, the costs other than treatment costs are borne by the sufferer alone, since it cannot be transmitted to others. Hence, the only issue is the impact of mammography or alternative procedures on outcomes. The epidemiological evidence suggests that this is more limited than is sometimes thought, in the sense that random selections of women receiving mammographies are not much less likely to die from the disease than controls who do not receive the treatment. Its effectiveness is stronger among women with a genetic predisposition, and among women aged less than 50. It is not risk free, and there is a non-trivial incidence of both false positives and false negatives. As a result, cost–benefit analysis indicates that subsidised access to mammography is hard to justify unless the recipients are in the higher risk categories.[3]

REGULATORY FAILURE

The object of regulation is to correct market failure. However, much theoretical and empirical literature has made clear that, as always, there is no free lunch. The cost of introducing regulation is that the economy is exposed to regulatory failure. By this is meant two possible problems: the first is that regulation is simply badly designed or executed. The second is that the regulatory mechanism can be diverted from its original purpose to serve other interests. The second is the problem of 'regulatory capture'. This refers to a state of affairs where in effect the regulatory mechanism is perverted from its original purpose so as to advance the interests of the agents being regulated. The first may be described as the blunder problem. This describes what happens when, based on inadequate understanding of the supposed market failure, or of the consequences government intervention, regulation results in unforeseen (other than by economists!) consequences that were not desired in the first place.

REGULATORY CAPTURE

In its extreme form this concept can be summed up by a quotation from one of the earliest writers on the subject, R.A. Posner:[4] 'Regulation is not about the public interest at all, but is a process, by which interest groups seek to promote their private interest. . . .' A less extreme version would hold that it is frequently the case that what started as a mechanism to improve economic efficiency tends to drift towards advancing the interests of the firms being regulated.

The extreme version holds that much, perhaps most, regulation, while using the rhetoric of protecting the public from some aspect of behaviour by firms in the market, is in reality sought and obtained in order to protect producer interests from competition. Typically, such regulation will restrict entry to a market or restrict competition between suppliers in the market, or lay down product standards that have consequences

[3] This naturalist reflects the conclusions of some medical researchers: see Epstein, Bertell and Seaman, 2001.

[4] Posner, 1974.

similar to those of restrictions on competition. Examples would include sellers of alcohol who argue for restrictions on the number of pubs because they are concerned that alcohol consumption is too great. In the 'liberal professions' regulation of behaviour (for example, restrictions on advertising, or disclosing of prices) can be seen in the same light. Governments all over the world colluded for years with the airline industry to restrict entry and control prices on the basis that this was necessary to ensure an adequate service network, the nonsense of which was revealed when deregulation occurred after the middle 1980s. A remnant of that persists today in the US. The internal air transport market is restricted to airlines in American ownership for 'strategic security' reasons.

A less extreme version, but in the long term just as worrying, concerns how regulators function. To understand this, consider the problem facing an energy regulator who has to determine the level and structure of prices to be charged by a monopoly producer/distributor of electricity. At its simplest, the regulator knows that price must cover average cost if the producer is to remain in business. But quantifying costs of supply to different customers at different times (electricity can't be stored) is not easy, and depends on good technical information on generation and distribution technology and the price sensitivity of demand. Imagine that for all practical purposes this is proprietary information in the hands of the firm being regulated. This means the regulator is dependent on the firm to supply reliable information. The firm, however, has a strong incentive to restrict the flow of 'damaging' information to the regulator, in effect to misinform the regulator. Although this is itself an extreme set of circumstances, the point remains generally valid: good regulation requires good information that may be costly to generate and may not be fully available from independent sources, while misinformation offers the potential to the firm to manipulate the regulations in the firm's interests.

Other observers have suggested that, in the long-term, interactions between regulator and the firm(s) being regulated lead to a change in the regulatory mindset, which becomes more sensitive to the needs of the firm(s) rather than the needs of customers.

Finally, and particularly the case where the regulated firm has market power, regulation that attempts to set price by reference to cost creates an incentive for the regulated firm to incur costs to justify prices. If regulation is based on acceptable return rates on capital employed, a firm may find that it pays to invest in unnecessary capacity simply to retain expected profits.

Any or all of the above point to regulatory failure: either the regulatory process is inefficient, or the implementation of regulation leads to unintended cost increasing effects, or both.

The second category of regulatory failure is, quite simply, bad regulation, regulation that either can't or shouldn't achieve what it sets out to achieve. By way of introduction to this consider the following story of seriously bad regulation by way of an introduction to the topic. Then, if you have time and are interested, read the appendix to this chapter in which we use the ideas developed in Chapters 12 and 14 to offer some insights into the economic crisis that has struck most of the world's economies since 2008.

REGULATORY BLUNDER: CHEAP OIL FOR CANADIAN CONSUMERS

Alberta in Canada's western provinces has been a major oil producer for decades (and this is likely to continue thanks to the Athabasca tar sands). It has always exported most of its production to the US because before the first oil shock the cost of a pipeline to the east was too high. Oil for the east of Canada was imported by sea. After the sharp price increase in the price of oil in 1973–4 the Canadian Government decided that Canadians should not have to pay more for oil, given that Canada produced more than it consumed. This was supported by the Government of Alberta, flush with oil revenues, and anxious to keep the locals happy. It was also supported in the east, especially when it was announced that a pipeline project from Alberta was to be accelerated. Pending the completion of the pipeline, the government introduced a subsidy to oil imports to make sure that prices didn't rise in the east. The price for oil in Canada was frozen. Alas, this resulted in oil being diverted to the US, where prices were higher. So the government moved to restrict oil exports, and introduced an export tax. The object of these interventions was to regulate the oil market to make sure that Canadians did not have to pay the world price for oil, but something closer to the cost of producing it in Canada. Then they discovered that, given the energy cost of investment in exploiting unconventional oil (i.e., the tar sands) while the price of oil was frozen, it became less and less feasible to develop that resource. So, they had to introduce a subsidy in 1980 to encourage investment in the development of the tar sands. The regulatory regime to freeze consumer prices was abandoned in 1985.

The trouble was it never could have made sense. The object was to prevent Canadians from having to pay the world price of oil. But this was impossible. Remember the concept of opportunity cost. What was the opportunity cost of a barrel of oil consumed in Canada? The answer is what it would have been sold for if it had been exported (obvious if you think about the real cost to Canadians of oil imported into the east when subsidised to consumers). Canadians may have paid less for each litre they consumed, but Canadians as a whole lost the difference between the domestic price of a litre and the world price. The loss took the form of lower real incomes in Canada because Canadians could afford to buy fewer imported goods from abroad. This was a glaring example of regulatory failure on a massive scale, because those responsible simply did not understand the basic economics of regulating markets. Or perhaps it was because politicians were convinced that they had to act as they did because consumers (voters) are intellectually incapable of understanding the issues.

SUMMARY ◆◆◆◆

- Governments intervene in the market economy in two ways (other than to redistribute income and wealth): they seek to correct *market failure*, and they produce a range of *goods and services*.
- Just as markets are prone to market failure, policy makers need to recognise the possibility of *regulatory failure*. This arises when regulation is badly designed, or when the regulatory process is captured by those it seeks to regulate.
- Regulatory design is exemplified by the issues involved in environmental regulation. An understanding of the forces that give rise to environmental pollution can help to identify those policy measures that will achieve a desired reduction in pollution at the lowest possible cost. Both the taxing of pollution and the sale of transferable pollution rights promote this goal. Each distributes the cost of the environmental clean-up effort so that the *marginal cost of pollution abatement* is the same for all polluters.
- A perennially controversial topic is the application of the Cost–Benefit Principle to policies involving public health, safety and security. Many critics feel that the use of cost–benefit analysis in this domain is not morally legitimate, because it involves putting a monetary price on human life. Yet the fundamental principle of scarcity applies to human health and safety, just as it does to other issues. Spending more on public health and safety necessarily means spending less on other things of value. Failure to weigh the relevant costs and benefits, then, means that society will be *less likely to achieve its stated goals*.
- One of government's principal tasks is to provide *public goods*, such as national defence and the criminal justice system. Such goods are, in varying degrees, *non-rival* and *non-excludable*. The first property describes goods for which one person's consumption does not diminish the amount available for others, while the second refers to the difficulty of preventing non-payers from consuming certain goods.

- Goods that are both highly non-excludable and non-rival are often called *pure public goods*. A collective good – such as pay-per-view cable television – is non-rival but excludable. Commons goods are goods that are rival but non-excludable.
- Because not everyone benefits equally from the provision of any given public good, charging all taxpayers equal amounts for the provision of public goods will generally not be either feasible or desirable. As in the case of private goods, people's WTP for public goods generally increases with income, and most governments therefore levy *higher taxes on the rich* than on the poor.
- The criterion for providing the optimal quantity or quality of a public good is to keep increasing quantity or quality as long as the marginal benefit of doing so exceeds the marginal cost. One advantage of using the government to provide public goods is that once a tax collection agency has been established to finance a single public good, it can be expanded at relatively low cost to generate revenue to finance additional public goods. A second advantage is that because government has the power to tax, it can easily assign responsibility for the cost of a public good. And in the case of goods for which non-payers simply cannot be excluded, the *government may be the only feasible provider*.
- One disadvantage to exclusive reliance on government for public goods provision is the element of coercion inherent in the tax system, which makes some people pay for public goods they don't want, while others do without public goods they do want. Many public goods are provided through private channels, with the necessary funding provided by donations, by sale of by-products, by development of new means to exclude non-payers and in many cases by private contract. A *loss in surplus* results, however, whenever monetary charges are levied for the consumption of a non-rival good.

REVIEW QUESTIONS

1. Why do economists believe that pollution taxes and effluent permits are a more efficient way to curb pollution than laws mandating across-the-board cutbacks?
2. Does it make sense to require more sophisticated and expensive safety equipment in large commercial passenger jets than in small private planes?
3. **a.** Which of the following goods are non-rival?
   Apples
   Stephen King novels
   Street lighting in college grounds
   Public service radio broadcasts
   b. Which of the goods in part (a) are non-excludable?
4. Give examples of goods that are, for the most part:
   a. rival but non-excludable
   b. non-rival but excludable
   c. both non-rival and non-excludable.
5. Why might even a wealthy person prefer a proportional income tax to a poll tax?
6. Can you explain why issuing tradable permits to pollute have the same effects as fining firms for polluting?
7. Can you list and describe the main sources of regulatory failure?

PROBLEMS

1. Two firms, Sludge Oil and Northwest Lumber, have access to five production processes, each one of which has a different cost and creates a different amount of pollution. The daily costs of the processes and the corresponding number of tonnes of smoke emitted are as shown in the table below.

Process (smoke)	A (4 tonnes/ day)	B (3 tonnes/ day)	C (2 tonnes/ day)	D (1 tonne/ day)	E (0 tonnes/ day)
Cost to Sludge Oil (€/day)	50	70	120	200	500
Cost to Northwest Lumber (€/day)	100	180	500	1,000	2,000

   a. If pollution is unregulated, which process will each firm use, and what will be the daily smoke emission?
   b. The city council wants to curb smoke emissions by 50 per cent. To accomplish this, it requires each firm to curb its emissions by 50 per cent. What will be the total cost to society of this policy?

2. The city council in Problem 1 again wants to curb emissions by half. This time, it sets a tax of €*T* per day on each tonne of smoke emitted. How large will *T* have to be to effect the desired reduction? What is the total cost to society of this policy?

3. Refer to Problem 2. Instead of taxing pollution, the city council decides to auction off four permits, each of which entitles the bearer to emit 1 tonne of smoke per day. No smoke may be emitted without a permit. Suppose that the government conducts the auction by starting at €1 and asking how many permits each firm wants to buy at that price. If the total is more than four, it then raises the price by €1, and asks again, and so on, until the total quantity of demanded permits falls to four. How much will each permit sell for in this auction? How many permits will each firm buy? What will be the total cost to society of this reduction in pollution?

4. The table below shows all the marginal benefits for each voter in a small town whose town council is considering a new swimming pool with capacity for at least three citizens. The cost of the pool would be €18 per week and would not depend on the number of people who actually used it.

Voter	Marginal benefit (€/week)
A	12
B	5
C	2

   a. If the pool must be financed by a weekly poll tax levied on all voters, will the pool be approved by majority vote? Is this outcome socially efficient? Explain.
   b. The town council instead decides to auction a franchise off to a private monopoly to build and maintain the pool. If it cannot find such a firm willing to operate the pool, then the pool project will be scrapped. If all such monopolies are constrained by law to charge a single price to users, will the franchise be sold – and, if so, how much will it sell for? Is this outcome socially efficient? Explain.

5. Two consumers, Smith and Jones, have the following demand curves for broadcasts of recorded opera on Saturdays:
Smith: $P_S = 12 - Q$
Jones: $P_J = 12 - 2Q$
where *PS* and *PJ* represent marginal willingness to pay values for Smith and Jones, respectively, and *Q* represents the number of hours of opera broadcast each Saturday.
   a. If Smith and Jones are the only broadcast listeners, construct the demand curve for opera broadcasts.
   b. If the marginal cost of opera broadcasts is €15 per hour, what is the socially optimal number of hours of broadcast opera?
6. Would a regulation requiring airlines to pay the overnight costs of passengers arising from cancelled flights increase the economic welfare of passengers?
7. According to some sources, snow-boarders cause more accidents to skiers than skiers do to snow-boarders or skiers to other skiers. Can you think of a test to see whether economic surplus would be increased by obliging ski resorts to segregate the two groups on the ski slopes?
8. Why might a monopolist whose prices are controlled by a regulator have higher production costs than if there were no regulation?.
9. If a regulator is seeking to regulate an industry with a large number of competing firms, why might the problem of regulatory failure be smaller than if the industry were monopolised?
10. Is it a good idea for governments to guarantee the liabilities of financial intermediaries such as banks?

REFERENCES

Cockburn, A. (2002) 'Somalia: a failed state?', *National Geographic Magazine*, July, www.findarticles.com/p/articles/mi_hb3343/is_200207/ai–n8059104.

Epstein, S., R. Bertell, and B. Seaman, (2001) 'Dangers and Unreliability of Mammography: Breast Examination is a Safe, Effective, and Practical Alternative', *International Journal of Health Services*, 31(3), 605–15.

Posner, R.A. (1974) 'Theories of Economic Regulation', *Bell Journal of Economics and Management Science*, vol. 5 (2).

Sorkin, A.R. (2010) *Too Big to Fail: Inside the Battle to Save Wall Street* (Penguin Books).

Chapter 15

The Credit Crunch and the Great Contraction: an Application of Some Microeconomics to Help Explain a Macroeconomic Crisis

Make unto you friends of the Mammon of iniquity. *(Luke, 16.9)*

Learning objectives

When you have read this chapter you should be able to:

1. Understand the importance of concepts such as information asymmetry, adverse selection and moral hazard as potential causes of economic dislocation;
2. Understand the potential consequences of regulatory failure;
3. Summarise the events that precipitated a major recession, said to be the most severe since the Great Depression.

INTRODUCTION

The Great Economic Contraction of 2008–2010 that hit virtually all major and minor economies is often seen as originating in problems in the US mortgage market. However, important as these problems were, they don't tell the whole story. Just because it started after those problems became serious doesn't mean that they explain the whole economic crisis. As John Kay asserted in an article in the *Guardian* newspaper of London, to state that the Great Contraction was caused by the so-called 'sub-prime crisis' in the US makes about as much sense as to argue that the First World War was caused by a navigational error by Archduke Franz Ferdinand's driver in Sarajevo in June 1914 (having lost his way, the driver brought the car once again close to the assassin, Gavrilo Princip, who had been unable to get close enough to his intended victims a little earlier).[1]

One should be careful not to confuse a 'tipping event' with the underlying forces building up to, and released by, the event.

[1] Kay, 2009.

Economic Naturalist 15.1
Was Gavrilo Princip more important than John Kay thinks?

This Economic naturalist is composed not in order to give a definite answer, but to provoke the reader to give some thought to how economics can be used to address historical questions.

While for most people the assassination of the Archduke is seen as the event that plunged Europe and the world into war, there is another view. It is possible to argue that the murder of the Archduke and his wife in Sarajevo on Sunday, 28 June 1914 was relatively unimportant. The basis for this is a belief that the outbreak of a general European war was an event the timing of which might be subject to debate, but was itself a more or less predictable consequence of a cumulative series of events and decisions going back at least as far as the Franco-Prussian war of 1870. From this standpoint the only thing, then, that flowed from the assassination was that a war that would have broken out anyway, sooner or later, started in August 1914.

In Chapter 7 we looked at the efficient markets hypothesis. John Kay's observation above makes us wonder as to just how efficient markets really are. The prospect of an outbreak of a general war would be expected to cause a significant fall in the market value of government bonds. The losers (e.g., Russia) might default while soaring inflation would reduce the value of even the winners' bonds. Consequently, if financial markets were efficient, and if new relevant information is generated ('Archduke Gunned Down By Balkan Extremist') that made war more likely, bond prices should have dropped the next day. What actually happened?

Niall Ferguson, Jesus College, Oxford and Harvard, has pointed out[2] that the prices of German and other bonds on the London market were steady for over three weeks after Sarajevo, while the dispute between Austria-Hungary and Serbia worsened, right up to a week before Austria-Hungary declared war on Serbia. Austria-Hungary issued an ultimatum to Serbia over Gavrilo Princip on 23 July. It was only then that prices started to fall. That implies that the imminent outbreak of a general war was a nasty 'surprise event' as far as the markets were concerned.

So, where stands the efficient markets hypothesis (EMH)? Start from the proposition that all Sarajevo affected was the precise timing of the war, the inevitable outbreak of which might indeed have been postponed if diplomacy had been more successful in brokering a compromise in the Balkans. If Sarajevo was truly unimportant, and markets were efficient, then prices should indeed have been unaffected by the news. Of course, if Sarajevo is really important, but EMH is not true and market participants are poorly informed, then you get the same result: prices remain stable until an ultimatum is issued.

What does not seem plausible is to assert that EMH applied in 1914 *and* that Sarajevo was much more than a mere tipping point.

sub-prime mortgage a mortgage that involves a loan to a person or household with a high risk of default and/or without evidence of ability to repay

recession loosely, when economic activity, output and incomes fall below full capacity output and income; defined as two or more successive quarters of economic contraction or negative growth in gross domestic product (GDP)

It is worth remembering that about twenty years before the **sub-prime mortgage** crisis a very similar crisis occurred in the same mortgage market in the US economy. This is usually described as the 'S&L Crisis' of the late 1980s. S&L refers to Savings and Loans institutions, the main source of housing finance in the US. Poor lending decisions caused failures among the S&Ls accompanied by a wave of small-bank failures. The world economy, however, did not enter a severe contraction as a consequence. There was, indeed, a **recession** which spread outside the US and played a part in the currency crisis of 1992 that forced the UK out of the European exchange rate mechanism, but nothing like the economic difficulties that have occurred in recent years.

Remarkably, while the level of bank failures in the US between 2007 and 2009 was much higher than in previous years, it did not even approach the peak value of the previous crisis (531 banks

[2] Ferguson, 2007, pp. 85–7.

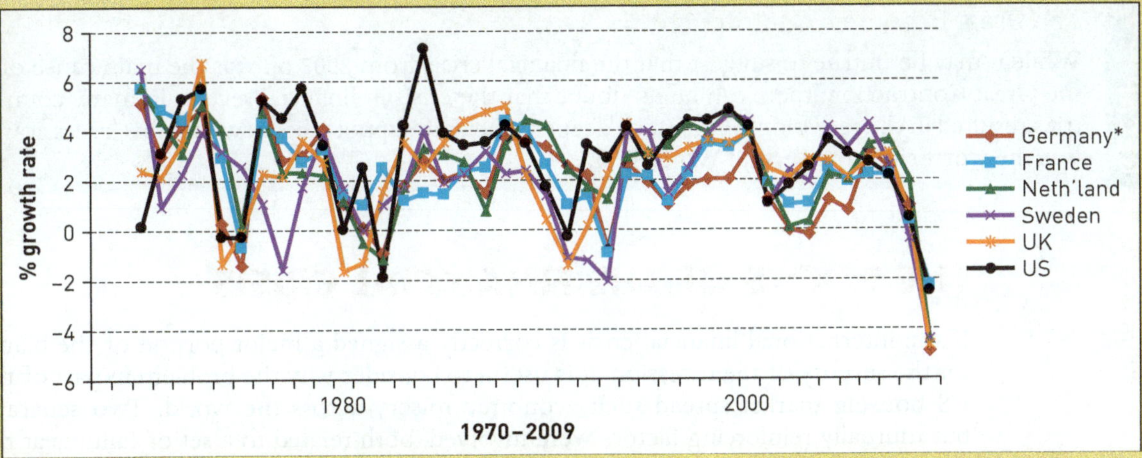

Figure 15.1 Annual Growth Rates for Six Countries, 1970–2009

Over a forty-year period the chart indicates there were five general economic contractions. In four of these at least some major economies entered into recession (more than two consecutive quarters of negative growth). In the earlier contractions the pattern of contractions varies as between countries in terms of both timing and depth. The last, our Great Contraction, is marked by a much deeper decline and uniformity of timing across all countries.

*Data for Germany are for West Germany up to 1990.

failed in 1989 alone).[3] One reason for the lower failure rate may have been the responses of the authorities as the storm gathered in the financial sector in 2008–9. The authorities moved to encourage shotgun marriages between institutions in order to avert failures.[4] These occurred when major 'too big to fail' institutions (more on this later) got into trouble. Examples are the forced sale of the banking operations of National Mutual (assets with a book value of $300 billion plus) to JP Morgan for $1.9 billion, the merging of Wachovia into Citigroup, costing the US taxpayer $42 billion, offset by $12 billion in shares in Citigroup and the merger of Merrill Lynch and Bank of America.

In retrospect we can see that some form of general slowdown affecting economies across the world was probably inevitable. Several of the larger OECD economies were experiencing a fall in the rate of growth of production. The explosive growth of the Chinese economy, averaging around 11 per cent per annum for several years, was clearly unsustainable. What was not inevitable was that the slowdown should take the form of the most severe contraction since the Great Depression (Figure 15.1) Put another way, a recession may have been unavoidable, but on top of these cyclical factors the economies of the world were hit by a credit contraction, resulting from the impact of property-related lending on bank balance sheets (the banking crisis). This implies that both the timing and the severity of the downturn in general reflected the crisis in the financial markets, originating in the US and spreading rapidly around the globe. In the case of the worst-hit economies in Europe, Iceland and Ireland, domestic banking sector blunders involving lending to property developers exacerbated the situation. The Irish banking sector collapse constituted, relative to GDP, the largest failure on record. The Irish banks were not significantly exposed to the US sub-prime market, but generated something even more toxic by excessive lending for investment in an already unsustainable domestic property market bubble, financed in large measure by selling bonds to financial institutions in other EU countries.

---

[3] There was a strong regional variation: in some states, particularly Georgia, there was a wave of collapses in what were very small banks, but this is probably best seen as an acceleration of the trend in the US towards concentration in the banking sector since the abolition of the ban on interstate banking.

[4] Sorkin, 2009 *passim*.

RECAP

The Great Economic Contraction

While it may be untrue to suggest that the financial crisis from 2007 on was the main cause of the Great Contraction, there can be no doubt that the crisis in financial sectors in many countries resulted in the recession being much deeper. The data support the view that this 'recession' was the worst since the Second World War.

THE ROOTS OF THE FINANCIAL CRISIS

If the international financial crisis is correctly assigned a major portion of the blame for the severity of the recession, it is useful to consider why the problem in part of the US housing market spread such economic misery across the world. Two separate, but mutually reinforcing factors were involved, both related to a set of failures at the microeconomic level, and which have been analysed in Chapters 12 and 14. These are regulatory failure and information asymmetries. The concepts developed in those chapters help us to understand how the crisis started and spread.

REGULATORY FAILURE AND FAILURE OF REGULATORY REFORM

First, there was serious regulatory failure. Regulation is in principle aimed at correcting market failure, but the cure, so to speak, can be worse than the disease, when changes in regulatory regimes have adverse effects and market failure is replaced by regulatory failure (see Chapter 14). Regulatory failure has been a feature of financial markets, and not just in recent years. In 1986 the UK Government deregulated the London Stock Exchange in order to restore London's pre-eminence as a global financial sector. This is described generally as London's 'Big Bang'. The consequences of deregulating the stock exchange spilled over across the entire financial sector and completely changed its operations, as the traditional boundaries between what the functions performed by the various categories of **financial intermediary** were weakened or else disappeared altogether. One important consequence was to change how banks operated. The old dividing line between banks that in effect operated the monetary system (deposit takers and low-risk lenders) and investment or merchant banks (borrowers of money market funds and investors in riskier assets) disappeared. Mergers and consolidations across sectors followed, and the financial sector became increasingly dominated by a small number of large multi-product financial institutions. Mutual funds were privatised as profit-seeking intermediaries made the traditional mutual form of organisation uncompetitive. Successful risk-taking became the goal of financial intermediaries in general rather than being the preserve of specialist risk-taking firms.

financial intermediary
a firm that accepts deposits or otherwise obtains funds in order to lend to firms (or households); examples are banks, credit unions, life insurance and pensions providers

The example of London was followed in New York, culminating in 1999 with the repeal of the Glass-Steagall Act of 1933, originally designed to avoid the risk taking that was seen as one of the causes of the Great Depression. Tokyo and Frankfurt changed, too, but German and Japanese banks had traditionally been heavily involved in direct investment in private-sector firms, so in some respects the deregulation impact in those centres was less than in London and New York.

The rationale for the wholesale deregulation of the financial sector was the belief that the sector had been beset by problems of regulatory failure by national governments. There was a widely held view at the time that banking suffered from being over-regulated, not that this necessarily damaged the interests of banks or their shareholders. As we know, regulatory capture is a source of protection from competition. The solution to all this was said to be radical deregulation and the integration of financial markets across the world.

However, replacing a regime where financial firms are subject to strict regulatory control and supervision to one of **light-touch regulation** carries its own potential disadvantages.

light-touch regulation a regulatory regime that lays down general rules affecting firms' operations, and excludes tight restrictions and refrains from day-to-day supervision and control of those operations

While it may be true that in 2008 the US had too many overlapping regulatory bodies overseeing the various parts of the financial sector, it is also true that they failed to foresee and try to avert the consequences of the expansion of business in the so-called 'sub-prime sector' (some of which was caused by political pressure to extend credit to higher-risk, lower-income borrowers).

In the UK (as will be discussed in Chapter 22) the Northern Rock crisis was in part a consequence of a financial intermediary financing its loan book by resorting to wholesale funding from short-term money markets rather than from more stable deposit finance. The UK Financial Services Authority did little or nothing to limit the use of such funding by lending institutions, effectively allowing the firms concerned to increase **gearing** (the ratio of borrowing to equity capital). In Canada, by way of contrast, a much tighter regulatory regime restricted the ability of banks to do this, and as a consequence, when the confidence crisis broke, Canadian banks were not as greatly affected by the collapse of inter-bank lending at the time of and after the Lehman Brothers collapse in 2008.

gearing the ratio of debt finance to equity finance on a firm's balance sheet; high gearing means the firm holds a high proportion of its assets by virtue of having borrowed to buy them rather than using shareholders' capital to do so

During the 1990s, under the Clinton administration, bank regulations were changed in order to persuade (force?) banks to provide low-cost mortgage finance to people with poor prospects as borrowers. This proved very popular (not, of course, with bankers) and hundreds of thousands of high-risk mortgages were the result. Lenders' loan books now contained a significant volume of what were later described as 'toxic' loans.

INFORMATION ECONOMICS AND THE CRISIS

Over-leveraged and over-extended, banks across the world were now hit by the second set of problems. We looked at these problems in Chapter 12, dealing with information in markets. Information is rarely 'perfect' in the sense that each side of a transaction possesses full access to all relevant information about the good or service in question and/or the other party to the transaction. Information is valuable and costly, and we saw that parties to a transaction will acquire information up to the point at which the marginal benefit from acquiring information equals the marginal cost of resources spent acquiring it.

Cost–Benefit Analysis

A core concept that arose here was that of information asymmetries. Insurance markets are particularly exposed to information asymmetries, but so, it transpired, were banks in the new light-touch-regulation era.

ADVERSE SELECTION AND MORAL HAZARD

Two consequences of information asymmetries are adverse selection and moral hazard, and there are cases where regulation or political intervention can exacerbate these. The sub-prime mortgage market is a good example of this, and the consequences that flowed from these effects were enormous.

The sub-prime market was a loan market for people who could not obtain credit on the favourable terms associated with a better credit record or demonstrable ability to service a loan. By definition, lending in that market is higher-risk than in 'normal' credit markets and the loans carry a compensating (to the lender) higher interest cost. This higher return is the cost of assuming the risk that the borrowers will default. At the expected rate of default it still is profitable for a lender to lend in the market.

The lender knows that some borrowers will indeed repay, but he also knows that if a 'good' borrower could get credit elsewhere at a lower price he would do so. He can assume that those seeking credit from him have a higher probability of defaulting than the population from which they came. That is, we are looking at an example of Adverse Selection (as in the case of used cars in the Market for Lemons, see Chapter 11).

Now, suppose the lender can pass on the risk to some one else. He bundles up the mortgages and sells them to another, larger financial institution that is looking for higher-yield assets (accepting higher risk) in its portfolio. In financial circles this is called **securitising** the loans. Banks such as Lehman Brothers 'bought' mortgages from mortgage providers, and 'bundled' them into parcels that were then used to back assets sold to investors carrying interest derived from the interest paid by the mortgage holders and whose capital value depended on the mortgages being repaid. The purchaser has less information that the original lender as to the quality of the loans, and decides to insure a proportion of their value with an insurer. At this stage the original lender has off-loaded the risk to two other institutions. The insurer may have funded the insurance contract in effect by seeking re-insurance from specialist firms. The bank that bought the mortgages may have funded the purchase in part of whole by borrowing from the international money market, the lenders in which are therefore assuming an element of risk. But at each stage the real risk cost being assumed in financing the purchase is becoming less and less clear as it is passed on to those who end up carrying it.

> **securitisation** the creation of a financial asset that can be sold to investors, where the issuer of the asset uses financial liabilities of other firms or of households as the asset backing the asset being created

Consider a lender in the sub-prime market who is unable to securitise his loans, compared with the lender in the example just given. Which of them will take more care about the repayment potential of a borrower? Assuming a lender is generally risk averse, the lender who must carry the risk that he has identified will take more care than one who can sell on the loan at a price that reflects the general riskiness of such loans. Bundles of loans that can be securitised will contain more 'toxic' loans (loans with a low probability of being repaid) than the average in the sub-prime market. Moral hazard strikes again. By increasing the demand for mortgages to bundle and sell on from larger banks further up the structure, securitisation made it possible for mortgage providers to accept increasingly risky loan propositions.[5]

REGULATION-BASED CHANGES IN THE STRUCTURE OF THE FINANCIAL SECTOR

What changed since the S&L crisis of the late 1980s is, in the first place, that mortgage securitisation by original lenders has been greatly extended. This in turn partly reflected regulatory regime changes that permitted banks to increase their exposure to securitized loans (and supply securitised loans themselves), while the market for these secondary assets and derivatives based on them expanded. Financial sector firms increasingly became **financial conglomerates**, straddling areas of financial activity that a generation earlier were dealt with by separate institutions. Inevitably, narrowly defined banks, as understood by the man in the street, changed radically. The public might become dimly aware of this as they realised that their bank could now be their mortgage provider, offer life insurance and direct clients to their stockbroking arm, while this last also operated as a market maker, buying and selling securities in order to increase the net worth of the bank that owned it, as well as advising clients on what to buy and sell.

> **financial conglomerates** financial sector firms that operate in several financial markets, e.g., day-to-day banking, insurance and stock exchange transactions

[5] The securitisation process under the new regulatory regime and its consequences are accessibly and wittily described by former Lehman executive, Larry McDonald (McDonald, 2009).

EFFICIENCY COMPATIBLE INCENTIVES: THE PRINCIPAL–AGENT PROBLEM

Here we see the potential for problems arising from the principal–agent relationship, where the interests of the agent, the adviser, may not be perfectly aligned with those of the principal, the client seeking advice on investment. In Chapter 9 we considered how this kind of problem can lead to market failure (the remote office game is an example; the question of how to sell your house is another).

The principal–agent problem also started to affect banking performance through internal remuneration structures which changed radically after deregulation. Payments by results (performance bonus payments are a case in point) on the face of it should align the interests of the management of the bank with those of the shareholders, and lead to a positive-sum game. However, much depends on whether the attitudes to risk-taking by executives reflect correctly the desire of shareholders to accept risk. In general, holding riskier assets should mean higher expected returns (but higher potential **volatility**), but if the calculation of profits permits them to be marked up into the accounts in terms of what is expected to happen the result can be higher bonuses without higher final profitability. As such this encourages a level of risk taking by the management that might not be what is really desired by the shareholders.

> **volatility** the degree of variability in the market price of an asset over time

This can cross the threshold between what is legal and what is effectively fraud only too easily. The collapse of the famous British bank, Barings, through the activities of one of its officers in Singapore in 1995, was an example of a bank that rewarded profitable trades extravagantly and fell down on internal supervision of officers' behaviour, all being made possible because it could be done through an overseas subsidiary.[6] The collapse of Enron, an energy and finance conglomerate, in the US followed a similar pattern, although there were more widespread problems than simply the performance of overseas branches.

We will return to this point later, but at this stage it is worth noting that many commentators believe that the question of incentives and structures in banking have to be addressed in a regulatory response to the financial crisis.

> **RECAP**
>
> **The roots of the economic crisis**
>
> In the globally interconnected financial world the contagious financial crisis can be seen to be connected to bungled regulatory reform and regulatory failure. These exposed the sector to a greater degree to endemic problems arising from information asymmetries. In particular, moral hazard and adverse selection played a central role in the development of the crisis.

A LIQUIDITY CRISIS?

The initial perception of the problems facing financial sector firms after the Lehman Brothers collapse was that they were suffering from a **liquidity** shortage. That is, while they had good long-term investments, they had a shortage of assets that they could easily sell and use to meet short-term obligations. Banks had used this market for liquidity to deposit funds surplus to requirements profitably with banks that were temporarily short of liquidity. After Lehman (and perhaps before it) the availability of funds from short-term, inter-bank lending simply disappeared, as banks became

> **liquidity**[7] the ease of realising a known capital value of an asset

[6] A simple and easily read account of this variant of the remote office problem can be found at www.riskglossary.com/link/barings_debacle.htm.

[7] In example, a household's savings in the form of a deposit in a bank is (normally) highly liquid (its value is fixed, and it can be drawn down immediately), while its accumulated investment in the house it bought on mortgage is highly illiquid (the value is uncertain, and selling a house is costly and takes time).

unwilling to lend funds to other banks with liquidity needs. This was explained as the consequence of a growing awareness of toxic loans (originating in the sub-prime market) buried away in the assets of banks that had invested in securitised mortgages or assets that were derivatives of these toxic assets. If Bank A needed funds because it was over-extended in the sense that it was short of liquidity, and Bank B loaned funds to Bank A, Bank B ran the risk that Bank A might not be in a position to return those funds if its assets turned out to be insufficient because the market value was less than the book value (since the assets contained toxic loans). Even if Bank B knew that Bank A held absolutely no assets exposed directly to the sub-prime problem, the latter might have loans out to, say, a hedge fund that had invested in assets that directly or indirectly contained toxic loans, and so on. To make things worse, the riskiness of assets containing potentially toxic loans was hard to calculate, especially after the original loans had been diced and chopped into derivative assets.

Short of liquidity, banks could only respond by reducing the size of their loan books. As loans were repaid, the banks reduced the volume of credit outstanding, using the repayments to replenish their liquid reserves. As a result, firms needing short-term credit or working capital found the supply drying up. While economies were already moving into recession (see above), the consequence of reduced credit availability was a further cut-back in output and employment in the broader economy arising from the reduction in credit availability. A snowball effect began to gather pace, and the recession started to look like a depression.

This is how the financial crisis was perceived in its early days. It had two implications. The first was that it was primarily a confidence crisis in banking that needed to be resolved to get the economies moving again. The second was that the provision of liquidity to the banking system and the removal of uncertainty were the necessary and sufficient solutions to the growing difficulties. Both were at best partly correct, and at worst a distraction from the underlying reality, and in at least one case led to a seriously misguided government response.[8]

RESPONSE TO A LIQUIDITY CRISIS

The immediate response of the monetary authorities in the US and the UK to the presumed liquidity crisis was to supply more liquidity to the banking system. This was followed by a similar decision by the European Central Bank. In classic monetary management mode, the authorities lowered the cost of funds to the banking system by lowering the **repo (rediscount) rate** so that banks could get access to liquidity from the central banks more easily. This did not result in a resumption of credit to borrowers. The authorities then began to aggressively buy securities from the markets to increase the monetary base. Credit growth still refused to resume. By late 2008 it was clear to most observers that the banking crisis was not simply a liquidity crisis in the sense of banks with plenty of funds refusing to lend to other banks. Bank share prices led a sharp slump on world stock exchanges. The crisis reflected a deeper problem, the involvement of the banks in financing property development.

> **repo** (or **rediscount**) **rate**
> this is the interest rate that the central bank charges on funds lent to banks who need funds and can offer certain securities as collateral; it is the base rate to which other interest rates are related

[8] The reference here is to the Irish Government's rushed decision to offer a blanket guarantee by the Irish state covering almost all the liabilities of the Irish banking system in September, 2008. This was a response to the imminent collapse of one bank that was hopelessly exposed to the collapse in property markets in Ireland and elsewhere in Europe, Anglo-Irish Bank plc. The guarantee exposed Irish tax-payers to a potential loss equivalent to more than two years' GDP, but also effectively tied the hands of the Irish Government in dealing with the evolving problems of the Irish banking system.

BANKS AND PROPERTY

We have noted that over the past 20 years the financial sector has changed significantly as the distinctions between different types of institution weakened or disappeared. One consequence of this was the increased involvement of retail banks in direct lending to finance real-estate development. Even when this was not done by retail banks themselves, the banks became exposed to property markets through subsidiaries or loans to investment funds. A significant proportion of this exposure in Europe reflected investment in US securitised mortgages. BNP Paribas had to suspend three property funds in summer, 2007, as a consequence of their large holdings of sub-prime assets. But apart from these 'toxic' assets, the banks had moved into providing finance for property developers. The value of these loans to the lending institutions depended on the value that could be realised from the assets on which they were secured, i.e., property prices.

By mid 2007 evidence was available that in Europe, as in the US, the decade of significant and continued price increases for real estate was at an end. Britain, Ireland, France and Spain led the field for price increases in Western Europe, while property prices had also been strong in many eastern European countries that benefited from foreign investment in property. Property company shares were weak on stock exchanges. Losses for banks on their loan portfolios were inevitable, and as a consequence of the involvement in property lending were likely to be large. If these losses were realised, the consequences for the banks were very serious, since losses on this scale would mean a collapse in their equity and reserves, on which rested their ability to maintain the credit extended to customers. In effect, the banks faced being bankrupt because they had made loans that were not likely to be repaid. That is not a liquidity crisis. It is a systemic asset-collapse crisis. What banks would need was not access to short-term funds for liquidity purposes but equity or equivalent injections of capital to cover losses on their loan books, only a fraction of which could be ascribed to the problems of the US sub-prime market.

This brings us to another aspect of the causality of the Great Contraction. The problems flowing from the property market can be seen as a proximate cause of the catastrophic losses of the banking sector when the property boom across so many countries collapsed. However, there is also a causal link between the activities of the banks and what happened in those property markets. Historically, high-risk property development (at least in traditional Anglo-Saxon capital markets) relied on intermediation by specialist finance houses rather than on the narrow banks (ordinary retail banks) that in recent years became involved by making loans financed by short-term borrowing in money markets.

Deregulation led to the emergence of broad-spectrum intermediaries based on the narrow banks. This meant that the equity of those banks (and their deposits) were now exposed to property market risks through the activities of subsidiaries. Since it was always open to developers to use the traditional sources of finance we can safely assume that using the retail banks, directly or indirectly, was more advantageous, involving lower financing costs or lower risks to developers.

Put another way, it is plausible to argue that the deregulated (or poorly regulated) banking system helped underpin the rising property prices of the decade up to 2007. Sub-prime crisis or no sub-prime crisis, increased use of bank finance for commercial development projects in property markets was something that was bound to end in tears sooner or later.

RECAP

A liquidity crisis?

The failure to recognise what was really happening was a serious problem for policy makers. The initial reaction, that the problem was simply one of risk aversion inducing a liquidity shortage on a huge scale, was incorrect. The financial sector crisis was not a liquidity crisis, but a solvency crisis, which in turn reflected changes in the organisation, remuneration and of financial-sector activities.

TOO BIG TO FAIL: SOWING DRAGON'S TEETH?

No monetary authority in Europe, Iceland excepted, or the US was prepared to contemplate a simple failure by one of the large clearing banks in the course of the crisis of 2007–09. Instead, various steps were taken to shore them up, varying from outright nationalisation (Northern Rock, Anglo-Irish Bank are examples) to recapitalisation by the tax-payer (Lloyds, RBS) to subsidised recapitalisation (the US Government permitted a number of banks to issue government-guaranteed bonds for a small sum to cover losses) and shotgun mergers (e.g., Lloyds and HBOS).

The reason for this set of responses was that in the authorities' eyes the banks involved were 'too big to fail'. This didn't simply mean too many depositors would lose their money; in general deposits were already covered by state insurance of one form or another. It meant that the liabilities of the banks concerned were a large proportion of the money supply. The scale of their activities was such that closure would seriously compromise the operations of the monetary system. The ripple-out effect on other banks could trigger cascade insolvency across the system. Hence, the costs of failure were simply too great to be accepted.

That argument is hard to rebut. The difficulty is that the sanction of potential failure is a major mechanism in ensuring that banks behave prudently. In the 'good old days' the costs of risky investments that brought down investment banks were imposed on shareholder and other creditors of the banks concerned, and (more or less) confined to them. Remove the threat of failure, because the institution is seen as 'too big to fail' and the downside associated with risk-taking is greatly reduced and moral hazard problems are increased. That is predicted to increase any financial institution's risk-taking.

Furthermore, the knowledge that a bail-out to avert failure is likely will encourage the management of a bank that has had a bad-loan experience to adopt a 'double or quits' approach to lending decisions. This is a classic incidence of the moral hazard problem, and points to the need for tighter regulatory control for banks that are deemed to be too big to fail.[9] In an era of financial conglomerates property-related loan losses exposed shareholders, bond holders and depositors in what had been 'conventional' banks to risks, and the decision that these could not be allowed to fail meant that someone else (i.e., the tax-payer) was being exposed to the consequences of poor management of the financial structure. There has been an increased incidence of failure events that trigger costly (to the tax-payer) bail-out exercises.

RE-REGULATION?

Assuming that permanent nationalisation of major banking institutions is ruled out (as opposed to temporary nationalisation as part of restructuring banks after failure events), the experience of the credit crunch and its consequences for economic activity create a case for going some way to reverse deregulation. One suggestion is that we should revert to a structure with 'narrow' banks, regulated and safe, and carrying out simple retail banking functions of a low-risk nature, and 'other' intermediaries that execute high-risk functions. This would in part reverse the 1986 Big Bang in London. These narrow banks would remain 'too big to fail', since they would constitute the main structure of a country's financial structure. Their liabilities would still constitute the major component of its money supply. However, their lending would be predominantly low risk and/or short term, and financed by deposits rather than by access to wholesale money markets. The remaining institutions would not be 'too big to fail' even if they were very big indeed. The idea would be that high-risk, high-return financial transactions would be confined to such banks, with those involved accepting the risk implications.

9 Wolf, 2009, points to the consequences for incentives and risk taking by banks with a small ratio of equity to total liabilities.

The difficulty with this suggestion is (a) defining what would be within the ambit of the 'narrow' banks, and (b) there would clearly be a loss of economic surplus by prohibiting multiple financial-service provision by financial intermediaries: we would lose much of the efficiency gains flowing from the 1986 deregulation.

However, this might be a price that is worth paying.

An alternative is to recognise that high-risk institutions need a large equity base both for solvency reasons and to reduce moral hazard problems. Consequently, regulation should first concentrate on ensuring that equity is sufficient to support the activities of all financial intermediaries. At the same time, recognising that failure is still possible, procedures will be needed for dealing with the failure of a 'too big' bank. These will have to involve keeping its 'good' operations functioning while forcing shareholders to shoulder the costs/losses and winding down the 'bad' business of the intermediary through a transfer to a 'bad bank'.

Common to both these positions is the need for a widening of the role of the regulators to include regulation based on dealing with **systemic risk**. Prudential regulation traditionally concerned limiting the individual banks' customer's exposure to risks to the banks' solvency arising from the activities of the banks. However, the Credit Crunch has highlighted the fact that we are exposed to systemic risk arising from the performance of individual bank behaviour. A major bank in trouble can undermine the entire system. Hence, regulators need to be empowered to supervise the behaviour of banks with a view to systemic consequences rather than simply to the implications for a particular bank's balance sheet. For example, even if a bank had plenty of room to lend to, say, the property sector given its loan-book profile, the regulator might need to be able to restrict such lending by reference to overall lending to that sector.

> **systemic risk** the possible impact of an adverse event on the entire financial system as opposed to the effect on the bank directly affected

At the end of June, 2009, substantial steps were taken to adjust the regulatory regimes in the US and Europe to the needs that have emerged as a consequence of the Credit Crunch. In the US the Obama administration proposed the following:

(a) establishing the Fed (the US central bank) as a systemic risk regulator, with special powers to oversee banks that are 'too big';
(b) extending a regulatory regime to cover derivatives, including retention by the issuer of any securitised asset of a minimum exposure to the risk associated (cf., the sub-prime securitisation problem);
(c) setting up procedures to permit winding-up and divestiture of the Assets of non-bank holding companies that control financial assets (i.e., orderly winding-up procedures).

The EU agreed to establish the European Systemic Risk Council to undertake macro- as well as micro-prudential regulation. This is to comprise the governors of the EU's central banks, and will probably be chaired by the president of the European Central Bank. However, its role is weaker than that of the Fed, since it will issue recommendations for actions to the central banks of the various countries rater than regulate directly. Supervisory authorities are to be set up to ensure regime harmonisation in regulation, and to resolve disagreements between home state and host state regulators (for example, disagreements between the Bank of England and the Banque de France concerning liquidity requirements for a British bank operating in France). Also, unlike the US, there is no equivalent power to that of the Fed to share the burden of a failure across the system. If a bank fails in Britain, the cost of cleaning up the wreckage will be confined to Britain.

In the UK the 2009 Banking Act requires that banks of systemic importance prepare plans for winding-down in the event of failure.

In the EU (including, with some amendments, the UK) as of 2011 a regulatory regime is being extended to cover hedge funds and similar alternative investment vehicles along the lines proposed in the US.

SUMMARY

- The economic contraction of 2008–2010 involved a cyclical downturn exacerbated by a financial crisis. The latter was made possible by regulatory changes over many years, including the Big Bang in London (1986) and the repeal of the Glass-Steagall Act in the US (1999), as well as the move to 'light-touch regulation'.
- Increasing exposure of financial intermediaries to risk that was difficult to quantify, itself in part at least the result of information asymmetries, increased the incidence of adverse selection and moral hazard in loan markets. In some cases changing incentive systems led to an increased appetite for risk taking.
- When the crisis broke, government and central bank reactions initially misdiagnosed the problem as a liquidity crisis, when in fact the financial crisis was a solvency crisis arising from exposure of banks to property price risks.
- A further problem was that the regulatory changes had resulted in these problems not being confined to specialist risk-taking intermediaries but to banks that were 'too big to fail' with attendant consequences for governments faced with the need to cover the losses. As a result, there has been a general move to tighten up regulation of financial systems.

REVIEW QUESTIONS

1. Why is information asymmetry so big a problem in the financial sector?
2. How did securitisation lead to increased risk-taking?
3. What is the difference between a liquidity crisis and a solvency crisis?
4. How did regulatory changes contribute to the crisis?
5. How did banks' reaction to the crisis deepen the recession?

PROBLEMS

connect

1. If deregulation was a major factor in the development of the financial crisis can you explain why re-regulation is not a 'free lunch'?
2. Can you explain why in many countries in the wake of the crisis governments have moved to restrict or eliminate bonus payments to decision makers in the financial sector?
3. Should governments make it easier for poorer people to borrow money?
4. What kind of regulatory changes in banking structures might reduce the probability of a repeat of the financial crisis?
5. A bank obtains funds by accepting deposits, selling bonds and issuing shares. Depositors, bond-holders and even shareholders can be seen as 'creditors' of a bank. Why should governments guarantee depositors, but not the others, against a bank failure?

REFERENCES

Ferguson, N. (2007) *The War of the World: History's Age of Hatred* (Penguin Books).

Kay, J.A. (2009) 'Taming the financial casino', *Guardian*, Comment is free, 23 March 2009. Accessed at www.guardian.co.uk/commentisfree/2009/mar/23/recession-globalrecession.

Mc Donald, L. (with P. Robinson) (2009) *A Colossal Failure of Common Sense* (Random House, Ebury Press).

Sorkin, A.R. (2009) *Too Big to Fail: The Inside Story of How Wall Street Fought to Save the Financial System – and Themselves* (Allen Lane).

Wolf, M. (2009) 'Reform of regulation has to start with incentives', *Financial Times*, 23 June.

Index

Note: Locators in **bold** indicate definitions

C

D

E

F

G

H

I

J

K

L

M

N

Q

R

S

T

U

V

W

X